ITALY AT THE PARIS PEACE CONFERENCE

ITALY AT THE PARIS PEACE CONFERENCE

BY

RENÉ ALBRECHT-CARRIÉ

ARCHON BOOKS
HAMDEN, CONNECTICUT
1966

FIRST PUBLISHED 1938 BY
COLUMBIA UNIVERSITY PRESS
FOR THE
CARNEGIE ENDOWMENT FOR INTERNATIONAL PEACE
IN THE SERIES
THE PARIS PEACE CONFERENCE — HISTORY AND DOCUMENTS

REPRINTED 1966 WITH PERMISSION
IN AN UNALTERED AND UNABRIDGED EDITION

LIBRARY OF CONGRESS CATALOG NUMBER: 66-13339
PRINTED IN THE UNITED STATES OF AMERICA

EDITORIAL FOREWORD

WHEN the series of which this volume forms a part was originally planned, some years ago, the Treaties of Peace at the end of the World War still stood as the accepted basis—if reluctantly accepted—of the polity of Europe. As President Butler pointed out in the Preface to the first volumes in the series, those on *The Origins of the International Labor Organization*, the Peace Treaties were in part "the register of events which had already taken place, the fall of great empires, the emergence of new nations and the recovery of long lost liberties, in part, the program for a far-reaching reform in the relations of nations with each other." He pointed out as well that "as for registering the effects of the War, the Paris Peace Conference had no alternative but to accept the already accomplished fact" of the disappearance of the Habsburg monarchy and the rise of new nations. With the defeat of the Central Powers the problem which confronted the Conference was not whether the outlying territories of the Habsburgs should go to the different claimants but how and to what extent their conflicting claims should be met. Never in all the history of diplomacy was there so difficult a task, for it involved more than a shifting of territories, it involved also the measurement of the forces of nationalism in a world the economic structure of which had been shaken to its base by the disasters of the War.

The belief has been widely shared in the post-war years that the Peace Settlement was responsible for what followed. Undoubtedly its mistakes did contribute seriously to that end. But the extent to which this was the case could only be established by an objective study of the problems of diplomacy as they confronted the negotiators, and this intensive work of analysis has as yet been only partially accomplished. Scholarship has not yet checked up on political opinion. The tribunal of history has only just begun to have the documents in the case laid before it. The present volume is an effort to supply some of this evidence. It is evidence most of which in one form or another is available to the researcher, but it has never been assembled or made available in the form given it here. As for the portions of it which come from unpublished sources, they do not violate confidences at any point but will be found to throw a helpful light upon phases of the negotiations which otherwise might easily be misconstrued. This is but another way of saying that the author has avoided the temptation to gain effect by either the partial use of authoritative sources or the exploitation of material that will not stand the test of criticism.

While the volume is primarily designed for scholars, more especially for students of international relations, it opens up to any thoughtful reader a clear perspective of one of the major problems of the Peace Settlement. Nowhere else did the new theories of international polity championed by President Wilson come so definitely to an issue with the elements of pre-war and war-time diplomacy. But it was more than theories that were at stake. The *sacro egoismo*, of which Orlando and Sonnino were the exponents, had behind it the commitments of the Treaty of London; and behind that ill-fated agreement lay the military necessities of the hard-pressed Allies. But the ideology under which the United States had entered the World War ran counter to all the implications of this kind of settlement, and the result was that at the Peace Conference the struggle for Fiume, in itself an insignificant item of contest, hardened into a diplomatic battle of prestige which ultimately brought gain to no one. Had it not been for the major issues involved, the question might well be dismissed by historians as relatively trivial, but its bearing upon the Peace Settlement as a whole, as well as upon the subsequent history of Italy, was of outstanding importance. Upon these major questions the present volume touches only incidentally. While it offers a general view of a history before and after the event, it concentrates upon the story of negotiations. Within this field the author has woven together the tangled threads of one of the strangest of all episodes in modern history. He has depicted with clarity and insight not only the problems themselves but the personalities who were involved in them; for only in this way would the events be understood.

While the ultimate task of publishing the complete records of the Paris Peace Conference will rest with the participating governments, it is to be hoped that this volume, along with other volumes in this series, will enable the reader to form a better judgment as to what really happened than has been possible heretofore.

New York　　　　　　　　　　　　　　　　　JAMES T. SHOTWELL
May 4, 1938

PREFACE

THE lapse of two decades has not detracted from the importance of the drama that had its inception at Sarajevo in June, 1914. Rather it tends to confirm the view that the war itself and the peace settlement which followed it will rank among the crucial events of modern history, while at the same time it enables us to obtain a more comprehensive view of those events. A vast literature has grown and is still growing around the subject, in which the element of controversy may be expected steadily to yield to that of historical analysis. The time has come to gather together the elements of the history of that period, to which the present work is intended as a modest contribution.

Not unnaturally, attention has been focused to a large extent on the various phases of the German settlement, but the importance of developments east of the Rhine and south of the Danube should not be underestimated. In that region the position of Italy is of prime importance. In 1919 as well as in 1914—albeit in a different way— Italy was in a unique position. That fact lies at the root of the well-nigh universal dissatisfaction with which the peace settlement was received in Italy, and it is well worth examining the manner in which the peace negotiations helped to produce this result, which has been one of the important elements in subsequent developments in that country.

The unexpected duration of the war and the unprecedented havoc which it wrought created a widespread desire to prevent the recurrence of a like catastrophe. Circumstances caused the United States, particularly its chief representative in the person of President Wilson, to become the spokesman for the hope that a new order of things, especially in international relations, might come into being. That hope—widespread though it was in Europe—could not help clash with the forces of tradition that were pushing the nations into an attitude of exclusive, and often short-sighted, concern with their own interests.

Italy, like the other European Powers, had a well-defined national policy, which she hoped to further as the result of victory. The ambitions of the Powers had found expression in a number of secret treaties, the provisions of which were in flagrant contradiction with the principles proclaimed by the American President. The collapse of Russia provided a convenient way of jettisoning these treaties, but, in actual practice, once the question was reopened, the substance of the same ambitions was pursued by the Powers, though no longer on the strength of treaty obligations. In the scramble that ensued Italy found herself in a particularly difficult position, for her territorial desires appeared to be in conflict, not with the claims of the former enemy, but with those of a country which—although consisting in large part of territory of the disrupted Austro-Hungarian Empire—appeared at the Peace Conference in the guise of an ally. In the end Italy fell back on the written pledge of her allies. Thus it was that, just as circumstances undreamt of in the earlier stages of the war made the United States the champion of the New Order, in large measure owing to circumstances, it fell to Italy to be cast in the rôle of defender of the Old. The result of this situation and of its handling by the Italian statesmen was the dramatic clash of April, 1919, when President Wilson issued his appeal to public opinion and the Italians temporarily withdrew from the Conference; and the unforeseen (before 1919) development that the negotiations with Italy resolved themselves, to a large extent, into a controversy between that country and the United States.

It has been our purpose to trace the development of these negotiations, as far as can be done at present; not to judge the merits of the case—an attempt that our proximity to the events would almost inevitably vitiate—but merely to fit their course into an intelligible pattern. In doing this, the Italian sources have been found regrettably meager; save, however, on one important point, for the minutes of the crucial meetings in April have been published in the form of a diary by Count Luigi Aldrovandi, then secretary to the Italian delegation. It is to be hoped that the English or French accounts of these same meetings and other meetings which the Italians did not attend at the time may soon be brought to light. On the other hand, the fact that the dispute was largely one between America and Italy, Great Britain and France remaining conveniently in the background, is responsible for our having a considerable amount of material of American origin, both documentary and in the form of personal recollections, while it is also possible to obtain

word-of-mouth accounts of the events from some of the participants.

The emphasis of the present work is definitely on the negotiations
between Italy and the other Powers. For that reason, certain phases
of the Italian settlement, though important, have not been dealt
with in great detail. This is particularly the case with the Treaty
of St. Germain, for there was no appreciable controversy that involved Italy in any special way in the framing of that Treaty. Once
President Wilson had agreed that the Italian frontier in the north
should be at the Brenner, the matter was essentially settled, for the
Austrians, like the other defeated Powers, were not consulted in the
drawing of their frontiers. On the other hand, it has been necessary
to go back to the origins of the conflict and the making of the
Treaty of London in order to provide an intelligible account of
Italian policy; the events of 1919 were only a momentary phase,
which should always be considered in the larger framework of the
policy over a longer period of time. However, the author wishes it
to be clearly understood that this introductory survey is given merely
to explain and to clarify subsequent events. It is not intended in
any sense to be an exhaustive account of Italian pre-war diplomacy
affecting the relations of Italy with Austria-Hungary and the outbreak of the World War. It is an outline of the diplomatic history
based upon documentary material, but it is definitely limited to
those elements of the problem which serve to throw light on the
question of the Italian negotiations at the Peace Conference, which
question is the subject of the present work. For the same reason,
the story has been followed beyond the adjournment of the Peace
Conference proper to the settlements of Rapallo and Sèvres, which
are but the conclusion of the same episode.

The author wishes to express his indebtedness to Professor James
T. Shotwell, who is primarily responsible for the inclusion of this
work in the present series. Professor Shotwell was a member of
The Inquiry and subsequently of the American Peace Delegation;
his consequent acquaintance with events and personalities has proved
invaluable and has been freely drawn upon. Professor Robert C.
Binkley, through his wide knowledge of the history of the Peace
Conference, has made important suggestions, both on questions of
major policy and on matters of detail; through him and thanks to
the courtesy of Dr. Charles Seymour, it has been possible to make

use of the correspondence between Ambassador T. N. Page and Colonel House. Dr. Bowman, Chief Territorial Specialist of the American Delegation, has been kind enough to read the original manuscript and has offered valuable suggestions.

In addition to the editors of the present series, Major Thomas H. Thomas, who was in Italy during the war and in Paris in 1919, has given freely of his time in reading the manuscript and offering numerous and valuable comments and suggestions. To Mrs. Gino Speranza are due special thanks for permission to make use of the Daily Reports drawn up for Ambassador Page by Gino Speranza and forwarded to Paris. Through the courtesy of the American Geographical Society, the author has had access to the maps drawn for The Inquiry under the direction of Professor Mark Jefferson. Mr. John Philip is responsible for the draftsmanship of the maps appearing in the present volume. Thanks are due to Miss Harriet J. Church for the compilation of the index.

The present work, it is hoped, may serve the twofold purpose of presenting a fair factual account of events, and, through this account, to assist understanding to take the place of what has been unfortunately too often, misunderstanding born of misinformation.

RENÉ ALBRECHT-CARRIÉ

New York
March 28, 1938

CONTENTS

INTRODUCTION

THE WAR

(*JULY, 1914–OCTOBER, 1918*)

PART ONE

THE ORLANDO-SONNINO MINISTRY

(*NOVEMBER, 1918–JUNE, 1919*)

CONTENTS

MAPS

INTRODUCTION: THE WAR

(JULY, 1914—OCTOBER, 1918)

I

THE TREATY OF LONDON

THE OUTBREAK OF WAR—ITALY AND THE
TRIPLE ALLIANCE

IN THE LATE SPRING of 1915 Italy joined forces with the Entente Powers against the Central European Empires. That step she took as the result of a carefully negotiated and definite understanding, the much discussed Treaty or Pact of London, which, despite later declarations and changed conditions, remained in 1919 the written charter of Italian aspirations. It is therefore essential to bear in mind the provisions of that agreement in any discussion of the course followed by the Italian representatives during the long-drawn-out controversy lasting from the autumn of 1918 to that of 1920. The peculiar circumstances which caused the issue of secret treaties and old diplomacy versus the new order to center around that treaty more than any other, enhance alike its interest and its importance. It is our purpose to trace the vicissitudes of that controversy from the evidence—bulky, though still incomplete—available at the present time.

The Treaty of London had its immediate origins in the situation created by the war; more remotely, it arose from the peculiar position of Italy in the general scheme of Europe. Without taking a completely deterministic view of a nation's foreign policy[1] or attempting to minimize the rôle and influence of contrasting social philosophies, it is true nevertheless that there is a large fixed residuum which no foreign office can afford to disregard, at least in its broader aspects.[2] In the case of Italy, geography tends to orient her policy with unusual clarity: the Italian peninsula is a more sharply defined entity, both physically and ethnically, than are many continental European states. Toward the sea, the capital fact is the complete dependence

[1] As, for instance, Toscano in his study on the origins of the Pact of London, *Il patto di Londra*, pp. 3-4.

[2] The continuity of French foreign policy under the Third Republic, among the kaleidoscopic succession of ministries, is a case in point. Even Soviet Russia, despite her thoroughgoing break with nationalist diplomacy, has gradually reverted to many of the traditional policies of the Czars.

of her trade routes on the exits of the Mediterranean, Gibraltar and Suez. Of even closer and more immediate interest must be the situation in the adjacent Adriatic waters and on the eastern shore of that sea, the Balkan peninsula. The Alps and the Mediterranean, merging in the Adriatic, must always be borne in mind in any discussion of Italian foreign policy.

The Pact of London was not born full grown out of chaos, but was rather the adaptation of a continuous line of thought to the circumstances of the time. For that reason, while this is not the place to embark on an exhaustive discussion of Italian foreign policy previous to 1918, it is necessary to follow, if only briefly, the thread of that policy through the negotiations from July, 1914, to May, 1915, to its culmination in the signature of the Treaty and the Italian declaration of war. That story cannot yet be told completely, owing to the lack of certain important documentary material. There is, however, sufficient evidence in the published archives of the Central Powers, the revelations of the Russian Foreign Office, and the *Italian Green Book* of 1915, in addition to numerous personal memoirs, to make it possible to speak with a fair assurance of accuracy.[3]

In 1914, Italy was a member of the Triple Alliance. That partner-

[3] For a critical description of the material published prior to 1930 see the discussion in *The Origins of the World War*, by Sidney B. Fay, I, 3-32. The Austrian documents were published in the collection *Oesterreich-Ungarns Aussenpolitik von der bosnischen Krise bis zum Kriegsausbruch 1914*, in 9 vols. (Vienna, 1930). The references to this collection in the following text are given under the abbreviation "Oe-U." Most of these will also be found in the *Austrian Red Book*, in 3 vols., published by Dr. Roderich Gooss, in 1919 (English translation, 1920). References to this source are abbreviated "A.R.B."; it extends to Aug. 27. whereas the former collection goes only as far as Aug. 1. Of particular value for this study is the publication, *Diplomatic Documents concerning the Relations of Austria-Hungary with Italy from July 20, 1914, to May 23, 1915*, a collection of 221 documents published by the Austro-Hungarian Government (Vienna, 1915). This source is referred to as "D.D." The German publication, *Die deutschen Dokumente zum Kriegsausbruch 1914*, in 4 vols. (Berlin, 1927), an enlarged edition of the 1919 publication of the same title collected by Karl Kautsky, is referred to as "K.D."

The *Italian Green Book*, of May, 1915, gives Italian documents for the period from Dec., 1914, to May, 1915. It is referred to as "I.G.B." Possession of the Italian cipher enabled the Russian Foreign Office to read communications between the Italian Foreign Office and its Ambassador in Petrograd. The material of Russian origin bearing on this study is conveniently collected in *Das zaristische Russland in Weltkriege* (Part IV, "Russland und Italien"), edited by von Wegerer (Berlin, 1927) and in the publication, *L'intervento dell'Italia nei documenti segreti dell'Intesa* (Rome, 1923). The French and British documentary collections do not extend beyond Aug. 4 and Sept. 1, 1914, respectively.

Probably the most complete study, to date, of the negotiations leading up to the Treaty of London is Toscano's *Il patto di Londra* (Bologna, 1934). There is, in addition, considerable periodical literature, which it is beyond the scope of the present work to analyze. On the use of the above-mentioned material in the following pages, see the statement in the author's preface.

ship, begun in 1882, had been renewed several times, with gradual modifications to keep it in harmony with changing conditions.[4] Perhaps the most striking element of the Alliance was the partnership between Italy and Austria-Hungary. The achievement of Italian unity, it must be remembered, had been the result of one long struggle against Austria; indeed the purposely unfavorable frontier of 1866 had left an Italian *irredenta* under Austrian rule. This situation was at once a source of strength and of weakness to the Alliance. On one hand, if relations were to remain peaceful, both countries had a common interest in covering up their differences under the cloak of friendship, which the very existence of the Alliance made it easier to do. On the other hand, the whole spirit of the *Risorgimento*, attenuated but not dead, had been strongly anti-Austrian, and there always remained the possibility that the latent Italian irredentism might flare up into open discord.[5] No less serious was the fact that the Dual Monarchy, in order to maintain its position, was led to seek an expansion of its influence, if not of its territory, in the Balkans. The naval situation of Italy in the Adriatic can only be compared with that of her unfavorable northeastern Alpine frontier. The Austro-Italian rivalry in the Balkans and the Adriatic was at least as real as the Franco-Italian rivalry in North Africa.[6]

Matters were not helped by such events as the annexation of Bosnia-Herzegovina in 1908, which upset the unstable balance in the Balkans in favor of Austria-Hungary, or the friction that had developed over Italian naval action against Turkey during the war of 1911-12.[7] Long before 1914 Italy had begun to flirt with the Entente; her relations with Great Britain had always remained cordial and,

[4] In 1887, 1891, 1902, and lastly in 1912. Shortly after the renewal of 1912 Italy informed Germany that political conditions would make it impossible for her to send troops to the Rhine, as provided by the agreement of 1888, in the event of war between Germany and France. In 1909 a special agreement supplementing Article VII of the Treaty of Alliance had been made between Italy and Austria-Hungary.

[5] Trento and Trieste remained the rallying cry of Italian nationalism, not incomparable to the cry for Alsace-Lorraine in France. There was this important difference, however, that whereas nationalistic agitation in France was—broadly speaking—mainly kept alive by the conservative elements, Italian nationalism, associated with the Mazzinian tradition, caused the liberal elements to have little enthusiasm for the Austrian association whose main support—again broadly speaking—was conservative and clerical. It must also be said that the cry for Nice and Savoy was not unknown in Italy.

[6] The establishment of the French protectorate over Tunis in 1881 had contributed to push Italy into the Triple Alliance. On the Tunisian origins of the Triple Alliance, cf. Salvatorelli, "La Triplice Alleanza," *Rassegna di politica internazionale*, May, 1936.

[7] On this point, cf. *Italian Green Book*, Document 6.

with the turn of the century, there had begun a *rapprochement* with France. With correct insight, Italian policy was alive to the potentialities of having a stake in each of two fairly evenly balanced groups of Powers.[8]

The Sarajevo murder in itself was no necessary cause for war, nor was it so interpreted generally in Europe, despite the sensation it created. But when Austria-Hungary took the position that it was a matter of life and death to her continued existence to administer a crushing and lasting rebuke to disruptive nationalist agitation, this naturally brought up the question of Italy's position under the Treaty of Alliance. Two points are of especial importance: the *casus foederis* and compensations. The first was covered by Articles III, IV, and V, which provided as follows:

Article III. If one, or two, of the High Contracting Parties, without direct provocation on their part, should chance to be attacked and to be engaged in a war with two or more Great Powers nonsignatory to the present Treaty, the *casus foederis* will arise simultaneously for all the High Contracting Parties.

Article IV. In case a Great Power nonsignatory to the present Treaty should threaten the security of the states of one of the High Contracting Parties, and the threatened Party should find itself forced on that account to make war against it, the two others bind themselves to observe towards their Ally a benevolent neutrality. Each of them reserves to itself, in this case, the right to take part in the war, if it should see fit, to make common cause with its Ally.

Article V. If the peace of one of the High Contracting Parties should chance to be threatened under the circumstances foreseen by the preceding Articles, the High Contracting Parties shall take counsel together in ample time as to the military measures to be taken with a view to eventual coöperation.

They engage, henceforth, in all cases of common participation in a war, to conclude neither armistice, nor peace, nor treaty, except by common agreement among themselves.

[8] The Franco-Italian *rapprochement* was made possible by the fall of Crispi, in 1896. A commercial treaty in 1899, ending a prolonged tariff war, was followed by an agreement in regard to North Africa (Morocco, Tunis, Tripoli) negotiated between Visconti Venosta and Barrère in 1900 and, two years later, by the Prinetti-Barrère exchange of Notes, whereby each country undertook to remain neutral even in the event that the other should take the initiative in declaring war in defense of its honor or security.

The annexation of Bosnia-Herzegovina, of which Italy had received no previous notification, served to revive anti-Austrian feeling in Italy and contributed to the signature at Racconigi in October, 1909, of the Tittoni-Izvolski agreement, one of whose aims it was to insure a common policy in regard to the European East and the Straits.

The subject of compensations was covered by Article VII:

Article VII. Austria-Hungary and Italy, having in mind only the maintenance, so far as possible, of the territorial status quo in the Orient, engage to use their influence to forestall any territorial modification which might be injurious to one or the other of the Powers signatory to the present Treaty. To this end, they shall communicate to one another all information of a nature to enlighten each other mutually concerning their own dispositions, as well as those of other Powers. However, if, in the course of events, the maintenance of the status quo in the regions of the Balkans or of the Ottoman coasts and islands in the Adriatic and in the Aegean Sea should become impossible, and if, whether in consequence of the action of a third Power or otherwise, Austria-Hungary or Italy should find themselves under the necessity of modifying it by a temporary or permanent occupation on their part, this occupation shall take place only after a previous agreement between the two Powers, based upon the principle of a reciprocal compensation for every advantage, territorial or other, which each of them might obtain beyond the present status quo, and giving satisfaction to the interests and well founded claims of the two Parties.[9]

The significance of Article VII for this study is that Italy desired to preserve the *status quo* in the Balkans: she did not wish them to fall under the predominant influence of either Austria-Hungary or Russia. There is no indication that she entertained any designs of territorial acquisitions in that area; her position was rather the defensive one of maintaining herself in the Adriatic.

As Austria-Hungary and Germany were not subject to attack by a Great Power early in July, 1914, the *casus foederis* was not in question at first. The situation clearly fell under the provisions of Article VII. Austria could and did claim that her security was threatened by Serbian intrigues. That claim raised the question of the existence of such intrigues, their connection, if any, with the Sarajevo murder, and what responsibility the Serbian Government could be held to have in them. Under the circumstances, Article VII called for consultation. Austria did consult with Germany on July 5, but, rightly suspecting that Italy would not favor drastic action against Serbia, she abstained from taking that country into her confidence. Germany approved this course. On July 6 the German Chancellor was reported to Vienna as considering "the present moment as more

[9] Treaty of the Triple Alliance of 1912. Text from Pribram, *The Secret Treaties of Austria-Hungary*, I, 244-59.

favorable [to action in the Balkans] than a later time; he agrees wholly with us that we need inform neither Italy nor Rumania beforehand of an intended action against Servia."[10] In accordance with this, Berchtold informed Mérey, his Ambassador in Rome, that "the Italian Government should not be informed, but placed in a situation that cannot be averted, by our grave *démarche* in Belgrade."[11] Two days later, Flotow, the German Ambassador in Rome, was informed that Germany would support whatever action seemed appropriate to Austria, and advised not to notify the Italians.[12]

Already on this date (July 14), the Italian attitude had begun to take shape. San Giuliano, the Italian Foreign Minister, maintained that a Government could not be held accountable for mere political propaganda, and expressed the fear that the Austrian attitude would run counter to the feelings of the Italian people and their liberal principles. He insisted that Italy could not oppose the principle of nationality.[13] Flotow correctly interpreted this speech as an indication that Italy was divorcing herself from Austrian action.

Article VII now began to come into play. In view of the turn of the situation, in particular the Russian attitude, Germany began to show concern over Italy. Jagow, the German Foreign Minister, was convinced that in the event of an Austro-Serbian conflict, Italian sympathies would be definitely on the Serbian side. It was therefore

of the utmost importance that Vienna should come to an understanding with the Cabinet in Rome on the aims that would be pursued by Austria in the event of conflict with Serbia, and place Italy on her side, or at least —since a conflict with Serbia alone *does not constitute a casus foederis*— make sure of her strict neutrality. By virtue of her agreements with Austria, Italy is entitled to compensations for any modification in the Balkans in favor of the Danube Monarchy. This subject of compensations could constitute the object and the bait of negotiations with Italy.[14]

It is important to notice that the initiative came from Berlin. Jagow further added that Italy did not seem to consider Valona suitable compensation, that she seemed to have no desire to acquire territory on the eastern shore of the Adriatic, and that only the Trentino

[10] Szögyény to Berchtold, July 6, 1914, *Oe-U.*, Doc. 10076.
[11] Berchtold to Mérey, July 12, *Oe-U.*, Doc. 10221.
[12] Jagow to Flotow, July 14, *K.D.*, Doc. 33.
[13] Flotow to Jagow, July 14, *K.D.*, Doc. 42.
[14] Jagow to Tschirschky, July 15, *K.D.*, Doc. 46. Author's italics.

would probably be regarded as sufficient compensation by her.[15] The idea of bribing certain newspapers to organize a press campaign in Italy in favor of the Central Powers was discouraged alike by the German and the Austrian ambassadors as impractical under the circumstances and likely to prove a boomerang.[16] Pending further developments, it was agreed between Berlin and Vienna that, in deference to the Alliance, San Giuliano should be informed twenty-four hours in advance of what action Austria proposed to take against Serbia.[17]

Germany and Austria did not see eye to eye in the matter of compensations to Italy under Article VII. Germany, who, in the last analysis, could not be called upon to make personal sacrifices, could afford to be more detached, and had no difficulty in seeing the similarity between the Austro-Serbian controversy and that between Austria and Italy of a century before, both having arisen out of the forces of nationalism.[18] Despite his own devotion to the Alliance, San Giuliano had a clear understanding both of Italian interests and of Italian opinion.[19] Jagow insisted that Vienna cherish no illusions on the score of the Italian attitude,[20] but apparently failed to induce Berchtold to act in accordance with this view.[21] In a conversation with Stolberg, councillor at the German Embassy in Vienna, Berchtold, emphasizing the futility of a mere diplomatic victory, said that he intended to face Italy with a *fait accompli*. Discussing the subject with Hoyos immediately afterwards, and asked whether the Germans were thinking of the Trentino as the object of compensations, Stolberg replied in the affirmative.[22]

[15] *Ibid.*

[16] Cf. *Oe-U.*, Docs. 10264, 10290, 10306, 10308; *K.D.*, Docs. 44, 47, 54, 59, 128.

[17] Berchtold to Mérey, July 15, *Oe-U.*, Doc. 10289.

[18] "If Austria intends to suppress by violence the aspirations of Serbian nationalism, it would be quite impossible for an Italian Government to follow her on that ground; all the traditions of the idea of nationality and of liberal principles prevent Italy from starting on that road." Flotow to Jagow, July 16, *K.D.*, Doc. 64; also Doc. 73.

[19] Flotow to Jagow, July 16 and 17, *K.D.*, Docs. 64, 60.

[20] Jagow to Tschirschky, July 18, *K.D.*, Doc. 68.

[21] It should be mentioned here that in this matter, and not without justification, Vienna was suspicious of Berlin. Mérey thought that San Giuliano had been informed by the Germans of the Austrian plans. Mérey to Berchtold, July 18; Berchtold to Mérey, July 20, *Oe-U.*, Docs. 10364, 10418.

Bülow, in his memoirs, makes the charge that Italy's repeated attempts, during the week before the twenty-third, to find out from Jagow Austria's real intentions were met by persistent evasion and misrepresentation. *Memoirs of Prince von Bülow*, III, 188.

[22] Stolberg to Jagow, July 18, *K.D.*, Doc. 87.

Two days later (July 20) Tschirschky, the German Ambassador in Vienna, again urged Berchtold to negotiate with Italy, but found him not very helpful; while recognizing Italian opposition, Berchtold thought Italy too weak to intervene actively and was also concerned over the possibility that information given to Italy might find its way to Russia.[23] He went so far as to send Mérey instructions showing that Article VII did not apply to the present situation but advised him to avoid being drawn into a discussion of the interpretation of this Article.[24] On the twenty-first, San Giuliano told Mérey that it was Italy's intention to support Austria-Hungary if the Austrian demands were such that they could be complied with, but that if it were otherwise he could not go against the feeling of the whole country. Mérey assured San Giuliano that Austria had no intention of territorial acquisitions, but made it clear that he could take no engagement to that effect.[25] Considering the way that temporary occupations have of becoming permanent (Cyprus, Bosnia-Herzegovina, Dodecanese, to cite only a few), San Giuliano could hardly feel reassured by such an announcement.

On July 23 the Austrian note was presented to Serbia without Italy having been notified of its contents even twenty-four hours in advance, as had been planned originally.[26]

On being apprised of the contents of the Austrian note, Salandra, the Italian Prime Minister, and San Giuliano agreed on the course to be pursued. This was outlined in a memorandum to the King, the main points of which were:

1. Insist that Italy has no obligation to take part in the war, owing to the fact that she has not been consulted by her Allies.[27]

2. Make sure that our Allies accept our interpretation of Article VII before giving them any support, even diplomatic.

[23] Tschirschky to Bethmann-Hollweg, July 20, *K.D.*, Doc. 94; cf. *Oe-U.*, Doc. 10398. In view of the Racconigi agreement, Berchtold's fears were not without foundation.

[24] Berchtold to Mérey, July 20 and 21, *Oe-U.*, Docs. 10420, 10458.

[25] Mérey to Berchtold, July 21, *Oe-U.*, Doc. 10458.

[26] The Italian Government was informed on the twenty-third by the Austrian Embassy that the Austrian note was being delivered in Belgrade that day. It was not until the next day that Salandra, who had gone to Fiuggi to meet San Giuliano, received communication of its contents by telephone from Rome, in the midst of a conversation between the two Italian Ministers and Flotow. Salandra, *La neutralità italiana*, p. 75.

[27] Compare Flotow to Jagow, July 24, *K.D.*, Doc. 156. Upon being informed by Jagow of the Italian situation, the Kaiser wrote the interesting marginal comment in reference to compensations, "The little thief always wants to gobble up something at the same time as the others." Jagow to the Kaiser, July 25, *K.D.*, Doc. 168.

3. Make sure of compensations for any territorial increase of Austria.

4. Make sure of compensations in the improbable event of our participation in the war, a decision which should be made deliberately and without precipitation.

5. Possibly secure some minor compensations, or at least the safeguard of our interests, in exchange for any diplomatic support of our Allies.[28]

Instructions to the same effect were sent to Bollati and Avarna, the Italian Ambassadors in Berlin and Vienna respectively.[29]

From that time the Italian attitude began to stiffen. San Giuliano was suspicious of the Austrian disclaimer of any intention to annex territory[30] and had already told Flotow that he considered the situation extremely serious.[31] Flotow analyzed the position of the Italian Government under three points: first, fear of public opinion; second, consciousness of military weakness; third, the wish to use the occasion to secure some advantage, possibly the Trentino. With an eye to European complications, San Giuliano maintained that "the Austrian action against Serbia was aggressive, that any possible intervention by Russia and France would not make the war a defensive one, and that the *casus foederis* did not therefore arise." From which Flotow correctly concluded that Italian assistance could not be counted upon, but that a wise attitude on the part of Vienna could prevent Italy from being hostile.[32]

Italy was pursuing a steady course. Avarna, in Vienna, informed the Austrian Foreign Office that Italy would press her demands for compensations under Article VII for even a provisional occupation of Serbian territory,[33] while San Giuliano told Flotow that, failing compensations, Italy would be forced to stand in opposition to Austria.[34] Tschirschky was endeavoring to bring Berchtold around to the view of Rome and Berlin,[35] but found his task such as to elicit the comment, "Austrians always will remain Austrians; a mixture

[28] Given by Salandra, *La neutralità italiana*, pp. 79-80.

[29] San Giuliano to Bollati and Avarna, July 24, Salandra, *op. cit.*, pp. 76-78; cf. Jagow to Tschirschky, July 24, *K.D.*, Doc. 150.

[30] Flotow to Jagow, July 23, *K.D.*, Doc. 119.

[31] Flotow to Jagow, July 22, *K.D.*, Doc. 109.

[32] Flotow to Bethmann-Hollweg, July 25, *K.D.*, Doc. 244.

[33] *Oe-U.*, Doc. 10680, July 25.

[34] Flotow to Jagow, July 26, *K.D.*, Doc. 211.

[35] Tschirschky to Jagow, July 26, *K.D.*, Doc. 212; *Oe-U.*, Doc. 10715.

of pride and folly is not overcome easily or quickly."[36] Germany
growing anxious, Tschirschky, on direct instructions from the Kaiser,
urged Berchtold "for Heaven's sake" to come to terms with Italy
over Article VII,[37] and again on July 30, Szögyény, the Austrian Ambassador in Berlin, repeated the German view of the absolute necessity of conciliating Italy by a liberal interpretation of Article VII.[38]
The preceding day San Giuliano had given a formal reply to the
Austrian advances: emphasizing that Italy was in agreement with
Germany on the question, he pointed to the fact that it was impossible for Italy to abet Austrian policy, pending a clear understanding
on Article VII.[39]

German insistence finally induced Berchtold to accept the Italian
interpretation of Article VII.[40] This was not taken, however, as
meaning the granting of the Italian claim to the Trentino, but merely
as an acceptance of the principle that an understanding should be
reached over that Article. This concession was, moreover, qualified
by the assumption that "Italy will fully do its duty as an ally in
the present conflict."[41] In view of the Russian attitude, Berchtold now
argued that the *casus foederis* arose under Article III of the Triple
Alliance Treaty,[42] but San Giuliano maintained that Italy had neither obligation nor interest in the matter;[43] he refused to entertain
the Austrian offer in regard to Article VII because of the qualifications that went with it, and informed Austria that the Government
had decided to remain neutral.[44]

In fact, Vienna and Rome had only become further estranged;
San Giuliano did not think that there was any prospect of securing
territorial concessions from Austria. His assumption was correct,

[36] Tschirschky to Jagow, July 26, *K.D.*, Doc. 326. On the Austrian side there was continued suspicion of Germany. Mérey to Berchtold, July 26, *Oe-U.*, Doc. 10750.

[37] Berchtold to Mérey, July 28, *Oe-U.*, Doc. 10909.

[38] Szögyény to Berchtold, July 30, *Oe-U.*, Doc. 11030.

[39] Mérey to Berchtold, July 29, *Oe-U.*, Doc. 10988. In 1913, during the second Balkan
war, when Austria-Hungary considered intervening in favor of Bulgaria in order to prevent
the possibility of too great a success by Serbia, San Giuliano and Giolitti, then Prime
Minister, agreed with the Germans in seeking to exercise a restraining influence upon
Vienna. The incident was first disclosed, by way of citing a precedent for the present
situation, by Giolitti speaking in the Chamber on Dec. 5, 1914. Cf. Giolitti, *Memorie della
mia vita*, pp. 502-3; 519-20. For a criticism of the interpretation of his own activity given
by Giolitti on this occasion, cf. Fay, *The Origins of the World War*, I, 448; 454-55.

[40] Berchtold to Mérey, Aug. 1, *A.R.B.*, III, Docs. 86, 87.

[41] Berchtold to Mérey, Aug. 1, *A.R.B.*, III, Doc. 86.

[42] Berchtold to Mérey, Aug. 2, *A.R.B.*, III, Doc. 106.

[43] Mérey to Berchtold, Aug. 1, *A.R.B.*, III, Doc. 88.

[44] On Aug. 1, Mérey to Berchtold, Aug. 2, *A.R.B.*, III, Doc. 109.

for Austria was aiming only at preventing a break by undertaking protracted negotiations. Both Vienna and Rome turned more and more to Berlin, especially as relations between San Giuliano and Mérey were far from cordial. The latter was opposed from the beginning to any concession, either of territory or of principle, and in the later stages described the Italian attitude as blackmail, pure and simple. That view has, in fact, received considerable credence, but, from the evidence just reviewed, must appear hardly justified at this time. That the initial dispute did not involve the *casus foederis* was clear. Austrian action in the Balkans did, however, definitely call for consultation—it was the very purpose of Article VII to provide for just such a situation as the present—and, by agreeing to ignore Italy, Germany and Austria were the first to violate both the letter and the spirit of the Treaty. That they did this because they correctly surmised that Italy would oppose their plans can hardly be held justification. The further Italian argument that the Austrian action was aggressive is on a somewhat different plane, for it implied judgment of responsibilities. Lacking sufficient evidence at the time, such a matter could easily be decided to suit convenience.[45] On the Austrian side it may be said that if what Italy really wanted as compensation was the Trentino, it would have been well-nigh impossible to grant that demand: the assistance of an Italy unprepared for war[46] would have been no compensation for the moral effect of such a transfer of territory at the outset of the war.

Behind the legal technicalities of the situation stands the more fundamental fact that in 1914 the Triple Alliance was no longer adequate to the existing conditions and could not survive the test of trial. To have joined Germany and Austria would have put Italy in the position of waging war in furtherance of interests inimical to her own. This she quite naturally declined to do. If any further inducements had been necessary to point her way clearly, the inva-

---

[45] Cf. San Giuliano's memorandum of July 24 to the King, see below, p. 18. The distinction should be pointed out between the positions of Austria-Hungary and of Germany with respect to Italy, since no mention of Germany occurs in Article VII. The fact remains, however, that as signatory of the whole treaty Germany had an important stake in the matter and could not dissociate herself from Austria-Hungary, as further shown by the fact of consultation between these two Powers.

[46] The Tripolitan war had been a considerable drain on Italian military and financial resources, and the deficiency—mainly for financial reasons—had not been made good by 1914. This situation was well known to Italy's Allies as well as to the Entente, and the purely military value of Italian intervention in 1914 should therefore not be overestimated. It was—or at least was thought to be—otherwise in the spring of 1915.

sion of Belgium, which aroused public opinion to a considerable extent, and the British intervention, amply sufficed to remove any hesitations. On August 3 Italy formally proclaimed her neutrality.

The whole situation can perhaps best be summed up in the words of her Prime Minister at the time:

> The behavior of Austria, with Germany's explicit approval, put us in a juridical position that was clear and sound and of which it would have been unforgivable for any Italian Government not to take advantage. We were free from obligations; we had well founded claims to put forward; we could freely choose our way.[47]

Italy was thus the only important Power in Europe outside the struggle, which put her in a very delicate position. The situation called for caution, for the consequences of backing the loser were not to be faced lightly. Having separated herself from the Central Powers, Italy could expect little profit from a victory of their arms; she was therefore committed in some degree to a triumph of the Entente or at least to a stalemate. Neutrality once decided upon, there was no question of joining her Allies at some later time, and the issue from that moment was solely between continued neutrality and active intervention on the side of the Entente, an issue to be decided exclusively on grounds of self-interest.

The declaration of neutrality naturally put an end, for the time, to negotiations between Rome, Vienna, and Berlin. With an eye to possible future developments, the Central Powers, especially Germany, decided to accept the inevitable with good grace and acknowledged the correctness of the Italian attitude.[48] Among the Entente Powers, Italian neutrality was naturally highly welcome, but it is none the less surprising that there were thoughts of the possibility of immediate Italian coöperation. The idea that Italy might join the Entente at once seems to have been primarily Russian, based apparently on a strategy analogous to that planned by Ger-

[47] Salandra, *La neutralità italiana*, p. 86. This, it should be noted, was written in 1928; presumably under the influence of events subsequent to 1914, Salandra makes the further comment: "The defeat of Serbia . . . and her reduction to the condition of an impotent vassal state, meant the definitive hegemony of Austria, and through her the triumphal invasion of Germanism in the Balkan peninsula: that is, the loss to us of any possibility of expansion; the loss of the Adriatic commercially and militarily." *Ibid.*, p. 87.

[48] Berchtold to Macchio, Aug. 28, *D.D.*, Doc. 49. Under the circumstances, this acknowledgment can hardly be quoted as evidence of the validity of the Italian attitude. Like that attitude itself, it was dictated exclusively by interest and convenience, quite independently of the merits of the case. That Italy had a sound legal position did not in fact lessen Austrian and German resentment against her, the evidence of which abounds.

many in the west—the crushing at the very outset of Austria-Hungary by simultaneous attack on three fronts.[49] As early as August 1 and again on the fifth,[50] Izvolski, the Russian Ambassador in Paris, communicated to Sazonov, at the Russian Foreign Ministry, the French willingness to have Italy receive the Trentino and Valona; the French preferred to have the negotiations conducted by Russia. Sazonov, with Paléologue and Buchanan, the French and British Ambassadors in Petrograd, were urging in pressing terms the favorable opportunity to the Italian Ambassador, Carlotti, the last two conveying a slight nuance of threat.[51] Grey, in London, thought that Trieste should also be offered to Italy,[52] then modified this by saying that England would not contest with Italy the possession of what she might herself acquire in the Adriatic.[53] Sazonov wanted the Entente Ambassadors in Rome to take up the question with San Giuliano, but was dissuaded on the ground that too overt pressure might hurt Italian sensibilities and have the opposite effect to the one desired.[54] On the tenth Sazonov was ready to propose an agreement on the following basis:

1. The Italian army and navy shall attack immediately the Austro-Hungarian army and fleet.

2. After the war, the Trentino and the ports of Trieste and Valona shall be annexed to Italy.[55]

But, despite Russian urgings, the British and French Ambassadors in Rome, Rodd and Barrère, only discussed the question in vague terms with Salandra and San Giuliano. Krupenski, the Russian Ambassador, went to visit the latter in Fiuggi; San Giuliano definitely stated the impossibility of immediate intervention but indicated the conditions under which it might be discussed in time:

[49] It has been suggested (Solmi, *Le origini del patto di Londra*, p. 132) that the French were reluctant to take the initiative in this negotiation, owing to the friction with Italy during the Tripolitan war, while Russo-Italian relations had remained distinctly cordial. The negotiation once begun, it was mainly pushed by Sazonov. Cf. Toscano, *Il patto di Londra*, p. 34.

[50] Izvolski to Sazonov, Aug. 5, *L'intervento dell'Italia nei documenti segreti dell'Intesa*, Doc. 3.

[51] Carlotti to San Giuliano, Aug. 6 and 8, *L'intervento*, Docs. 4, 9.

[52] Benckendorff to Sazonov, Aug. 6, *L'intervento*, Doc. 5.

[53] Benckendorff to Sazonov, Aug. 8, *L'intervento*, Doc. 8.

[54] Benckendorff to Sazonov, Aug. 8; Doumergue to Paléologue, Aug. 11, *L'intervento*, Docs. 10, 16.

[55] Aug. 10, *L'intervento*, Doc. 12.

1. Negotiations must be conducted with the greatest secrecy, and for that reason must take place in London and in London only;

2. The French, British, and Italian fleets must act in agreement;

3. The four Powers must undertake not to make separate peace.[56]

It proved difficult to convince Sazonov, and San Giuliano found it necessary to state formally that he would refuse to discuss the matter any further and that he wished not to have it mentioned again by the Entente Ambassadors.[57]

Such an attitude on San Giuliano's part was only natural, especially if opinion in Italy is taken into account. On the strength of treaty obligations, it might have been possible for the Government to drag the country into war on the side of her Allies. The country's interest and Austro-German tactics provided a good case for neutrality, which was accepted with relief. On the other hand, pending the uncertain outcome of the struggle, Italy certainly was not subject to an immediate and direct menace which would make her intervention appear a matter of self-defense. Salandra was quite correct in emphasizing the need for slow and careful preparation, both material and spiritual, if Italy were to take part in the conflict.[58] Her intervention late in August could not have stopped the German drive on Paris. If that drive were to result in a quick victory for the Central Powers, as seemed conceivable at the time, that intervention would have been merely foolish. Temporizing was the only sensible course.

In September the first military stalemate was reached, and as it appeared that the final outcome would be remote and doubtful, the disadvantages of neutrality became more apparent: in the event of an Austro-German victory, Italy's Allies would hardly be friendly toward her, while the Entente would have neither power nor cause to give her support; if the Entente were to triumph, it would have no reason to take Italy into account. In either case, she would be a loser from the new balance that would be established in the Balkans and

---

[56] Krupenski to Sazonov, Aug. 15, *L'intervento*, Doc. 25. Although San Giuliano did not respond to the Russian advances he had nevertheless formulated a fairly definite program as shown by the communication received by Grey from Imperiali on Aug. 12 and which contained a demand for the Brenner frontier and for Trieste. In addition, San Giuliano wanted the Italian concessions at Adalia confirmed but would relinquish the Dodecanese if Turkish integrity were preserved (otherwise he would claim a share of the Mediterranean provinces of Turkey); he would also consent to the partition of Albania and to the placing of Valona under a status similar to that of Tangier. Imperiali made it clear to Grey, however, that this was a mere tentative outline of San Giuliano's personal views. Grey to Rodd, Aug. 12, given in Trevelyan, *Grey of Fallodon*, pp. 331-32.

[57] San Giuliano to Carlotti, Aug. 17, *L'intervento*, Doc. 30.

[58] Salandra, *La neutralità italiana*, Chaps. IV, V.

the Adriatic. With these thoughts before him, Salandra definitely made up his mind that Italy would, in all probability, have to go to war on the side of the Entente, and undertook in earnest the task of preparing the country for the event.[59]

The very fact that Italy could choose her way called for skill in the handling of her diplomacy. She should not, on the one hand, make it obvious that she was preparing to go to war against Austria and Germany, for that would give those Powers time to prepare— possibly to take the initiative against her—while it would weaken her bargaining position with the Entente. On the other hand, the risks of war were not to be taken lightly, and the attempt, at least, must be made to secure concessions from Austria by playing the threat of intervention. That policy has been characterized as blackmail, and scorn has been liberally heaped on it by Italy's Allies before and after 1915 alike. In a sense it was. But it was also sane and sound national policy—even patriotic policy from the Italian point of view. Italy was after all only preparing to take advantage of the favorable situation in which she was thrust by circumstances, in order to maintain at least, and possibly to enhance, her position—a state of affairs not very different from Britain's traditional continental policy—nor can she be accused in this attempt of having put forward inordinately large claims. With the lapse of a hundred years, we shall no doubt be able to look upon this episode dispassionately, much in the same light that we now consider Talleyrand's activities, for example. It is equally natural, on the other hand, that her behavior should have caused resentment on both sides. *Realpolitik* is not an application of Christian morality, and no nation likes to be dealt with by others as it has dealt with them, least of all by a nation which it has been wont to think of as of inferior status.

RENEWED NEGOTIATIONS WITH AUSTRIA-HUNGARY

There was now a comparative lull in diplomatic activity,[60] while Salandra went on with the task of building up the army and of edu-

[59] "We of the Government could not indeed be certain of the duration or final outcome [of the war]. We drew the conclusion that, with the failure of the attempt to crush France at the outset, the war would be prolonged, with growing probabilities of victory for the Entente, less prepared but much richer in men and resources. We drew the conclusion that, sooner or later, our intervention would be inevitable and must be prepared with every effort." Salandra, *op. cit.*, p. 190.

[60] Toscano reports the existence of a treaty with Rumania on September 23, the main purpose of which was to insure common action by the two countries. Like Italy, Rumania was bound by treaty to Germany and Austria-Hungary, and like Italy she had declined to

cating public opinion in preparation for any possible developments and probably for war. He reviewed the situation at length and with clarity in a memorandum to the King on September 30.[61] San Giuliano, who had long been ill, but insisted in keeping his post to the last, died shortly after on October 16, and Salandra took charge of the Foreign Ministry, pending the appointment of a new incumbent. It was on this occasion, while addressing the officials of the *Consulta,* that he used the famous phrase *sacro egoismo.*[62] The phrase achieved a fame unsuspected by its author and much has been made of it since as an avowal of selfish and cynical policy.[63]

During his brief personal direction of the Foreign Office, Salandra had occasion to intervene in Albania. The Prince of Wied had found it expedient to abandon his insecure throne at the end of August and, faster than ever, the little state drifted into chaos, a fertile ground for intrigues on the part of the various interested Powers. Italy was mainly concerned with the activities of irregulars in Northern Epirus and derived but little comfort from Venizelos' assurances that no attempts would be made against Valona. Sonnino, consulted by Salandra, was in favor of outright occupation by Italy, judging that the signatories of the London Convention[64] had their hands too full to offer any opposition,[65] but Salandra seems to have preferred a more formally correct procedure and, without great difficulty, secured the consent of the Powers, though he found the Austro-Ger-

---

join her Allies. The two countries were often dealt with together in the calculations of the Central Powers, as well as of the Entente. Rumania, however, did not go to war until 1916.

The information about the nature of this purported treaty is largely derived from an article by Diamandy, Rumanian minister in Petrograd at the time ("Ma Mission en Russie," *Revue des deux mondes,* Nov. 15, 1930). Salandra, in his memoirs, makes no reference to this treaty. The corroborating evidence is analyzed by Toscano, *Il patto di Londra,* pp. 55-60. The existence of this agreement is mentioned by Pribram, *Austrian Foreign Policy, 1908-18,* p. 74.

[61] Salandra, *op. cit.,* pp. 330-39.

[62] On October 18. "The guiding principles of our international policy will be tomorrow what they were yesterday . . . we need daring, in actions not in words; we need a spirit free from any preconceived idea, from any prejudice, from any sentiment save that of exclusive and unlimited devotion to our country, of 'sacro egoismo' for Italy." Salandra, *op. cit.,* pp. 377-78.

[63] Not least among those to share this view were some of the Americans in Paris in 1919. When later reproached for the words, Salandra pointed out that they were a declaration of neutrality policy, not of war policy, not incomparable to the words "An exclusively American sentiment," used by President Wilson in August, 1914, when describing America's neutrality policy. Salandra's letter to the *Messaggero,* Jan. 9, 1919.

[64] This created the independent state of Albania in 1913.

[65] "They would swallow anything rather than risk pushing new forces into the arms of their enemies." Sonnino, quoted by Salandra, *op. cit.,* p. 396.

mans somewhat more amenable than the Entente.[66] On October 29 an Italian "sanitary mission" landed at Valona and the next day marines took over the islet of Saseno.[67]

Salandra had no intention of remaining at the Foreign Office; he was also in need of a Finance Minister who would be more willing to support the large army expenditures in prospect than the present holder of that office. He decided therefore to reorganize his Cabinet as soon as he had induced Sonnino to take over the foreign portfolio. Sonnino had been one of the few leading Italian statesmen who, in the first days of August, had expressed doubts as to the wisdom on Italy's part of not adhering to her Alliance. However, Sonnino was not swayed by feeling; his policy was and remained thoroughly and exclusively Italian, to the point of blindness perhaps, but certainly marked by considerable firmness.[68] He assumed office on November 5.

When Parliament met in December, Salandra pointedly remarked that "Italy has vital interests to safeguard, justified aspirations to assert, a position of Great Power to maintain and she has to see that that position shall not be relatively impaired through possible increases of other states."[69] The hint could not be lost on Vienna. Using the pretext of the Austro-Hungarian offensive against Serbia, Sonnino repeated now the argument presented by San Giuliano in July that, under the terms of Article VII of the Treaty of Alliance, Italy was entitled to compensations for even a temporary occupation of Serbian territory, pointing in addition to the further disturbance in the Balkans caused by Turkish participation in the war.[70] Berchtold's first reaction was wholly negative, and he tried to draw a fine distinction between "temporary" and "momentary" occupation.[71] However, the lack of success of the Austro-Hungarian offensive gave the discussion a setback.

[66] Salandra, *op. cit.*, p. 399. For a detailed account of the negotiations in regard to Valona, cf. Toscano, *Il patto di Londra*, pp. 60-64; also, Stickney, *Southern Albania*, pp. 52-54.

[67] The "sanitary mission" soon found that it needed armed protection and troops were landed at Valona in December.

[68] Sonnino was the son of a Jewish father and a Scottish mother. The family's fortunes had their origin in Egypt, under the reign of Mehemet Ali, when many people found that country a fertile ground for investment and speculation.

[69] Speech of Dec. 3, 1914. Salandra, *op. cit.*, p. 441. Cf. *Atti del Parlamento, 1913-19, Camera, Discussioni*, VI, 5533.

[70] Sonnino to Avarna, Dec. 9, *I.G.B.*, Doc. 1; cf. Berchtold to Mérey, Dec. 12, *D.D.*, Doc. 74.

[71] Avarna to Sonnino, Dec. 12 and 13, *I.G.B.*, Docs. 2, 3; Berchtold to Macchio, Dec. 21, *D.D.*, Doc. 78.

Germany now intervened actively by sending Bülow on a special mission to Rome in replacement of Flotow,[72] in an endeavor definitely to secure Italian neutrality by bringing Vienna and Rome to terms. Bülow went to see Sonnino and Salandra at once[73] and the discussion turned immediately to the Trentino. In Salandra's words, "about the Trentino we can talk; for Trieste, impossible." On his side, Bülow seems to have found conditions worse than he had expected and urged in Berlin the importance of Austrian concessions. The slow-moving Austrian Foreign Office still insisted on talking about Albania while Bülow was already discussing with Sonnino the actual extent of concessions in the Trentino: he suggested the former bishopric of Trent, to spare the feelings of the old Emperor, very sensitive on the subject of the Tyrol, and wished the eventual agreement to be kept secret.[74]

Internal Italian politics intervened at this time in the negotiations. Opinion was still very much divided on the issue of neutrality and war, and all the elements advocating the first course rallied around Giolitti, generally recognized as the greatest political power in the country, who had made no secret of his views on the subject. Rumor accused him of dealing with Bülow behind the scenes and, in a purported attempt at denial, a letter of Giolitti was published, wherein he stated that "it would not seem improbable that, in the present condition of Europe, *parecchio* might be obtained without war."[75] The letter merely gave rise to further controversy and to the charge that Giolitti knew the extent of the German offer, and associated him definitely with the Austro-German, or neutrality, party.

[72] Bülow was eminently qualified for the task. He knew Italy well from long residence in that country; his wife belonged to the Italian aristocracy and he had an easy entrée to social, political, and financial circles.

[73] Sonnino to Avarna, Dec. 20, *I.G.B.*, Doc. 8. Salandra, *op. cit.*, pp. 466-70.

[74] Sonnino to Avarna, Jan. 15, 1915, *I.G.B.*, Doc. 11. No one seemed to be very clear on the boundaries of the bishopric. On the Austrian position, cf. Berchtold to Macchio, Jan. 7, and Burián to Macchio, Jan. 14, *D.D.*, Docs. 91, 96.

[75] Giolitti's letter to Peano of Jan. 24, published in the *Tribuna* of Feb. 2, 1915. The word *parecchio* conveys the idea of an undetermined but substantial amount. In his memoirs, Giolitti reproduces the letter, using *molto* (much) in place of *parecchio* (Giolitti, *Memorie della mia vita*, p. 529). The term became associated with Giolitti, who was often subsequently referred to as "the man of the *parecchio*."

Giolitti, in his memoirs, denies all contact with the German Embassy or Bülow who, in turn, makes no reference to any contact with Giolitti in his own memoirs. Both men give a very unsatisfactory account of their activity during this period, and against their negative evidence, we have the statement: "The German Ambassador, in conformity with his instructions, to-day read me two long reports by Prince Bülow from Rome. They referred to his conversations with Baron Sonnino and Giolitti on Italy's attitude toward the Dual Monarchy." Berchtold to Macchio, Jan. 4, *D.D.*, Doc. 88.

In Vienna, Burián who had succeeded Berchtold on January 14, continued the latter's tactics of delay.[76] He professed to be highly indignant at Sonnino's contention that Italy, as a neutral, could not be satisfied with cessions at the expense of a third party (meaning other than Austria), for that would give her a stake in the conflict;[77] he sought to counter the Italian claim to compensations under Article VII by entering counterclaims for the Italian occupation of the Dodecanese and of Valona.[78] Sonnino's reaction was one of impatience, and he threatened to withdraw from the discussion leaving Austria-Hungary responsible for the consequences.[79] He went a step further by insisting that the "previous agreement" of Article VII must precede any military action.[80] It was not until March 9 that the persistent pressure of Rome and Berlin—and the Russian advance in Galicia—finally induced Burián to consider the cession to Italy of territories belonging to the Monarchy.[81] However, this was again no more than an acceptance of principle, and, when it came to the actual cession to be made, the same dilatory recalcitrance was encountered in Vienna. The Italians remained highly skeptical of the value of a promised cession of territory which would not become effective until the end of the war and, for that reason, insisted on immediate cession in the event of agreement.[82] Salandra was, in fact, quite convinced of the futility of the negotiation, but induced Sonnino to keep it alive in order to gain time to complete military

[76] Cf. Avarna's dispatches of Jan. 18, 28, Feb. 9, 12, *I.G.B.*, Docs. 12, 16, 20, 21.

[77] Burián to Macchio, Jan. 20, *D.D.*, Doc. 98. The first definite intimation that Italy wanted Austrian territory was made to Macchio on January 6 when Sonnino "hinted that Italy's territorial aspirations could be satisfied in *one* direction only." Macchio to Berchtold, Jan. 6, *D.D.*, Doc. 90.

[78] Burián to Macchio, Feb. 4, *D.D.*, Doc. 104. Sound as the claim may have been, one may well question whether this was a skillful move; it could serve to complicate the negotiations, hardly to promote their success, when Italy had the whip hand, as Burián himself recognizes. Cf. Burián, *Austria in Dissolution*, pp. 28 ff.

[79] Sonnino to Avarna, Feb. 12, *I.G.B.*, Doc. 22; Burián to Macchio, Feb. 15, *D.D.*, Doc. 106.

[80] Sonnino to Avarna, Feb. 17, *I.G.B.*, Doc. 24; Burián to Macchio, Feb. 23, *D.D.*, Doc. 109.

[81] Avarna to Sonnino, March 9, *I.G.B.*, Doc. 41; Burián to Macchio, March 9, *D.D.*, Doc. 115.

[82] Even Germany's offer to guarantee the execution of the agreement at the end of the war did not change his attitude. Cf. Sonnino to Avarna and Bollati, March 17; Sonnino to Avarna, March 20, *I.G.B.*, Docs. 48, 49. Bülow, on the other hand, still thought that a compromise could be arranged, on the purely territorial extent of the cession at least, unless, as he told Sonnino, "you should already have made up your minds for war in March." Sonnino to Avarna and Bollati, March 15, *I.G.B.*, Doc. 46.

preparations.[83] It was true, as Sonnino repeatedly pointed out, that Article VII spoke of "previous agreement based upon the principle of a reciprocal compensation" before any action in the Balkans. However, to have insisted on immediate benefits, especially under the circumstances, and when the compensations which would accrue to Austria were doubtful to say the least, was perhaps stretching a point. Certainly it was insisting on the letter rather than the spirit of the Treaty, and one can understand the painful position of Burián well aware that he was fighting a losing diplomatic battle. It had been Austria's mistake to put Italy in her initial advantageous position of which the latter took advantage to the full. Burián himself recognizes that "each of the allies was entitled to regard the arrangement [the Alliance] from the point of view of its utility to himself."[84]

Only at the end of March did Burián finally "assent to a cession of territories situated in Southern Tyrol, including the city of Trent,"[85] and, when Sonnino declared that this was insufficient, asked the latter to formulate his own definite proposals.

In reply to Burián's suggestion, Sonnino submitted a definite statement of the Italian demands.[86] In the north, the new frontier was to be that of Napoleon's kingdom of Italy of 1810, eliminating the whole salient of the Trentino (art. 1). In the east, the existing frontier was to be shifted eastward so as to include Gorizia and Gradisca in Italy, joining the sea at Nabresina (art. 2). At that point was to begin a small autonomous state of Trieste consisting of the city of Trieste itself together with some surrounding territory (art. 3). In the Adriatic, Italy claimed the islands of the Curzolare group (art. 4) and Valona with a sufficient hinterland (art. 6). Cession of the territories mentioned in articles 1, 2, and 3 was to take place immediately, and the territory of Trieste was to be evacuated at once (art. 5). In addition, Austria-Hungary was to relinquish all interest in Albania

---

[83] Salandra, L'intervento, p. 116. Salandra's feelings were matched by Burián's conviction of the hopelessness of reaching a satisfactory understanding. Cf. Burián, Austria in Dissolution, pp. 35 ff.

[84] Burián, op. cit., p. 32. Under the circumstances, the question may well be raised whether it would not have been to Austria's advantage to come to terms with Italy at an early date. Difficult as the situation was for Austria, the Italian claims were, after all, essentially confined to Italian territory. The belated and reluctant yielding on the part of Austria enabled Italy to negotiate with the Entente and to raise her terms progressively.

[85] On March 27. Burián to Macchio, March 28, D.D., Doc. 131.

[86] Sonnino to Avarna, April 8, I.G.B., Doc. 64. For the full text of the Italian demands, see below, Document 2.

(art. 7), to release at once all soldiers and sailors from the ceded and evacuated areas, and to amnesty all persons condemned for military or political acts in these same areas (art. 8). In exchange for these advantages, Italy would undertake to maintain absolute neutrality for the duration of the war (art. 10), pay Austria-Hungary 200,-

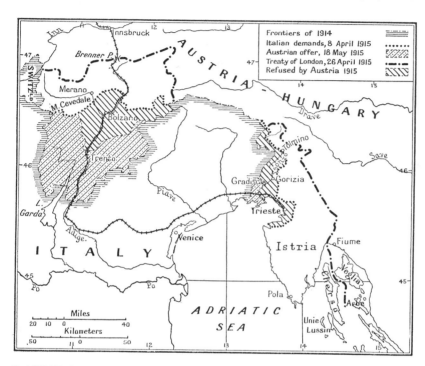

I. NEGOTIATIONS IN 1915: ITALIAN DEMANDS FROM AUSTRIA-HUNGARY, AUSTRIAN OFFER; TREATY OF LONDON

The lines in this map are taken from Temperley, *A History of the Peace Conference of Paris;* Toscano, *Il patto di Londra.*

000,000 gold lire (art. 9), and renounce the right to make any further claims under Article VII, while Austria-Hungary was to undertake a similar engagement in regard to the Italian occupation of the Dodecanese (art. 11).

These demands represented the minimum program for the fulfillment of the aims of Italian policy: redemption of the Italians under Austria; security on land and in the Adriatic.[87] Sonnino and Salandra

---

[8] There was a good deal to be said in favor of the Italian demands. The frontier proposed by Italy would have eliminated the Italian irredentist problem, without creating in its

were afraid for a moment lest their demands be accepted,[88] but their minds were soon set at rest, for Burián's reply was wide of acceptance. The only real concession was in the Tyrol, where a line south of Bolzano was offered.[89] For the rest, substantially a complete refusal.[90] The real and irreconcilable difference was over Trieste and the issue of immediate cession.

This refusal practically ended the negotiation, for Italy was having better success in London than in Vienna.[91] After some further futile exchanges, her military preparation sufficiently advanced, summing up her irreconcilable differences with Austria-Hungary, she took the final step of formally denouncing the Alliance on May 3, 1915.[92]

NEGOTIATIONS WITH THE ENTENTE

The Treaty of London

It is now necessary to go back in time and to survey the negotiations which took place between Italy and the Entente. Our purpose is not so much to write a complete history of these negotiations—still an impossible task—as to follow the continuity of Italian policy and to bring out the main outlines of that policy as the background to the events of 1919.

We have seen how San Giuliano firmly dismissed the attempt to draw Italy in on the side of the Entente in August, 1914.[93] With the

---

place a German and Slav irredentism. Strategically, it was not so good as the line eventually obtained by Italy, especially in the east, but it would have been a vast improvement on the existing frontier. It is a curious commentary that a frontier drawn "according to clearly recognizable lines of nationality" could hardly have improved upon Sonnino's proposal at this time. See Maps IV and V.

[88] In that event, Salandra proposed the following course: "We shall have of course to renounce going to war for the moment; but we shall remain in arms. I shall leave the government. You [Sonnino] will appoint me Minister Plenipotentiary at Trieste and give me an undated decree authorizing me to become Royal Commissioner. Then we shall see." Salandra, *L'intervento*, pp. 120-21.

[89] For the lines proposed by Italy and Austria in the Trentino, see Map I.

[90] Avarna to Sonnino, April 16, *I.G.B.*, Doc. 71.

[91] Italy had been negotiating actively with the Entente since the beginning of March; and signed the Treaty of London on April 26. See below for an account of these negotiations.

[92] Sonnino to Avarna, May 3, *I.G.B.*, Doc. 76. For text see below, Document 4. As a general commentary on the negotiations just reviewed may be cited Sforza's remark: "When . . . I read Sonnino's *Green Book*, I felt a burning pang of sorrow greater than any experienced later on during the dark hours of the war." Sforza, "Sonnino and his Foreign Policy," *Contemporary Review*, Dec. 1929, p. 725; also, *Makers of Modern Europe*, p. 291. For Salandra's defense of Sonnino, cf. Salandra, *L'intervento*, p. 194 n.

[93] See above, pp. 15-16.

Entente, as with the Central Empires, Italy maintained an attitude of reserve for a time.[94] There were, however, some further attempts to commit Italy. On October 24 a Russian offer was made to free Austrian prisoners of Italian nationality, provided Italy should undertake to prevent their return to Austria.[95] Rather more subtly, when Turkey was about to declare war, Great Britain inquired whether Italy would consider lending her assistance in keeping open the Suez Canal in the event of a land attack against Egypt.[96] However, it was not until February, 1915, that Italy began to push the negotiations in earnest. By that time it may be said that the Government had virtually made up its mind to join the Entente. It was only a question of not giving the impression that intervention was a foregone conclusion, lest the Entente should not give Italy sufficiently favorable terms: a position which may fairly be described either as normal and legitimate defense of Italian interests or as selling to the highest bidder, according to one's preference.[97]

Between August, 1914, and February, 1915, there had occurred, however, a shifting of positions. Broadly speaking, it was now Italy that took the initiative, while Russia, who had been the prime mover on the earlier occasion, no longer seemed very anxious for Italian assistance. Sazonov attached less importance to the value of Italy's military coöperation than formerly, while he feared that her participation would tend to complicate the peace settlement and act as an element of discord among the Allies.[98] It was he who now restrained Great Britain and France and thought that his offers of the preceding August should be revised.[99] As early as February 16, Imperiali, Italian Ambassador in London, received from Rome an outline of the Italian demands, which however he was not authorized

[94] On September 25, however, San Giuliano went so far as to draw up a fairly detailed, though not very precise, outline of agreement. San Giuliano to Carlotti, Sept. 25, 1914, *L'intervento dell'Italia nei documenti segreti dell'Intesa*, Doc. 51.

[95] Salandra, *La neutralità italiana*, pp. 387 ff. Not very skillfully, Krupenski gave out news of the offer to the press.

[96] Salandra, *La neutralità italiana*, pp. 411-12.

[97] "Supreme interests were at stake, in some respects the very life of the nation. Who ever would have dared to neglect them on account of more or less elegant and sentimental scruples of personal correctness?" Salandra, *L'intervento*, p. 151. Our proximity to these events tends to color any account of them. Perhaps the only safe thing to do for the present is to refrain from moralistic judgment. Salandra's further comment, "Let them who have acted differently cast stones," does not seem inappropriate.

[98] *L'intervento*, Doc. 81.

[99] Aide-mémoire to the British and French Embassies in Petrograd, Feb. 22, *L'intervento*, Doc. 82.

to present to Grey until March 3.[100] Grey received the Italian memorandum on the fourth, and subsequently (on the tenth) read its contents to Cambon and Benckendorff. From the nature of the *démarche*, Grey inferred the failure of Bülow's mission in Rome; he agreed with the two Ambassadors that the Italian claims were excessive, but thought that they deserved careful consideration and should be met with counter-proposals.[101]

The Italian memorandum has been published by Salandra.[102] Italy claimed the so-called natural frontier of the Alps, i.e., the Trentino and Southern Tyrol to the Brenner in the north; all Istria to Volosca in the east; complete control of the Adriatic through the annexation of Dalmatia as far as the Narenta, and the possession of Valona with a sufficient hinterland, in addition to neutralization of the remaining parts of the coast (see Maps I and II); recognition of the Dodecanese in full sovereignty and a share of Turkish territory in the event of partition of that country, as well as compensation in case the German colonies should be taken over by the Allies.[103] On her part, Italy would use all her resources against Austria-Hungary and Turkey and any Power that should lend them military or naval assistance.[104] She would be ready to go to war in the middle or at the end of April.

As Imperiali told Grey, these demands were motivated by the pursuit of four essential aims: the liberation of the Italians under foreign rule; the obtention of a secure Alpine frontier; the securing in the Adriatic of sufficient guarantees against the danger of leaving too extensive a stretch of coast in the hands of the Slavs; and finally, the safeguarding of Italy's interest as a Mediterranean Power.[105] The Italian memorandum of the fourth marked the beginning of a close negotiation, with Italy and Russia at the opposite extremes, while Great Britain and France endeavored to bridge the gap by securing concessions from both. The majority of the Italian demands (frontier of the Alps, Albania, Dodecanese, Turkey) were accepted without much difficulty; from the first, the discussion centered about Dalmatia. Sazonov insisted that the granting of the Italian demands on

[100] Salandra, *L'intervento*, p. 149.

[101] Benckendorff to Sazonov, March 10, *L'intervento*, Docs. 85, 86; von Wegerer, *Das zaristische Russland im Weltkriege*, (Part IV, "Russland und Italien"), Docs. 57, 58.

[102] Salandra, *L'intervento*, pp. 156-60. For text, see below, Document 1.

[103] In regard to the demand for Jibuti, see below, p. 311.

[104] It is of interest that Germany was not specifically mentioned, and in fact Italy did not declare war on Germany in 1915.

[105] Salandra, *L'intervento*, p. 164.

that coast would merely invite conflict at some future time between Italy and the Serbs and Croats; for that reason, he thought that the share of Serbia and Montenegro along the coast should be determined. According to his views, Montenegro should include Ragusa, Serbia

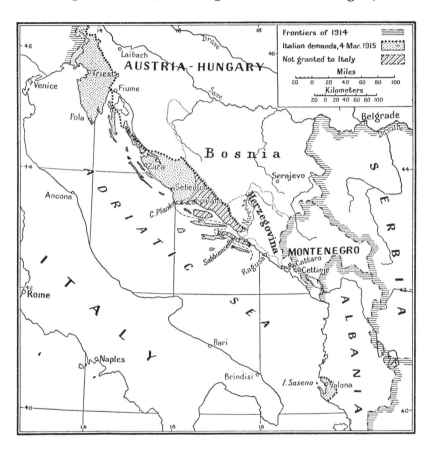

II. NEGOTIATIONS FOR THE TREATY OF LONDON IN THE ADRIATIC: ITALIAN DEMANDS, OFFER OF THE ENTENTE

The lines in this map are taken from Toscano, *Il patto di Londra*.

should have the coast and the islands from there to the Kerka, and the rest of the coast to Volosca should belong to Croatia.[106] In short, he would have excluded Italy entirely from the Eastern Adriatic.

However, Sazonov promptly retreated from his extreme position

[106] Sazonov to Benckendorff and Izvolski, March 15, *L'intervento*, Doc. 89; Sazonov to Krupenski, March 15, von Wegerer, *Das zaristische Russland*, Part IV, Doc. 60.

by yielding Zara and Sebenico, with the intervening coast and islands, himself informing Carlotti of this concession.[107] Striking a middle course, Grey proposed to signify to Sonnino the Entente's acceptance of the majority of his demands, while asking him to reconsider the matter of the Eastern Adriatic.[108] He gave Imperiali the reply to the Italian memorandum on March 20.[109] Imperiali came back three days later hinting that Italy could obtain the majority of her desiderata in exchange for mere neutrality; if she were to face the risks of war, she must therefore obtain some worth-while additional advantage; security in the Adriatic was her main motive in going to war, and nothing would be gained from her point of view by merely replacing Austrian by Slav supremacy in that quarter.[110]

Owing to the importance which he attached to Italian intervention, both for its own sake and for the influence which it might have on other neutral Powers (e.g., Rumania), Grey thought that the demand for control of the Adriatic should essentially be granted.[111] But Sazonov insisted that Spalato at least was indispensable as an outlet for Serbia, and he did not think that the military situation warranted setting such a price to Italian assistance.[112] For some time the tussle went on, Grey defending the Italian point of view in the Adriatic and insisting on the importance of drawing Italy in on the side of the Entente,[113] Sazonov defending the interests of the Slavs, but gradually yielding.[114] On March 29 a second Italian memorandum was forthcoming, in which Italy relinquished Southern Dalmatia from Cape Planka to the Narenta, but neither the islands nor the Sabbioncello peninsula.[115] The difference was thus brought to the vanishing point. Sazonov, under the influence of the Russian capture of Przemyśl, remained very reluctant; he would give Italy

[107] Sazonov to Grey, March 18; Buchanan to Grey, March 20, *L'intervento*, Docs. 92, 93.

[108] Grey to Buchanan, March 16, *L'intervento*, Doc. 90.

[109] *L'intervento*, Doc. 96. In the course of the interview, Imperiali denied that Italy was negotiating with Austria at the same time, though, as he put it, the latter could not be prevented from making offers. To this, Grey hinted at knowledge that the generosity of the Austrian concessions was due only to the determination to take back at the first opportunity what had been given. Grey to Buchanan, March 21, *L'intervento*, Doc. 95.

[110] Aide-mémoire from Buchanan, March 24, *L'intervento*, Doc. 98.

[111] Aide-mémoire from Buchanan, March 24, *L'intervento*, Doc. 99.

[112] Aide-mémoire to Buchanan and Paléologue, March 25, *L'intervento*, Doc. 100.

[113] Aide-mémoire from Buchanan, March 28; Benckendorff to Sazonov, March 28, *L'intervento*, Docs. 101, 103.

[114] Aide-mémoires to Buchanan, March 28 and 29, *L'intervento*, Docs. 102, 104, also Doc. 106.

[115] *L'intervento*, Doc. 105.

only four islands in Southern Dalmatia (Lissa, Busi, Cazza, and Lagosta),[116] and his own Ambassador in London had to point out that "we cannot compel the British and French Governments to prolong this war considerably for the sole benefit of Serbia."[117] On April 1 Sazonov's objections were reduced to Sabbioncello,[118] and that same day Asquith gave Imperiali a memorandum listing the extent of the Entente concessions: the islands mentioned by Sazonov and the Dalmatian coast and islands from Cape Planka north, to Italy; from Cape Planka to the Montenegrin frontier, to Serbia; neutralization of the islands from Zara to Cattaro.[119] Sonnino was for holding out for better terms, but Salandra was now willing, if necessary, to give up Sabbioncello.[120] After some further debate over points of detail, agreement was finally reached on April 14.[121] The matter was not quite ended, however, for Sazonov had renewed qualms over Albania and the month's delay which Italy deemed necessary before she could begin her campaign,[122] and it was only under strong pressure from Grey[123] and owing to Poincaré's direct appeal to the Czar[124] that with great reluctance and only in deference to the wishes of Russia's Allies, his consent was finally given.[125]

At last the Treaty of London was signed, on April 26, by Grey, and the Italian, French and Russian Ambassadors in London, Imperiali, Paul Cambon, and Benckendorff respectively. The territorial clauses of the Treaty granted Italy her desiderata in regard to the continental frontiers of the country itself: the so-called "line of the Alps" from Switzerland, over the Brenner, and to the Gulf of Fiume, including all Istria (art. 4). Only in Dalmatia had she been forced to compromise, yielding about half her original claim (art. 5); the specific mention that the remaining Adriatic territory from Volosca to the Drin "shall be assigned by the four Allied Powers to Croatia, Serbia and Montenegro" (note to art. 5) is especially important in view of subsequent events. Parts of Albania

[116] Aide-mémoire to Buchanan and Paléologue, March 31, L'intervento, Doc. 109.
[117] Benckendorff to Sazonov, March 30, L'intervento, Doc. 108.
[118] Sazonov to Buchanan, April 1, L'intervento, Doc. 112.
[119] Aide-mémoire from Buchanan, April 3, L'intervento, Doc. 114.
[120] Salandra, L'intervento, pp. 171-72.
[121] Aide-mémoire from Buchanan, April 15, L'intervento, Doc. 123. The Italian acceptance referred to Grey's memorandum of the tenth, slightly different from that of the first.
[122] L'intervento, Doc. 124.
[123] Grey to Buchanan, April 19, L'intervento, Doc. 128.
[124] Poincaré to Nicholas II, April 20, L'intervento, Doc. 130.
[125] Sazonov to Buchanan and Paléologue, April 21, L'intervento, Doc. 134.

were to be assigned to Italy, Serbia, and Greece respectively, leaving a small autonomous state (arts. 6, 7). In the Dodecanese and in Libya her demands for full sovereignty were granted (arts. 8, 10). Her remaining colonial ambitions in Africa and in Asia Minor were the subject of what can only be described as surprisingly vague language (arts. 9, 12, 13).

In addition to these purely territorial clauses, Italy was to receive a loan of £50,000,000 (art. 14), a proportionate share of any eventual war indemnity (art. 11), and the assurance that her opposition to the participation of the Vatican in the peace negotiations would be supported by her Allies (art. 15). Military and naval conventions were to ensure Russian military coöperation and Anglo-French naval coöperation against Austria-Hungary (arts. 1, 3). In exchange for these benefits, Italy pledged the use of "her entire resources for the purpose of waging war" (art. 2). The Treaty itself was supplemented by a declaration on Italy's part—which was to remain secret like the Treaty itself—that she subscribed to the joint Anglo-Franco-Russian undertaking of September 5, 1914, not to make separate peace. Upon Italy's entrance into the war, this declaration alone was to be renewed and made public by the four Powers.[126]

From the account of the negotiations just presented, it appears that Italy did not secure her original demands unquestioned, nor did she obtain in the end all that she had claimed at first. She did, however, secure the major part of her demands, for she had the whip-hand in the negotiations, and once the Entente Powers, or rather Great Britain and France, had made up their minds that they must have Italian assistance, they clearly were not in a position to haggle over details. Realistically, Grey recognized the situation from the start. Furthermore, the Entente were not asked to contribute any but enemy territory, and naturally found it easier than Austria-Hungary to be generous in the matter.

The real basis of the Treaty of London must be seen as an application of the doctrine of the balance of power. In 1915 the total dismemberment of the Hapsburg Empire was an ultimate possibility, but hardly an immediate prospect. The Treaty, therefore, did not attempt to go beyond a division of spoils on the basis of a new balance. Austria-Hungary was to retain an outlet on the Adriatic and

---

[126] For the text of the Treaty and Declarations, see below, Document 3.

Serbia was to become the Greater Serbia favored by Russia.[127] To compensate for this modification of the Balkan balance—the presumable increase of Russian influence through the aggrandizement of Serbia—Italy was to have secure control of the Adriatic through the possession of Pola, Valona, and Northern Dalmatia.[128] As an application of the theory of the balance of power, such an arrangement does not seem unreasonable; one may rather wonder, in fact, at the vagueness of the terminology through which Italy sought to safeguard her further Mediterranean interests.

That is not to say that there were not other elements in the question, or that the terms of the Treaty were welcomed by the Entente. As to the latter, their feelings are perhaps best summed up in Benckendorff's report of the final act of signature on the twenty-sixth:

The feeling of satisfaction which presided at the signature of the Treaty of September 5 was absent the day before yesterday. Even Imperiali inwardly felt qualms about the future. Cambon alone, very disturbed by the Italian hesitation of the last few days, seemed relieved of a great burden. The faults of the Treaty from the Slav point of view were evident to all, more painfully so to me than to the others. . . . To negotiate in time of peace the conditions of a possible war is altogether different from negotiating during the critical time of war with a Power who is dealing with both sides and to whom circumstances give a weight out of proportion to its real force.[129]

If the Allies wanted Italy, they must pay her price; Italy, on her side, certainly was under no obligation to assist the Entente. It was a clear case of interest on both sides.[130]

Those "faults of the Treaty from the Slav point of view" cannot be denied. The principle of nationality, itself at the root of the war, certainly was ignored. It had fallen to Russia—not for any unselfish devotion to that principle on her part—to take up its defense in the Adriatic, with the result that the Treaty contained the ambiguous

[127] That is, have access to the Adriatic by the annexation of Bosnia-Herzegovina and Southern Dalmatia. Incorporation of Croatia-Slavonia was definitely not envisaged; it was, in fact, looked at askance in Petrograd.

[128] From the point of view of land defense, Northern Dalmatia was a liability to Italy. Its possession was deemed necessary, however, as protection to the naval base of Pola, which, on the other hand, did not constitute a threat toward Dalmatia.

[129] Benckendorff to Sazonov, April 28, L'intervento, Doc. 149.

[130] If Italy drove a hard bargain with the Entente, the Entente on its side did not neglect to do the best it could under the circumstances. It was Grey who insisted on keeping secret the previous agreement among the Allies in regard to Turkey, on the plea that once Italy had committed herself, she could then be faced with a fait accompli.

phraseology, "the following Adriatic territory shall be assigned by the four Allied Powers to Croatia, Serbia and Montenegro" (note to art. 5), opening the door to future dissensions. Even without the events of the following three years—events undreamed of at the time—the Treaty of London contained potential seeds of discord between Italy and her new Allies.

Italy Declares War

With the signature of the Treaty of London, the stage was set for Italy's entrance into the war "at the earliest possible date and within a period not exceeding one month," presumably, therefore, some time after the middle of May. The short interval proved to be one of considerable anxiety for the Austro-Germans, for the Entente, and for the Italian Government as well. It is worth dwelling for a moment on the events of this last period, most of all perhaps, on account of the light which they throw on the internal situation in Italy; for the cleavage between the elements then in conflict—reconciled, in part at least, during the war period—was to reappear soon after the Armistice and to have a considerable influence on the events of 1919.

As already indicated, Italy denounced the Triple Alliance on May 3. That step, however, did not put an end to negotiations, but rather coincided with a renewed and intensified activity on the part of Germany in a last effort to preserve Italian neutrality. To supplement Bülow's work in Rome, Erzberger, leader of the German Centrist party, arrived in Rome on May 2. He was received by Sonnino the next day and by Salandra on the fourth.[131] In their predicament, the Central Powers sought assistance in all available quarters. Salandra, his mind once made up, had been pursuing a steady course of military preparation and educative propaganda of public opinion. Even without his intervention, public opinion and the press had shown a tendency to take sides with increasing vociferousness, and had become divided more and more between the rival camps of *interventisti* and *neutralisti*. For entirely different reasons, the latter group drew its main support from the Catholics and the Socialists.[132] In Parliament, Giolitti may be said to have been the

---

[131] Salandra, *L'intervento*, p. 231.

[132] Among the latter there was not complete unanimity. Bissolati and Mussolini both favored intervention. Mussolini, editor of the *Avanti*, the party organ, resigned his editorship in the autumn and founded his own newspaper, the *Popolo d'Italia*, which carried on a very vocal and effective campaign of propaganda.

leader of this movement, which had there greater relative support than in the country at large. Parliament was to meet on May 12, but, at a meeting of the Cabinet on the seventh, it was decided to defer this meeting to the twentieth,[133] and to inform Giolitti of the situation. The Austrians meantime came forward with some further minor concessions, which were not considered. The nature of these offers was known in those parliamentary circles thought to be favorable to continued neutrality, and also apparently at the Vatican.[134] Bülow, distrustful of Sonnino, insisted on seeing the King, in order to be certain that the latter knew of the Austrian proposal.[135]

Giolitti arrived in Rome on May 9 and was greeted at the station by a hostile demonstration. Under the circumstances, he could not help becoming associated in the public mind with the Austro-German party, and it was in fact the only remaining hope of the Central Powers that by connecting the now famous *parecchio* with a judiciously spread knowledge of their offers, a movement might be created in Parliament that would overthrow Salandra and put Giolitti in his place. According to Salandra,[136] Giolitti, when informed, approved of the manner in which the negotiations had been conducted with Vienna and Berlin, but he was both appalled and incensed when told that the Alliance had been denounced[137] and that Italy was formally committed to the Entente. His proposal, which he explained both to the King and to Salandra the next day (May 10), was to withdraw from the Treaty of London under the cover of a large vote in the Chamber, which he undertook to guarantee.[138]

That same day brought a joint proposal from Bülow and Macchio,[139] offering the entire Italian Tyrol, the right bank of the Isonzo (see Map I), and the promise of friendly consideration for the remaining Italian demands (islands and Gorizia).[140] This offer was supplemented the following day by a further joint memorandum

[133] Mainly for military reasons, according to Salandra, and in order to reduce as much as possible the interval between the opening of the session and the declaration of war. Salandra, *L'intervento*, p. 242.

[134] Salandra, *op. cit.*, p. 245.

[135] Salandra, *op. cit.*, p. 246.

[136] Salandra, *op. cit.*, p. 250.

[137] The denunciation of the Alliance was not made public at the time.

[138] This is Salandra's account (*L'intervento*, pp. 252 ff.). Giolitti's own account of these events (*Memorie della mia vita*, pp. 537 ff.) is rather sketchy. On some points it is directly at variance with Salandra's.

[139] Baron Macchio had replaced Mérey at the Austro-Hungarian Embassy.

[140] Also Valona and the Austrian renunciation of any interest in Albania. Salandra, *L'intervento*, pp. 257-58.

indicating the method of procedure. Bound by the Treaty of London as he was, and uncertain of Giolitti's course,[141] Salandra decided to force the issue at once, without giving the opposition an opportunity for parliamentary maneuvers. This he did by resigning on the thirteenth. The news was nothing short of sensational. It was naturally received with dismay at the Entente capitals, while Berlin and Vienna thought to have triumphed. At home, it took the opposition by surprise, and the too-close immixture of the German and Austrian Embassies in internal Italian politics proved a boomerang. Giolitti refused to assume office,[142] and it was announced on the sixteenth that the King had refused to accept his Government's resignation.

One more attempt was made from Vienna. On May 19 Macchio submitted a draft agreement,[143] substantially not very different from the last Austro-German offer, save in one important respect. Article 14 provided for the cession of the territories in question, within a month of the ratification of the decisions taken by the mixed commissions that were to settle the details of agreement. Three months earlier that offer might perhaps have secured Italian neutrality, but once more Austria had arrived too late.

On May 23, 1915, Italy formally declared war on Austria-Hungary and severed diplomatic relations with Germany.[144]

[141] Over three hundred deputies and senators had left their cards at Giolitti's residence as a token of their support.

[142] As the result of his generally assumed connection with the Austro-German maneuver, Giolitti remained under a cloud for a long time and wisely kept in retirement throughout the war. He seems to have been genuinely opposed to war, but his later attempt to appear to have been more patriotic than the Government at the time in question can only be described as unconvincing. Cf. his *Memorie*, pp. 541 ff.

[143] Salandra, *L'intervento*, pp. 292-96. For the text of this last and most extensive Austrian offer, see below, Document 5.

[144] She did not declare war against Germany until August, 1916. On the controversy that arose over this circumstance, see below, p. 236, n. 10. The reasons for this distinction remain obscure, as it does not seem that anything was gained by this action.

II

THE WAR PERIOD

DESPITE THE CARE and deliberation which had preceded Italy's declaration of war, she did not enter the field under very favorable auspices. From the military point of view, it was important to coördinate the three fronts—Russian, Italian, and Serbian—surrounding Austria-Hungary. Realizing this need as well as the divergence of interests between the three countries, Italy had signed with Russia a military convention on May 21. The main provisions of this convention were as follows:

Art. 4.—In the present conditions, the first aim of the Italian army and of the Russian forces concentrated in Galicia will be to defeat the enemy in the common Austro-Hungarian theater of war, especially in the region between the Carpathians and the Alps forming the Italian frontier.

In order to achieve this purpose, the Russian and Italian armies mutually undertake:

1. To concentrate on those fronts the maximum possible of their forces, keeping on all the other fronts only the forces strictly necessary in order not to compromise the strategic position of each army;

2. To choose in agreement, at the beginning and during the course of operations, the best directions to give to both armies.

The Serbian and Montenegrin armies must lend their assistance to reach the above-mentioned goal; in particular, it will be desirable that the Serbian army take the offensive, preferably toward the northwest, in order to connect its action as soon as possible with that of the right wing of the Italian army, the latter moving toward Laibach.

When the Serbian army shall take the offensive in that direction, Italy engages herself to assist as much as possible in supplying it.[1]

This optimistic and ambitious plan did not even begin to be carried into execution. The Russians had suffered a severe reverse in the early part of May, the extent of which only became more apparent with time. There could be no question of their taking the offensive. In the south, the Serbs, less than friendly toward the new Ally, showed no signs of activity, moving instead into Northern Albania,

[1] Salandra, *L'intervento*, pp. 323-24. The complete text of the Russo-Italian military convention is not available.

to the extent that Sonnino remarked to the Serbian Minister in Rome: "If Serbia had been allied with Austria, she would not have acted differently."[2] In any case, whether or not as the result of this situation on the Russian and Serbian fronts, the Austro-Hungarians were soon able to bring the Italian offensive to a standstill, after some initial gains had been made.

This is not the place, however, to follow the checkered course of military operations as they affected Italy, from May 24, 1915, to the conclusion of the Armistice of Villa Giusti on November 3, 1918. It will suffice to say that the allied hopes of prompt victory, as the result of Italian intervention, failed to materialize. One more front was added to those already in existence, and the struggle went on with varying fortunes. Under the stress of war, Italy, much the weakest of the western Allies, became a fertile ground for discontent and defeatism; social unrest, which had been acute before 1914, began to reappear and the Government had to cope with disaffection and riots on the home front. This situation contributed to the rout of Caporetto, when, for a time, the whole Italian front seemed in danger of collapsing. The army managed, however, to stage a rally in the Venetian plain, and the outcome internally—similar to that in the other Allied countries—was the formation of a union ministry, at the end of October, 1917, under the presidency of Orlando. Sonnino remained at the Foreign Office, Nitti had the Treasury, and Bissolati, as Minister without portfolio, represented a section of the socialists. Under this set-up, Italy carried on to the end.

More important, from our point of view, than the vicissitudes of war, are certain circumstances and conditions, in existence before the war or growing out of it, which were to have a profound influence on the Italian peace. The problem of the South Slavs and the American intervention are among the most important of these.

AMERICAN INTERVENTION AND THE DISCUSSION OF WAR AIMS

As it turned out, the deciding factor in the victory of the Entente was the throwing on its side of the vast resources of the United States, which more than made good the loss of the Russian Ally. Both sides in the war had endeavored to influence world opinion in their behalf and to secure allies wherever they could find them. In

---

[2] Reported by Salandra, *L'intervento*, p. 325.

doing this, much stress was laid on the justice of their cause and the aims pursued by the belligerents, and the Allies had far greater success than the Central Empires, culminating in the addition of America to their forces.

The events of the second half of 1917, Caporetto, and the Russian Revolution, ending in the complete withdrawal of that country from the struggle against the Central Powers, together with the revelations of secret treaties and imperialistic aims, put the Allies on the defensive in both the military and the moral sense. To counteract the bad effects of these events at home and outside, it became imperative to set in a better light the war aims of the Allied Powers. In response to this need, on January 5, 1918, Lloyd George, in a carefully prepared speech, presented the most comprehensive statement of British war aims yet made.[3] Disclaiming any aggressive desires, the British Empire, said Lloyd George, was fighting essentially for the righting of wrongs and a settlement based on the consent of the governed. As to Austria-Hungary, there was no desire to destroy that country; in the case of the Italians subject to Austrian rule, however, their transfer to Italy was deemed legitimate, but for the other nationalities genuine self-government on true democratic principles was alone contemplated; a somewhat vague statement, hardly clarified by the proclaimed determination to press for justice "to men of Rumanian blood and speech in their legitimate aspirations." Sharply reversing the Allied position of a year previous,[4] Lloyd George denied any intention of driving Turkey out of Europe; as to the subject lands of Turkey, their separate national conditions should be recognized, and the Russian collapse had reopened the question of their future disposition.[5]

But, owing to its great power and unique position, America was destined to take the leadership in this discussion of war aims and to

[3] In August, 1917, Pope Benedict XV sent to the various belligerents a Note (dated Aug. 1 and published Aug. 15) which, except for suggesting disarmament and arbitration, proposed essentially a return to the *status quo ante bellum*. Cf. Temperley, *A History of the Peace Conference of Paris,* I, 56. Although Italy would naturally tend to be suspicious of such a move (cf. art. 15 of the Treaty of London), she had no cause to exert active opposition to the Pope's proposal which had no results. Temperley's work is referred to hereafter simply as "Temperley."

[4] Allied Note to the United States, of Jan. 10, 1917. This Note spoke of "the turning out of Europe of the Ottoman Empire as decidedly foreign to Western civilization." Cf. Temperley, I, 428-29.

[5] No attempt is made here at a comprehensive analysis of Lloyd George's speech, those statements alone which, directly or indirectly, bear on Italian problems being referred to. Cf. Temperley, I, 190.

become the spokesman of the Allies, for it sought no conquests and pursued no selfish ends, but rather entered the conflict "to make the world safe for democracy."[6] Under the leadership of Wilson, great stress was laid on the new principles that were to govern international relations in the future and those that would be followed in the peace settlement. These principles took concrete form in the declaration of war aims of January, 1918, the famous Fourteen Points, which drove into the background the Lloyd Georgean statement of three days before.

In view of the importance of Wilson's statement, it is worth recording those of the Fourteen Points which, in their general or specific provisions, have a bearing on Italian problems. They are the following:

Point IV.—Adequate guarantees given and taken that national armaments will be reduced to the lowest point consistent with domestic safety.

Point V.—A free, open-minded, and absolutely impartial adjustment of all colonial claims, based upon a strict observance of the principle that in determining all such questions of sovereignty the interests of the populations concerned must have equal weight with the equitable claims of the government whose title is to be determined.

Point IX.—A readjustment of the frontiers of Italy should be effected along clearly recognizable lines of nationality.

Point X.—The peoples of Austria-Hungary, whose place among the nations we wish to see safeguarded and assured, should be accorded the freest opportunity of autonomous development.

Point XI.—Rumania, Serbia, and Montenegro should be evacuated; occupied territories restored; Serbia accorded free and secure access to the sea; and the relations of the several Balkan states to one another determined by friendly counsel along historically established lines of allegiance and nationality; and international guarantees of the political and economic independence and territorial integrity of the several Balkan states should be entered into.

Point XII.—The Turkish portions of the present Ottoman Empire should be assured a secure sovereignty, but the other nationalities which are now under Turkish rule should be assured an undoubted security of life and an absolutely unmolested opportunity of autonomous development, and the Dardanelles should be permanently opened as a free passage to the ships and commerce of all nations under international guarantees.

[6] Exception may be taken to this statement, and indeed much has been and is still being said on that score. One would hesitate, in 1938, to defend the thesis that democracy has gained as a result of the war; but that the slogan was a powerful reality in 1918 can hardly be gainsaid.

Point XIV.—A general association of nations must be formed under specific covenants for the purpose of affording mutual guarantees of political independence and territorial integrity to great and small states alike.

The genesis of the Fourteen Points is of interest. Wilson's declaration had been prefaced by discussions which had taken place between the Allied leaders and the American Mission in Europe, especially Colonel House, at the close of 1917. During these conversations, House found the Italians, and particularly Sonnino, strongly opposed to a statement of war aims and very insistent upon the Treaty of London.[7] House was back in the United States in the second half of December and when Wilson set to work on his speech, he supplied him with a complete territorial program drawn up by The Inquiry.[8] There seems to have been no particular discussion of the Italian claims between House and Wilson, but the latter, according to House, aware of the extent of British and French commitments to Italy and wishing to make it plain that the United States was not in agreement with these, wrote in the margin of the Inquiry Report the sentence which became Point IX: "Readjustment of the frontiers of Italy along clearly recognized lines of nationality."[9]

A Serbian mission was visiting the United States at this time, and the advice of its leader, Vesnić, was sought in regard to Point XI (Balkans), an area of prime interest to Italy. Vesnić proved to be in total disagreement with Point XI and, at House's request, wrote the following comment on it:

There will and there cannot be in Europe any lasting peace with the conservation of actual Austria-Hungary. The nations kept in it, as well

[7] "November 30, 1917: Baron Sonnino was as difficult today as he was yesterday. He is an able man, but a reactionary. . . . If his advice should carry, the war would never end, for he would never consent to any of the things necessary to make a beginning towards peace." Seymour, *The Intimate Papers of Colonel House,* III, 283; see also 280. Hereafter referred to as "House."

[8] House, III, 320. The Inquiry was the group of men, drawn for the most part from academic life, which House began to gather together in the autumn of 1917 with a view to making a preliminary study of the problems which would have to be solved at the peace. Although its function was primarily to supply information, it came to have far greater importance than originally expected, and many of its members played an important part in the actual peace negotiations. Cf. Shotwell, *At the Paris Peace Conference,* Chap. I.

[9] House, III, 323. "recognized" was changed to "recognizable" in Wilson's speech of Jan. 8. This statement amounted to a denial of the Italian claims to the German portion of the Tyrol and to the Eastern Adriatic; it is important to bear this in mind when we come to considering the rôle played in the Italian negotiations in the Spring of 1919 by various members of The Inquiry.

Serbians, Croats and Slovenes, as Tchecs and Slovaks, as Rumanians and
Italians, will continue to combat the German-Magyar dominations. As to
Bulgaria, Serbia stands firm on the Treaty of Bucharest. The Allied Powers
have guaranteed to her these frontiers. It will be morally and materially
impossible to get so rapidly an understanding of Balkan nations, which is
of course desirable, and which may come. Bulgarian treachery can and shall
not be rewarded. I sincerely believe that serious negotiations for the peace
at this moment of the war would mean the complete failure of the policy
of allies and a grave collapse of the civilization of mankind.[10]

The Serbian commentary had apparently no effect, for Point XI
was retained essentially unaltered in its rather vague and meaning-
less phraseology. No particular significance should be attached to
the fact that Vesnić's opinion was sought on this occasion, but the
fact is worth noting in view of the activity of Yugoslavs and Italians
in the United States.[11]

There were further declarations and statements of policy in
1918, none of which achieved the fame of the Fourteen Points.
Among these, however, the Four Principles, formulated by Wilson
in a speech on February 11, deserve special mention, for, although
relatively uncommented upon at the time, they clearly revealed a
state of mind on Wilson's part which was to be of the utmost

[10] House, III, 335. It is perhaps worth while to quote the Inquiry Report in regard to the
Balkans: "No just or lasting settlement of the tangled problems confronting the deeply
wronged peoples of the Balkans can be based upon the arbitrary treaty of Bucharest. That
treaty was a product of the evil diplomacy which the peoples of the world are now determined to end. That treaty wronged every nation in the Balkans, even those which it
appeared to favour, by imposing upon them all the permanent menace of war. It unquestionably tore men and women of Bulgarian loyalty from their natural allegiance. It denied
to Serbia that access to the sea which she must have in order to complete her independence.
Any just settlement must of course begin with the evacuation of Rumania, Serbia, and
Montenegro by the armies of the Central Powers, and the restoration of Serbia and
Montenegro. The ultimate relationship of the different Balkan nations must be based upon
a fair balance of nationalistic and economic considerations, applied in a generous and
inventive spirit after impartial and scientific inquiry. The meddling and intriguing of
Great Powers must be stopped, and the efforts to attain national unity by massacre must be
abandoned.

"It would obviously be unwise to attempt at this time to draw frontiers for the Balkan
states. Certain broad considerations, however, may tentatively be kept in mind. They are in
brief these: . . . (4) that the best access to the sea for Serbia is through Saloniki; . . . (6)
that an independent Albania is almost and certainly an undesirable political entity.

"We are strongly of the opinion that in the last analysis economic considerations will
outweigh nationalistic affiliations in the Balkans, and that a settlement which insures economic prosperity is most likely to be a lasting one." House, III, 333-34, n. 2. The points
omitted do not affect Italian interests in the Balkans.

[11] On this point, see below, p. 46.

importance to the Italian case and which ought to have been a clear warning to the Italians as to the tactics that should be adopted in dealing with Wilson. The Four Principles were stated as follows:

First, that each part of the final settlement must be based upon the essential justice of that particular case and upon such adjustments as are most likely to bring a peace that will be permanent;

Second, that peoples and provinces are not to be bartered about from sovereignty to sovereignty as if they were mere chattels and pawns in a game, even the great game, now forever discredited, of the balance of power; but that,

Third, every territorial settlement involved in this war must be made in the interest and for the benefit of the populations concerned, and not as a part of any mere adjustment or compromise of claims amongst rival states; and

Fourth, that all well defined national aspirations shall be accorded the utmost satisfaction that can be accorded them without introducing new or perpetuating old elements of discord and antagonism that would be likely in time to break the peace of Europe and consequently of the world.

Clearly the Italians could not afford to express outright opposition to the Fourteen Points. Their reaction is therefore of particular importance, especially in view of future developments. In a speech before the Chamber on February 12, Orlando, though not referring specifically to the Fourteen Points, emphasized the similarity of purpose pursued by Italy and by the nationalities that sought their emancipation. "Italy," said he, "wants no more and no less than this: the completion of her national unity and the security of her frontiers on land and on sea." He did refer at the same time, however, to the defenselessness of the Italian coast in the Adriatic.[12] Referring to the Fourteen Points a few days later, he paid homage to the loftiness of the Wilsonian ideal, but only to emphasize as a worthy example to his own country Wilson's pledge to use all the resources of America in the prosecution of the war to a successful conclusion.[13] The same ambiguity appeared in a speech before the Senate. Italy's policy toward the subject nationalities of Austria-Hungary was one of sympathy and coöperation in the accomplishment of their aim, but this did not imply "that it is necessary to decide at once what influence this attitude must have on the

[12] Speech of Feb. 12, 1918. *Atti del Parlamento, 1913-19, Camera, Discussioni*, XV, 15493.
[13] Speech of Feb. 23, 1918. *Ibid.*, XV, 16093.

aims of war."[14] Sonnino likewise, in his capacity of Foreign Minister, was called upon to comment on the Fourteen Points and Italy's war aims. He was even more guarded than Orlando in his language and laid stress on the element of security and the need of compensations in the eastern Mediterranean to preserve the balance of power.[15]

At the same time, Count Macchi di Cellere, the Italian Ambassador in Washington, finding little comfort in the Wilsonian program, sought clarifications from Wilson himself. Received on January 21, according to his own account, he could obtain little more than an insistence on the value of the future League of Nations as a guarantee of Italian security.[16]

THE SOUTH SLAVS AND THE PACT OF ROME

Despite this inauspicious ambiguity, there seemed for a time to be fair prospects of an amicable arrangement between the Italians and the Yugoslavs. The relations of Italy with the South Slavs were of particular importance and delicacy. The South Slav problem, as manifested by Serbian nationalism, had been the immediate cause of the war; South Slav or Yugoslav nationalism had existed for some time, but had failed to crystallize before the war. Various schemes had been proposed to meet the difficulty. The setting up of the South Slavs as a third partner in the Austro-Hungarian Monarchy was a device supposed to have been favored by the murdered Archduke; it was opposed with equal vigor by the Hungarians within the monarchy and by the Serbs without. The enlargement of Serbia by the incorporation of what corresponded roughly to the provinces of Bosnia and Herzegovina was another solution. This Greater Serbia scheme was considered seriously by Belgrade, which dared not cast eyes as far as the upper Adriatic; Russia was the main advocate of this solution among the Great Powers. It is the one hinted at in the Treaty of London. Finally, there were some who dreamed of the union of all the South Slavs, Croats, Slovenes, and Serbs.[17]

[14] Speech of March 4, 1918, Orlando, *Discorsi per la guerra e per la pace*, p. 162.

[15] Speech of Feb. 23, 1918. *Atti del Parlamento, 1913-19, Camera, Discussioni*, XV, 16066-71.

[16] Bernardy and Falorsi, *La questione adriatica vista d'oltre Atlantico*, pp. 35-36. "It would be puerile to insist that the security of Italy should and could be entrusted to a hypothetical League of Nations," wrote di Cellere.

[17] For an account of these various schemes, cf. Temperley, IV, 172 ff.

The similarity may be pointed out here between the rôle and position of Serbia in the Yugoslav national movement and those of Piedmont in the unification of Italy. At the same time the differences should not be ignored: while the languages are closely related, different alphabets (Latin and Cyrillic) are in use in the north and the south respectively; more

Italy had no objection to an enlarged Serbia. She had, indeed, an interest in the preservation at least of that country; that had been one of the reasons for her neutrality in 1914. But the prospect of an entirely new Yugoslav state, reaching to the gates of Trieste and in control of the eastern Adriatic, was quite a different matter.

With the collapse of Russia, the Greater Serbia scheme lost much of its support among the Powers, and although this collapse did not tend to brighten Allied prospects, it served to unify Yugoslav nationalism. As early as December, 1914, the Serbian Government had spoken of the liberation of the Croat and Slovene brothers.[18] In the early days of the war, Ante Trumbić, a Dalmatian deputy, had emigrated to London, where he organized the so-called Yugoslav Committee. At the same time, although the Treaty of London was secret, there seems little doubt that from the very time it was being negotiated, a fair knowledge of its stipulations percolated, probably from Petrograd, to the Serbian Government and to the Yugoslav Committee.[19] The result was to create suspicion of Italy and to solidify against her the Slav elements of Austria-Hungary. Italy on her side, or at least the *Consulta*—for the question did not yet arouse much public interest in Italy—reciprocated both suspicion and dislike. She sought to protect her interests by playing a lone hand; in June, 1917, she proclaimed the independence of Albania under her "protection." She maintained 100,000 troops in that country, but, owing to the conflict between her own aspirations and those of Serbia and Greece in Northern and Southern Albania, respectively, her coöperation on the Macedonian front remained a reluctant one.

---

important is the difference in religion, Roman Catholic in the north, Orthodox in the south; and finally the fact that while Piedmont was the most progressive part of Italy, precisely the reverse was true of Serbia in the prospective state. This difference was best evidenced by the contrast between the behavior of the rulers of Piedmont and that of the Belgrade Government.

[18] Declaration of the Serbian Government in the Skupshtina. Adriaticus, *La Question adriatique,* Document I. Russia was supposed to favor the enlargement of Serbia, not, however, to include the Croats and Slovenes, mainly Catholic in religion. For this attitude she was denounced by the Croatian leader Supilo, as a betrayer of the Slavs. Her collapse, with the result that the South Slavs could no longer depend upon her for support, hence need not consider her wishes, left the field clear to the agitation for the union of all Southern Slavs.

[19] Early in 1916 the Yugoslav Committee published a map showing the line of the Treaty of London, with only minor deviations. Cf. Temperley, IV, 183.

The Yugoslav Committee was an unofficial group, like similar Czech and Polish organizations, active in carrying on propaganda among the Allies for its ideal of national unification.

She also displayed a marked difference in her treatment of Czechs on the one hand, and of Southern Slavs on the other.

The Yugoslav Committee, under the leadership of its president, Ante Trumbić, nevertheless went on with its propaganda and issued manifestos and declarations with a view to keeping alive the agitation for the formation of a Serb-Croat-Slovene state.[20] Finally, as the result of discussions between representatives of the Serbian Government, temporarily transferred to Corfu, and of the Yugoslav Committee, the so-called Manifesto of Corfu was issued, in July, 1917, over the signature of Pašić, the Serbian Prime Minister, and Trumbić.[21] This official declaration proclaimed the desire of union of the three branches of the South Slav family as a single state under the Karageorgević dynasty, on the basis of the principle of self-determination.

The war, meantime, was continuing as a stalemate and the leaders of the Allies, casting about for new resources, began to pay more attention than had hitherto been the case to the potentialities of disruptive propaganda among the subject nationalities of the Hapsburg Monarchy. Under the stimulus of the Russian defection and the defeat of Caporetto, Italy, whose suspicion of the Slavs was the main stumblingblock to coöperation, began to take a more sympathetic view of Yugoslav aspirations. She remained, in addition, fearful of the recurrent suggestion of a separate peace with Austria-Hungary[22]—a possibility not wholly displeasing to some of Italy's Allies, more interested in Germany and devoid of ill feeling toward the Danube Monarchy—which might rob her of a large part of her expected gains. With the assistance of some Englishmen, notably Seton-Watson and Wickham Steed, unofficial negotiations were initiated in the summer of 1917. Signor Torre, an Italian deputy advocate of conciliation with the Yugoslavs, met Trumbić in London.[23] The two signed a preliminary agreement on March 7, 1918,[24] and in April was held in Rome the Congress of Oppressed Nationali-

---

[20] Manifesto of May, 1915, to the British Nation and Parliament. Declaration upon the accession of Charles of Hapsburg in December, 1916. Adriaticus, *op. cit.,* Documents III, IV.

[21] Text in Temperley, V; Adriaticus, *op. cit.,* Document V.

[22] Soon after his accession to the throne, Emperor Charles I began a secret negotiation with Paris through the intermediary of his brother-in-law, Prince Sixte of Bourbon-Parma, then serving in the Belgian army.

[23] Torre was accompanied by other Italians in these discussions.

[24] Temperley, IV, 294; Adriaticus, *op. cit.,* p. 24.

ties, the outcome of which was the so-called Pact of Rome.[25] In this declaration, the representatives of the various nationalities, Italians, Poles, Rumanians, Czechoslovaks, and Yugoslavs, subject, totally or in part, to Austro-Hungarian rule, mutually recognized their right to achieve or complete their national unity as independent states and the need of common action to that end. Regarding Italy and Yugoslavia in particular, the Pact of Rome explicitly placed the unity and independence of the two nations on the same footing, and stated the desirability of an amicable territorial settlement between the two countries on the basis of nationality and self-determination, allowing for the possibility of having to include nuclei of one nationality within the frontiers of the other, with proper guarantees.[26]

This agreement was of course not an official treaty, no member of the Italian Government having set his signature to it. But a moral obligation, at least, resulted from the fact that Orlando welcomed the gathering and expressed approval of its purpose. It is worth noting, however, that in addressing the Congress, Orlando quoted from his speeches in Parliament of February 12 and March 7 passages wherein he had declared that Italy pursued as her aims the protection of all the "gente italica" and the obtention of "defensible frontiers."[27]

The Pact of Rome was highly welcomed by Italy's Allies and by the Slavs, not least by those in the United States who indulged in congratulatory addresses.[28] In Italy itself it had considerable support from the liberal elements; such men as Bissolati and Salvemini and as important a newspaper as the *Corriere della sera* carried on a steady propaganda, aiming to define more concretely the rather vague terminology of the Pact through a clear territorial understanding.[29] But the Government remained skeptical.

[25] Orlando deemed it politic to assume the leadership of the movement for independence of the subject nationalities of Austria-Hungary, in order better to keep it under control; this is the reason why the Congress was held in Rome. Cf. Paresce, *Italia e Jugoslavia*, p. 39. The Italian delegation at the Congress was by no means of one complexion; in it we find such names as Federzoni, Forges Davanzati, Mussolini, and Salvemini, among others, representative of wholly divergent tendencies.

[26] For the text of the Pact of Rome, see below, Document 7.

[27] Speech to the Congress of Oppressed Nationalities, April 11, 1918. Orlando, *Discorsi*, p. 171.

[28] Bernardy and Falorsi, *La questione adriatica*, pp. 50-52.

[29] While territorial questions were excluded from the Pact of Rome, according to some of the Italian participants in the Congress, the Yugoslavs were ready to come to terms with Italy, granting her the following:

1. The County of Gorizia, and Istria to Monte Maggiore;

In Washington, di Cellere sought to explain away to House and to Lansing the seeming inconsistency in adhering at the same time to the Treaty of London and to the Pact of Rome.[30] Slav propaganda meantime continued actively, and on the whole successfully, in seeking to enlist the sympathy of the Allies and of the United States; Masaryk was leading the movement in that country, and though primarily interested in his own Czech countrymen, associated himself with the Yugoslav cause, in opposition to the Treaty of London.[31] But Sonnino persistently held back from definite commitments. In August Masaryk scored an important success in the formal recognition of the Czechoslovaks by the British and the French, followed in September by recognition by the United States. The news was not welcome to Sonnino, who realized the significance of the precedent, and di Cellere emphasized to Lansing the distinction between Czechoslovaks and Yugoslavs.[32]

The high water-mark of Italo-Yugoslav conciliation was reached when, under pressure from Bissolati, the Italian Government gave out a statement on September 8, declaring that "Italy considers that the movement of the Yugoslav people for independence and for the constitution of a free state corresponds to the principles for which the Allies are fighting and to the aims of a just and lasting peace."[33] But there was little reason to think that Sonnino and Bissolati could be reconciled so easily;[34] victory once achieved, proclamations of friendship were soon to be forgotten.

---

2. The Albanian protectorate;

3. Fiume and Zara, free cities with guarantees;

4. Respect of national minorities;

5. Military conventions and economic treaties;

6. In the islands, concessions between a minimum consisting of the use of certain naval bases and a maximum amounting to sovereignty over some small or even some larger island. Amendola-Borgese-Ojetti-Torre, *Il patto di Roma*, p. 105.

[30] On April 24 and 25. Bernardy and Falorsi, *La questione adriatica*, p. 53.

[31] In May the Italian Embassy was advised by the State Department that some statement in support of the aspirations of the subject nationalities seemed opportune. Sonnino insisted, however, that no declaration should be made which would imply an abandonment of the rights of Italy. Bernardy and Falorsi, *op. cit.*, p. 56. At about this time, also, Sonnino and di Cellere sought to prevent the recruiting of a Slav legion in the United States. Bernardy and Falorsi, *op. cit.*, p. 83.

[32] On Sept. 17. Bernardy and Falorsi, *op. cit.*, p. 59.

[33] Temperley, IV, 295.

[34] It was not long, in fact, before the conflict between the two came out into the open and was resolved through Bissolati's resignation. See below, p. 71.

It is not without interest, in connection with the declaration just mentioned, to record that "Baron Sonnino opposed with all his strength the proposition of Signor Bissolati, but at last had to give way. But, as the *Corriere della sera* points out, Baron Sonnino, in for-

The whole episode of the Pact of Rome served no useful purpose in the end, save perhaps as a "negligible expedient of war propaganda." It can perhaps best be appraised in the words of a recent Italian commentator: "From the time . . . in which a profound divergence between Italians and Yugoslavs manifested itself, the problem should have been clearly posed of whether the Yugoslavs should be considered really and effectively as enemies and as such should be fought with all military and political means available, or whether it would have been advisable to make a definite agreement with them."[35] The Pact of Rome only gave rise to false hopes and paved the way for future recriminations.

Sonnino's course in connection with it may well be thought disingenuous; the Slavs would be justified in taking this view. In his defense it may be pleaded that he himself never subscribed to it and only yielded, even to the extent that he did, to the pressure of his colleagues in the Cabinet. Perhaps a bold policy of conciliation might have been rewarded, although one should not forget the difficulty of defending at home the hardships of three years of war for results which could have been achieved substantially by remaining at peace: the whole issue of Italy's wisdom in going to war is here at stake. Perhaps again the problem might have been solved by Italy's receiving some compensation elsewhere, and in this Italy's Allies might have had some contribution to make.[36] But none of these things happened at this time; the fatal ambiguity which was to deadlock negotiations at the Peace Conference was fully in the making.

THE YUGOSLAV REVOLUTION AND THE ARMISTICE OF VILLA GIUSTI

The war was now fast drawing to a close. In mid-September the Allied offensive on the Macedonian front resulted in the complete collapse of that front, followed within two weeks by the Bulgarian armistice, tantamount to unconditional surrender. The victorious Allies continued their northward push, overran Serbia, and by November 1 the Serbs entered their capital. The internal situation

---

warding the statement to the Italian ambassadors at the Entente capitals, interpreted it as a negligible expedient of war propaganda with no subsequent value." [London] *Times*, Jan. 10, 1921, quoted by Temperley, IV, 295.

[35] Paresce, *Italia e Jugoslavia*, pp. 43-44.

[36] Sonnino seems to have considered this very possibility in a communication to di Cellere of Feb. 1, 1918. Bernardy and Falorsi, *La questione adriatica*, p. 80.

of Austria-Hungary, long critical, became chaotic and events began
to move at an ever-accelerated pace toward the inevitable disintegration. The rulers of the once proud Empire continued for a time to
go through the motions of their offices, but they could not even
compose their own internecine quarrels, Budapest proving more unyielding than Vienna in its attitude toward the subject nationalities.
The schemes of reorganization proposed at the time might have
saved the day at an earlier date, but the end was too near and
obvious; genuine national feeling—to say nothing of the desire to
abandon a sinking ship—swept all obstacles in its path, sealing the
fate of the Hapsburg Empire.[37]

As early as August, a Slovene National Council had been set up
in Laibach, under the presidency of Korošeć, as the avowed pre-
lude to the formation of a similar Yugoslav Council. On October
5-6 a conference of all the Yugoslav parties from the Parliaments of
Austria, Hungary, Croatia, and Bosnia, meeting at Zagreb, elected a
Yugoslav National Council.

At the same time (October 7), following an earlier exchange in
the middle of September, an Austro-Hungarian Note was sent to
Wilson offering "to conclude . . . an armistice on every front, . . .
and to enter immediately upon negotiations for a peace" on the
basis of the Fourteen Points, the Four Principles, and Wilson's
declarations in his last speech of September 27.[38] In his reply to
this Note, which did not come until the nineteenth, Wilson found
the offer unacceptable on account of new conditions which had
arisen to modify Point X. "Autonomous development" of the subject
nationalities was no longer sufficient, in view of the fact that the
United States had recognized the Czechoslovak National Council as
a belligerent government (September 3) and had also recognized
the justice of the Yugoslav aspirations (June 28).[39]

Wilson's reply was promptly accepted by Austria-Hungary,[40] who
wished to enter into immediate *pourparlers* regarding an armistice.

[37] It is outside the province of the present work to enter into details over the demise of
Austria-Hungary. An account of the events of this period may be found in Temperley, IV,
89-119; 194-206; 262-66. For a more detailed account, with special emphasis on the Austrian side of the story, cf. Glaise-Horstenau, *The Collapse of the Austro-Hungarian Empire*,
Chaps. VII-XI.

[38] Austro-Hungarian Note of Oct. 7, 1918. See below, Document 8.

[39] Wilson's Note of Oct. 19, 1918. See below, Document 9. On the pressure exerted by
Italy to tone down this latter declaration, cf. Bernardy and Falorsi, *La questione adriatica*,
p. 56.

[40] Austro-Hungarian Note of Oct. 27, 1918. See below, Document 10.

By the subject nationalities, Wilson's reply was taken as definitely sanctioning the movement for independence. On the twenty-ninth the Parliament at Zagreb unanimously denounced all connection with the Hapsburg crown, proclaimed the union of Croatia with Slovenia and Serbia, and recalled the Yugoslav troops from the Italian front. While much confusion ensued, the revolution was essentially peaceful. Powerless to stem the tide, Emperor Charles gave his sanction to the *fait accompli* on October 31.[41]

While these events were taking place, Korošec went to Geneva, where he met Trumbić, head of the Yugoslav Committee, who was further entrusted with the task of representing the National Council with the Allies. They were joined by Pašić and representatives of the various parties in the Skupshtina, and the conference which was held laid the basis for the organization of the future Serb-Croat-Slovene state in accordance with the declaration of Corfu; Pašić instructed the Serbian representatives in the Allied capitals to seek recognition of the new state. Finally, on December 1, the National Council offered Prince Alexander the Regency over all Yugoslavs. Upon his acceptance, the Council proclaimed the Kingdom of the Serbs, Croats, and Slovenes, and the action was ratified on the sixteenth at the joint session of the Skupshtina and the National Council.[42]

[41] The final disintegration of the Hapsburg Empire received its final sanction when Emperor Charles recognized in advance the decision which German Austria might make in regard to her future constitution (Nov. 11), and made a similar declaration with respect to Hungary (Nov. 13). Republics were proclaimed in German Austria and in Hungary on Nov. 12 and 16 respectively. It is of interest that Emperor Charles never executed a formal instrument of abdication for himself or his heirs.

[42] A word may be said here in regard to Montenegro. With the break-through on the Macedonian front, the Italians continued to advance northward in Albania, and Montenegro rose against the Austro-Hungarians in occupation; the Montenegrins were also supported by the arrival of Serbian troops. At the end of October was issued a proclamation by King Nicholas of Montenegro (then residing in France) expressing the wish for a federal union with Yugoslavia in which "each State shall preserve its rights, its institutions, its religion, its habits and customs, and no one claim supremacy."

Meantime, however, a temporary National Government had been organized, hostile to King Nicholas. On Nov. 26, a so-called National Assembly, meeting at Podgorica, deposed King Nicholas and voted for union with Serbia. This resolution, presented by a delegation of the National Assembly to the Serbian Regent, was embodied by the Yugoslav Assembly in an Act passed on December 16. King Nicholas refused to accept his deposition and doubts may well be cast on the regularity of the election of the National Assembly. Disturbances continued in the country and the situation remained obscure—nor was it cleared up by the Peace Conference—but from this time Montenegro remained in fact a part of Yugoslavia. King Nicholas died in March, 1921, and his son Danilo declined to claim the succession. There are numerous references to Montenegro in the communications sent by the American Embassy in Rome toward the end of 1918. Cf. also, Temperley, IV, 202-4.

Contemporaneously with these political developments, ending in the formal organization of the new Yugoslav State, the Italians had taken the offensive on their front, toward the end of October. They met with stout resistance at first and it is a curious fact that the Austro-Hungarian army retained its effectiveness almost to the very last, presenting the strange phenomenon of a country that continued to fight after it was politically dead, to all intents and purposes. After a few days, however, the Austro-Hungarians began a retreat which became a rout. The collapse was final and irretrievable, for there was nothing to fall back upon at home.

Without waiting for further developments, the Austro-Hungarian command asked for an armistice directly from the Italians. General Diaz referred the request, together with his own proposed conditions, to Orlando and Sonnino, then attending the meetings of the Supreme War Council at Versailles. These were discussed at the meeting of October 31,[43] and, with slight changes, became the terms of the Armistice which was signed at Villa Giusti, near Padua, on November 3. The military and naval clauses of the Armistice amounted to unconditional surrender of Austria-Hungary, and it is of interest that no mention was made of the Fourteen Points during the discussions of October 31.[44] At this meeting, also, Vesnić sought, somewhat obliquely but without success, to secure recognition of the Yugoslavs as Allies. Of greatest interest from our point of view is the fact that Article III, describing the armistice line, is a textual reproduction of Articles IV and V of the Treaty of London.[45]

Orlando, from Paris, took this occasion to make a friendly gesture toward the Yugoslavs, declaring in an interview to the *Matin* that "it is the fault neither of the Italians nor of the Yugoslavs if we have had to face them in their enforced rôle of our enemies, which resulted from the fact that they were unwillingly a part of the enemy State," and expressing the hope that the old enmities would soon be buried and forgotten.

But Orlando's soothing words could not prevent two conflicts from appearing at once between Italy and the Yugoslavs as the result of the Armistice. Realization that the line of occupation of the Italian armies was identical with the line of the Treaty of London caused no little dismay among the Yugoslavs, in particular among

[43] For the Minutes of this meeting of the Supreme War Council, see below, Document 11.
[44] On the discussions of the previous day, see below, p. 61.
[45] For the text of the Armistice, see Temperley, I, 481-91.

the Slovenes and the Dalmatians, who were immediately concerned, especially when the occupation showed signs of being a mere pre-liminary to permanent settlement. On November 5 the National Council at Zagreb asked for Serbian troops, who arrived shortly; a Serb battalion occupied Fiume on the fifteenth, and on the twenty-fourth all the Yugoslav military forces were merged in the Serbian army, preliminary to the formal political union at the beginning of December. The Croats and the Slovenes, by virtue of their union with Serbia under the Karageorgević dynasty, claimed the quality of Allies of the Entente. In this capacity they wanted to be left in control of the debated territory held by the Italians since the Armis-tice of November 3, or at least to have this territory occupied by Powers neutral in the dispute. However, the Yugoslav State failed to secure recognition at this time and the Italians remained in occu-pation.

The conflict over Fiume also threatened to become acute at this time. As early as October 18, Andrea Ossoinack, the representative of Fiume in the Hungarian Parliament, had declared before that body that, inasmuch as Austria-Hungary had adopted the Wilsonian principle of self-determination in her peace proposals, Fiume, by virtue of its status of *corpus separatum*, claimed the right to avail itself of this principle without restrictions of any sort.[46] Two weeks later, on October 30, the Italian National Council of Fiume, by vir-tue of this right of self-determination, proclaimed the union of the city to Italy.[47] The danger inherent in the Serbian occupation of Fiume of November 15 was averted when the Serbs consented to withdraw. A compromise was arranged, whereby the occupation was to be international rather than purely Italian. On November 17 the Allied troops entered Fiume; the preponderance of the occupying force, as well as its command, were Italian. The Italian National Council took unto itself all powers of administration, and Ossoinack was sent to Paris as its representative.

[46] Benedetti, *La pace di Fiume*, pp. 24-25.

[47] Benedetti, *op. cit.*, p. 26. As to the value of this resolution, much depended on the status of the Italian National Council. While the Italian preponderance in Fiume proper is an established fact, this Council was none the less a self-appointed body and not the outcome of a regular election. (See below, p. 245, for the recommendations of the Com-mission of Inquiry into the incidents of July, 1919.) There existed, in fact, an autonomous party in Fiume, and the very unanimity of the Council argued against its being truly repre-sentative. At the same time, it must be considered that at this time (Oct. 30), four days before the Italian Armistice, there was little likelihood that Italian agents had been active in Fiume.

The other difficulty was over the Austro-Hungarian navy. A mutiny had taken place at Pola on October 30, and the crews, in large part Yugoslav, had declared their allegiance to the National Council at Zagreb. Emperor Charles recognized this arrangement the next day, at the same time that he acknowledged Yugoslav independence. Clearly this solution could have no binding value, so far as the Allies were concerned, and it could hardly be expected that they would give up the prize of the Austro-Hungarian fleet through such a subterfuge. Favored by the confusion, some Italians managed to slip into the harbor of Pola and torpedoed the dreadnought "Viribus Unitis" during the night of October 31, whereupon the Yugoslav naval command broadcast a request, addressed to Wilson and to the American naval command in Europe, to put the captured vessels under the protection of the American or of one of the Allied fleets.

The situation thus created was unexpected and somewhat embarrassing, for the terms of the Austro-Hungarian Armistice, just discussed, had provided for surrender of certain units of the Austro-Hungarian fleet and disarmament of the rest. The Yugoslav offer was considered at the Supreme War Council meeting of November 1. Not unskillfully Vesnić endeavored to put it in the light of the friendly act of an ally, a view which Lloyd George was rather inclined to accept. But Sonnino saw in it nothing but a last Austrian ruse, and Orlando pointed out the indefiniteness which surrounded both the offer itself and its source.[48] The issue was postponed, and the Yugoslavs decided to comply with the terms of the Austro-Hungarian Armistice in the matter. On November 5 an Italian naval force appeared before Pola, when the surrender of the fleet to the Allies was arranged, eliminating for the time this further potential source of Italo-Yugoslav friction.

ITALY VIS-A-VIS THE ALLIES AND THE UNITED STATES

From now on the scene was to shift to Paris, the center of negotiations, whither the various delegations went. Before tracing the course of the debates that took place, it may not be inappropriate to emphasize the special position of Italy, deriving in great part from her peculiar position in the war and, more generally, from her position in Europe. Especially after the defection of Russia and the

[48] Minutes of the meeting of the Supreme War Council, Nov. 1, 1918. See below, Document 12.

entrance of the United States into the war, the main scene of military activity became the Western front—or at least so it was in the eyes of the United States, Great Britain, and France; that is, for all the Great Allied and Associated Powers with the exception of Italy —and more than ever Germany became the principal enemy, again for all except Italy. As a consequence of this situation, Italy found herself relegated to a comparatively secondary position. She was considered in a sense to be apart from the main current of events by the other Allies, and she herself took a comparatively secondary interest in the happenings on the Western front. She thought of the war as her war, *la nostra guerra,* connected almost incidentally with the struggle of the other Allies against Germany. There was a tendency among the other Powers to come to decisions among themselves, then as if by afterthought to remember Italy and to ask her acquiescence.[49]

One illustration of this is to be found in the recurrent idea of separate peace with Austria-Hungary, which met a favorable response in British, French, and American quarters.[50] In 1918 the movement for independence among the subject nationalities had made sufficient headway to require its being taken into consideration. This movement could work to Italy's disadvantage—as eventually it did—in two ways: the desire for self-preservation might induce Austria-Hungary to separate herself from Germany, and this bait in turn might lure the Allies into being lenient with her; or again, if the cause of nationalities were to be espoused by the Allies,. the claims of these nationalities would be likely to clash with those of Italy. Faced with this dilemma, Italy thought it best to take the movement under her patronage, in the hope of retaining a measure of control over it. Less understandable are the secret agreements for the partition of the Near East, entered into between Great Britain, France, and Russia, both before and after the signing of the Treaty of London. It was only by insisting upon it that Italy secured a definition of her share at St. Jean de Maurienne in 1917.[51]

The relations between Italy and her Allies varied according to the peculiar characteristics of the different countries and their posi-

---

[49] As, for instance, during the discussions of Point IX in connection with the German Armistice. See below, pp. 60 ff.

[50] The United States did not declare war against Austria-Hungary until Dec., 1917.

[51] The origin and nature of this agreement will be examined in connection with colonial questions (Chap. VIII).

tion with respect to Italy. Officially, France was the Latin sister, and there was between herself and Italy some very real community of culture and feeling; but the strain deriving from the fact that the former was an older, wealthier, and long-established national state, while the latter was younger, poorer, and still struggling to establish herself, was never completely overcome. Great Britain, on the other hand, had a tradition of sympathy and friendship for the young nation, dating from the days of the *Risorgimento*, though her attitude was perhaps not devoid of a certain patronizing element. But most delicate of all were the relations with the United States. America was acquainted, in some degree at least, with Great Britain and France, with both of whom she had historical and cultural connections. But Italy was rather the object of prejudice than of knowledge. The fact that American troops were quartered almost exclusively in France did not contribute to create the impression that Italy was an active partner in the war as were the other Allies. All this tended to magnify the discrepancy arising from the fundamental fact that for all that she was classed as a Great Power, Italy was certainly not in the same category as the United States and Great Britain, or even France.

Nor were the Italians unaware of the situation. The reports of Count Macchi di Cellere give evidence of his efforts "to put Italy on the map," of self-conscious accounts of minor incidents and happenings tending to show that Italy was being considered and treated with due regard.[52] Colonel House noticed this too; in April, 1917, for instance, he wrote in his diary:

The Japanese, Russians, and Italians are being left out of English, French, and American calculations. As far as one can see, they do not appear at any of the functions in Washington except the larger ones, and there is a lack of Russian, Japanese, and Italian flags which might easily hurt sensibilities.[53]

On the heels of the British and French missions to the United States, Italy also sent a mission, late in May, 1917, mainly because the others had done so, and the Italian mission spent much of its time in America playing Italian internal and personal politics.[54] Nitti, who was a member of the mission with ministerial ambitions,

[52] *All'Ambasciata di Washington*, pp. 98, 162. Published posthumously from di Cellere's papers. Hereafter referred to as "di Cellere."

[53] House, III, 54.

[54] Di Cellere, pp. 66-68. For the Nitti-di-Cellere feud, see below, p. 251.

was also strongly opposed to Sonnino, and apparently sought to convey the impression that the latter was the principal obstacle to an Italian policy of conciliation.[55] Di Cellere informed Sonnino of this, while he endeavored to mitigate the bad effect of the public exhibition of family quarrels. In America, also, Italy had to contend with an active Slav propaganda; Wilson had definitely espoused the cause of small nations, a cause which, under the general slogan of "justice," held a traditional appeal for American opinion, little informed of or interested in the complexities of the European balance of power —a doctrine presented to it as belonging to the evil past which America was fighting to abolish. No one contested Italian irredentist aspirations, but security in the Adriatic, based on strategic considerations, could not appear in a very favorable light by comparison with the professed wish of the Slavs to rejoin their brothers. To emphasize the differences among these Slavs, by way of counter propaganda, might have seemed somewhat ungracious. Italy was in the difficult position of associating herself formally with the aspirations of the Oppressed Nationalities while opposing some of these aspirations; at the same time, she also felt it somewhat beneath her dignity as a Great Power to appear to be on a par with these smaller, in some cases unborn, states.

Di Cellere was aware of the delicacy of the situation and called insistently for a more effective Italian propaganda; but Sonnino, personally a very reserved and uncommonly silent man, was rather contemptuous of such devices, the effectiveness of which he underestimated. When a foreign propaganda office was organized in Italy, it was not placed under his direction, and furthermore its head was not a partisan of the Sonninian policy. On his part, di Cellere, an avowed disciple and admirer of Sonnino, while doing his best to defend the Italian case in the United States according to his own and Sonnino's ideas, did not tend to create a favorable atmosphere by sending reports to his Foreign Office deprecating American idealism as either deliberate or naïve self-deception, and depicting Wilson as on the whole a self-seeking politician, primarily concerned with his own reputation, the fortunes of his party, and the interest of his country.[56] Much could have been done to remedy these impressions

[55] Bernardy and Falorsi, *La questione adriatica,* p. 17.

[56] The following passage, sent shortly after America's entrance into the war, will serve as an illustration:

"The contribution of America, fatally useful to the Allied cause, is a usurer's mortgage

on the occasion of Wilson's visit to Rome at the beginning of 1919; but as chance would have it, the attempted discussions at that time only created further misunderstanding.[57]

on the peace conditions which the vaunted, but not true, disinterestedness only serves to conceal. Wilson's ambition to dictate the peace does not date from today. For two months he has subordinated his policies and the interests of the country to the hope of mediating and arbitrating as a neutral. This game having failed, and with a clear vision of the inevitable consequences of continued isolation, he has entered the war in the name of high principles and with an apparently noble disinterestedness, but in reality in order to insure as far as possible the future security of the country and to exert the desired influence on the Peace Congress." Di Cellere, p. 59. (April 19, 1917.)

An informative account of Italian foreign propaganda activities during the war may be found in the *Relazione della commissione parlamentare d'inchiesta per le spese di guerra,* pp. 51-75.

[57] On this point, see below, pp. 81-85.

Part One

THE ORLANDO-SONNINO MINISTRY

(NOVEMBER, 1918—JUNE, 1919)

III

THE PRE-CONFERENCE PERIOD

FROM THE PICTURE just outlined of what might be called the psychological atmosphere, it should not be inferred that there was ignorance of fact in the American delegation. For a year and longer before the conclusion of the Armistices, Colonel House had gathered together a group of technicians—usually known as The Inquiry—in the various fields of law, history, ethnography, and geography, who quietly proceeded to collate all the information that would be relevant to the drafting of the eventual peace treaties. So-called experts have been subjected to a good deal of criticism, derision, and scorn; that their mental processes are apt to differ from those of politicians no one would deny; that their absorption in their own sphere is not always unaccompanied by a certain narrowness and an inability properly to weigh the various elements of a complex problem, is equally true. However, it was not the task of The Inquiry to draft the treaties of peace, but merely to have at hand in organized form whatever information might be required. This they did successfully, and the American delegation was second to none in the quality of its technical staff. Whenever needed, the Crillon[1] could always produce statistics and maps, physical, political, and ethnographical.

On the other hand, Wilson himself was not acquainted with the details of the European complex. Himself a historian of distinction, his interest had centered primarily in the development of his own country, where the forces of European nationalism were relatively inoperative. Whatever the qualities of his intellect, it is important to emphasize the difference between abstract knowledge and what, for want of a better term, may be called the "feeling" for a situation. This was of prime importance when it came to redrawing the map of a Europe torn by warring nationalisms. It was therefore natural that the Fourteen Points should have emphasized general principles rather than specific territorial readjustments. What is more, such equally desirable things as national self-determination, eco-

---

[1] Residence of the American delegation in Paris.

nomic interest of a given territory, and security might, and often did, come into conflict with one another. It was a comparatively simple matter, in a good many cases at least, to draw lines on a map of Europe according to the dictates of either strategy or language, for instance; but these lines would seldom coincide. What could be done in such a situation but effect some compromise between the various principles at stake? As to what would constitute "justice" in the particular instance, that would naturally depend upon the interests or preferences of those who made the decision. When such situations arose, all the maps and statistics bearing on the problem were no longer sufficient, and, as it turned out, even "experts" differed among themselves, according to the importance which they attributed to this or to that consideration. When such an issue was joined, the element of power could no longer be kept out of the deliberations. The problems of the Peace Conference would have been arduous enough had they been wholly in the hands of a disinterested group of men, free from the pressures and passions of the moment; they were, instead, immensely complicated by all the devices of press and propaganda.

THE FOURTEEN POINTS AND THE GERMAN ARMISTICE

Inasmuch as "the Fourteen Points and subsequent declarations" were to be the bases of the Armistice and the peace treaties, it was of vital importance that the meaning of these rather general statements of principle should be made specific and precise before replying to the German request. The proclamations of war aims could no longer be regarded in the light of war propaganda, now that peace was in sight.

This task of definition took place at the meetings of the Supreme War Council held from October 30 to November 4, 1918, as the result of which the Armistice terms were drafted.[2] As indicated, the terms of the Austro-Hungarian Armistice were decided upon with comparatively little discussion at the meeting of October 31, no formal connection being established between them and the Fourteen Points; it was otherwise with the German Armistice. Two reservations were introduced; in regard to Point II (Freedom of the Seas), which was open to various interpretations—some of which the Brit-

---

[2] In addition to the formal plenary sessions, there were other informal and preparatory meetings.

ish could not countenance—the Allied Governments "must, therefore, reserve to themselves complete freedom on this subject when they enter the peace conference." Further, in order that no misunderstanding might arise as to meaning of *restoration*, the Allied Governments declared that "by it they understand that compensation will be made by Germany for all damage done to the civilian population of the Allies and their property by the aggression of Germany by land, by sea, and from the air."[3] The text of these reservations was discussed at the meeting of November 1.[4]

In the case of Italy, Point IX, as mentioned before, called for "a readjustment of the frontiers of Italy . . . along clearly recognizable lines of nationality." It would be idle to attempt to reconcile this statement with the provisions of the Treaty of London. We have mentioned the guarded response which the Fourteen Points elicited from Orlando and Sonnino before the Italian Parliament, as well as the strained attempt—a reflection of the divergent tendencies held together only by the war in the Orlando Cabinet—at professing devotion at one and the same time to the Fourteen Points, to the Pact of Rome, and to the Treaty of London. It did not tend to clarify the issue.

During the pre-Armistice discussions, Sonnino, following the British example in regard to Point II, thought it time to make formal reservations. This he did by reading a statement saying that

the Italian Government considers that the "readjustment" mentioned in Point IX does not imply a mere rectification of frontiers; but that it means that Italy shall obtain the liberation of the provinces whose nationality is Italian, and at the same time shall establish a frontier between Italy and Austria-Hungary, or the other states which until now have formed part of Austria-Hungary, that offers the essential conditions of military security sufficient to assure independence and the maintenance of peace, in view of geographic and historic factors, and with the application of the same principles as those affirmed in the case of Germany in the matter of territorial delimitation consequent upon the present war.[5]

The attempt to cover all possible contingencies made Sonnino's reservation too sweeping and indefinite. Under pressure of the other Prime Ministers, and on the plea that Point IX was not relevant

[3] Wilson's Note of Nov. 5, 1918. *Foreign Relations of the United States*, 1918, Supp. 1, Vol. I, 468-69.
[4] Mermeix, *Les Négociations secrètes et les quatre armistices*, pp. 226 ff.
[5] On Oct. 30. House, IV, 173.

to the German Armistice, Orlando finally consented to drop this reservation, despite Sonnino's insistence on the danger of his course.[6] Meantime the Austrian Armistice was being negotiated, and it likewise contained no mention of Point IX, although the Austrians had also asked for an armistice on the basis of the Fourteen Points. In a cable to Lansing on October 31, House construed this silence as implying acceptance.[7]

At the meeting of November 1, while discussing the draft of the reservations to be sent to Wilson, the following exchange took place:

Orlando.—I wish to remind you that during the meeting of the Heads of Government during which we have prepared this Note, the Italian Government had made reservations in regard to Point IX, which lends itself to various interpretations; I was told at the time that the note referred to Germany only and that Point IX was therefore not under discussion.

Since this note is now being examined in Plenary Session, I wish to insist on the reservations which I have previously made in regard to Point IX.

Clemenceau.—Mr. House will give explanations on the whole Fourteen Points.

Lloyd George.—I think that Points IX, X, XI and XII have nothing to do with the document we must send to Germany. Would it not be preferable to add a paragraph stating that we do not wish to discuss with Germany clauses which do not concern her?[8]

Once more, on November 3, Orlando tried to insert a reservation in regard to Point IX and again failed, this time on the plea that it was best to have as few exceptions as possible to the Fourteen Points.[9] Thus it came to pass that despite the Italians' awareness of the situation and their attempt to protect themselves, in large part owing to circumstances, no trace of this appears in any of the exchanges, either between the Allies and Wilson, or between him and the Central Powers.[10]

---

[6] House, IV, 173-74.

[7] House to Lansing, Oct. 31, House, IV, 178. The importance which House attached to these pre-Armistice discussions is evidenced by his remark in a letter of Dec. 18 to the Attorney General: ". . . the thing I did that was of value to the President, to the United States, and I dare hope, to the world, was the incorporating in the armistice the American war aims." House's papers, Yale University.

[8] Minutes of the meeting of the Supreme War Council, Nov. 1, 1918, Mermeix, *Les Négociations secrètes,* p. 228.

[9] House, IV, 177.

[10] However Wilson himself was kept informed. "The Belgians are protesting Articles III

At the beginning of these discussions, in order to avoid ambiguity and to have a concrete basis on which to proceed, House had caused to be prepared a detailed commentary on the Fourteen Points.[11] This commentary was cabled by House to Wilson for his approval on October 29. Wilson replied the next day that the commentary was "a satisfactory interpretation of the principles involved," adding, however, "that the details of application mentioned should be regarded as merely illustrative suggestions."[12] This approval of Wilson gave the commentary the character of an official document. It must be pointed out that the fact that he replied immediately precludes the possibility of his having consulted The Inquiry on the specific recommendations made.[13] Presumably with this in mind, he qualified his acceptance. In view of its importance, it is worth quoting the commentary on the issues affecting Italy.

IX. *A readjustment of the frontiers of Italy should be effected along clearly recognizable lines of nationality.*

This proposal is less than the Italian claim, less of course, than the territory allotted by the Treaty of London, less than the arrangement made between the Italian Government and the Jugo-Slav State.

In the region of Trent the Italians claim a strategic rather than an ethnic frontier. It should be noted in this connection that Italy and Germany will become neighbors if German Austria joins the German Empire. And if Italy obtains the best geographical frontier she will assume sovereignty over a large number of Germans. This is a violation of principle. But, it may be argued that by drawing a sharp line along the crest of the Alps, Italy's security will be enormously enhanced and the necessity of heavy armaments reduced. It might, therefore, be provided that Italy should have her claim in the Trentino, but that the northern part, inhabited by Germans, should be completely autonomous, and that the population should not be liable to military service in the Italian army. Italy could thus occupy the uninhabited Alpine peaks for military purposes, but would not govern the cultural life of the alien population to the south of her frontier.

The other problems of the frontier are questions between Italy and Jugo-Slavia, Italy and the Balkans, Italy and Greece.

---

and V of the Fourteen Points. The Italians are protesting Article IX." House to Wilson, Nov. 3, 1918, House, IV, 175.

[11] Frank Cobb was given this task by House, but Seymour makes the comment: "Internal evidence indicates that the actual drafting of the commentary was largely the work of Walter Lippmann." House, IV, 153, n. 1.

[12] House, IV, 153.

[13] The Inquiry was doing its work in New York.

The agreement reached with Jugo-Slavs may well be allowed to stand, although it should be insisted for the protection of the hinterland that both Trieste and Fiume be free ports. This is essential to Bohemia, German Austria, Hungary as well as to the prosperity of the cities themselves.

Italy appears in Balkan politics through her claim to a protectorate over Albania and the possession of Valona. There is no serious objection raised to this, although the terms of the protectorate need to be vigorously controlled. If Italy is protector of Albania, the local life of Albania should be guaranteed by the League of Nations.

A conflict with Greece appears through the Greek claim to Northern Epirus (or what is now Southern Albania). This would bring Greece closer to Valona than Italy desires. A second conflict with Greece occurs over the Aegean Islands of the Dodekanese, but it is understood that a solution favorable to Greece is being worked out.

(Italy's claims in Turkey belong to the problem of the Turkish Empire.)

X. [*Austria-Hungary*]

. . .

4. JUGO-SLAVIA. It faces the following problems:

a. Frontier question with Italy in Istria and the Dalmatian Coast; with Rumania in the Banat.

b. An internal problem arises out of the refusal of the Croats to accept the domination of the Serbs of the Serbian Kingdom.

c. A problem of the Mohammedan Serbs of Bosnia who are said to be loyal to the Hapsburgs. They constitute a little less than one third of the population.

. . .

The United States is clearly committed to the programme of national unity and independence. It must stipulate, however, for the protection of national minorities, for freedom of access to the Adriatic and the Black Sea, and it supports a programme aiming at a Confederation of Southeastern Europe.

XI. [*Balkans*]

Albania could be under a protectorate, no doubt of Italy, and its frontiers in the north might be essentially those of the London Conference.

XII. [*Turkey*]
[No mention is made of Italian claims under this section.][14]

In most instances the commentary did not attempt to lay down

[14] "Official American Commentary on the Fourteen Points." House, IV, 197-200.

definite frontier lines. It is not clear what was meant by "the arrangement made between the Italian Government and the Jugo-Slav State," since there was yet no such state, and the Pact of Rome, undoubtedly referred to, was not an agreement between governments and did not consider the question of actual frontiers. However, the Brenner frontier was mentioned specifically and, despite the qualifications, the commentary created at least a strong presumption in favor of granting this claim to Italy. Certainly the Italians would be warranted in taking this interpretation, and Wilson could hardly take refuge behind the phrase "illustrative suggestions" in denying it to them.[15]

The situation thus created was confusing and unfortunate in the extreme. Later on, the Italians claimed to have made reservations to the Fourteen Points,[16] of which, in fact, no record appeared in the outstanding correspondence. On the one side, it may be said that they had yielded on their reservations, albeit for rather irrelevant and extraneous reasons; certainly Orlando was easily put off and could have made a stronger stand at the time. He could hardly plead ignorance, in view of the commentary on the Fourteen Points; in House's words, "these interpretations were on the table day after day when we sat in conference in Paris while the Armistice was in the making."[17] On the other hand, the Italian arguments were never met by a frontal attack and discussed on their merits, and House's tendency was to put off such discussion in order to expedite acceptance of the Wilsonian program with as few reservations as possible. In this he succeeded, but only at the cost of causing greater trouble in the future. Furthermore, while the commentary was used during these pre-Armistice discussions, apparently it remained in House's hands and was not known to The Inquiry. Thus it came about that when the American Report on Territorial Claims was drawn up, the question of the Tyrol, among others, was taken up in

[15] This is, in fact, what happened, and the issue of the Brenner frontier was never raised by Wilson in the Council. It is only fair to say, on the other hand, that granting this claim to Italy implied at least a moral obligation on her part to accept the rest of the commentary. Wilson steadily insisted on this point (cf., e.g., Wilson's Note of Feb. 24, 1920), and what he considered an unfair unwillingness on the part of the Italians in accepting a *quid pro quo* contributed not a little to his stiffness on the Yugoslav issue. His acceptance of the Brenner frontier in the first place must be set down as an oversight, due to the haste of his approval of the commentary.

[16] Council of Four, April 20, 1919. Tittoni's Note of July 7, 1919.

[17] House, IV, 153-54.

great detail.[18] It caused considerable surprise, not to say indignation, among the American experts, particularly in the case of Douglas Johnson, who was largely responsible for drawing the Italian frontier, to discover that the Brenner issue had practically been settled in advance of their recommendations.

To be sure, the Italians could probably not have got very far with their reservations had they been more insistent, for House held the trump of the threat of a separate American peace,[19] but it never came to that in connection with Point IX. It would have been better if it had, and if the situation had been definitely clarified at the start, instead of later providing both Italians and Americans with the excuse that each had given the other false impressions.

THE SITUATION IN ITALY

There was growing tension, meanwhile, between the Italians and the Yugoslavs. The Italian occupation of Dalmatia was very high-handed in its treatment of the local population. Local authorities were summarily dismissed by the military, to be replaced by more amenable appointees of their own; suppression, imprisonment, and exile were visited upon the land, reminiscent of the Hapsburg domination from which it had just freed itself.[20] Indeed it could hardly be otherwise: as was correctly pointed out later in the Italian Parliament, it was only by such coercive measures that order could be maintained among an alien and unwilling population.[21] At the time, however, there seems to have been little or no protest in Italy against this state of affairs; on the contrary, there were numerous and loud complaints against the treatment of the Italian minorities in Southern Dalmatia at the hands of the Yugoslavs, some of which were undoubtedly justified.[22]

The Italians felt tricked by the circumstance that through a mere change of name, some of their most tenacious enemies should escape the consequences of defeat. Whole units of the former Austrian army, without so much as changing their uniforms, simply shifted their allegiance from Vienna to Zagreb. Croats, Slovenes, and Dal-

[18] See below, p. 90 and Doc. 16.
[19] House, IV, 165.
[20] See below, Document 40.
[21] E.g. by Salvemini during the discussion of the Treaty of Rapallo. *Atti del Parlamento, 1919-21, Camera, Discussioni*, VI, 5837-38.
[22] Cf. Speranza's Reports to Ambassador Page, *passim;* in particular, the reports for Nov. 14, 19, 30, Dec. 19, Jan. 18, 21. On Speranza, see below, p. 68, n. 27.

matians felt no particular cause to display friendly feelings toward Italy, or toward the Italian population which happened to find itself in such places as were left in their possession along the coast. Something in the nature of a race had developed between the Italians moving northward in Albania, and the Serbians and the French, to reach points along the coast and in Montenegro. The fact that the Serbo-French troops were under French command tended to turn Italian resentment against France as much as against the Slavs.[23] In the middle of December a French base was established at Fiume to supply the Armée d'Orient operating in the Balkans and in Hungary; the matter was arranged in agreement with the Italian Government and the National Council of Fiume, but proved a source of endless bickering and much ill-feeling.[24]

The Italian feeling toward France may perhaps best be described as one of hypersensitivity. The frequent talk in Italy about the Latin block, in opposition to Germanic, Slav, and even Anglo-Saxon blocks, found little or no response across the Alps. France intended the Entente Cordiale to continue, reinforced by American support; as to the Slavs, their very existence was predicated on German powerlessness, and they should therefore be supported, even against Italy if necessary. The assertion of Italian claims under the circumstances was, from the French point of view, in the nature of an annoyance, magnified into actual opposition and resentment owing to the fact that Italy had, to say the least, considerable nuisance value, if not overwhelming power of her own. Late in October, just before the Armistices, Page urged House to pay a visit to Italy "before you get your impressions of Italy out of the French atmosphere."[25]

[23] Just how far the French may have been following a deliberate anti-Italian policy at this time is impossible to tell. Italian complaints were numerous and loud, but concrete evidence is scarce; there can be little doubt, however, that the French were pursuing an active policy in the Balkans and in southeastern Europe.

[24] The tenseness of the situation is attested by Miller's report to House: "In the matter of the Adriatic I am told that the position is really dangerous and there may be a clash between Italian and Jugo-Slav forces unless we take hold of the situation." Miller, *My Diary at the Conference of Paris*, Dec. 5, I, 33. Miller's work in 20 volumes is, for the most part, a documentary collection, the Diary itself being wholly contained in Vol. I. This work is referred to hereafter as "Miller," to which the notation "Diary" is added when the reference is to the Diary proper as distinguished from the documentary part.

House reports requests from both Orlando and Korošec to send American troops to the disputed areas, a course which he was in favor of adopting. House to Lord Derby, Nov. 21, 1918. House's papers, Yale University.

[25] Page to House, Oct. 22, 1918. "I suggest this," went on Page, "not only because Italy has felt very neglected in the past, and there is always danger that such a feeling may

A month later, referring to Wilson's prospective arrival in Europe, Page insisted that he must come to Italy, for

it would never do for him to come to France and not to come to Italy. . . . Italy has stood our not sending troops here without charging us with un-friendliness, because she has charged it against France, just as she has charged against France the chief part of the failure to provide her with what she deemed her just proportion of the materials necessary for con-ducting the war.[26]

Instances and quotations could be multiplied; it can safely be said that, as the opening of the Conference drew near, the Italian attitude was one of guarded and suspicious reserve and indecision, which the political situation in the country only served to intensify.

This political situation in Italy during the two months between the Armistices and the opening of the Conference, and the trends of opinion must be borne in mind.[27] After the celebrations and re-joicings which naturally followed the Armistice of November 3, there seems to have been a momentary hesitation in formulating a policy. The incident of the Austro-Hungarian fleet, taken over by the Yugoslavs, caused considerable indignation in all quarters in Italy, and, although the fact itself tended to recede into the back-ground, there developed an increasingly violent anti-Yugoslav press

deepen into an idea that she is intentionally slighted, but because she has been neglected and she does feel isolated." House's papers, Yale University.

[26] Page to House, Nov. 19. House's papers, Yale University. Cf. also Speranza's special Report of Dec. 16, "Some Views Showing the Growing Dissatisfaction with the Attitude towards Italy of Certain Elements in France." To be sure, there was in France a considerable range of opinion, which it is not our purpose to examine. What matters here is not so much what was, as what was thought to be, and how it appeared in Italy.

[27] No attempt has been made at an exhaustive survey of the press throughout this period— a task beyond the scope of the present work. However, the British War Office weekly publication, *Daily Review of the Foreign Press, Allied Press Supplement,* has been found of great value for a concise analysis of the main events and trends, as they appeared at the time in the Italian press.

Equally useful have been the detailed daily reports on all phases of Italian activity drawn up for Ambassador T. N. Page by Gino Speranza, Attaché to the American Embassy in Rome. Speranza was an American of Italian parentage—his father had been professor of Italian in Columbia University—whose background particularly qualified him to present for American use a sympathetically fair view of the Italian scene. These reports are unpub-lished, and the author is indebted to Mrs. Speranza for permission to make use of them.

The political section of Speranza's "Daily Report" was forwarded to the American Mission, later Delegation, in Paris. In addition, Ambassador Page sent voluminous reports of his own, which he further supplemented with frequent letters to House. It should be pointed out that, in view of the mass of problems which had to be dealt with, the very bulk and completeness of the reports emanating from Rome impaired their usefulness to the American Delegation.

campaign. Quite naturally, the leadership in this campaign was taken by the nationalist press, which soon began to heap abuse on the Pact of Rome as an expression of weakness dictated by "paroxysms of cowardice."[28] What is perhaps more remarkable is the relative supineness of the more liberal, or *Mazzinian*, press.[29] Organs such as the *Corriere della sera* continued to defend the Pact of Rome, but for a time at least—roughly until mid-December—in a rather half-hearted and apologetic way.[30] The result of this was that, although Italian opinion was by no means unanimously nationalistic immediately after the Armistice, the fact that the nationalist press was by far the most vocal, having the field largely to itself, tended to create and crystallize such opinion.

Special mention should be made of Sonnino and the *Giornale d'Italia*. This newspaper, which was often regarded as Sonnino's mouthpiece,[31] was prominent in the anti-Yugoslav campaign. As early as November 6, Sonnino, addressing the functionaries of the *Consulta*, had referred to the necessity of overcoming the opposition to the attainment of Italian ideals, which should therefore be stated loudly and forcibly.[32]

The *Giornale d'Italia* was also responsible, with others, for spreading the false impression that the Italian claims were recognized by Great Britain and France; hence that the united front of the three Allies would easily secure these demands.[33]

[28] *Giornale d'Italia*, Dec. 8.

[29] So-called from its advocacy of the Mazzinian principle of nationality. It should be borne in mind, when speaking of the press, that in a country of many parties and political opinions like Italy, divisions are by no means clear-cut, and epithets qualifying sections of the press, while often convenient, can be used only in a loose sense, as indicative of a broad tendency.

[30] On Dec. 3 there appeared in the *Secolo* a lengthy interview with Pribicević, Vice President of the Yugoslav National Council. It was a sane discussion of the Italo-Yugoslav problem, but received surprisingly little attention, even in the liberal press.

[31] Owing to the fact that he was its largest shareholder. Certainly many things were printed in the *Giornale d'Italia* which Sonnino himself would never have said, and it would be a mistake to consider this newspaper as an official mouthpiece of the *Consulta*. None the less the very fact of the actual connection and the popular and often reasserted belief in it, coupled with Sonnino's lack of denial, are of importance. It is another instance where one must be careful in judging the connection between certain press organs and personalities.

[32] *Avanti*, Nov. 8.

[33] After the meeting in London at the beginning of December. On Dec. 7 the *Giornale d'Italia* bore the tendencious headline: "Treaty of London Recognized." Even if true of Great Britain and France, the American attitude, known to Sonnino, could obviously not be ignored. Nothing was known in Italy of the pre-Armistice discussions and the American Commentary on the Fourteen Points.

Parliament met again on November 20 and the Government had generally smooth sailing. True to form, Orlando confined himself to generalities that could mean all things to all men and give comfort to the most diverse opinions. In reply to a query as to his attitude toward the Fourteen Points, he professed to subscribe to them, but had to point out that "from their very broadness, every one of these principles would require, when it comes to their application, such lengthy considerations that I should have to ask you to remain a couple of months to exhaust the matter"; Orlando would go to the Peace Congress "with an Italian spirit"; that Italy entertained no imperialistic designs against anyone could have no better proof than "to recall that the sympathy of Italy for the peoples oppressed by Austria was proclaimed in this House." At the same time, as further evidence of Italy's motives, it should be pointed out, according to Orlando, that those very agreements cited as proof of imperialistic intent "themselves represented a compromise, since by them Italy spontaneously renounced a city whose *italianità* no one could deny."[34] Speaking before the Senate on December 15, Orlando remained equally vague as to what his program at the coming Peace Conference would be, confining himself to an assurance—in reply to a speech by Tittoni—that whatever principles were adopted would be applied to Italy equally with the other Allies.[35]

The Government, it must be remembered, had been born of and held together by an emergency. Victory now secured, the tendency soon reappeared among the political parties to reassert their separate existences. Within the Cabinet, Sonnino and Bissolati represented hopelessly irreconcilable points of view. The former, a forthright conservative and nationalist, a believer in the traditional European system of balance of power; the latter, favoring a peace of compromise with the Slavs, a sincere devotee of the Wilsonian ideal, and one who placed high hopes in the future League of Nations—an idea which, to Sonnino, was little more than a Utopia of which he was rather impatient.[36] Between the two stood Orlando, skilled in

[34] Speech of Nov. 27, 1918. *Atti del Parlamento, 1913-19, Camera, Discussioni*, XVI, 17777-79. The speech delivered on Nov. 20 was in large part a timely oration in celebration of victory.

[35] Speech of Dec. 15, 1918. *Ibid., Senato, Discussioni*, V, 4793-97. On the whole, this lack of a definite program at this time was well received by the press.

[36] The headline in the *Giornale d'Italia* (Jan. 12): "Two distinct formulas: 1. Italy for the Italians; 2. The Society of Nations," whether inspired by Sonnino or not, expressed rather well his point of view.

It is of interest that, as far back as the summer of 1918, Sonnino was reported as realizing "that much of what he claimed under the London Pact, relating to the Istrian-

the art of florid, noncommittal words, a man of not-too-deep personal convictions, who could easily be drawn by one current or another, depending on which seemed stronger at the moment. His wartime rôle had been useful in persuading his disparate team to pull together, but there are times—and this was one—when clear and strong direction is required.[37] Sonnino and Bissolati had had many differences in the past, but the higher necessity of conducting the war, together with Orlando's suasion, had held them in collaboration. Now, however, the paramount question was peace demands—specifically the status of the Treaty of London—and no common purpose could be found to reconcile the fundamental divergence. After a Cabinet meeting on December 27, at which the course of Italy at the Conference was discussed, Bissolati handed in his resignation. The resignation was welcomed by the "Sonnino" press as indicative of a victory for the latter and his policy of adherence to the Treaty of London. The *Epoca*, which was supposed to be close to Orlando, attempted to minimize the importance of Bissolati's resignation, while the liberal and socialist press took the occasion to launch attacks against Sonnino, sounding warnings of the danger of his ideas, which ran counter to Wilson's.[38]

Bissolati's views appeared in the *Morning Post* of London (Jan. 6),[39] and he presented them again in greater detail, or rather attempted to do so, in a speech at the Scala in Milan on January 11.[40] In view of the fact that Bissolati was the foremost exponent of the tendency which he represented, a tendency which had no mean support in Italy for a time, and in view of the further fact that this was the first specific statement of a peace program given by a re-

---

Dalmatian coast, would not be conceded to Italy in the final arrangement; but held on to it still because he would not permit France to say that she had forced Italy's concession and use it in dealing with the Balkan people on her own account." Page to House, Oct. 29, 1918. House's papers, Yale University.

[37] On Nitti's rôle and position, see below, p. 89.

[38] For an account of the situation following Bissolati's resignation, see Ambassador Page's report from Rome of Dec. 30, 1918. See below, Document 14.

[39] The fact that Bissolati's views appeared in a foreign newspaper, especially a Tory organ like the *Morning Post*, when his own resignation was due to his opposition to supposed imperialism in his own country, naturally created an unfavorable impression in Italy and reacted against him. Bissolati told Speranza that he had expressed his views to the *Morning Post* correspondent in a private capacity, and that the latter had written the article in question without submitting it first to Bissolati as was the custom. He did not deny, however, the accuracy of the report—though he would have used different wording—and was, in general, quite candid about his opinions. Later he sought to state his case in the American press. Cf. Speranza's "Confidential Report for the Ambassador" of Jan. 24, 1919.

[40] A well-organized opposition prevented him from speaking, but his statement appeared in the press the next day.

sponsible Italian statesman, Bissolati's views warrant examination. Mazzinian idealism, very real to him, impelled him to subscribe frankly and whole-heartedly to the concept of a new order, of which the Wilsonian League of Nations was the concrete symbol and expression; the success of such an enterprise was in turn contingent upon a settlement that all peoples could accept without reservations. From these premises the territorial settlement followed logically:

1. German unity, i. e., the union of German Austria with Germany, should not be opposed and, while the Brenner line was the best strategically, he would be content with a line north of Bolzano which would include a minimum of German population.

2. In the Adriatic he would renounce the Treaty of London and with it Dalmatia, Slav in population and strategically difficult to defend. By renouncing the Treaty of London, Italy would have a sound claim to Italian Fiume and could make an amicable arrangement with Yugoslavia for the protection of the Italian groups in the eastern Adriatic.

3. The Dodecanese was of no economic value and this unnecessary source of irritation should be given to Greece.[41]

Bissolati's program was totally at variance with Sonnino's ideas, and his influence and that of the *rinunciatari* was on the wane, giving place to a desire to participate in the scramble for territory. There was, in fact, some point to the criticism that to offer to yield Dalmatia without previously having secured Fiume, was to play into the hands of Yugoslav nationalists and their supporters among Italy's Allies. Bissolati's position may best be characterized in the words of Speranza's Report: "Bissolati's only fault is this: that he believes seriously in the democratic and revolutionary function of the war, and that he actually thought that the Italian governing classes would understand the new epoch and would become modernized, and cast into the fire the appetites and the systems of the past."[42]

A few days after Bissolati had spoken in Milan, General Gramantieri, who had attended the meeting and made a plea for giving Bissolati a fair hearing, was put on the retired list. At about this time, also, some of the Italian contributors to the *New Europe* were sending in their resignations on account of the anti-Italian tendency

[41] The *Morning Post* interview and the speech of January 11 are both summarized at length in the *Daily Review of the Foreign Press.* The latter also in Speranza's Report of Jan. 12-13.
[42] Report of Jan. 12-13.

of this periodical.[43] Small incidents, no doubt, these incidents were nevertheless straws in the wind, indicative of the trend of Italian policy and of the steadily decreasing likelihood of an amicable Italo-Yugoslav settlement.

PRELIMINARY DISCUSSIONS—WILSON'S ARRIVAL

The two months' interval between the signature of the German Armistice and the formal opening of the Peace Conference is of considerable importance. The Armistices had successfully brought the war to a close by making it impossible for the enemy Powers to resume active warfare against the Allies—a fact the implications of which have sometimes been lost sight of in postwar discussions. The war ended, the question of peace terms became paramount. In view of the magnitude of the task, matters of organization and procedure of the coming Congress were of the first importance, for they could have a considerable influence on many vital issues. Awareness of the need of some sort of program was not lacking in many quarters,[44] but it seems—at least from what evidence is available at the present time, and it is likely that some trace at least would appear of other plans if such had existed—that the French were the most active in seeking to devise some concrete plan of procedure immediately following the German Armistice.[45]

It may be stated by way of preface that at this time (November-December, 1918), it was generally taken for granted that a quick preliminary peace would be made. We are here primarily concerned

[43] The *New Europe* was an English weekly, generally sympathetic to the new nationalities, though not necessarily anti-Italian, except in so far as Italian policy might be anti-Yugoslav. The Italian contributors were in general followers of Bissolati's policy.

[44] House, for instance, took up the matter with Wickham Steed. Steed, *Through Thirty Years*, II, 264-65.

[45] These French plans have been analyzed by Binkley, "New Light on the Paris Peace Conference," *Political Science Quarterly*, Sept. 1931, pp. 335-61; Dec. 1931, pp. 509-47. The question has been debated of the eventual effect of some sort of plan or lack of plan on the peace settlement. Tardieu regrets the fact that the agenda which he devised (growing out of these plans) failed of adoption by the Council in January, charging the failure to "the instinctive repugnance of the Anglo-Saxons for the systematized constructions of the Latin mind." (Tardieu, *La Paix*, p. 101.) Binkley takes issue with the claim, deeming the Tardieu plan neither comprehensive nor systematic, save "as an attempt to bring the French claims under principles which the Conference would accept." (Binkley, *op. cit.*, p. 359.) Without entering the much-abused field of national characteristics, and granting that Tardieu's proposal was drawn up with a purpose, the question would seem to remain whether the earliest possible systematization of the jungle that the Peace Congress was about to enter was not desirable. It would seem either that the early French plans could have been modified or some more acceptable proposal brought forward.

with the French proposals, in so far as they touched the Italian position; in this respect they offer some points of interest. The first French draft appeared on November 15.[46] Under a section headed "Principles and Bases of Negotiations," we find the following:

a. Right of peoples to decide their own destinies by free and secret vote (combined with the principle of a certain homogeneousness of the States, principle applicable to Bohemia, Tyrol, Istria, Dalmatia, Luxemburg).

. . .

b. Release from treaties concluded between them of such groups of States which by the fact of their admission to the Congress shall waive their right thereto: this principle is entirely in accordance with the ideas of President Wilson.

Such a declaration has the advantage of freeing the Allies from any previous imperialistic aims: the necessity of abolishing the agreements with Russia (which would comprise the cession of Constantinople to that Power) would in itself exact the adoption of such a measure.

As to Italy, should she not adhere thereto, it would be difficult to see how she could be admitted into the discussion: having previously to her entry into the war presented to the Allies minutely detailed conditions for the advantages she desired to derive therefrom, she would only be entitled to discuss the affairs of the others if she herself allowed discussion upon her own extensions.

And further, the somewhat surprising statement:

One single basis seems to exist at the present time: it is the solidary declaration of the Allies upon their war aims, formulated January 10th, 1917, in answer to the question of President Wilson, but it is rather a programme than a basis of negotiation.[47]

What, indeed, had become of the Fourteen Points and subsequent declarations, the pre-Armistice exchange of Notes, and the discussions of the Supreme War Council between October 30 and November 4?

A revision of this first draft appeared on November 21.[48] It contained no essential changes in regard to Italian problems.[49] A week

---

[46] At least this is the date of House's cablegram transmitting it to Washington.

[47] Miller, II, Document 5. The cablegram was not a wholly accurate summary; it had, indeed, some important lacunæ which, however, do not affect this discussion.

[48] Received by Miller on the twenty-first. The French text of this draft is given in Miller, II, Document 4.

[49] Save the addition, "combined with the principle of the guarantee of the rights of Minorities," in the first paragraph cited above. Istria was omitted from the areas listed in

later, on the twenty-ninth, a third edition of the French draft was given by Jusserand, the French Ambassador in Washington, to the State Department.[50] This third draft made no mention of the denunciation of the secret treaties. Still speaking of peace preliminaries, it definitely stated that

The examination will first apply to Germany and Bulgaria, with which it is to our interest to negotiate at once in order to promote on the one hand the disassociation of the countries which compose the first named: and on the other hand, as to the second country, avoid the dangerous Bulgarian intrigues at home and abroad.

Of equal or greater importance is the following paragraph:

It may be remarked that a certain number of the questions that are raised have to be settled directly amongst the great powers without calling upon any committee to discuss them; this also applies to colonial affairs which essentially concern England and France. It also applies to indemnities, for outside of the torpedoing from which the British fleet mainly suffered, Belgium and France alone are entitled to indemnities on account of the systematic devastation suffered by them. (The states which have become independent and those which have secured considerable territorial enlargement would have but a slight claim to indemnities.) . . .

Taken together, these French plans throw valuable light on France's Italian policy. Much could be said for the proposal to renounce secret treaties, which were to prove in the end such a source of annoyance and ill-feeling. From Italy's own point of view, it is very much a question whether she would not have had as strong a case—certainly a more appealing one—by adopting a bolder and more generous policy, instead of bogging herself in the futile attempt to reconcile the irreconcilable. At the same time, it is only fair to point out that France could well afford to appear generous in this matter, for she was giving up only the worthless Russian guarantee of a free hand on the Rhine.[51] Whether this was a deliberate attempt to court Wilson's favor at the expense of Italy, we must leave to surmise and interpretation;[52] later on, Orlando did claim, as a ground

this same paragraph, and the Tyrol was qualified in the phrase, "perhaps the Tyrol, south of the Brenner."

[50] Reproduced in Baker, *Woodrow Wilson and the World Settlement*, III, Document 7.

[51] Giving up the Near Eastern treaties would not necessarily weaken her claims in that area, for they would still remain on the same level as those of Great Britain and Italy, while it had the advantage (as the French drafts recognized) of disposing of the Russian problem.

[52] The French drafts were increasingly outspoken in their objection to the Fourteen Points.

for gratitude from Wilson, his support of the League of Nations. It was, in any case, a convenient way of torpedoing the Treaty of London, for which neither the French nor the British ever professed affection.

The giving of precedence to the German and Bulgarian settlements was evidently the result of the fact that France was first and foremost concerned with the former, as were all the important Allies with the exception of Italy; in addition, it would be comparatively easier to deal with the two enemy states which had survived as political entities than to plunge into the jungle of the former Danube Monarchy, whose status of enemy or ally was not even clear in places, bordering on the further chaos that was Eastern Europe at the time. As to Turkey, save for the Straits, she was essentially extra-European. These considerations would afford little consolation to Italy, however, for her interest was precisely in those two disintegrated empires, and her diplomacy—quite rightly from her point of view— held it as a cardinal principle that the German settlement must not be given precedence over the Austrian. It is important to bear in mind the divergence as much as the conflict of interests between Italy and her Allies, France in particular.

The comment on the subject of indemnities can only be understood as a manifestation of the absorption of the French in the magnitude of their losses. The restoration of Alsace-Lorraine was strictly taken as restitution, and in no sense an acquisition that could be written off against indemnities. Belgian priority was universally and properly recognized, but in French eyes Italian increments were unqualified gains; perhaps it would not be inappropriate to make a distinction in this respect between "clearly recognizable lines of nationality," even qualified by strategic considerations, and the line of the Treaty of London. Economically, Alsace-Lorraine was of considerably greater value than the proposed Italian acquisitions; from the standpoint of security, Italy's gain would be much the greater. That the physical devastation of France was far the greater was not debatable when one considers that the bulk of French industry is situated in the north; the Italian industrial equipment was essentially untouched. Despite this, the drain of the war on the whole Italian economy was greater than appeared in the confused financial condition of the time.

Taken as a whole, the French proposals of November were highly unfavorable to Italy. Whether they were the result of a carefully planned anti-Italian policy or of a careless tendency to treat Italy as a second-rate Power, the result was the same from the Italian point of view; in any case they were hardly a manifestation of vaunted French tact. The plea of war psychology must seem hollow in this instance; it may serve as an alibi for popular feeling, not for a foreign office whose task it is not only to defend the country's interest, but to do so intelligently; the Quai d'Orsay showed neither a lack of information nor of energy in pursuing its policies at the Peace Conference.

Just what knowledge the Italians had of the French proposals we cannot tell. By December there were signs in Italy of growing dissatisfaction with France, the general complaint being that the latter was opposing the former and not treating her as an equal;[53] about this time also there appeared in the Italian press a sudden interest in colonial questions, which, however, was not sustained.[54] General Bliss heard rumors of these proposed French Plans, which he communicated to Miller[55] on December 12, in the form of a memorandum which he had received.

I have received information, from a source I believe to be trustworthy, that the French government has made certain proposals to the Italian government suggesting a method of procedure at the Peace Conference and outlining, in certain respects, the French attitude. These propositions I have not been able to see myself, but I am informed that their gist is as follows:

The principle of reparation and indemnity shall apply to France and Belgium alone.

At the Peace Conference Germany shall be first dealt with. After the German question has been disposed of the problem of the new states to be formed out of Austria-Hungary shall be considered.

The London agreement will be denounced by the French government.

It is believed that the British government is already in agreement with the French government with regard to the above points. There is also reason to think that France and Great Britain have reached an agreement regarding the partition of Africa and with reference to all Asiatic questions.

The Italians, I am told, feel that Italy is being excluded from the fulfillment of any colonial aspirations and from the reception of indemnity.

---

[53] Cf. Speranza's Report of Dec. 16, 1918.
[54] See *Daily Review of the Foreign Press* for December.
[55] Miller had joined House as legal adviser on Nov. 19.

The attitude of the Italian government toward the French propositions is said to be uncompromisingly negative.[56]

Miller, however, thought some of this, particularly the comment on reparations, highly improbable.[57] The entry in his *Diary*,

Davis . . . frankly rejected the efforts of the Italians to obtain control of the relief in such a way as would coerce the Jugo-Slavs. I told Mr. Davis something of the informal efforts that were going on to induce the Italians to abandon the Treaty of London, which I thought might be successful,[58]

throws light on the activity and spirit of the time.[59] It is somewhat surprising, in the light of all this, to find reports in the Italian press that the London Conference at the beginning of December had essentially recognized the Italian claims, which the Allies were agreed to support.[60]

Wilson, meantime, put into effect his decision to attend the Peace Conference in person. The results of his highly personal conduct of affairs and of his choice of personalities to make up the United States delegation have been widely discussed and are too well known to need comment. He sailed on the "George Washington" on December 4, taking with him the staff of The Inquiry; on this voyage he also brought with him the French and the Italian Ambassadors, Jusserand and di Cellere. That he had great hopes and expectations was plain at the time; his central thought seems to have been the setting up of a new order to govern the relations among peoples, presided over by the ideals of democracy and law. On technical questions of detail he was not informed and, as he told di Cellere, he would rely on his experts.[61] Wilson had not had time before his departure to consider the French draft of November 29, and it was presented to him by Jusserand during the voyage, but apparently

---

[56] Miller, II, Document 61.

[57] Miller, II, Document 63. One would hardly think, in fact, that the matter would be put quite so bluntly to the Italians.

[58] Miller, "Diary," Dec. 13, I, 44. The Italians made similar complaints that the Serbians were using the distribution of relief in Montenegro for political purposes. Cf. Page to House, Feb. 4 and 20, 1919. House papers, Yale University.

[59] This may be compared with the incident of Orlando's visit to Clemenceau on Dec. 7, on which occasion he begged the latter in most earnest fashion "on no account to sanction any recognition of the Yugoslav National Council." Steed, *Through Thirty Years*, II, 263.

[60] See above, p. 69.

[61] Di Cellere's Diary, Dec. 12. Reproduced in Bernardy and Falorsi, *La questione adriatica*, p. 200.

without concrete results.[62] The ocean crossing afforded good opportunities for informal exchanges, of which di Cellere availed himself; in particular, he had several conversations with Mezes, Head of The Inquiry, whom he thought to have convinced of the validity of the Italian claims in regard to the Yugoslavs.[63]

On December 14 Wilson arrived in Paris, and that very evening Miller received a call asking for the text of the Treaty of London, indicating that the question was under consideration at the time.[64] Quite a controversy has raged over the question of whether Wilson had knowledge of the secret treaties among the Allies. During the course of the debate in the United States over the ratification of the Treaty of Versailles, Wilson denied, before the Senate Committee, having had such knowledge before his arrival in Europe. It is quite possible that the text of the various secret treaties had not come to Wilson's knowledge in any official way before this time. However, the existence of these treaties was a matter of public knowledge and they had even been published, albeit in somewhat garbled fashion, by the Bolsheviks, as early as 1917. Certainly House was not ignorant of such commitments, as Balfour had broached the question during his visit to America with the British Mission in 1917; the Commentary on the Fourteen Points, which House had caused to be drafted at the end of October, also implied knowledge of the terms of the Treaty of London. According to Seymour,[65] Wilson, too, was informed of the nature of the secret treaties and fully aware of the fact that they were at variance with his own program, but counted on the Allies' dependence on America to make his views prevail.[66]

---

[62] In reply to an inquiry by di Cellere, Lansing replied that no plan existed for the work of the Peace Conference. Di Cellere's Diary, Dec. 9, Bernardy and Falorsi, *La questione adriatica*, p. 199.

[63] Di Cellere's Diary, Dec. 6-12, *passim*, Bernardy and Falorsi, *op. cit.*, pp. 197-201.

[64] Miller, "Diary," Dec. 14, I, 45.

[65] House, III, 51.

[66] There is also extant a letter of Jan. 30, 1918, from Balfour to Wilson, in which the following passages occur:

"I gather from a message sent by Wiseman that you would like to know my thoughts on the Italian territorial claims under the treaty of London concluded in 1915.

"That treaty . . . bears on the face of it evident proof of the anxiety of the Allies to get Italy into the war, and of the use to which that anxiety was put by the Italian negotiators.

"Personally, however, I am in doubt whether Italy would really be strengthened by the acquisition of all her Adriatic claims. . . . Of the three west-European belligerents she is certainly the most war-weary; and if she could secure peace *and 'Italia Irredenta'* she would, I believe, not be ill satisfied. . . ." (Cited in House, III, 50-51.)

Whatever may be said of secret treaties, it must be remembered that they were engage-

Also bearing on the American attitude toward the Treaty of London is a letter which Miller wrote to Bliss on December 13, in which he stated as his opinion,

that the Note of the Allies quoted in the communication of the President of 5 November, 1918 to the German Government . . . must be considered to have modified the Pact of London in any respect in which the same is inconsistent with the Fourteen Points of the President; for the Note of the Allies is signed on behalf of the British, French, and Italian Governments, the parties to the Pact of London.[67]

Aware of Wilson's attitude and of the impending conflict, di Cellere, upon his arrival in Paris, began to exert himself with members of the American delegation. He spoke with House and Miller on different occasions during the latter part of December, taking the position that America ought to support the Treaty of London, which merely gave Italy the frontiers necessary to protect her from invasion.[68]

On December 21

the President, Orlando, Sonnino, and I [reports House] were together from ten until twelve o'clock. The President talked well but he did not convince the Italians that they should lessen their hold on the Pact of London. On the contrary, Sonnino convinced the President that from a military point of view Italy was pretty much at the mercy of the nations holding the Dalmatian coast.[69]

Just how far Wilson committed himself or may have given to the Italians the impression of committing himself at this time, it is impossible to determine. In an anonymous article which appeared in the *Revue des deux mondes*[70] the author—who, from other internal evidence, seems to have been well informed—claims that when Orlando and Sonnino went to see Wilson in Paris, Sonnino expounded the Italian claims, but, following the advice given him

---

ments representing a promise of payment for value, in some cases at least, received. It was hardly to be expected that the beneficiaries would renounce their gains merely on the plea of a new order in international relations. The Treaty of London is the best and most clear-cut illustration of the conflict, for, unlike the other Allies, Italy had joined the war, not on a plea of self-defense, but deliberately and with a clear agreement as to what the price of her assistance was to be.

[67] Miller, II, Document 65.

[68] Miller, "Diary," Dec. 16 and 25; I, 46, 56.

[69] House, IV, 253.

[70] "L'Aventure de Fiume," *Revue des deux mondes*, Jan. 15, 1921, p. 365.

by Page, did not mention the Treaty of London.[71] Wilson is stated to have granted then that the Brenner frontier was justified but made reservations in regard to the eastern frontier. It should be noted that the above quotation from House makes no specific mention of the northern frontier—of even greater importance to the Italians than the Adriatic—nor of the Commentary on the Fourteen Points to which one would naturally expect the Italians to make reference.[72]

Whatever the precise facts, the Italian claims and the Treaty of London were among the few questions which were considered by Wilson immediately after his arrival in Paris.[73] Complaints were, in fact, beginning to be heard as December was passing into January, and the Conference showed no signs of getting under way, even though the pretext of awaiting Wilson no longer held. A variety of reasons contributed to this delay: the lack of agreement on a prearranged program was one; the very magnitude and complexity of the settlement to be made, with the consequent cumbersome machinery which it necessitated, was another. Wilson himself was somewhat of a problem. His position among the Allied leaders was unique, and he had been hailed by the people somewhat in the guise of a savior and a prophet; his dual rôle of Head of State and Foreign Minister was perplexing, while his enormous prestige counseled caution. For these reasons, the Allied leaders were not averse to letting some time elapse until they could feel surer of their ground in dealing with him. Wilson thus had time to pay official visits, first to London and then to Rome.

When Wilson set out for Italy, both he and the Italian Government, certainly Orlando and Sonnino at least, were clearly aware of the difficulties they would have to face over the Treaty of London; his visit would have seemed an excellent opportunity to make a further attempt at reaching an understanding. Unfortunately, as it happened, his visit was remarkably barren of results. On the cir-

[71] This need not be a contradiction of House's statement, for the Italian policy was to ask, in effect, for the terms of the Treaty of London on the combined grounds of strategy and nationality, but without resting their demands on the legal basis of treaty obligations. House may well have used the term "Pact of London" for the sake of convenience in referring to the Italian demands.

[72] For further evidence on this point, see below, pp. 84-85, 104.

[73] By December 24, according to Beer, quoting a report from Bullitt, the Adriatic question was the only one which had been taken up seriously by Wilson. (Beer, Diary, Dec. 24.) Beer was the American expert on colonial questions.

cumstances of Wilson's visit to Rome, we cannot do better than quote two entries from the Diary of Gino Speranza; the flavor of the reaction to events as they appeared at the moment to an informed observer is best preserved by quoting these entries in full.

December 29th, 1918.

Late last night I read that Minister Bissolati had resigned. A...., his personal secretary, was coming to lunch with me today; so after getting off a telegram on Bissolati's resignation to our Mission in Paris, I made my plans for the day, in order not to be interrupted during his visit. He telephoned to say that he would be late for luncheon, as he was going personally to deliver Bissolati's resignation to Orlando.

A.... trusts me as a friend. He told me an infinite lot of *retroscena*, really nauseating, of political life. Bissolati's move undoubtedly embarrasses Orlando, who, I gather, is the chief offender in Bissolati's eyes. The last straw for Bissolati was the discovery that Orlando had told Wilson that the entire Cabinet shared his—Orlando's—views on the Adriatic question. But the dissension is deeper. Bissolati is enough of an idealist and humanitarian to be unable to put up longer with the insincerity of the Orlando-Sonnino "support" of Wilsonian principles. Bissolati wants to talk to Wilson, and there is no reason why he shouldn't. I told A.... that if he would get from Bissolati a frank, full statement of his case, I would give it to the Ambassador. A.... is an honest soul, not "closed." I think, but this is a mere "think," that the King is near—if not behind—Bissolati; and certainly Bissolati is a strenuous and faithful admirer of the King.

This afternoon I went to the Embassy, all fussed and fussy over plans for the President's visit. What miserable and endless and pitiless vanities; what worthless and ridiculous much ado about nothing! Wilson will arrive by royal train at 2 P.M. on Saturday, stay two or three days in Rome, then go to Naples perhaps.

From the Embassy I drove Richardson to the Capitol, where preparations are in progress for the reception to the President, at which he will be made a citizen of Rome. Richardson has been told that the floor of the great hall where the function will take place isn't strong enough to bear the crowd that will be present! From the Capitol we drove back to the Embassy. Bruce, Post, Buckey, Lane, Anderson, and Train—I don't know whom I didn't see.

At six o'clock the Ambassador came to call on me, and we were closeted for almost an hour, talking over the Bissolati resignation and its effect on the Wilsonian movement in Italy. Mr. Page told me of incidents that had happened during his stay in Paris and of his interview with Wilson and Sonnino. I can't put them down here. I think the Ambassador has clear, broad, right views of what Italians really want and should have, and no more.

January 17th, 1919.

I simply cannot keep up even a skeleton daily record. Events are too many, visitors too numerous, and work too hard and absorbing. As I try to look back at events that have happened since my last entry, I find only a few that stand out for record. I saw little of the President's visit to Rome, except his arrival at the Quirinal, which I watched with Florence[74] from the windows of the Foreign Office—a fine and dignified spectacle, but not over-enthusiastic. Florence attended the reception at the Capitol, escorted by Anderson, as I am not allowed to go out at night, and, together, we saw his arrival at Queen Margherita's palace, opposite our hotel. My part, however inglorious, was to try and break through the "social" program and beg—almost threaten—the Ambassador to arrange for some representative Italians outside of official and social circles to meet the President. We had almost high words. I was tense over Bissolati's resignation and disgusted with "society" for stepping all over the "rights of men." Page asked me to prepare a list of representative Italians, which I did—a very short one—and meanwhile I did what I could to make sure that Wilson would see Bissolati in Rome and Albertini in Milan, the latter having long-distance 'phoned D'Atri to ask me to arrange for him to see the President. Bissolati had asked me, if he had an interview with the President, to interpret for him. After his resignation, he let me know that, since he was no longer a member of the Cabinet, he could not make any move to see the President. He could not go unless he were invited. Late in the second day of the President's stay in Rome, Bissolati was summoned, and next day Wilson saw Albertini; so that much was accomplished.

Meanwhile, Palazzoli, agitator and agent of the "people of Rome," was planning for Wilson to address them. I wish I could record (I should as a matter of historic duty!) all the obstructive measures taken by the Italian Government to prevent the President from speaking to the people. It succeeded! More's the pity. Page told me that, when Sonnino first heard of the plan, he said, *"Porcheria! Porcheria!"* The officials in charge of the visit even lied to him. They told him that, on the way to the Chamber of Deputies, his motor would stop in Piazza Venezia, so that he might speak to the people, but instead they whisked him off to Montecitorio. When he asked if it were there that he was to speak to the citizens, they replied, "No, it is now too late." Meanwhile the Ambassador in his car and thousands of persons were waiting in the Piazza. Even the plan for the President to stop a moment in the Piazza on his way to the reception at

[74] Mrs. Speranza.

the Capitol was frustrated; and finally, on the evening of his departure, as he started to go out on the balcony of the Quirinal, from which it had been arranged for him to say a few words, he was informed that there was no audience—quite true for a cordon of troops on the Piazza in front of the palace prevented any one from coming into it. After the President left Rome, the Government circulated reports that Wilson had a *fobia* for crowds; also that it feared some one might throw a bomb. All rot. The people really trust Wilson, almost too much, I think. The "antis" of the Regular Socialist Party have all they can do to prevent the party from going over to him. In fact, at Milan, the Socialist Mayor, Caldara, disregarded the Party resolution and went to greet the President.

The Presidential visit showed me the strength of social privilege and the hopelessness of breaking through it, except by violence. It was a pitiful spectacle of favoritism, "climbing," and lack of responsibility on the part of those in authority to the times and the Country. I'm through with them! The trouble is that government today, *everywhere*, is *class* government, and it is so entrenched, if not behind physical force, then behind sentiments, "respects," habits of mind, and human vanities, that you can't hope to change it "constitutionally."

Lest it be thought that this is too strong language, it should be remembered that Speranza was by no means a revolutionary, but was sincerely devoted to the Wilsonian ideal, with the qualification that his intimate connection with things Italian made him sympathetic to the Italian case and anxious to make sure that what was sound and reasonable in it should receive a fair hearing from Wilson. It is rather the reaction of an "honest soul" driven to exasperation by the feeling that its efforts were blocked at every turn by the blank wall of reaction and narrow prejudice.

Later on, much was made in Italy of the fact that Wilson had singled out Bissolati to discuss Italian problems, and hints were dropped that this gesture was a manifestation of his sympathy for a policy in opposition to that of the Italian Government. There was nothing in the nature of a plot in the fact of Wilson's interview with Bissolati, and if he did not have an opportunity to speak with other leaders of Italian opinion—with Salandra, for example—that was merely due to the lack of open time left by the crowded schedule of official and social engagements. Even from the Italian point of view, it should be considered that the fact that Bissolati was strongly sympathetic with the Wilsonian outlook in such matters as the League of Nations, would have tended to create in Wilson's mind a favorable predisposition toward the Italian case, instead of strengthening his conviction that he was more representative of the wishes of the people than their own Governments. Such a policy would have required boldness and imagination on the part of the Italian Government, and the very fact that Bissolati had just deemed it necessary to resign indicates that Orlando was committed not to follow such a course.

The Italian Government was anxious, none the less, to discuss its claims with Wilson. It must be remembered that at this time, neither popular nor Government opinion had yet definitely crystallized in Italy. If Sonnino had a definite program, Orlando had not; his main concern was to do whatever was politically feasible. When the question of Italian territorial claims was broached to Wilson, he gave the candid and truthful answer that he was not in a position to discuss such matters, being himself uninformed on specific territorial issues, which he had left to his experts to study and report upon. Such was in fact the case, but the Italians shared the general belief that Wilson had reached fairly definite conclusions at this time on the subject of the European territorial settlement; his answer was therefore interpreted as indicating unwillingness to discuss the matter, and in turn created among the Italians an attitude of reticence and suspicion.[75]

What would have happened had Wilson held frank and open discussions with the Italians at this time, must remain a matter for speculation; it is safe to say, however, that nothing could have been worse than the vicious circle of mistrust upon which Italian-American relations entered from the very start. It may also be pointed out that Orlando realized—as he asserted later on—that the whole question of Italian claims could easily have been settled in the early stages before Italian opinion had become crystallized,[76] and also that American opinion on its side was still open on the subject of the new Yugoslavia.

[75] For some of the facts mentioned in this paragraph the author is indebted to a letter from Maj. Thomas H. Thomas, who was in touch at the time with Speranza and with happenings at the American Embassy in Rome. As later developments showed, the Brenner frontier was not questioned by Wilson who, however, evinced the greatest tenacity in denying the Italian claims in Istria and in the Adriatic. It would therefore seem safe to draw the conclusion that Wilson committed himself to the Brenner frontier at the end of December but declined to give an opinion on the rest of the Italian claims at that time.
[76] See below, pp. 101-2, 123.

IV

THE PROBLEM OF THE ADRIATIC STATED

WILSON'S RETURN from Rome marked the end of the round of official visits. The various delegations had for the major part by now been appointed and, almost two months after the Armistice, the Conference could at last get under way. The Allies had had time to become acquainted with the American President and to prepare themselves for the coming discussions. Two things were now clear. Wilson had set his heart on the creation of an association of nations to prevent a recurrence of the events of the past four years; it may be said that he attached more importance to this than to the specific details of the forthcoming treaties. As he had optimistically told House at their first meeting (December 14), he intended

making the League of Nations the center of the whole programme and letting everything revolve around that. Once that is a *fait accompli*, nearly all the very serious difficulties will disappear.[1]

The European Allies on the other hand were at best open-minded on the question of a League of Nations. Clemenceau, for one, had openly declared that he pinned his faith on the system of alliances to preserve the peace.[2] This statement was in reply to Wilson's speech in London,[3] wherein he had taken issue with the system of balance of power, and Wilson in turn took up Clemenceau's challenge at Manchester.[4] However, Clemenceau realized that, under proper conditions, a League might be useful to France, with the result that instead of a sterile opposition, a French scheme was elaborated for such a League. A British scheme had been likewise produced and, under the impetus of these proposals, Wilson was prompted to define his own ideas, heretofore confined to the realm of generalities.

Wilson's interest in a League of Nations was not such, however, as to make him lose sight of the specific questions which were of greater interest to the Europeans. On the contrary, his position was

---

[1] House, IV, 251-52.
[2] Speech of Dec. 29 in the French Chamber, *Daily Review of the Foreign Press,* Dec. 23-31.
[3] Guildhall speech of Dec. 28, Temperley, III, 58-59.
[4] Manchester speech of Dec. 30, Temperley, III, 59.

that a fair settlement was a prerequisite to the success of the League. He insisted that the American people could not be asked to approve a settlement which violated the high ideals for which they had gone to war, as stated in the Fourteen Points. He was thus led to take a very definite position on the various issues that came before the Conference. America's decisive rôle in the ultimate victory, and even more the extent to which Europe was dependent upon her for continued economic and financial assistance, are all important in this respect. The mere possibility of reprisals, or the threat of withdrawal, furnished unanswerable arguments, as the event was to prove before long. The definite adoption of unanimity, rather than majority rule, on January 17 gave Wilson the power of veto, even in purely European questions.

We have seen evidence that Wilson had had the Italian problem in mind from the very time of his arrival in Paris.[5] Despite this interest on his part and the Italians' eagerness to have their frontiers ratified by the Conference, the Italian question did not become a prime concern of the Conference until April.[6] A variety of reasons made for delay. One was that, as mentioned before, Germany was the most important enemy Power, and the settlement of the German question took first place for all the principal Allies, except Italy. Another was the unforeseen outcome of the war in the former Austria-Hungary. While Germany remained as a definite entity, there was no longer an Austria-Hungary, but various bits of territory whose status ranged all the way from that of enemy to that of ally. The Republics of Austria and of Hungary were easily classified as enemies; Czechoslovakia, almost wholly within the limits of the defunct Empire, was recognized as an ally. In the southwest a peculiar situation had developed. There was Serbia, unquestionably an ally, but territories larger than Serbia herself had suddenly joined with her. These territories were not claimed by Serbia by right of conquest, in virtue of existing treaties, or as redeemed lands, as Transylvania, for instance, was claimed by Rumania. Instead an entirely new entity had come into existence, which called itself the Kingdom of the Serbs, Croats, and Slovenes. Of this new creation, the larger part in territory and population had been enemy, some of it loyal

---

[5] See above, p. 79.

[6] Much preliminary work was done, however, in reports, informal discussions, and meetings.

to the Hapsburgs almost to the very last. The matter clearly called for careful consideration: how much reality was there in the new state and was it likely to hold together?[7] These considerations, which the Italians naturally did not fail to emphasize, lay behind the refusal of the Allies to recognize the Serb-Croat-Slovene State until a later time.

The Yugoslav delegation in Paris was a clear reflection of this state of affairs. There was Pašić, the old Serb, who understood Serbian ambitions in Macedonia, Albania, and Bosnia-Herzegovina, but who was rather a stranger to the Upper Adriatic.[8] There was Trumbić, the Dalmatian Croat, President of the Yugoslav Committee, and in that capacity most representative of the reality of Yugoslav unity. There was Zolger, the Slovene, turned overnight from an Imperial Austrian official into a delegate of an Allied Power. Little wonder that the Yugoslav—officially Serbian—delegation was looked at askance. No better evidence of this could be given than the opinion expressed by Wilson to Orlando in the course of a conversation on January 30. Wilson thought that

Yugo-Slavia might be divided into one, two or three States. He was pre-pared to admit two Yugo-Slav States to the League of Nations but, if it were found advisable to separate them into three parts, he would prefer to place the more unformed and less developed of the new States under the mandatory of the League of Nations.[9]

The impatience expressed by Beer, of the American delegation,[10] was shared by many of his colleagues, and it was not until the arrival of Professor Pupin, more qualified to understand and be understood

---

[7] The seeming reality of the new state may almost be said to have varied in direct pro-portion to the distance from Belgrade. In Croatia-Slovenia there was a definite opposition party, highly suspicious of Serbia. In Italy, in part owing to the knowledge deriving from proximity, and in part from wishful thinking, there was much doubt as to the viability of the new Yugoslavia. In Great Britain and in Amercia the new formation was much more readily accepted. In the latter country it almost appeared as an entity on a par with Italy, at least among certain groups.

[8] Pašić always thought in terms of the Old Serbia. He had no objections indeed to terri-torial acquisitions, but the idea of a federation in which Serbia would merely be one of the units was essentially repugnant to him. He remained suspicious of the Manifesto of Corfu and of the Pact of Rome alike, and there had been friction between him and the Yugoslav Committee. Cf., for instance, Steed, *Through Thirty Years,* II, 235-37.

[9] "Notes of a Conversation between President Wilson, Signor Orlando, Colonel House, and Signor Scialoja," Miller, IV, Document 268.

[10] Beer, Diary, Feb. 19: "Dined with Delegation of the Kingdom of Serbs, Croats and Slovenes . . . Nothing especially new. These small nations with their intense national feel-ings bore me."

by the Americans, that a marked change of heart was experienced by some of them.[11] This situation, together with the extensive Italian claims in the Adriatic, was one of the elements that contributed to a postponement of the consideration of the Adriatic problem.

The political situation in Italy also made for delay and hesitation. Bissolati's resignation at the end of December, instead of removing an element of discord from the Cabinet, opened the way to intrigues and realignments. The Italian delegation was not even complete when the Conference first assembled on January 12. Instead Orlando had to return to Rome to cope with a more important ministerial crisis, brought about by the resignation of his Finance Minister, Nitti. Nitti was commonly credited with the desire to supplant Orlando, and in fact owned to the American Military Attaché in Rome that he would head the Government whenever he chose, which would be a few weeks after the elections;[12] he disagreed with Orlando's labor policy at home, as well as with his foreign policy, but mainly with the former. On the other hand, Salandra thought that Orlando had forced Nitti's resignation because he did not trust him in charge of the Government during his absence.[13] Whatever the actual facts, the situation bore witness to the confused and complicated play of parliamentary politics. Orlando, skilled in that game, did not attempt to form a strong ministry; deprived of Nitti's support, he took into the cabinet Facta, whose principal recommendation was his close connection with Giolitti.[14] Altogether, the new ministry was a patchwork affair which established a nice balance between the various parties in the chamber, but which, from the point of view of foreign affairs—of necessity the dominant issue during the coming months—did not represent any definite line of policy.[15] This too large preoccupation with domestic party politics was to prove a

[11] Conversation with Professor James T. Shotwell, then a member of The Inquiry. Professor Pupin as an American citizen was of course not a member of the Yugoslav delegation.

[12] Report of the American Military Attaché, Feb. 24. It was thought in Italy at this time that a general election was in the offing. House's papers, Yale University.

[13] Speranza's Report of his interview with Salandra, Jan. 17.

[14] However the *Stampa*, generally considered a Giolitti paper, remained hostile to the Government. Giolitti, too, was biding his time for a come-back.

[15] Sonnino remained at the Foreign Office, but Orlando kept the thread of negotiations in his own hands. In addition to Orlando and Sonnino, the Italian delegation consisted of Salandra, Barzilai, and Salvago-Raggi, the last named versed in colonial questions. On the whole it was not a strong delegation and the last three members played a wholly insignificant part in the negotiations.

serious handicap to Orlando, who was to conduct the coming negotiations with an ever-watchful eye on the home situation.

Preliminary meetings began at the Quai d'Orsay on January 12, and the following week was spent in organizing the working of the Conference; the arrangements made were ratified at the first Plenary Session on the eighteenth. Between this time and the time of Wilson's departure for the United States on February 14, the groundwork was laid for the majority of the territorial settlements. This was done by the appointment of commissions to study and report on the various territorial problems. Italian problems, like those affecting the other major Powers, the Powers with "general interests," were reserved by the Council as its own province. There were, besides, countless meetings and interviews among delegates and minor representatives.

THE REPORT OF THE AMERICAN TERRITORIAL EXPERTS

There was little doubt by this time as to Wilson's position in regard to the Treaty of London. The Armistice discussions had made that clear, while creating at the same time an unfortunate misunderstanding. However the matter had not yet come before the Conference. The American attitude had been stated again by Miller in his letter of December 13 to Bliss,[16] and once more he now expressed the view "that any provisions of the Pact of London . . . which may be inconsistent with the agreement [Wilson's Note of Nov. 5, 1918] . . . were by that agreement abrogated and are no longer in force."[17] Wilson adhered to this view throughout the negotiations.

Much depended, therefore, on the specific proposals that would be made in regard to the future Italian frontiers. The Report of the American Territorial Experts was ready in the latter part of January. In regard to matters affecting the Italian settlement, it made the following recommendations:

1. *Northern frontier.*—The report recommended a line between the purely ethnic line and that of the Treaty of London. This line, which would include in Italy 161,000 Germans, was admittedly not as good strategically as the line of the Treaty of London, but represented a considerable amelioration of the intentionally bad frontier

---

[16] See above, p. 80.
[17] Miller's letter to House, Jan. 11, 1919. See below, Document 15.

imposed on Italy by Austria in 1866. Such a concession was deemed necessary to give Italy a defensible frontier if she were to enter the League of Nations with a feeling of security, especially in view of the possibility of her having a powerful German state on her northern border (see Map IV).

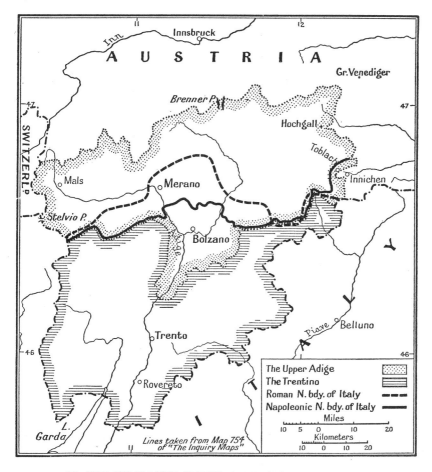

III. THE TYROL: THE TRENTINO AND THE UPPER ADIGE

2. *Eastern frontier.*—Here also a deviation was proposed from the ethnic principle. The suggested boundary ran along the main watershed of the Carnic and Julian Alps, then following the high ridges down the Istrian peninsula. Three hundred and seventy thousand Yugoslavs out of a population of 715,000 would thus be given to

Italy, as against 75,000 Italians left in Yugoslavia. In this case again this was presented as a reasonable compromise and a concession to

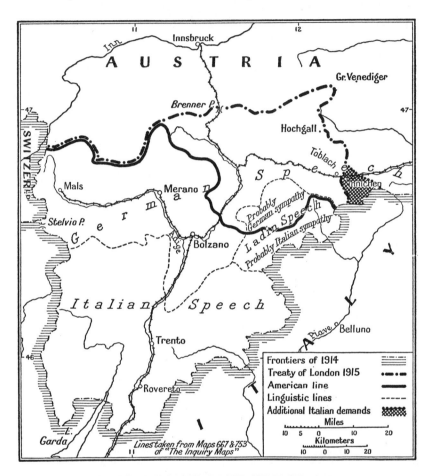

IV. LINES PROPOSED IN THE TYROL IN 1919

Note that the linguistic line is practically identical with the line of the Austrian offer of 1915 (see map, I). The law of the Austrian Republic of November 22, 1918, and the decision of the Austrian Staatsrat of January 3, 1919, also described a line very closely following the linguistic line, the Ladins being included in Austria (cf. map in Almond and Lutz, *The Treaty of St. Germain*). For the linguistic line in this map and the following, cf. also the map given by Marinelli, "The Regions of Mixed Population in Northern Italy," *Geographical Review*, March 1919, pp. 144-45.

the necessity of giving an adequate hinterland to Trieste and Pola for economic and strategic reasons (see Map V).

As to Fiume, while the city had a sizable Italian majority, which

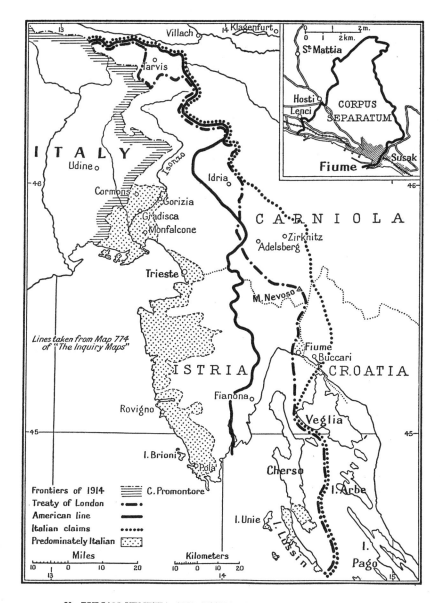

V. JULIAN VENETIA AND ISTRIA: LINES PROPOSED IN 1919

Three remarks should be made in regard to the line of the Treaty of London as it appears in this map: (1) The extreme northern segment extends West of Tarvis (cf. map I); (2) between Istria and Monte Nevoso, instead of running in a straight northwest-southeast direction, the Treaty of London line is curved toward the west so as to cut the Fiume-Laibach railway at the San Pietro junction (cf. maps I, VI); (3) in the extreme south it curves around the island of Lussin, and excludes Pago, which was assigned to Italy in the Treaty of London. The boundary of the *corpus separatum* is taken from Bowman, *The New World;* and from Benedetti, *Fiume, Porto Baross e il retroterra.*

the addition of Sušak would reverse into a small Croat majority, its retention was vital to Yugoslavia. There would be the additional advantage to the Danubian hinterland of competition between it and Trieste if the two ports were under different sovereignties.

3. *Eastern Adriatic.*—The entire coast from the Italian frontier in Istria to Albania and all the islands were to go to Yugoslavia.

In regard to this last country, the report recommended its recognition, to consist of Serbia, Montenegro, and the Serb-Croat-Slovene territory of the former Austria-Hungary.

4. *Albania.*—In consideration of Italy's "doubtful claim," it was recommended that she should be given Valona with its immediate hinterland, as a mandatory of the League, however, and not in full sovereignty. The north was to go to Yugoslavia.[18]

5. *Dodecanese.*—Rhodes and the Dodecanese islands, overwhelmingly Greek in population, should go to Greece.

6. *Colonies.*—Libya should be given an adequate hinterland.

Finally the report suggested that the mandatory principle should be applied to Anatolia, but no recommendation was made of specific mandatories.[19]

These recommendations of the American Territorial Experts may perhaps best be characterized as a sane and fair-minded analysis of local situations. As to the physical and ethnographical facts which lay behind them, there could not be much dispute.[20] The American Report took into account first ethnographical, then economic and strategic considerations, and struck a moderate compromise between them. In the north, Italy was to have a frontier better than that drawn along a purely linguistic line, but not the best strategically. Likewise in the east, for economic and strategic reasons, a substan-

[18] For Central Albania the Report recognized that nominal autonomy under a League mandatory would be the best solution. Having ruled out Italy, whose presence would be a source of friction with both Greece and Yugoslavia, the Report added the somewhat unexpected commentary, which would have made strange reading to Italian eyes: "These are obstacles which can only be faced under the protection of a great Power like England or the United States, and then only by a Power sufficiently imbued with the missionary spirit to be willing to spend its efforts unselfishly."

[19] This is merely a brief condensation of the recommendations of the American Report. For a full statement, see below, Document 16. See also Maps III, IV, and V.

[20] The figures used in the American Report were based, in the main, on the Austrian census of 1910. There was naturally any amount of propaganda and misinformation, deliberate and otherwise, in circulation, but no serious discrepancy among responsible sources. Whatever discrepancy there was would not have invalidated the recommendations of this report. Even the differences caused by the so-called process of denationalization, of which much was made by all claimants, would alter statistics only by rather negligible amounts. For the Italian view, see below, p. 100, n. 33.

tial number of Slavs was to be incorporated into Italy. Economic considerations dictated that Fiume should go to Yugoslavia, despite an Italian nucleus, and its railway connection with Laibach was not to be cut by the Italian frontier. Again in Dalmatia, the small proportion of Italians was held to be no argument against its full attribution to Yugoslavia. Historical arguments as such, Roman frontiers, quotations from Dante, and the glory that was Venice made no noticeable impression on the Americans. Characteristically, to them Italy and Yugoslavia were on the same footing, and the arguments that held for the one must apply to the other. Considerations rooted in the idea of balance of power, as for instance that Italy should have undisputed control of the Adriatic because France would receive a privileged position on the Rhine, and Great Britain would secure advantages somewhere else, carried no weight whatsoever with them. Those were distinct and independent problems, to be settled on their own merits; of far more importance was the welfare of the populations involved. In short, the very ideas which lay at the foundation of the Treaty of London were deliberately disregarded, nor was any mention made of that Treaty as creating any claims for Italy. It could hardly have been otherwise if the Wilsonian principles were to guide the peace settlement, and the idea of the League of Nations was the corner stone of the American Report.

Here was clearly a potential source of difficulty. On the basis of the Fourteen Points, it is difficult to criticize the proposed American settlement, and any attempt to do so and to justify larger acquisitions while professing to abide by these principles must needs be strained and appear disingenuous, as indeed it often was. If, however, exceptions were to be made in favor of Great Britain (freedom of the seas[21] and colonies), and of France (the Saar, colonies), and in a host of other cases (e.g., Poland, Czechoslovakia, etc.), it might appear somewhat strange that strict "justice" should be adhered to when it came to Italy. *Summum jus, summa injuria,* and one may understand the feeling which became prevalent in Italy of being cheated by comparison with the other Powers.[22] Dependent as she was upon

---

[21] The doctrine of freedom of the seas may have been difficult of definition, and the British objection correctly founded on this lack of definiteness; the fact remains that Great Britain succeeded in disposing of the troublesome (to her) question completely.

[22] This real or supposed discriminatory treatment of Italy has been and remains one of the most valuable talking points of the present Italian régime.

her Allies, and powerless to block the German settlement, Italy could indeed fall back on the Treaty of London, as she eventually did, but she hesitated before putting herself in so invidious a position before Wilson.

The American Report was of course not made public in January, and the Italians were preparing a statement of their own.

THE ITALIAN MEMORANDUM OF CLAIMS

This memorandum, drawn up by Barzilai, was the first formal statement of the Italian position, and is worth analyzing in some detail. It bore the date of February 7, and a résumé of it was given out by the Stefani Agency[23] on March 12. The original document[24] is a lengthy, not to say verbose, disquisition.

The purpose of this memorandum was to give "a statement of Italy's claims on the territories of the former Austro-Hungarian Monarchy." It set forth "in their whole the various reasons upon which the Conventions regulating Italy's entrance into the war were based." It is important to notice two things: the memorandum confined itself to the *former Austro-Hungarian territories*; instead of taking a legalistic view of the Treaty of London, it wisely sought to go back of that Treaty to the foundation of the Italian claims.

By way of introduction the memorandum pointed out, like the American Report, the need of security as a sound basis for creating a League of Nations. Stressing the concept of "natural boundaries," it insisted that violent displacement of the original population could not create a valid claim, pointing out that, for that matter, the numbers of alien population which Italy claimed to annex would constitute a smaller percentage of the country's population than was the case with any of the succession states or with France.

Coming to specific frontier questions, the memorandum presented the following claims:

1. *Northern frontier.*—The line proposed in the north was essentially the line of the Treaty of London, with two small additions:

(a) A rectification in the neighborhood where the Treaty of London line joined the frontier of 1914, by the addition of Innichen and the Sexten Valley;

---

[23] The official Italian news agency.
[24] See below, Document 17. Maps IV and V.

(b) At the point where Carinthia bordered on the Küstenland, the addition of Tarvis, important as a railway junction.[25]

This claim was presented as a moderate demand, based on the geographical unity of the Trentino and the Upper Adige (Southern Tyrol), and strategic considerations, with a passing touch on the historical connection.[26] As to the population, the Italians claimed 180,000 German-speaking inhabitants (220,000 according to the Austrian statistics), making the area in its entirety 70 percent Italian.

2. *Eastern land frontier.*—Here also the frontier now proposed deviated from the Treaty of London line. Following that line to a point east of Idria, it then diverged from it, continuing in a south-easterly direction so as to include Adelsberg and Zirknitz, then following the watershed between the Quarnero and the Canale di Maltempo instead of the administrative boundary between Istria and Croatia, included Fiume, reaching the coast east of Buccari, and joined the Treaty of London line between the islands of Cherso and Veglia (see Map V).

This frontier, according to the Italian memorandum, would merely restore the unity of Julian Venetia, artificially divided under separate administrations, thus giving Italy its natural boundary in the east. As to population, this would bring into Italy 482,000 Italians as against 411,000 Slavs; stress was laid on the cultural factor, the definite Italian preponderance in the urban centers, Trieste, Gorizia, Pola, Fiume, in the civil administration throughout, and the essentially Italian character of the whole region, whose Italian culture even the Slavs had in large part adopted.[27]

3. *The Adriatic and Dalmatia.*—The line of the Treaty of London was claimed in Dalmatia, emphasis being placed on the moderation of this demand which constituted a threat to no one, while it was

[25] The map given in Temperley, IV, 298, shows a further rectification between Switzerland and the Brenner, eliminating the pocket formed by the Vent Valley, by bringing the frontier over the Wildspitze. No evidence of this claim appears in the Inquiry maps. The Italian map submitted with the memorandum is not available. See Maps III and IV.

[26] The historical argument was weak. Neither the Roman frontier nor the short-lived Napoleonic Kingdom of Italy had reached as far north as the Italian claim. If anything, the fact that Napoleon had considered strategically sufficient a frontier closer to the linguistic line was an argument against the line of the Brenner. See Map III.

[27] The precise extent of Julian Venetia, in particular the status of the coastal region from Fianona to Fiume (Liburnia) and its past connection with Italy, were the subject of considerable debate. Without going into the details of this question, we may refer to a scholarly study of it by Maranelli and Salvemini, *La questione dell'Adriatico*, Chap. I.

absolutely essential for Italian security in the Adriatic. Even with this protection, Italy would have to demand neutralization of the coast and islands not attributed to her. The Austrian statistics, which recognized only 12,000 Italians in a population of 287,000 in the part of Dalmatia claimed by Italy, merely bore testimony to the continued suppression of the Italian element;[28] but, even so, no more than 50,000 Italians were claimed to live in this area. As in the case of Julian Venetia, the historical and cultural background was emphasized (see Map II).

4. *Fiume.*—The importance attached to this point was borne out by the fact that as much space was devoted to it in the Italian memorandum as to any of the other areas considered, although it had already been included in the claim for Julian Venetia.

Fiume, it was pointed out, was necessary to the system of land defenses in the east; Italy had particularly felt the weight of the Russian defection, not having been compensated like her Allies by the assistance of American troops, and had thus more than lived up to her engagements of 1915. But the burden of the argument was nationality and the right of self-determination: Fiume had 33,000 Italians, 10,927 Slavs, and 1,300 Magyars, and had herself proclaimed her wish to be united to Italy on October 29, 1918. Other considerations were adduced: the importance of preventing Fiume from becoming, under a Yugoslav façade, a base of Germanic expansion toward the Adriatic; also the fact that Fiume's hinterland was Central Europe, while Croatia supplied only a small fraction of its commerce. Italy, a better equipped and better qualified maritime nation than the prospective Yugoslavia, and already in control of Trieste, was its natural possessor.

In view of the situation at the time, it was natural that this statement of the Italian case should be directed mainly to the Americans, even though they were not singled out in the memorandum. Hence the stress on the moderation of the claims made and the endeavor to show their consistency, or at least to disprove their inconsistency, with the Wilsonian principles; it was good tactics to pass lightly over the Treaty of London. There was no attempt at concealing the annexation of Slavs and Germans, but that in itself need not be objectionable—to a certain extent it was admitted even in the Amer-

[28] The further claim that Italian was the dominant language in Dalmatia would tend to contradict the weight of this suppression. In fact the Austrian rule had been mild by comparison with the methods of its successors, whether Italian or Yugoslav.

ican Report—and, where it occurred, it was justified on grounds of military necessity and economic welfare. The frontier demanded by Italy was no doubt a favorable one from the standpoint of security, but the point might well be made that Italy's neighbors were also entitled to their own security. A question might also be raised over the fact that during her negotiations with Austria-Hungary in 1914-15, Italy had apparently considered satisfactory a frontier well on this side of the one she now claimed to need. To be sure she had fought a costly war since 1915, but if the spoils of victory and compensations were the real bases of her claim, that was somewhat of a departure from the Wilsonian principles. Did she need greater protection against a weaker Yugoslavia than against a stronger Austria-Hungary? The question points to the difference between the situations on her northern and eastern frontiers respectively. If, as seemed possible at the time, Austria was to be absorbed by Germany, Italy would be confronted with a powerful neighbor on the north; it was this consideration which underlay the recommendation to give Italy the Brenner frontier, contained in the "Official American Commentary on the Fourteen Points" at the end of October, 1918.[29] Yugoslavia could hardly be called a strong Power, and there was everything to be said in favor of avoiding the creation of a Yugoslav irredentism. The simple solution might have seemed to be to allow the Slavs to join the new Yugoslavia, and from there argue that the outlets to the sea should follow the hinterland, rather than the opposite, as was the Italian contention. Certainly Italy could not complain of a dearth of good ports.

As to the question of nationalities, while it was quite true that, even if all her claims were granted, Italy as a whole would have a smaller percentage of aliens than any of the succession states,[30] that argument in itself need not carry undue weight. It so happened that both in the Tyrol and in Julian Venetia the linguistic line could be traced with rather unusual definiteness. On the other hand, the Italians' claim of superior culture, as manifested by their dominance in the towns and the general character of the culture of Julian Venetia and Dalmatia, could not be ignored;[31] in fact, the American

[29] See above, pp. 63-64.

[30] The Italian figure of 4 percent in the case of France was apparently obtained by counting as German the entire population of Alsace-Lorraine, an argument which might require more detailed consideration.

[31] There seems little doubt that the statement of the Italian memorandum, that the

Report took cognizance of this argument, and it was rather a difference of degree than of principle as to the extent to which it should be taken into account.

In the Adriatic, the claim to a part of Dalmatia, save on the basis of the Treaty of London, could not but appear weak. The military defense of this isolated over-sea possession was likely to be more of a liability than an asset in the event of war. It is difficult to escape the impression that what Italy really wanted in the Adriatic was not only security but as much as possible a *mare clausum*. That had been the aim of Salandra and Sonnino in 1915, an aim of which the former was still in favor.[32]

But the most striking feature of the Italian claim was the demand for Fiume, specifically allotted to Croatia in the very Treaty of London. This particular provision may well have been the result of Russian influence, and there is no denying that the Russian collapse had put a grievous burden on Italy, as on the other Allies for that matter. Italy did emphasize this fact, but she might well hesitate to put it forward as a justification for further compensation. She did therefore decide to fall back on arguments of nationality and defense.

The facts about Fiume were fairly simple. According to the census of 1910, the city proper had 22,488 Italians and 13,351 Slavs; if, however, the suburb of Sušak were included, there were 23,988 Italians and 24,351 Slavs.[33] Sušak is separated from Fiume proper only by

---

visitor to Dalmatia could only get the impression of an Italian land, was correct. Italian was commonly spoken along the coast and currently used even by many Slavs. It is still commonly understood if one can overcome the suspicion which its very use arouses, though it is losing ground among the younger generation.

[32] "As regards the Adriatic, his [Salandra's] position was that Italy was not and could not under any circumstances be strong enough to defend two frontiers at the same time, or as he put it, Italy could not fight Austria and France at the same time, either on land or sea, and must, therefore, try to have as much as possible, at least a single naval frontier. This he explained by saying that Italy could not keep a defensive fleet in the Adriatic and also one in the Mediterranean so that, as a result of this war, to whose success she has materially contributed, she is entitled to be assured that the fleet of no State shall be in the Adriatic as a menace to Italy." Speranza's Report of his interview with Salandra, Jan. 17.

[33] Juridically, all citizens of Fiume were subjects of the Hungarian Crown. This fact should be borne in mind, as well as the fact that Fiume was a town whose main activity was maritime trade; a certain latitude in its choice of nationality—especially in times of stress—could naturally be exercised by a portion of the population, for whom the element of economic interest would be an important factor.

A census taken during December by the National Council of Fiume gave the following results for the city proper: Italians, 19,684; Slavs (Croats, Slovenes, Serbs), 6,576; others (Hungarians, Germans, etc.), 4,834. The census did not extend to Sušak, outside the jurisdiction of the National Council. Speranza's Report of Feb. 21.

a narrow stream, the Recina (Eneo), and is in every respect part of the same agglomeration. The main port facilities belong to Fiume; Sušak has only a small harbor, Porto Baross, used primarily for the wood commerce of Croatia. Fiume proper, without Sušak, was not part of the Kingdom of Croatia-Slavonia, but a *corpus separatum*, directly under the Hungarian Crown. This distinct status of Fiume dated from 1868 and was the result of a falsification of article 66 of the Hungaro-Croatian compromise of that year. The Italians, on the other hand, claimed that Fiume had enjoyed a special status from time immemorial and that this status had been confirmed by Maria Theresa in 1779.[34] Much was made of the situation by both Italians and Yugoslavs. As to the country surrounding Fiume, no one denied that it was solidly inhabited by Slavs.

The economic considerations adduced by the Italian memorandum warrant critical examination. No doubt Italy was a great maritime nation, better equipped than Yugoslavia; on the other hand, Austria-Hungary, while not a major sea power, had had a navy and a mercantile marine both manned in substantial part by Croats and Dalmatians.[35] It was also true that Italian control of both Trieste and Fiume would give Italy a strangle hold on Central European trade; but for that very reason it might be best to encourage competition between the two ports. As against this might be set the prospect of leaving under Yugoslav sovereignty a port whose hinterland was largely Hungary and Czechoslovakia, bearing in mind the feeling between Hungarians and Yugoslavs, and the lack of Balkan political aptitude.[36] The anti-German rôle of Italy might appeal greatly to the French, but less to the Americans; in any case, it would depend

[34] The two statements are by no means contradictory, for the compromise of 1868 was the result of the new organization of Austria-Hungary, the Ausgleich of 1867, as the result of which Croatia was left to deal directly and solely with Hungary.

There is a whole literature on the subject of Fiume, much of it propaganda and of little use. The following works, among the more serious treatments, may be mentioned: G. Benedetti, *Fiume, Porto Baross e il retroterra;* C. Maranelli and G. Salvemini, *La questione dell'Adriatico* (an excellent and scholarly survey of the whole Adriatic problem); E. Susmel, *Fiume attraverso la storia;* S. Tchiritch, *La Question de Fiume;* F. Šišić, *Abridged Political History of Rieka (Fiume)* (this gives a facsimile of article 66 of the compromise of 1868, showing the alteration made in it).

[35] As in the army, the officer class had a larger representation of Germans and Magyars. There were also Italians among the crews and Italian as a language was widely used.

[36] Already at this time Hungary showed signs of gravitating toward Italy; Czechoslovakia could be expected to lean toward Yugoslavia, although her relations with Italy remained cordial. These considerations point to the overwhelming importance of the economic factor in the case of Fiume.

upon Italy remaining in the anti-German camp, a doubtful prospect for the longer future. These were essentially political considerations, just as political considerations of power were behind some of the Italian claims, and this is what—from Wilson's point of view— vitiated the Italian argument.

Just why Fiume should have been added to the Italian claims, when Wilson's opposition even to the terms of the Treaty of London was well known, is hard to tell. Before and during the war, the slogan of Italian irredentism had been: Trento and Trieste. It would hardly be an exaggeration to say that Italian opinion had been unaware of the existence of such a city as Fiume. The cry for Fiume was of very recent origin; certainly the Government had done nothing to discourage it and it is worth noting that even Italian moderates, such men as Bissolati and Salvemini, who favored compromise with the Slavs in other places, insisted on the Italian character of Fiume.[37] It is also of interest that Sonnino steadfastly adhered to the written letter of the law and always demanded the terms of the Treaty of London, no more and no less. The responsibility must therefore fall to Orlando for this further demand. Possibly, not to say probably, he had in mind a transaction whereby Italy could secure Fiume in exchange for yielding Dalmatia. Such an arrangement would have made it possible for him to appear before home opinion not to have suffered a defeat at the Conference. The exigencies of politics at home should also be remembered: the cry for Fiume was exploited for purely political purposes by some at least of the Giolittian following.[38] At this time, in fact (second half of January), the situation was still sufficiently fluid so that a compromise might have been successful. Page reported that the press in Italy was

showing considerable impatience at the prospect of protraction in the Peace Negotiations indicating dangers that will arise from such protraction. . . . The people will follow the Conference now in any firm decision it may make.[39]

Later on, Orlando, too, expressed the opinion that all might have

[37] Cf. Bissolati's speech of Jan. 11; Salvemini's reply to Wilson's Manifesto quoted below, pp. 146-47.

[38] Some even thought that this pressure was the determining factor which caused Orlando to espouse the demand for Fiume. Cf. Steed's Memorandum of March 22, 1919, Document 30 below.

[39] Page's Report of Jan. 24, Miller, IV, Document 232.

been well if a settlement could have been made just after the Armistice, for then "Fiume would never have been injected into the terms by the Italians";[40] it was perhaps already too late in January to give up Fiume and survive politically, but Fiume for Dalmatia might still have been acceptable. However, this demand for Fiume proved the source of endless complications and difficulties for Orlando, for, as time passed and national feeling became exasperated in Italy, he found it increasingly difficult to retreat from the position which he had originally taken, and when at last he fell back on the written obligation of Great Britain and France, these Powers faced him with the retort that he had been the first to depart from the Treaty.

Finally, it should be noted that the Italian memorandum of claims did not attempt to concern itself with any but former Austro-Hungarian territories. This is important as evidence of a lack of connection between the Adriatic problem and the other Italian claims (Near East, colonies). Whether deliberate or otherwise, it shows at least that the two were distinct categories for the Italians.[41]

The course of negotiations from this time until the climax of April we now propose to trace.

FIRST TERRITORIAL DISCUSSIONS IN THE COUNCIL

Mention has already been made of some meetings and discussions among the principals in the Italian settlement, Wilson, Orlando, Sonnino, and others.[42] In his daily memorandum to Lord Northcliffe, Steed reports on January 27 that Wilson had

had a stormy interview with Sonnino, who seems to have lost his temper and to have gone to the length of telling Wilson not to meddle in European affairs but to stick to his American last. When referring to Sonnino, Wilson clenched his fist and used unparliamentary language.[43]

The report may well be exaggerated; it is none the less indicative of the coming friction over the Italian problem. The next day Pro-

[40] During a conversation with House on April 3. House, IV, 441.

[41] The very suggestion of a transaction between the Adriatic and colonies, coming from the Italians, would no doubt have tended to weaken their claim in the former region. But, without hinting at such a possibility, it might have been well, from the Italian point of view, to enter colonial claims on the record. The idea was rather vaguely suggested in the *Corriere della sera.*

[42] See above, pp. 80 ff.

[43] Steed, *Through Thirty Years,* II, 273.

fessor Herron had an interview with Sonnino, who proved no more yielding than Wilson.[44]

On the thirtieth, during the course of a conversation between Wilson and Orlando, while discussing the draft of the League Covenant, Orlando incidentally raised the question of the possibility of the Trentino and Trieste being given to Italy in mandate, a solution which he could not accept. Wilson replied that such an idea was far from his mind and that "the Trentino and Trieste had, as far as he was concerned, already been ceded to Italy."[45]

Steed himself was brought into the negotiations at this juncture, according to his account. On February 2 Major Bonsal, of the American delegation, asked him "to extract from the Yugoslavs their final terms so that, if these terms were just, the President might insist upon Italian acceptance of them."[46] When Steed set out to do this, he did not at first find Trumbić very conciliating, but the following morning one of the Yugoslav delegates brought him a map with six different lines showing the extreme Italian and Yugoslav claims, and suggested that something between the two central moderate lines would be acceptable. This middle portion was Central Istria. Seton-Watson, of the British delegation, copied these lines and took them to House and Johnson. The Americans were delighted, according to Steed, and proposed to take the map to Wilson, who was to see Orlando shortly. When Frazier told him this, Steed suggested that Wilson see Trumbić first, and accordingly Frazier arranged for the latter to be received an hour before Orlando was due.[47]

Trumbić said he was willing to leave the final decision to Wilson and would accept his arbitration. Wilson replied that both parties

[44] Steed, *op. cit.*, II, 275.

[45] "Notes of a Conversation between President Wilson, Signor Orlando, Colonel House and Signor Scialoja, Held on January 30, 1919," Miller, IV, Document 268. This may account for the reports in Italy at the beginning of February (*Giornale d'Italia*) that the Brenner and the Treaty of London line to Fiume had been recognized to Italy. The expression "the Trentino and Trieste," usually synonymous with Italian Irredentist claims, is rather vague, and whether Orlando and Wilson meant the same thing by it is a question. It should be considered in the light of the American Commentary on the Fourteen Points.

[46] Steed, *Through Thirty Years*, II, 278.

[47] Steed, *op. cit.*, II, 279-80. By this time Steed had become definitely pro-Yugoslav. He had been instrumental in bringing together in London in 1917 the Italians and the Yugoslavs who eventually devised the Pact of Rome (see above, p. 44), but subsequent developments had convinced him that Orlando was not sincere (*Through Thirty Years*, II, 261-63).

Steed was foreign editor of the [London] *Times*, controlled by Lord Northcliffe, together with other British dailies. Through the powerful Northcliffe press, Steed had considerable influence on British opinion, which accounts for the frequent attacks against him in the Italian press.

would have to agree to this, and suggested that Trumbić make an official proposal to this effect to Clemenceau. Orlando, again according to Steed, accepted arbitration in principle, but said he would have to consult his delegation before committing himself definitely.[48] This apparently is the origin of the proposal which was made by Pašić to Clemenceau on February 11.[49]

The early days of February brought before the Council a number of territorial questions. These were in general referred to commissions for reports. On February 3 Venizelos made an exposition of the Greek claims, among which were Southern Albania (Northern Epirus) and the Dodecanese. The Banat was among the questions that came up at this time, and its treatment is of interest because of the attitude taken by the Italians and the Yugoslavs in this connection. The secret treaty of August, 1916, which had preceded Rumania's entry into the war, attributed the entire region to Rumania. Owing to Rumania's separate peace of Bucharest and her subsequent reëntry into the war, the Allies (Great Britain and France) considered the treaty of 1916 superseded and Bratianu had been informed of this in advance of his appearance before the Council on February 8.[50] On that occasion, he put in a claim for the whole Banat. The Yugoslavs, who had neither been a party to nor informed of the treaty of 1916, had taken the position, when presenting their own claims on January 30, that they could not recognize secret treaties to which they had not been parties, and asked for a division of the Banat on the basis of nationality.[51] The Italians, on the other hand, with an eye to precedent in regard to their own secret treaty of 1915, tended to uphold the validity of the Rumanian treaty.[52] Despite Italian opposition, the Banat question was referred to the Rumanian commission.

It was at this time, on February 5 to be exact, that the United States officially recognized the new Serb-Croat-Slovene State. As mentioned before, the Yugoslavs had been seeking recognition ever since December, 1918, but had failed, in part or largely owing to

[48] Steed, *op. cit.*, II, 280.
[49] See below, p. 107.
[50] Temperley, IV, 225.
[51] Temperley, IV, 225.
[52] Temperley, IV, 227. They maintained this attitude in the commission on Rumanian claims. Another motive was the possibility of future coöperation with the Rumanians against the Yugoslavs. This is merely one instance of the machinations going on in Paris; the Italo-Rumanian scheme had its counterpart in the Franco-Yugoslav *rapprochement*.

Italian opposition. This opposition had come into the open at the first Plenary Session of the Conference on January 18, with the result that the Yugoslav delegates were officially recognized as Serbian representatives. It was by way of retaliation for this attitude on the part of the Italians that Wilson had decided upon immediate recognition.[53]

This action was naturally not welcomed in Italy, but was received with apprehension and disappointment rather than violent objection; it was still thought that an understanding would be reached with Wilson, whose stature was moreover increased in Italian eyes for what was considered his skill in having secured British support.[54] One point which recognition tended to settle—if we bear in mind the recommendations of the American Territorial Report—was the fate of Montenegro. The situation in that country remained very confused, and appeared in Italy as being in the main a Franco-Italian contest. Of little consequence economically, the tiny state was of importance for its position, dominating the excellent naval base of Cattaro. Before the war Italy had steadfastly resisted Austrian encroachments in that area.[55] According to an American report,[56] there were three parties in Montenegro: a small group, estimated roughly at 20 percent, in favor of independence with the return of the King; another, of about 35 percent, in favor of federal union with Yugoslavia, with a very large measure of independence; about half the population was thought to be in favor of incorporation into Yugoslavia, with some measure of autonomy. The French were in favor of Montenegro being absorbed by Yugoslavia, and Radović, who represented this tendency, went from France to Montenegro and took an active part in the "election" which ratified this course. The French General Venel, who took command at Cattaro shortly thereafter, seems to have assisted the policy of union.[57] Whatever the facts, at this time and subsequently—in any case difficult to as-

[53] Temperley, IV, 297.

[54] See *Daily Review of the Foreign Press*, Feb. 8-16.

[55] She had moreover a sentimental and dynastic interest in the fate of Montenegro. Queen Elena is one of the daughters of King Nicholas of Montenegro.

[56] Major Scanland's report sent by Page to House on Feb. 7. House's papers, Yale University. Major Scanland had gone to Cattaro as part of a small Italo-American contingent sent from Fiume in Nov., 1918. He had therefore been in a position to observe events at first hand.

[57] Or at least was charged with doing so in Italian reports. All military activity in the Lower Adriatic was technically under the command of General Franchet d'Esperey, head of the Allied forces formerly on the Macedonian front.

certain—Montenegro did not secure recognition from the Peace Conference and its union with Yugoslavia was allowed to stand, so to speak, by default.[58]

THE YUGOSLAV PROPOSAL OF ARBITRATION
THE YUGOSLAV CLAIMS

Following the suggestion of a few days previous, on February 11 the Yugoslavs sent a letter to Clemenceau, stating that the delegation of the Kingdom of the Serbs, Croats and Slovenes, "having full confidence in the high spirit of justice of Mr. Wilson, President of the United States, and being formally authorized by the Royal Government, . . . is ready to submit the territorial dispute between the Kingdom of the Serbs, Croats, and Slovenes and the Kingdom of Italy to President Wilson's arbitration."[59] A similar communication was sent to Wilson at the same time.

In view of conditions at the time and of Wilson's known opposition to the Treaty of London, the offer was undoubtedly a skillful move on the part of the Yugoslavs. Whatever the outcome of their proposal, they could only benefit by having made it. If it was accepted, they could rest assured that the Treaty of London was a dead letter and that most of their claims would be satisfied. If refused, it must put the Italians in the position of acknowledging, at least by implication, either that their demands would not bear impartial examination or that they did not consider Wilson to be possessed of such impartiality. In either case, the rather flattering appeal to Wilson tended to put him in the position of champion of the Yugoslav cause. This is precisely what he came to be in Italian eyes; nor would the Yugoslavs, one may rest assured, have made the offer had they not felt confident that Wilson's decision, had it been left to him alone, would, on the whole, have been favorable to them.[60] The Yugoslav proposal of arbitration, for some reason, was not commented upon in Italy until the nineteenth. It was unanimously condemned—much as the French condemned the suggestion of a plebiscite in Alsace-Lorraine—and generally considered not to have been made in good faith.[61] It is perhaps a case where the value

[58] In view of the comparative unimportance of Montenegro, a surprising amount of material in regard to it—some of Italian source and some from American observers—was forwarded by Page to House.

[59] See below, Document 18.

[60] Trumbić admitted as much to Miller. Miller, "Diary," March 5, I, 152.

[61] Cf. Speranza's Report of Feb. 19.

of a "just" settlement might be weighed against the dangers of the grievance to which such a settlement would give rise.

The arbitration proposal was taken up in the Council of Ten on February 17, when Clemenceau announced the receipt of Pašić's letter, which he gave to the Council without comment. Sonnino thought it his duty to state that "the Italian Government regretted that it could not accept any proposal for arbitration on any question for the solution of which Italy had engaged in war, and waged it for three and a half years in full agreement with her Allies, and the examination of which by the Peace Conference was pending."[62]

Later at the same meeting, Clemenceau announced that the Serbians would be heard by the Council the next day if there was no objection. Sonnino pointed out that the position of his Government in relation to the Serbs was a delicate one. They (the Italians) did not wish to enter into a polemic at the Conference and he therefore suggested that either the Serbs should be heard in the absence of the Italian delegates, or that, if heard in their presence, no discussion should ensue. Clemenceau declared the last proposal in accordance with precedent, and it was accordingly adopted as the procedure for the next day.[63]

When the Yugoslavs appeared before the Council on February 18, Vesnić spoke first by way of introduction to their various territorial claims. He traced the antecedents of the war, German expansion in the Balkans, the systematic oppression of the Slavs, and the rôle of the Yugoslav troops in the Austro-Hungarian army, putting the Yugoslav claims on the basis of the principles for which the Allies had been fighting: nationality, self-determination, and the freedom of small nations. Any agreement disposing of the Yugoslav people without its consent he must regard as null and void. In the matter of the Italian frontier, he asked that they should be treated on a footing of equality with Italy. This introduction over, the various frontiers were taken up individually and in detail. It was Trumbić who spoke on the western frontier.[64]

The frontier demanded by the Yugoslavs can be stated very simply: it was the frontier of 1914 between Italy and Austria, from the point where Italy, Austria, and Yugoslavia would come together south-

[62] Minutes of the Council, Feb. 17, B.C. 34. Miller, XIV, 465.
[63] Minutes of the Council, Feb. 17. *Ibid.*
[64] Minutes of the Council, Feb. 18. See below, Document 19.

ward to the Adriatic, with a small modification. A line through Monfalcone, Gradisca, and Cormons was to replace the old frontier between that last-named locality and the sea, giving Italy a small triangle of territory inhabited by Italians. Everything else to the south and the east, all Istria and the Dalmatian coast with all the islands, without exception, were to go to Yugoslavia.

To defend this claim, Trumbić pointed out that from Monfalcone to the southern extremity of Dalmatia the coast and the hinterland were solidly inhabited by Yugoslavs. He recognized the existence of Italian majorities in some towns such as Gorizia, Trieste, the towns of the western coast of Istria, Lussin, Fiume, and Zara; but these were isolated instances of Italian nuclei in an otherwise solidly Slav countryside and they did not even border on Italian territory.

Expanding on the age-old oppression of which the Slavs had been victims, first under Venice and later under Austria, he pointed out that the Slav national awakening dated from the Constitution of 1861, from which time had begun the struggle with the Italian element. When universal suffrage had been introduced in Austria in 1907, the first elections had shown the Yugoslav element to be much stronger than it had seemed. He then took up in greater detail the various parts of the territory in question.

For Eastern Istria from Cape Promontore, and Dalmatia, in addition to an overwhelmingly Slav population, there was the fact that this region, economically poor, could not be separated from the mainland, of which it was the natural outlet and whose trade was the main resource. The deliberate Austrian policy, which had developed communications with a view to Balkan penetration, could then be corrected.

Fiume belonged to Croatia, of which it was the only sea outlet, and it would be unthinkable that it should be separated from her when so much was done in other places to secure an outlet to the sea for landlocked countries.

Coming to the land frontier, the province of Gorizia-Gradisca, east of the proposed line, contained 142,500 Slovenes and 17,000 Italians, 14,000 of whom—half the population—were in the town of Gorizia. Gorizia itself, the economic and intellectual center of this Slovene country, though half Italian in population, would hardly be sufficient reason for turning the entire district over to Italy. Trieste was two-thirds Italian and one-third Slav and would not be claimed were it contiguous to Italian territory; but the whole country around it was Slav and, in addition, Trieste, whose main function was maritime and commercial, did not have an Italian hinterland. Under Italy it would be politically separated from its hinterland.

Istria, taken as a whole, had 223,318 Yugoslavs and 147,417 Italians. The eastern and central portions were solidly Slav, and the Italians were concentrated on the western coast in discontinuous groups. Finally, in regard to the population statistics, the fact that the census was compiled by the communes, together with the urban nature of the Italian population, which gave it an undue municipal representation, would tend to make the figures favorable to the Italians.[65]

Several facts are noteworthy in this exposition. First of all, the union of the component parts of the new state was assumed as definite and final, no attempt being made to defend its justification. This was legitimate enough, in view of the fact that Yugoslavia had been recognized by the United States, Great Britain, and France; but the existing opposition to unification which, instead of decreasing with recognition, continued and even grew, could not quite be ignored.[66] The Yugoslav exposition made no mention of strategic considerations, so prevalent in the Italian memorandum; it was wholly confined to ethnic and economic facts. This was indeed the best line for the Yugoslavs to follow, for here they were on solid ground. The land frontier with Italy, claimed by the Yugoslavs, was purely ethnic, and it was taken for granted that the area between the line drawn by the Americans and the line claimed by Italy was to go to Yugoslavia. A number of Italians—small in comparison with the number of Yugoslavs claimed by Italy—was to go to Yugoslavia, and this claim we may assume to have been put forward for purposes of a transaction.[67]

The ethnic facts about Trieste, Istria and Fiume were, within fairly narrow limits, incontrovertible. Nevertheless the claim to

---

[65] This exposition is taken from the Minutes of the Council of Feb. 18. In addition, the Yugoslavs submitted to the Conference a general memorandum covering the totality of their claims, as well as specific memoranda on: 1. *The Frontiers between the Kingdom of the Serbians, Croatians and Slovenes and the Kingdom of Italy;* 2. *The Dalmation Question;* 3. *The Town of Riyeka (Fiume);* 4. *The Territories of Goritza and Gradisca and the Town of Goritza;* 5. *Istria;* 6. *The Town of Triest.* Cf. Hoover War Library, *A Catalogue of Paris Peace Conference Delegation Propaganda.*

[66] Cf. a report of Dr. Kovacević, representative of the Croatian independence party, sent by Page from Rome on Feb. 14. House's papers, Yale University. Montenegro was likewise ignored in the Yugoslav presentation. According to Italian reports, Montenegro was in a state of active revolt against the Serbs.

[67] See above, p. 104, on the Yugoslav willingness to compromise.

Trieste may be considered too extreme, as no one, even among the Yugoslavs, thought that it might not go to Italy; putting forward such a claim tended to create the impression that the Yugoslavs were merely bent on making the widest possible demands, whether in or out of reason, and to that extent it weakened their whole case. It was different with Fiume, where the arguments which applied in favor of giving Trieste to Italy held for leaving the former town in Croatian territory. Some provision was no doubt indicated to protect the rights of the Italians in Fiume as well as in Dalmatia. In regard to this province, the Yugoslav case would seem difficult to answer. Possession of the entire eastern coast by the Yugoslavs would undoubtedly have prevented Italy from having secure control of the Adriatic; but the value of security resting on resented military occupation may well be questioned.

Finally, no specific mention was made of the Treaty of London beyond the general statement that the Yugoslavs could not be bound by arrangements to which they had not been a party. The Treaty of London, for all that it was well known, had not been officially communicated to the Yugoslavs,[68] and their tactics were sound in ignoring it. What they did, in short, was to transform their immediate quarrel with Italy into a much larger issue between Italy and her Allies, Great Britain and France, and even more, between Italy and the United States, or at least Wilson. For this reason the Yugoslavs played an almost minor rôle in the negotiations regarding the Italian problems at the Conference. In its first phase, the key to the Italian question was in Wilson's hands; later, as America gradually withdrew, it was in London and Paris. Only after two years of weary discussions was the Adriatic dispute nearly settled, by direct negotiations between the two principals.

Their exposition concluded, the Yugoslavs retired to let the Council discuss the question. Balfour pointed out that similar questions had been referred to committees for report, but that in this case treaty commitments (the Treaty of London) were in the way. Sonnino declared that Italy would not enter into a discussion of its claims outside the Council; he did not object to the Yugoslav claims being examined by a committee, provided Italo-Yugoslav questions were excluded from the competence of such a committee. Clemenceau agreed that the question was analogous to that of the Rhine, and must be dealt with in the Council. On a resolution of Balfour,

[68] It was only given to them a year later, in Jan., 1920.

Sonnino's solution was adopted and the questions raised by the Yugoslavs, excluding those in which Italy was directly concerned, were referred to a committee. The same committee that was already investigating the Banat problem was designated to do this.[69]

Wilson was on his way to America when this session of the Council took place.[70] In his absence, the Council naturally devoted more attention to the specific details of the European settlement and, in response to the general popular demand, endeavored to expedite the drafting of the Treaty. On February 22 Balfour offered a resolution with this end in view, wherein he mentioned the German Treaty only. A long discussion ensued, caused by Sonnino's objection to having the German settlement put ahead of the Austrian; pointing to the condition of unrest and dissatisfaction in Italy and the danger of revolution if she had to remain armed longer than her Allies.[71] The Council, none the less, directed the various commissions to submit their reports not later than March 8.[72]

The two guiding principles of Italian diplomacy were now apparent. First, insistence that the Austrian settlement be pushed ahead simultaneously with the German, lest Italy find herself isolated and consequently weakened. In this attempt, she was at a distinct disadvantage for, in the eyes of the United States, Great Britain, and France, the German settlement came far ahead of the Austrian in urgency and importance. The fact that whatever discussions of Italian problems had taken place had shown only a wide divergence between Italians and Americans, with no apparent prospect of compromise up to this time, could only make her isolation greater. Second, the Yugoslavs must not be allowed a status of equality in the discussion of Italian problems, which must be dealt with exclusively in the Council. This would give Italy a free hand in bargaining with her Allies. As Clemenceau had pointed out, a similar privilege had been claimed by the French in regard to Germany, and no doubt technically Italy was entitled to like treatment. Unfortunately for her, whereas there was no question about Germany being an enemy Power, and a dreaded one at that, the feeling was quite different toward the Yugoslavs, who appeared in Paris as allies rather than enemies. And the fact that Italy was standing on legalistic ground

---

[69] Minutes of the Council, Feb. 18, Document 19 below.

[70] Orlando, too, was away, having gone back to Italy.

[71] Minutes of the Council, Feb. 22; B.C. 37. Miller, XV, 6-19.

[72] Thompson, *The Peace Conference Day by Day,* p. 223. There was still at this time talk of making a preliminary peace treaty.

in her objections, rather than on grounds of "justice," may not have been without influence in putting Wilson in the position of champion of the Yugoslavs—though this need not necessarily have been deliberate and conscious on his part—especially as the Yugoslavs had taken care to base their claims strictly on his cherished principles of nationality and self-determination.

The official position of the Italians, the Americans, and the Yugoslavs has been stated in detail. The British and the French tended, on the whole, to remain on the side lines of the dispute, for the simple reason that they considered this the most advantageous course to follow, rather than for lack of interest in the issue. They could not very well repudiate the Treaty of London, but they certainly would shed no tears over its demise, for they looked upon it as a hard bargain driven by Italy in their hour of need.[73] The British had no direct conflict with Italy and would be content to safeguard their commercial interests. The French were in a somewhat different position. French foreign policy was traditionally opposed to a strong Italy as much as to a strong Germany; now Italy sought control of the Adriatic and was in a position to fall heir to much of the Austro-German influence in Central Europe, the Balkans, and the Near East. It is not very surprising, therefore, that in 1919 the French should be thinking of the possibilities of a stronger Italy, rather than of the assistance she had rendered in the war; just as the Italians conveniently forgot the Pact of Rome and the concessions to the Slavs which they had been willing to make when threatened by a common danger.[74] Under the circumstances, a community of interest was the basis of French support of the succession states of Central Europe, and this led naturally to a conflict with Italy.[75] The conflict was not open and, in general, it may be said that both the French and the British were content to let Wilson bear the burden of the Italian quarrel, while they endeavored to remain on good terms with both him and the Italians.

[73] See, for instance, Balfour's letter to Wilson of Jan. 30, 1918, quoted above, p. 79, n. 66.

[74] This is not to say that there was not in Europe widespread support for the League of Nations and the Wilsonian ideals. But, in general, it may be said that the devotion of the various foreign offices to the League varied in direct proportion to the value they considered the League would have in furthering their respective national policies. The British and the French, unlike the Italians, mainly concerned with maintaining their acquired position, naturally favored a League that would crystallize the *status quo*.

[75] Which is the reason why Italian animus was directed mainly and more consistently against France. Specific grievances may have been imagined at times, but there is no denying the anti-Italian tendency of French foreign policy from the Italian standpoint.

V

THE CLASH WITH WILSON

WITH THE OPENING of the Conference, there had been a tendency in Italy to abandon the more violent type of polemics for a calmer attitude of expectancy, pending some indication of the course which it would adopt. Up to the time of Wilson's departure (February 14), two important questions had been dealt with by the Council: Colonies and the League. The mandatory principle had been adopted in regard to the former German colonies and the Italians seemed to be content, for the most part, with the rather vague but oft-repeated assurance that Italy would receive a just share in the final distribution; moreover the problem of the former Turkish possessions, where lay the more important Italian expectations, had not yet been approached.[1] As to the League of Nations, it was a novel idea which, in Speranza's words, had found Italian opinion "essentially perplexed and uncertain."[2] In any case, achieving their war aims and security was a prerequisite to sincere participation of the Italians in the League. As to the exact definition of these war aims, there was not yet complete agreement; opinion was still divided on the score of Dalmatia, but increasingly solid on the subject of the eastern land frontier which must include Fiume in Italy. Relations with the Yugoslavs were not improving with time. Emphasis was placed on reports of Croat discontent with Serbia and on the treatment of Italians at the hands of the Yugoslavs. The Italian mission at Laibach was invited to leave after the United States had granted recognition to the Serb-Croat-Slovene Kingdom; incidents occurred at Spalato on February 23 which brought the intervention of the Allied Admirals in the Adriatic; there was trouble again in the first half of March, and the list could be lengthened at will.

The rest of the work being done in Paris was still in the prepara-

[1] Interest in colonial matters was revived for a time by the Colonial Congress held in Naples in January.

[2] Speranza's special Report of March 8, "What do Italians Really Think of the League of Nations?" This report is a good succinct analysis of the Italian reaction to the idea of the League. It is borne out by contemporary comment in Italy (cf. *Daily Review of the Foreign Press*).

tory stage and offered no basis for judgment. The course of the Italian delegation toward the Yugoslavs was generally approved. The Italian memorandum of claims, of which a résumé was not given out in Italy until March 12, evoked surprisingly little comment. The political situation remained likewise in abeyance. There was much talk of impending general elections, but the parties were somewhat at a loss for an issue, hoping that events might provide a useful, if not a real, one. This general attitude of expectant uncertainty is best described in a contemporary editorial, written on the day after Orlando returned from Paris:

Yesterday the President of the Council returned to Rome and today there begins to function again in Italy a domestic and parliamentary policy. Among us everything is focussed around the head of the Government; the Parliament, the Cabinet, Constitutional guarantees, the political and economic life of the country—everything stagnates when the Premier is away because no one attempts to move a finger . . . without knowing what the Premier thinks. The arrival of the head of the Government is made manifest not so much by the news of his reception at the station as by the change of attitude in all the organisms of the State; the police become either more monstrous or more reasonable, the censorship more foolish or more intelligent, the semi-official press more liberal or more reactionary, and yet the present head of the Government is neither a tyrant nor a daring statesman with the capacity to impress his stamp on all the functions of the State. He is not at all such a man; his unaggressive temperament, his indecision, his desire to please God and the devil, his habit of procrastinating, of flanking rather than facing questions—all this is well known, but so ingrained is the Italian political habit of attempting nothing without seeking a refuge under the mantle of whosoever bears the chief responsibility that even a man like the honorable Orlando has actually to be on deck in order to steer along the somewhat unseaworthy Ministerial boat. What is sought especially is that the boat will be steered without new Cabinet crises, because now it seems the custom that the return to Italy of the Premier always marks the announcement of the resignation of one or more Cabinet Ministers. . . . There is no question that Orlando's activity in Italy is largely taken up in stopping up the holes in the Ministerial boat, and preventing any of the Ministers who wish to leave it from getting off . . .[3]

Orlando made a brief address before the Chamber on March 1

[3] *Avanti,* Feb. 17. Taken from Speranza's Report of Feb. 18. The somewhat facetious and irreverent tone of the article is due to the political coloration of the *Avanti.*

and surpassed himself in the art of saying nothing. Pointing to the achievements of the Conference in its brief month of activity, he went on to explain that "Italy is all the more happy to have been able, not only to accept, but to coöperate in the assertion of this new spirit [creation of the League of Nations] . . . that she feels and knows that every one of her particular aspirations is strictly in accordance with the principles of the most rigorous justice"; he did moreover insist on his faithfulness to "the most Italian gem of the Quarnero."[4] In other words, matters stood precisely where they had been from the beginning, so far as Italian problems were concerned; of the difficulties which he had already encountered and which he was certain to meet again upon his return to Paris, not an inkling. Parliament was really more interested at the moment in the question of general elections and in the much-discussed electoral-reform law. Orlando took an attitude of opposition to any reform "for constitutional reasons," and asked for postponement of the discussion until April. The proposal of postponement, strangely enough, was eagerly seized upon by all groups, even by those whose speakers had been most urgent in advocating the reform, and Orlando disposed of the possibility of further debate by leaving for Paris.[5]

During his absence, on March 3, Clemenceau had informed the Yugoslavs that, owing to Italian opposition, their offer of arbitration had been rejected by the Council.[6]

During the course of a meeting between House, Lloyd George, and Clemenceau on March 10, the latter two showed themselves in agreement with the American line, in preference to the line of the Treaty of London.[7] The Italian question came up again in the Council on the eleventh, when Clemenceau read a letter from Pašić in which the latter complained of the rumored decision to exclude the Italo-Yugoslav frontier from discussion outside the Council. Sonnino insisted that the small Powers could be heard in the territorial commissions, but could have no voice in the final decisions of the Council. Orlando then spoke up to explain that this was not a problem affecting Serbia, but a question of the boundary of Italy with an enemy state. A new state had been formed which he did not recognize; other Powers could recognize it, although that would be an

[4] Atti del Parlamento, Sessione 1913-19, Camera, Discussioni, XVII, 18076-77.
[5] Cf. Daily Review of the Foreign Press, March 3-9; Speranza's Report of March 9-10.
[6] For Clemenceau's reply to the Yugoslavs, see below, Document 20.
[7] House, IV, 359-60.

unfriendly act toward Italy. For him, the Croats and the Slovenes had merely taken the place of Austria, and it was a great concession to have heard them at all. Lloyd George pointed to the difficulty of making a distinction between Pašić and the other Serbian delegates; it was merely a case of Serbia having acquired new territory, according to him. Clemenceau suggested the adoption of Orlando's proposal as amended, meaning that the Serbs should be admitted to the discussion when their frontiers were under consideration. Under the circumstances, Orlando thought it best to propose a postponement of the question which, after some further discussion between Sonnino and Lansing, was finally agreed upon. Later at the same meeting, in reply to an inquiry of the Greek committee, it was decided that this committee should not deal with the Albanian-Yugoslav frontier, because Italy was also interested in Albania.[8]

INTERVENTION OF THE AMERICAN EXPERTS

From this time on, instead of moving toward a compromise, the situation steadily deteriorated. The issue became drawn with increasing sharpness between the Italians and the Americans, both of whom drifted more and more into a defense of their respective positions, until the climax of April. March and April produced a wealth of reports, memoranda, and recommendations.

When Wilson returned to Paris (March 14), he found that the Italians had just submitted to the Council a new memorandum in which they extended their claim in Dalmatia to reach Spalato.[9] Another Italian memorandum[10] painted a dire and rather overdrawn picture of the situation of inferiority which confronted Italy in the Adriatic.[11]

[8] Minutes of the Council, March 11; see below, Document 21. The session seems to have been a stormy one, especially when Lansing proposed that neither the Italians nor the Yugoslavs should participate in the discussion; but the Minutes were subsequently revised to delete any trace of this. Cf. Steed, *Through Thirty Years*, II, 327-28.

[9] This memorandum is not available. The only direct evidence of its existence is the reference to it in the report of the American Experts of March 18 (see below, Document 28). According to Steed, on March 15 "apparently upon the advice of Clemenceau," the Italians sent to House "a memorandum demanding Fiume and the greater part of Dalmatia." Steed, *op. cit.*, II, 328.

[10] See below, Document 22.

[11] Complaints were often heard in Italy in regard to the ineffectiveness of Italian propaganda. The complaint has a familiar ring; few are the countries which have not made a similar one. It is true that the Yugoslavs carried on a very active propaganda and it is also true that the Italian Bureau of Foreign Propaganda had been abolished in January and foreign propaganda taken over by the Foreign Office. Sonnino himself seems to have had little opinion of propaganda as such; however there was no dearth of Italian "litera-

The American Territorial Experts examined the Italian and the Yugoslav claims and reported unfavorably on both. Their report pointed out that:

1. In the north, the American line gave Italy sufficient protection and was economically sounder than the line of the Treaty of London. The American line represented a concession to strategic considerations and, in view of the hostile feeling of the Tyrolese, it was suggested that the region between the ethnic line and the actual frontier be given to Italy in mandate.[12]

2. The district of Tarvis was wholly inhabited by Germans and Slovenes.

3. In Julian Venetia too the ethnic line was quite clear, and the Fiume-Laibach railway should be left in Yugoslav territory. Here too concessions had already been made to Italian security, and in fact the Yugoslavs had a natural, if not a just, grievance in view of the more generous treatment of the Czechoslovaks and the Rumanians.

4. Fiume, in addition to the ethnic facts, was essential to Yugoslavia, which had no other port with railway connections north of Spalato, and it was important to Central Europe.

5. In Dalmatia the situation was clear. Save in Zara, the population was Slav and wanted union with Yugoslavia.[13]

Such comments were only what should be expected. The American Territorial Report had been drawn up as a result of careful study and with a general knowledge at least of the rival claims. There was little likelihood that additional facts would be brought to light which would modify its conclusions. The American experts could only, as they did in fact, stand upon their recommendations; their report was, after all, no more than a basis of discussion which political or other considerations might modify in some respects. Even the experts were aware of such possible considerations, and as a concession to them they envisaged the possibility of three solutions for the Fiume problem, applicable, however, only to Fiume proper:

ture" in circulation at the Peace Conference. To a certain extent it defeated its own purpose by creating the impression that Italy was resorting to the tactics of a secondary Balkan nation instead of maintaining the dignity of a Great Power. This was unfortunate, especially in regard to some of the Americans whose prejudices such tactics tended to confirm.

[12] This shows that the American experts were not informed of Wilson's position on the Brenner. Cf. above pp. 65, 80 ff., 104.

[13] See below, Documents 24, 25.

1. Cession to Italy;

2. Municipal autonomy, with or without a mandate to Italy (this was considered rather too complicated);

3. An Italian mandate for a free city and port.[14]

Such further recommendations were no doubt based in part on reports from observers on the spot.[15]

A British memorandum on Italy's northern frontier indicated two alternative lines: one close to the ethnic line; the other, better strategically, would have included 160,000 Germans who should have been granted in that case substantial autonomy.[16]

Mezes' Recommendations

It is at this time that division began to manifest itself within the American delegation. Technical experts and others took a more direct part in the controversy than heretofore. On one side, House and Miller, with some assistance from Beer, felt that the Yugoslavs were pursuing negative tactics, and that the only hope of solution lay in reaching an agreement between the Italians and the Americans first, of which there would be little difficulty in securing Yugoslav acceptance. In doing this, they were willing to make substantial concessions to Italy; their attitude is perhaps best summed up by Beer, who thought that the territorial questions were being dealt with in too narrow a technical spirit.

Germans, Magyars and Italians [wrote Beer] were being sacrificed to people whose cultural value was infinitely less. The Poles and Jugo-Slavs may become a nationality but as yet they are merely a potential one. It is far preferable to have Poles under Germans and Jugo-Slavs under Italians than the contrary, if there is no other good alternative.[17]

On the other side, the territorial experts who had drafted the report on territorial claims took the view that the Italians would give way if only they could be convinced that there was no room for compromise.

On March 16 Mezes sent a letter to House which, in view of the

[14] See below, Document 25.
[15] Summary of Report from Lt. Col. Sherman Miles from Fiume. See below, Document 29.
[16] See below, Document 23.
[17] Beer, Diary, March 16. On Miller's attitude, cf. Miller "Diary," I, 172, 190, 198. This episode has been mentioned as the beginning of the much-debated House-Wilson estrangement.

consistent attitude of the territorial experts, can only be described as a curious document.[18] Mezes' letter proposed the following:

1. The Treaty of London line in the north—providing ample guarantees for the Germans included in Italy—which would be an inducement for Italy to disarm.

2. Small changes in the Treaty of London line along the Julian and the Carnic Alps to provide a better defensive frontier to both Italy and Yugoslavia and better railroad communication between both these countries and Austria.

3. Fiume to Italy, making it a free port and ensuring fair treatment in it and on the railroad to the nations concerned.

4. The Dalmatian islands asked by Italy to be given to her, providing generous autonomy to them and to the mainland.

5. Italy to give up the Dodecanese and abandon or abate her claims in Asia Minor and Albania.[19]

On March 17 Beer asked to lunch some of the Italian delegates and suggested that his American colleagues join them. Only Westermann and Seymour accepted, while Frazier and Johnson refused, on the ground that it would merely serve to reinforce the Italian belief that the American delegation was divided, and thereby complicate the negotiations.[20]

Almost on the heels of Mezes' letter to House, there came, on March 18, a further report from the Chiefs of the Austro-Hungarian, Balkan, and Italian divisions, and Johnson, recalling that

every memorandum hitherto submitted to the Commissioners, about which any of the heads of the above-mentioned divisions have been consulted, recommends that Fiume and all of Dalmatia should go to the Jugo-Slavs. We are still unanimously of that opinion. . . .

[18] Mezes, House's brother-in-law and president of the College of the City of New York, was officially head of The Inquiry, though he himself took little part in its work (cf. Shotwell, At the Paris Peace Conference, pp. 5, 18). Mezes' recommendations are totally at variance with those of The Inquiry; they read rather like quotations from the Italian Memorandum of Claims.

Whether Miller had any part in this maneuver cannot be ascertained. However, on this very date (March 16), he discussed the Italian situation regarding the Trentino, Dalmatia, and Fiume and "talked in favor of the Italian claims in all three places." Miller, "Diary," March 16, I, 172. Cf. also Miller, "Diary," March 25, quoting House on Mezes.

[19] See below, Document 26. The general tenor of this letter is very reminiscent of the Italian arguments in general, and in particular of the memorandum entitled "The Military Problem of the Adriatic" (Document 22), which concluded to the necessity of an Italian base in the middle Adriatic, and mentioned the possibility of an exchange between Fiume and a part of Dalmatia.

[20] Beer, Diary, March 17.

The arguments used were the now-familiar ones. In Dalmatia, the population was now and had long been Yugoslav; Italy had no historic right to this territory, whose development had been hindered by Austria-Hungary. As to the strategic claims, the Italian naval experts agreed with the United States Naval Advisory Staff that Pola, Valona, and a base in the middle Adriatic were sufficient. In regard to Fiume, taken with its district, it was Yugoslav; the Yugoslavs needed it economically while Italy did not, and competition between it and Trieste would redound to the benefit of Central Europe.[21]

Reinforcing these views, Johnson sent a memorandum to House, explaining that he understood that the French and the British were in general agreement with the Americans and wanted the Americans to insist upon a full discussion of the problem.[22] In agreement with the Chief of the Italian division, Johnson recommended that such discussion be insisted upon as a prerequisite to American participation in the peace treaties involved. This insistence, he wrote, could be based on the modifications of the Treaty of London implied in the acceptance of the Wilsonian principles, on the moral obligation of the Pact of Rome, and on the technical fact that Italy herself had departed from the Treaty of London by making additional demands. This last point suggested that a compromise might be arranged by granting Italy certain concessions outside the Treaty of London in exchange for her acceptance of free discussion of the rest.[23]

Throughout this period, however, the Italian question was not before the Council, whose activity centered on the task of drafting the German Treaty in general, and, more particularly, of finding a common ground between the French demands on the Rhine and in the Saar, and the American views on these subjects. Agreement was finally reached on these points, but not without difficulty and not until the Conference had come close to disruption. The strain of this crisis and the consequent exhaustion and fraying of tempers should be borne in mind as we follow the vicissitudes of the coming Italian crisis. Nor did the passage of time, without a solution of the Adriatic question, make such a solution easier to reach; for,

[21] See below, Document 28.
[22] On the British view regarding the northern frontier of Italy, see below, Document 23; also House, IV, 359-60.
[23] See below, Document 27.

naturally enough, opinion in Italy was growing impatient over the continued uncertainty, and the Slavs on their side were equally restive under continued Italian occupation. Petty irritations multiplied; Italy, in charge of requisitioning Austro-Hungarian shipping for the Allies, insisted on treating the Yugoslavs as former enemies in this respect.[24] The Yugoslavs also complained of the continuing blockade resulting from the fact that the Salonika railway line was destroyed and that Fiume was in the hands of the Italians. They submitted their grievances to Wilson and to the Council.[25] The Italians, in turn, complained that their communications with Hungary through Croatia were interrupted.[26] An entry in Miller's Diary reports Mezes as saying that Wilson was in agreement with Lloyd George's opposition to giving Danzig to the Poles "because he did not want Fiume to go to the Italians, and if Danzig went to the Poles he would have to consent to Fiume being Italian."[27] Accurate or not, the statement is indicative of the current talk and belief, second in importance only to actual facts.

With the French crisis surmounted, the Italian problem was at last to be approached at the beginning of April, in this none-too-favorable atmosphere. On April 2 Wilson asked House to explain to Orlando the frontier proposed by the Americans: the Treaty of London line in the north; Eastern Istria, Fiume and Dalmatia to the Yugoslavs. "I do not relish the job," records House who was to see Orlando on the fourth.[28]

Quite unexpectedly, Lloyd George raised the Adriatic question at the Council meeting of April 3. It appeared then that Wilson, Lloyd George, and Clemenceau were agreed that Fiume should not go to Italy, and it was decided to hear the Yugoslavs in the afternoon. In his isolation, Orlando, caught unprepared, elected to absent himself from "the Italian funeral."[29] He wrote a letter to Wilson explaining that in "the very delicate matter of giving a further hearing to the representatives of the Slovenes and Croats—against whom Italy has been at war for four years—I would not insist against it, just as I would not exclude the advisability of giving a hearing to the repre-

[24] See below, Document 31.
[25] On March 28; see below, Document 31.
[26] Minutes of the Council of Foreign Ministers, March 28. See below, Document 32.
[27] Miller, "Diary," March 28, I, 208. The statement was originally made by Wilson to Headlam Morley and Bowman; the latter told Mezes, from whom Miller had it in turn.
[28] House, IV, 439.
[29] House, IV, 441. The comment is House's.

sentatives of any other enemy people on whom it is a question of imposing conditions." Lest his absence give rise to the impression that there was a misunderstanding between Italy and the other Powers, he chose to take the view that "the meeting this afternoon is not the meeting of the representatives of the four Powers, but a conversation between the President of the United States and the Prime Ministers of Great Britain and France with those Gentlemen."[30]

Instead of going to the Council meeting, Orlando went to see House, and the two went over the maps. No conclusions were reached; Orlando's main difficulty was about Fiume. He expressed regret that the settlement could not have been made just after the Armistice, for then, said he, "Fiume would never have been injected into the terms by the Italians."[31] More and more the controversy was centering on Fiume.

First Appeal of the American Experts to Wilson

Mezes' proposed scheme of settlement, outlined above, caused not a little indignation among the American territorial experts, for his official position at their head tended to imply their support of a settlement of which they completely disapproved. Besides restating their views in the memoranda referred to,[32] they now addressed themselves to Wilson directly, rather than to the American Commissioners collectively. In a memorandum dated April 4,[33] they repeated once more the usual arguments. The most interesting part of this memorandum is the last, which gave a list of conditions necessary to safeguard Yugoslav interests if Fiume was to be, for other reasons, made a free city. It contained the germ of the idea which was to become the basis of a later negotiation and indicated the extent to which Wilson would eventually be willing to compromise. The general idea of an independent city or state, centering around Fiume, was discussed between Miller and Johnson on April 5.[34]

For the next two weeks the Italian question was the object of intense activity and came increasingly to the front. The rumor circu-

[30] Orlando to Wilson, April 3, 1919. See below, Document 33.
[31] House, IV, 441.
[32] See above, pp. 118 ff.
[33] See below, Document 34.
[34] Miller, "Diary," April 5, I, 225; see also below, Document 35.

lated that Orlando would withdraw from the Conference, but was denied by House on the fourth;[35] the next day it was definitely announced that he would attend the meeting of Monday, April 7.[36]

It is worth noting that during this period the thread of negotiations on the Italian side was almost wholly in Orlando's own hands. He had private meetings with Lloyd George on the eighth and with Wilson on the eleventh.[37] Little, if any, mention occurs of Sonnino. The reason for this is to be seen in the fact that the situation, as it had developed, called for a compromise, and it was difficult to bargain with Sonnino, stolidly entrenched behind the Pact of London. The other Italian delegates seem to have been equally inactive, at least to judge from the purely negative evidence.[38] Orlando was then and subsequently much criticized for this state of affairs, and it is what gave rise to the reports of division within the Italian delegation.[39] If not actual divergence of aims, there was unquestionably difference in manner, method, and outlook between the two chief Italian delegates.

According to Miller, on April 11 Johnson broached to him the possibility of informal discussions between the Italians, the Serbs, and some Americans (Miller, Johnson, and Young). Miller approved of the idea, subject to Wilson's consent, which was obtained; but apparently Orlando vetoed it for the reason, reported Frazier, "that Orlando preferred to put responsibility on the President in view of the political situation in Italy, as he believed that his Government would shortly fall in any event."[40]

The idea was revived on April 13 by di Cellere, who came to see Miller and told him that "Trumbić would welcome a decision against him by America, so that he could go back and say that he had acted under compulsion, but on the other hand would not dare to offer what he would be glad to have taken away."[41] It was di Cellere's idea throughout that any Italo-American agreement would be accepted by the Yugoslavs, from which he drew the logical corollary

---

[35] Thompson, *The Peace Conference Day by Day*, p. 286.

[36] Thompson, *op. cit.*, p. 288.

[37] Aldrovandi, "La Settimana di passione adriatica a Parigi," *Nuova Antologia*, May 16, 1933, p. 162.

[38] Salandra returned to Italy at the beginning of April, supposedly for reasons of health, but his return was taken as a sign of dissatisfaction. He came back to Paris later in the month.

[39] Di Cellere, *passim*.

[40] Miller, "Diary," April 11, I, 240.

[41] Miller, "Diary," April 13, I, 247-48.

that the issue was to bring Wilson around to the Italian point of view. The day was spent in conversations between Miller and di Cellere, and Miller and House, who said that Miller, Johnson, and Mezes were to represent the Americans in the proposed discussions.[42] All was ready for the next day when the matter was postponed on House's advice, because it was being taken up directly between Wilson and Orlando.[43]

When Orlando had returned to Paris, preceding Wilson by a few days, it was hoped in Italy that the Italian question was about to enter its final phase, and that a decision would at last be forthcoming. The report that Wilson had suggested submitting the Italian claims to the League was received with such a unanimous outburst of condemnation in the Italian press as to give the impression that "something like a word of order must have been passed around" to be prepared to put the blame on the United States if the Italian claims failed of recognition or of settlement contemporaneously with the French territorial claims.[44] The prevalent atmosphere of nervousness and uncertainty lent itself to obscure political maneuvering. The *Stampa* and the *Tempo*, generally regarded as expressing the Giolittian point of view, adopted the seemingly inconsistent policies of berating the Government for its laxity in pushing the Italian demands, while playing up at the same time the social unrest of which the Socialists were the chief promoters.[45] There was no basis in fact for such a *rapprochement*; the maneuver was wholly political. Much comment was aroused at this time by the reappointment of Corradini to his former position of *Chef de Cabinet* at the Ministry of the Interior.[46] This obscure political game, further complicated by the play of personalities, would be highly confusing to any one not thoroughly familiar with the nature and intricacies of Italian politics, and Speranza rightly emphasized the distinction between the very real popular feeling in regard to the Italian aspira-

[42] *Ibid.*

[43] Miller, "Diary," April 14, I, 249.

[44] Speranza's Report of March 18.

[45] Cf. *Daily Review of the Foreign Press*, March 17-23.

[46] Corradini had been ousted by Salandra with much difficulty. Although he had quarreled with Giolitti, he had retained the confidence of the large Giolittian following in Parliament. His appointment (giving him control of the secret service), put him in a position to exert considerable influence in *making* the coming elections, and was considered a surrender by Orlando in an attempt to secure Giolittian support. Cf. *Daily Review of the Foreign Press*, March 17-23; Speranza's Report of March 20.

tions and the artificial propaganda of certain press organs.[47] Unfortunately, the very few newspapers which issued occasional and cautious warnings were in the nature of voices crying in the wilderness, and there was an increasingly loud clamor for Spalato, instead of a tendency to moderation and compromise. From the distance of Paris, and especially in American eyes, it might easily seem as if the Italian Government were deliberately working up opinion at home in an effort to exert pressure on the decisions of the Conference. The strained feelings which had been produced by the French crisis, and the repeated comments in Italy about an Anglo-Saxon peace, enforced by commercial and financial interests at the expense of the Latin nations—a convenient oversimplification based on a small foundation of fact—tended further to poison the atmosphere in which Orlando and Wilson were about to make a final effort to reach an understanding.

ORLANDO-WILSON MEETING OF APRIL 14
WILSON'S MEMORANDUM

Italian and American accounts of the events of this date are somewhat at variance. According to the former, Orlando brought with him to the meeting Ossoinack, former representative of Fiume in the Hungarian Parliament, who gave in English a detailed exposition of the case for giving Fiume to Italy. His arguments were based in the main on the overwhelming Italian preponderance in Fiume— from 70 to 80 per cent—and the fact that the *corpus separatum* had always enjoyed a special status—it was part of Hungary proper and not of Croatia—in virtue of which the principle of self-determination should be applied in its case. The wishes of Fiume had found expression in his own (Ossoinack's) declaration of October 18, 1918, in the Hungarian Parliament, and in the vote of the Italian National Council of Fiume of October 30, 1918. As to the economic question, he pointed to the small contribution of Croatia to the commerce of Fiume and to the fact that, the Yugoslav railroad system being narrow-gauge in the main, the standard-gauge line to Fiume would be of little use to Yugoslav trade, which would have to be diverted to other Dalmatian ports in any event. After showing some signs of

[47] "This sentiment of anxiety among the people is real and deep and must be sharply distinguished from the artificial sentiment whipped up by the press and allowed by the Government in order to save those in the Government who may have to defend themselves before the Italian people should certain Italian claims be excluded at Paris." Speranza's Report of March 20.

impatience at the lengthiness of the explanation, Wilson assured Ossoinack that the Conference would do justice to Fiume.[48]

On this occasion Wilson gave Orlando a memorandum summing up and restating his views on the Italian claims in the Adriatic. The burden of it was that he did not feel at liberty to use different bases for the Austrian and for the German peace. Personally, he agreed to the Pact of London line in the north, but did not feel that the same criterion could be applied in the east; he then stated the usual arguments in defense of the proposed American line. As to Fiume, it was an international, not an Italian, port; for that reason, while included in the Yugoslav customs system, it should have a large degree of autonomy. Italy could probably have Lissa and Valona; this, with the demilitarization of the islands and guarantees for the Italians in Yugoslavia, would give Italy complete fulfillment of her national aspirations and all the security she could reasonably expect.[49] Wilson wished in addition that Orlando should make his memorandum known to the Italian Parliament.

While these arguments were not novel, this was the first formal communication of them to the Italians. The weakness of conceding the Treaty of London frontier in the north while denying it in the east is at once apparent. To Wilson it meant that, having departed from his principles in one place, the Italians in turn should yield in the other. To the Italians it simply meant that the Wilsonian principles did not always apply; if liberties could be taken with them in one place, for reasons of strategy, or when dealing with former enemies, they insisted that both these reasons applied to the eastern frontier as well. At the same time, Wilson, in agreement with the position taken by his experts, was still disposed to accept some degree of compromise, as evidenced by the statement which he made during the course of a meeting with these experts: "I am ready to fight for the line you gentlemen have given me, with one possible exception: It may seem best to make Fiume an independent port."[50]

According to House, Wilson found the interview with Orlando extremely painful.[51] Aldrovandi, secretary of the Italian delegation, reports that it was actually stormy and that Orlando declared the

[48] Benedetti, *La pace di Fiume*, Document I, pp. 237-42. No mention of Ossoinack's participation in the meeting occurs in American accounts.
[49] See below, Document 36.
[50] Baker, *Woodrow Wilson and the World Settlement*, II, 146.
[51] House, IV, 443.

same day that Wilson's proposed scheme could not even be taken as a basis for discussion.[52]

House's Attempt at Compromise

On April 15 Orlando made calls on House, Clemenceau, and Balfour.[53] House, ever hopeful and conciliating, asked him not to be discouraged, pointing to the greater difficulties which had been overcome in the case of the French settlement. He felt sure that the Italian difficulty could be surmounted if all sides would yield a little; the main obstacle was Fiume.[54] Accordingly, Miller, Warrin, and Johnson set to work and drew up for House the draft of a settlement whereby Hungary would renounce the *corpus separatum* in favor of Italy. The district was to be governed by a commission, appointed by the League of Nations, to consist of three members chosen by the Council of the League: one Yugoslav, one Italian, and one from a third state.[55]

At the same time, Warrin prepared for Mezes an outline of a similar settlement for Dalmatia, which proposed its transfer to the Allied and Associated Powers, and in this case also called for the appointment of a League of Nations' commission, this time of five members, to be chosen by the Council of the League. In addition, after ten years there was to be a plebiscite with the two alternatives: maintenance of the existing régime, union with Yugoslavia.[56]

The suggestion of resorting to a plebiscite to settle all the outstanding differences between Italy and Yugoslavia appears also in a letter of Pašić to Clemenceau of April 16.[57]

None of these suggestions met with any success. Johnson himself, despite his connection with the last Fiume proposal, wrote to Miller asking him, in order to avoid possible misunderstandings, to "make clear that in common with all our territorial specialists who have studied this problem, I am most strongly opposed to the proposed compromise solution on the grounds that in principle it is fundamentally unjust to a small and weak nation, in practice unworkable,

---

[52] Aldrovandi, "La settimana di passione adriatica a Parigi," *Nuova Antologia*, May 16, 1933, p. 163.
[53] *Ibid.*
[54] House, IV, 441-42.
[55] See below, Document 38.
[56] See below, Document 39.
[57] See below, Document 37.

and from the standpoint of the future fraught with gravest danger to the prestige and even to the ultimate success of a League of Nations which can afford to guarantee only those arrangements which are inherently righteous."[58]

Second Appeal of the American Experts to Wilson

Johnson's views were, as he said, in agreement with those of the American territorial experts. Taking a none-too-friendly view of what they considered the unwarranted interference of outsiders among their colleagues, and holding this very interference responsible in part for Italian intransigence, the same five who had sent a letter to Wilson on April 4, with the addition of Isaiah Bowman, the chief territorial specialist, sent a new and urgent appeal to Wilson to shun any compromise. This document is worth quoting, as a clear statement of what might be termed the extreme American view.

En route to France, on the *George Washington* in December, the President gave the territorial specialists an inspiriting moral direction:

"Tell me what's right and I'll fight for it. Give me a guaranteed position."

We regard this as a noble charter for the new international order. We have been proud to work for that charter. At this critical moment we should like to take advantage of the gracious invitation of the President to address him directly on matters of the gravest importance, and in accordance therewith beg to submit the following observations:

The Italian representatives demand Fiume and part of Dalmatia in order to emerge from the Conference with loot for their people. These districts belong to Jugo-Slavia, not to Italy. In our opinion there is *no* way —no political or economic device, of a free port or otherwise—which can repair to Jugo-Slavia the injury done if any outside Power prevents Fiume from being made an integral part of the Jugo-Slav organization. It would be charged that we had betrayed the rights of small nations. It would be charged that the principle, "There shall be no bartering of peoples" had been publicly and cynically thrown aside.

Italy *entered* the war with a demand for loot. France and England surrendered to her demand. Of all the world's statesmen the President alone repudiated a war for spoils and proclaimed the just principles of an enduring peace. The belligerent nations, including Italy, agreed to make peace on the President's principles. Italy now insists that she must carry home an ample bag of spoils or the government will fall.

If Italy gets even nominal sovereignty over Fiume as the price of sup-

[58] Johnson to Miller, April 19, 1919, Miller, VIII, Document 818.

porting the League of Nations, she has brought the League down to her level. It becomes a coalition to maintain an unjust settlement. The world will see that a big Power has profited by the old methods: secret treaties, shameless demands, selfish oppression. The League of Nations will be charged with the acceptance of the doctrines of Talleyrand and Metternich.

If Jugo-Slavia loses Fiume, war will follow. When it comes, the League will be fighting on the wrong side. Ought we to hope that it will be strong enough to win? Will the people of the world send armies and navies and expend billions of dollars to maintain a selfish and aggressive settlement?

Better a League of Nations based on justice than a League of Nations based on Italian participation bought at a price. The Italian government may fall, but the Italian people cannot long withstand the opinion of the world.

Never in his career did the President have presented to him such an opportunity to strike a death blow to the discredited methods of old-world diplomacy. Italian claims are typical of the method of making excessive demands in the hope of saving a portion of the spoils in subsequent compromises. To the President is given the rare privilege of going down in history as the statesman who destroyed, by a clean-cut decision against an infamous arrangement, the last vestige of the old order.[59]

In the light of the present day the above statement is not devoid of profound irony. Be that as it may, it was unquestionably a skillful appeal, through its reminder of the "George Washington" phrase and its insistence on the foundations of the League in right and justice; as such it could not fail to strike a responsive chord. It hardly concealed its bitterness at the tactics which the Italians in their predicament, and with complete misjudgment of American idealism, had ill-advisedly thought it expedient to adopt.[60] With the best intentions and the highest motives—for certainly the Americans had no prejudged intention of being unfair to the Italians—it was as far removed from being a technical statement of local conditions,

[59] Letter of Isaiah Bowman, W. E. Lunt, Clive Day, D. W. Johnson, Charles Seymour, and A. A. Young to the President, April 17, 1919. Baker, *Woodrow Wilson and the World Settlement*, III, Document 36.

[60] "The Italians pushed their intrigues tirelessly throughout the interval [March-April]. . . . No one connected with the American delegation was free from their importunities." Baker, *op. cit.*, II, 150.

"T. . . . . . comes to see me and shows me telegrams which show that the Italians are intriguing everywhere, Epirus, Thrace, Turkey, Hungary." Nicolson, *Peacemaking*, p. 283. To be sure, neither of these writers is overcritical. Baker, especially, is given to dramatizing and should be taken *cum grano salis*.

the primary task of the territorial experts, as some of the provisions of the German Treaty were removed from the Fourteen Points.

House, more supple than Wilson and the American experts, realized the futility of the increasingly acrimonious discussion. For all his friendliness to the Italians and his own readiness to give them a large measure of satisfaction, he was anxious to preserve unity in the American camp. Discussing the question with Wilson on April 18, he "urged him to settle it [Fiume] one way or the other." He had "about come to the conclusion that since we cannot please the Italians by compromise, we might as well do what seems best in the judgment of our experts, and that is to give it directly to the Jugo-Slavs." This solution appealed to Wilson and House "urged him to take it up with Lloyd George and Clemenceau and commit them in order to present a united front."[61]

THE ITALIAN QUESTION IN THE COUNCIL: APRIL 19-24

The Italian question was now the outstanding issue of the Conference. The French problem once out of the way, it had been decided on April 13 to send an invitation to the Germans to come to Paris. In order to placate the Italians, the announcement of this invitation was accompanied by a statement that the other questions would be expedited, in particular the Italian settlement.[62] This was the reason for the meeting between Wilson and Orlando the next day and for the subsequent attempts at a settlement just outlined.

The Italians were, in addition, spurred to activity by disturbing news of unrest at home,[63] and on the seventeenth Orlando wrote a letter to Wilson urging the necessity of settling the Italian question, and proposing that the meeting of Saturday, the nineteenth, be devoted to it. The proposal was accepted at the meeting of the Council of the eighteenth.[64] For the better part of a week the Italian controversy held the center of the stage. Although the Council Minutes for the meetings of these six days are not available in full, it is nevertheless possible to obtain a fair knowledge of what went on: Vol. XIX of

[61] House, IV, 444.

[62] According to Baker, Orlando refused to approve the invitation unless assured that consideration of the Italian claims would not be deferred until the German settlement was complete. Baker, *op. cit.*, II, 78.

[63] Aldrovandi, "La settimana di passione adriatica a Parigi," *Nuova Antologia*, May 16, 1933, p. 165. Page's reports at this time gave the impression that the growing campaign against Wilson in Italy was inspired by the Italian delegates in Paris. Page to House, April 14, House's papers, Yale University.

[64] Aldrovandi, *op. cit.*, p. 166.

Miller's work contains an account of all discussions relating to Italy;[65] in addition, Aldrovandi has published his Diary for the period from April 17 to April 27, which includes in full the Minutes of the meetings at which the Italians were present.[66]

The meeting on the morning of the nineteenth was attended by the Four, with the addition of Sonnino. Orlando, speaking first, proceeded to state the Italian case in detail. In deference to American wishes, he said that he would not base his argument on the Treaty of London, to which the United States was not a party, and that he preferred to argue each point on its merits. In the north and east Italy claimed the natural frontier for reasons of defense and security. As to Fiume, while it fell within the natural frontier to the Quarnero, the main consideration in its case was the city's own expressed wish to be united to Italy; in reply to the contention that Fiume belonged to Yugoslavia, he pointed out that, in a similar case, Danzig, far more necessary to Poland than Fiume was to Yugoslavia, had not been given to Poland. Dalmatia and the islands he claimed for reasons of strategy and historic connection. In short, Orlando asked once more for the Treaty of London and Fiume in addition.

Wilson replied that he could only repeat what he had already told Orlando and Sonnino, namely that he could not depart from the principles of the German Treaty. He granted the force of the strategic argument in the north, but, beyond Trieste, Pola, and most of Istria, he thought that the argument ran the other way. When it had been thought opportune during the war, the Yugoslavs had been treated as friends. Fiume, because of its position should be internationalized. The case of Danzig was precisely the opposite: despite its use to Poland, the principle of nationality had prevailed in its case; Fiume was a mere island of Italian population, not contiguous to Italy. As to Dalmatia, Sonnino had used strategic arguments, but it could only be a menace to Italy in case Yugoslavia should be allied with another Power, and the League of Nations would take care of such a possibility. Moreover, it was precisely the interference of the Powers which had been the cause of strife in the Balkans.

Sonnino insisted that the strategic value of Dalmatia was purely

[65] Miller, XIX, 531-39. Subsequent references to Council proceedings occurring in this chapter, unless otherwise specified, are drawn from this account.
[66] Aldrovandi, op. cit., May 16, 1933, pp. 161-86; June 1, 1933, pp. 354-82. The relevant parts of Aldrovandi's articles have been reproduced below, Document 41. Aldrovandi was Sonnino's Chef de Cabinet and acted as secretary of the Italian delegation.

defensive; Northern Dalmatia was outside the Balkans for that matter. He claimed that, after having fought the war, Italy would receive less than Austria had offered her for mere neutrality. As to the League, a treaty would hardly suffice to make it effective.

Clemenceau shared Wilson's point of view, but recognized that the Treaty of London was binding on France. However, he pointed out that that very Treaty assigned Fiume to Croatia, and Italy could not claim the benefit of some clauses while rejecting others. He hoped Italy would not break with her Allies on that score.

Lloyd George agreed with Clemenceau. Either self-determination should be applied from Trieste to Spalato, or not at all; he pointed to France yielding her claim on the Rhine, and urged the Italians to consider the situation which their withdrawal would create.

Orlando indicated that if the Treaty of London were recognized and the case of Fiume reserved, he would consider the proposal, but Wilson insisted that he could not recognize the Treaty; he was prepared to make public his objections.[67]

The meeting had lasted three hours, but had brought the problem no nearer to a solution. That night the Italian delegation held a very stormy meeting, during the course of which it was decided to stand on the Treaty of London.[68]

In accordance with this decision, at the meeting on the morning of the twentieth, Orlando read a statement wherein he pointed out that, if the primary purpose of the Conference was to insure peace, the denial of Fiume to Italy would achieve precisely the opposite end, owing to the resentment which it would arouse among the Italian people, and concluded:

However, since the English and French Allies declared yesterday that they do not recognize the right of Italy to break the Alliance unless she be not granted what is guaranteed to her by the Treaty. . . . I therefore formally declare that in the event of the Peace Conference guaranteeing to Italy all the rights which the Treaty of London assured to her, I should not be obliged to break the Alliance, and I would abstain from any act or deed which could have this significance.[69]

According to Aldrovandi's account, Wilson made some rather

[67] Minutes of the Council, April 19, I.C. 171D; Aldrovandi, *op. cit.*, pp. 167-79.
[68] Aldrovandi, *op. cit.*, p. 180.
[69] This statement is taken from Aldrovandi, *op. cit.*, p. 180. See Document 41. Miller makes no mention of it, but it is also given in part by Baker, *Woodrow Wilson and the World Settlement*, II, 163.

damaging admissions in the course of this meeting: he granted that his attitude would have been different had Austria-Hungary subsisted, and also recognized that Italy was not bound by the Fourteen Points, resting his case solely on the moral obligation deriving from the fact that the Fourteen Points had been the basis of the German Treaty.[70]

Orlando pointed out that he had fallen back on the Treaty of London only with the greatest reluctance and because of the position taken by Lloyd George and Clemenceau. Sonnino repeated that the policy of the Treaty of London was purely defensive; if Italy were threatened by Serbia she would have to ally herself with Bulgaria.[71]

The meeting proved as inconclusive as that of the previous day; the only constructive suggestion came from Lloyd George, who proposed that the signatories of the Treaty of London hold a separate meeting.

Although he was beginning to entertain doubts, House had written to Wilson on the evening of the nineteenth, suggesting that he make a proposal along the following lines:

1. The line of the Treaty of London as far as it touched the old Austro-Hungarian boundaries (meaning to the Quarnero).

2. Fiume and the Dalmatian territory in dispute to the south to be held by the five Powers in trust for the League which would dispose of it at some future more opportune time.[72]

Wilson thought the proposal too great a concession, but told House that he would consider it if Lloyd George and Clemenceau would assume sponsorship of it.[73]

---

[70] Aldrovandi, *op. cit.*, pp. 181, 183. See Document 41.

[71] Minutes of the Council, April 20 I.C. 174A; Aldrovandi, *op. cit.*, pp. 180-85. See Document 41.

[72] House to Wilson, April 19, 1919; House, IV, 445. "I proposed this," went on House, "to the other Commissioners after you left and they all agreed. At White's suggestion, it was decided to draw this up in the form of a letter for us all to sign. I asked Lansing to prepare it, but since I cannot lay hands on him for the moment, I am sending this in advance." This statement should be compared with the following: "In April Colonel House proposed a compromise which would give eastern Istria to Italy and place Fiume and northern Dalmatia under a temporary League administration until their sovereignty was determined; a proposal which filled White with indignation." Nevins, *Henry White, Thirty Years of American Diplomacy*, p. 426.

White believed that the Italians would have accepted the solution of their eastern frontier advocated by Wilson had they not been encouraged in their resistance by the attitude of other members of the American delegation. Cf. *Ibid.*, p. 427; also pp. 475-76, citing a letter from White to Lansing of Nov. 8, 1919, in which White expressed himself very strongly on the subject of House's activity at the Peace Conference.

[73] House, IV, 446.

Following Lloyd George's suggestion, the three Allied Prime Ministers, accompanied by their respective Foreign Ministers, met on the morning of the twenty-first.

Lloyd George and Clemenceau were willing to abide by the Treaty of London. The former was impressed by the dangers of a break with America; the latter thought the basis of a compromise might be found in an exchange between Fiume and Dalmatia. But Sonnino pointed out that Wilson would give neither; in the absence of Wilson he felt free to express his distrust of the League, in which he did not believe, and whose meaning nobody knew. Orlando returned to the danger of revolution in Italy, to which later Balfour remarked that, inasmuch as Italy could not dispense with either Fiume or American economic assistance, she was apparently fated to have a revolution in any event. In reply to Clemenceau's insistence that he could not take Fiume away from the Yugoslavs, Sonnino remarked that when the Allies had entertained the idea of offering parts of Macedonia to Bulgaria in an effort to bring her into the war on their side, and of compensating Serbia in Bosnia and Croatia, they had apparently not felt bound to the Croats by the Treaty of London. The discussion led to no conclusion, as Orlando kept insisting on Fiume; however, Lloyd George thought that he and Clemenceau might try to induce Wilson to yield the islands.[74]

While this meeting was taking place, Wilson had gone to the Crillon and read to the American Commissioners a statement which he proposed to make public. House suggested that he consult Lloyd George and Clemenceau and follow their advice in the matter.[75]

In the afternoon Lloyd George and Clemenceau resumed the discussion with Wilson. Clemenceau hazarded the suggestion of a compromise in Asia Minor, but Wilson did not think well of it, because "the Greeks and everybody else appeared to dread the Italians as neighbors," and, besides, they lacked the colonial experience of the British. Lloyd George said that he had proposed giving to Italy the islands only; but Trumbić, according to Wilson, objected to yielding Cherso. Sir Maurice Hankey was sent over to ask the Italians if they would come back to discuss the cession of certain islands, and brought back a negative reply. Wilson then brought up the matter

[74] Aldrovandi, *op. cit.*, pp. 354-60. See Document 41. The account of this meeting is missing in Miller.

[75] House, IV, 446.

of his proposed statement, but Lloyd George and Clemenceau thought it premature, and he agreed to wait.[76]

The Italians, meantime, drew up a letter to the effect that the German Treaty being practically complete, they would be ready to sign it as soon as the question of their frontiers would be settled, and reminding their Allies of the undertaking not to make separate peace.[77]

On the twenty-second, negotiations took a new lease of life, and it seemed for a while that the deadlock might be broken. Orlando went to see Lloyd George at 2 o'clock and read him the letter which he proposed to send. After some discussion, Lloyd George said that he would see if he could get Wilson to accept the following basis of discussion: the Treaty of London line to Volosca; Fiume, under a régime similar to that of Danzig, within the Italian customs system, and with its diplomatic representation to Italy; the strategically more important islands to Italy; Zara, Sebenico, Trau, and Spalato free cities with a plebiscite after a period.[78]

Leaving Orlando, Lloyd George went to the Council meeting and informed his colleagues that the Italians would not be represented when the Germans came to Paris unless their claims were conceded; to this Lloyd George said he had countered that, in that event, Italy's claim for reparations could not be put forward. Wilson wanted to publish his statement; he realized what its immediate effect would be, but believed that "when the people realized the dangers of the position, as they might in the course of a week or so, opinion would probably change." However, Lloyd George was to make this proposal to Orlando: Fiume, a free city; the strategic islands to Italy; Zara and Sebenico, free cities under the League.[79]

At 6:30 Orlando and Aldrovandi went to see Lloyd George, who told them that, in addition to the line of the Alps (to Volosca) and the outer islands, he had succeeded in inducing Wilson to make Fiume, Zara, and Sebenico free cities under the League. Orlando indicated that these concessions were not sufficient, but evidently thought that they offered a serious basis of discussion. He therefore drafted the following counterproposal:

[76] Minutes of the Council, April 21, I.C. 175A.
[77] Aldrovandi, *op. cit.*, p. 361.
[78] Aldrovandi, *op. cit.*, p. 363. See Document 41.
[79] Minutes of the Council, April 22, I.C. 175D.

1. The line of the Alps (Brenner) to the sea, East of Volosca.
2. Fiume under the Sovereignty of Italy.

Italy will establish in the port of Fiume free zones in accordance with the terms of articles 8, 9, and 10 of the Peace clauses drawn up by the Commission of Ports, Waterways and Railways and will extend to Fiume those facilitations which may be arranged for later on in a general convention with reference to free ports.

3. Italy will have all the islands mentioned in the Pact of London except Pago.
4. Zara and Sebenico will be placed under the League of Nations with Italy as mandatory Power.[80]

Just how this proposal ever saw the light of day is somewhat difficult to understand, for it would have implied a fairly complete capitulation on the part of Wilson, especially in eastern Istria; it can only be that the Italians were laboring under a misapprehension. The Italian insistence on Fiume was apparently not very convincing to the Americans. Miller himself, despite his Italian leanings, admitted that he could not see why they wanted it. House comments on the developments of the day:

The whole world is speculating as to whether the Italians are "bluffing" or whether they really intend going home and not signing the Peace unless they have Fiume. It is not unlike a game of poker.[81]

By the following morning House had apparently decided that the time had come to call Italy's "bluff," if such it was, for he advised Wilson to issue his statement—not, however, before he had conferred with Lloyd George and Clemenceau.[82]

However, di Cellere took the Italian counterproposal to Miller late on the night of the twenty-second, presenting it as the utmost limit of the Italian concessions,[83] and the next morning Aldrovandi took it to Kerr, Lloyd George's secretary.[84] Kerr thought that the demand for Fiume might prevent agreement; the Italians said that they would attend the afternoon meeting of the Council in the

---

[80] Miller, IX, Document 842; Aldrovandi, *op. cit.,* p. 364. See Document 41. Also Minutes of the Council, April 23, I.C. 175F, Appendix I.

[81] House, IV, 446.

[82] House, IV, 446-47.

[83] Miller, "Diary," April 22, I, 268.

[84] At the same time, Miller took the statement to House and discussed it also with Wiseman, who promised to take it up at once with Balfour. Miller, "Diary," April 23, I, 268-69. Aldrovandi, *op. cit.,* p. 364.

event of a favorable answer.[85] Precisely what happened then is not entirely clear. At a meeting of the Three, Lloyd George himself declared that the Italian counterproposal offered no basis for discussion, and Wilson announced his intention of publishing his statement that very evening.[86] According to Italian accounts—di Cellere's report to Miller that same evening,[87] and Aldrovandi's[88]—at three o'clock in the afternoon Kerr brought notice to the Italians that, except for point 2 (Fiume), their proposal was acceptable. Thereupon, as time was pressing—Wilson's statement was expected to appear the next morning in the event of failure to agree—di Cellere and Imperiali were dispatched to see Wilson and Lloyd George, respectively, to seek clarification on the status of Fiume. Imperiali saw Lloyd George for a moment during a meeting of the Council, but di Cellere could not see Wilson at once, and, while the Italians were waiting for an answer, there appeared an edition of the *Temps* with the text of Wilson's statement.[89] Out of these circumstances arose the claim that Wilson's Manifesto interrupted a promising negotiation.[90] The misunderstanding was not cleared up—in part at least —until the following day, and it would seem that Lloyd George, not always any too precise and careful, must bear a large share of the blame for it. It remains, nevertheless, difficult to understand how so wide a divergence as that between Wilson and the Italians could appear to be composed while it still remained complete.[91]

When Wilson's statement appeared, the Italians decided to send the letter which they had prepared the preceding day but had held in abeyance pending the outcome of the negotiation with Lloyd George.[92]

Apparently undismayed, Lloyd George made an appointment with

---

[85] Aldrovandi, *op. cit.*, p. 364.

[86] Minutes of the Council, April 23, I.C. 175F.

[87] Miller, "Diary," April 23, I, 268-69.

[88] Aldrovandi, *op. cit.*, p. 365.

[89] Wilson's statement appeared in the press generally on the twenty-fourth. See below, pp. 141 ff.

[90] Miller subscribes to this view. Cf. "The Adriatic Negotiations at Paris," *Atlantic Monthly,* Aug., 1921.

[91] This does not warrant, however, subscribing to Baker's highly dramatized account of Lloyd George's perverse intriguing. Cf. Baker, *Woodrow Wilson and the World Settlement,* II, 166 ff. Wilson's statement to House in connection with the latter's suggestion of the nineteenth should be borne in mind; it would not seem that Wilson himself had made his position quite plain.

[92] Aldrovandi, *op. cit.*, p. 366. The letter was redrafted to include a recital of the events of the afternoon.

Orlando for the next morning. On that occasion he insisted again upon the dangers of a break with America and wanted to continue negotiations so that their resumption might be announced contemporaneously with the publication of Wilson's statement in Italy, in order to offset the effect of that statement. Orlando consented to remain for a while if invited to do so. At the same time Kerr handed to Aldrovandi a letter explaining that "he had been instructed by Lloyd George to state that an agreement was impossible so long as Italy asked for sovereignty over Fiume but that he (Lloyd George) believed that a compromise might be reached on the other points."[93] This put a somewhat different complexion on the happenings of the twenty-third.

Lloyd George went back to meet Wilson and Clemenceau and notified them of the imminent publication of Orlando's reply to Wilson's message. Wilson complained that the press had already been conveying the impression that the signatories of the Treaty of London were standing together, leaving the United States isolated. It had been necessary for him to issue his statement, for he could not "let the Italian people get their version of what had occurred from a poisoned press." However, the Three sent Orlando a joint invitation to remain for a few days, while Lloyd George and Clemenceau were to prepare a joint letter to Orlando, once more recognizing the validity of the Treaty of London which, however, gave Fiume to Croatia.[94]

The Four were together again for the first time in four days on the afternoon of the twenty-fourth. The meeting was naturally dominated by the new situation, created by the publication of Wilson's Manifesto. In the face of this new situation, Orlando felt that he must go back to Rome in any case to reassert his authority, but he did not mean to break with the other Powers. He did not know that he was in a position either to accept or to refuse any proposal at the moment. Wilson hoped that he would make clear in Italy the position of the United States. Lloyd George and Clemenceau wanted to know the position of the Italians in regard to the German Treaty, and how the Italian claims could be put forward. Orlando was willing to let the Allies look after Italian interests in this respect, but

[93] Aldrovandi, *op. cit.*, p. 368.
[94] Minutes of the Council, April 24, I.C. 176B.

could not give any assurances as to what Italy would do; he repeated that the Allies were pledged not to make separate peace.

Sonnino wanted to know where they stood, and if there was an offer on which the other Powers were agreed. This produced a clarification of the misunderstanding which had apparently occurred. Wilson had never modified his views on Istria and had merely asked Lloyd George to find out if the Italians would enter a discussion. Lloyd George recognized it was his fault; he had been under the impression that Wilson, too, was prepared to make concessions, but apparently had neglected to make sure about Istria.

Sonnino said that the preceding afternoon they had received a message from Lloyd George to the effect that the question of sovereignty over Fiume was the only remaining difficulty, and that Imperiali, sent to see Lloyd George, had brought back the reply that it could be made a free city under the League. Wilson knew nothing of this; all that he knew was that Lloyd George had left the room to see Imperiali; neither he nor Clemenceau had sent a message to the Italians. None too convincingly, Lloyd George explained that there had been a misunderstanding in connection with mandates for Zara and Sebenico. There was nothing to be gained, however, by pressing that point.

Sonnino insisted that it would be desirable to have some concrete proposal from the other Powers when the Italians met their Parliament. Lloyd George and Clemenceau agreed with him in this; but Wilson and Orlando were content, the one to trust to the righteousness of his position, the other to see how the situation would develop in Italy. The only definite result was, as Wilson said, that the three Powers were agreed in denying Fiume to Italy.[95]

The meeting adjourned with all parties standing essentially on their previous positions, and Hankey gave Aldrovandi a copy of the joint Franco-British letter referred to before, which stated the position of Great Britain and France in agreement with Wilson.[96] There was nothing left for Orlando but to leave for Italy, which he did

[95] Aldrovandi, op. cit., pp. 370-81 (see Document 41); Minutes of the Council, April 24, I.C. 176C. Unfortunately Miller's account of this session is very sketchy; it makes no mention of the explanations in connection with the misunderstanding which grew out of Lloyd George's attempt at compromise.

[96] Aldrovandi, op. cit., p. 381. The Franco-British Memorandum, drawn up by Balfour, is given in the Minutes of the Council, April 24, I.C. 176C, Appendix I. See below, pp. 149 ff., for an analysis of this document.

that very evening. Sonnino, so disturbed that he would see nobody the next day, left in turn two days later.

WILSON'S MANIFESTO

The publication of Wilson's statement naturally created an enormous sensation, not so much on account of its content, as because it signalized an open break in the Conference and a radical departure from its methods. This sudden appeal to public opinion in the midst of negotiations, hitherto much criticized for the secrecy in which they had been shrouded, was indeed a novelty.[97]

The Manifesto itself[98] presented no new arguments. It was essentially an earnest appeal to Italy to subscribe whole-heartedly to the new order of things, of which the League of Nations was the embodiment, and, more immediately, to the settlement outlined in the Fourteen Points. Entirely new circumstances, it was pointed out, had come to prevail since the Treaty of London had been signed. That Treaty could not be binding on the non-signatory Powers, who had entered the war subsequently and without knowledge of its existence; moreover, it had been directed in the main against Austria-Hungary, which Power had ceased to exist and whose menace had therefore disappeared. The United States, on the other hand, was bound by definite commitments expressed in the Fourteen Points. These were the basis on which the German peace had been conceived, and Wilson did not feel at liberty to depart from their application in the case of the former Austro-Hungarian and Balkan territories.

Coming to the specific points in dispute, Fiume and Dalmatia, the Manifesto repeated the familiar argument that the former was primarily not an Italian port, and that to give it to Italy would be to put it under a sovereignty alien to its essential economic function. As to Dalmatia, the main reason for its attribution to Italy in the Treaty of London had been strategic, but that argument no longer held, in view of the disappearance of Austria-Hungary and the creation of the League of Nations, under whose auspices, moreover, fortifications would be dismantled in the Adriatic, armaments re-

---

[97] To be sure, much use had been made of the press by the various governments, but there was a vast difference between those back-stage maneuvers and Wilson's formal and direct appeal to a public opinion not of his own country.

[98] Despite the availability of this document, in view of its importance the full text is reproduced below, as Document 42.

duced, and Italian territorial integrity guaranteed, along with
that of the other members. The League would likewise insure the
safeguard of Italian minorities in Dalmatia.

In view of these considerations and of the advantages already secured by Italy, "it is within her choice," said Wilson, "to be surrounded by friends; to exhibit to the newly liberated peoples across
the Adriatic that noblest quality of greatness, magnanimity, friendly
generosity, the preference of justice over interest." The appeal concluded with the restatement of America's unyielding adherence to
the principles for the defense of which she had gone to war.

The compulsion is upon her to square every decision she takes a part
in with those principles. . . . These, and these only, are the principles for
which America has fought. These, and these only, are the principles upon
which she can consent to make peace. Only upon these principles, she
hopes and believes, will the people of Italy ask her to make peace.

With the statements of fact—taken by themselves—regarding
Fiume and Dalmatia, little quarrel could be found. But, as the Manifesto clearly recognized, the conclusions arrived at were based on the
implicit assumption that the new order would become a workable
reality. The issuance of Wilson's Manifesto was a climax in the evolution of the Conference: an issue was joined far transcending the
local disputes over Fiume and Dalmatia, or indeed the whole Italian
problem, which only the accident of circumstances made the occasion and the symbol about which the opposing ideologies clashed.
The first concrete formulation of war aims in the Fourteen Points,
the acceptance of his principles by the Allies, the position taken in
the debates of the past four months, constituted for Wilson a logical
sequence of which his appeal was but a consistent culmination.
Clearly and unequivocally, he stood on ground where there could
be no compromise, for compromise would mean surrender of principle, and principles could not be surrendered in part.

Nor is it difficult to understand how, despite practical objections
and possible consequences, Wilson came to adopt so novel a procedure. To him and the advisers on whom he most depended, the
Italian question was a comparatively simple issue. He had definitely
recognized the right of the subject nationalities of Austria-Hungary
to organize their independent political life; the Fourteen Points had
been freely discussed and accepted, save for one reservation, in mak-

ing the Armistices. He had been generous to Italy in granting the demand for the Brenner frontier and was willing to make reasonable concessions to her in the east at the expense of the Slav population; beyond that, the Italian demands could have but one interpretation: in the words of his experts, "a demand for loot," which could carry no weight against the principle of nationality to which the Slavs made appeal. Even more, it would be to Italy's own future interest to avoid creating a Slav irredentism. The idea of appealing to public opinion was ever-present in his mind; he was thoroughly convinced —and not wholly without reason—that public opinion, if properly informed, would, in general, support him, and that its backing was his greatest source of strength. On the "George Washington," he had expressed the belief to the members of The Inquiry that America was the only disinterested party, the statesmen of Europe did not represent their peoples. The experience of his visit to Rome could only tend to confirm this conviction. He had threatened before, with successful results, to resort to the same device when attacked in the French press. As indicated previously, the news from Italy which reached the American delegation tended to create a picture of a press largely controlled from the source of the Italian delegation in Paris, while it failed to convey the change which had taken place in Italian opinion as the result both of the actual developments in Paris and of the manner in which those developments were presented to it. This impression could not have been more clearly expressed than by Wilson himself when he said that "it had not been possible for him to let the Italian people get their version of what had occurred from a poisoned press." The personal attacks on Wilson hit a sensitive spot. The recurrent mention in Italy, at first, of the Anglo-Saxon block;[99] then, as the issue gradually became more sharply drawn between Orlando and Wilson, the attempt to isolate the United States by insisting that Great Britain and France supported the Italian claims,[100] when, actually, Wilson had the backing of Lloyd George and Clemenceau in the Council; and, worst of all, the

[99] The report is of interest that the campaign against the Anglo-Saxon Powers was of French origin, and had become intensified with the return to Paris of Barrère, who worked assiduously to create and maintain a Franco-Italian *rapprochement*. Cf. Page to House, April 18, House's papers, Yale University.

[100] Page to House, April 22, *Ibid*. Page's reports, while not essentially inaccurate, by concentrating on the phase of the Italian reaction toward America, tended to give an oversimplified and one-sided view of the situation in Italy. Page himself had, by this time, become somewhat irritated with the Italian press.

endeavor to dissociate Wilson from the United States—all this was psychological preparation for the unexpected procedure adopted by Wilson.

And yet, much as we may understand the background which made this action possible, it cannot be described otherwise than as a capital error in judgment. Without going into the merits of the case presented by Wilson, the fact remains that his Manifesto could be interpreted only as an appeal to Italian opinion, against the Italian delegation. If, as Wilson himself believed, that opinion was molded by a poisoned press, it is difficult to understand his thinking that a mere statement on his part would suffice to put the American position in its true light before Italian opinion.

Orlando's Reply and the Reaction in Italy

Be that as it may, the actual appearance of Wilson's Manifesto on the evening of the twenty-third was a complete surprise to the Italians. Under the circumstances, Orlando could hardly let it pass unquestioned, and his answer appeared accordingly on the twenty-fourth.[101] Whereas Wilson's appeal was earnest and based on high principle, Orlando preferred the lighter touch of irony, which he used not without skill: such assertions as that Italy must abide by the spirit of the new order as it was manifested in the German Treaty did, after all, lend themselves to this sort of treatment. The first part of Orlando's reply[102] is the most interesting and important. It began by expressing surprise at the publication of Wilson's statement, which had interrupted a promising negotiation, and went on to declare its adherence to this "innovation in international intercourse," which doubtless "will aid in granting the different peoples a broader participation in international questions," which participation was "a sign of a newer era." With a view to his home opinion, Orlando felt that he had to protest, however, against the derogatory implication toward Italy that such an appeal might be directed to the Italian people outside, or even against, the Government which it had elected as its representative. "To oppose, so to speak, the Italian Government and people, would be to admit that this great free nation could submit to the yoke of a will other than its own, and I

---

[101] Wilson's Manifesto and Orlando's reply were published simultaneously in Italy.
[102] See below, Document 43.

shall be forced to protest vigorously against such suppositions, unjustly offensive to my country."

Coming to the specific issues raised by Wilson, Orlando went on to repeat and to summarize the customary Italian arguments. He regretted having been unable to convince Wilson of the soundness of his case, but, at best, that must be set down as an honest difference of opinion. Once more he insisted on the justice of the Italian demands, which were moderate by comparison with others; the demise of Austria-Hungary did not imply a reduction of the Italian aspirations, for Italy needed security in the east as much as in the north. As to Fiume, rather speciously, he argued that its size should not prevent the application to it of Wilson's cherished principle of self-determination. For Dalmatia, "this boulevard of Italy throughout the centuries," the precedent of Poland was adduced.

This presentation suffered from the usual weakness of Orlando's arguments, a weakness inherent in the attempt to reconcile the demand for the Treaty of London plus Fiume, with the Fourteen Points. But if Wilson's Manifesto was directed to Italian opinion, Orlando's reply was even more so, and, when the two statements appeared side by side in Italy, there could be little doubt as to which would arouse the more favorable response.

The immediate reaction in Italy was violent in the extreme and quite unanimous: an emotional outburst of unreasoning nationalism and injured pride, which joined in heaping maledictions on the head of the American President; and, what was more unfortunate, it put for a moment in the same camp, the most aggressive and irreconcilable annexationists, the type of the followers of d'Annunzio, with those saner elements who, like Bissolati, advocated a just and reasonable peace of compromise with the Yugoslavs. Nor can the outburst be explained away as having been engineered by the Government, though the latter was at least tacitly sympathetic toward it. The dominant note was not so much perhaps anger or disappointment at the prospect of being thwarted in Fiume—the Fiume agitation, as such, was, to a large extent, a comparatively recent and artificial development—as resentment against unfair discrimination where Italy was concerned, heightened by touchiness over anything that might seem to raise a question as to Italy's position among the Powers.[103] (Wilson had threatened, but had not used, such methods

---

[103] Cf. *Daily Review of the Foreign Press*, April 20-27.

when Great Britain and France, more powerful nations, were concerned.)

Salvemini, like Bissolati, had, for a long time, been one of the leading advocates of a policy of compromise and of abandonment of the Treaty of London. Yet even he was moved at this time to an impassioned protest. Representing the most moderate element, one which had earned for itself the rather deprecatory epithet of *rinunciatari*, to quote an article of Salvemini's will serve to give an idea of the hopelessness of Wilson's appeal—so far, at least, as it was directed to the Italian people. Incidentally, this article constitutes also an excellent statement of the case for the failure of Wilson at Paris:

Not today [wrote Salvemini] but two months ago, and not only to the Italian people, but to all the peoples of the Entente, should President Wilson have addressed himself to recall them to a greater realization of the dangers that threatened peace. . . . Not from the Adriatic negotiations alone, but from all negotiations, should he have withdrawn in time, without ever giving up any essential point from the system of ideas on which the hope of the world was focussed. . . .

President Wilson dared not, perhaps never contemplated accomplishing so bold an act. . . . From the ground of right, he shifted to that of opportunity. But in this field the wolves and the foxes of the old European diplomacy were stronger than he.

And the wolves and foxes of old Europe had their counterpart in young America: the industrialists of steel and war, the traders in human blood. They brought up against him the Monroe doctrine and the question of the yellow race, that is, all the mental inertia, all the prejudices and suspicions of his own country. . . . The Man, of whom up to now all had been asking for something, had in turn to ask for something from others: he asked for an exception for his country from the law of the League of Nations which was to have been equal for all. He was no longer an arbiter.

Under these conditions, President Wilson came to disagree with the Italian delegation. And when he wanted to speak to the Italian people, he found it disillusioned, hostile and irritated.

Why does he want to impose what he considers absolute justice on the Italian people alone? Why does he not first issue a message to the English people to deny it the German colonies and ask that they be all entrusted to the League? Why does he not send a message to the French people, denying it the right to violate the principle of nationality in the Saar basin? Why does he not send a message to the Yugoslav people, to tell it that the claims of M. Trumbić to Trieste, Gorizia and Pola are absurd and unhealthy? Why does he not send a message to the American people, to explain to it that the Monroe doctrine cannot be reconciled with a League of Nations that claims to insure equality of rights to all civilized nations?

The statute of the League of Nations being rudimentary as it is, it is natural that President Wilson should not ask England to give up Gibraltar, Malta and Suez, but instead should recognize the English protectorate in Egypt. But why not recognize then the right of Italy to protect herself also in the Adriatic by occupying those Dalmatian islands which would make her coasts secure? . . . Italy has no right in Dalmatia, because it is Slav country; but why should not the Slavs renounce Fiume which is 2/3 Italian? The Slavs need the port of Fiume for their commerce, but does not the Covenant of the League, art. 21, make the states assume the obligation "to guarantee and maintain the freedom of passage and a just treatment of the commerce of all the states members of the League?" Should not this article be sufficient to insure the Slavs that their commerce will not be interfered with at Fiume? Or could it be that the Slavs have a right to distrust the League when it comes to guaranteeing freedom of transit in Fiume under Italy, but that Italy must trust the League for the treatment of the Italian population of the city?

It is against this discrimination in treatment that Italy has revolted.[104]

Bissolati also, in a message given to the press on April 25-26, made it clear that his advocacy of renouncing Dalmatia was based on the understanding that Fiume would go to Italy and Zara be made autonomous.[105]

However, while there was unanimity in condemning Wilson's tactics, there shortly began to appear in the press comments expressing the view that, inasmuch as Wilson's appeal was a complete failure, the problem remained essentially where it had been before that appeal had been issued.[106]

After the noisy welcome which had greeted him upon his return, Orlando stated his case on April 29 in a speech before the Senate, in which he took the position that Wilson had appealed to the Italian people over and even against their Government, and that he must therefore secure a formal renewal of his mandate from Parliament before proceeding with further negotiations. In this speech he gave his version of the events leading up to Wilson's Manifesto,

---

[104] Salvemini, *Dal patto di Londra alla pace di Roma,* pp. 270-74. Reprinted from the *Unità* of May 3, 1919.

[105] Bissolati, *La politica estera dell'Italia dal 1897 al 1920,* p. 415.

[106] *Giornale d'Italia,* April 26; *Corriere della sera,* April 25, 26, among others.

all the more unexpected because, as he said, after his interview with the latter on the fourteenth, "I had always been assured that the American delegation had not yet reached final conclusions in regard to our claims." Also, Wilson had told him on that same occasion that "he would have his experts reëxamine the question with a view to finding what, if any, further concessions could be made to the Italian demands." The difference between Lloyd George and Clemenceau on the one hand, and Wilson on the other, was stressed again. Insisting on the necessity of maintaining the Alliance, he (Orlando) was still ready to make reasonable concessions to that end, but had found it difficult to arrive at anything concrete, for, in the conversations of the twenty-fourth, "there appeared a divergence not only from our point of view, but also between that of our Allies and of the Associated Power."

"So that Italy is not confronted with a solution . . . or a compromise to which they [the Allies and the United States] all agree; but rather she is faced with a disagreement among them which precludes the possibility of including a territorial settlement for Italy in a treaty acceptable to all the Powers."[107] In other words, failing agreement with Wilson, a bid to Italy's Allies to exert pressure on him to produce a settlement.

Curiously enough, Wilson's outburst gave the Orlando Cabinet a new lease on life. None too successful at home, it had continued more or less on sufferance, for no one among the politicians in Italy wished to put himself in the invidious position of stabbing the delegation in the back without at least apparently sufficient cause. Orlando had thus been driven more and more into a position of relying on the outcome in Paris to save himself at home. The rather suddenly developed nationalism of the Giolittian element in politics was a maneuver to corner him in that position. But, as the result of the peculiar turn of events in the form of Wilson's Manifesto, these elements found themselves caught at their own game, and could not consistently do otherwise, at the moment, than give Orlando a rousing vote of confidence. Everything then conspired at this time—popular feeling as well as the parliamentary situation—to put Orlando in the position of true champion of a united Italy; even the taciturn Sonnino experienced for a day the unwonted feeling of being a

[107] Speech of April 29, 1919. *Atti del Parlamento, 1913-19, Senato, Discussioni,* V, 4888-91.

popular hero.[108] But in fact the situation was little changed, for, if Wilson's appeal had failed to achieve its purpose, neither was the reaction in Italy likely to change Wilson's views on the Italian problem.

The Balfour Memorandum

The position of Great Britain and France, rather of Lloyd George and Clemenceau, remained essentially what it had been. Officially, it was stated in Balfour's able and sober memorandum, given to Orlando just before his departure on the twenty-fourth. This memorandum pointed out that the situation in 1918, with Germany defeated and Austria-Hungary destroyed, was entirely different from what had been foreseen when the Treaty of London had been made in 1915. Also the attempt to organize peace would be vitiated from the very start if the new boundaries ran counter to the wishes of populations.

Admittedly it was often difficult to draw these boundaries, owing to the divergence between the factors (race, language, economics, and so forth) that had to be taken into consideration, and a compromise was usually necessary. France and Great Britain were bound by the Treaty of London, and any request for a change in the terms of that Treaty must come from Italy herself. But this same Treaty gave Fiume to Croatia. True, the population had expressed its wish to join Italy, but even this applied to Fiume proper, that is, without Sušak, which in fact formed part of the same agglomeration. And, with Sušak, the majority of the population was Slav.

Examining the arguments drawn from history, territorial contiguity with Italy, and economics, Balfour found all these militating against the Italian demand. As to the argument that Italy had a right to the fruits of victory, it could hardly be applied to a friendly power like Yugoslavia.

The British and the French did not think that the possession of Dalmatia would be strategically advantageous to Italy, and certainly with the control of Trieste and Pola, there could be no possible reason to fear Fiume either commercially or as a naval base.

Balfour went on to point out the very real gains which were

[108] A popular demonstration greeted his arrival at the station in Rome, and he had reluctantly been induced to address crowds at various points on the railway journey.

already assured to Italy. With no cause to fear her neighbors, she had every reason to cultivate their friendship, to which a badly drawn frontier would be the greatest obstacle.

It was for Italy to decide whether it was the best policy for her to insist on the Pact of London. But in the case of Fiume, the Pact, as well as justice and policy, were against her, and it was the considered opinion of Great Britain and France that it should not be separated from the country to which it belonged economically, geographically, and ethnically.

The memorandum concluded by calling attention to the effect on the League of Italy's separation from her partners, and appealing to Orlando to reconsider his action.[109]

Actually, Lloyd George and Clemenceau agreed with Wilson's point of view, but they would not associate themselves with it publicly. Despite Wilson's urgings, they refused to allow the Balfour note to be published, on the ground—not unreasonable—that to do so would merely serve to alienate Italy completely and would tend to shut the door irrevocably to the possibility of future compromise. Out of sympathy as they were with the Italian demands, they did not see their way to denouncing the Treaty of London, and took refuge behind the convenient, but none too convincing, contention that they were bound by that Treaty to give Fiume to the Croats.

At the same time, they did not care to antagonize the Italians too violently. This was especially true of the French, concentrating their energy on the German danger and anxious to achieve dependable security on their Alpine frontier: they endeavored throughout to appear to the Italians as their best hope of mediation; with few exceptions—among them the *Journal des débats*—the tone of the French press was distinctly pro-Italian.[110] As Aldrovandi put it, the suggestion of the Quai d'Orsay to the French press was: *"Roses sur l'Italie; ménager l'Amérique."*[111] In the French Chamber a resolution of sympathy for Italy was presented by a group of deputies. None the less the French and the British Foreign Offices were not blind to the potential danger to the influence of their respective countries in the Danube Valley, the Balkans, and the Near East, of an Italy too

---

[109] See below, Document 44.

[110] Cf. Noble, *Policies and Opinions at Paris, 1919*, pp. 333 ff. In part, at least, this was due to the use of Italian subsidies.

[111] Aldrovandi, "La settimana di passione adriatica a Parigi," *Nuova Antologia*, June 1, 1933, p. 382.

firmly in control of the Adriatic. Under the circumstances, it was doubly convenient to take shelter behind Wilson, hoping that his insistence would suffice to invalidate the Treaty of London without involving their own responsibility.

As to the Yugoslavs, the soundest thing for them to do was to stay out of the controversy. From their point of view, they had a good case on any grounds, and they were ready, besides, to accept a reasonable compromise. They could point out with justice that even the American line handed over some 300,000 Slavs to Italy; that the Italians in Dalmatia constituted at most a few urban islands in a solid Slav country; and that Fiume, whose hinterland was their own country and Central Europe—non-Italian territories in any event— was their only northern outlet to the sea. Italy had all the security she could reasonably demand in the Adriatic with the possession of Pola and Valona, especially if the eastern coast were demilitarized, as had been proposed. They could easily give their consent to any scheme for future settlement, based on consultation of the wishes of the inhabitants—provided, of course, small areas should not be separated from the surrounding countryside—secure in the knowledge of an overwhelming Slav majority. They, too, were aware of Great Power rivalries in the Danube Valley and the Balkans, but could not afford to forget that it might be dangerous for them to be isolated in front of a stronger Italy; hence the desirability of a settlement, even at the cost of some concessions on their part. This last consideration is what made the Italians feel that if they could first reach a settlement satisfactory both to themselves and to the Americans, such a settlement would undoubtedly be accepted by the Yugoslavs—an opinion shared by some Americans. From this derives the Italian endeavor to procure such an arrangement; and, for the same reason, the reliance of the Yugoslavs on Wilson and their appeal to his principles.

The Yugoslavs also had to remember their internal problems, arising from the very fact of the formation of a new state from elements separated for centuries, under the influence of widely divergent cultures and political régimes; the incipient rivalry of culture and religion; the tendency of the established Serbian state machinery to regard the Croats and Slovenes as secondary adjuncts to itself, if not quite as conquered peoples; and the corresponding suspicion of the latter. All this, still further complicated by the danger that the Serbs might be accused by the Croats and Slovenes of being generous at their expense in the matter of territorial settlements, especially after the Allies had been generous to Serbia where Bulgaria and Hungary were concerned, while these same Allies showed signs of greater leniency toward Austria, and the Italian boundary remained wholly problematic.

VI

THE MILLER-DI CELLERE PLAN

SUCH WAS THE general situation immediately after the appearance of Wilson's proclamation. Much as one may sympathize with his point of view and understand the motives which led him to issue his appeal on the evening of the twenty-third, there is no denying that it failed utterly to achieve its purpose. In Italy, it had merely served to solidify opinion while irritating it, as shown by the reaction of even the most moderate and conciliating elements. It had provided the Government with an easy triumph and incidentally let loose a campaign of vilification in the press, and hardened the Adriatic quarrel into one between the Italians and the Americans. Comparing its results with its purpose, it cannot be described otherwise than as a false move. None the less the question remained, and the need for a solution was no less urgent, for all the added difficulty and bad feeling.

The danger to Italy of being isolated was quite as great and as real as that of not securing her demands. Italy was too vulnerable economically to face such a prospect with equanimity.[1] There was therefore no desire for a break on either side, but rather an attitude of watchful waiting. On the one hand, how far would the Italians carry their withdrawal? And, on the other, what inducements would be offered them to return? However, the Conference had survived other and more serious storms, and this one would blow over too. As Seymour remarks, "the inner circle of the Peace Conference was not seriously disturbed."[2]

Orlando, ever reluctant to resort to extremes, had indicated in his speech before the Senate his unreadiness to break with the Allies.

[1] "Mr. Auchincloss said that the Italians have had a cable saying that they are being delayed in their financial arrangements with the United States; that the Treasury is only doing what it must, and that the Guaranty Trust Co. has turned suddenly very cold on the proposition for a $25,000,000 credit, and that they believe that this is due to the action of our Government, which of course it is, as Davis sent a cable a few days ago directing it, or at least suggesting it." Miller, "Diary," May 12, I, pp. 300-301.

[2] House, IV, 449. As early as April 26, Prince di Scordia, Orlando's secretary, went to see House and, rather to the latter's surprise, expressed Orlando's regret that he had left Paris without saying good-by. Ibid.

When the Committees of the Senate and the Chamber visited him on April 27, he had obtained from them—though not without some difficulty—the promise that the two houses would be content with simply voting the Order of the Day, rather than any motion committing him in advance to a specified course. He was thus secure for the moment and had carte blanche to resume and pursue negotiations. Throughout the country there were numerous manifestations, and patriotic societies urged the simple solution of annexation.[3] On April 26 the National Council of Fiume had decreed annexation of the city to Italy and had asked General Grazioli to take command, which of course he was unable to do.[4] The general attitude in Italy, which was at first that she could resume her place at the Conference only in exchange for at least a large measure of recognition of her rights, soon yielded to an undertone of apprehension as it became increasingly apparent that the Conference was going on with its work, unmindful of the absence of the Italian delegation. The point was made that the Allies could not make peace with Germany without Italy's participation, for that would constitute on their part a breach of the undertaking—contemporaneous with the Treaty of London—not to make peace separately.[5] Irritation was caused by the contrast between the expressions of sympathy for Italy —especially in the French press—and the behavior of the Allied Governments.[6] Even the *Giornale d'Italia* had to admit that the situation was disquieting, as no favorable news was forthcoming from Paris.[7]

On May 4 Barrère, who had been in Paris for some time, returned to Rome, apparently giving rise to great expectations.[8] He was received at once by Orlando, who was also, like Sonnino, in touch with Page. No doubt Barrère was the bearer of some message, but, in the absence of documentary evidence, the events behind the scenes during the first few days of May must remain obscure. According to the anonymous writer in the *Revue des deux mondes*, the Italians were alarmed by the intention of the Conference—announced by Clemenceau to the Italian Ambassador in Paris—to summon the

[3] Cf. *Daily Review of the Foreign Press*, April 28-May 4.
[4] Benedetti, *La pace di Fiume*, p. 32.
[5] *Giornale d'Italia*, May 3.
[6] *Corriere della sera*, May 4.
[7] *Giornale d'Italia*, May 4.
[8] To the extent that comment on his arrival was censored at first.

Austrian representatives for the middle of May.[9] Be this as it may, Orlando and Sonnino left Rome quite precipitately on the evening of the fifth, in such secrecy that the news of their departure was not allowed to be published until the following evening. The impression in Italy was that Great Britain and France had finally taken the position that they would stand by the Treaty of London, and hence that if Italy persisted in absenting herself from the Conference, it was she who was breaking the Treaty and not her Allies, who would consequently be at liberty to proceed with the German and Austrian negotiations. Whether or not this was the deciding factor, a similar argument was used in the Council.[10] From the British and French standpoint, it had the advantage of extricating them from responsibility while putting the Italians in a very uncomfortable dilemma: it was cold comfort to the Italians to know that their Allies were willing to live up to the Treaty of London, for that meant fighting it out with Wilson on the old line; on the other hand, trying to secure Fiume by giving up the Treaty of London also meant going back to the old unsuccessful arguments. What seems clear is that having gone through the motions of withdrawal was a gesture totally barren of results.

From the point of view of the situation in Italy, the recent events had made Fiume more than ever a political necessity. The secrecy and precipitateness of the return to Paris of Orlando and Sonnino could only accentuate the feeling of uneasiness in the country, and the recent enthusiasm quickly turned into skepticism and resentment. The well-nigh unanimous approval of Parliament and country had not been so much approval of Orlando's handling of the negotiations as a manifestation of national unity in the face of outside interference. Actually, Orlando's position was badly shaken, and unless he could secure a satisfactory agreement, and that quickly, it may be said that his fate was sealed from the time of his return to Paris.

DISCUSSIONS IN THE COUNCIL: APRIL 30-MAY 6

The Council, reduced to the Three by Orlando's absence, did not allow its work to be interrupted by his departure. Its activity during this period, and in particular its treatment of Italy and of

[9] "L'Aventure de Fiume," *Revue des deux mondes*, Jan. 15, 1921, p. 378.
[10] May 2-5; see below, pp. 156-57.

questions touching upon Italian interests, are of the greatest importance. There was naturally a lull at first,[11] pending clarification of the Italian situation, lasting until April 30, when the Three discussed the effect of Italy's absence from the Conference upon her claims in the German Treaty, and agreed that her presence would be a prerequisite to the entry of these claims. Wilson rejected Lloyd George's view that the Italian demand was essentially for security. At this same session, Clemenceau announced the dispatch of Italian warships to Smyrna,[12] a rather futile irritant to the Allies.

By way of exerting pressure on the Italians, the Three decided the next day that the Italians should be notified of the expected date of the meeting with the Germans.[13] On May 2, the Three had a long discussion on how best to secure the return of the Italians, who showed no signs of coming back. Wilson was unrepentant and favored using threats; he wanted the Balfour memorandum of the twenty-fourth published, to counteract the impression of public opinion that the United States was isolated in this matter, instead of being supported by the French and the British;[14] but Lloyd George again pointed out that this would tend further to estrange Italy, while he emphasized the danger of an Italian Government headed by Giolitti, whose tendency would be anti-Entente.[15] In fact, while he was ready enough to agree with Wilson, he did not wish, any more than Clemenceau, to create a solid front against Italy. Wilson wanted to exert pressure on the Italians by making a declaration; the Austrians had been sent for, and "if they [the Italians] did not come back they would be out of it altogether."[16]

Clemenceau suggested that the Italians should be told that their withdrawal broke the Pact of London, and it was finally agreed that the terms of the German Treaty would be redrafted to leave out all mention of Italy if her withdrawal proved permanent.[17] The dispatch of Italian warships to Asia Minor was again touched upon at this meeting.

[11] As far as Italian questions went; the Plenary Session, at which the Covenant of the League was accepted, and the Japanese crisis intervened in this period.

[12] Minutes of the Council, April 30, I.C. 177E. This and subsequent references to Minutes of the Council occurring in this section are taken from the account given in Miller, XIX, 539-42.

[13] Ibid., May 1, I.C. 179A.

[14] Ibid., May 2, I.C. 179B.

[15] Ibid.

[16] Ibid.

[17] Ibid., May 3, I.C. 179C.

Clemenceau's suggestion of notifying the Italians that their departure broke the Pact of London was taken up again the next day, when three drafts were proposed and discussed in turn.[18] Wilson was not in favor of doing this, for it tended to imply recognition of the Treaty of London, and thus isolate the United States; he wanted, instead, publication of the Franco-British memorandum showing agreement with his views. Lloyd George acknowledged that they were agreed on Fiume, but his position and that of the French was different from Wilson's, for they were bound by the Treaty of London. Balfour also thought that the only way was to make Italy agree that she had broken the Treaty.[19] The essential point of the validity of the Treaty of London remained unsettled and this vital ambiguity remained then, as indeed throughout the whole Peace Conference, one of the major stumblingblocks in the way of a settlement.[20]

Two days later, on the fifth, Pichon was able to inform the Council that he had heard from Sonnino, and that the Italians were coming back to be present at the presentation of the German Treaty.[21] This news came too late to relieve the tension. That day and the next there was considerable discussion of the Italian propensity to send troops on their own initiative, wherever they had potential interests at stake. Lloyd George appeared somewhat unstable and given to hearing rumors. One day the Italians were going to stand

[18] *Ibid.,* May 3, I.C. 180A. Appendices I, II, III.

[19] *Ibid.,* May 3, I.C. 180A.

[20] Referring to the Minutes of the Council for this meeting, Baker says that "it has been assumed by certain writers that this assignment of Fiume to Croatia at the time [of the London Treaty] was made with Italy's free consent, but this, as the secret records clearly show, is not correct. Italy had coveted Fiume from the beginning of the war and was only restrained from claiming it in the London treaty through a complicated diplomatic intrigue then going on with the object of bringing Bulgaria into the war on the side of the Entente. Fiume was to be offered to the future Jugoslav state as compensation for certain sacrifices of Serbian territory to Bulgaria. This whole intrigue fell through, leaving Italy's renunciation of Fiume as its only trace." Baker, *Woodrow Wilson and the World Settlement,* II, 134. This statement seems open to doubt. Even the initial maximum Italian claims presented to Grey on March 4, 1915 (see Document 1), before Sazonov had intervened and begun to whittle down these claims, contained no demand for Fiume. Indeed, the complete disruption of Austria-Hungary, while it had been a subject for speculation, was hardly in the realm of diplomatic considerations at the time any more than was the formation of Yugoslavia, and the Italians were quite prepared to leave her Fiume as an outlet to the sea. Sonnino's statement during the meeting of the Italians with the British and the French on April 21 (see above, p. 135) gives a totally different impression from that conveyed by Baker. The nearest approach to Baker's statement is the reference to Fiume in connection with Russian pressure, in the Italian Note of July 7, 1919 (see below, p. 239).

[21] Minutes of the Council, May 5, I.C. 181B.

on the Pact of London, then make a bargain for Fiume with the Croats; he said that the Italians had broken the Treaty by their occupation of Fiume, until Clemenceau reminded him that the occupation was not exclusively Italian.[22] The next day they were going to ask for a mandate for Fiume under the League. This last information caused Wilson to ask "how long it would take the Italians to realize that they could not get Fiume under any circumstances," and further to comment that "the only advantage in letting the Italians have Fiume would be that it would break the Treaty of London, which he was disturbed to find allotted the Dodecanese to Italy."[23] Wilson's irritation was profound and apparently sufficient to allow him to become a party to the sorry scheme of a Greek expedition to Asia Minor.[24] The refusal to grant the Italian request for a day's postponement of the meeting with the Germans perhaps evinces best the temper of the Three on that day.

RETURN OF THE ITALIANS

The Italians, Orlando and Sonnino at least, returned on May 6. They were coming back empty-handed and if they had ever expected that their return would be bought by concessions, their move had been a distinct failure, which left them, if anything, in a weakened position. Their return gave them an opportunity to appraise the work accomplished in their absence, and in which they could find little cause for cheer. The German Treaty was now complete and some last minute changes had been introduced, one in particular, in response to the French wish to prevent then, and for all future time if possible, the union between Austria and Germany. Italian opinion was far less unanimous than the French and, in general, more objective on this point. French activities in Vienna are rather obscure and seem to have been influenced by conflicting desires. From the French point of view, the Southern Tyrol in Italian hands would have the combined advantages of fulfilling the Treaty of London, satisfying Italy, and, not least important, creating a deepseated grievance between Italy and Germany—the best sort of insurance against the future possibility of an Italo-German *rapprochement*. On the other hand, the very real antagonism between the

[22] *Ibid.*
[23] *Ibid.*, May 5, I.C. 181C.
[24] This episode is taken up in detail in Chap. VIII.

Tyrolese and Vienna had to be taken into account. But the Tyrolese were at least as strongly opposed to being put under Italian rule as to being ruled from Vienna; from their point of view, it looked for a time as if Vienna might abandon them to Italy for the sake of *Anschluss*. In that event they might prefer the lesser of two evils and give up their support of *Anschluss* to keep clear of Italian annexation.[25] Thus by this devious route, they might find themselves unexpectedly supporting French policy; and we find the strange report that Allizé, Head of the French Mission in Vienna, had stated to representatives of the Tyrol that the question of the Austro-Italian frontier had by no means been settled.[26] Hope was further aroused among the Tyrolese after Orlando had left Paris, by statements made by Cunningham, Head of the British Military Mission in Vienna, which led them to believe that "the two Entente Powers [Great Britain and France] might actually be prepared to compensate Austria on her boundaries towards Czechoslovakia, Hungary and Yugoslavia, and even to abandon the Tyrol, if she would definitely renounce union with Germany."[27] This proved to be a false alarm, but it is significant as an indication of the possibilities that were entertained.

Modifications had also been made, during the absence of the Italians, in the reparations clauses of the German Treaty, and, when it was submitted to the Conference on May 6, Crespi thought it advisable, in the absence of the chief Italian delegates, to reserve Italy's consent in regard to the changes which had been introduced. The general tenor of the German Treaty became known publicly on that day; it was not well received in Italy, where comment on it was, in general, sane and enlightened, and some of the more glaring faults were pointed out.[28] The announcement of the American and British treaties of guarantee to France—even though it had nothing to do with the Italian controversy—was rather resented, and contributed to heighten the feeling that Italy was isolated and ignored.

However, the returning Italians seem to have taken the attitude that they had sufficient difficulties of their own, showing a comparative lack of interest in the fate of the German Treaty. After their

---

[25] Herre, *Die Südtiroler Frage*, p. 89.
[26] *Corriere della sera*, April 28.
[27] Herre, *op. cit.*, p. 97.
[28] *Daily Review of the Foreign Press*, May 5-11; in particular, *Corriere della sera*, May 8 to 10.

return, in view of the widely publicized positions taken by them and by Wilson respectively, there was little likelihood of an agreement resulting from the discussions in the Council. The Council did not in fact concern itself primarily with such an attempt, but went on to consider mandates. It touched upon the Italian problem rather incidentally, albeit in an important way, owing mainly to a scheme of Lloyd George.

Considerable activity was displayed, however, in an attempt to come to an understanding, but largely through direct negotiations and discussions among various members of the Italian and the American delegations; discussions which came so close to a solution of the difficulty that one can only regret their ultimate failure.

Resumption of Negotiations

Completely defeated in their attempt to secure concessions in the Adriatic in exchange for their return to Paris, the Italians nevertheless did not mean to yield completely. They had lost a move in the game, but the essential disagreement remained. As negotiations could not very well be resumed directly, either in the Council or outside, between Wilson and Orlando, some compromise solution had to be put forward from another source.

What message Barrère may have brought to Rome we do not know. The anonymous writer in the *Revue des deux mondes* believes that the French took the initiative in proposing a transactional scheme along the following lines: The League of Nations to take over Fiume, pending the completion of a port to be built for Yugoslavia at Buccari, and of a railway connection between this new port and the Fiume-Laibach railway; after the completion of the port and railway connection within a specified time, Fiume to go to Italy, Dalmatia to the Yugoslavs, except Zara and Sebenico (one of these towns to go to Italy, the other to the League of Nations). Italy to have the islands assigned to her in the Treaty of London.[29] The American, British, and French Ambassadors were active in Rome, and on May 5 Page sent a telegram to Paris likewise suggesting the construction of a Yugoslav port at Buccari.[30]

This suggestion evidently ran counter to Wilson's views on Fiume;

[29] "L'Aventure de Fiume," *Revue des deux mondes,* Jan. 15, 1921, p. 378.

[30] This telegram from Page is mentioned in Johnson's Memorandum of May 8, see below, p. 162.

nevertheless, granted the physical possibility of such a port at Buccari, it did tend to dispose of the economic argument for giving Fiume to Yugoslavia. The idea that some port other than Fiume might serve as an outlet for Yugoslav trade was not new. It had been hinted at in the statement of Italian claims, where such places as Buccari, Porto Re, the island of Veglia, Segna, and so forth, were mentioned.

When it comes to considering the building of a port, two sorts of conditions are essential to its usefulness. First, conditions depending upon the locality itself: sufficient depth of water, such, however, as not to preclude anchorage; adequate space both to accommodate the prospective tonnage and to install suitable land facilities, such as docks, warehouses, railway terminals, and so forth; proper shelter for ships. Second, conditions depending upon the hinterland: there must be proper railway connections, and the port must be naturally related by physical geography to the territory it is intended to serve.

It so happens that the mountain barrier of the Alps is narrowest and easiest to negotiate toward the head of the Gulf of Fiume, say from Volosca to Segna, and Fiume, the existing port, had been the outlet of the broad plain that corresponds roughly to the former Hungary. Beyond Segna, the coast somewhat bulges out into the Adriatic beyond a line that would run from Fiume to Ragusa, while, at the same time, the northern edge of the mountains extends more nearly in a west to east direction, paralleling the course of the Save River. Thus the mountain massif, quite narrow at the head of the Istrian peninsula, broadens out considerably to the south. Moreover, as this region, corresponding to the provinces of Dalmatia, Bosnia and Herzegovina, is relatively poor and thinly populated, there are very few railroads through it connecting the coast with the interior. The two main lines run, one from Spalato northward, roughly parallel to the coast some distance from it, until it joins the Fiume-Zagreb line at Ogulin; the other, from the bay of Cattaro, past Ragusa and up the valley of the Narenta to Sarajevo, and eventually to the main Orient Express line. Even these are very inferior from the point of view of equipment: single track, narrow gauge with numerous tunnels, even resorting to rack and pinion in one instance. Running through such difficult country as they do, the cost of transforming these lines into roads adequate to carry Central European freight to such ports as Spalato or Ragusa would be enormous, to say nothing of the longer haul that would be entailed, and of the fact that the territory traversed would not offer the compensation of any substantial local trade. All this would be reflected in a heightened cost of transportation, which disqualifies the ports from Sebenico southward from competing with those at the head of the Adriatic, even though some of them would make excellent harbors, especially Spalato and Sebenico.

There is no adequate locality between Volosca and Segna, outside of Fiume itself, owing to local conditions: smallness of the bay, lack of space between the water and the cliffs immediately behind, or insufficient shelter. These conclusions were presented as early as March 27 in a memorandum submitted by Johnson.[31]

Johnson's Memorandum of May 8

In the light of these conclusions, it would seem that the latest suggestion contained in Page's telegram of May 5 had little hope of being accepted by Wilson. However, it was not rejected flatly, but was instead examined by the American experts, and their conclusions were embodied in a memorandum written by Johnson. This memorandum did not confine itself to a technical examination of the feasibility of constructing a port at Buccari, but took the form of a survey of the entire Italian question. It made the following suggestions:

1. In the north, Italy should be granted, in addition to the Treaty of London, her claims in the Sexten Valley and in the Tarvis district.

2. In the east, the frontier should be the American line, and the Italian troops should withdraw west of that line. However, a plebiscite should be held within a fixed period in the area between the American line and that claimed by Italy.

3. Italy should receive the islands of Unie, Lussin, Sansego, and Asinello, and the Pelagosa group. As a concession to Italian sentiment, a plebiscite might be held in the rest of the islands and the part of Dalmatia claimed by Italy. Zara should be made a free city.

4. Italy should receive Valona with a sufficient hinterland and whatever mandate might be agreed upon.

[31] Memorandum on the "Possibility of Substituting Another Adriatic Port for Fiume, as the Commercial Outlet for Jugo-Slavia," Miller, VII, Document 628. This memorandum gave a description of the Adriatic ports from Fiume to Cattaro. It was based on the Austrian Coast Survey Charts and the official French sailing directions and descriptions of ports, supplemented by personal inquiries.

The most interesting part of this memorandum is the arrangement which it proposed for Fiume. The Italian troops were to be withdrawn and the city and district were to be administered by the League, pending the outcome of a plebiscite. In the event of the plebiscite turning out in favor of annexation to Italy, such annexation was to take place only after the completion by Italy, within a specified period, of a port at Buccari which, together with its facilities and railway connections, should in no way be inferior to the port of Fiume. If any of these requirements remained unfulfilled after a specified time, Fiume should be placed under Yugoslav sovereignty.

In the meantime, Johnson had an interview with Trumbić, as the result of which he added the provision that the entire Yugoslav coast should be neutralized.[32]

Finally, in order to find out Wilson's reactions to the idea, Johnson suggested the offer of an American loan to Italy on favorable terms.[33]

Italy's chances of securing Fiume under these conditions were the subject of no illusions on the part of Johnson, and the preamble accompanying this memorandum clearly showed his real views which may be taken as those of the territorial experts with whom he collaborated, as well as of Wilson himself. The formula just outlined

might offer to the Italian plenipotentiaries a means of emerging from a difficult situation without humiliating the Italian people. *Adoption of the formula* would result in the solution supported by the American territorial specialists and proposed by the President in his public memorandum of April 22nd, and hence *is not a compromise solution*;[34] but the ends sought would be attained without needlessly wounding Italian sensibilities.

Enlarging on this point, Johnson thought that the combination of a substantial Slav element and of economic interest would insure the outcome of the plebiscite being favorable to Yugoslavia. But even if that should not be the case,

the practical impossibility of constructing an adequate port at Buccari would be forced upon the Italian Government as soon as it began to study the problem and to count the cost. . . . Since Italy claims that Fiume has already manifested its unanimous desire to be Italian, and also

[32] Trumbić made the same offer of neutralization to Steed at this time. Steed, *Through Thirty Years*, II, 331.

[33] Johnson's Memorandum of May 8. See below, Document 45.

[34] Author's italics.

claims that Buccari can serve Jugoslavia as well as Fiume, the formula is fair to the Italian claims.

The Italians may well have brought this retort upon themselves by their loose assertions. However, it may be doubted whether this solution, for all its face-saving devices, was not rather too transparent for acceptance by Italy. In substance, it really amounted to a double guarantee that Fiume would ultimately belong to Yugoslavia.

THE AUSTRO-YUGOSLAV FRONTIER IN THE COUNCIL OF FOREIGN MINISTERS: MAY 9-12

Things seem to have been quiescent for a few days, until the twelfth, when negotiations were resumed in earnest. During this interval, the frontier between Austria and Yugoslavia was under discussion in the Council of Foreign Ministers. These discussions are important as evidence of the attitude of Italy toward her two northeastern neighbors, in particular of Sonnino's obstinate defense of his country's interests.

Two points were under consideration: Marburg and Klagenfurt. In regard to the first, the Americans, the British, and the French were in favor of giving the district to Yugoslavia, while the Italians felt that it should not be detached from the Austrian economic system of which it was a part.[35] The same argument was used by the Italians for Klagenfurt, and the other three delegations felt likewise that the Austrian frontier should be set along the Karawanken Mountains bounding the region in the south; they were also in favor, however, of holding a plebiscite in the region to ascertain its wishes, a suggestion opposed by the Italians.

The question of Klagenfurt brought up that of the Italian claims in that vicinity, for the frontier had been considered only up to the Klagenfurt-Laibach railway line, inasmuch as the determination of the point where the frontier between Italy and Yugoslavia was to join the Austrian frontier was the province of the Supreme Council. Sonnino was willing to consider the frontier beyond the point where it had been left off, and sought to bring out that the Committee had been guided by the principle that the railway line between Klagenfurt, Assling, and Trieste should be "free, that is to say, outside the territories allotted to Jugo-Slavia." (See Map VI.) This of course

---

[35] In population the district was predominantly Slovene, but the town of Marburg itself was largely German.

would imply that the Austro-Yugoslav frontier, delimited up to the Klagenfurt-Laibach road, should then turn south, remaining east

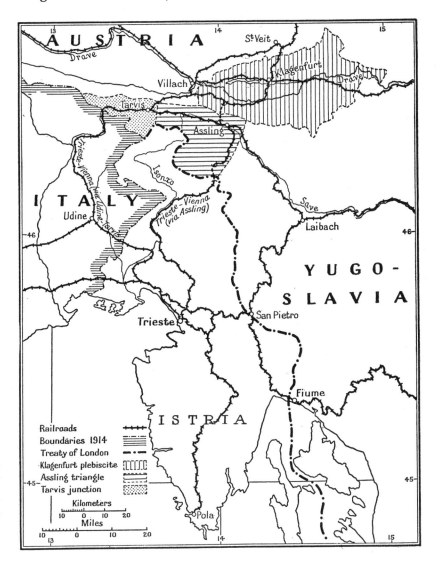

VI. RAILROAD CONNECTIONS: ISTRIA, TARVIS, ASSLING, KLAGENFURT

of Assling until it joined the Italian frontier. Sonnino was not proposing to examine the latter frontier nor to settle the final attribution of the territory in question, but simply to secure recognition of the principle that the railway from Klagenfurt to Trieste via Assling should, in any event, be wholly outside Yugoslav territory. Lansing pointed out that there was nothing in the report that warranted Sonnino's interpretation. After some further discussion of the extent of the competence of the Committee in this matter, the Committee was directed to submit recommendations, based on ethnic and economic considerations, in regard to the frontier between Austria and Yugoslavia up to the Italian frontier.[36]

The report of the Committee was circulated the next day. In reply to the economic argument (the undesirability of having a section of the Klagenfurt-Assling-Trieste road in Yugoslav territory), and to the strategic argument (the railway constituted a military threat against Italy from an enemy attacking from the east), the Americans, the British, and the French thought that:

1. Special arrangements could be made for customs regulations and the free use of the railway;

2. A link from Tarvis to Tolmino could be constructed without jeopardizing the commerce of Trieste.

The Committee was unanimous on the ethnic facts—50,000 Slovenes would be annexed to Austria—and in declaring itself incompetent to pass judgment upon the strategic considerations. It concluded its report by proposing a formula whereby the Austrian frontier would be extended westward from the point where it had been left off, and the districts of Tarvis and of Assling would simply be ceded by Austria to the Allied and Associated Powers for future final disposition.[37]

The report was taken up by the Council of Foreign Ministers on the afternoon of the tenth. Sonnino once more explained his point of view, and Balfour replied, making, with his wonted clarity, an analysis of the various factors in the case, and showing why he was unable to share the Italian point of view as against that of the other three Powers. Some further discussion ensued, in the course of which the oft-debated question of whether the Yugoslavs were enemies or friends came up between Sonnino and Lansing, and the Committee's report was finally adopted with Sonnino's amendment to the effect that the territory whose ultimate disposition was re-

[36] Minutes of the Council of Foreign Ministers, May 9. See below, Document 46.

[37] "Report Submitted to the Council of Foreign Ministers by the Committee of Jugo-Slav Affairs." Minutes of the Council of Foreign Ministers, May 10, F.M. 14, Annexure A. Miller, XVI, 264-67.

served should be so bounded as not to include the western line from Trieste through Tarvis.[38]

Two days later, the Council, unable to make a final decision in regard to the reserved area, ratified the solution just indicated.[39]

The question of Mandates, more particularly of the disposition of Turkey in Asia Minor, was before the Council at various times during this period (late April-early May) and is of considerable interest for two reasons. First, because of Italy's special claims in Asia Minor, her treatment of the situation and the manner in which the Council handled it in turn, throw much indirect light on the general question of Italian claims and the spirit in which they were dealt with at the Conference; secondly, because the fact that Italy left the Conference nearly empty-handed in the way of colonial compensations must be considered one of the keys to subsequent developments of Italian policy down to the very present.

The details of these discussions will be considered in a later chapter, together with other colonial questions.[40] For the moment it will suffice to say that, in order to forestall an Italian occupation of Smyrna, the Council decided upon the immediate dispatch of an expedition to that region, which it assigned to Greece.[41] This was done on May 6, in the absence of the Italians, and in great secrecy lest they get wind of what was happening. When they came back to Paris, the Italians found themselves faced with a *fait accompli*, in which they eventually acquiesced.[42]

DIRECT NEGOTIATIONS BETWEEN THE AMERICANS AND THE ITALIANS

House had always been sympathetic to the Italians and thought that a definite break with them must be avoided at all costs. He had been active before April 24 in trying to bridge the difference between their claims and the position taken by Wilson, and, as the latter proved immovable, realized that if an agreement were ever to be reached, someone else in the American delegation would have to lead the negotiations. For this reason, he again took the initiative, after the Italians had returned, in trying to work out some form

[38] Minutes of the Council of Foreign Ministers, May 10. See below, Document 47.

[39] Minutes of the Council, May 12, B.C. 61. Miller, XVI, 269-72.

[40] See below, Chap. VIII.

[41] Baker, *Woodrow Wilson and the World Settlement*, II, 187; Sforza, *Makers of Modern Europe*, pp. 160 ff.

[42] In the Council, on May 12.

of compromise. He did not do this without Wilson's knowledge, but his general sympathy for the Italians and the extent to which he kept the thread of negotiations in his own hands were not perhaps without some effect in the cooling of the President's feelings toward him.

House at first had no hard and fast scheme in mind; rather some form of compromise based on the general idea of the League of Nations taking over, temporarily at least, the disputed territory, especially Fiume: something along the lines of Page's telegram. With a view to reëstablishing contact and by way of smoothing things out, Sonnino had an interview with him on the afternoon of the eighth which House reported to Wilson as follows:

> Sonnino came to see me this afternoon to ask that I say to you that he and Orlando were exceedingly sorry because of the intemperate things that had been said in Italy both in public speeches and in the press. He said they did their best to curb it and that they would like you to know that they in no way sympathized with it. He spoke in a very conciliatory tone and hoped that a way out would be found.

However, adds House, "he had nothing to suggest."[43] Something of a personal apology, pending the result of the latest suggestion.

The idea of settling all the Italian claims at once, rather than piecemeal, on the local merits of each individual issue, had always been favored by some of the Americans. Among them Beer, for one, thought that in their totality the Italian demands were the most moderate of any of the Allies, and that the main issues were being lost sight of by concentrating too narrowly on a small and relatively unimportant point like Fiume, or a few miles of railroad line.[44] For a few days, beginning with May 12, he and Miller, on the American side, were active in attempting to produce a settlement.

On that day, House had to lunch Sonnino and di Cellere, and Orlando came to see him just after Sonnino had left. House spoke to them of Miller, whom he intended to use as intermediary. It was arranged that Miller should see di Cellere, who was to be the Italian

---

[43] House, IV, 462.

[44] Beer, Diary, *passim*. It may be mentioned that Beer was one of the few among the Americans who had a thorough and personal acquaintance with Italy and things Italian, of which he had long been an admirer. His general point of view and his knowledge of the language account for his being brought into this negotiation, despite the fact that it was outside his immediate province.

intermediary in this particular negotiation; Orlando made an appointment with House for the next morning. About six o'clock that evening, Wilson came in to see House, who told him of his general idea of placing Fiume and Dalmatia under the League until passions had cooled; White, present at the meeting, supported House's view. Wilson, while not actively opposed to the project, remained noncommittal.[45]

After seeing House, Miller called di Cellere in order to prepare the ground for the meeting between House and Orlando the next morning. Miller outlined this general solution: definite settlement of the Italian frontiers not touching upon Yugoslavia; postponement of the Italo-Yugoslav settlement by turning over to the League for a period of five years the territories in dispute, except those islands which were to go to Italy at once. For Fiume, a régime analogous to that of the Saar; Zara and Sebenico also under the League, possibly with a mandate to Italy. As his own idea, Miller suggested that, in regard to the future disposition of these territories, some formula might be drawn up to the effect that the League should take into account the wishes of the population, the necessity of access to the sea for the hinterland, and the security of Italy in the Adriatic. Miller also let di Cellere understand that the proposal was supported by House and that Wilson was informed of the present discussion.[46]

Di Cellere took this proposal immediately back to the Hotel Edouard VII, headquarters of the Italian delegation, where he spoke to Sonnino first, then to Orlando. After the last two had conferred together, they told di Cellere that he could report to Miller that they would consider the idea, Orlando adding that if it represented the extreme and final concessions of the Americans it was unacceptable, but that, with certain possible modifications, it could be used as a basis for further discussion. This answer was brought back to Miller late that night, when he and di Cellere had a long talk on the general Italian question and that of Italo-American relations. Di Cellere complained of Great Britain and France, who were dividing the German colonies exclusively between themselves.[47] The Italians were also complaining of difficulties which they were having in their ar-

---

[45] House, IV, 463.
[46] Miller, "Diary," May 12, I, 301; di Cellere, "Diary," May 12, pp. 191-92.
[47] Miller, "Diary," May 12, I, 302.

rangements with the United States Treasury and of the sudden coldness of the Guaranty Trust Company in the matter of a $25,-000,000 credit, difficulties which they rightly suspected of originating with the American delegation in Paris.[48]

Until now, di Cellere had been playing the rôle of an idle by-stander in the Italian delegation. In his capacity of Ambassador to the United States, he not unnaturally resented having been thrust into the background while negotiations were being carried on between the American and the Italian delegations. An admirer and follower of Sonnino, his immediate chief, and perhaps not immune to departmental jealousies, he blamed the difficulties encountered by the Italians on Orlando's tendency to centralize the conduct of negotiations in his own hands and on his lack of firmness and consistency in adhering to one line of policy.[49]

The charge was not, perhaps, devoid of justification; on the same day (May 12), Orlando was sounding out other possibilities. Beer had Piacentini, one of the Italian colonial experts, to lunch, during which they discussed colonies, their own immediate province. Piacentini voiced the same regret at being deprived of almost all share in Africa beyond some extension of the existing Italian colonies; then they went on to discuss the Adriatic problem. Piacentini thought that Italy was ready to make a settlement on the following basis: Fiume, without Sušak, a free port under Italian sovereignty; in Dalmatia, Zara and Sebenico free cities; three or five islands.[50] Piacentini insisted that this proposal, or rather feeler, be kept wholly unofficial, as Orlando might change his mind. He (Orlando) wanted to remain free to commit himself to one scheme or another, depending upon the turn of negotiations.[51]

This proposal, inspired by Orlando, is further evidence of his almost hypnotic concentration on Fiume, entirely out of proportion to its real value. This fixation is undoubtedly one of the main reasons for the failure to reach a settlement at the Peace Conference, when, in all likelihood, had the Italian problem been considered as a whole, much more favorable terms for Italy could have been obtained than was eventually the case.

[48] See above, p. 153, n. 1.
[49] Di Cellere, pp. 188-89.
[50] Beer, Diary, May 12.
[51] Beer, Diary, May 13.

Miller's "Definitive Solution"—Beer-Piacentini Proposal

The next morning Miller reported to House his conversation of the previous day with di Cellere. After this, Orlando came to see House, who arranged for him to have a talk with Miller later in the morning.[52] House notified Miller of the arrangement by telephone, adding that he had communicated with the President, and that the latter "would consider any solution which was reached by Orlando and myself [Miller]."[53]

Di Cellere received Miller and they were joined shortly by Orlando, returning from a meeting with Lloyd George.[54] Orlando repeated his wish to reach an agreement and not to have to fall back on the Treaty of London, which he would do only as a last resort. Miller, after making it clear that this current negotiation had House's backing but did not commit Wilson, emphasized the desirability of avoiding an Italo-American breach, especially as this would only be too welcome to certain other parties. He then went on to outline the solution which he had proposed the previous day to di Cellere. But Orlando still hesitated and played for time; without rejecting the scheme, he found flaws in it. To include the railway connection between Fiume and Vienna in Yugoslav territory would leave Fiume without land connection with Italy, in the event of this city becoming Italian; to speak with complete frankness, he must admit that Fiume was of no real importance to Italy, but urged that feeling on the matter had become so strong in Italy that he could not be sure that, if he ordered its evacuation, the order would be obeyed by the army. Would it not be just as well to make Fiume a free city politically, while giving a mandate to Yugoslavia for the Dalmatian coast, except Zara and Sebenico? As another feeler, he hinted at the possibility of maintaining the *status quo*, i. e., Italian occupation; but Miller made it clear that there was little hope of such a solution finding favor with the Americans. They separated to meet again the next day.[55]

In brief, Orlando did not like a postponement under League auspices; his heart was still set on Fiume and, failing immediate pos-

[52] Miller, "Diary," May 13, I, 303; House, IV, 463.
[53] Miller, "Diary," May 13, I, 303.
[54] Di Cellere, "Diary," May 13, p. 192.
[55] Miller, "Diary," May 13, I, 303-6; di Cellere, "Diary," May 13, pp. 193-94.

session by Italy, he must at least prevent its going to the Yugoslavs. On the other hand, Miller felt convinced "that the Italians realize perfectly that they cannot and will not have Fiume and that no negotiation is possible which does not admit this."[56] He felt that things had made sufficient progress to warrant putting in writing a concrete outline to serve as a basis of discussion the following day. This "Definitive Solution" recommended the following:

1. Fiume will become an independent city and free port under the protection of the League of Nations.

2. The frontier of Italy in Istria shall exclude the railroad running from Fiume to Vienna.

3. The Dalmatian coast is assigned to the Jugo-Slav State except the Italian towns of Zara and Sebenico which are to be under the sovereignty of Italy as free ports.

4. The whole Dalmatian coast is neutralized, including Zara and Sebenico. No fortifications shall be erected, no bases established, and no military, naval, or air operations shall be conducted. The inhabitants shall not be subject to military service except for purposes of local order.

5. Pago shall be considered as part of the Dalmatian coast assigned to Jugo-Slavia. The other islands in the Adriatic claimed by Italy are assigned to her.

6. Valona shall be Italian and any mandate of the League of Nations in respect of Albania shall run to Italy.[57]

He brought this to House in the evening, but advised against sending a memorandum to Wilson so that any changes might be made more easily. House, too, felt confident; as he told Miller, "if the Three would keep their hands off and let me [House] go on with Orlando it could be ended."[58] House did advise Wilson, who showed concern lest Orlando interpret the proposal as an offer coming from himself, which caused House to feel that Wilson *was* perhaps a trifle punctilious.[59]

Perhaps House and Miller were overoptimistic about the probability of the Italians yielding on Fiume. Beer, told by Mezes—who had heard it, in turn, from House—that the deadlock continued, again met Piacentini on the thirteenth. Piacentini repeated the pro-

[56] Miller, "Diary," May 13, I, 308.
[57] Miller, IX, Document 946.
[58] Miller, "Diary," May 13, I, 307.
[59] House, IV, 463.

posal of the preceding day in a somewhat more specific form, reported by Beer as follows:

1. Fiume to be under Italian sovereignty. Sušak not to be included. Fiume to be a free port with an International Commission for the regulation of the port. Full guarantees to minorities as regards language, schools, etc.

2. In return Italy to give up all her rights under the Treaty of London in Dalmatia except that Zara and Sebenico to go to Italy on the same terms as Fiume and, if necessary, international commissions to be established there. Piacentini, however, said that Italy might be satisfied if these towns were made free cities with native Italian commissionaries.

3. The island of Veglia must go with Fiume, but they would not insist upon Arbe.

4. In addition, Italy wants the four islands Curzola, Lissa, Lesina and Lagosta.[60]

Although the proposal came from Orlando, Piacentini insisted that it be kept strictly unofficial and that no names be mentioned. Beer thought the plan entirely reasonable and took it to Kerr, who thought likewise and promised to speak to Lloyd George about it. Kerr emphasized the difficulty arising from Wilson's obstinacy on the subject of Fiume, and, on the other hand, the irritation created by the Italian landings in Asia Minor, where they had gone on their own initiative. Beer reiterated the advisability of settling the entire Italian question, pointing to the moderation of the official claims made by the Italians in Africa.[61]

Orlando's Scheme of Direct Italo-Yugoslav Agreement

Beer saw House the next day. He felt optimistic about the prospects of agreement on the basis of the Piacentini proposal, and advised House against seeing the Yugoslavs before he had come to an agreement with the Italians.[62] The reason for this advice seems to lie in a new idea which Orlando brought out that morning.

When Miller and di Cellere went to see Orlando on the fourteenth to resume the discussion of the preceding day, the latter, instead of proceeding on the basis of Miller's "Definitive Solution," waived it aside with little comment, and took up an entirely different sugges-

[60] Beer, Diary, May 13.
[61] Beer, Diary, May 13.
[62] Beer, Diary, May 14.

tion. According to Orlando, between April 14 and April 24 two Italians (Quartieri and Bensa) had, in the course of purely private conversations with some Yugoslav friends of theirs, outlined the following as a possible solution:

1. The complete line of the Alps to Italy.
2. Fiume politically to Italy, who would grant Yugoslavia real privileges in the port.
3. For Dalmatia two solutions: either Zara with a hinterland reaching to the bay of Sebenico to Italy; or Zara, Sebenico, and Spalato free cities.
4. Nearly all the islands to Italy.[63]

These conversations had been wholly unofficial, neither Government having committed itself, and they had been interrupted in any case by the events of the twenty-fourth.[64] However, Orlando thought the above a possible basis of discussion and, inasmuch as Wilson had always advocated a good understanding between Italians and Yugoslavs, he wanted to know whether Wilson would agree to such a direct compromise being reached under the auspices of some Americans, even though the outcome might be at variance with the solution favored by Wilson. Miller was very skeptical of the value of this attempt;[65] he tried, without success, to bring Orlando back to a discussion of his "Definitive Solution," but finally agreed to do what he could.[66]

He reported the result of the meeting to House and drafted for him the following letter to Wilson:

Signor Orlando has suggested the possibility of an agreement being reached between Italy and the Yugo-Slavs on the whole Adriatic question, including Fiume. This agreement if it was in the form suggested would give Fiume politically to Italy but would give the Yugo-Slavs commercial advantages.

The two questions which Orlando asks are these: First, would the President oppose an agreement freely reached between the Italian and Yugoslav Governments, assuming that they reached a solution different

[63] Di Cellere, "Diary," May 14, p. 195. Cf. Miller, "Diary," May 14, I, 308-9.

[64] This is confirmed by Steed, who reports that on April 12 he was approached by two Italians with a semi-official request from Orlando that he act as umpire between them and two Yugoslavs. Steed was then about to leave for London, but found on his return (April 22) that conversations had taken place between the Italians and the Yugoslavs. Steed, *Through Thirty Years,* II, 328-29.

[65] "I regarded this tangent of Orlando as being his supreme mistake." Miller, "Diary," May 14, I, 309 (a).

[66] Miller, "Diary," May 14, I, 309.

from that which he would lay down; second, if the President's answer to the first question is favorable, would the President be willing that conversations between the Italian and Yugoslav Governments be carried on through the friendly medium of a representative of the American Government.[67]

Wilson replied immediately, his answer, written on the letter itself, being "yes" to both questions, but he had underscored the words "freely reached."[68] Miller conveyed the result to Orlando that same evening.[69]

This is the day (May 14) on which Lloyd George took up in the Council the idea of solving the whole Italian problem, proposing to grant larger concessions to Italy in Asia Minor in exchange for concessions on her part in the Adriatic, where he saw no prospect that Wilson would yield.[70]

In accordance with the latest proposal of Orlando, House presented to Trumbić, in the course of a long interview on the morning of the fifteenth, the idea of direct Italo-Yugoslav conversations under American auspices. It did not appeal to Trumbić, who reserved his answer till the next day, after he would have had a chance to take it up with his own delegation that evening. House had taken care to present the scheme as of American rather than Italian origin.[71] Beer called to see House immediately after Trumbić and asked how it stood with the Piacentini proposal; that proposal had been shelved for the time being, and he was told, instead, of the plan to have Miller and himself work with the Italians, while Frazier and Johnson would work with the Yugoslavs. Beer did not think well of the idea and would have preferred it "if our people and the British accepted the Italian proposal and told the Jugo-Slavs that it was a fair arrangement which they must accept."[72]

During the afternoon, Orlando had an interview with House, of which Miller drew up a résumé for Wilson.[73] They first discussed the matter of the former Austrian shipping, over the distribution of

---

[67] Miller, IX, Document 952; House, IV, 464. The last sentence in the first paragraph was omitted in the letter as sent by House.

[68] Miller, "Diary," May 14, I, 311; House, IV, 464.

[69] Miller, "Diary," May 14, I, 311-12.

[70] See below, p. 222, for an account of this meeting.

[71] Cf. Miller, IX, Document 957.

[72] Beer, Diary, May 15.

[73] "Memorandum of a Conversation between Col. House and Premier Orlando," Miller, IX, Document 957.

which House suggested a joint protest of the Italians and the Yugo-slavs, backed by the Americans (this common interest being a pos-sible point of Italo-Yugoslav *rapprochement*). They went on to the question of mandates in Anatolia, where Orlando thought it would be difficult for Italy to secure further concessions, in view of the French demands and of the difficulty of knowing how Clemenceau felt (amicable at a first meeting that day, he had been the very oppo-site later on). Finally, they returned to the Adriatic and Fiume. In the latest proposal suggested by Miller, the latter had expressed him-self as being personally in favor of having the Italian frontier run near Fiume. Orlando would take this as a basis of discussion with the Yugoslavs; the question for him was, what would Italy have to give up in order to secure Fiume politically; he was willing to make large concessions to the Yugoslavs for the use of the port. We see here the three current negotiations dovetailing into Orlando's plan: the Miller-di Cellere solution, the Beer-Piacentini proposal, and the idea of direct negotiations with the Yugoslavs. Orlando was also insistent on the desirability of procuring a settlement with the short-est possible delay; he pressed House to obtain an answer from the Yugoslavs and, failing their agreement, he would fall back on Miller's proposal.[74]

We also see at this point the members of the American delegation sympathetic to the Italian case, House, Miller, and Beer, coöperating with the Italians in trying to evolve a favorable compromise. Beer, favoring an Italo-American agreement in the first place, was urging House not to see the Yugoslavs before such a result had been achieved, while House took it upon himself to present the project as of American origin. Miller and di Cellere both thought Orlando's latest suggestion a false move; discussing the matter at dinner on the fifteenth, they agreed that House's way of putting the suggestion to Trumbić retrieved the situation from the Italian point of view, placing the Yugoslavs in the position of opposing the Americans rather than the Italians in case they turned it down.[75] Miller's diary of that date does not conceal a certain irritation at what he considered the unwarranted irreconcilability of Johnson, with whom he talked about Fiume that day.[76] Albeit with good intentions and excellent

[74] Miller, IX, Document 957.
[75] Di Cellere, "Diary," May 15, p. 197.
[76] Miller, "Diary," May 15, I, 313.

reasons from their point of view, and though it be called honest differences of opinion, there is no gainsaying that the American delegation was divided, and that even a certain amount of feeling was aroused among its members. To Johnson and those who shared his point of view, Orlando's tactics were disingenuous. He would fall back on the excuse that feeling in Italy made it impossible to yield on the subject of Fiume, when that feeling had, in their opinion, been largely engineered by Government propaganda; or again, he would extract from Miller a concession in Istria—and that through a diversion—and the next day would take that concession for granted and speak of the new line as a possible basis from which to begin discussions.[77] The very same acts or words, coming from a person who has antagonized us, or from one with whom we are disposed to sympathize, are likely to produce wholly different reactions. In fact, to a degree, the whole regrettable controversy and its even more unfortunate handling may be attributed to faulty psychology, though it would be idle to attempt to apportion among the parties involved the blame for lack of perspicacity.

The Crillon Meeting

Friday, May 16, found the situation little, if at all, clearer, despite House's optimistic entry of the day before that "the situation is different from what it formerly was. The Italians are now talking sense."[78] Orlando, very anxious for an immediate settlement, sent for Miller, who found him "somewhat agitated and rather depressed." Miller expected to hear from the Yugoslavs momentarily and told Orlando that they would probably use the American line as a point of departure in the discussion. Orlando declared it unacceptable and thought that there was little hope of a direct agreement.[79] Apparently he had made this suggestion in the first place, thinking that House would give the Yugoslavs to understand that the Americans were in favor of some such compromise as Miller had proposed, as a starting point for the discussion; in that event, the discussion might have centered on Fiume, for the sake of whose political control Orlando would have made some concessions in Dalmatia and the islands. The scheme would have had some fair

[77] Miller, "Diary," May 16, I, 315.
[78] House, IV, 464.
[79] Miller, "Diary," May 16, I, 313.

prospect of success, had House been willing to commit himself to that extent and had the Yugoslavs not felt that they could depend on the support of Wilson and his territorial experts. And there is good reason to think that House would have considered such a course, had it not been in flagrant opposition to Wilson's position.

Miller reported to House, who was having a meeting with Trumbić. House found the latter recalcitrant and inclined to make a stand on something like Johnson's proposal; House brought to bear whatever pressure he could, but Trumbić would not yet commit himself definitely. Nevertheless, House went ahead to prepare a meeting for that afternoon.[80] While waiting, Miller discussed the proposal with Johnson, who still stood on his memorandum of the eighth. Pending Trumbić's final answer, Miller went back to Orlando, who was willing to go to the meeting in the afternoon, but had quite given up hope of any results from it. So much so, that in the meantime he and Sonnino had drafted a reply to Miller's "Definitive Solution" of two days before and had given it to di Cellere to take back to Miller.[81] Miller, informed of this, returned to his hotel, where he had lunch with di Cellere, who handed him the Italian paper. This consisted of two parts; the first, a somewhat modified version of Miller's proposal, may be summarized as follows:

1. For the Alps: Armistice line from the Brenner till the boundary with Fiume.[82]

2. Fiume (*corpus separatum*) free and independent city and free port guaranteed by the League.

3. Zara and Sebenico to Italy.

4. The Dalmatian hinterland neutralized.

5. The islands claimed by Italy to Italy except Pago.

6. Valona to Italy. If mandate for Albania, Italy to have it.

The second part consisted of Italian acceptances, variations, and additions, as follows:

1. Alpine frontier accepted.

2. Fiume to be free to entrust Italy with its diplomatic representation.

---

[80] House, IV, 464; Miller, "Diary," May 16, I, 314.

[81] Miller, "Diary," May 16, I, 314-15; di Cellere, "Diary," May 16, p. 198.

[82] On the score of the first item, Miller made the following entry in his diary: "What they call my proposals are not strictly such, for . . . I had added verbally that if the only point was Istria I should recommend concession to the Italians." Miller, "Diary," May 16, I, 315.

3. Accepted. An adequate territory (e.g., political district) to go with Zara and Sebenico.

4. 5. 6. Accepted.

The Italian Government expects the support of the American Government on the following questions:

A. The Italians of Traù and Spalato to have a year's option for Italian citizenship. Reciprocal treatment for the Slavs of Zara and Sebenico.

B. The two railway lines between Trieste and Vienna to run outside Yugoslavia.

C. Elimination of all special customs clauses conducive to a special customs system in the former Austria-Hungary.

D. Reconsideration of the decisions in regard to Adriatic tonnage.

E. The whole of Anatolia in mandate to Italy except Smyrna and the territory that goes with Constantinople.[83]

Miller did not hide from di Cellere a certain annoyance at the turn of events, for he found himself in the position of having to contend with three elements: the Italians, Wilson, and Trumbić.[84]

He saw House once more and was told that the meeting had been arranged for 5:30. Orlando and di Cellere were notified and went to the Crillon, where the meeting took place. Orlando and di Cellere were in one room with Miller and Beer, "two perfect and convinced friends of ours," in di Cellere's words;[85] in another, Trumbić with Frazier and Johnson, who might be similarly qualified by the Yugoslavs; between the two groups, House, in another room, acted as intermediary. Although the meeting lasted four hours, at no time did the Italians and the Yugoslavs come into direct contact. The meeting[86] unfortunately did not open under very good auspices; Orlando's plan of using an agreement with the Americans as a basis from which to start and exert pressure on the Yugoslavs had gone awry, and he came to the meeting only because it was the outcome of his own initiative, but without expectations. In Istria, the kernel of the disagreement, the Italians and the Yugoslavs stood essentially on their original positions: the Treaty of London line and the Wilson line respectively; it could hardly be expected that this difference could be reconciled in one such meeting. As to the Americans acting as seconds, while they naturally did not feel as strongly as the Ital-

[83] Miller, IX, Document 967.
[84] Di Cellere, "Diary," May 16, p. 199.
[85] Di Cellere, "Diary," May 16, p. 200.
[86] Miller, "Diary," May 16, I, 315; di Cellere, "Diary," May 16, pp. 199-201; Beer, Diary, May 16; House, IV, 465-66.

ians or the Yugoslavs, they had nevertheless committed themselves to the extent of appearing as supporters of the opposing delegations —each at least in the eyes of the other—thus losing the prestige of disinterested arbiters. What is more, they had little common ground left among themselves. Miller and Beer thought Johnson blinded by technicalities to the higher interest of reaching an agreement; to which Johnson could retort that he too wanted an agreement, but a just one, and that had it not been for the encouragement Miller and Beer had given to the Italians—all the more culpable in that it ran counter to Wilson's position—such an agreement would have been reached. They almost came down to the level of advocates pleading the case of their own clients.

After some time, Miller was called out, then came back to the Italians, having drafted a paper which summarized the points of agreement and those still in dispute. This paper read as follows:

1. Italy to receive Sexten Valley.
2. Italy to receive Tarvis District.
3. Fiume, including Sušak, to be an independent city and free port under the protection of the League of Nations. The Great Powers will see that Fiume will, if necessary, secure a loan for the improvement of the port. The independence of Fiume shall be under the guarantee of the League of Nations.
4. Dalmatia to be neutralized.
5. Pago to go to the mainland.
6. Lussin and Lissa and Pelagosa, etc. to go to Italy.

Questions unsettled:

1. Eastern part of Istria.
2. Zara and Sebenico.
3. Remaining islands within the line of London.[87]

The Italians asked that the phrases "including Sušak" and "under the protection of the League of Nations" be struck out from item 3 of the first group, and that item 4 be restricted to Yugoslavia. With an eye to possible eventualities, they bore in mind that the *corpus separatum* had an Italian majority, whereas Fiume including Sušak had not; they also wanted the other Powers as much out of Fiume as possible. With the same idea in mind, di Cellere objected to the provisions for an international loan.[88]

[87] Miller, IX, Document 968.
[88] Di Cellere, "Diary," May 16, p. 200.

Returning to the other group, Miller found Trumbić unwilling to make any further concessions, and Orlando thought that the attempt had better be given up as a failure, when Johnson intervened in an attempt to convert Orlando to the idea of plebiscites in Istria, Dalmatia, and the islands, under League of Nations auspices. But Orlando was unyielding, and, as he told House, he did not think well of turning the disputed areas over to the League; he did not want France and Great Britain in the Adriatic.[89]

With this the meeting ended. If House's comment, "we got them so nearly to an agreement that it was a matter of deep regret that we could not bring them all the way,"[90] is perhaps more optimistic than the facts warranted, nevertheless some progress had been made and the situation further clarified. It was safe to assume that there was only one remaining essential point of disagreement, namely, the boundary of eastern Istria; this, mainly owing to the fact that the Italians were bent on maintaining a land connection with Fiume, whether they secured the city in full sovereignty, or whether it was given some sort of independent status. If that point could be settled, it was neither Zara, Sebenico, nor the islands, that would ultimately stand in the way of complete agreement.

End of House's Attempt

Having tried and failed to reach a solution by this method, it was agreed to proceed as between the Italians and the Americans, and see if they could definitely come together. However, the failure of the Crillon meeting could not but have a somewhat depressing effect, especially on those Americans who had exerted themselves in trying to bridge the difference. House saw Wilson that day and again early the next morning, and told him what he was doing, but found Wilson completely unmoved and unyielding.[91] Realizing that the Yugoslavs would not yield, Beer was confirmed in his belief that the only way out was to have the Americans agree with the Italians in the first place, and then force the solution upon the Yugoslavs.[92]

The next morning (May 17) Orlando, di Cellere, Miller, Frazier, and Beer were again with House for an hour and a half. Orlando

---

[89] Di Cellere, "Diary," May 16, p. 200; Miller, "Diary," May 16, I, 315.
[90] House, IV, 465.
[91] House, IV, 466.
[92] Beer, Diary, May 16.

yielded something in Istria, though not all, and would not consent to a plebiscite. House telephoned to Wilson during the meeting, but to no avail.[93] The Italians were by now beginning to feel mistreated, and the feeling was shared by some of the Americans.[94] True, Wilson had made a stand and proved quite immovable; in effect, what some of the Americans were doing, for all their friendly helpfulness, amounted to extracting piecemeal concessions from the Italians. This was, in fact, Wilson's view of their activity: he would be glad to see an agreement with the Italians, but such agreement could occur only through their coming around to his position, and even of this activity he was rather suspicious. The Italians could not understand that Wilson should insist "on an integral application of his principles on the Italian sector, when he had given way on so many others," or in the picturesque if somewhat crude quip credited to Sonnino, "he provoked among the Italians the impression that he wanted to retrieve his virginity at our expense."[95]

Under the circumstances, little more could be done, even though House pursued a forlorn hope that Wilson might be induced to move a little way to meet the Italians.[96] Beer suggested that he himself might see Kerr and try to have Lloyd George use his influence on Wilson.[97] It was arranged that Miller, Johnson, and Beer meet Wilson the next day and explain to him how the matter stood.[98] As Beer was taken ill, only Miller and Johnson went to this meeting.[99] Wilson was adamant, especially on the question of the Fiume-Laibach railway; in fact, he still favored strong tactics toward the Italians and wanted to send word to them that he would not make any concessions whatever. Miller succeeded in dissuading him, pointing out that, after all, the Italians had conceded a great deal already and saying that he thought they would yield still more. Wilson agreed to let Miller continue his conversations, rather than issue an ultimatum. Evidently there was little hope in that quarter and Miller naturally felt discouraged. He went on to see di Cellere mainly in order, as House put it, "to keep the negotiations going

[93] House, IV, 468; Miller, "Diary," May 17, I, 316; di Cellere, "Diary," May 17, p. 201; Beer, Diary, May 17.

[94] House, IV, 468.

[95] Sforza, Makers of Modern Europe, p. 297.

[96] Miller, "Diary," May 17, I, 316.

[97] Beer, Diary, May 17.

[98] Miller, "Diary," May 17, I, 316; Beer, Diary, May 17.

[99] Miller, "Diary," May 18, I, 317; Beer, Diary, May 18.

and in our own hands," rather than with any thought of achieving any results.[100]

Orlando went to see Lloyd George that same day, May 18, with the text of Miller's "Definitive Solution" and the Italian reply thereto. According to di Cellere, Lloyd George thought the proposal entirely reasonable and, when Orlando spoke of Anatolia, hinted that Fiume, a direct addition to the national territory, was perhaps more important than an Anatolian mandate.[101] Having propounded this very idea of an Anatolian mandate in the Council four days earlier, he had thought better of it since.[102]

Nothing further came of this attempt. An interview between Miller and Sonnino served only to show that the latter was as unyielding as Wilson when it came to the Italian line.[103] With it closes a chapter in the course of which the Italians and the Americans had come as close to meeting each other as they ever were. More than a year was to elapse before the Treaty of Rapallo was to consecrate a direct Italo-Yugoslav agreement not very dissimilar to the one proposed by Orlando at this time.

[100] Miller, "Diary," May 18, I, 317-18.

[101] Di Cellere, "Diary," May 18, p. 202.

[102] Baker, *Woodrow Wilson and the World Settlement*, II, p. 198. See Chap. VIII for the Council meetings from May 14 to May 17, and the discussion of Lloyd George's schemes, the Nicolson plan, and the Balfour memorandum.

[103] Miller, "Diary," May 19, I, 319.

VII

FALL OF THE ORLANDO CABINET

ALL THE EFFORTS and negotiations since the Italians had returned to Paris had failed to produce an agreement. The attempt to come to an understanding between the Italians and the Americans (the Miller-di Cellere plan sponsored by House), had had no more success than the even more abortive effort to arrive at a direct Italo-Yugoslav understanding. Lloyd George's short-lived attempt at connecting the Adriatic with Asia Minor had merely succeeded in adding a little more confusion to problems that were sufficiently complicated when taken separately.

Even the negotiations between the Italians and the Americans, for all the activity which was displayed, were somewhat outside of the main current of events. The German Treaty, more than ever, held the center of the stage, and, during the necessary lull while the Germans were examining the Treaty handed to them on May 7, the Council spent much time in considering colonies and mandates.[1] With an eye to the possibility that Italy might withhold ratification of the German Treaty even after signing it, a clause was introduced in that Treaty on May 12, making it effective upon ratification by three Powers.[2] This registered the definite failure of the persistent Italian endeavor to link the progress of the German Treaty with that of the Austrian Treaty. To be sure, the latter Treaty was being drafted at this time, but the prevalent feeling among the American, British, and French delegations was that the signature of the German Treaty would settle the major problem of the Conference.

Nothing, then, was settled for the Italians, and even the progress of the Austrian Treaty gave little cause for cheer from their point of view. The very different reception given to the Austrians from that given to the Germans not unnaturally aroused suspicion in Italy, and comment appeared upon the alleged fact that Allizé had hand-picked the Austrian delegation, which had been induced to

[1] See Chap. VIII for a detailed account of colonial questions.
[2] This provision would also take care of possible American failure to ratify. In fact, the Versailles Treaty became effective upon ratification by Great Britain, France, and Japan.

forego the idea of union with Germany in exchange for a promise to support the scheme of a Danubian customs federation.[3] Not a few people in Italy could countenance the prospect of *Anschluss* with equanimity, but anything that might tend to a revival of the Hapsburg Empire aroused feelings not very different from those which any threatened revival of German power aroused among the French; it was considered particularly ungrateful on the part of the latter to lend their support to any such scheme, after the Italians had given them practically a free hand in dealing with the German problem.[4] The uncertainty of the Italians extended to their northern frontier; di Cellere reported a rumor of an attempt to force a solution of the Adriatic question by linking it with that of the Brenner frontier.[5] The rumor persisted of a suggested modification of the Tyrol frontier, in exchange for economic concessions to Italy in Austria and Czechoslovakia.[6]

Quite naturally, then, the Italians felt isolated—which in fact they were—and the feeling grew into uneasiness and, to a certain extent, apathetic discouragement. The delegation in Paris could show nothing to combat this feeling and was subject to considerable criticism, both from those who considered that it had mishandled the Italian case through faulty tactics,[7] and from those who saw in the situation possibilities of political advantage for themselves. However, the tone of a substantial part of the press in Italy was now very different from what it had been formerly; those organs in particular which were close to the Government (*Giornale d'Italia, Epoca*), instead of arguing more or less vociferously in favor of the Italian claims, undertook to defend the delegation and its work, while hinting at the likelihood of moderate compromises. The attempt was rather belated and could not restore confidence in the country.

On the twenty-first Orlando went to meet his cabinet at Oulx in response to the growing clamor for more information, and to discuss the situation in Italy and in Paris.[8] Under the circumstances, Orlando's political life was none too vigorous and his succession was

[3] Cf. *Daily Review of the Foreign Press*, May 12-18.

[4] *Giornale d'Italia*, May 16; *Corriere della sera*, May 15. The *Corriere della sera* remained particularly active throughout, in fighting any form of restoration of Austria-Hungary.

[5] Di Cellere, "Diary," May 25, p. 207.

[6] Di Cellere, "Diary," May 26, p. 208; *Corriere della sera*, May 25; cf. above, p. 159.

[7] Bissolati, for instance, in the *Giornale del popolo*, May 20. Also *Unità*, May 17.

[8] It was also necessary to replace Salandra and Salvago Raggi, who had definitely resigned from the delegation. They were replaced by Crespi and Imperiali.

again under discussion;[9] however, one more attempt was to be made at the Conference before the demise of his Cabinet.

THE TARDIEU PLAN

Two Council meetings were held on May 26, at which the familiar ground was gone over. At the first, Wilson stood on his principles, with which the French and the British expressed sympathy and agreement, while recognizing themselves bound by the Treaty of London. At the same time, they pressed upon Orlando the necessity of not disrupting the Alliance.[10] At the second meeting, Clemenceau appealed for an early settlement of the Adriatic question and asked Orlando to make a proposal. Orlando agreed that he wanted a general settlement, pointing out, however, that he must fall back on the Treaty of London in the event of failure to reach an agreement. Wilson appealed to him again on the oft-reiterated ground of the new order, the principle of self-determination, the value of the United States guarantee under the League Covenant, and the suggestion of demilitarizing the Eastern Adriatic. Orlando defended the Treaty of London as being itself a compromise and, as before, turned down any suggestion of plebiscites, to which, however, Wilson returned. Clemenceau once more pointed out that Orlando had not made a proposal and asked him to suggest a feasible solution, which Orlando agreed to do.[11]

In the evening, di Cellere was called upon to formulate the Italian counter-proposal to the Miller project.[12] At lunch that day he had surveyed the situation with House, who agreed that the Yugoslavs ought to be confronted with a proposal to which the Italians and the Americans had previously agreed among themselves; but Wilson's insistence on the Yugoslavs' freedom of decision precluded such an arrangement.[13] Orlando took with him to the Council meeting the next day the Italian proposal formulated by di Cellere, but apparently other matters were discussed and he merely handed the draft to Kerr.[14]

[9] *Epoca,* May 17 (warning Nitti).

[10] Minutes of the Council, May 26, C.F. 32. This and subsequent references to Minutes of the Council occurring in this chapter are taken from the account given in Miller, XIX, 545-52.

[11] Minutes of the Council, May 26, C.F. 34.

[12] Di Cellere, "Diary," May 26, p. 208.

[13] *Ibid.*

[14] *Ibid.,* May 27, p. 209.

On leaving this meeting, Orlando took Tardieu aside and, according to the latter, told him:

I am asked to make a proposal: I cannot. I understand that France hesitates to make one, for if it fails, she will receive the blame. However I

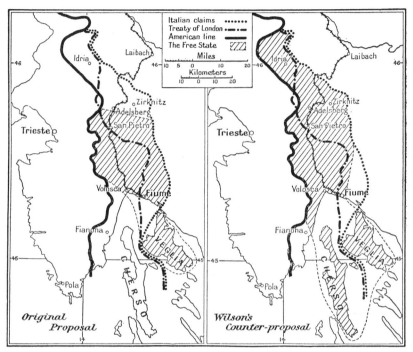

VII. MAP ILLUSTRATING THE TARDIEU PLAN

The boundaries of the proposed Free State are drawn from the description of the original proposal and Wilson's Counterproposal.

ask you to take this risk and to take the responsibility of suggesting a solution.[15]

The idea was not as sudden as may appear. Already on the twenty-fifth di Cellere had reported that Crespi, dissatisfied with the temporizing tactics of Orlando and Sonnino, was preparing a general plan of solution[16] and, according to Tardieu, as early as the end of April he himself had, with Clemenceau's knowledge, been in touch with Crespi[17] and Bonin Longare on precisely such an undertaking.[18]

[15] Tardieu, La Paix, pp. 432-33. This account lends color to the claim that the Tardieu Plan was in reality an Italian scheme, presented under Tardieu's name and sponsorship.
[16] Di Cellere, "Diary," May 25, p. 207.
[17] Crespi had remained in Paris after April 24.
[18] Tardieu, op. cit., p. 432.

According to his own account, having consulted Clemenceau, Tardieu set to work at once and took a draft proposal to Crespi that same evening, May 27. The two discussed it far into the night, and, although Orlando himself was not present, Crespi reported to him at various times, and finally secured his approval of it as a basis for negotiations.[19]

The outline of this proposal, which became known from its author as the Tardieu Plan, was as follows:

1. Formation of an independent State of Fiume under the League, with the following boundaries: in the West, from Volosca to a point Northwest of San Pietro, the American line;[20] from there to the Schneeberg (Monte Nevoso) in the North; in the East, the Italian line including the island of Veglia.

This state to be administered by a body of five members: two named by Italy, one by Fiume, one by Yugoslavia and one by the League. Fiume to retain the municipal autonomy it had enjoyed under the statute of Maria Theresa; its port to be a free port. The citizens of the new state to be exempt from military service. After fifteen years a plebiscite by communes to decide the future status.

2. Zara and Sebenico to Italy. The rest of Dalmatia to Yugoslavia who will neutralize it.

3. All the islands, except Pago, to Italy.

4. An Italian mandate for Albania where a railroad will be constructed with Italian and Yugoslav capital, each participating to the extent of 40% and the rest mixed.

5. At Tarvis and Bistriza the frontier to be drawn as requested by Italy.

6. The Austrian mercantile fleet to be apportioned in accordance with Italian wishes.

7. The Assling triangle to Austria.[21]

Early the following morning, Tardieu obtained Clemenceau's approval of the project;[22] then went to see House,[23] who was personally favorable; and finally Lloyd George,[24] whose backing he likewise secured. House, Lloyd George, and Orlando talked the

---

[19] Tardieu, *op. cit.*, p. 433.

[20] What is meant by this is not clear; the American line did not come to Volosca. This is reminiscent of the misunderstanding which arose when Lloyd George was negotiating between the Italians and Wilson previous to April 24.

[21] *Politica*, IV, 272-73. This text was given originally in the *Messaggero* of June 21, which apparently had obtained it from Tardieu himself. See Map VII.

[22] Tardieu, *La Paix*, p. 433.

[23] Tardieu, *op. cit.*, p. 433; House, IV, 470.

[24] Tardieu, *op. cit.*, p. 433.

matter over, and the three joined Wilson and Clemenceau.[25] The Tardieu Plan[26] was officially before the Council. Wilson wanted the matter of Albania reserved, pending a report by a commission. He also suggested that the Fiume delegate to the governing body be elected by the state as a whole.[27] As to Zara and Sebenico, Lloyd George proposed that they be made free cities, while House renewed Hankey's suggestion that they be attached to Fiume. Orlando was hesitant and not enthusiastic about either alternative; he also wanted to consult his naval experts. Wilson still favored leaving the question of acceptance of the Plan to the Yugoslavs, but Lloyd George and House succeeded in convincing him that the only feasible course was to present to them a solution recommended by the other Powers.[28]

The scheme might have succeeded if accepted at once by all sides, but hesitation doomed it. House wanted to be hopeful, but had to admit that Wilson was very reluctant.[29] Orlando's uncertainty is easy to understand, in view of the situation in Italy; Piacentini, just back from Rome, told Beer that the concessions made by Orlando and Sonnino had sealed their fate, and that, as soon as the German Treaty was signed, a Nitti-Tittoni Cabinet would be formed with Giolitti's support.[30] Beer himself thought that the scheme was "an absurd settlement and cannot last"[31] and, according to Piacentini, considered it best for the Italians to fall back on the Treaty of London.[32] This was also the view of di Cellere, who recognized that the proposed state would be almost entirely Slav in population.[33]

There was further discussion of the project in the Council on the twenty-ninth. Orlando wanted a mandate for Zara and Sebenico; he was willing to give up three islands in the southern group (Lesina, Curzola, and Meleda), but wanted Cherso. Wilson, on the other hand, thought that both Veglia and Cherso should go to the Yugo-

[25] House, IV, 470.
[26] Miller refers to it as the House-Tardieu Plan.
[27] Since the state would, as a whole, be overwhelmingly Slav in population, this would put on the governing body two Italians and two Yugoslavs, thus giving the deciding vote to the League delegate.
[28] Minutes of the Council, May 28, C.F. 37A.
[29] Miller, "Diary," May 28, I, 328; Tardieu, La Paix, p. 433; House, IV, 471.
[30] Beer, Diary, May 28.
[31] Ibid.
[32] Di Cellere, "Diary," May 28, p. 210.
[33] Ibid.

slavs; he was willing to have the plan offered to the Yugoslavs, but drew back from exerting any pressure on them.[34]

On this day (May 29) Italy won an important point. The Austrian delegation, who had been waiting to receive the terms of the Austrian Treaty, were pressing the Council for them. These had been promised for the twenty-ninth, and it was found necessary to postpone the date once more; but the Austro-Italian frontier was definitely set at the Brenner on this occasion,[35] thus eliminating the potential threat of refusal to grant this line to the Italians in retaliation for the failure to settle their eastern frontier.

The Tardieu project was presented by House to the Yugoslav delegation on May 30.[36] He seems to have made it clear to them that Wilson would not have any objections to an agreement between them and the Italians on the basis of this scheme, but that he was not urging its acceptance.[37]

After studying the project, the Yugoslavs decided to accept the principle of a buffer state, and Trumbić told Johnson on what terms the compromise would be acceptable to them, which were as follows:

Jugoslavia to accept the "American line" as the western boundary of the proposed Free State, which should include the districts of Volosca and Albona and the Island of Cherso.

Sušak and, if possible, Veglia, to go to Jugoslavia.

Zara and Sebenico to be given autonomy under Jugoslav sovereignty.

A settlement of the islands claimed by Italy either by plebiscite (after from three to five years) or by decision of the League of Nations.[38]

The outline of the Tardieu Plan had meantime become public. Under the optimistic title, *L'Accord est fait,* it appeared in the *Temps* of May 30[39] and it was also known in Italy. The Italians were apparently willing to accept the compromise and were exerting themselves in preparing public opinion in Italy to be content with it. The *Giornale d'Italia* professed to be very pleased with the Austrian

---

[34] Minutes of the Council, May 29, C.F. 38.

[35] Temperley, IV, 392.

[36] Adriaticus, *La Question adriatique,* p. 52.

[37] According to Adriaticus, *op. cit.,* p. 52.

[38] On June 2. Cf. Minutes of the Council, June 6, C.F. 49A, Appendix I. A slightly different version is given by Giannini, "Il compromesso Tardieu per la questione adriatica," *Aperusen,* July, 1922, p. 343.

[39] According to Giannini (*op. cit.,* p. 342), the article was written under Tardieu's inspiration. The *Temps* article gave a less complete account of the Tardieu plan than the one above.

Treaty and the excellent frontier which it gave Italy in the north; it asserted that Italy had control of the Adriatic and played down the remaining minor differences over Fiume; it even found pleasant things to say about Lloyd George and Clemenceau for the assistance they had given the Italian delegation;[40] other newspapers amenable to Government influence followed the same lead.[41]

As valuable time was passing and the Yugoslav counter-proposal was known, on June 5 Orlando sent to Clemenceau a map showing the boundaries desired by the Italians for the free state, and urged the need of reaching a conclusion. Clemenceau agreed that he and Lloyd George would take up the matter with Wilson.[42]

Wilson's Counter-proposal

The discussion of the Tardieu Plan was resumed in the Council on June 6. Wilson said that a new difficulty arose from the Italian claim to revise the boundaries of the free state (the Italians wanted the boundary farther east than the American line); he thought that the latest Yugoslav proposal was in line with the other settlements, whereas the Italian was not. He was also impressed by the consideration that the Slovenes were going to be divided among three states, whereas, under the Austrian régime, they at least were under only one. Lloyd George spoke of the importance of the islands to Italy and mentioned the Pan-Slav danger, to which Wilson replied that the French had not secured the Rhine frontier, despite Foch's excellent strategic arguments. Besides, said Wilson, the strategic argument should apply to Yugoslavia as well, and he pointed out that Cherso would bottle up Fiume. Lloyd George thought that the coast was the natural defense. Clemenceau was of the opinion that Zara could go with the islands, i. e., to Italy, but that Sebenico should be Slav. An Italian suggestion of a hinterland for Zara was promptly set aside by Lloyd George and Clemenceau. Finally, after some further discussion, Wilson agreed to prepare a proposal which "would include the creation of a Free State in Fiume commencing in the north from the point where the line of the Treaty of London joined the Ameri-

[40] *Giornale d'Italia,* May 31, June 1.
[41] Cf. *Daily Review of the Foreign Press,* May 26-June 1.
[42] Giannini, *op. cit.,* p. 343.

can line and extending the Tardieu line so as to include the Islands of Cherso as well as Veglia."[43]

The next day this proposal was jointly presented to Orlando by Wilson, Lloyd George, and Clemenceau. It may be summarized as follows:

1. Boundaries of the free state: the American line beginning on parallel[44] 14 (just North of Kirchheim) down to Fianona; thence southward around Cherso; northward around Veglia, joining the mainland just West of the bay of Buccari; thence northwestward to the Treaty of London line at a point East of Adelsberg or Zirknitz and from there along that line to the starting point.

2. The state to be governed by a commission consisting of two Italians, one Yugoslav, one representative of the free state and one representative of the League Council. Fiume to have the same local autonomy as under Hungary.

3. Guarantees of economic freedom for the port of Fiume.

4. After five years a plebiscite with the alternatives of Italy, Yugoslavia, or continued status under the League.

5. Islands to Italy.[45]

6. Reciprocal safeguards for national minorities.

7. Zara to be a free city under the League. Italy to have its diplomatic representation.

8. The Assling junction to Yugoslavia.[46]

Wilson said that he had agreed to this reluctantly and that any further concession on his part would be impossible. Orlando, likewise, considered the original Tardieu Plan his furthest concession, and if this proposal were less favorable he could not accept it. He repeated that the Italian boundary should not be along the Istrian ridge, but farther east along the crest of the Alps. Save for a small American concession in Istria between the mouth of the Arsa and Punta Fianona, the difference between the Italians and Wilson over the Italian frontier in Istria remained what it had been. Orlando's reply, therefore, amounted to a rejection of Wilson's counter-pro-

---

[43] Minutes of the Council, June 6, C.F. 49A.

[44] Obviously "meridian" is meant.

[45] These appear on a map not given in the Minutes. According to Giannini ("Il compromesso Tardieu," p. 345), they were the same as mentioned before, save for those in the immediate vicinity of Sebenico, and neither Italy nor Yugoslavia were to fortify the islands attributed to them or to build naval bases on them.

[46] Minutes of the Council, June 7, C.F. 52, Appendix IV. See Map VII.

posal; however, he agreed to consult his delegation, who merely confirmed the rejection.[47]

That evening Orlando left for another Cabinet meeting at Oulx, where the question was examined—among others—and returned to Paris at once. He submitted his reply to the latest proposal in the form of a memorandum pointing out that the original plan offered by Tardieu had received several modifications, all of them to Italy's disadvantage.

1. The Eastern frontier of Italy had been pushed to Punta Fianona, instead of starting west of Volosca, thereby dividing Istria.

2. The Northern extremity of the free state had been shifted from San Pietro to the neighborhood of Kirchheim.

3. Fiume was to have the same status it had had under the Hungarian régime instead of the status given it by Maria Theresa.

4. The plebiscite was to be for the whole state as a unit, instead of by separate zones as proposed originally, and as was to be the case in such places as the Saar and Klagenfurt.

5. Only Zara, and that without its district, was assigned to Italy instead of Zara and Sebenico, both with their districts.

6. The Italians had renounced the islands of Meleda, Curzola and Lesina assigned to them in the original Tardieu Plan. It was now proposed in addition to withhold Cherso and the islands around Sebenico.

7. Neutralization was restricted to the islands instead of applying to the mainland as well.

8. The Assling triangle was assigned to Yugoslavia.[48]

In view of all these modifications, Orlando declared himself unable to accept the new plan offered him by the three Powers.

The kernel of the issue was still the Italian frontier in Istria. In this region, the Italians and the Americans stood essentially on the positions which they had assumed at the beginning of the controversy. That difference could not be disguised by any proposal to erect the disputed territory into a distinct entity, so long as the Italians kept thinking of it in terms of a temporary device that would merely postpone their securing Fiume, and while Wilson kept looking upon it as a means to achieve the exact opposite. The project could be taken as a basis for discussion, but the irreconcilable purposes were bound to show themselves over the details, whether it was the exact

[47] Giannini, *op. cit.*, p. 345.
[48] Giannini, "Il compromesso Tardieu," pp. 345-46. This statement is somewhat condensed.

location of a frontier, the freedom of the railway from Fiume to Laibach, or the modalities of plebiscite.

For this reason the Tardieu compromise failed of acceptance, like its numerous predecessors. Nevertheless, it cannot be said to have been wholly fruitless, for the idea of a buffer state was to be the starting point of further discussions after the signature of the German Treaty and the change of ministry in Italy. Moreover, even though an agreement had not been reached, the various parties involved had moved a long distance toward one another from their original extreme positions.

THE AUSTRIAN TREATY—KLAGENFURT

In Paris, the Conference was fully occupied during this time with other matters than the Italian settlement. First in order of importance was still the German Treaty. After it had been handed to the Germans in May, they promptly set to work drafting memoranda, objections, and counter-proposals, which had to be examined by the Council. As time passed, doubts arose as to whether the Germans would sign the Treaty, doubts which manifested themselves in divergences among the Four. Lloyd George in particular became concerned, thought the Treaty too harsh, and wanted to make changes in it. Clemenceau and Wilson also had grounds for dissatisfaction: the former considered the Treaty imperfect but thought it the best he could secure for France under the circumstances, while the latter admitted that many of its provisions were bad, but pinned his faith on the League to secure their modification when passions had cooled. However, both agreed that after the work of half a year and much discussion, some of it carried to the verge of an open break, the task of revision was hopeless. This view prevailed and, faced with Allied unity, the Germans, after much hesitation and with many qualms, finally produced a Government that sent a delegation to Versailles to sign the Treaty on June 28.

Work on the Austrian Treaty was proceeding apace, and a first draft, though incomplete, was given to the waiting Austrians on June 2. It had at least the merit of defining the frontiers of the new Austria.[49] By it, Italy secured the Brenner frontier promised her in the Treaty of London, with further rectifications in her favor, definitely in the Sexten Valley, and in all likelihood in the Tarvis

[49] Except Klagenfurt, which was reserved by the Conference.

district as well.[50] Owing to the fact that the frontier between Italy and Yugoslavia was still unsettled, the former Adriatic lands of Austria were handed over by that country to the Allies and the United States, who would later decide on their ultimate disposition. As the result of this, Italy lost her point in regard to the Assling junction. This and the adjoining Klagenfurt area were the cause of much debate and some disturbance. The root of the difficulty, in this case as in many others, lay in the conflict between economic considerations on the one hand, and ethnic and strategic ones on the other. The Assling triangle is a small area included between what was known as Point 1370,[51] the section of the Vienna-Trieste railroad through Assling, and the Treaty of London line (see Map VI). The Klagenfurt area, adjacent to it in the northeast, forms the basin of the Drave, bounded on the south by the Karawanken Mountains. Ethnically both districts were predominantly Slovene, although Klagenfurt itself, the principal town of Carinthia, had in 1910 an overwhelming German population;[52] and there was the further point that an American mission, which had investigated the question on the spot in January, had reported that, while the inhabitants were Slovene in the majority, there would not be a majority in favor of joining the new Serb-Croat-Slovene State.[53] The importance of these areas derived from the railroads, so that economically their disposition was of concern to the three states involved: Italy, Austria, and Yugoslavia. The main railway line from South Germany to Trieste ran through Villach and Assling;[54] another important line from Villach to St. Veit, and thence to Vienna, bounded the Klagenfurt area in the north.

The Assling area was unquestionably Slav, but the difficulty was that if the Klagenfurt district went to Austria, and Assling did not, a small segment of the railway line would run through the territory of a third nation, with all the attendant possibility of complication and sources of friction. For this reason, and because this area outside of

[50] See above, pp. 164 ff., for the discussions in the Council of Foreign Ministers in regard to Tarvis, Assling, and Klagenfurt.

[51] Point 1370 was the spot where the Italian frontier, as set by the Treaty of London and extended by the inclusion of Tarvis, would presumably turn south, diverging from the Austrian frontier, which continued eastward.

[52] 25,582 out of a total of 28,958; cf. Temperley, IV, 370.

[53] Colonel Miles' mission; cf. Temperley, IV, 370.

[54] The other railway, through Udine-Tarvis, would presumably be in Italian territory, but it was a less important line.

the London line at all events was unlikely to be given to Italy, Sonnino had stoutly maintained that the railroad should be "free," and Assling given to Austria. If, on the other hand, Sonnino's solution were adopted, it had the disadvantage, to say nothing of the ethnic question, of bringing the Austrian frontier over the Karawanken Mountains, thus giving Austria a controlling position in the Save Valley and opening a way to the sea, a situation strategically undesirable.

At the time of the Austrian Armistice, the Italians occupied the line of the Treaty of London, and the territory to the east was held by the local Slovene troops. That Armistice, however, made no provision for an Allied occupation in Carinthia and Styria. In the latter province, the Allied armies, coming up from the south, eventually settled on a line set by Gen. Franchet d'Esperey, roughly following the ethnic frontier and the line of the Austrian frontier as eventually established by the Conference. But it was otherwise in Carinthia. There the fighting continued sporadically, neither side paying much heed to the Conference, which for that matter did not set any definite line of occupation. At the end of April, Yugoslav irregulars moved over the Karawanken into the Klagenfurt area; repulsed at first, they were later successful with the assistance of regular Serbian troops. This brought the Conference into the scene, and on May 31 the Four sent warnings to both the Austrians and the Serbs, ordering the evacuation of the district. An armistice was signed on June 6, only to be disavowed two days later by the Austrians. Finally, in virtue of a clause in the armistice of Villa Giusti, which allowed the Italians to safeguard the routes to Vienna,[55] Italian troops occupied the Villach-St. Veit railway line. This caused the Yugoslavs to stop at a line along the Wörther See, and continuing from there to Klagenfurt, where they remained. The news of the Italian advance was not received with complete satisfaction in Paris.[56] The Council finally came to a decision, when it decreed, June 23, that a plebiscite should be held in the Klagenfurt area.[57]

When the terms of the Austrian Treaty were considered at the Plenary Session of May 31, it appeared that the succession states,

[55] Armistice of Villa Giusti, Article IV.
[56] This advance, like the landings in Asia Minor, took place without consultation with the other Powers. Franco-Italian rivalry and playing for position in the Danube Valley should also be borne in mind.
[57] This account is drawn in the main from Temperley, IV, 370-71, 393.

Czechoslovakia, Poland, Rumania, and Yugoslavia, were expected to sign definite engagements for the protection of the racial minorities which the Treaty was to include in their boundaries.[58] Italy, likewise, was to receive a solid block of Germans in the Tyrol and, in all likelihood, although the matter was not yet definitely settled, several hundred thousand Slavs within her new borders. However, she was not expected to take any written engagements in regard to these minorities, the Powers being satisfied with her verbal declarations of policy as stated in Parliament.[59] Considering that Italy had sat throughout at the Council table from which the small Powers had been excluded—an exclusion strongly resented and bitterly complained of—these same Powers were incensed at what seemed to them, not unnaturally, gross discrimination. Their grievance was voiced with vehemence by Bratianu,[60] and, as it turned out, it was only with great difficulty that they were eventually induced to subscribe to the minorities clauses of the various treaties.[61]

ORLANDO'S RESIGNATION

The provisions of the Austrian Treaty had been made known in Italy on June 3-4 and there was an attempt, mainly on the part of the Government press, to play up the advantages thereby definitely secured to Italy, as a counterweight to the disappointment at the failure to reach an equally favorable settlement in the east and in the Adriatic. But it was too late. The Tardieu Plan proved to be but a momentary ray of hope, and the enervating wait since the preceding November, when it was thought that peace would quickly follow victory, gave rise to a widespread feeling of disillusionment among the mass of the people. The nationalist press exploited this feeling, insisting that Italy had been defrauded of the fruits of her victory and relegated among the vanquished powers. So much had been said about the Adriatic, and especially about Fiume, which came to assume in Italian opinion an importance wholly out of proportion to its real value, that even the announcement of the very satisfactory northern frontier elicited no enthusiasm.

[58] Draft Austrian Treaty of May 29, Article 57 for Czechoslovakia, Article 51 for Yugoslavia, Article 60 for Rumania.
[59] Reply of the Allied and Associated Powers to Austria, Sept. 2, 1919. Cf. Temperley, IV, 138, 284.
[60] Temperley, IV, 137. Poland and Yugoslavia followed suit.
[61] Yugoslavia and Rumania would not sign the Austrian Treaty until December.

Equally, if not more, important was the social unrest prevalent in the country. The readjustment from war to peace proved uneasy in all countries, but nowhere more so, among the victorious nations, than in Italy, owing to the comparatively greater strain on her economy. Strikes multiplied in alarming proportion in June; they were economic in their ultimate foundation, owing to the rapidly rising cost of living, but tended to assume an increasingly political complexion. It was as much owing to the internal situation as to the negotiations in Paris that Orlando had held hurried Cabinet meetings at Oulx on May 21 and again on June 7. Within his delegation in Paris there were disagreements and recriminations. He himself refused to attend a banquet given by Crespi to the delegates on the economic commissions, a gesture which did not pass uncommented upon.[62] Di Cellere openly blamed his vacillations and his misunderstanding of Wilson for his lack of success, and hinted at personal intrigues.[63] Di Cellere's own view, which was also Sonnino's, was that it was best, under the circumstances, to leave the question unsettled, while still holding the trump card of military occupation of the territories assigned to Italy by the Treaty of London.[64] He himself greatly resented having been pushed into the background, while others, with less understanding of things American, had carried on most of the negotiations; with an author's pride, he thought that the Miller compromise would have been accepted if only Orlando had forced the Allies to put pressure on Wilson by holding over their heads, in a convincing fashion, the threat of the Treaty of London.

In his predicament Orlando had already put off the scheduled meeting of Parliament, making use of royal decree to meet immediate financial demands.[65] When Parliament reassembled, he was naturally called upon to give an account of his Ministry's handling of affairs since the crisis of April. His policy in foreign affairs, he explained to the deputies, had been guided by two principles: first, insistence on the Italian claims, sole guarantee of a just peace; and second, maintenance of the war-time alliance, which aim precluded a blind obstinacy fatal to friendly relations. Italy, he pointed out, had definitely secured the Brenner frontier; for her eastern and Adriatic frontiers she still claimed fulfillment of the Treaty of Lon-

[62] Di Cellere, "Diary," June 1, p. 212.
[63] *Ibid.*, June 2, p. 212.
[64] *Ibid.*, June 5, p. 214.
[65] *Ibid.*, June 6-7, p. 215.

don, whose validity the Allies did not question.[66] The Chamber was not satisfied with this purposely vague statement and wanted greater details, but Orlando, arguing that a public debate would be dangerous at this time, moved a secret session for a discussion of foreign affairs. Several deputies, among them Nitti, spoke against the motion, but, Orlando insisting, a division was taken in which he received only 78 votes against 262 in opposition.[67]

As a result of this vote, Orlando's Cabinet resigned, and the formation of its successor was entrusted to Nitti, who gave the Foreign Ministry to Tittoni. The signing of the German Treaty, Wilson's departure for the United States, and ᵗhe almost simultaneous fall of Orlando clearly mark the end of one period.

It is not easy to appraise the work of the first Italian delegation, but certain things nevertheless stand out quite clearly. First of all, we would stress the difficulty of the task which confronted it. The peculiar position of Italy *vis-à-vis* the Allies and the United States, and the unexpected importance which this last named Power came to assume in the Peace negotiations, are all important in this respect. Toward the Americans, the British had the enormous advantage of a common language and cultural background; the French benefited from the generally accepted belief that they had been the innocent victims of aggression, and the impression—prevalent out of all proportion to actual fact—that their country had been *the* battleground, the evidence of which one did not have to go far from Paris to see. The Italian front was known to but very few of the negotiators in Paris, and Italy certainly could not pose as a victim of aggression. She had come into the war as the result of careful deliberation and practically on her own terms, and her military effort had had no essential effect on the outcome in any obvious way; at least such was the prevalent impression among the other nations. In Europe, where the nationality principle was most important, the British claimed no territory; the French claims to the Rhineland might be understood in the light of French experience; but even so, Clemenceau—a far stronger personality than Orlando—found it expedient to yield them for a somewhat dubious guarantee. Only the

[66] This slurred over the vital point made by the Allies, that the Italian claim to Fiume constituted itself a breach of the Treaty of London.

[67] Orlando's speech of June 19, 1919. *Atti del Parlamento, 1913-19, Camera, Discussioni,* XVII, 18866-67, 18870-72. It was freely hinted that Orlando had deliberately chosen to be defeated on a technicality, rather than face a debate (*Stampa,* June 19, 21).

Saar was left, and that by way of reparations and not definitely annexed. Under the circumstances, the Treaty of London could easily take on the appearance of Shylock's pound of flesh.

What were the Italians to do then? To give up the Treaty would have been a bold gesture, but a risky one, especially in view of the prevalent feeling toward Italy, unless she could secure in advance definite compensations elsewhere from her Allies. It was a difficult case at best, and one may well doubt whether either Sonnino or Bissolati could have come out better than Orlando. At the same time, there is no question that the Italians committed serious blunders. The first of these was the extraordinary case of Fiume; it may well have had the element of a bargain in Orlando's mind, but the manner in which it was allowed to become a symbol in Italy soon destroyed the Government's freedom of action, while it had the very damaging psychological effect of antagonizing Wilson. The complete misunderstanding of Wilson in particular and of the Americans in general seems a fault which might have been avoided. Even such a document as the Italian memorandum of claims, with its florid, verbose, and involved style—the English version is particularly unfortunate in this respect—beclouded rather than clarified the Italian case. This, and Orlando's irresolute tactics, easily created the impression that Orlando was disingenuous, and produced high indignation among the American experts. With Wilson tired by his other struggles, and urged on by his own experts, the highly complex Italian problem gradually took on the simple garb of an issue between right and wrong. This is not to say that the Italians were alone guilty of faulty psychology, but the fact that they were in the position of demandants put the burden of failure on them. When the German Treaty was signed, the deadlock was still complete and they were truly isolated.

VIII

COLONIAL QUESTIONS

(To June, 1919)

BASES OF THE ITALIAN CLAIMS

THE ORIGINAL BASIS of Italy's colonial claims at the Peace Conference lay in the Treaty of London,[1] which sanctioned and enlarged the existing colonial interests and aspirations of Italy. Her conquests in the Turkish war of 1911-12 were consolidated through her acquisition of the Dodecanese in full sovereignty (Article 8) and the abolition of whatever rights the Sultan had retained in Libya (Article 10). Most important was Article 9, which recognized that Italy had an interest in the maintenance of the balance of power in the Mediterranean and, as a consequence, promised her "a just share" in the "region adjacent to the province of Adalia" in the event of partition of Turkey. This Italian share was to be delimited "at the proper time," and Italy was recognized the right to occupy it in the event that the other Powers occupied territory in Asiatic Turkey during the war. Italy also associated herself in the declaration of her newly joined Allies in favor of an independent Moslem power in Arabia (Article 12). Finally, in Africa she might "claim some equitable compensation" for any increase of British and French colonial possessions at the expense of Germany (Article 13).

The main characteristic of the provisions just outlined is their extreme vagueness. In particular, the phrase, "the Mediterranean region adjacent to the province of Adalia," could and did lead to a wide divergence of interpretation; nor was it clarified by the qualification of "just share." Likewise the "equitable compensation" in Africa might mean anything from relatively minor frontier rectifications of the existing Italian possessions to an extension of the Libyan hinterland as far as Lake Chad. The balance of power is at best a rather general phrase; did it mean that the various Powers should maintain their present relative ratios of power and possessions (naval

[1] See below, Document 3.

ratios are a good example of this sort of balance), or that their acquisitions should be equivalent in value? What weight would be given to the efforts expended by the various nations in the actual conquest of the territories in question? This proved to be, in large measure, the determining factor in the end. The reasons for this lack of definiteness are to be seen in the unwillingness of Italy's Allies to commit themselves any more than they could help, and in the Italian absorption in problems nearer home: the frontier with Austria and control of the Adriatic.

It was two years before Sonnino could secure a promise of more specific gains; this was finally embodied in the so-called agreements of St. Jean de Maurienne. That story involves the tangled tale of negotiations over the Near East, negotiations in the course of which the various Allies displayed a remarkable lack of common spirit, save perhaps in their mutual distrust and in seeking to secure advantages at each other's expense. The account of these negotiations has been given elsewhere in detail,[2] but, owing to its important bearing on later developments, it is necessary to sketch it here, if only in barest outline.

The entrance of Turkey into the war in November, 1914, revived in acute form the age-old problem of Constantinople and the Straits. On March 4, 1915, Sazonov presented to Buchanan and Paléologue a memorandum wherein he definitely demanded the annexation of Constantinople and the Straits to Russia, while promising to guarantee British and French interests in that zone, and to give favorable consideration to the claims of these Powers elsewhere in the Ottoman Empire. This was the very day on which Grey received Imperiali's memorandum of Italian demands. Opposition to Russian control of the Straits had been for a century one of the cardinal principles of British diplomacy, but under the pressure of war both Grey and Delcassé, French Foreign Minister at the time, acceded to the Russian request.[3] The negotiations with Italy were proceeding at

[2] For the negotiations and agreements between Russia, Great Britain, and France, cf. Howard, *The Partition of Turkey, 1913-1923,* Chaps. IV-VI; also Toscano, *Gli accordi di San Giovanni di Moriana.* This last named work gives a very full account of the negotiations between Italy and her Allies. It is the most satisfactory treatment of that particular phase, although it presents a somewhat overdrawn picture of an innocent Italy, struggling for a bare recognition of her "rights" against the duplicity of her Allies. Without seeking to minimize the latter, the fact that Italy was relatively a newcomer in the field, as well as the "rights" of the other Powers, should also be borne in mind.

[3] Great Britain would have preferred to put the Greeks in Constantinople, but Venizelos, who favored Greek intervention on the side of the Entente, was forced to resign on March 6.

the same time. Having won his point, Sazonov wanted Italy to be informed of the agreement and her adherence to it secured, but Grey was definitely opposed to doing this before Italy had definitely committed herself. Italy was therefore kept in ignorance of the Constantinople agreement, and, to reassure Sazonov on the score of possible future objections from her, notes were exchanged in London by the Russian Ambassador with Grey and Cambon on April 27 reasserting the validity of the tripartite agreement.[4] This procedure gives a measure of the mutual confidence of the Allies.

In this same year, 1915, Great Britain was carrying on negotiations with the Sherif of Mecca, the basis of which was that, in exchange for his active participation in the war against Turkey, Great Britain would undertake to support the formation of an independent Arab state wherein she would enjoy special privileges.[5] The French, meantime, were pressing the British for a definition of their "rights" in the Ottoman Empire; lengthy discussions took place between Sir Mark Sykes and Georges Picot as the result of the French request. On March 9, 1916, a joint Franco-British memorandum, embodying the result of these discussions, was submitted to Sazonov by Sykes and Picot, who had gone to Russia, while an exchange of notes in London between Grey and Cambon ratified the arrangement, known from its authors as the Sykes-Picot Treaty. The outstanding provision of this Treaty, for our purpose, was the one whereby France obtained the coastal strip of Syria, the vilayet of Adana, and a zone extending to the future Russian frontier (Russia was to receive the four Armenian vilayets of Erzerum, Trebizond, Van, and Bitlis); Alexandretta was to be a free port.[6] As the result of these various understandings, Great Britain found herself bound by rather inconsistent—in spirit if not in letter—commitments. The three Allies had been in agreement on one point, however, and that was in completely ignoring Italy. Doubtless to have brought Italy into these negotiations would have complicated them, for she was bound to ask for a definition of her share of booty, and it would have been awkward to have to inform her of the earlier Constantinople agree-

[4] Cf. Howard, *op. cit.*, p. 147; Toscano, *op. cit.*, pp. 40-46.

[5] The final agreement did not take place until Jan., 1916. Cf. Howard, *op. cit.*, pp. 188-92.

[6] A zone of French influence was to include Mosul. The British favored this buffer between their own and the Russian sphere, but, after the collapse of Russia, laid claim to the Mosul district.

ment; however, the issue was bound to arise sooner or later, and the more secret agreements were made without her, the more awkward was their disclosure bound to be. The Italian complaint that this was a violation of the spirit of the Alliance—to put the matter in its most favorable light—is unquestionably justified.

Italy declared war on Turkey in August, 1915, and Sonnino, who had heard rumors of agreements affecting the Near East among Italy's Allies, used the occasion to seek clarifications from Grey. Grey was very reserved, and there followed a long series of consultations and postponements, during which Italy was accused by her Allies of not living up to the spirit at least of the Treaty of London, in that she was not actively participating in the war against Turkey and had failed to declare war on Germany. Italy finally declared war on Germany on August 27, 1916, and once more Sonnino requested to be informed of all the agreements concluded among the Allies without Italy's participation. It was not until two months later that the texts were finally communicated to him by Grey.[7] They could hardly be a pleasant discovery for the Italian Foreign Minister, and, in his reply, which he gave on November 4, Sonnino quite properly took the position that Italy was equally interested with her Allies in the disposition of the Straits and that, by virtue of Article 9 of the Treaty of London, she must have an equal voice in the future of the Ottoman Empire. In consequence of this, he entered a claim for the three vilayets of Konia (containing the region of Adalia), of Adana, and of Aidin, the latter containing Smyrna.

This request was the beginning of a protracted discussion, for, now that Italy was at war, her Allies proved far from eager to accede to her wishes. In December, Sonnino was induced to exchange notes with Giers, the Russian Ambassador in Rome, giving Italy's sanction to the Constantinople agreement of March, 1915; but, even after this, Russia continued her opposition to putting Smyrna in the Italian zone: she wanted to preserve a none-too-strong but viable Turkish state in Asia Minor, and insisted that that port was essential to its existence. In the east, the Italian claim came into conflict with the French. Under persistent pressure from Sonnino, the matter was taken up in London in January-February, 1917, but Imperiali con-

---

[7] For the details of these negotiations between Italy and her Allies and the exchanges between Great Britain, France, and Russia, cf. Toscano, *Gli accordi di San Giovanni di Moriana*, Chap. III.

sidered the offer presented by Balfour[8] so wide of the Italian demands (it excluded Smyrna as well as Adana and Mersina) that he would not even discuss it.[9] More delay ensued[10] until Ribot, the new French Premier, met Lloyd George at Folkestone on April 11, after which he invited Sonnino to meet him and the British Prime Minister.

VIII. THE PARTITION OF TURKEY ACCORDING TO THE WAR-TIME
SECRET TREATIES

The lines in this map are taken from Temperley, *A History of the Peace Conference of Paris*, and Toscano, *Gli accordi di San Giovanni di Moriana*.

The meeting[11] took place at St. Jean de Maurienne on April 19, and agreement was reached quite promptly on the subject of the Italian zone in Asia Minor. The terms of the agreement were set in a joint memorandum[12] signed by Lloyd George, Ribot, and Boselli, Prime Ministers respectively of Great Britain, France, and Italy. By

[8] Balfour came to the Foreign Office in Dec., 1916.

[9] A detailed account of these discussions in London is given by Toscano, *op. cit.*, pp. 209-27.

[10] The first Russian Revolution (March, 1917) intervened here. In France a new ministry under Ribot took the place of the Briand Cabinet on March 19.

[11] One of the purposes of this meeting was to discuss the Austrian peace overtures, made through Prince Sixte of Bourbon Parma.

[12] St. Jean de Maurienne Agreement, see below, Document 6.

it, Italy adhered to the previous agreements concluded between her Allies in regard to Asia Minor and Arabia, and they in turn recognized the Italian share (Articles 1, 7). France retained Adana and Mersina, but the latter was to be a free port, and Italian goods, going to or coming from, the Italian zone were guaranteed freedom of transit over the railroad connecting it with Mersina; Italy, on her side, agreed to make Smyrna a free port (Article 2). In general, the three parties guaranteed one another equality of treatment in their respective zones (Articles 5, 6). The region under Italian administration comprised the southern part of Anatolia, bounded by the French zone in the east and, in the north, by a line running due east from Smyrna, which it included. In addition, there was a zone of Italian influence, analogous to the zones assigned to Great Britain and France, to the north of Smyrna, extending to the railroad through Afiun-Karahissar, which railroad was not included (see Map VIII).

From the Italian point of view, Sonnino had indeed done his job well, for the agreement did rather more than maintain the equilibrium in the Eastern Mediterranean; it marked a decided advance in Italian colonial policy. To be sure, Italy had interests in the region, but they were both more recent and smaller than those of Great Britain and France, being almost exclusively confined to trade rather than investment.[13] The Straits for Russia, and the routes to the East for Great Britain, were matters of the highest importance to those countries; this explains the feeling toward Italy that she was somewhat of an intruder and the tendency to exclude her from previous arrangements, which in turn accounts for the quite natural Italian resentment at such proceedings. Sonnino's experience in dealing with his Allies on these questions goes a long way toward explaining his distrust of new ideas (self-determination, League of Nations) and the reluctance to abandon the fruit of his hard-won treaties which he was to evince at the Peace Conference. Nor, in view of his experiences with the Allies, can such an attitude be called totally unwarranted.

In view of later developments, it is essential to point out that no definite treaty was concluded at St. Jean de Maurienne. No Russian representative attended the meeting, and the tripartite memorandum

[13] She had a substantial and growing share in the commerce of Turkey, and if she were to acquire Trieste, her share would become predominant.

opened with the phrase: "Subject to the consent of the Russian Government," and closed with the provision: "It is understood that the present memorandum shall be communicated to the Russian Government in order to enable it to express its opinion" (Article 9). Miliukov, Foreign Minister in the Provisional Russian Government, strove to maintain the policy of his predecessors in the office in regard to the Straits and Asia Minor,[14] and there followed further consultations among Italy's Allies. However, Russia became increasingly wrapped up in her internal difficulties and correspondingly less capable of pursuing an active foreign policy; but it was not until August, after further exchanges, that Sonnino succeeded in obtaining an exchange of notes in London (August 18) and in Paris (August 21-22), embodying the memorandum drafted four months earlier. Russia continued on the path of disintegration and never ratified the St. Jean de Maurienne agreement; once in power, the Bolsheviks published and denounced the secret treaties, while renouncing all the imperialist schemes of expansion of the czarist government.

The Russian withdrawal reopened the question of the fate of the Ottoman Empire, in particular that of the Straits and of the portion which had been assigned to Russia. Two solutions were possible. One was to maintain the provisions of the partitioning agreements as they applied to Great Britain, France, and Italy, while disposing anew of the Russian share; the other, which received its principal support from American participation in the war, was to ignore the secret agreements altogether and to deal with Turkey afresh on the basis of the Fourteen Points.

Neither solution was adopted at first. In October, 1918, Great Britain declared that she considered nonvalid the St. Jean de Maurienne agreement, owing to the lack of Russian consent, and France took the same position.[15] If technically sound, the argument was in fact very weak, for Russia's power of veto in the matter was evidently contingent upon the performance of her duty in the Alliance, which she had been the one to break. The denunciation of the agreement could, therefore, be little more than an attempt to be rid of Italian competition, under cover of a technicality. It may well be that

[14] Partly for that reason he was forced to resign and the Government adopted the slogan of a peace without annexations or indemnities.

[15] Toscano, *Gli accordi di San Giovanni di Moriana*, p. 357. Cf. also Anglo-French Declaration of Nov. 8, 1918 (see below, Document 13).

Great Britain and France resented the Treaty of London and did not feel kindly disposed toward Italy; that argument, however, seems rather beside the point, especially in view of the behavior of these Powers in the Near East. Now that Russia was gone as a rival imperial Power, Great Britain did not seem to feel the need of a French buffer between her possessions and Russia; in December Lloyd George managed to secure Clemenceau's renunciation of the Mosul region in favor of Great Britain, and his consent to putting Palestine under a British rather than an international régime.[16] No doubt the British had furnished the bulk of the military effort in the Near East and this arrangement foreshadowed the principle that was to prevail, more than any other, in the attribution of extra-European territory at the Peace Conference.

Of the Fourteen Points there were two[17] which referred directly to colonies and to the Ottoman Empire. Point V provided for "a free, open-minded, and absolutely impartial adjustment of all colonial claims," giving equal weight to the interests of the populations involved and of the claiming Power. Point XII promised a "secure sovereignty" to the Turkish portion of the Ottoman Empire, "security" to the other nationalities of that Empire, and freedom of the Straits.

Save for the last item, these were very broad declarations of principle, susceptible of varied interpretations. The principle of self-determination may be quite commendable, but even in a highly nationalized and nationalistic Europe, where presumably the wishes of populations could be ascertained with comparative ease, it was not possible to draw a map on the sole basis of nationality. How then could the wishes and the interests of the populations be determined in Africa? These populations might be dissatisfied with German rule—as was asserted and largely believed in Paris—but how determine who their new rulers should be? Their only spokesmen, if such they might be called, were evidently those who had ousted their former masters. As to Turkey, where it might be possible to determine national or religious allegiance, such phrases as "secure sovereignty" offered a wide latitude of interpretation. Almost the only thing that could be foretold with certainty was that the Turks would object to foreign rule, whether by one or by several Powers.[18]

[16] Howard, *The Partition of Turkey,* pp. 210-12.
[17] Points V and XII, see above, p. 38.
[18] The British position did not appear to be very definite. The Allied Note of Jan. 10, 1917,

As indicated before, the element of military conquest and actual occupation proved to be of the highest importance. The German colonies and portions of the Ottoman Empire were in 1919 in the hands of Great Britain, the Dominions, and France, with Belgium and Japan participating to a smaller extent. Italy, on the other hand, had not taken any part in any of the African or Near Eastern conquests; on the contrary, she barely maintained herself on the Tripolitan coast. While it might be argued that conquests, like resources, ought to be pooled, since the war had been a joint enterprise, the tendency prevailed that he who had provided the effort of conquest had a prior claim to possession, and, in effect, the final attribution of mandates followed, with few exceptions, the factual occupation as it stood at the end of the war.[19]

Such was the not-very-promising situation which confronted Italy before the opening of the Peace Conference. Great Britain and France did not recognize the validity of the agreement of St. Jean de Maurienne, and the French had expressed quite bluntly their opinion that colonial affairs were essentially the concern of Great Britain and themselves.[20] This may well have been a reflection of the feeling that Italy had failed to bear her share of the common burden during the war; certainly Bliss's report that the Italians felt that they were "being excluded from the fulfillment of any colonial aspirations"[21] was amply justified. As to Wilson and the Americans, their feeling toward the secret treaties was already well known, and the Italians realized the importance of their attitude.[22]

THE ITALIAN COLONIAL PROGRAM

There is no evidence that, at this time—during the period intervening between the cessation of hostilities and the opening of the Peace Conference—the Italians did anything to improve the very unfavorable circumstances under which they would have to present

spoke of "the setting free of the populations subject to the bloody tyranny of the Turks; and the turning out of Europe of the Ottoman Empire as decidedly foreign to Western civilization"; while in his speech of Jan. 5, 1918, Lloyd George declared that the Allies were not fighting "to deprive Turkey of its capital or of the rich and renowned lands of Thrace, which are predominantly Turkish in race." Cf. Temperley, I, 190, 428.

[19] Syria, conquered in the main by Arab and British forces, might be called the exception that proves the rule, for its attribution to France was the source of much controversy.

[20] French Draft of Nov. 29, 1918, given by Jusserand to the State Department; see above, p. 75.

[21] Miller, II, Document 61; see above, pp. 77-78.

[22] See above, pp. 80 ff.

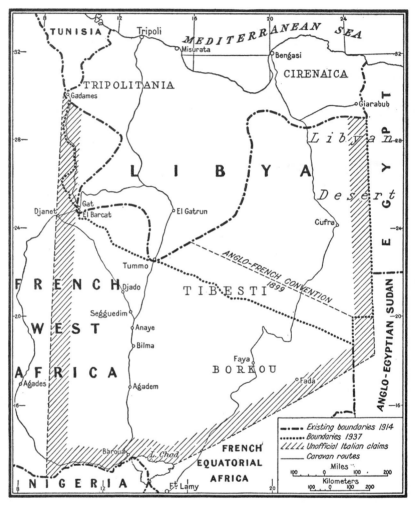

IX. MAP ILLUSTRATING THE ITALIAN COLONIAL PROGRAM IN NORTHERN
AFRICA: LIBYAN CLAIMS AND CONCESSIONS FROM GREAT BRITAIN
AND FRANCE

The lines of the unofficial Italian claims are taken from Piazza, *La nostra pace coloniale*.

their colonial claims.[23] Presumably, they thought it safer to concentrate their energy on their eastern frontier and on the Adriatic, which provided ample cause for concern. What is more, it is very difficult to obtain a clear idea of Italian colonial policy at the Conference, assuming that such a policy existed.[24] The evidence is wholly negative, which is all the more surprising in view of the persistence and tenacity which Sonnino had displayed in securing the St. Jean de Maurienne agreement. One is forced to the conclusion, tentatively at least, that colonial matters were of comparatively secondary interest to the Italians at Paris.

If such was the official position, that is not to say that there was lack of interest in colonial questions in Italy.[25] Groups and societies interested in colonial questions, such as the *Società africana d'Italia*, the *Istituto coloniale italiano*, the *Istituto orientale di Napoli*, the *Società italiana di esplorazioni*, etc., as well as many publicists, had kept the issue alive.[26] It is from these that we can form an idea of Italian aspirations.[27] These came under two main heads: Africa and Asia Minor. The situation in the latter region has been outlined. In Africa, Italy possessed the colonies of Eritrea and Somaliland, evidences of greater hopes and frustrated ambitions; and, since 1912, she had succeeded to the Sultan in the vilayets of Tripoli and Cyrenaica (Libya). Her claims naturally grew out of these possessions.

As to Libya, the principal contention was that it lacked a suitable hinterland. It was claimed that Libya was the natural outlet for a large part of the trade of the Sudan, which was diverted to Algeria and Tunisia, to the West Coast of Africa via Nigeria and Senegal, and to the Red Sea via the Anglo-Egyptian Sudan, thus making

---

[23] There is a conspicuous lack of comment on colonial questions in the press during this period. Cf. *Daily Review of the Foreign Press.*

[24] On the subject of Italian colonial policy, Dr. Bowman, who was in a good position to know, has the following to say: "It should also be noted that Italy's imperial policy shifts with every breeze of suggestion. In truth, the country cannot be said to have a policy at all, and it is difficult to see how one could be framed that would meet the expressed need for additional territory when all the territory that could possibly be obtained is not worth obtaining from an economic point of view." Bowman, *The New World*, p. 246.

[25] In certain circles at least. From the nature of the question, such matters are of interest to comparatively restricted groups. For the colonial agitation during the war, see the *Franchetti memorandum* presented to the Boselli Government in April, 1917 (*Politica*, IV, 217-19) and Toscano, *Gli accordi di San Giovanni di Moriana*, pp. 24-29, 135-44, 265-69.

[26] For references to specific articles, cf. Beer, *African Questions*, pp. 392 ff.

[27] "It should be remembered, of course, that these are non-official views. Some of the claims are undoubtedly exaggerated, and have been criticized by Italians themselves, but there is substantial unanimity on the main points." Beer, *op. cit.*, pp. 392-93.

Libya a rather worthless possession. To redress the situation in its favor, it was proposed to extend the boundaries of Libya as follows: in the west, a line running from Gadames roughly along the ninth meridian of east longitude to the Nigerian border; then along that border to Lake Chad, and from there in a general northeasterly direction, by the heights of Ennedi, to the twenty-fifth meridian of east longitude, which would form its eastern boundary as far as the Mediterranean at the bay of Sollum.[28] This arrangement would give Italy control of the caravan route from Lake Chad to Tripoli, and of the branch between Gat and Gadames, separated at the time by French territory.[29] It would involve the cession by France of Borku and Tibesti, though leaving her Wadai, thus cutting in two the French possessions in Central Africa. On the side of Egypt, some territory would also have to be given up; in particular the whole Senussi territory would fall to Italy.[30] This Libyan claim was also based on the contention that the vilayets of Tripoli and Cyrenaica, to which Italy had fallen heir, included the Oasis of Kufra as well as Borku and Tibesti (see Map IX).[31]

East Africa had been the scene of the earliest Italian attempts at colonization. These had come to grief at Adowa, leaving Italy the two possessions of Eritrea and Somaliland. During her Sudan war, Great Britain had made a treaty with Italy (in 1891) allowing her to occupy, in case of military necessity, the Kassala district to the Atbara River. This treaty specified that such temporary occupation would not abrogate Egyptian rights. The territory was occupied by Italy in 1894, but when she prepared to withdraw, after the Adowa reverse,

---

[28] Beer, *op. cit.*, pp. 393-94; Piazza, *La nostra pace coloniale*, pp. 45-47.

[29] Tripoli was the northern terminus of the central caravan route, running from Barroua, on the Nigerian border, through Agadem, Bilma, and Tummo. The section as far as Tummo was in French hands; the branch between Gat and Gadames was cut by a French salient into Tripolitania.

[30] The Senussi were the most powerful Moslem sect in northeast Africa. As the result of the war of 1911-12, their activity, from having been anti-British and anti-French turned anti-Italian. They successfully fought the Italians and, by the end of 1914, they held the whole interior of Cyrenaica (Beer, *African Questions*, p. 395 n.). Eventually this led, in July, 1916, to an Anglo-Italian agreement for joint action against them.

[31] The Tunisian boundary from the sea to Gadames had been determined by a Franco-Turkish convention (Jan., 1910), but beyond that point French territory was bounded by the line of the Franco-British convention of 1899, to which Turkey was not a party. Italy, succeeding to the Sultan in the vilayet of Tripoli, questioned the validity of this convention, or at least claimed the right to be a party to the definition of frontiers. This argument is developed at length by Piazza, *La nostra pace coloniale*, pp. 38 ff., 59.

The French occupation of Baracat, at the beginning of the war, had been withdrawn at Italy's request. Piazza, *op. cit.*, p. 41.

Great Britain requested her to delay the evacuation until she could send Anglo-Egyptian troops. On the strength of these precedents, a claim was made to the Kassala district, one of the most fertile areas

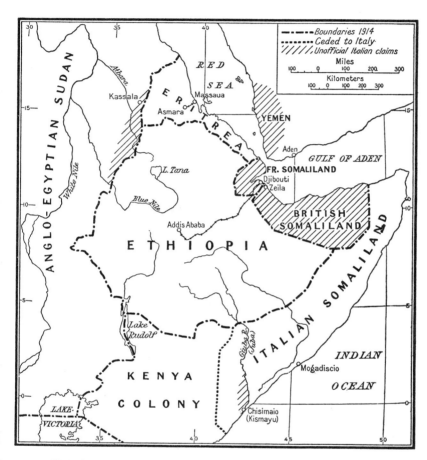

X. MAP ILLUSTRATING THE ITALIAN CLAIMS IN EAST AFRICA

The lines in this map are taken from Piazza, *La nostra pace coloniale.*

of the Anglo-Egyptian Sudan and adapted to the cultivation of cotton (see Map X).[32]

By another Anglo-Italian Treaty of 1891, the port of Kismayu and the territory on the right bank of the Juba River were declared British. By a subsequent agreement of 1905, Italy obtained a lease to a plot of ground in Kismayu, useful to her on account of the dearth

[32] Beer, *op. cit.,* pp. 395-96.

of good harbors in Italian Somaliland. Possession of Kismayu was now declared necessary to the development of this colony (see Map X).

According to Beer,[33] the claims just outlined had the unanimous support of the colonial party in Italy. Beer himself, in the paper which he wrote for the guidance of the American delegation, considered the principle of the Libyan claim for an adequate hinterland entirely reasonable, provided it were confined to limits which would not in turn interfere with the development of the French possessions and of the Anglo-Egyptian Sudan.[34] He was inclined to favor the claim to Kassala[35] and lacked information about the Juba district.[36] From certain quarters in Italy[37] there were also demands for the British and French possessions in Somaliland; for an abrogation of the tripartite agreement of 1906, by which Great Britain, France, and Italy guaranteed the integrity of Abyssinia;[38] and even for a sphere of influence on the coast of Yemen (see Map X).[39]

FIRST COLONIAL DISCUSSIONS

The question of the disposition of the German colonies was among the first to be considered by the Council. Wilson's draft for the League of Nations of January 10, 1919, contained the statement that the League should be "the residuary trustee with sovereign right of ultimate disposal" of the territories formerly belonging to Turkey, and of the German colonies.[40] During a discussion on the twenty-eighth, Orlando declared himself willing to accept any principle of distribution, provided it were equally applied and that it assured Italy's participation. He did not wish to appeal to Article 13 of the Treaty of London—owing to Wilson's attitude toward the secret treaties—as the principle therein stated would apply as a matter of course, even if that Treaty had not existed.[41] He made the same point two days later, in connection with the discussion of mandates for

---

[33] *Ibid.,* p. 397.

[34] *Ibid.,* pp. 451-52.

[35] *Ibid.,* p. 396.

[36] See below, for the position taken by the French and the British.

[37] *Istituto coloniale di Napoli;* Piazza, *op. cit.,* pp. 87 ff.

[38] This claim grew out of the disturbances which had followed the death of Menelik in 1913.

[39] This claim was based on arguments similar to those given for the possession of Valona.

[40] Wilson's First Paris Draft. Miller, *Drafting of the Covenant,* II, Document 7, p. 88.

[41] Minutes of the Council, Jan. 28, B.C. 14. This and subsequent references to Minutes of the Council occurring in this chapter, unless otherwise specified, are taken from the account given in Miller, XIX, 557-67 (Asia Minor), and 572 (African questions and mandates).

the Ottoman Empire.[42] Wilson did not feel, on that occasion, that the time had come to discuss the partition of Turkey. The meeting closed with the adoption of a resolution declaring that the Allies and the United States were agreed that "Armenia, Syria, Mesopotamia and Kurdistan, Palestine and Arabia must be completely severed from the Turkish Empire." However, this was to be "without prejudice to the settlement of other parts of the Turkish Empire."[43] Thus were reconciled Wilson's demand for a "free, open-minded, and absolutely impartial adjustment of all colonial claims" and the more concrete desire of Great Britain, the Dominions, and France to hold what they had secured by military conquest or had promised one another in the secret treaties. From the Italian point of view, the situation is reminiscent of that which existed before Italy had secured a definition of her share in Asia Minor, while Great Britain, Russia, and France had mutually recognized one another's portions. The difference is highly significant between the definite exclusion of certain regions where the British and French interests lay, and the vague formula covering the zone which was of interest to Italy. It is only surprising that a more determined protest was not registered by the Italians.

On February 3 Venizelos appeared before the Council to make an exposition of Greek claims. With his wonted tact, he chose to humor the Council rather than to bore them with a lengthy recital of the past glories of Greece, and he made an excellent impression.[44] Among other things he entered a claim for Northern Epirus and Koritsa (Southern Albania), and for all the islands of the Eastern Mediterranean.[45] The latter demand, especially, was in direct conflict with the Italian claim to retention of the Dodecanese[46] which had been recognized by the Treaty of London (Article 8). Continuing his presentation the next day, Venizelos now laid claim to the western part of Anatolia, on the grounds of nationality and on the

---

[42] Minutes of the Council, Jan. 30, B.C. 17.

[43] Minutes of the Council, Jan. 30, B.C. 18. Miller, XIV, 130-31.

[44] Nicolson, *Peacemaking,* pp. 255-56; House-Seymour, *What Really Happened at Paris,* p. 159.

[45] Minutes of the Council, Feb. 3, B.C. 21. Miller, XIV, 190-91.

[46] Nicolson reports a rumor, prior to this date, of an attempted deal between Sonnino and Venizelos, on the basis of Italian support for the Greek claim to Smyrna and the Dodecanese, in exchange for the Greeks yielding Northern Epirus to Albania (Nicolson, *op. cit.,* pp. 246, 248). Comments appeared in the Italian press at the end of January on the frequent interviews between Orlando, Sonnino, and Venizelos. Cf. *Daily Review of the Foreign Press,* Jan. 25-31.

basis of Wilson's Twelfth Point.[47] This claim also cut across Italian ambitions, expressed in general form in the Treaty of London and more concretely at St. Jean de Maurienne. The meeting on February 4 ended, as other similar meetings, by turning over the Greek demands for study and report to a committee.

The Greek Committee held a number of meetings over a period of a month, but failed to reach unanimous agreement. A threefold division manifested itself, with the French and the British at one extreme, the Italians at the other, and the Americans generally holding a middle position. The differences between the French and the British on one side, and the Americans, were, however, debated amicably and without creating friction. But it was otherwise with the Italians, who evinced a tendency to resort to dilatory and obstructive tactics and, as a result, tended to isolate themselves. When Venizelos was to appear before the Committee on February 24, Cambon, who presided, refused to allow some of the questions which the Italians proposed to ask mainly for the purpose of embarrassing the Greek statesman.[48] Some of their contentions, which were not in accordance with facts, merely served to create a bad impression.[49] Other arguments failing, the Italians would claim that they lacked instructions, or would simply refuse to discuss subjects covered by the secret treaties, as being outside the competence of the Committee.[50] Such tactics were no doubt unfortunate and contributed not a little to create that feeling of antagonism to and annoyance with the Italians, of which Sonnino complained to Balfour on one occasion.[51] Yet, indefensible as they may be, one ought to bear in mind the peculiarities of the Italian position. Great Britain and France displayed a strange readiness to make light of the engagements which they had taken toward their Ally, and to regard the whole Near Eastern question as subject for a fresh settlement. Much, indeed, could be said in favor of this attitude, but the case for it certainly would have been stronger had it been adhered to with consistency and in a spirit of fairness. It was at least awkward, for example, to ask the Italians

[47] Minutes of the Council, Feb. 4, B.C. 22. Miller, XIV, 199-209.

[48] Nicolson, *Peacemaking*, p. 268.

[49] Nicolson reports an incident of Castoldi seeking to pass, as a unanimous recommendation of the Albanian delimitation commission of 1913, his lone dissent in that commission, and of the contention being disproved by immediate reference to the proceedings, much to the embarrassment of the Italians. Nicolson, *op. cit.*, p. 265.

[50] Nicolson, *op. cit.*, pp. 266, 274.

[51] Nicolson, *op. cit.*, p. 331.

to give up the Dodecanese to Greece, while the British delegation decided that it must retain Cyprus. Koritsa may have been of vital importance to Greece—opinions differed on that score—but the motive for assigning it to her, rather than to Albania, seems somewhat peculiar.[52] On March 6 the Greek Committee presented its report to the Council. The report contained three sets of recommendations: the Franco-British, the American, and the Italian, with the result that the problems which had been examined by the committee were thrown back into the Council for final settlement.[53]

ATTRIBUTION OF MANDATES—ASIA MINOR

It was not until April 21, as the discussion of the Adriatic problem was approaching its climax, that mandates were mentioned again in the Council. During the afternoon meeting,[54] Lloyd George and Clemenceau, seeking a way out of the Adriatic impasse, brought up the suggestion of a compromise in the Adriatic on the basis of an Anatolian mandate to Italy, a large territory, as proposed by Clemenceau. The proposal did not find favor with Wilson, for the Greeks dreaded the Italians as neighbors—as the Patriarch of Constantinople had told him—and besides, the Italians, he thought, lacked the colonial administrative experience of the British. He agreed, however, that the Turks were not fit to rule. Lloyd George was mainly interested in the railroads.[55]

Then came the explosion of the twenty-third in the form of Wilson's Manifesto, and there the matter rested for a time. During their absence from the Conference, the Italians took it upon themselves to send warships to various points in Asia Minor without consulting the Allies and the United States. Subsequently, in a speech before the Chamber of Deputies,[56] Orlando sought to justify these expeditions on the somewhat specious ground that they had taken place without

[52] "It is terribly bad luck on Albania, who has Italy imposed upon her as a Mandatory Power, and then gets her frontiers cut down merely because none of us trust Italy in the Balkans." Nicolson, *op. cit.*, p. 276.

[53] "Report of the Committee on Greek Territorial Claims," Miller, X, 285-92; Annexes to the Report, 293-310. By comparison with the problem of the Yugoslav frontier, Southern Albania was a relatively minor issue for the Italians, which is the reason why the question has not been considered in greater detail. A good account of these negotiations may be found in Stickney, *Southern Albania*, pp. 75-76, 107-12.

[54] Orlando was not present at this meeting.

[55] Minutes of the Council, April 21, I.C. 175A.

[56] On September 28, 1919. *Atti del Parlamento, 1913-19, Camera, Discussioni*, XIX, 21399.

violence, merely in order to protect Italian nationals;[57] and further that, inasmuch as other Allied troops had been landed, his action—while perhaps not quite formally correct—had at least the merit (from the Italian point of view) of having secured actual physical representation on the spot.[58] Whatever the reasons, the fact could hardly be expected to mollify the Three, in the already tense and not over-friendly atmosphere.

Clemenceau mentioned the dispatch of Italian warships to Smyrna on April 30,[59] and Wilson referred to it again on May 2, on which occasion Lloyd George also spoke of Italian intrigues, aiming at stirring the Turks against the Greeks. Lloyd George suggested the sending of troops by all the Allies, but nothing was decided at this meeting.[60] On the fifth, Lloyd George announced that the Italians had occupied Marmaris as a coaling station and said that they had gone to Adalia without consulting the Allies, while General Wilson reported an unconfirmed landing at Alaya. Lloyd George and Wilson also had news of Greeks killed by the Italians at Rhodes. Lloyd George wanted to reallocate the Allied troops in Asia Minor; he was willing to let the Italians go into the Caucasus (where there was oil) so that he might have British troops more easily available in Constantinople, ready to counteract any Italian move; he was also anxious to have the matter settled before the return of the Italians.[61]

Something in the nature of a *coup de théâtre* was to happen on the sixth. The atmosphere in which the Council met is perhaps best expressed in Nicolson's words: "They [the Italians] can rely only on sympathy, not upon their inherent force: and they have sacrificed that sympathy by incessant ill-temper, untruthfulness, and cheating."[62] Continuing the discussion of the previous day, it appeared that Wilson could not send American troops to Turkey, for the United States was not technically at war with that country. However, he thought that if the Italians occupied Anatolia they would have to leave, for they depended on the United States for credits for

[57] Count Sforza—at the time Italian High Commissioner in Constantinople—reports that the Grand Vizier, Damad Ferid Pasha, hinted to him that the Italians, rather than the Greeks, ought to go to Smyrna. But, as Sforza correctly points out, this was merely another instance of the time-honored Turkish policy of playing the Powers against one another. Sforza, *Makers of Modern Europe*, pp. 353 ff.

[58] On the importance of this point, see above, p. 209.

[59] Minutes of the Council, April 30, I.C. 177E.

[60] Minutes of the Council, May 2, I.C. 179B.

[61] Minutes of the Council, May 5, I.C. 181B.

[62] Nicolson, *Peacemaking*, pp. 326-27. The point is not so much that this was a correct appraisal, as that it was the prevalent feeling at the time.

essential purposes.[63] Convinced that an Italian mandate in Asia Minor would cause friction, and irritated as he was by the actions and the attitude of the Italians, while, on the other hand, Venizelos had known how to make a very favorable impression upon him, Wilson consented to the giving of Smyrna to the Greeks and to the immediate dispatch of an expedition to that city—there were already seven Italian warships there—to forestall an Italian occupation of Smyrna. As there was no time to be lost, Venizelos was called in and asked whether he could land such an expeditionary force at once, "within two or three days."[64] Rather taken aback by the shortness of the notice, but sensing a unique and perhaps transitory opportunity of realizing the *megala idea*, Venizelos grasped the offer.[65] The whole affair was arranged in great secrecy lest the Italians get wind of what was happening.[66] It is difficult to avoid the feeling that all parties were resorting to rather undignified tactics; certainly this was a far cry from open covenants, openly arrived at.

To round out the day's work, the Council, still without Orlando, took up the question of the distribution of the former German colonies[67] and, for all practical purposes, the selection of mandatories took place the next day.[68] The actual attribution was largely determined by the fact of conquest and occupation, which in turn depended mainly on geographical contiguity to the various German colonies.[69] Italy had taken no active part in these colonial conquests; on the contrary, by the end of the war, she was barely maintaining

[63] Minutes of the Council, May 6, I.C. 181C.

[64] Sforza, *Makers of Modern Europe*, p. 164. Cf. Baker, *Woodrow Wilson and the World Settlement*, II, 192.

[65] Venizelos had claimed Smyrna as early as February, and had circulated reports of trouble in that region in April, but the offer made to him at this time was none the less rather unexpected.

[66] Baker, *op. cit.*, II, 187.

[67] Temperley, II, 240.

[68] *Ibid.*, VI, 503-4.

[69] The distribution was as follows:

1. *Togoland and Cameroons*. France and Great Britain to make a joint recommendation to the League of Nations as to their future. (This was eventually done, on the basis of a modification of the provisional agreements of 1914 and 1916.)

2. *German Southwest Africa*. In Mandate to the Union of South Africa.

3. *German East Africa*. In Mandate to Great Britain.

4. *German Pacific Possessions*. In Mandate to the British Empire, Australia, New Zealand, and Japan.

Owing to minor difficulties and readjustments, the Mandates were not issued at this time and the Treaty of Versailles simply contained a clause (Article 119) whereby Germany renounced title to her overseas possessions, in favor of the Principal Allied and Associated Powers. The eventual distribution conformed to the outline just indicated, save for a modification in East Africa (Ruanda and Urundi), in favor of Belgium.

herself on the Tripolitan coast. However, Orlando just back from Rome, attended the meeting of May 7 and remarked, not inappropriately, "that if mandates were a burden Italy was ready to accept them. If mandates had advantages, then Italy has a right to share in them." He agreed, on that occasion, to the formation of a special committee of Great Britain, France, and Italy to consider the application of Article 13 of the Treaty of London.[70] Thus, while Great Britain and France had already secured definite acquisitions, Italy, for the time at least, had to be content with a rather vague promise, the fulfillment of which obviously depended to a large extent on the good will of her Allies.

It was not until May 12 that Clemenceau informed Orlando of the decision taken by the Council during his absence in regard to Smyrna, and, after some awkward explanations, induced him to accept it on the assurance that "the landing was without prejudice to the ultimate disposal of Smyrna."[71]

The Nicolson Plan for the Partition of Turkey

Turkey had been the subject of informal discussions among the British,[72] and between the British and the Americans.[73] On March 27, after a talk with Balfour, Nicolson reports continuing to work on a partition scheme;[74] he refers to a scheme of Lloyd George on April 30.[75] By May 13, Asia Minor was again to the fore, both in the Council and in the British delegation. Lloyd George took up in earnest the idea of solving the Italian problem on the basis of compensations in Asia Minor. He asked his advisers what he could offer the Italians, and Nicolson suggested the Adalia zone, but was not supported by the others (Milner, and so forth). Orlando and Sonnino then came to see Lloyd George, who indicated to them on a map drawn by Nicolson what he proposed to offer.[76] The Italians seemed inclined

[70] Minutes of the Council, May 7, I.C. 181G.

[71] Baker, op. cit., II, 194.

[72] Toynbee, Nicolson, Temperley. Cf. Nicolson, Peacemaking, pp. 289-90, 312.

[73] Nicolson, op. cit., pp. 288, 291, 317; also, Howard, The Partition of Turkey, p. 224.

[74] Nicolson, op. cit., p. 290.

[75] Ibid., p. 318.

[76] According to Nicolson (op. cit., p. 333), this is the occasion on which Lloyd George carried on the discussion for some time in the belief that the map was an ethnographical map, thinking "the green means Greeks instead of valleys, and the brown means Turks instead of mountains."

This statement is somewhat surprising in view of the fact that British interests in Asia

to accept a mandate over the Adalia region, but they wanted also Scala Nova and the mines at Eregli. Milner's reminder of the article of the Covenant which provided for "the consent and wishes of the people concerned" apparently evoked considerable mirth. However, Balfour took a different view and, after leaving, dictated a memorandum to the following effect:

a. Greek Zone.

b. An Independent Turkey embracing all Anatolia, but put under International Control in the shape of foreign advisers in all the key ministries.

c. A zone of commercial and immigration interest for Italy in the region of Adalia.[77]

The Three met in the afternoon of that day (May 13),[78] and Lloyd George, bent on forwarding his scheme, assumed the rôle of advocate for Italy. He stressed the Italian resentment at not being treated as a first-class Power and argued for an Italian mandate in Asia Minor. He proposed to have the United States in the Straits and in Armenia, a Greek zone as suggested by Wilson, and France and Italy in Northern and Southern Anatolia respectively. Wilson could not be certain that the United States would accept a mandate and questioned whether Anatolia ought to be divided. The necessity of a port in the Italian zone and the various possibilities, Scala Nova, Makris, Mersina, were discussed. As to the coal mines, Lloyd George thought that the German shares could go to Italy as reparations. Wilson was in favor of giving to Greece the Dodecanese, Smyrna and its district, and a mandate for the rest of Venizelos' claim. Nicolson was then called in and told of the tentative agreement; he pointed out that Konia was being included in the Italian zone and the Baghdad railway was being cut, but his objections were brushed aside.[79]

On the basis of the instructions given him, Nicolson drew up the following plan for the partition of Turkey:

1. The United States to have a mandate for Constantinople and Armenia subject to the approval of the Senate.

Minor were neither small nor recent. Lloyd George himself had attended the meeting of St. Jean de Maurienne, at which the final partition of Turkey had been arranged on the basis of a British map. Cf. Toscano, *Gli accordi di San Giovanni di Moriana*, p. 272.

[77] Nicolson, *op. cit.*, p. 334.

[78] Balfour did not attend this meeting and therefore could not present his views.

[79] Minutes of the Council, May 13, C.F. 10A; Nicolson, *Peacemaking*, p. 335.

2. Greece to have in full sovereignty the Dodecanese, Castellorizzo and the Smyrna-Aivali zone, and a mandate for the rest of the vilayet of Aidin.

3. A mandate for Italy over Southern Asia Minor from Marmaris to Mersina.

4. A mandate to France for the rest, i. e. Northern Anatolia.[80]

This plan was presented in the Council—Wilson, Clemenceau, and Lloyd George—by Lloyd George on the fourteenth. Wilson spoke of a Turkish state in Northern Anatolia under a loose French mandate, rather than a Turkish state including the whole region (Anatolia without Armenia and the Greek zone), in order to avoid the undesirable situation of France and Italy both having advisers at the capital. Nicolson was summoned again and told to make some minor alterations in his map—Marmaris to be left out of the Italian zone—and the scheme was provisionally adopted.[81]

After this meeting, Lloyd George left for a visit to the battlefields. In the meantime, on May 15, the expeditionary force—Allied officially, but Greek in practice—landed at Smyrna. Lloyd George's scheme was far from having the united support of his own delegation. Nicolson himself, who had done the drafting, thoroughly disapproved of it and kept urging Balfour to do something to prevent its adoption.[82] Balfour, seeking to do the best he could with what he considered a bad job, wrote a memorandum[83] for the Three, defending and amplifying his suggestion of the thirteenth. This proposal, which, he endeavored to show, did not constitute a condominium, was designed, he wrote, "to do two things: to maintain something resembling an independent Turkish Government, ruling over a homogeneous Turkish population; the other is to find a position for the Italians within this Turkish State which will make a sufficient appeal to the ambitions of the Italian Government." He admitted that, "from every other point of view, the plan . . . is a bad one," but, under the circumstances, something had to be done for Italy. He defended it further on various grounds: it was essentially a mere extension of the prewar system of foreign advisers to the Sultan; if Italy were granted special privileges in the south, the rest of the country would be barred to her intrusion; more speciously, he pointed

[80] Minutes of the Council, May 14, C.F. 13A, Appendices I, II; Nicolson, *op. cit.*, p. 335. This outline is reconstructed from the summaries given by Miller and Nicolson.

[81] Minutes of the Council, May 14, C.F. 13A; Nicolson, *op. cit.*, p. 336.

[82] Nicolson, *op. cit.*, pp. 338-39.

[83] Minutes of the Council, May 17, C.F. 15A, Appendix. See below, Document 48.

out that the general principle of equal opportunity to all nations in a mandated area was not violated, since this was not a mandate.

Lloyd George handed out this memorandum of Balfour at the Council meeting of May 17. No action was taken then, except an agreement to make a joint remonstrance to Italy for her military actions in Asia Minor.[84]

Meantime, Lloyd George's partition scheme aroused something of a storm among the British. We have just indicated Balfour's attempt to prevent the partition of Turkey; but more serious than that was the revolt in Lloyd George's own Cabinet: there were even rumors of threatened resignations.[85] Realizing that he had gone too far, Lloyd George was not slow in making a complete about-face. When Orlando went to see him the next day, he asked for a mandate for the whole of Anatolia: if he could not get Fiume, he must have something else to show in its place. Lloyd George countered by explaining that the acquisition of Fiume, situated in Europe and constituting an addition to the national territory, was of greater importance to Italy than a distant mandate; he thought matters could be arranged.[86]

With this idea very much in mind, Lloyd George, at the Council meeting of May 19, began by explaining that Orlando had asked for all of Anatolia, but that he really did not care about it if he could get Fiume. He also said that Mohammedans objected to an Italian mandate in Turkey.[87] In fact, he wanted to withdraw his previous scheme, in order to "get the Italians out of Asia Minor altogether."

[84] Minutes of the Council, May 17, C.F. 15A.

[85] Curzon, Montagu, Bikanir, and even Balfour. Nicolson, *op. cit.*, p. 342.

To be sure, the Near Eastern situation, while of greatest concern to Curzon, was not the only cause of dissension, nor did differences appear suddenly. As the German Treaty was taking shape, increasing doubts appeared, and were expressed, as to the wisdom of some of its provisions. The Near East was merely the immediate occasion that served to crystallize the opposition. The slowness of reply or even the complete lack of response from the British delegation in Paris to inquiries and memoranda from London (e. g., Curzon's memoranda on the Near Eastern question) was also one of the elements in the formation of the situation that had developed among the British. Cf. Nicolson, *op. cit., passim*.

[86] Di Cellere, "Diary," May 18, p. 202. This is one of the not-infrequent reversals of Lloyd George, which earned him a name for unreliability.

[87] The Indian delegation had been summoned to Paris by Lloyd George. Whether he did this to cover his retreat behind the screen of Mohammedan feeling, as has been suggested, seems doubtful. Mohammedan loyalty to the Sultan should not be taken for granted. Certainly the Turkish alliance with Germany had not prevented the Moslem world from dividing its allegiance, and one should also bear in mind divisions within it, not incomparable to those among Christians. However, the Mohammedan peoples, like others, naturally objected to being objects of barter. Cf. Temperley, VI, 27; Nicolson, *Peacemaking*, pp. 342-43.

Wilson agreed about Mohammedan feeling and wondered whether the Sultan could be left in Constantinople with the French as advisers. In that event, Lloyd George pointed out, the whole question of mandates for the Turkish Empire would have to be reopened. He returned to the idea that it was worth concessions in Fiume to get the Italians to give up Asia Minor.[88]

A meeting that day of a large part of the British Cabinet who had come to Paris, alarmed by the Anatolian partition scheme of Lloyd George, while it produced no concrete plan, revealed a strong feeling in favor of leaving the Turks alone in Asia Minor, except for the zone of the Straits and the Greek zone.[89]

At a second meeting of the Council on the nineteenth, Orlando was still absent, but Sonnino took his place. The Italian intervention in Asia Minor was again discussed in connection with Orlando's note of the seventeenth[90] which tried to justify it on grounds of military necessity, and reiterated the hope that the Mediterranean problem would be solved in accordance with the agreements made on Italy's entrance into the war. Sonnino defended the landings as being within the zone of the Treaty of London,[91] but Lloyd George would have none of it and wanted the Italians to withdraw before discussing the matter. Sonnino insisting that Scala Nova was included in the 1917 agreement, Lloyd George retorted that the validity of that agreement was contingent upon Italy making active war against Turkey, which she had failed to do.[92] The Greeks, whose landing at Smyrna had been accompanied by much disorder and bloodshed, also had to be cautioned not to move beyond the line assigned to them.[93]

Two days later, on May 21, Lloyd George had a new plan[94] which he presented to the Council. According to it, the United States was to have a mandate for Constantinople, the Straits, Armenia, and Cilicia. Anatolia, save for the Greek zone, was to remain undivided, under a "light mandate" to the United States, or else wholly independent. France was to retain Syria, pending the report of the commission on that region, and Great Britain would stay in Mesopotamia

[88] Minutes of the Council, May 19, C.F. 18B.

[89] Nicolson, *op. cit.*, p. 343.

[90] Minutes of the Council, May 19, C.F. 19, Appendix I.

[91] Sonnino also mentioned Rhodes as a reason for Italian interest in the Adalia region, to which Wilson observed that Rhodes had not yet been ceded to Italy.

[92] Minutes of the Council, May 19, C.F. 19.

[93] Nicolson, *op. cit.*, p. 344.

[94] Minutes of the Council, May 21, C.F. 20A, Appendix III.

and Palestine. The Caucasus was to be included in the Armenian mandate, pending stabilization of the Russian situation. Wilson was doubtful about the likelihood of the United States accepting an Anatolian mandate,[95] and Clemenceau objected to the ousting of France from Anatolia. A long discussion of the Syrian question ensued, but no decision was reached.[96] Except for a reference on May 28 to the ever-recurring topic of Italian landings in Asia Minor,[97] other matters held the attention the Council until the signing of the German Treaty.

The Turkish question came up once more, however, before Wilson's final departure. On June 17 Damad Ferid Pasha was heard by the Council, and on the twenty-fifth, when Lloyd George brought up the matter, Wilson suggested a procedure similar to that resorted to in the case of Austria-Hungary: a definition of the frontiers of the new Turkey, with the severed portion of the Empire remaining to the Allies collectively. It is an indication of the feeling toward Italy at the time that when Clemenceau inquired what would be done about the Italians in Asia Minor, Lloyd George replied that

the district in question either belonged to the Turks or it did not. If it did, the Turk would say: "What are the Italians doing here?" And the Allies could only reply that the Italian occupation had been made without their knowledge or consent.[98]

Further reference to Turkey the next day emphasized the isolation of the Italians. Wilson blamed them, rather than differences among the Powers, for the difficulties in Asia Minor, and thought that they should be asked to state clearly whether or not they remained in the Alliance. Clemenceau was inclined to refuse all discussion of the subject with Italy, and Lloyd George was concerned over the effect of the Italians' actions on Mohammedan feeling.[99] The Turkish question was still far from a solution when the German Treaty was signed on June 28.

AFRICAN NEGOTIATIONS

If the Italians had failed to achieve anything concrete in Asia Minor, their policy in regard to Africa seems to have been pursued

[95] Wilson favored extending the Greek zone to include the mainland opposite the Dodecanese.
[96] Minutes of the Council, May 21, F.A. 20A.
[97] Minutes of the Council, May 28, C.F. 37B.
[98] Minutes of the Council, June 25, C.F. 92. Miller, XVI, 459-61.
[99] Minutes of the Council, June 26, C.F. 93A.

with even less vigor. For all its lack of definiteness, Article 13 of the Treaty of London clearly recognized Italy's right to participate in a division of the German African colonies, or to receive compensations elsewhere in Africa in the event of such a division among the other Powers. Even if this Treaty were to be disregarded, a strong case could be made by Italy for receiving compensations, for, as had often been pointed out, the war had been a joint enterprise. Orlando did, in fact, make this point on two occasions,[100] but he seems to have been content with this general statement of principle. The Italians were handicapped by the lack of a committee to discuss African questions. As mentioned before, the African mandates were, in effect, distributed on May 6, in the absence of the Italians, and it was not until the following day, with Orlando just back from Rome, that the formation of such a committee was arranged.[101]

The result was that the Italians were left to deal directly, as best they could, with the British and the French, and their colonial delegates had time and energy to spend on the endless series of Adriatic compromises. Beer, who was familiar with the subject and sympathetic toward the Italians, tried to help them, even if only in establishing contacts. He mentioned his own views with respect to Libya, Somaliland, and Abyssinia to Louis Aubert and Lionel Curtis, of the French and British delegations respectively, as early as January 14.[102] It was only two months later that Piacentini explained to him the Italian colonial program, which Beer found "far more moderate than the unofficial one of Piazza and his associates."[103] Beer suggested the possibility of exchanging Jibuti for something else in Africa.[104] At lunch with a group of Italian delegates, he found, rather characteristically, that the "conversation was not very illuminating" as to the Italian claims.[105] Piacentini wanted to be put in touch with the British, but, when the meeting took place, the question discussed seems to

---

[100] On Jan. 28 and on May 7.

[101] Minutes of the Council, May 7, I.C. 181G. The Belgians, as a result of their protests, quickly came to terms with the British, and obtained a mandate for Ruanda and Urundi. To be sure, the feeling toward the Belgians was more sympathetic than toward the Italians, and the Belgians, besides, had actually taken part in the military conquest of the area assigned to them. The Italians did eventually obtain some concessions, but only minor ones and at a later date.

[102] Beer, Diary, Jan. 14.

[103] Ibid., March 14. For a statement of this programme, see above, pp. 209 ff.

[104] Ibid., May 17. Beer came to realize that the French would not be likely to give up this possession, of little value in itself, but important because of its situation.

[105] Ibid., March 20.

have been the extent to which the mandate system invalidated the Treaty of London.[106]

It was not until May 12 that Piacentini, discussing African questions with Beer, told him that the Italians were then taking up their colonial claims with the French and the British. Beer gathered the impression that the Italians had given up hopes of either French or British Somaliland, that they thought there was a small possibility of obtaining Kismayu, and that, in the end, they would get only a hinterland for Libya.[107] Again the Adriatic held the center of the stage in Italian eyes,[108] and Africa was of very secondary interest. The idea of colonial compensations to Italy in Africa received but scant attention from the Three. On May 13 Wilson threw out the suggestion that concessions in Somaliland might ease the situation with Italy,[109] but the next day Clemenceau reported that the French colonial experts would not hear of any concessions in Jibuti.[110]

During the course of a conversation with Lord Milner, Beer found the latter averse to giving up anything at the expense of Egypt. He thought, nevertheless, that a hinterland would have to be given to Libya, and did not seem opposed to concessions in Somaliland.[111] At a "colonial conference,"[112] Piacentini found Milner well disposed, but the French unwilling to concede much;[113] again it seems there were no concrete results. In the Council, Lloyd George mentioned that he understood that the French were not willing to make any concessions in Africa, but that Milner was willing to give the Italians 40,000 of the 60,000 square miles for which they were asking.[114]

When the German Treaty was signed at the end of June, the Italian colonial problem was hardly nearer a settlement than at the beginning of the Conference. In Europe, Italy had at least secured some definite advantages, even if all her requests had not been

---

[106] *Ibid.,* March 24.

[107] *Ibid.,* May 12.

[108] See above, p. 173, for Piacentini's Adriatic scheme.

[109] Minutes of the Council, May 13, C.F. 10A.

[110] Minutes of the Council, May 14, C.F. 13A.

[111] Beer, Diary, May 14.

[112] Presumably a meeting of the committee whose formation had been agreed upon on May 7.

[113] Beer, Diary, May 15.

[114] Minutes of the Council, May 22, C.F. 22B. The account just given is of necessity very sketchy, owing to the lack of information. This very lack of evidence is in itself significant, however, as an indication of the comparative importance to the Italians of colonial and of European questions.

granted, but in the colonial field she still had nothing definite to show. This in spite of the fact that she had, in many respects, a stronger case in that realm than in the Adriatic. To be sure, the St. Jean de Maurienne agreements had never been ratified by Russia, but the most that can be said of the Anglo-French contention that this lack of Russian ratification invalidated the agreement, is that it was legal, not to say legalistic. The peculiar difficulty of the Italian position at this point was that, even on such high grounds as the principles embodied in the Fourteen Points, a strong case could be made for detaching the non-Turkish portions of the Ottoman Empire from the rest of Turkey, while these same principles would militate in favor of the formation of an independent Turkish state in Anatolia. This made it possible to enlist, in general, the support of the United States for the Franco-British claims and its opposition to the Italian ones. Having once agreed that the non-Turkish areas needed the guidance of some more advanced Western Power, it would be difficult for the Italians to encroach upon the British and French mortgages on these same areas. Thus was achieved the curious result that a plausible case was built up for denying the Italian claims in Asia Minor while recognizing those of Great Britain and France in the Near and Middle East. In direct proportion to the plausibility of this case, there was irritation with the Italians for resorting to any and all possible devices to obstruct agreement or to secure a hold on some territory—whether by having it recognized to them, or by the act of military occupation—and, correspondingly, there grew up in Italy a deep-rooted resentment at what came to be looked upon as a deprivation of rightful claims, a resentment all the deeper for its having been caused by something in the nature of sleight of hand.

An attempt might have been made to form a common front with the French, who were having an uphill struggle in securing recognition of their claims in Asia Minor, but, while the idea was suggested,[115] its possibilities were never seriously explored. Very possibly nothing would have come of it, for the French preferred, on the whole, the support of the Anglo-Saxon Powers; certainly the policy of alternately blowing hot and cold on the French Alliance was least calculated to secure support from the French.

[115] Cf. for instance, *Secolo*, May 27, which gives a clear analysis of the Near Eastern situation as it stood at the time.

Sending a few detachments here and there in Southern Anatolia was legally (on the basis of Article 9 of the Treaty of London) in the same category as the argument for the non-validity of the St. Jean de Maurienne agreement, but it was nevertheless a mistake on Italy's part, for she was not in a position to dispense with the good will and assistance of the Allies and the United States, whom she thus provided with an easy argument against herself. To do so at the height of the Fiume controversy was to choose the most psychologically unfavorable moment, and, in fact, this only served to precipitate the dispatch of the Greek expedition to Smyrna. One may well have no sympathy for the Italian claim in Anatolia, or even feel that the Italians were seeking rewards to which their military effort did not entitle them; the real point is that, behind the phraseology of high principle, a very real competitive struggle was taking place over the Near East, and that the Italians were comparative newcomers in the field. It was as natural for the British and the French to resent the intrusion as it was for the Italians to seek to force their way in. Looking back to 1919, the surprising thing is that no more determined effort was made by the Italians, either to secure more definite results in the colonial field, or to link their colonial ambitions with the European settlement.[116] It can only be taken as further evidence of the too narrow—and one can hardly help feel, mistaken—concentration on the Adriatic issue, not to say on the mere city of Fiume.

With the signing of the German Treaty, the major problem of the West was solved, and this tended to emphasize the special position and the isolation of Italy, whose main interests lay wholly in Central Europe, the Balkans, and the Eastern Mediterranean. Great Britain and France had, no doubt, important interests in these regions, but, while Italy had, up to now, definitely secured only the northern frontier with Austria, France had disposed of her Eastern problem, secured her share in German reparations, and disarmed her main enemy, while Great Britain had eliminated the German naval and commercial fleets and driven Germany completely out of Africa. In that continent, Italy had as yet secured nothing more definite than a promise from Great Britain and France of minor readjustments,

---

[116] The idea did appear, mainly as Lloyd George's suggestion, but was not seriously pursued. See above, p. 220.

but had received no share in any of the German colonies. This is one of the elements which helped to develop in Italy a psychology of defeat and frustration, all the more dangerous in that it followed a technical victory.

Part Two

THE NITTI MINISTRY

(JUNE, 1919—JUNE, 1920)

IX

THE SECOND ITALIAN DELEGATION[1]

THE FALL OF the Orlando Cabinet had come somewhat unexpectedly; there had been not so much active opposition to it as general weariness over its continued inability to break the deadlock in Paris, and Orlando himself apparently had chosen to be defeated on a technicality rather than in open debate. Certainly there was no trace left of the momentary unanimity which Wilson's Manifesto had produced in April. While there were some who recognized the difficulty of Orlando's task, many criticized his vacillating policy, which had gained Italy nothing but suspicion and ill-will from her Allies;[2] some even discovered that the unbridled nationalistic propaganda of the earlier months and the undiscriminating attacks against the Allies had served to antagonize rather than to impress them.[3] There was still fairly unanimous insistence on the Italian claims, but the dominant note was rather one of frustration, in which the advantages already secured by Italy were nearly forgotten.

The fundamental problem of Italian foreign policy was at stake. Even before 1914, Italy had not been an overenthusiastic partner in the Triple Alliance; rather she looked upon her membership therein as giving her a strong bargaining position. Her real interest lay in the balance of power on the Continent, and how valuable her position had been needs no better illustration than the terms of the Treaty of London, where her demands were almost granted for the asking. Now that she found herself among the victors, with Germany thoroughly crushed and impotent for some time to come and Austria-Hungary completely destroyed, she had lost that bargaining position and she was merely the weakest among the Great Powers.

[1] With the signing of the Versailles Treaty, there is a very sharp drop in the extent of our sources of information. The Chief delegates and a large part of the delegations returned to their respective countries after June 28; as a result, most of the personal accounts of events end at about this time. Of necessity, therefore, the account of negotiations becomes rather sketchy after June, 1919. This is especially the case for the period from July to November. After November, the British and American official publications covering the period from Dec., 1919, to March, 1920, and the *Italian Green Book* on the Treaty of Rapallo fill the gap to some extent.

[2] *Corriere della sera,* June 20; *Secolo,* June 20.

[3] *Giornale d'Italia,* June 27.

At best she could attempt to counteract French influence in the Danube valley and in the Balkans, but the potential threat of joining the enemy camp had, for the time at least, quite evaporated. She did not relish the prospect of French security guaranteed by Great Britain and the United States, and looked upon this arrangement as an endorsement of French hegemony on the Continent, far more preponderant than German influence had ever been. She would have preferred an alliance with France—the Anglo-Saxon Powers reverting to their traditional policy of no formal commitments—which she could increasingly exploit as Germany regained her position in the councils of Europe. Little wonder that there had been such recurrent outbursts of anti-Allied and especially anti-French feeling throughout the Peninsula.

At the moment, however, interest naturally focused on the new Cabinet, rather than on the shortcomings of the outgoing one. Nitti was accepted at first in none-too-friendly fashion, except by the Giolittian elements, which had substantial representation in his Government.[4] Nitti himself was fully aware of the difficult situation that confronted him. His first decision was to leave foreign questions wholly in charge of Tittoni, a decision which was generally well received, while he devoted his undivided attention to internal affairs —a more immediately pressing necessity. In doing this he displayed considerable activity and made a good start. Perhaps the single most important issue which he had to face was that of the high cost of living, which was the fundamental cause of increasingly numerous food riots and of growing labor unrest, overflowing into the political field. Without going into the details of internal affairs, it will suffice to say that, when he met Parliament for the first time on July 9, his declaration of policy was far better received, both in Parliament and outside, than the first announcement of the formation of his Ministry had been. On the foreign situation he was rather reserved; with the internal problems he proposed to deal by returning as quickly as possible to the status of peace, by taking effective measures to lighten the cost of living, by shortly introducing the necessary economic and financial reforms to deal with that problem, and to reorganize Italian economy with a view to increased productivity.[5]

[4] *Corriere della sera* (June 24) lists the affiliations, past and present, of some of the members.

[5] Nitti's speech of July 9, 1919. *Atti del Parlamento, 1913-19, Camera, Discussioni,* XVII, 19053-60. For the sections dealing with the Fiume incidents, see below, p. 237. For comments on Nitti's declaration, cf. *Daily Review of the Foreign Press,* July 6-13.

The Government received a comfortable majority (257 against 111).

Meantime the foreign situation remained stationary. With the German Treaty about to be signed, a chapter was closing in Paris, and naturally nothing could be done in regard to Italian matters until a new delegation had been appointed and had arrived. The change in Ministry had not essentially altered the outlook, and the new Cabinet had to be careful not to lay itself open to the charge that it was ready to sacrifice Italian interests, even though it may have realized the necessity for compromise.[6]

Tittoni appeared before the Senate on June 25 and indicated briefly the state of affairs at the time: the Austrian frontier drawn as Italy wanted it, but the Adriatic question still hanging fire, owing to the failure of the last attempt at a compromise, embodied in the Tardieu Plan. No decision had yet been made about Albania, although Serbia was, in fact, in occupation of the northern portion. In Asia Minor, Smyrna, promised to Italy at St. Jean de Maurienne, was occupied by the Greeks. In Africa, having secured possession of the German colonies, Great Britain and France were offering Italy compensations which were, on the whole, satisfactory in the case of Great Britain, but should be somewhat increased in the case of France.

For the rest, Tittoni confined himself to generalities. He recognized the disadvantage ensuing from the fact that Great Britain and France, having secured the terms of peace they sought, could now devote their energies to the task of reconstruction, while Italy still labored under the handicap of uncertain frontiers. However, he had great faith in the justice of the Italian cause, which, he thought, could not fail of recognition. As to a program of action, if he had formulated one, he did not divulge it; he instead assured the Senate of his patriotism, as a guarantee that he would defend Italian interests. Only in reference to Fiume was he specific to the extent of proclaiming that its right of self-determination could not be denied.[7] Even that formula left the door open to compromise. The speech did not elicit great enthusiasm, but, in view of Tittoni's reputation,

[6] Nitti was attacked in the *Giornale d'Italia* (June 28), which quoted articles from American newspapers *(New York Herald, New York Sun)*, describing him as opposed to the aspirations of Fiume. He was also attacked in Parliament for his activities while in the United States.

[7] Tittoni's speech of June 25, 1919. *Atti del Parlamento, 1913-19, Senato, Discussioni,* V, 4910-12.

the tendency was to trust him to handle the Italian case as could best be done under the circumstances.

RENEWAL OF NEGOTIATIONS

The Balfour Memorandum of June 28

Tittoni then left for Paris with Scialoja, who had second place on the Italian delegation,[8] and arrived just as the Versailles Treaty was about to be signed. He was immediately confronted with a memorandum drawn up by Balfour and intended for Orlando, had the latter continued to represent Italy at the Conference.

The main point of this memorandum[9] seems to have been an endeavor to impugn the validity of the Treaty of London. Italy herself, according to the memorandum, had not lived up to that Treaty, in that she had delayed for a year her declaration of war on Germany,[10] and had not participated in the war against Turkey; she had, of her own accord, proclaimed a protectorate over Albania in 1917; finally, she was demanding Fiume, which the Treaty specifically assigned to Croatia. The memorandum laid great stress on, and strongly condemned, the continued landings of Italian troops in Asia Minor in disregard of the Council's admonitions. Also, conditions were wholly different from what they had been at the time of the conclusion of the Treaty: Russia had collapsed and withdrawn from the struggle; Austria-Hungary had ceased to exist, and the United States refused to recognize the secret treaties. All these, it was felt, were strong reasons for modifying an ill-kept agreement,

---

[8] The other delegates were Maggiorino-Ferraris, and Crespi and Imperiali, who were kept from the former delegation.

[9] The text of this memorandum is not available, but a fair idea of its contents may be gathered from the Italian reply of July 7 (see below, pp. 238 ff.) and from the Minutes of the Council for June 28, C.F. 99A, when it was discussed and approved by Wilson, Lloyd George, and Clemenceau. This and subsequent references to Minutes of the Council occurring in this chapter, unless otherwise specified, are taken from the account given in Miller, XIX, 553-56, 567-69.

[10] A controversy arose in Italy on this point. In a speech during the electoral campaign in October, Giolitti adhered to the view that the delay constituted a breach of the Treaty (Giolitti's speech at Dronero, Oct. 12, 1919). Salandra, who had been responsible for this delay, on the other hand boasted of it as a service rendered to his country (Salandra's letter to his electors, Oct. 19, 1919, in reply to Giolitti's speech). Article 2 of the Treaty of London pledged Italy to fight all the enemies of Great Britain, France, and Russia, but these Powers do not seem to have objected to the Italian behavior until Italy began to make specific demands in Asia Minor.

Cf. also Temperley, IV, 310. (Temperley incorrectly attributes Giolitti's remark to a speech in the Chamber of Deputies, which was not in session at the time.)

and it was therefore proposed to reëxamine the whole situation in the light of the Treaty of London, the Anglo-French declaration of November, 1918,[11] and the Fourteen Points. Finally, the note warned Italy that she would lose the support of her Allies if she persisted in such tactics as maintaining her troops in Asia Minor.

The Fiume Incidents

Tittoni went immediately to see Lloyd George and Clemenceau,[12] who had signed the note, but found himself confronted with a different task from what he had expected. For the Franco-Italian friction had just then come to a head in Fiume. The French had established in this port a base of supply for the army operating in the Balkans and Hungary under General Franchet d'Esperey. The Italian party in Fiume did not take kindly to what it considered interference on the part of the French, whom it suspected of having ulterior motives. French cordiality toward the Slavs was equally objectionable, and relations were not very amicable, despite the fact that an Italian general was in command of the Inter-Allied troops in Fiume. Young enthusiasts of the Italian party organized a volunteer force, which was armed without, it would seem, interference from the Italian Supreme Command. Some trouble occurred on June 29, and on the night of July 2-3 the Croat club was attacked and wrecked and a French officer wounded. Finally, during further affrays on July 6 and 7, in which some Italian regulars took part, nine French soldiers were killed and fifty-eight wounded.[13] These incidents naturally created quite a sensation and put the Italian Government in an embarrassing position. On his first appearance before the Chamber on July 9, Nitti, referring to the events of Fiume, attempted to pour oil on the troubled waters by counsels of coolness and moderation,[14] and Tittoni, making a brief visit from Paris spoke to the same effect. Their task was made easier by the attitude of the French. The French press on the whole, while regretting and condemning the incidents, adopted a moderate attitude,

[11] See above, p. 207.

[12] Cf. Scialoja's speech of July 20, 1920. Giannini, *L'Italia alla conferenza della pace*, p. 73.

[13] This outline of facts is drawn from Temperley, IV, 307. Numerous accounts of all colors are to be found in the contemporary press.

[14] Nitti's speech of July 9, 1919. *Atti del Parlamento, 1913-19, Camera, Discussioni*, XVII, 19057.

in contrast with a section at least of the Italian press.[15] Clemenceau, who had received a report on the incidents from the French general in Fiume, laying the blame on the Italians, brought the situation to the attention of the Council.[16] However, he did not wish to make an issue of the matter, and, on Tittoni's suggestion, the question was disposed of through the appointment of an Inter-Allied Commission of Inquiry on July 8.[17] Both the French and the Italian Governments agreed in feeling that the incidents were of secondary importance and must not be allowed to interfere with the more essential task of finding a settlement.[18]

The Italian Note of July 7

Meanwhile Tittoni had entrusted to Scialoja the task of drafting a reply[19] to the Franco-British memorandum of June 28. Point by point, this Italian reply sought to confute the arguments of the Balfour memorandum.

1. As to the declaration of war on Germany, no time limit was specified in the Treaty of London, and Italy had declared war as soon as she had been sufficiently prepared. Despite her lack of preparedness, she had not hesitated to declare war promptly on Austria-Hungary. At that time she had failed to receive the expected support of the Serbian army, which had remained inactive. Italy had sent an entire army corps and many (61,000) military workers to the Western front.

2. Article 1 of the Treaty of London stated that a military convention was to establish the minimum number of forces that Russia was to use against Austria-Hungary "in order to prevent that Power from concentrating all its strength against Italy." The very argument

[15] On the attitude taken by the press of the two countries, cf. Nitti's speech of July 9, 1919, and Scialoja's speech of July 29, 1921. *Ibid., 1921-23, Senato, Discussioni*, I, 200.

[16] Cf. Tittoni's speech of Sept. 28, 1919. *Ibid., 1913-19, Camera, Discussioni*, XIX, 21420. In this speech Tittoni stated that he had received at the same time the Italian report tending to opposite conclusions, and that, as a result, instead of offering apologies, he had agreed to an investigation. For the Report of the Inter-Allied Commission of Inquiry, see below, p. 245.

[17] Minutes of the Council, July 7, 8, H.D. 1, 2. According to "L'Aventure de Fiume," *Revue des deux mondes*, March 1, 1921, p. 176, the suggestion came from Clemenceau.

[18] Regrettable as they may be, happenings of this nature, which have occurred before and since, should not be given undue weight. They can often develop out of the merest trifles, such as an overheard derogatory remark.

[19] The Italian Note, referred to as Tittoni's Note, owing to the fact that he signed it, is given in full (in French) by Giannini, *L'Italia alla conferenza della pace*, Document 1, pp. 117-23, from which source the following summary is drawn.

of the Russian collapse presented in the Franco-British note would have justified Italy in seeking greater compensations for the added burden thrown upon her as the result of this collapse. However, she had refrained from doing this. In the elaboration of the German Treaty, Italy had loyally collaborated with her Allies and had recognized the attribution to them of the fruits of victory; she could not believe that doubts would begin to arise when it came to recognizing to Italy her due share.

3. Italy had declared war on Turkey on August 20, 1915. She was not in a position to send troops against Turkey, but she had sent 47,000 troops to Macedonia, in addition to the 100,000 already in Albania. It was Italians who, to a large extent, had built and kept up the land communications of the Allied armies. After the Dardanelles expedition, the war against Turkey had been prosecuted in Mesopotamia and Palestine. In the former region, Great Britain would not have welcomed an Italian contingent, but Italy had offered several times, particularly in August, 1917, to send assistance to Palestine, which was to have an international régime. Italy had maintained 40,000 men in Libya, thereby diverting possible raids against Egypt and Tunisia.

4. It was true that the proclamation of June 3, 1917, spoke of the "unity and independence of all Albania under the protection of the Kingdom of Italy." But this proclamation, issued by the military authorities, had been explained and interpreted by Sonnino, in his speech before the Chamber of Deputies on June 20, 1917, to mean protection of Albania against her neighbors, and not a protectorate. Moreover, Article 7 of the Treaty of London declared Italy's assent to the partition of Albania.

5. Fiume was attributed to Croatia in the Treaty of London, when Croatia was thought of as a separate entity, and in deference to Russian wishes. Croatia, now joined to Serbia, would have the use of the southern Adriatic ports. In any case, the question of Fiume was independent of the Treaty of London, inasmuch as the Powers were confronted with the expressed wishes of the population. Italy had always been willing to give all facilities in Fiume to Croatia and to the other interested countries.

Italy had not interfered in Fiume. What had been done by the National Council of Fiume was merely evidence of the local feeling. As to the number of Slavs that would be incorporated into Italy, it was far smaller than that of the alien populations assigned by the Peace Conference to Poland, Czechoslovakia, Rumania, and Yugoslavia.

6. In regard to Anatolia, Italy must assert her right to maintain her position as a Mediterranean Power. This had been one of her principal aims in participating in the war. But, aside from general considerations of justice, there were definite commitments: Article 9 of the Treaty of London; the St. Jean de Maurienne agreements of April 19, 1917; the Italo-French agreement of July 26, 1917; and the Anglo-Franco-Italian agreement of August 18, 1917.

The British note of October 30, 1918, stated that the validity of the Treaty of London was not called in question. The British Government had questioned, however, the validity of the agreement of August, 1917, because of the lack of assent of the Russian Government. Russia had ceased to be an Ally and had lost her voice in the councils of the Allied Powers; this fact could not destroy the value of the agreement among the other parties to it.

The note of June 28 stated that any spheres of influence would not be held in full sovereignty, but only in trust or as mandates from the League of Nations, and seemed to imply that Italy intended to secure by the use of force what she considered as falling to her share. Italy had no designs of conquest or annexation in Anatolia and firmly adhered to the principles proclaimed by President Wilson, as evidenced by the Italian note of November 16, 1918, to the Foreign Office.

The Italian military occupations in Anatolia, in particular that of Scala Nova, were the subject of very sharp expressions in the note of June 28. A perusal of the Minutes of the meeting of the Council of Four of May 19 gave the painful impression that the Italian representative had been treated as might have been that of an enemy Power, called upon to account for criminal acts. It must be pointed out that the occupation of Scala Nova had taken place for the sole purpose of maintaining order, and was the direct result of the Greek occupation of Smyrna. To be sure, this Greek occupation had been sanctioned by the Council, but in the absence of the Italian delegation. Moreover, it should be remembered that Article 9 of the Treaty of London stated that "if France, Great Britain and Russia occupy any territories in Turkey in Asia during the course of the war, the

Mediterranean region bordering on the Province of Adalia . . . shall be reserved to Italy, who shall be entitled to occupy it."

7. The note of June 28 stated that the Treaty of London, the Franco-British declaration of November, 1918, and the Fourteen Points should all be taken into account.

Italy fully adhered to the declaration of November, 1918. As to the Fourteen Points of President Wilson, it should be recalled that formal reservations had been made in due time by Italy with respect to the formula used in reference to certain Italian interests. But the Treaty of London, in contradistinction to the other two acts, was a formal Treaty. Changed conditions might be taken into account, but could not justify alterations in the spirit of the Treaty at the expense of one of the participants.

In conclusion, said Tittoni, who signed the note,

I am quite willing to examine the whole Turkish question with the Allied and Associated Powers, in the firm conviction that legitimate Italian interests will receive due consideration from these Governments. But it is my duty to reject the threat of "the loss of all claim to any further assistance." The meaning of this phrase is not clear. Could it refer to the possibility of withholding food supplies from Italy, if she did not renounce her rights and her legitimate interests, recognized in solemn treaties, and her national dignity? Even if such lengths should be resorted to, after having voluntarily thrown herself into the maelstrom of this long war, after having sacrificed to the common cause the best of the present generation and her entire national wealth, Italy could not consent to renunciations contrary to her honor, and History would pronounce its infallible verdict on the injustice of which my country would have been a victim.[20]

For all its determined language and somewhat grandiloquent conclusion, Tittoni's note may fairly be described as playing for position. Aside from the episode of the Fiume incidents, which was handled through the device of an investigation, Tittoni's first task in Paris was to clear the atmosphere of the accumulated recriminations and misunderstandings of the past three months. The question of Asia Minor in particular have been poorly handled. For all the provocation that Italy may have furnished in this quarter, the Allies had shown a decided lack of statesmanship in the petty revengefulness which they had allowed to sway their decisions. In this respect, Tit-

[20] Tittoni's note of July 7, 1919. Giannini, *L'Italia alla conferenza della pace*, Document I, p. 123.

toni's statement tended to put the question back in its proper light. The note carefully avoided shutting the door to compromise. Between the Allied claim of nonvalidity of the Treaty of London and Tittoni's insistence that the Treaty must be acknowledged, while admitting that changed conditions might be taken into account, the quarrel was more of language than of substance, especially when one considers that Orlando himself had previously shown willingness to make wide concessions in the Adriatic. The question of the validity of the Treaty of London, at least so far as Great Britain and France were concerned, was little more than an argument to be used as expediency might dictate, now in putting pressure on Italy, later to the same effect on the Yugoslavs.[21]

The Tittoni-Venizelos Agreement

Pending further developments in Paris, Tittoni went back to Rome. He was again in Paris and in London later in the month, in an attempt to formulate definite proposals of settlement. One of Tittoni's first moves in Paris was to see Venizelos, with a view to coming to a direct agreement with him in the spheres where Italian and Greek interests came in contact, in Southern Albania and in Asia Minor. The result was an agreement signed by the two in Paris on July 19, after it had been presented to the Council and approved by it on the eighteenth.[22]

"In order to facilitate a settlement in the Eastern Mediterranean and in the Balkan Peninsula," Tittoni and Venizelos, were to "collaborate in defending before the Peace Conference the following points of view":

1. Italy will fully support the Greek claims in Eastern and Western Thrace presented in the Greek memorandum of December 30, 1918.

2. Italy will likewise support the Greek claim to Southern Albania (Northern Epirus) within an indicated line.

3. Greece undertakes to support before the Conference the Italian claim to the Albanian Mandate and to sovereignty over Valona with the necessary hinterland.

The Canal of Corfu shall be neutralized as well as the region from Cape Stylos to Aspri Ruga, including the islands and a 25 kilometer zone from the coast.

[21] In Jan., 1920. See below, pp. 268-69, for the Nitti compromise of Jan. 14, 1920.
[22] Minutes of the Council of Heads of Delegations, July 18, H.D. 10.

4. In the event that the Greek claims in Thrace and Northern Epirus are recognized, Greece will renounce in Asia Minor, in favor of Italy, the area South of an indicated line (from Otousbir-Kaya on the coast, eastward, then south and to Balachik on the Smyrna-Aidin railway; thence along the line separating the Sanjaks of Smyrna and Saroukhan on the North from those of Aidin and Denizli on the South). This concession is to be made even if, owing to American opposition, Koritsa is not attributed to Greece.

Greece will lease to Italy for 50 years a free zone in the port of Smyrna.

5. Italy renounces in favor of Greece the sovereignty of the islands which she occupies in the Aegean Sea with the exception of Rhodes.

6. Mutual guarantees by each Power for the subjects of the other that will be within its administrative zone in Asia Minor.

7. In the event that Italy does not secure her claims in Asia Minor, she will resume full freedom of action in regard to all the provisions of the present agreement.

The same holds for Greece if she fails to secure her claims as stated in art. 4.

8. Inasmuch as Italy and Greece cannot guarantee the fulfillment of the conditions of this agreement, which is only intended to lay a common line of action before the Conference, it shall be kept secret in view of the fact that it is not a formal treaty.[23]

For a small concession around Scala Nova, Italy was willing to give up the Dodecanese and to recognize Smyrna to Greece, while she accepted the partition of Albania. This was in line with the Italian policy of disposing of other quarrels in order better to concentrate her efforts on the Northern Adriatic.[24] It is also a measure of how far she had retreated from even her moderate position of a few months earlier, to say nothing of the more ambitious claims of November, 1918.

THE THREE TITTONI PROJECTS

After the diversion produced by the Fiume incidents, and while the commission of Generals was investigating the situation on the spot, Tittoni resumed negotiations for a settlement of the Adriatic

---

[23] This is a summary of the Tittoni-Venizelos agreement of July 19, 1919, taken from the French text given in Giannini, *I documenti diplomatici della pace orientale*, pp. 27-30. The text of the agreement is also in the Minutes of the Council of Heads of Delegations, July 18, H.D. 10.

[24] This agreement was repudiated the following year by the Giolitti-Sforza Ministry; see below, p. 297. On the Tittoni-Venizelos agreement and the reaction to it in Albania, cf. Stickney, *Southern Albania*, pp. 113, 123.

dispute. The last concrete proposal for a settlement had been the Tardieu-Crespi plan of the end of May and Wilson's modification of this plan, discussed at the meeting of the Council of June 7.[25] Taking up the discussion where it had been left off, Tittoni used this plan as the basis for his first definite proposal.

Tittoni's First Project

On August 12, after a visit to Lloyd George in London, Tittoni presented in Paris, at a meeting at the Quai d'Orsay attended by Clemenceau, Balfour, and Polk,[26] the following scheme:

1. Fiume, with its hinterland and Veglia, to form a neutralized free state under the protection of the League.

2. Dalmatia, save Zara and its district, to Yugoslavia.

3. The Vienna-Trieste railway to be left outside of Yugoslavia, by means of a slight modification of the Wilson line.

4. Likewise a rectification towards Assling, without, however, including that town in Italy.

5. Eastern Istria with Cherso and Lussin (which should both go to Italy) to be neutralized.

6. A mandate over Albania included in the frontiers of 1913, leaving Italy and Greece to come to an agreement about the Southern frontier.[27] The coast of Epirus and the Canal of Corfu to be neutralized.[28]

Clemenceau accepted this proposal of Tittoni as a basis of discussion. He himself had considered the possibility of giving the city of Fiume proper to Italy outright. But, after consultation with Lloyd George, then vacationing in Brittany,[29] Tittoni decided not to take up Clemenceau's suggestion, and the project was sent to Wilson as outlined.[30] Lloyd George and Clemenceau both sent telegrams to Wilson in support of the proposal.[31]

---

[25] See above, Chap. VII.

[26] Acting head of the American delegation after Lansing's departure.

[27] See above, pp. 242-43, for the Tittoni-Venizelos agreement. The result would have been to exclude Yugoslavia from Albania.

[28] "L'Aventure de Fiume," Revue des deux mondes, March 1, 1921, p. 177.

[29] At Clairefontaine, on Aug. 31. Cf. Tittoni's speech of Sept. 27, 1919.

[30] Temperley mentions the existence of a scheme of American origin—published on Aug. 25—which proposed giving the city of Fiume to Italy, Sušak to Yugoslavia, and placing the port and the inland communications in the hands of the League (Temperley, IV, 310). We find no reference to this in Tittoni's projects, perhaps because this scheme maintained the Wilson line, thus separating Fiume from Italy.

[31] "L'Aventure de Fiume," Revue des deux mondes, March 1, 1921, p. 178. The memorandum of Dec. 9 refers to a Franco-British Note to Wilson of Sept. 10.

D'Annunzio in Fiume

While Tittoni's project was being discussed, the commission of Generals presented its report on the Fiume incidents.[32] Its recommendations were as follows:

1. Dissolution of the "National Council" which is to be superseded by a municipality regularly elected and constituted under control of an Interallied Commission that shall supervise the electoral lists and the balloting in order to insure fairness.

2. Immediate dissolution of the League of Volunteers of Fiume.

3. Reduction of the Italian forces to one brigade of infantry and one squadron of cavalry; only one battalion of these forces may be permanently stationed in the Fiume-Sušak zone.

4. Replacement of the present personnel of the French Naval Base—which should be disbanded as soon as possible—owing to the hostile feeling of the citizenry.

5. Constitution of an Interallied Commission, consisting of one American, one Italian, one French and one British representative, that shall have ample control of the administration of the city—which should retain its autonomy—and supervise political matters.

6. Maintenance of public order to be entrusted to an American or British police force.

7. Inquiries to be instituted into the conduct of the Commander of the Carabinieri, of the Commander of the navy who ordered the invasion of the stores of the French Base, and of other officers who may have proceeded arbitrarily to make arrests.

8. A searching inquiry to determine the author and the circumstances of the killing of a French soldier.

9. It is recommended that these provisions, and the consequent measures that will have to be taken, be carried out without disturbing the relations of sincere cordiality which—outside of Fiume—have always obtained between the French and Italian armies and peoples.

10. It is recommended that facilities be granted for the supply of food and goods to Italy who has given so much assistance to the Allied cause during the war and who needs them for the return to normalcy of her industry and trade.[33]

[32] Minutes of the Council of Heads of Delegation, Aug. 25, H.D. 38.

[33] *Politica*, IV, 279-80. The document was first given out by the *Vedetta d'Italia* (Sept. 3, 1919), which obtained it from the English section of the Interallied Command in Fiume. Points 1-6 are given in full; the last four are summarized. Adriaticus (*La Question adriatique*, p. 53), gives the first six points only. In the version of Point 4 given by Adriaticus it is stated that the French personnel should be replaced by a British or American personnel.

The report was accepted by the Council; General Grazioli, the Italian commander in Fiume, was replaced by General Pittaluga, and it was arranged that a British force should take charge in Fiume on September 12.

The Italian party in Fiume realized that a repetition of local incidents would only aggravate matters, and on September 6 d'Annunzio, who was in Venice organizing a force,[34] wrote a letter to the *Vedetta d'Italia*[35] asking whether the hour was ripe for his projected *coup de main*.[36] Disturbing articles by d'Annunzio were published in Fiume on September 9 and 11. On that day the city was restless and full of rumors. General Pittaluga, disturbed, was unable to locate the mayor. Late at night he heard from the British Command that an attempt on the city was to be made that very night. He sent some troops to guard the British and French Commands, but was unable to disarm a group of volunteers. He sought to secure instructions from Abbazia, headquarters of the Twenty-fourth Army Corps, but, according to his own account, General Gandolfo, in command there, would not take the matter very seriously. The next day General Pittaluga was informed that a body of *Arditi* was marching on Fiume. He went out to meet them and, after some theatrical gestures on both sides, unwilling to resort to force, he let d'Annunzio enter the city and surrendered his command the next day. He then left the city and reported the situation in person to General di Robilant at Abbazia.[37] D'Annunzio had very successfully stage-managed the episode, and the news of his raid created the proper amount of sensation in Italy as well as outside.

One may wonder how such an extraordinary performance could ever take place unless with the complicity of some at least of the responsible authorities, for certainly the preparations of an adventure involving, as it must, a fairly large number of people, and the doings of so well-known a character as d'Annunzio could hardly proceed without arousing suspicion. The answer to this question is to be found, not in governmental complicity, but in the very unsettled and

[34] Others of the Italian party, in and out of Fiume, were working toward the same end. Cf. Benedetti, *Fiume, Porto Baross e il retroterra*, p. 16.

[35] Associated with this newspaper were some of the leaders of the Italian party.

[36] Facsimile of this letter in Benedetti, *op. cit.*, pp. 13 ff.

[37] Benedetti, *La pace di Fiume*, Document VII, pp. 252-58. This narrative was published by General Pittaluga in the *Rivista d'Italia* of Sept., 1923.

fluid situation in Italy; Government authority was weak at the time, organized groups of various descriptions being allowed far greater latitude than they would under normal conditions. The territory around Fiume was still under military rule and it is easily conceivable that under the circumstances the persons in authority, somewhat doubtful of their allegiance to begin with, would prefer to shun the responsibility for interfering in a potential hornet's nest and would take the easier course of allowing events to develop unhindered.

However, d'Annunzio's coup did not solve the problem of Fiume, but rather created an extremely embarrassing situation for the Italian Government. Before the Allies and the United States it could only take the position that this was an act of military insubordination, to be dealt with as such. But the matter was not so simple as that; d'Annunzio's contingent contained a goodly number of regular troops, and he knew that he had considerable support among the armed forces, not least among the higher commanders. As to public opinion in the country, it was almost unanimously convinced by now of the *italianità* of Fiume, and if there was some apprehension at the thought of possible consequences, between the unexpected and picturesque gesture of d'Annunzio and the everlasting bickerings of diplomats working behind closed doors, there could be no question as to which had the greater appeal for the populace. The Government had to be cautious lest it appear in the light of fighting patriotic Italians in subservience to unpopular Allies.

Tittoni's Second Project

Nevertheless, the last sensation at Fiume seems to have had little effect on the diplomatic negotiations. The Adriatic question was taken up in the Council on September 15. Clemenceau apparently did not think well of the idea of creating a buffer state of Fiume, and reverted to the suggestion of giving the city of Fiume proper to Italy, while leaving the port and the railway under League supervision, and turning the hinterland over to the Yugoslavs. Polk pointed out that no reply had yet been received from Wilson on the first proposal of Tittoni sent in August, but Tittoni replied that he had come to an agreement with Clemenceau. Lloyd George was willing to have the Italians and Wilson settle the matter in any way that would be acceptable to both sides.[38]

At a second meeting the same day, Tittoni presented a written memorandum explaining his new proposal, which may be summarized as follows:

1. Instead of a large independent state, Italy to have the *corpus separatum* and Yugoslavia the rest (but not Albona). The territories of the proposed state to be demilitarized. The League to take over the port of Fiume and its appurtenances, and to make whatever arrangements it saw fit in regard to the city and the hinterland. Guarantees for the ethnic minorities.

2. Dalmatia to Yugoslavia, except Zara which would be a free city under League guarantee and whose representation Italy would have; facilities for the commerce of its hinterland. Guarantees for Italian minorities and economic interests in Dalmatia.

3. Lussin, Unie, Lissa and Pelagosa to Italy.

4. An independent Albania under Italian mandate.

5. Valona with the strictly necessary hinterland to Italy.

6. Italy abandons the Assling railway route and will be satisfied with guarantees for its use. No cession to Yugoslavia in the Drin Valley, but similar guarantees for the use of the railway to be constructed there.

7. Neutralization of the coast and islands from Cape Promontore to Cattaro.

8. Formation of an expert commission of Allied and Associated Powers to settle the details.

Polk asked what the difference was between this proposal and the former one sent to Wilson, and Tittoni went on to explain that the difficulty with an independent state was Wilson's insistence on a plebiscite, which his new proposal would obviate. Polk thought the coexistence of the two plans would not be understood by Wilson, but Tittoni replied that Wilson had a choice between two projects and that, while he, Tittoni, preferred the second, he would accept either one. However, he would not agree to a plebiscite. Tittoni also insisted that the question of the Assling triangle and the Yugoslav demand for a railway in the Drin valley be both treated alike, that is, answered in the negative.[39]

[38] Minutes of the Council of Heads of Delegations, Sept. 15, H.D. 53.

[39] Minutes of the Council of Heads of Delegations, Sept. 15, H.D. 54, Appendix A. See below, Document 49. Lloyd George suggested that Zara might have its own representation.

Again the crux of the matter was the possession of Fiume, and d'Annunzio's recent occupation of the city had this result, that it made this possession more than ever a necessity for the Italian Government. For the rest, there were no irreconcilable differences. Like the first project of Tittoni, this one was supported by a letter from Clemenceau to Wilson, dated September 18.[40]

Tittoni then returned to Rome, and in a very long speech before the Chamber of Deputies, on September 27, traced the course of the negotiations from their very beginning. Somewhat apologetically, he defended his own compromises. The root of the difficulty, according to him, lay in the decision, as early as January, to adopt the unanimity rule in the Council. This gave to Wilson, who had declared that he did not recognize the Treaty of London, the power of veto. Great Britain and France had become more favorably inclined toward Italy since Wilson's departure from Paris and the arrival of the second Italian delegation; but even so, they would support Italy only up to the point where they would themselves come into conflict with Wilson. Under the circumstances, it had become necessary to modify the Pact of London, but this was no more than had been forced upon the other Allies (e.g., Rumania deprived of part of the Banat, and France of the Rhine frontier). By way of compensation, he pointed to the valuable results already secured by Italy: Fiume not given to the Yugoslavs, the coast neutralized, the Albanian mandate.[41]

The temper of the Chamber reflected the puzzled and irritated mood of the country and manifested itself in a stormy session on the twenty-eighth. As a result, the Government resolved upon dissolution, which was announced the next day, together with the decision to hold a general election.[42]

Toward the end of the month, Wilson seems to have indicated his unwillingness to separate Fiume-city from the state of Fiume; in other words, he rejected Tittoni's second project.[43]

[40] "L'Aventure de Fiume," *Revue des deux mondes*, March 1, 1921, p. 178.

[41] Tittoni's speech of Sept. 27, 1919. *Atti del Parlamento, 1913-19, Camera, Discussioni,* XIX, 21292-308.

[42] A Crown Council, attended by former Prime Ministers and parliamentary leaders, had been held on the twenty-fifth, to consider the situation. Like other war-time legislatures, the Italian House had outlived its normal mandate.

[43] "L'Aventure de Fiume," *Revue des deux mondes*, March 1, 1921, p. 191. This is the only evidence available.

Tittoni's Third Project

Under the auspices of the military occupation of Fiume, a "plebiscite" was held in the city on October 30, which proclaimed the annexation of the city to Italy.[44] The conditions of such a plebiscite evidently made it of little value so far as the Conference or Wilson were concerned. Nevertheless, the *de facto* government of the city drew up a project, the main points of which were:

1. Full recognition of the plebiscite of October 30. The city, the port, the railway station and the territory are annexed to Italy.

2. In recognition of the importance of the port of Fiume to its hinterland of Croatia as well as to Hungary, Austria, Czechoslovakia and Rumania, the city, the port, the docks, the railway station and the territory will be under the régime of a free port. Italian sovereignty shall imply unbroken territorial connection with Italy.[45]

The project was sent to Deschanel, then President of the French Chamber of Deputies, through a French sympathizer, Achille Richard, together with a personal appeal from d'Annunzio to Deschanel. The latter acknowledged receipt of the letter and document, which he said he had given to Clemenceau. While this project is of minor importance, and its authorship militated against a favorable reception, it contained the germ of the idea which Tittoni used as the basis for a third project, which he presented to the Conference at about the same time—first half of October.[46]

The main points of this new project were as follows:

1. Annexation to Italy of a strip of coast from the Wilson line to Fiume, so as to establish the contiguity of Fiume with Italian territory.

2. Fiume to be detached from the free state and to be wholly independent.

3. The free state, under League supervision, to retain control of the port and railway.

4. Italy to receive the island of Lagosta, in addition to Lussin, Unie, Lissa and Pelagosa, already granted to her.

[44] Benedetti, *La pace di Fiume,* p. 31.

[45] *Ibid.,* p. 52.

[46] This is not to say that d'Annunzio and Tittoni were working hand in hand. However, d'Annunzio was in touch with the Italian Government, as shown by the *modus vivendi* mentioned below.

5. Zara to be independent under the protection of the League of Nations; Italy to have its diplomatic representation.

6. The whole Dalmatian coast to be neutralized.[47]

Like the previous proposals, this new one of Tittoni's was supported by the French Government.[48]

Tittoni was exerting his influence at the same time in Fiume and in Washington. In Fiume, he was trying to induce d'Annunzio to withdraw by the offer of a *modus vivendi* on the following terms:

1. Italy has secured from the Conference the consent to occupy Fiume with exclusively Italian troops until such time as a definite settlement shall be arrived at.

2. Formal agreements with the Allies and the United States definitely exclude the possibility that Fiume shall be given to Yugoslavia.

3. The Government undertakes to continue the current negotiations aiming at the annexation to Italy of a strip of territory that shall establish the contiguity of the territory of Fiume with Italy, and to make this a condition of agreement.

[4, 5, and 6. Various promises concerning details of organization.]

7. No sanctions shall be taken against officers, soldiers or citizens as a result of the occupation of September 12.[49]

In Washington, di Cellere, returned to his post, received instructions to press with Lansing the last proposal of Tittoni, by emphasizing the consequences of the persistent refusal to give Fiume to Italy.[50] Matters were complicated by the fact that di Cellere, inherited from the previous ministry, was no longer *persona grata* in Rome.[51] Di Cellere prepared a memorandum for Lansing, but before

---

[47] This statement is reconstructed from "L'Aventure de Fiume," *Revue des deux mondes,* March 1, 1921, p. 191; and from Scialoja's speech of Dec. 20, 1919, *Atti del Parlamento, 1919-21, Camera, Discussioni,* I, 496.

[48] "L'Aventure de Fiume," *Revue des deux mondes,* March 1, 1921, p. 191.

[49] Condensed from *Politica,* IV, 284-85. First published by the *Vedetta d'Italia,* Dec. 31, 1919.

[50] Benedetti, *La pace di Fiume,* pp. 54-55; di Cellere, p. 238. Tittoni's communication was apparently not quite clear and di Cellere asked for further instructions. What Tittoni was really seeking seems to have been the annexation of Fiume, together with sufficient territory to give it territorial connection with Italy, in exchange for turning over the rest of the proposed independent state to Yugoslavia. He was also willing to undertake the construction of a port at Buccari.

[51] The friction appears to have been between Nitti and di Cellere. Their differences dated back to 1917, when Nitti had gone to the United States with the Italian Mission. As early as July, 1919, rumors had appeared in the Italian press announcing di Cellere's imminent recall, owing to unsatisfactory reports of his activity in the United States. He was, in fact, notified of his recall on Oct. 12, in the very midst of the current negotiation. Evidently these circumstances did not make his task any easier nor help the Italian case in Washington. See above, p. 54.

he had time to take up the question with him, he was suddenly taken ill, and he died on October 20.[52]

In the midst of this exchange of correspondence, Nitti, perhaps because he did not depend on his Ambassador, himself took a hand in the matter by sending directly to Lansing a note in support of the last project of Tittoni. The burden of this communication was that if Wilson persisted in his refusal to give Fiume to Italy, in view of the present condition of the country the responsibility for a crisis in Italy would fall upon America.[53] In view of all that Wilson had said in the past, the outcome of Tittoni's third project, and of his and Nitti's appeals, could have been foretold.

The American Note of October 27

Wilson was still willing to give Fiume the same local autonomy which it had enjoyed under Hungarian rule, but refused to detach it from the autonomous state; he rejected likewise the idea of a corridor linking Fiume to Italy. On October 27 Polk handed to Tittoni a detailed reply from Lansing, stating anew the American position. It is worth while to quote this memorandum at some length, for it will serve as a survey of the whole Italian question at this time, and it marks the end of Tittoni's activity in the matter, as he resigned shortly thereafter. The American memorandum runs as follows:

1. The eastern frontier of Italy shall begin at the River Arsa, West of Fianona, and follow the so-called American line northward to the Karawanken with such modification as will make it possible to include the city of Albona in Italy. The coastal strip thus attributed to Italy (from the Arsa to the boundary of the free state) shall be completely neutralized, as well as the strip of coast reaching southward to Cape Promontore.

2. The independent State of Fiume shall be contained within the boundaries set by President Wilson, including the city and its immediate hinterland. The southwestern boundary shall be modified in accordance with 1.

The League of Nations shall have absolute control of the free state and shall also control the port and railways. These shall be used in accordance with the interests of the city and of the countries whose natural outlet they are. After five years, a plebiscite shall take place, the population

---

[52] Di Cellere, p. 239; Benedetti, *La pace di Fiume*, p. 55.

[53] Benedetti, *op. cit.*, pp. 55-56. Published by the *Vedetta d'Italia* on Feb. 6, 1920.

voting as a whole. If Italy should not accept this plebiscite, the League of Nations shall remain in charge of the free state.

3. If this solution is accepted, the so-called *corpus separatum* could retain the same autonomy which it enjoyed under Hungarian domination; but Italian sovereignty shall never be exercised in any form.

The Serb-Croat-Slovene State shall have Dalmatia in full sovereignty, but the city of Zara shall have a special régime. It shall be declared a free city and the local authorities shall establish in agreement with Yugoslavia the modalities of government. The League shall guarantee this freedom and decide in case of any dispute between the city and Yugoslavia. The city shall choose its own diplomatic representation.

4. The following islands to Italy: the Pelagosa group, Lissa and adjacent islets to the west, Lussin, and Unie.

The Slav population in the Lissa group shall have complete local autonomy under Italian sovereignty.

5. Italy shall have the Albanian mandate, in such terms, however, as to prevent economic and military exploitation of the country or its colonization. The territory around Valona shall be neutralized and the Yugoslavs shall have the right to build and operate railways north of latitude 41° 15'. They shall also have the right to improve the navigation of the Boyana River.

6. The city of Valona, with a very limited hinterland, sufficient only to provide for its essential economic needs and security, shall go to Italy in full sovereignty.

7. Italy shall have the unrestricted right of transit, with adequate guarantees, over the Yugoslav section of the Assling railway.

8. A strip of territory, east of the American line in Istria, shall be neutralized under guarantee of the League. This zone shall include, besides the free State of Fiume, a strip reaching to the Karawanken in the north and including the Assling triangle. The eastern boundary of this strip shall begin at the Austrian frontier, and follow a line running 6 kilometers east of Assling and from there southward to Eisnern, thence towards Poller, Lutschana and Podlipa (running east of these towns), then eastward to join the frontier of the free state, where it is cut by the Laibach-Trieste railway.

All the Dalmatian islands and waters shall be neutralized. There will thus be a neutral strip of islands, sea, and land between Yugoslavia and Italy, extending from Ragusa to the Karawanken. The Italian islands mentioned in 4. shall be included in the neutralized zone.

The American Government considers that no reason of any kind has appeared to modify the above-mentioned points of view, so often and emphatically maintained by President Wilson.

The American Government notes with deep regret that the Italian Government does not seem to realize that the acceptance of an agreement on the basis of the above-mentioned generous and just terms corresponds to its interest; the Italian Government should realize that these are absolutely the last conditions which the American Government is prepared to accept and that the concessions of Albona, Lussin, Unie, and the Albanian mandate are conditional upon the acceptance by the Italian Government of the above terms, without further modifications, as complete and final.

The proposal that Fiume shall have its own status with the changes suggested by Italy, that Italy shall have the diplomatic representation of Zara and the possession of the island of Lagosta (as well as the most recent suggestion of the cession of a strip of land to establish territorial connection between Italy and Fiume) are completely inadmissible, and the suggestion of such modifications has produced the most painful impression on the American Government.[54]

To make even plainer the finality of this communication, Wilson sent a note directly to Nitti in terms which can hardly be called amicable.

I cannot conceal my surprise [said the note], in regard to the new project[55] which the Italian delegation to the Peace Conference has submitted to me. You know that my views on the problem of Fiume are not susceptible of modification. . . .

Any solution of the problem of Fiume at variance with the one which I have advocated, would run counter to the foreign policy which I have pursued. I firmly believe that your doubts in regard to the reaction of the Italian people to a solution of the problem of Fiume other than that advocated by an imperialistic minority have no foundation in fact. The Italian people are not seriously interested in the question of Fiume, but rather in the solution of their major social and economic problems. In any case I regret to have to say that our attitude is not susceptible of any change. I should rather ask of you and your colleagues of the Peace Conference that, for the good of mankind, the Adriatic problem be resolved without further delay. The need of a European readjustment is felt by all the peoples of the world and that country which would prevent this readjustment would compel my country to take unsympathetic measures dictated solely by the irrevocable decision of the Government of my country to

---

[54] *Politica,* IV, 285-87. Condensed and translated by the author; the original English text is not available.

[55] The last project of Tittoni.

assist in the task of economic reconstruction only those countries which adhere to its program.[56]

The last proposal of Tittoni could not have been more decisively disposed of and, in view of this attitude, the negotiation was abandoned.

The attitude of the Allies in regard to the events of Fiume was, on the whole, that they constituted a purely Italian quarrel.[57] Rather than insist on maintaining the Inter-Allied character of the occupation of the city, at Italy's request, the Allies withdrew their troops, the continued presence of which would certainly have led to further friction and regrettable incidents. The naval vessels were likewise withdrawn and, when a cry was raised in Italy because a French vessel remained in the vicinity, it too was ordered away.[58] Toward the beginning of October, however, the British seem to have urged the Italian Government to put an end to the situation in Fiume.[59]

In Fiume itself, d'Annunzio managed to keep up a state of excitement and issued numerous proclamations to the people of the city and of Italy, which often bear witness to his literary skill, if not to his good judgment and taste. On September 20 he notified the country that the National Council of Fiume had "for the third and last time, proclaimed the annexation" of Fiume to Italy.[60] A blockade was enforced at first which soon became existent only in name, so that people came and went without much difficulty from Fiume to Italy and from Italy to Fiume. The situation remained, nevertheless, fraught with danger, especially as an incident might easily occur between d'Annunzio's forces and the Yugoslavs. On October 24 the Belgrade Government issued a decree annexing Sušak, as an indication of its growing impatience. On two occasions d'Annunzio sought to extend his influence beyond Fiume; once at Zara,[61] where he had a friendly reception from Admiral Millo, governor of Dalmatia, and again at Traù. This last town was within the American

---

[56] *Politica*, IV, 287-88. Published in the *Vedetta d'Italia*, Nov. 29, 1919. The Note was dated Nov. 13.

[57] Temperley, IV, 308; "L'Aventure de Fiume," *Revue des deux mondes*, March 1, 1921, pp. 185-87.

[58] Scialoja's speech of July 29, 1921; *Atti del Parlamento, 1921-23, Senato, Discussioni*, I, 200. "L'Aventure de Fiume," *Revue des deux mondes*, March 1, 1921, pp. 185-86.

[59] "L'Aventure de Fiume," *Revue des deux mondes*, March 1, 1921, p. 186.

[60] Benedetti, *La pace di Fiume*, p. 44.

[61] In November. Cf. Temperley, IV, 308.

Armistice zone,[62] and d'Annunzio was given two hours in which to withdraw by the American commander, with which request he found it politic to comply.[63]

The electoral campaign was meantime going on in Italy, and naturally, under the circumstances, the foreign situation played an important part in it. The Adriatic became the rallying cry of the nationalists, but many people were beginning to weary of the continued agitation and uncertainty. To a great extent the press showed signs of assuming a more moderate tone than it had on some previous occasions in the spring and summer. The balloting took place on November 16, under the recently revised and rather complex electoral law. The most interesting feature of the result was the emergence of two large parties: the Socialists increased their membership from 52 to 155, and the newly formed Catholic *Partito Popolare* secured 101 seats; between them, these two parties controlled just over half the total membership of the new chamber. It is not without interest that the nationalists made a very poor showing in the election.

Toward the end of the month, Tittoni, supposedly for reasons of health, relinquished the direction of foreign affairs and the leadership of the Italian delegation at the Peace Conference. Scialoja, who had from the beginning been closely associated with him, took his place. The new chamber convened on December 1, when the King was greeted with a hostile demonstration from the Socialists. However, the Nitti Ministry was continued in office.

Tittoni had had no more success than his predecessor in breaking the deadlock of the Italian question, and the conflict remained as much as ever an Italo-American dispute. The last communication from America showed no trace of yielding on Wilson's part, but rather an increasing impatience which found expression in the blunt statement that "the Italian people are not seriously interested in the question of Fiume," and the plain hint of possible economic reprisals. Tittoni recognized from the first the situation which confronted him, and exerted himself in creating better relations with Great Britain and France. This he did successfully, despite the events

[62] At the time of the Armistice with Austria-Hungary, the Adriatic had been divided into three zones. In the north, the Italians held the coast as far as Cape Planka; the Americans held the middle zone from Cape Planka to east of Slano, and the Southern Adriatic was left to the French.

[63] Temperley, IV, 308.

of Fiume, as is clearly shown by the difference between the note which greeted his first arrival in Paris and the support which his successive projects received from the Allies. However, as he said himself, the Allies would support him only up to the point where they themselves would come into conflict with the United States, upon whose favor they too were dependent. Since Wilson would not move, Tittoni was willing to make concessions, and there was little left in November of the original provisions of the Treaty of London. The difference was clearly and definitely whittled down to Fiume itself. But that last obstacle proved insuperable and, even had Tittoni been disposed to yield on it, the seizure of the city by d'Annunzio shut the door on that possibility, for the Government did not have the necessary strength to take the risks of military action.

X

THE NEGOTIATIONS FROM DECEMBER, 1919, TO MAY, 1920

SCIALOJA WAS IN a good position to resume negotiations, having been second ranking member of the Italian delegation while Tittoni was its head. The final touches were being put to the Hungarian Treaty when he arrived in Paris; the frontiers of the new Hungary had been announced long since, with the natural implication that Hungary was to be deprived of the territories which lay outside of these frontiers. In the case of areas which had not been definitely assigned to another state, the customary formula adopted by the Council had been renunciation of sovereignty in favor of the Principal Allied and Associated Powers, who were consequently free to decide the ultimate disposition of the territories in question. However, in view of the special circumstances in the case of Fiume, the American representative proposed that Hungary renounce her sovereignty in favor of the Principal Allied and Associated Powers and of the Serb-Croat-Slovene Kingdom. Scialoja definitely refused to accept this variation. Finally, a compromise solution was proposed by Scialoja and accepted by the Council, in the form of renunciation pure and simple.[1] Scialoja's reasoning was that, by such a renunciation, without specific transfer of sovereignty, the *corpus separatum*, endowed as it was of separate autonomous status, became a sovereign entity. This would, in turn, enable it to choose its own sovereignty.[2]

THE MEMORANDUM OF DECEMBER 9, 1919

Lansing had rejected Tittoni's last proposal and, when Scialoja arrived in Paris—Nitti was detained in Rome—he found that Polk

[1] Treaty of Trianon, Article 53: "Hungary renounces all rights and title over Fiume and the adjoining territories which belonged to the former Kingdom of Hungary and which lie within the boundaries which may subsequently be fixed."

[2] Actually, this was intended to bolster the juridical significance of Fiume's demand for annexation to Italy, and to strengthen the contention that there was no inconsistency in the Italian demand for Fiume in addition to the Treaty of London. The one was an application of the principle of self-determination, the other merely the fulfillment of a contract.

The weakness of the contention need not be emphasized; the issue remained between the Fourteen Points and the secret treaties as bases of the Peace Treaties, and Scialoja's legal fiction did not carry much weight with the Allies. Cf. Scialoja's speech in the Senate of July 29, 1920; also, Giannini, *Fiume nel Trattato di Trianon*.

was about to return to America,[3] leaving the American Ambassador in Paris more as an observer than as a plenipotentiary, and that Great Britain was suggesting adjourning the Conference. Under these circumstances, the representatives of the United States, Great Britain, and France had decided to draw up a memorandum summing up the Italian negotiations to date, partly to keep the issue alive, and, to some extent, in the hope that the Italian problem might be settled before the Conference should break up. Clemenceau mentioned this memorandum to Scialoja, adding that it was not intended by way of exerting pressure on Italy.[4] Scialoja then went to London, where, on December 8, he and the Italian Ambassador had a meeting with Lord Curzon. At this meeting, Curzon indicated the contents of the proposed memorandum and expressed the hope that it might lead to a solution. Scialoja pointed out that no essential concession was being made to the Italian point of view in regard to Fiume, and that Italian security would be jeopardized by leaving Cattaro and Sebenico in the hands of the Yugoslavs. Curzon explained that it was desirable to clarify the issue by a definite statement, which was the purpose of the note, rather than to have Scialoja travel from one capital to another in search of compromises. Scialoja finally acceded, but made three requests: (1) That the note itself and even the fact of its presentation be kept secret, lest opinion in Italy regard it as an ultimatum; (2) That his Government be at liberty to reply; (3) That the note be regarded as a step in the discussion and not as a last word. Curzon transmitted these requests to Crowe in Paris, instructing him that he was "at liberty to sign and to join in the presentation of the note on these conditions; if your colleagues disagree you should abstain."[5] Crowe reported that Clemenceau and Polk found no difficulty in accepting Scialoja's conditions, and Clemenceau gave instructions to prevent any divulgations.[6]

[3] He left on December 10.

[4] Scialoja's speech of Dec. 20, 1919. *Atti del Parlamento, 1919-21, Camera, Discussioni,* I, 496. The note grew out of discussions between members of the American and British delegations and of exchanges between the former and Washington. A first draft was agreed upon by Bowman and Leeper, to which the consent of Lloyd George and Clemenceau was obtained, and the final text was finally approved after Clemenceau had made some minor alterations in it and changed a paragraph that might have hurt Italian sensibilities.

[5] Curzon to Crowe, Dec. 8, 1919. This and subsequent documents in this chapter are quoted from the United States State Department publication, *The Adriatic Question,* issued April 12, 1920. There occur in this publication several instances of careless editing; however, the same documents are also to be found in a British White Paper (Cmd. 586, Parl. Papers. Misc. No. 2, 1920). The Italian version is given by Giannini, *L'Italia alla conferenza della pace.*

[6] Crowe to Curzon, Dec. 9, 1919. *The Adriatic Question,* p. 49.

Lloyd George himself gave Scialoja the same assurances, that the note was merely intended to make a fresh start, and they were repeated once more when the note was delivered in London on December 9.[7]

The note[8] stated that the move was prompted by a desire to reach an agreement on the Adriatic question before adjourning the Conference. Great Britain and France had refrained from offering any advice to Italy during the Tittoni negotiations, in the hope that these would lead to a direct agreement with Wilson. This having failed to materialize, they felt that the differences had, in the meantime, been so whittled down that they were justified in hoping that a complete accord would now be reached. The note went on to summarize what it described as the points of agreement "embodied in the American memorandum communicated to the Italian delegation in Paris on October 27."

These were:

Istria.—The frontier to run from the River Arsa to the Karawanken Mountains, incorporating in Italy more than 300,000 Yugoslavs. President Wilson had consented from the first to this infringement of the ethnic principle, on account of strategic and economic considerations. He was further willing to move the frontier eastward so as to include in Italy the region of Albona, despite its considerable Slav population.

State of Fiume.—To give Italy still further protection, President Wilson and the Italian Government had agreed to the formation of a buffer state of Fiume including some 200,000 Yugoslavs and 40,000 Italians, under the control of the League of Nations. The three Governments had agreed that the Assling triangle should be permanently demilitarized and their representatives would be happy to know whether the Italian Government desired any modification of the demilitarized zone between the Arsa River and Cape Promontore.

Despite the overwhelming Yugoslav majority of the free state of Fiume, which would demand that its population be allowed to express its wishes through a plebiscite, it was agreed, in deference to Italian representations, that the future of the state should be left in the hands of the League of Nations, which would further insure

[7] Clemenceau had gone to London. Cf. Scialoja's speech of Dec. 20, 1919. A further account of the discussions was given by Scialoja in a speech before the Senate on July 20, 1920. Giannini, *op. cit.*, pp. 53-54.

[8] *The Adriatic Question*, pp. 2-11.

Fiume the same degree of autonomy it had enjoyed under Austro-Hungarian rule.

Dalmatia.—The three representatives were glad to record the abandonment by Italy of her claim to Dalmatia. However, Zara was to be given complete freedom to control its affairs under the League, provided it were left within the Yugoslav customs union.

Islands.—The same wisdom that prevailed in regard to Dalmatia had recognized the necessity of political union of the islands with the Yugoslav State. However, for strategic reasons, the following islands had been accorded to Italy on a demilitarized status: (1) the Pelagosa group, (2) Lissa and adjacent islets, (3) Lussin and Unie. These were to be under full Italian sovereignty, and Italy was to grant their Slav population local autonomy.

Albania and Valona.—Italy was to receive the Albanian mandate. (A suggested form of the mandate was attached to the memorandum.) In the north and east, the frontiers should be those fixed by the London Conference of 1913; the southern frontier was still subject to negotiation. However, to avoid delaying a general settlement, a provisional line of demarcation was indicated.

The city of Valona, together with such hinterland as might be strictly necessary for its defense and its economic development, was to be given to Italy in full sovereignty.

"The above six points . . ." said the note, "are those on which, after many months' negotiation, the Italian Government have happily reached an agreement with the President of the United States."[9] Pointing to the magnitude and value of the concessions made to Italy, who had achieved her historic national aspirations, as well as security from aggression, the three representatives asked the Italian Government to reflect on these great advantages.

Beyond that, "anxious to give the most sympathetic consideration to every Italian interest or sentiment, the three representatives have carefully examined in all their bearings certain further demands which the Italian Government have presented."

The note went on to consider these further demands under four heads.

1. Control by Italy of the diplomatic relations of Zara.

This ought to offer no difficulty, since it was already conceded

---

[9] This statement seems rather surprising, in view of the rejection of the last two Tittoni proposals. Albania and Valona account for the last two points.

that—except for incorporation in the Yugoslav customs union—the city would be completely independent under the League of Nations. If, as claimed, the city was completely Italian, its own choice would therefore meet this demand.

2. An arrangement by which the *corpus separatum* of Fiume should be dissociated from the free state of Fiume and made completely independent, although its port and railway should be left to the free state.

This demand has been found seriously perplexing. The creation of a buffer state had the double object of safeguarding Italian security and the prosperity and development of Fiume.[10] To separate Fiume from the rest of the free state would result in crippling both, and would open to question the very creation of a buffer state wholly inhabited by Yugoslavs. With this in mind, as well as the sentimental attachment to Fiume, it was proposed to give the city the same degree of autonomy as it had under Austro-Hungarian rule. Sovereignty vested in the League—on the Council of which, Italy would, moreover, be represented—should suffice to guarantee full protection to the Italian ethnic and cultural interests in Fiume.

3. Direct connection of the city of Fiume with the Italian province of Istria by the annexation to Italy of a long narrow strip of coast from Fiume to Volosca between the railway and the sea, the Italian frontier being pushed eastward so as to include the whole peninsula within Italy.[11]

This demand was said to have been made for purely sentimental reasons. It was pointed out that Italy had a long land frontier with the proposed free state, which was created, in part, with the object of safeguarding the position of Fiume. The physical difficulty and the uselessness of cutting off a barren sand beach—since the railroad ran for a considerable distance along the coast—thus causing great injury to the free state, which would be deprived of its coast line, was emphasized. Summing up, "the plan appears to run counter to every consideration of geography, economics, and territorial convenience and it may perhaps be assumed that if these considerations

[10] Strictly speaking, this was hardly correct. The idea of a buffer state represented a compromise between the Italian determination that Fiume should not be Yugoslav—if it could not be Italian—and Wilson's equally firm resolve that it should not be Italian—if it could not be Yugoslav.

[11] This very demand was a confutation of the agreement on Istria, mentioned earlier in the memorandum.

were overlooked by the Italian Government this was due to their having connected it in their mind with the question of annexing to Italy all that remains of the Jugoslav portion of the peninsula of Istria."

4. Annexation of Lagosta.

This demand, like the demand for a strip of coast adjacent to Fiume was not justified by either economic or strategic reasons. As to the latter, Italy had secure control of the Adriatic with the possession of Trieste, Pola, the islands facing Fiume, Pelagosa, and Valona, besides the proposed demilitarization of the free state and of a zone to the north of it. This demand could only arise from a desire for further territory, as these territories were admittedly Yugoslav and contained practically no Italian elements. This being so, the demand was met by a reference—in the form of a quotation from Lansing's last note to Tittoni of November 12—to the way in which President Wilson, with the cordial approval of Great Britain and France, had met every successive Italian demand for the absorption into Italy of territories not Italian and not in favor of being absorbed.

The note went on to remind Italy of the achievement of her own national unity, which had been followed with sympathy by liberty-loving peoples, and pointed out that "to annex as the spoils of war territories inhabited by an alien race, anxious and capable to maintain a separate national state, [. . . would be to create within the Italian borders a compact body] of irredentism exactly analogous in kind to that which justified the demand of Italia Irredenta for union with the Italian State."[12] For this reason, "the three representatives venture with all deference to express the opinion that in declining to agree to the incorporation of more Jugoslav territory, they are acting in the highest interest of the Italian nation itself." The recent attitude of moderation of the Italian Government led the three representatives to believe that their appeal for a prompt settlement would not pass unheeded.

The last part of the note was taken up with Albania.

The three Governments were anxious to give Italy the Albanian mandate, under the conditions implied in the covenant of the League of Nations. They considered that these conditions should be incorporated in a convention to be concluded between the Italian Gov-

---

[12] Quotation restored from the British paper; several lines are missing in the American version.

ernment and the Governments of the Principal Allied and Associated Powers, under the following heads:

1. Albania to be recognized as an independent state (its frontiers were indicated in a covering memorandum). However, it should be left free to negotiate with Yugoslavia rectifications of frontiers for local ethnic or economic reasons.

2. Yugoslavia should have the right to construct and to operate railways through Northern Albania north of latitude 41°15′.

3. The right to control the development of the Boyana River should be vested in the Council of the League of Nations, which might delegate the work either to Italy or to Yugoslavia. It was assumed that Montenegro would form a part of Yugoslavia.

4. A commission should be established consisting of one representative each of the Italian Government, the League of Nations, and Albania—this last named to be designated by the Principal Allied and Associated Powers—for the purpose of elaborating: (a) the terms of the mandate; (b) the organization of the future state of Albania. This commission should terminate its labors within five months of the signature of the present convention and should report to the Council of the League of Nations, which should decide by majority vote on the terms of the mandate and the organization.

5. The commission should also base its deliberations on the following principles:

(a) Freedom of conscience and worship, and complete liberty in education and linguistic matters for all the inhabitants.

(b) The organization, so far as possible, of legislative and administrative bodies representative of all sections of the population.

(c) Prevention of the exploitation or colonization of the country in a manner injurious to the interests of the population.

(d) Eventual creation of a *gendarmerie* whose senior officers might be nationals of the mandatory Power. After a period of two years Albania should be permanently demilitarized and no Power should be allowed to maintain regular forces in the country without the sanction of the Council of the League of Nations.

The note was signed by Clemenceau, Crowe, and Polk.[13]

[13] *The Adriatic Question*, pp. 2-11. Owing to the length of the memorandum, only the above condensation is given. It will be noticed that this memorandum deals solely with the Adriatic. Colonial questions were the object of direct negotiations between Italy and Great Britain and France respectively, while Asia Minor was on the agenda for the near future.

Despite Scialoja's request for secrecy, the fact that he had received a note became known and, in the absence of precise information, the rumor was spread in Italy that the Allies were exerting pressure on her for a settlement. The note was indeed, on the whole, an espousal of the American position, and Scialoja would have been hard put to it to defend it at home had its contents been made public. To allay disquiet, one of his first tasks on his return to Rome, on December 18, was to give the Chamber an explanation. He recited the circumstances of his conversations in London and laid stress on the verbal assurances given him by Lloyd George, Clemenceau, and Curzon, which, he claimed, had equal weight with the written memorandum—he insisted that it was merely an *aide-mémoire*, not a formal note—and were evidence of the fact that Great Britain and France were willing to make some departure from the American position in meeting Italy's demands. From the nature of the case, his defense was weak, and his assurances were received with only moderate satisfaction by the deputies. Skillfully, he took refuge behind a formula that satisfied Italian *amour-propre* without excluding the possibility of compromise. The Italian demands were, he said: a guarantee of the *italianità* of Fiume; protection (*tutela*) of the Italians of Dalmatia, and security in the Adriatic.[14] All these demands were evidently susceptible of various definitions.

Some difficulty was caused by Clemenceau's account in the French Chamber on December 24. Clemenceau referred to the note as an important document and the greatest effort up to that time to solve the Adriatic question.[15] This aroused much comment in Italy, and Scialoja had to enlarge his defense before the Senate on December 30. He again sought to minimize the importance of the note and explained away Clemenceau's statements by saying that they referred, not only to the contents of the note, but also to the verbal discussions which had taken place in connection with its delivery; and these discussions, he insisted, modified considerably the contents of the note. For that reason, he said, the note had taken largely the form of a recapitulation of the American and the Italian positions.[16]

[14] Scialoja's speech of Dec. 20, 1919. *Atti del Parlamento, 1919-21, Camera, Discussioni*, I, 497.

[15] Clemenceau also repeated the charge of inconsistency between the Italian demands for both Fiume and for the Treaty of London.

[16] Scialoja's speech of Dec. 30, 1919. Giannini, *L'Italia alla conferenza della pace*, pp. 61-65.

The Italian Reply

Eventually, an equally lengthy and closely reasoned memorandum was submitted by the Italians, under date of January 10, 1920, in reply to the memorandum of December 9.[17]

By way of introduction, the Italian note remarked that, while various proposals had been made with a view to reaching a compromise, failing agreement, no understanding had been arrived at between the Italian Government and the Allied and Associated Powers. It then went on to consider the individual items of the memorandum of December 9.

Free State of Fiume.—Such a proposal had never been offered by the Italians; rather, they had always considered that this state would consist of two unrelated elements, the Italian city of Fiume and the Slav remainder. For this reason, special guarantees were necessary for the protection of Fiume, greater than the mere status it had had under Hungary. The American refusal to grant such guarantees had made agreement impossible.

Istrian frontier.—The so-called American line, even if shifted to include Albona in Italy, would be totally inadequate to secure the military defense of Trieste, Istria, and Pola against the range of modern artillery. The line was only eighteen kilometers from Trieste and twenty-two kilometers from the advanced defense of Pola.

Fiume.—The Note to Article 5 of the Treaty of London—quoted in the memorandum—foresaw the attribution of certain territories to the three distinct states of Croatia, Serbia, and Montenegro. The formation in their place of a large single Yugoslav State altered the terms of the problem. The specific mention of the "Port of Fiume" suggested that special treatment was intended for the city. Large sections of Hungary had been taken away from that country, on the basis of the principle of self-determination. The application of this principle could not be denied to Fiume. The Italian Government was obliged to voice the will of Italian Fiume, and this had nothing to do with the Treaty of London.

Contiguity of the corpus separatum with Italy.—The arguments presented in the note of December 9 did not seem sufficient to out-

---

[17] Drafted by Scialoja of Jan. 3, but not presented until the tenth. *The Adriatic Question,* pp. 39-47. Like the memorandum of Dec. 9, this Italian Note is summarized in the following.

weigh the consideration that Fiume and the *corpus separatum* needed such a direct contact lest they be wholly surrounded by Slav populations, not to mention the sentimental considerations which the note of December 9 acknowledged. Moreover, Article 4 of the Treaty of London itself provided for the contiguity of the *corpus separatum* with Italy. The latest Italian proposal, by confining its claim to the territory between the railroad and the sea, constituted the relinquishment of a large section of territory north of that strip. As to the objections based on the physical configuration of the area, they related only to modalities and could be taken care of by special arrangements.

Again it was pointed out that Italy had made no official waiver of her claims under the Treaty of London.[18]

Dalmatia and the islands.—The suggestion of the note of December 9 that the Italian claim was based on an unwarranted desire for territory was rejected. The claim was rather founded on strategic considerations. The offer of the Allied and Associated Powers would improve the situation only in the northern Adriatic, and even then, the proposed frontier in Istria would destroy the value of Pola as a naval base, for Monte Maggiore, Cherso, and Lussin were an essential part of the defensive system of Pola. The Treaty of London gave Cherso to Italy for this very reason. As to Valona, while useful in controlling the entrance to the Adriatic, it could not serve as a base from which to defend the Italian coast, which would be at the mercy of Cattaro and Sebenico. Lissa could not become a naval base, even if exempted from the demilitarization demanded by Mr. Lansing. It must also be pointed out that neutralization and demilitarization—especially if limited to the islands and waters—were by no means synonymous, as the drafters of the note of December 9 seemed to think. The latter would not preclude preparations for attack on the mainland. Moreover, demilitarization ceasing north of Ragusa, Cattaro would still remain a menace. The Italian delegation must therefore insist on neutralization.

[18] Scialoja had made the same point in his speech of Dec. 30: the offer of certain concessions in the course of a discussion did not amount to relinquishment of a claim. The fact remains that the making of such an offer is an indication of what the maker will yield; on the other hand, such yielding is evidently contingent on the acceptance of the remainder of the claim by the other side. Both sides had evidenced a tendency to disregard this element in the negotiations between the Italians and the Americans during the spring of 1919, each considering as settled any suggested concession by the other, and attempting to extract piecemeal concessions by this method.

Albania.—There was agreement except for the southern frontier. Here it was proposed that a representative of Greece and one of Albania be allowed to argue the case before the representatives of the United States, Great Britain, France, and Italy who could then make an award or resort to a plebiscite. Any Albanian territory and coast ceded to Greece should be neutralized.[19]

THE NITTI COMPROMISE

From the beginning of 1920, the Peace Conference may be considered adjourned. However, there remained not a few matters calling for negotiation and consultation among the Powers, not least the Adriatic question. The Council of Foreign Ministers continued in existence, but it was evidently not practical for the various Foreign Ministers to remain indefinitely away from their respective capitals. Henceforth, the work was to be done in a long series of numerous conferences, meeting at intervals in a variety of places. The first of these took place in Paris in January, and concerned itself to a considerable extent with the Italian problem.

After receiving the note of December 9, Scialoja had returned to Rome to consult with Nitti on the course to be adopted. While he drew up the reply just outlined, Nitti himself went to London at the beginning of January, and, after a meeting with Lloyd George on January 6, sent him the following memorandum:

Italy asks for the fulfillment of the Pact of London.

In order to eliminate the difficulties subsequently arisen and to reach a general agreement without any further delay the Italian Government is prepared to accept the following compromise:

1. Free state of Fiume according to Wilson's plan, but with the frontier of the Pact of London in its southwestern part towards Italy.

2. But in the free state, the city of Fiume with its district *corpus separatum*, must be guaranteed by a statute efficaciously safeguarding its 'italianità,' which, owing to the great Slav majority in the free state, would be more threatened than it was under Hungary.

3. To the *corpus separatum* of Fiume within the free state must be assigned the road to the west with the surrounding strip of territory up to the Italian frontier.

4. The islands of Cherso and Lagosta, besides those already assigned by Wilson, to be assigned to Italy.

5. Zara, free town, with freedom to select its diplomatic representation,

[19] Italian memorandum of Jan. 10, 1920. *The Adriatic Question*, pp. 39-47.

guarantees for the relations of the citizens of Zara with the Dalmatian territory.

6. Effective neutralization of the islands and also of the whole coast and of the ports of the eastern Adriatic coast from Fiume down to the mouth of the Vojussa.

7. The Italians of the cities of Fiume and Dalmatia to have the freedom of choosing Italian citizenship without leaving the territory.

8. Guarantees for the existing economic enterprises in Dalmatia.[20]

Nitti's note was promptly answered by a joint memorandum of Clemenceau and Lloyd George, dated January 9.

This memorandum stated that Great Britain and France

are prepared, should the Italian Government require it, to abide by the terms of the Treaty they have signed. If, however, the Italian Government agree in thinking that, owing to the disappearance of the Hapsburg monarchy, the rise of national states in its place, the great uprising of Italian feeling in Fiume, and the other great events which have occurred since 1915, the Treaty of London no longer constitutes a satisfactory settlement of the Adriatic question, they are willing, subject to the amendments set forth below, to adopt as the basis of settlement the memorandum presented to Signor Scialoja by the representatives of France, the United States of America, and Great Britain, on December 9, 1919, and modified by proposals made to them by Signor Nitti on January 5, 1920.

The eight points of Nitti's communication were then answered as follows:

1. There should be constituted a "free state of Fiume according to President Wilson's plan," but the southern end of the western frontier of this state should be moved eastward in accordance with the Italian demand. The railway must be left wholly within the free state.

2. The city of Fiume with the *corpus separatum* should be guaranteed by a statute safeguarding its 'italianità.' This would be attained by giving the *corpus separatum* the same degree of autonomy it had had under Austro-Hungarian rule. The privileges of the free state, of the *corpus separatum*, and the international character of the port should be guaranteed by the League of Nations.

3. Cherso, owing to its predominantly Slav population, should not be separated from the free state. However, Lagosta could be ceded to Italy if it were a strategic necessity.

4. The free state of Zara should be governed by a high commissioner, advised by a council representative of the population, which should

select its diplomatic representation. It should be within the Yugoslav customs union.

5. The islands should be neutralized. However, neutralization of the Dalmatian mainland could hardly be imposed on a friendly state as it would interfere with measures of self-defence.

6. The Italians of Dalmatia should be free to choose Italian citizenship without leaving the territory, but the arrangement could not be extended to the citizens of Fiume.

7. Existing economic enterprises in Dalmatia should be safeguarded by international convention.

8. The boundaries of Albania should be discussed.

After pointing to the magnitude of the concessions forced upon Yugoslavia, the note concluded:

The British and French Governments are prepared to ask the Serb-Croat-Slovene state to make these great concessions for the sake of an amicable and prompt settlement of a question which now threatens the peace and progress of southern Europe. But they can go no further and they earnestly trust that the conference and the Italian Government will accept them.[21]

A considerable step forward had now been made. Great Britain and France had taken the matter in their own hands, justifying Scialoja's contention that they were willing to depart to some extent from the American position, in the hope that Wilson would not refuse to recognize an agreement come to by all the European states involved.[22] The two Governments formally recognized the validity of the Treaty of London, but with the tacit implication that its strict enforcement was incompatible with concessions in Fiume.[23] On the other hand, they were willing to grant the main debated point of territorial contiguity of Italy with the *corpus separatum*, and to sponsor such an arrangement in Belgrade. The prospects of agreement must therefore have seemed promising at this time.

In accordance with these developments, the following proposals, somewhat condensed here, were presented by Clemenceau to the Yugoslav delegates[24] in Paris on January 13:

[21] Franco-British memorandum of Jan. 9, 1920. *The Adriatic Question*, pp. 11-13. The statement of the answer to the eight points is condensed.

[22] Scialoja's speeches of Dec. 20 and 30, 1919.

[23] Scialoja's speech of July 20, 1920, implies that the reservation was stated during the discussions.

[24] Pašić, Trumbić, and the Prince Regent Alexander were in Paris at this time.

1. The *Corpus Separatum* of Fiume shall be under Italian sovereignty. Sušak shall go to Yugoslavia. The whole port with the facilities for its development as well as for that of the railway shall be handed over to the League who shall take into consideration the interests of the Serb-Croat-Slovene State as well as those of Hungary, Transylvania and the city itself.

2. The proposed free state of previous proposals shall disappear. The boundary between Italy and Yugoslavia shall be drawn so as to satisfy the following conditions:

(a) to provide a road connection with Fiume along the coast within Italian territory, but leaving the railway from Fiume through Adelsberg within Yugoslavia.

(b) a readjustment of the Wilson line in the region of Senosecchia to provide for the protection of Trieste.

(c) the boundary line indicated on attached map.

3. Zara, within the limits of its municipality, shall constitute an independent state, under guarantee of the League of Nations, with the right to choose its diplomatic representation.

4. Italy shall retain Valona and receive the mandate over Albania. Northern Albania (shown on an attached map) shall constitute an autonomous province of Yugoslvia under a régime similar to that of the autonomous provinces of Czechoslovakia.[25] The southern boundary of Albania shall be the line proposed by the French and British in the commission on Greek affairs, leaving Koritsa and Argyrokastro to Greece.

5. The following island groups to Italy: Lussin, Lissa, and Pelagosa.

6. All Adriatic islands shall be demilitarized.

7. Special provisions allowing the Italians in Dalmatia to choose Italian nationality without leaving the country.

8. An international convention safeguarding the security of existing economic enterprises in Dalmatia.[26]

The salient points of this scheme, known from its originator as the Nitti Compromise, were the abandonment of the buffer state and the partition of Albania.

[25] This was to enable Yugoslavia to build and operate the railroad from Prizrend to Scutari and San Giovanni di Medua. Cf. Temperley, IV, 343.

[26] Adriaticus, *La Question adriatique*, Document XXIV. On Jan. 8 the Yugoslavs had sent to the Conference a note containing their observations on the arrangements proposed in the memorandum of Dec. 9, and offering their own suggestions. Cf. Adriaticus, *op. cit.*, Document XXI. This note was, however, superseded by the proposal just outlined and their reply thereto.

The Yugoslav Replies

The next day, January 14, Pašić and Trumbić submitted their reply. It may be summarized as follows:

1. Italian sovereignty over the *corpus separatum* cannot be accepted. Neither the Tittoni project nor the last vote in the Italian Parliament demanded it.

2. Fiume should not be joined to Italy by a corridor. The memorandum of December 9 rejected this demand. The Wilson line must be the Italo-Yugoslav frontier.

3. The city of Zara (not the municipality) will receive, under Yugoslav sovereignty, wide local autonomy under an international convention and will be under protection of the League.

4. In the event that Italy receives Valona and the Albanian mandate and Southern Albania goes to Greece, Yugoslavia should have, besides Northern Albania, a rectification of the Serbo-Albanian frontier in the east.

5. The islands could be demilitarized if they are attributed to Yugoslavia. However, war vessels may freely enter their waters.

6 and 7. Accept 7 and 8 of the Council's proposals.

8. Italy shall guarantee the protection of the nationality, language, and of the economic and cultural development of the Yugoslavs in her territory.[27]

This Yugoslav reply practically amounted to complete refusal, and there could be little hope of bridging the difference between it and the Council's offer in a short time. However, the Yugoslavs were dealing at the moment with a united British-French-Italian front. In the afternoon of the same day a set of "revised proposals" was handed to them by Clemenceau. These were identical with the offer of the preceding day save on one point. The *corpus separatum*, instead of being under Italian sovereignty, was to form an independent state with the choice of its diplomatic representation.[28] Undoubtedly as the result of pressure during the next few days,[29] another reply was forthcoming from the Yugoslavs, still wide of

[27] *Ibid.*, Document XXV.
[28] *Ibid.*, Document XXVI.
[29] According to Temperley (IV, 319, n. 1), Professor Sišić's work, *Jadransko Pitanje na Konferenciji mira u Parizu*, gives accounts of the conversations with Pašić and Trumbić on Jan. 13, 14 and 20.

acceptance of the Nitti Compromise, but couched in an entirely different tone.

1. The independence of Fiume was accepted in principle. However, it emphasized the points that the port and railway must be the property of the League of Nations, and it was demanded that they be placed under Yugoslav management, with the right to develop them. Sušak and Porto Baross would go outright to Yugoslavia.

2. The claim for an extension eastward of the Italian frontier was rejected. The American line, starting at the Arsa River, already put 40,000 (*sic*) Yugoslavs in Italy, and as to the proposal for the annexation of a strip of land between the railroad and the coast, the memorandum of December 9 had sufficiently emphasized the difficulties which such an arrangement would create. Moreover, the fifty kilometers of coast line from the Arsa to Volosca would give Italy control of the Gulf of Fiume, an essential outlet of Yugoslav trade. The proposed rectification in the Senosecchia region was wholly in Yugoslav territory and would bring the Italian frontier within five or six kilometers of the St. Peter junction, thus constituting a menace to the Vienna railroad.

3. The independence of Zara was accepted, but for the city only, not for the whole commune. The diplomatic representation of Zara as well as of Fiume should be left to the League of Nations, for giving it to Italy would amount to a disguised annexation.

4. For Albania, it would have been preferable to maintain it as an autonomous state with the boundaries of 1913 and without the interference of any outside Power. However, if partition were insisted upon, the frontiers of Northern Albania would have to be modified (as shown on an attached map). The districts thus detached from Albania would have the same status as the autonomous province of Ruthenia.

5. The demilitarization of the islands was agreed to, provided Lissa should be Yugoslav. Italy would receive Lussin and Pelagosa, which should also be demilitarized. Demilitarization should mean the interdiction of fortifications, but allow the free movement of war vessels.

6 and 7. The option of Italian nationality for Italian residents of Dalmatia, and the guarantee of their economic enterprises were accepted.

8. Protection was demanded for the Yugoslavs in Italy in regard to nationality, language, economic and intellectual development.

9. Italy and Yugoslavia should be authorized to proceed immediately to the division of the Austro-Hungarian commercial fleet on the basis of the decision of the Supreme Council of November 22, 1919. As to the war fleet, certain ships mentioned in letters of June 2, 1919, and January 8, 1920, should be attributed to Yugoslavia.[30]

For all practical purposes, the Yugoslavs had taken no part in the Adriatic discussions since the arrival of the second Italian delegation, in June, 1919, until the current negotiation. Even before Wilson's return to the United States, the discussion had been largely an Italo-American debate, with occasional French and British intervention. Thereafter, Tittoni had had some success in bringing the French and the British closer to his position, but first Lansing, then Polk, had still defended the American point of view. With Polk gone and Wilson ill in Washington, Nitti had proceeded on the assumption that the problem could be settled between the three main European Allies, and had at last succeeded in coming to terms with Great Britain and France. However, this did not prove sufficient to end the resistance of the Yugoslavs, as shown by their reply to the Nitti Compromise.

The Council's Attempted Ultimatum

This reply was taken up at once by the Council. At the afternoon meeting on January 20, Clemenceau, in the presence of Lloyd George and Ambassador Wallace, told Pašić that the Yugoslav objections could not be entertained. He seems to have defended the proffered compromise in strong terms, and gave the Yugoslavs four days in which to declare their acceptance, failing which Great Britain and France had authorized Italy to enforce the Treaty of London.[31] Thus pressed, the Yugoslavs played for time. The original delay of four days was extended to eight, at the end of which came their reply. It was skillfully couched in conciliatory but evasive language. The Yugoslav Government considered the communication of January 20 as a friendly proposal rather than as an ultimatum to be

[30] Wallace to Lansing, Jan. 23, 1920. *The Adriatic Question*, pp. 15-18. The memorandum, of which the above is a condensation, was submitted by Trumbić on Jan. 20. The figure 40,000 in point 2 is obviously a misprint for 400,000.

[31] Temperley, IV, 318-19; Franco-British note to Wilson of Feb. 17, 1920; Adriaticus, *La Question adriatique*, p. 116.

answered immediately. This was the first official proposal submitted to them since the beginning of the Conference, and it would hardly be reasonable to demand an immediate answer to proposals of such far-reaching consequences. The Yugoslav Government therefore pleaded for more time, while pointing out that the proposed settlement was somewhat at variance with the principles proclaimed by the Peace Conference, whereas the Yugoslavs had always shown a spirit of conciliation in their repeated offers to submit to arbitration or plebiscite, solutions which they were still ready to accept. But, in any event, the Yugoslav Government failed to see how it could be presented with the alternative of a settlement negotiated by other parties and of the terms of which it had not even been informed.[32] The request for the text of the Treaty of London could hardly be refused. Meanwhile Clemenceau's public career came to an end,[33] and internal complications in the form of a cabinet crisis in Belgrade afforded an opportunity for further delays. The Yugoslavs were not, perhaps, without hope that what had been their best defense in the past might once more be brought into play.

THE LAST AMERICAN INTERVENTION

For, as it turned out, the absence of an American delegate from the Council sessions did not mean that Wilson had renounced intervention in European questions. On January 19, Ambassador Wallace received instructions from the State Department to inquire from Clemenceau and Lloyd George what was being done about the Russian and Italian problems, and whether it was the intention of Great Britain and France to dispose of European problems and merely communicate the results to the United States. "There are features in connection with the proposed Fiume settlement which both M. Clemenceau and Mr. Lloyd George must realize would not be acceptable to the President."[34]

The reply to this inquiry was given by Lord Derby[35] to Ambassador Wallace for reference to Washington. It disclaimed any inten-

[32] Adriaticus, op. cit., Document XXX. The nature, even the text, of the Treaty of London were matters of public knowledge. The request of the Yugoslav Government was technically justified, however, by the fact that the Treaty had never been officially published, nor formally communicated to them.

[33] He resigned at this time and was succeeded by Millerand.

[34] Lansing to Wallace, Jan. 19, 1920. The Adriatic Question, p. 14. While we have no documentary evidence of this, it is not unreasonable to assume that the Yugoslavs had been active in Washington.

[35] British Ambassador in Paris.

tion of ignoring the United States, but pointed out that Nitti had made certain proposals in reply to the joint note of December 9, and explained that the presence of the Prime Ministers in Paris had made it possible to carry on discussions. To refer every step to Washington and wait for a reply would simply have nullified the value of the Paris Conference, while there was every reason to proceed with dispatch. There was no other solution but to proceed as they had done and inform the United States as soon as definite conclusions had been reached. They felt that their proposal was the best available reconciliation of the Italian and Yugoslav points of view. Moreover, they claimed, only two features of the memorandum of December 9 had been modified, and these to the advantage of Yugoslavia.

1. By abolishing the free state and modifying the Italian frontier, some 18,000 additional Yugoslavs had been incorporated into Italy, but, as against this, three-quarters of the 200,000 Yugoslavs who would have been in the proposed free state would now be definitely united to Yugoslavia.

2. As to Albania, the proposal represented a compromise, attempting to satisfy the requirements of all the parties concerned. The details of administration had still to be settled, and, in the process of doing this, the feelings and interests of the Albanian people would not be lost sight of.[36]

This was clearly an understatement. While it was true that Nitti had made some concessions, the Yugoslavs had been confronted with what was essentially an Anglo-Franco-Italian agreement, and certainly the Albanian people had not been consulted. Nor, as we have seen, were Wilson's misgiving as to the method of procedure wholly without foundation.[37]

Wilson's Note of February 9

Both Italy and Yugoslavia now dropped out of the picture and the Adriatic problem turned into a controversy between the United

---

[36] Wallace to Lansing, Jan. 23, 1920. *The Adriatic Question*, pp. 18-20.

[37] This, of course, did not impair the contention that such an agreement was the only way of ever reaching a settlement, a view held by many since the beginning of the controversy. The alternative of unqualified espousal of the American point of view by Great Britain and France was hardly practical, with the Italians in occupation of Dalmatia and d'Annunzio in Fiume. On the other hand again, these arguments had little to do with abstract "justice" in the case.

States on one side and Great Britain and France on the other. The Franco-British reply of January 23 did not prove at all satisfactory and drew from Wilson a plain-spoken statement of his views. The President noted with satisfaction the assurance that there was no intention of settling the Adriatic question without consulting the American Government, especially as he understood that Mr. Lloyd George and M. Clemenceau, in agreement with Sig. Nitti, had decided upon a solution which included provisions previously rejected by the American Government, and that they had called upon the Yugoslavs to accept this solution under threat of enforcing the Treaty of London. He then proceeded to tear to shreds the Franco-British contention that the Nitti Compromise modified only two features of the memorandum of December 9, and both these to the advantage of Yugoslavia. The view that very positive advantages had been conceded to Italy was borne out by the fact that Italy had rejected the joint memorandum, but was willing to accept the new proposals. The earlier memorandum rejected the device of connecting Fiume with Italy by a narrow strip of coast; the latter accepted it. The former rejected the demand for the annexation of all Istria; the latter agreed to it. The memorandum of December 9 carefully excluded every form of Italian sovereignty over Fiume; that of January 14 opened the way to Italian control of Fiume's foreign affairs and to possible annexation. The memorandum of December 9 gave proper protection to the railway from Fiume northward; that of January 14 gave Italy dominant military positions at a number of critical points. The memorandum of December 9 maintained to a large degree the unity of Albania; it was now proposed to partition it among three alien Powers.

These and other provisions, negotiated without the knowledge or consent of the American Government, completely altered the nature of the settlement, and, even if the Yugoslavs were coerced into acceptance, both the settlement and the manner of its enforcement constituted a denial of the principles for which America had entered the war. It would be different if there had been any real divergence of opinion, but, on the contrary, "the opinions of the French, British, and Americans as to a just and equitable territorial arrangement at the head of the Adriatic Sea were strikingly harmonious." There was now, however, "a difference of opinion as to how firm[ly] Italy's friends should resist her importunate demands for alien territories to which she can present no valid title," and the American Government did not feel that it could connive in purchasing peace at the price of a future conflagration.

Passing on to more general considerations, the note went on:

It is a time to speak with the utmost frankness. The Adriatic issue as it now presents itself raises the fundamental question as to whether the American Government can on any terms coöperate with its European associates in the great work of maintaining the peace of the world by removing the primary causes of war. This Government does not doubt its ability to reach amicable understandings with the Associated Governments as to what constitutes equity and justice in international dealings; for differences of opinion as to the best methods of applying just principles have never obscured the vital fact that in the main the several Governments have entertained the same fundamental conception of what those principles are. But if substantial agreement on what is just and reasonable is not to determine international issues; if the country possessing the most endurance in pressing its demands rather than the country armed with a just cause is to gain the support of the powers; if forcible seizure of coveted areas is to be permitted and condoned, and is to receive ultimate justification by creating a situation so difficult that decision favorable to the aggressor is deemed a practical necessity; if deliberately incited ambition is, under the name of national sentiment, to be rewarded at the expense of the small and the weak; if, in a word, the old order of things which brought so many evils on the world is still to prevail, then the time is not yet come when this Government can enter a concert of powers the very existence of which must depend upon a new spirit and a new order. The American people are willing to share in such high enterprise, but many among them are fearful lest they become entangled in international policies and committed to international obligations foreign alike to their ideals and their traditions. To commit them to such a policy as that embodied in the latest Adriatic proposals, and to obligate them to maintain injustice as against the claims of justice, would be to provide the most solid ground for such fears. This Government can undertake no such grave responsibility.

The President desires to say that if it does not appear feasible to secure acceptance of the just and generous concessions offered by the British, French, and American Governments to Italy in the joint memorandum of those powers of December 9, 1919, which the President has already clearly stated to be the maximum concession that the Government of the United States can offer the President desires to say that he must take under serious consideration the withdrawal of the treaty with Germany and the agreement between the United States and France of June 28, 1919, which are now before the Senate and permitting the terms of the European settlement to be independently established and enforced by the Associated Governments.[38]

The Franco-British Reply of February 17

The importance of this communication transcended by far the mere Adriatic dispute which was its immediate cause, for it laid down in the form of a near ultimatum the American—or at least the Wilsonian—line of policy in regard to relations with Europe. Its immediate effect was to put a stop to the current discussion of the Italian question, for it would have been hardly practical to ignore so threatening an intervention. Consequently, Lloyd George and Millerand replied at length to the communication in a note dated February 17.

This reply attempted to justify the Nitti Compromise, as offered to the Yugoslavs on January 20, by minimizing the nature of the concessions made to Italy. The American criticism of the proposed settlement bore mainly on four points: the cession to Italy of a coastal strip; the fact that the way was open for the annexation of Fiume to Italy; the modification of the Istrian frontier at the expense of Yugoslavia, and the partition of Albania.

It was explained that the proposal had its origin in the fact that neither the Italians nor the Yugoslavs cared for the formation of a buffer state; the proposal was therefore a compromise abolishing the free state and incorporating 150,000 of its Slav population of 200,000 definitely into Yugoslavia. As to the assertion that the proposal paved the way for the annexation of Fiume to Italy, it implied that the League of Nations guarantee was of no value. The railway was commercial and not strategic, and could easily be cut in the event of war, no matter what solution was adopted. As to Albania, the details of administration, as had been pointed out, were not settled; in any case, the proposed arrangement would provide an outlet for Southern Yugoslavia, a demand expressed by the Yugoslavs.

"The Governments of Great Britain and France, therefore, must repeat that they find difficulty in understanding the present attitude

[38] Lansing to Wallace, Feb. 9, 1920. *The Adriatic Question*, pp. 21-25.

of the United States Government towards the proposals, and they hope that in view of these explanations that Government will see its way to reconsider its attitude." However, the proposal would not be pressed pending a reply. The difficulty of reaching an understanding in the absence of an American representative in Europe was again emphasized.

As to the Treaty of London, while recognizing the altered circumstances and preferring a settlement based on other considerations, nevertheless, in view of the circumstances of Italy's entrance into the war and her very considerable losses and sacrifices, Great Britain and France had always made it clear that they were not at liberty to renounce it. The enforcement of this Treaty, as an alternative to the acceptance of their proposals, was not an ultimatum to Yugoslavia, for by the terms of that Treaty Italy would have to relinquish Fiume definitely to the former. Since she was as reluctant to do this as was Yugoslavia to give up Dalmatia and the islands, this declaration was meant to exert pressure on both parties by putting them face to face with the fact that, if they could not agree to a reasonable compromise, they would both have to accept a less palatable arrangement.

The French and the British professed to be deeply disturbed by the possibility of American withdrawal from European councils, and hoped their explanations would remove any misunderstanding. To these explanations they added the consideration of the inescapable conflict between existing treaties, made under the stress of war, and the newly arisen national aspirations. It must be remembered that the war began with an effort to enforce upon Germany respect for a treaty she had signed eighty years before. Moreover, the imperfection of some settlements was fully recognized, and Article 9 of the League Covenant had been designed for the special purpose of mitigating this condition. The President himself had recognized the impossibility of strict adherence to ethnographic frontiers, as evidenced by his agreement to the inclusion of 3,000,000 Germans in Czechoslovakia and 3,500,000 Ruthenes in Poland. Although the British had objected to this arrangement, the British Government had not thought it a reason for reconsidering their membership in the League of Nations.[39]

[39] Davis to Lansing, Feb. 17, 1920. *The Adriatic Question*, pp. 25-30.

Wilson's Note of February 24 and the Franco-British Reply of February 26

Progress of the negotiations was naturally held in abeyance pending the issue of the controversy between Great Britain and France on one side and the United States on the other. The last Franco-British communication was promptly answered with a refusal on the part of Wilson to modify his position. Wilson's reply did, however, offer a suggestion that was eventually to be the basis of the final settlement. After restating the fundamental principles which had guided the peace settlement, the American note went on to consider the various arguments presented in the Franco-British memorandum. If, as was stated, the projected Free State of Fiume had been abandoned because the Italians and the Yugoslavs both objected to it, the consent of both these Powers should have been secured for the new proposal. Instead, the consent of Italy alone had been obtained, and it could hardly be argued that because the Yugoslavs had not been satisfied with the proposal of December 9 they should now be offered a less satisfactory arrangement. However,

the President would, of course, make no objection to a settlement mutually agreeable to Italy and Jugoslavia regarding their common frontier in the Fiume region, provided that such an agreement is not made on the basis of compensations elsewhere at the expense of nationals of a third power. His willingness to accept such proposed joint agreement of Italy and Jugoslavia is based on the fact that only their own nationals are involved. In consequence, the results of direct negotiations of the two interested powers would fall within the scope of the principle of self-determination.

The danger of annexation of Fiume, as a result of the proposed arrangement, did not lie in distrust of the value of the League of Nations guarantee, but in the fact that its peculiar conditions would invite strife in Fiume, out of which annexation might result. In regard to the proposed partition of Albania, it might be quite satisfactory to Yugoslavia, but the American Government was just as opposed to doing injustice to the Albanian people for the sake of Yugoslavia as it was opposed to doing injustice to the Yugoslav people for the sake of Italy.

As to the alternative of enforcing the Treaty of London, the usual arguments of changed conditions were repeated. The American Government was surprised at the suggestion, since it considered that it had come to a definite understanding with Great Britain and France in the memorandum of December 9. Moreover, the American Government had always understood that the previous negotiations, some of them resulting in the cession to Italy of territory not included in the Treaty of London (Sexten and Tarvis), had been conducted on the assumption that a better basis than that Treaty was to be found for an understanding.[40]

This last American communication, received February 25, was answered the very next day by Lloyd George and Millerand in a joint memorandum to the American Ambassador in London. After repeating that they had never intended to arrive at a settlement without consulting the American Government, and touching anew on the difficulty created by the absence of an American representative, the memorandum continued:

> They [the British and French Prime Ministers] note as a fact of the greatest importance that the President of the United States expressed his willingness to accept any "settlement, mutually agreeable to Italy and Jugoslavia, regarding their common frontier in the Fiume region, provided that such an agreement is not made on the basis of compensations elsewhere at the expense of nationals of a third power."

This would be the ideal solution and they were ready to withdraw the proposals of December 9 and January 20, for Italy and Yugoslavia would be more likely to come to terms if the other Powers were not committed to any particular solution. The American Government was therefore invited to join the British and French Governments in making a formal proposal to this effect to both the Italian and the Yugoslav Governments.

In the event, however, that this failed, the United States, Great Britain, and France should once more examine the question, with a view to formulating their own proposals. On the subject of the Treaty of London, Lloyd George and Millerand added that the Italian Government had loyally coöperated in endeavoring to find a substitute acceptable to themselves and to Yugoslavia alike. They would welcome, as cordially as President Wilson, an agreement which would naturally supersede the former Treaty, but in default

[40] Lansing to Wallace, Feb. 24, 1920. *The Adriatic Question*, pp. 31-34.

of such an agreement they must admit that the Treaty which they had signed in 1915 would be the only alternative.[41]

The Nitti Compromise Definitely Abandoned

But Wilson refused to accept the implications of this last communication. In his reply, dated March 4, he showed surprise that his expressed willingness to leave the settlement of the frontier in the region of Fiume to a joint Italo-Yugoslav agreement should be interpreted to mean willingness on his part to withdraw the memorandum of December 9. That memorandum clearly stated the chief points on which the French, the British, and the Americans had reached agreement after deliberate consideration, and should remain the basis of reference for future negotiations. The American Government would not object to the limitation of the free state to the *corpus separatum*, if it were put under League sovereignty without either Italian or Yugoslav control.

Albania was extraneous to the issue and the memorandum of December 9 made adequate provision for economic outlets for Yugoslavia in the south. As to the Treaty of London, the American Government had consistently maintained that it refused to be bound by secret treaties of which it had not even been informed. In conclusion, the President agreed with the British and French Prime Ministers on the urgency of the Adriatic settlement,

but he cannot accept as just the implied suggestion of his responsibility for the failure to reach a solution. He has merely adhered to the provisions of a settlement which the French and British Governments recognized as equitable in the joint memorandum of December 9, and has declined to approve a new settlement negotiated without the knowledge or approval of the American Government, which was unacceptable to one of the interested Governments and which in his opinion was in direct contradiction of the principles for the defense of which America entered the war. These views he has fully explained in his note of February 10, and he ventures to express the earnest hope that the Allied Governments will not find it necessary to decide on a course which the American Government in accordance with its reiterated statements would be unable to follow.[42]

In other words, Wilson refused to move from his position as ex-

[41] Davis to Polk, Feb. 26, 1920. *The Adriatic Question*, pp. 35-37.
[42] Polk to Davis, March 4, 1920. *The Adriatic Question*, pp. 47-49.

pressed in the memorandum of December 9. His last communication did therefore amount, in a sense, to an ultimatum. At the most, the free state could be altered, but the Italian frontier must not be moved eastward of the American line. Not only would he not modify his position, but he insisted on retaining his power of veto.

After the delivery of the memorandum of December 9, and the departure of Polk immediately thereafter, Italy, Great Britain, and France had agreed on one thing at least: the urgency of reaching a settlement to avoid prolonging the dangerous situation in the Adriatic. In January Nitti had taken negotiations in his own hands and had speedily come to terms with Great Britain and France. There is reason to believe that the Yugoslavs, however reluctantly, would not have been able to withstand the pressure of the three Allies; nor is there any question that the alternative of the Pact of London, offered on January 20, was a means of exerting pressure on them. For the terms of this alternative, the loss of Fiume on one hand, and the loss of a substantial part of Dalmatia with the Italian frontier at the gates of Fiume on the other, hardly bear comparison. Italy *was* willing to make substantial concessions for the sake of Fiume. The Yugoslavs' only hope, therefore, lay in turning their defense over to Wilson, and their dilatory tactics had had precisely this result of turning the debate into one between Wilson on the one hand, and Great Britain and France on the other. The last two named Powers had a difficult case, further weakened by the fact of their previous adherence to the memorandum of December 9. They found themselves in the position of *advocatus diaboli*, defending a cause the merits of which they themselves had often questioned in the past. Their main argument was necessity in the face of a choice of evils, but it failed to dent Wilson's logically, if not practically, sound position. The argument that the Nitti Compromise was in two respects more advantageous to Yugoslavia than the offer of December 9 was too tortuous and far-fetched to carry much weight, especially when one of the advantages to Yugoslavia was the partition of Albania. This last, if it was sound *Realpolitik*, was particularly unfortunate from Wilson's point of view, for, as he said, he was just as opposed to doing injury to Albania for the sake of Yugoslavia as to doing injury to Yugoslavia for the sake of Italy. To point out to Wilson that in other cases he had departed from principle could achieve no useful end, and merely served to irritate him.

But what was more important was America's position of prestige and power, and the vital necessity of continued assistance from her. In the face of Wilson's determined threat of withdrawal from the councils of Europe,[43] there could be but one result, abandonment of the Nitti Compromise. This is in fact what happened, adding one more failure to the long series that had extended over more than a whole year.

DIRECT ITALO-YUGOSLAV NEGOTIATIONS

The Nitti Compromise of January was dead, but the suggestion of the American note of February 24 of direct negotiations between Italy and Yugoslavia, eagerly taken up in the Franco-British reply of the twenty-sixth, indicated the new trend that the Adriatic problem was to take. To be sure, the last American communication insisted that such negotiations should take place within the framework of the joint memorandum of December 9. Nevertheless, the general situation was changing in favor of Italy, for Great Britain and France had definitely indicated their willingness to support her demands.[44] If left alone to face Italy, there was little doubt that the Yugoslavs must ultimately come to terms with her. Their mainstay had been American support, still sufficiently strong to block Nitti's last proposal. But, in view of the changing situation in America, the growing doubts regarding the fate of the Peace Treaties in the American Senate, and the general tendency in America to revert to the traditional isolationism of the past, Italy stood to gain by playing a waiting game.

Realizing this, the Yugoslavs were no longer averse to direct negotiations with the Italians, and Nitti oriented the negotiations in this direction: In March, Scialoja and Trumbić met in Paris on various occasions, and matters were far enough advanced toward the end of April for Nitti to announce at the last meeting of the San Remo Conference (April 17-28) that he definitely accepted the American suggestion of direct negotiations.[45] In fact, the preliminary discussions had made sufficient progress for Trumbić to arrange to meet Nitti at San Remo. However, he was prevented from doing so and

---

[43] Particularly in view of the very uncertain fate of the Versailles Treaty and of the French reinsurance Treaty in the American Senate.

[44] They had definitely abandoned the suggestion of the note of June 28, 1919, of nonvalidity of the Treaty of London.

[45] "L'Aventure de Fiume," *Revue des deux mondes*, April 1, 1921, p. 659.

asked that another meeting be arranged.[46] To this Nitti acquiesced,[47] and eventually it was decided that Trumbić and Pašić would come to Pallanza to discuss the question with Scialoja.

The first meeting took place on May 11; it was agreed that no public statements would be issued during the negotiations, that both Governments would defend before their Allies any agreement that was reached, and that only a territorial settlement (not a commercial treaty as well) would be sought for at the moment. Then, for two hours, Trumbić expounded the Yugoslav case. Failing an agreement, the Yugoslavs would be willing to accept the memorandum of December 9.[48]

As to Fiume, Trumbić was willing to recognize Italian sovereignty over the city but not over the district (*corpus separatum*), since the city alone contained an Italian population. The city and district should be demilitarized. The railway, the station and the port should be under Yugoslav sovereignty lest Italian influence, firmly established in the city, become dominant over them as well. A special agreement, guaranteed by the League of Nations, would protect international interests in the port. Sušak and Porto Baross should go to Yugoslavia in full sovereignty. In view of the heavy sacrifices entailed in the cession of Fiume, Yugoslavia should have compensations elsewhere in the Adriatic. For the Istrian frontier, Trumbić insisted on the Wilson line, which, he said, represented a considerable sacrifice for Yugoslavia. He could not accept the Italian arguments for the protection of Pola and Trieste, for a small shift in the frontier would not improve the strategic situation, and much too great a shift would be required to remedy this condition effectively. Trumbić proposed, instead, to demilitarize a zone of equal extent on either side of the American line.

All the islands should go to Yugoslavia. Trumbić proposed self-determination for Lussin and Lissa.

Zara should not be separated from Dalmatia, of which it was economically an integral part. However, it could have autonomy under international guarantee.

The Yugoslavs were willing to accept demilitarization of the

[46] Trumbić to Nitti, April 25, 1920. Adriaticus, *La Question adriatique,* Document XXXVI. There was a railroad strike in Yugoslavia.

[47] Nitti to Trumbić, April 25, 1920. Adriaticus, *op. cit.,* Document XXXVII.

[48] This was a concession on their part, since they had previously rejected it.

islands, with the exception of those which formed part of the system of coast defense.

Montenegro had in fact been absorbed into Yugoslavia, and had been refused recognition at the Peace Conference. Formal recognition of this situation by Italy would help to create good feeling.

As to Albania, the Yugoslavs preferred an independent state within the limits of 1913, on account of the danger to Yugoslavia of a Great Power established in that country. However, failing this, Yugoslavia claimed a section in the north, to which it would give an autonomous status.

Finally, guarantees were asked for the protection of the 400,000 Slavs included in Italy. The Italians of Dalmatia could remain there while opting for Italian nationality.[49]

Scialoja replied to Trumbić's exposition at a second meeting the same day. He noted that Trumbić had expressed his readiness to recognize Italian sovereignty over Fiume, to which Trumbić immediately objected that that was merely a proposal in the course of negotiations, not a definite commitment. Scialoja went on to point out that the Yugoslavs were asking many compensations for this supposedly great concession. Italian sovereignty, it had been pointed out before, should extend to the whole *corpus separatum*. However, the Slav nucleus in the north and the Italians residing at Cantrida[50] might form the object of an exchange. Fiume could not exist without contiguity to Italy.

As to the port, in view of its international character, a commission on which the various interested states would be represented would be preferable to the League of Nations, an untried organization.

In view of the divergence of opinion in regard to the Istrian frontier, and the desirability of a good frontier for both states, Scialoja proposed that the question be turned over for study to the experts of the two countries (General Badoglio and Admiral Acton of the Italians were due to arrive at Pallanza momentarily).

In regard to the islands, even Wilson was willing to give Italy Lussin, Unie, Lissa, and Pelagosa. An exchange could take place between Lissa, wholly Slav in population, and Cherso, evenly di-

---

[49] Scialoja to Nitti, May 11, 1920. *Italian Green Book* of June, 1921, Doc. 1.

[50] A suburb to the west of Fiume proper.

vided; moreover, Cherso was necessary lest Fiume be separated from Italy by both land and sea in Yugoslav hands.

Demilitarization of the continental frontier, as well as of the islands and the coast, was turned over to the technical experts by common agreement. Scialoja would have preferred an undertaking not to fortify Cattaro and Sebenico.

Autonomy within Yugoslavia would not be sufficient for Zara.

The question of Montenegro must remain open; the other Powers had yet made no decisions. Moreover, Wilson had insisted that an agreement must not be reached through compensations at the expense of a third party. This might apply to Montenegro, and certainly applied to Albania. In regard to the latter, Wilson was willing to recognize an Italian mandate within the frontiers of 1913. Scialoja further claimed that this Albanian mandate would be more of a burden than an advantage. Possession of Valona was a defensive need, not the acquisition of a base for expansion in the Balkans, and its hinterland would be made as small as possible. Pašić here insisted on the need of a strategic frontier in the north of Albania.

Finally, Scialoja ended by urging the conclusion of a commercial agreement, to supplement and to facilitate the acceptance of the territorial one, which would inevitably be criticized in both countries.[51]

From this account it would appear that the Nitti Government was moved by a really conciliatory attitude. In fact, it might be doubted whether the terms it seems to have been willing to accept would have been ratified by the Italian Parliament. Very possibly, Nitti was urged toward a settlement at all costs by the increasing difficulties of the internal situation.[52]

The Yugoslav claims may seem rather far removed from what Nitti was willing or able to concede; however, their demands were made to some extent as bargaining points, and, on May 15, Scialoja

[51] Scialoja to Nitti, May 11, 1920. I.G.B., Doc. 2.

[52] In addition to the bad financial situation, there was increasing social unrest and violence, owing to the growth of parties on both extremes. The Government was loath to resort to the use of force to maintain order; nationalistic and army circles were, to a considerable extent, affected by d'Annunzio's activity in Fiume. It is interesting in this connection to note Nitti's letter to Clemenceau, asking for a minor change of wording in the proposal of Jan. 14, as given to the Yugoslavs, and his circular of April 24 to the Italian prefects, urging that demonstrations must be prevented at all costs when the San Remo Conference would announce a decision in regard to the Adriatic. Cf. Benedetti, *La pace di Fiume,* pp. 63-64.

was able to report that their intentions were conciliatory.[53] There is, therefore, every reason to believe that the long dispute would have been brought to a close at Pallanza, and, if it had, the Yugoslavs would have secured better terms than they were to obtain some months later under conditions which, in some respects, might seem more favorable to them.[54] Unfortunately, the negotiations were abruptly interrupted by a Cabinet crisis in Rome, which caused Scialoja to leave Pallanza. He asked Trumbić and Pašić to wait for a few days, but, as he was unable to return, they left for Paris with friendly expressions of regret at the interruption and of hope that negotiations might soon be resumed.[55]

[53] Scialoja to Nitti, May 15, 1920. *I.G.B.,* Doc. 3.
[54] See below, p. 293, for Giolitti's comments on the Treaty of London.
[55] *I.G.B.,* Doc. 4.

THE FINAL SETTLEMENT

XI

THE SETTLEMENT OF 1920

THE TREATY OF RAPALLO

Giolitti's Programme—Albania

THE CRISIS which interrupted the Pallanza negotiations did not cause the immediate fall of the Nitti Ministry. Nitti attempted to carry on by means of a reshuffling of his Cabinet, but was able to survive only another month, when Giolitti once more took the helm. For a long time the most powerful leader in Italian political life, he had played no part in the events of the war and the Peace Conference. He had, from the beginning, been a determined partisan of strict neutrality, considering that Italy could secure some worthwhile compensations, the famous *parecchio*, without the expenditure of blood and treasure. His attitude and, even more, his connection with the negotiations of 1915 between Berlin, Vienna, and Rome—despite his denial of such connection[1]—proved to be a political error. Even though a majority of the Chamber of 1915 were his followers, Salandra had remained in power and had carried out the undertaking of the Treaty of London. Once Italy had thrown in her lot with the Allies, Giolitti had adopted voluntarily the wise course of keeping in the background throughout the whole duration of hostilities. The war had justified his forecast, in the matter of duration and cost at least, and now that Orlando and Nitti had tried and failed in the peace settlement, it was quite natural that the old leader should resume his former position in name as well as in fact.

His views were no secret, having been fully aired during the election of the preceding autumn.[2] On the particular subject of the Treaty of London, he had expressed the opinion that Italy herself had not lived up to the terms of that Treaty.[3] That admission, from

---

[1] Giolitti, *Memorie della mia vita,* pp. 535 ff. See above, p. 20, n. 75.

[2] Dronero speech of Oct. 12, 1919. See above, p. 236, n. 10.

[3] Dronero speech; Giolitti, *Memorie,* pp. 541-42. It should be considered, however, that the position taken by Giolitti in this respect was prompted by the exigencies of internal politics and by his own feelings toward Salandra, at least as much as by the intrinsic merits of the case.

the man now in charge of directing Italian policy, might at first seem a considerable asset to the Yugoslav case, for, in the past, the Italians had always fallen back on the written pledge of Great Britain and France when other things had failed. What was more, they had finally secured the support of these two Powers in their contention, and it was only an eleventh-hour American intervention that had saved the day for the Yugoslavs in January.

However, to assume that Giolitti came to power prepared to meet the Yugoslavs on their own terms, or even on any such terms as those contained in the memorandum of December 9, would be to misjudge the man. It must be remembered that it was he who had led the country during the Tripolitan war. It is equally essential to bear in mind Giolitti's position in the Italian political scheme of things, his own particular preserve to a far greater extent than Foreign Affairs. During the spring of 1919, when Orlando was waging a losing fight for the Italian claims, caught between the pressure of his own home opinion and Wilson's finality of decision, Giolitti had been quite willing to use the cry for Fiume as a convenient stumblingblock in Orlando's path. His own press and that influenced by those who looked to him as likely to return to office, had not been backward in discovering in themselves a sudden overwhelming love for the *italianissima città*.[4] When Orlando had left the Conference as the result of the publication of Wilson's Manifesto, these elements, which might be described as the Giolittian following in Parliament, could do little else but support the Government. The result was to make Giolitti, quite as much as his predecessors, a prisoner of the agitation which he had encouraged. If this had not been sufficient, d'Annunzio's continued occupation of Fiume made it out of the question to give that city a status which would have put it under any sort of Yugoslav control. Opinion in Italy may have been divided on the score of d'Annunzio's tactics and pronouncements, but to take a position which might be presented in the light of an alliance with Belgrade against Italian Fiume would have been simply unthinkable for any Italian public man.

On the other hand, Giolitti recognized realities, in particular the difference between the situation in 1915 which had led to the Treaty of London, and the new situation created by the outcome of the

[4] See above, pp. 102, 125.

war. Within the limits of internal political necessities, he was therefore quite willing to adjust himself to changed conditions. In this
he was ably seconded by the man he chose for his Foreign Minister,
Count Carlo Sforza. Sforza's background was diplomatic, and particularly appropriate in the present circumstances. He had personal
knowledge of the leaders in Belgrade, with whom he had become
acquainted while representing his Government; in Corfu he had had
occasion to discuss with Pašić the future settlement. He was in favor
of a policy of coöperation with the new Yugoslavia, being intransigent only on the question of the Istrian frontier.[5] During 1919 he
had been Italian High Commissioner in Constantinople.

With a clearly outlined foreign policy in mind, Giolitti did not
show himself anxious to resume negotiations with the Yugoslavs at
once, but turned his attention to the home situation; it was troublesome enough to demand all his energies. Like other Continental
countries, Italy had become accustomed to the war-time scale of
reckoning in billions, and, the war long over, was still, to a large
extent, living on the printing-presses. The financial disorder went
hand in hand with increasing costs of living, which, in turn, were
the single greatest cause of social unrest. The palliative of fixing the
price of certain staples, mainly bread, only postponed for a little
while the inevitable day of reckoning. Little had been done under
the preceding Ministry to break the vicious circle; conditions in the
country had become rather chaotic and the enforcement of law very
weak: to such a degree that railroad unions took it upon themselves
to decide whether or not to allow the transport of armed forces to
quell riots. Though not blind to the gravity of the situation, Giolitti
felt that the storm would blow itself out if only the Government
gave signs of pursuing a firm, though not necessarily unduly repres-
sive, policy. With a combination of suasion and of a moderate use of
force in certain instances, he made some progress toward restoring
more orderly conditions in the country.

In agreement with him, Sforza, while desirous to reach an agreement as soon as possible, pursued the policy of carefully preparing
the ground before undertaking definite formal negotiations. As the
result, the Giolitti-Sforza Government turned its attention in the

---

[5] Sforza outlined his policy in speeches in the Chamber on July 22 and Aug. 6. *Atti del
Parlamento, 1919-21, Camera, Discussioni,* IV, 3775-85, and V, 4983-88. Cf. also, Sforza,
Makers of Modern Europe, pp. 151-52.

foreign field, not to the eastern land frontier at first, but rather toward Albania.

The Treaty of London of 1915 had outlined the partition of Albania between Italy, Serbia, and Greece. That solution was reverted to during the negotiations of December, 1919-January, 1920, but Wilson's intervention caused the proposed compromise to be stillborn. During the discussions of the spring of 1919, it had been found impossible to come to an agreement over the actual frontiers of Albania among the French and the British on one side, and the Americans on the other;[6] but, in any event, it was understood throughout the negotiations that Italy was to receive the mandate over Albania within whatever frontiers might eventually be agreed upon. The Tittoni-Venizelos agreement of August, 1919, confirmed the idea of partition, at least between Italy and Greece.[7]

The Italians had proclaimed a protectorate over Albania as early as 1917.[8] In reply to this Italian move, the French had set up an independent Republic of Koritsa around the town of that name. The Republic was short-lived, but the French remained in occupation and administered the district until May, 1920, when they withdrew.[9] Upon their withdrawal, Albanian troops occupied the region and eventually secured control of the territory up to the frontier of 1913 with Greece. The Albanians manifested equal opposition to the Serbs and to the Italians.[10] The former had occupied some sections beyond the frontier of 1913 in the north and the northeast, and managed to maintain themselves against Albanian attacks.

In view of the internal situation in Italy, the Government had not seen its way to engaging in war in Albania. The result was that the Italian troops had gradually evacuated the country until they were concentrated around Valona. The conditions of the army in Albania were notorious, and the mortality from malaria particularly high; a

---

[6] The British and the French favored giving all of Northern Epirus to Greece, while the Italians wanted it left to Albania. The Americans advocated a division of the region, giving Argyrocastro to Greece and Koritsa to Albania. Eventually the Italians ceased to take part in the discussion. Cf. Stickney, *Southern Albania*, pp. 107-13; Nicolson, *Peacemaking*, pp. 265-78; Haskins and Lord, *Some Problems of the Peace Conference*, p. 280; and see above, pp. 216-17.

[7] See above, pp. 242-43.

[8] The Italian proclamation spoke of "protection," not of protectorate. On the explanations in connection with this distinction, cf. Tittoni's note of July 7, 1919, above, p. 239.

[9] Stickney, *op. cit.,* p. 126.

[10] They set up their own Government in Feb., 1920. Cf. Stickney, *op. cit.,* p. 123.

regiment of *bersaglieri*, stationed at Ancona, mutinied when ordered to embark for Valona.[11]

The views of Giolitti and Sforza on the Albanian question were that the break-up of Austria-Hungary had removed the cause of rivalry between that country and Italy in the Lower Adriatic. Confident that Albania, in its own right, could constitute no threat to Italy, they thought that the best interest of Italy in that region lay in maintaining an independent state, free from encroachments on the side of either Greece or Yugoslavia. As to the merits of a base in Valona, Giolitti felt that, in view of modern developments in artillery, submarines, and aircraft, far too large an area would be necessary for the effective protection of such a base. If Italy did not have control of the sea, Valona would be a mere liability, a beleaguered outpost that could not be relieved; if she were the stronger, it would be sufficient for her to prevent its being of use to an enemy; this objective could be achieved just as effectively through the possession of the islet of Saseno.[12] Sforza could not see the point of attempting to create an independent state while depriving it at the same time of Valona. Neither could he see any merit in the Tittoni-Venizelos agreement, which he considered detrimental to Italian dignity.[13]

These considerations prompted the Giolitti-Sforza Ministry to adopt a radical solution, namely, complete evacuation of Albania. Giolitti spoke of the independence of Albania at the end of June, and on July 22 Sforza sent a note to Venizelos denouncing the Tittoni-Venizelos agreement.[14] Direct negotiations were taking place, in the meantime, between Italy and the Tirana Government, as the result of which an agreement was signed on August 2, 1920, whereby Italy recognized the independence of Albania in the frontiers of 1913 and retained possession only of Saseno.[15]

[11] Giolitti, *Memorie*, p. 568. This was one occasion on which troops to quell the mutiny had to be transported by lorries, owing to the refusal of the railroad workers to allow them to be moved by rail.

[12] These are Giolitti's views, as he expounds them in his *Memorie*, p. 571. A question might well be raised as to the effectiveness of a base at Saseno against enemy artillery and aircraft on the mainland.

[13] Sforza, *Makers of Modern Europe*, p. 161. Cf. Stickney, *op. cit.*, p. 124.

[14] At the Spa Conference which both attended. Sforza's speech of Aug. 6. *Atti del Parlamento, 1919-21, Camera, Discussioni*, V, 4985-86.

[15] Stickney, *op. cit.*, p. 125. This agreement, of course, could not, and did not, settle the question of Albanian frontiers, for the Yugoslavs were still in occupation beyond the line of 1913 in the north and the east. Eventually Albanian independence was recognized by the Powers, and Albania was admitted to the League of Nations, though with still undefined frontiers, on Dec. 17, 1920.

This arrangement might be looked upon as a sign of weakness on the part of Italy and be so interpreted, especially in Belgrade. That it was not such will appear presently. Undoubtedly, on the other hand, it weakened the case of Yugoslavia for a share in the north and east of Albania, in so far as that case was based on the general idea of compensation for Italian acquisitions. Incidentally, it also disposed of one of the objections raised by Wilson to the Nitti Compromise.[16]

Preliminary Exchanges with the Yugoslavs

As already mentioned, with the coming into force of the Treaty of Versailles in January, 1920, the Peace Conference proper formally came to an end. The numerous questions which called for frequent consultation between the various Governments were dealt with, besides through the ordinary channels of diplomatic intercourse, in a series of conferences. The first of these, held in Paris in January, 1920, considered the Adriatic question and, in the form of the Nitti Compromise, produced a scheme of settlement which, in all likelihood, would have been accepted by all the interested parties, had it not been for the last American intervention. As the result of this intervention, the Italian Government seized upon the suggestion of direct negotiations between itself and Yugoslavia. However, these negotiations had not made sufficient progress for Nitti to make an announcement on the subject at the San Remo Conference in April, as he had thought that he would be able to do.[17] The meeting at Pallanza, opening auspiciously, had been interrupted by the crisis in Rome and the subsequent fall of the Nitti Cabinet. The Giolitti Government preferred to let the matter rest for a time.

The successive Conferences of the year 1920, therefore, did not attempt to deal with the Adriatic issue, which was now supposed to be the subject of direct negotiations between the two principal parties. These meetings were mainly concerned with the Turkish settlement and with reparations. The former will be considered below; for a variety of reasons that settlement was stillborn and can be said, in a sense, to have played a secondary rôle in Italian policy. In the case of German reparations, likewise, Italy, whose original share was

[16] Sforza stated his views on Albania in his speech of Aug. 6.
[17] See above, pp. 285-86.

small, did not feel that this was a vital matter to her; these discussions were, in the main, a Franco-German controversy, with Great Britain apparently unable to pursue and enforce a consistent policy, often supporting German hopes, only to frustrate them whenever it came to a test. In this matter, Italy used her influence for conciliation, and, for herself, was primarily interested in obtaining an adequate supply of raw materials, chiefly coal.[18]

However, these frequent meetings of the Prime Ministers and the Foreign Ministers afforded them an opportunity of discussing any matters of interest among themselves, whether or not these were on the agenda of the Conference. In this way contact was maintained between the Italians and the Yugoslavs: in this case between Sforza and Trumbić, the respective Foreign Ministers. Throughout this period (June-November), it is important to bear in mind that there took place a steady disintegration of the Franco-British alliance, which actually continued to exist only in name. Relations with Germany and the Near Eastern settlement were the main points of difference, and the two countries pursued diametrically opposite policies. A semblance of unity was maintained toward Germany, but, in the case of Turkey, the difference could not be glossed over by mere declarations of common policy, and culminated eventually in a separate treaty between France and Turkey, preliminary to the military assistance which the French were to give to the Turkish nationalists. Italy followed, on the whole, a policy akin to, though more open than, the French, and the resulting Franco-Italian *rapprochement*, largely in opposition to British policy, was reflected in the markedly pro-Italian attitude of the French Foreign Office on the score of the Adriatic, as compared with a relatively neutral British position.

The Yugoslavs were naturally anxious, on their part, to make a settlement. That they could count on no further assistance from London and Paris against Italy had been established in January; with the passing of time, it also became increasingly clear that their mainstay in Washington would, in all probability, be definitely swept from the scene. Under the circumstances, Italy held a valuable trump card in the occupation of Dalmatia. In June Millerand notified Sforza through Barrère, who had returned to his post in Rome, of this

---

[18] At the Spa Conference, Sforza secured a slight improvement in the Italian percentage of reparations.

eagerness of the Yugoslavs to resume negotiations. Sforza, in turn, notified Belgrade of the continued conciliatory intentions of his Government, but insisted on the avoidance of incidents and reckless talk on the part of the Yugoslavs.[19] A few days later, Sforza and Trumbić were both at the Conference of Spa (July 5-16). They had a meeting on the fifth, and again on the twelfth, going over the debated issues, now confined, for all practical purposes, to the Istrian frontier. Popular feeling in both countries was, however, still agitated. On July 4 a skirmish occurred near Fiume; a few days later anti-Italian riots took place in Spalato, the reply to which came in the form of similar anti-Slav incidents in Trieste. The Yugoslavs were, or pretended to be, concerned over recurring reports of expeditions planned in Fiume by d'Annunzio, and Sforza kept repeating to both Trumbić and to Belgrade his insistence on calm on the part of the Yugoslavs, and his assurances of good will and readiness to come to terms if only the Yugoslavs would be reasonable.[20] On July 17, just before leaving Spa, Sforza indicated to Trumbić the main lines of the settlement which Italy was prepared to accept.[21]

According to Bonin Longare, Italian Ambassador in Paris, Trumbić, after visiting that capital, went to seek assistance in London, considering the French attitude too favorable to the Italians, Millerand having given him a curt reception.[22] Perhaps as the result of his *démarche* in London, the British urged the Italians to reopen negotiations, pointing to the dangers of continued delay.[23] But Giolitti and Sforza refused to be hurried. At the same time, news was forthcoming from Belgrade that the Serbian element in the kingdom, led by Pašić, was inclined to come to terms with Italy.[24]

Giolitti, in agreement with Sforza, had clearly defined for himself the terms of settlement, which were to be as follows:

1. A secure land frontier. This could not be obtained by any minor alterations of the Wilson line; it meant possession of Monte Nevoso and something approximating the line of the Treaty of London.

2. Fiume, meaning the *corpus separatum*, could be an independent state, but without interference of the League of Nations. This state

---

[19] Sforza to Galanti (Italian Minister in Belgrade), June 28, 1920. *I.G.B.*, June 20, 1921, Doc. 6.

[20] *I.G.B., passim,* in particular, Docs. 7, 8.

[21] Sforza to Galanti, July 21, *I.G.B.*, Doc. 13; see also Doc. 11.

[22] Bonin to Sforza, July 23 and 24, *I.G.B.*, Doc. 14, 15.

[23] Giolitti, *Memorie*, p. 572.

[24] Galanti to Sforza, July 25, *I.G.B.*, Doc. 16.

should be contiguous to Italy, either by moving the Italian frontier eastward to reach the independent state, or by incorporating in that state the intervening strip of land.

3. Italy must have Cherso and Lussin.

4. Yugoslavia could have the rest of the islands and Dalmatia, except Zara, and should give adequate guarantees for the protection of the Italians of Dalmatia.[25]

Save for possibly minor details, this represented an absolute minimum program, not a basis for transaction. In the event of failure, Giolitti was prepared to cut the Gordian knot by simply annexing the territories in question, and continuing the military occupation of Dalmatia and the islands, while declaring that Italy was ready to discuss their ultimate fate in return for international recognition of the independence of Fiume.[26] With this in mind, he approached the final negotiations. There was therefore little room for debate, and the decision rested with the Yugoslavs. No doubt, however, Giolitti preferred a negotiated agreement to unilateral action on his part, and, for that reason, he carefully prepared the ground with the assistance of his Foreign Minister. His assertion that there had been no previous discussions and exchanges when the Yugoslavs came to Santa Margherita[27] is a gross understatement. The strategy of Giolitti and Sforza was to put the Yugoslavs in a position of complete and unmistakable isolation.

At the end of July, Imperiali, the Italian Ambassador in London, expressed to the British Foreign secretary, Lord Curzon, the hope that, in his conversations with Trumbić, he would give no encouragement to the claims hitherto advanced by the Yugoslavs; to which Curzon replied that, already at Spa, he had let Trumbić know that Great Britain was determined no longer to intervene.[28] To make assurance doubly sure, Giolitti himself went to visit Lloyd George, then vacationing in Lucerne, in the latter part of August. According to Giolitti, Lloyd George made no comments on the details of the Italian program, but said that he had already urged the Yugoslavs to make a settlement.[29] At the end of the month Sforza instructed

[25] Giolitti, *Memorie*, p. 579.
[26] *Ibid.*, p. 581.
[27] *Ibid.*, p. 580. Cf. *I.G.B.*, Docs. 13 and 20.
[28] Imperiali to Sforza, July 28, *I.G.B.*, Doc. 18.
[29] Giolitti, *Memorie*, p. 573. Bonin to Sforza, Sept. 22, *I.G.B.*, Doc. 29. There was a change of Government in Belgrade in August, which, however, did not affect the issue. Trumbić remained at the Foreign Ministry.

the Italian Ambassador in Paris to speak to Trumbić, who was passing through that city on his way back from London to Belgrade,
to the same effect that he himself had spoken at Spa, emphasizing
that, in view of her concessions at Fiume, Italy could yield no further on the Istrian frontier. Trumbić was also to be told that Sforza
was ready to meet him at any time in the future and hoped that,
when they met, Trumbić would be invested with full powers to
negotiate.[30]

Pursuing his tactics, Giolitti had a meeting with Millerand at Aix-
les-Bains in September. According to his account, Giolitti found
Millerand willing to go further than Lloyd George in the way of
exerting pressure on the Yugoslavs.[31] Despite some remaining hesitation on the part of the Yugoslavs, both sides were ready to meet
at the end of September. There was some further delay, however,
in the matter of making minor adjustments and preparations, which
lasted throughout October. In September, in connection with the
elections for the Yugoslav Constituent Assembly, it appeared that
the electoral law provided for the election of deputies from the districts claimed by Italy, even such places at Gorizia, which the Yugoslavs could not hope to obtain under any circumstances.[32] This
indirect reassertion of the most extreme Yugoslav claims caused not
a little furore in Italy. The matter was smoothed over, eventually,
and, as Sforza pointed out, it did little more than tend to force the
Italian Government into a less conciliating position.[33]

The Yugoslav readiness to come to a final understanding with
Italy was further enhanced by the events of October, without immediate connection, but not without influence, on their decision. It
was during October that the plebiscite in the Klagenfurt area was
held, and, much to the chagrin of the Yugoslavs, the voting turned
out in favor of union with Austria. The reaction of the Yugoslavs
to this disappointment—the ethnic majority in the zone where the
plebiscite had been held was admittedly Slovene—was to occupy the
district with their troops. This gesture only brought them a sharp
joint ultimatum from Great Britain, France, and Italy, giving them
forty-eight hours in which to withdraw. They could do little else

[30] Sforza to Bonin, Aug. 31, *I.G.B.,* Doc. 20.

[31] Giolitti, *Memorie,* pp. 575 ff.

[32] On the other hand, as the Yugoslavs explained, to have acted otherwise would have been
tantamount to an implicit recognition of the Italian claims.

[33] Sforza to Galanti, Oct. 9, *I.G.B.,* Doc. 36.

but comply.[34] Close on the heels of this blow came the equally dis-heartening results of the American presidential election at the begin-ning of November: complete defeat for their great champion at the Peace Conference. Under the sting of these events, the Yugoslavs could not but feel thoroughly isolated. As Vesnić put it: "We realized the difficulty of our situation after the Carinthian plebiscite and the American election, and what counts much more, we felt our big Allies had left us to our own destiny and simultaneously put upon our shoulders the responsibility for the peace of Europe."[35]

The Meeting at Santa Margherita Ligure[36]

Under these circumstances, the Yugoslav delegates left for Santa Margherita Ligure to meet the Italians on November 8. Knowing the situation, it is reasonable to assume that they came prepared to accept the Italian conditions. To make quite certain of London and Paris, Sforza had instructed the Italian Ambassadors in these capitals to outline the Italian proposals and to hint at the advisability of their exerting some pressure on Belgrade.[37] He also forwarded to these same Ambassadors identical telegrams from Giolitti to Millerand[38] and to Lloyd George, expressing Giolitti's "personal trust and hope that your high authority may efficaciously intervene in Belgrade in favor of that peace of conciliation . . . which we are seeking."[39] In London, Curzon refused to commit himself to any action until he had precise knowledge of the terms proposed by Italy.[40] Lloyd George, in simpler language, told Imperiali, "You wish to create an atmosphere which will make the Yugoslavs realize that England is with you." In very friendly but vague terms, he too, avoided com-mitting himself.[41] However, he finally acquiesced in the Italian re-quest, after receiving a definite statement of the Italian terms,[42] al-though he said that his information made him doubtful that the

---

[34] Cf. Temperley, IV, 374 ff. for this plebiscite.

[35] Temperley, IV, 330.

[36] Although the name of Rapallo is usually associated with the meeting and the Treaty, the discussions were held in the neighboring town of Santa Margherita Ligure.

[37] Sforza to Imperiali and Bonin, Oct. 31, *I.G.B.*, Doc. 44.

[38] Millerand had become President of the Republic and Leygues had succeeded him at the Foreign Office in September.

[39] Sforza to Bonin and Imperiali, Oct. 31, *I.G.B.*, Docs. 45, 46.

[40] Imperiali to Sforza, Nov. 1, *I.G.B.*, Doc. 47.

[41] Imperiali to Sforza, Nov. 4, *I.G.B.*, Doc. 49.

[42] Imperiali to Sforza, Nov. 4, *I.G.B.*, Doc. 53.

Yugoslavs would be found accommodating.[43] In Paris matters went more smoothly. Barrère was there supporting the Italian case, and both Millerand and Leygues assured Bonin that they would forward an urgent appeal to Belgrade.[44]

The Yugoslav delegates, having arrived at Santa Margherita, met the Italians[45] on the morning of the eighth. They still spoke of the Wilson line and of international guarantees for the zone between that line and the line demanded by the Italians. Sforza discreetly hinted at the possibility of unilateral action on the part of Italy, in the event of failure to come to an agreement.[46] At the afternoon meeting, Vesnić proposed a demilitarized zone on both sides of the frontier. The Italians had no objection to such a formula, but it could not affect the line of the frontier itself, which must include Monte Nevoso;[47] this demand was backed by Giolitti from Rome.[48] The next day, the entire set of Italian proposals (Istria, Fiume, Zara, and the islands) was communicated to the Yugoslavs.[49] Further pressure from Paris was brought to bear by both Millerand and Leygues.[50] On the tenth, Sforza made a minor concession by yielding Lissa and agreeing to make the strip of land from Fiume to the Italian frontier part of the territory of Fiume. Trumbić agreed to this, and shortly thereafter accepted the whole Istrian frontier.[51] The news of this favorable turn brought Giolitti himself to Santa Margherita, and, after working all day on the twelfth, the final Treaty was drawn up and signed late that very night.[52]

The principal provisions of the Treaty were as follows:

Istrian Frontier (Article 1).—The frontier was to run from the point (Mount Pec) where Italy, Austria, and Yugoslavia came together, in a general southeasterly direction to Monte Nevoso, and thence to the sea, which it was to join just south of Castua. This town was left in Yugoslav territory.

[43] Imperiali to Sforza, Nov. 5, *I.G.B.*, Doc. 54; see also Docs. 57, 59.

[44] Bonin to Sforza, Nov. 2, *I.G.B.*, Doc. 48. A second and more pressing appeal was sent a few days later, *I.G.B.*, Doc. 56.

[45] The Italian delegates were Giolitti, Sforza, and Bonomi, but Giolitti remained in Rome and was to join the others only in the event that the negotiations proved successful.

[46] Sforza to Giolitti, Nov. 8, *I.G.B.*, Doc. 61.

[47] Sforza to Giolitti, Nov. 8, *I.G.B.*, Doc. 62.

[48] Giolitti to Sforza, Nov. 8, *I.G.B.*, Doc. 63.

[49] Sforza to Giolitti, Nov. 9, *I.G.B.*, Doc. 65.

[50] Bonin to Sforza, Nov. 11, *I.G.B.*, Doc. 69. Giolitti, *Memorie*, p. 581.

[51] Sforza to Giolitti, Nov. 10, *I.G.B.*, Doc. 67; see also Doc. 68.

[52] An account of the Rapallo meeting is given by Sforza, *Makers of Modern Europe*, pp. 236-38.

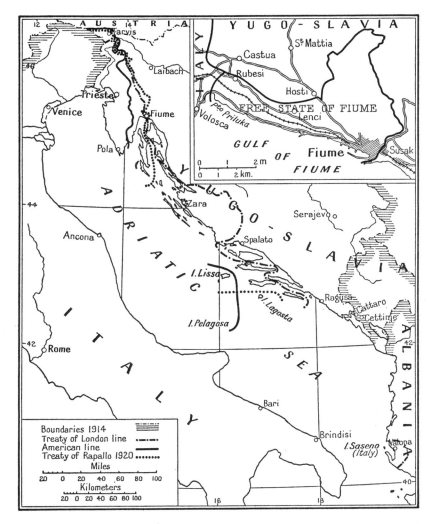

XI. THE ADRIATIC SETTLEMENT OF 1920: THE TREATY OF LONDON LINE OF
1915, THE AMERICAN LINE OF 1919, THE LINE OF THE TREATY
OF RAPALLO OF 1920, AND THE FREE STATE OF FIUME

The boundary of the Free State of Fiume is taken from Bowman, *The New World,* and
from Benedetti, *Fiume, Porto Baross e il retroterra.*

This was practically identical with the line of the Treaty of London, save for a slight shift eastward of that line between Idria and Castua.

Zara (Article 2).—The commune of Zara and portions of some neighboring communes, amounting roughly to a radius of seven kilometers around the city, "are recognized as forming part of the Kingdom of Italy." A special convention was to regulate the relations between the territory assigned to Italy and the surrounding Yugoslav territory, and the just division of provincial and communal property and archives relating thereto.

Islands (Article 3).—Cherso and Lussin with adjacent islets were to form part of Italy. Likewise Pelagosa and Lagosta. The rest of the islands went to Yugoslavia.

Fiume (Articles 4 and 5).—Italy and Yugoslavia recognized and undertook to respect in perpetuity the full liberty and independence of the State of Fiume.

The State of Fiume was to consist of:

(a) The *corpus separatum* as it was delimited at the time.

(b) The coastal strip extending to the Italian frontier, which it was to reach outside of Mattuglie—which remained in Italy—south of Castua (Preluca). (See Map XI.)

A mixed Italo-Yugoslav commission was to trace the boundaries on the ground. In case of disagreement, the President of the Swiss Republic would be asked to arbitrate without appeal.

Italian Minorities (Article 7).—In regard to Italians and Italian interests in Dalmatia:

(a) Yugoslavia was to respect and to maintain economic concessions, granted by states or public bodies to which the Serb-Croat-Slovene Government had succeeded, to Italian citizens or companies, and legally held by the latter up to November 12, 1920.

(b) Italians belonging to that territory of the former Austro-Hungarian Monarchy which had been recognized as Yugoslav territory by the Treaties with Austria and Hungary and the present Treaty, were to have the right of opting in favor of Italian citizenship within a year of the coming into force of the present Treaty, without being obliged to transfer their domicile. They would retain the free use of their language and religion.

(c) Degrees and university diplomas obtained by Yugoslav citizens in universities and other institutions of higher learning of the

Kingdom of Italy were to be recognized by the Serb-Croat-Slovene Government as valid in its territory and as conferring equal rights with degrees and diplomas obtained in equivalent institutions of the Serb-Croat-Slovene Kingdom. The validity of higher studies completed by Italian subjects in the Serb-Croat-Slovene Kingdom and by Serb-Croat-Slovene subjects in Italy was to form the subject of a further agreement.

Trade and Cultural Relations (Articles 6 and 8).—Within two months of the coming into force of the present Treaty a conference of competent authorities was to be convoked, in order to place before the two Governments concrete proposals on all the plans for establishing the most cordial economic and financial relations between the two countries.

A convention was to be established between the two Governments with the object of intensifying the intimate reciprocal development of the cultural relations between the two countries.

Finally, Article 9 provided that the Treaty be drawn up in both Italian and Serbo-Croat, but that, in case of disagreement, the Italian text was to be considered official, that language being known to all the plenipotentiaries.[53]

At the same time, the Italian and Yugoslav negotiators signed a convention whereby the two Governments

undertake to see to the strict observance of the Treaties of St. Germain and Trianon. In particular they will take in common accord all political measures apt to prevent the restoration of the House of Hapsburg to the throne of Austria and Hungary.

To this end, the two Governments would lend each other diplomatic assistance and exchange information on any moves in Austria and Hungary against their mutual security. This convention was to be brought to the knowledge of the Czechoslovak Government, who, the Italian Government was happy to learn, had already made an agreement with Yugoslavia to the same effect.[54]

The Treaty signed, no time was lost in securing its ratification. In Yugoslavia, the Cabinet having approved it, it was signed by the Prince Regent Alexander on November 22.[55] In Italy, it was pre-

[53] *I.G.B.*, Doc. 72. This is the first instance of the use of Italian as an official language.
[54] *I.G.B.*, Doc. 73. In marked contrast with subsequent Italian policy, Giolitti and Sforza were willing to coöperate with, rather than oppose, the Little Entente.
[55] Korošeć, the Slovene Minister, however, abstained from signing it.

sented to the Chamber on the sixteenth, promptly examined and reported on by the Foreign Affairs committee, and, after three days' debate, approved by the large majority of 212 favorable votes to 15 against it and 40 abstentions. It was presented in the Senate on December 15 and, on the seventeenth, received 262 votes for ratification against 22 in opposition. Royal assent was given on the nineteenth, and final ratifications were exchanged on February 2, 1921.[56]

Despite the large favorable vote in Parliament, considerable criticism of the Treaty had been voiced during the debates, as well as in the press,[57] and there remained one thorny issue in the form of d'Annunzio's continued occupation of Fiume. Clearly, it was up to Italy to secure his departure. Hopes that he would accept the settlement of Rapallo were soon found to be vain. Under the name of Italian Regency of the Quarnero, an independent state had been proclaimed in Fiume, a solution not very different from the one sanctioned at Rapallo. But d'Annunzio refused to recognize that Treaty,[58] which he insisted should be modified. Reluctant to use force, save as a last resort, the Government allowed him for a time to continue in his self-appointed dictatorial rôle, while it secured ratification of the Treaty in Parliament. On December 1, d'Annunzio declared war on Italy, then proceeded to seize the islands of Arbe and Veglia. He was clearly powerless, however, to achieve anything of consequence if the Government was resolved to enforce the settlement, which it was now determined to do. Having made the necessary military and naval preparations, the city was surrounded; but, even then, d'Annunzio would not leave until some skirmishes had taken place and shells had been dropped on the city. Realizing at last the hopelessness of his position, he left, on December 29, after declaring that "Italy is not worth fighting for," and he let the municipality come to terms with General Caviglia, which they did on January 1, 1921.[59]

The Treaty of Rapallo did not completely settle the fate of Fiume,

---

[56] The debates in the Italian Parliament have been conveniently collected by Giannini, *Il trattato di Rapallo al parlamento italiano*. The figures quoted here are taken from this work. Temperley (IV, 334) gives slightly different figures—253 to 14 in the Chamber.

[57] Cf. Giannini, *Il trattato di Rapallo nei comenti della stampa*.

[58] The text had been communicated to him by the Italian Government.

[59] A good account of the last days of d'Annunzio in Fiume may be found in Zoli's *Le giornate di Fiume*. Zoli bore the impressive title of Under Secretary for Foreign Affairs of the Italian Regency of the Quarnero. Cf. also "L'Aventure de Fiume," *Revue des deux mondes*, April 1, 1921, pp. 662-69.

but, except for a stretch of about one mile between Fiume and Porto Baross, it did put an end to the irritating and dangerous uncertainty of an undefined frontier.[60] The division of territory finally agreed upon unquestionably represented substantial concessions on the part of Italy, in view of the promises made to her in the Treaty of London. And the decision to evict d'Annunzio from Fiume, by force if necessary, for all that it was justified, was a thankless task and an unpopular undertaking, which betokened courage and a sincere desire for agreement on the part of the Government. On the other hand, the Yugoslavs, and in particular the Croat and Slovene elements of the triune Kingdom, were disappointed at seeing nearly half a million of their numbers annexed to Italy. How far the Treaty was an openly consented agreement must remain an open question, for, having lost the support of the United States, Great Britain, and France, the Yugoslavs had little choice left. Again, it should be pointed out, the very fact that Great Britain and France supported Italy in her demands may be taken as an indication that they did not consider the settlement an unreasonable one. In Yugoslavia, the Treaty introduced, to a certain extent, a further element of discord between north and south, for the Croats and Slovenes could feel that they had been sacrificed by the Serbs. Much would depend upon the future relations of the two countries and the reciprocal treatment of their minorities: enlightened coöperation might soften what rivalry would turn into a deep-rooted grievance.[61] The frontier secured by Italy was an excellent one: it gave her the valuable mercury mines of Idria, uninterrupted rail communication between Trieste and Fiume through the St. Peter junction, and, with the possession of Monte Nevoso, command of the road to Ljubljana (Laibach). Perhaps the best commentary on the Treaty at the time was the amount of criticism which it aroused in both countries.

[60] A violent debate arose in Italy when it was found that Giolitti and Sforza had given Porto Baross to the Yugoslavs, the question being whether it was part of the *corpus separatum* or not, as claimed by Giolitti (*Memorie*, p. 585) and by Sforza (*Makers of Modern Europe*, pp. 239-40). Cf. also Benedetti *Fiume, Porto Baross e il retroterra*.

The difficult position of the independent state, created at Rapallo soon became apparent, and the question was not definitely disposed of until its annexation to Italy in 1924. Even d'Annunzio was eventually justified in Italy, and received the title of Prince of Monte Nevoso.

[61] Italo-Yugoslav relations since the Treaty of Rapallo have fluctuated, but, on the whole, may be said to have been anything but cordial. Of the latest developments in the shifting sands of European diplomacy, it is too early to speak. As to the city of Fiume, center of the controversy, economically it had been killed.

THE COLONIAL SETTLEMENT

African Questions

Save for a later modification of the status of the independent State of Fiume,[62] the Treaty of Rapallo may be considered as the final liquidation of the Italian territorial settlement resulting from the war. This was the case at least in Europe. But Italy had extra-European interests, mainly in Africa and in the Eastern Mediterranean, explicitly recognized in the Treaty of London and the subsequent agreements growing out of that Treaty. None of the Italian colonial problems were settled by the Peace Conference itself; however, to bring the story up to date, it is necessary to examine the fate of these agreements and the arrangements made with respect to these areas up to the end of 1920.[63]

The negotiations in this field, up to the time of the fall of the Orlando Cabinet, have been examined before.[64] The outstanding characteristic of Italian colonial policy during the first phase of the Peace Conference was its passivity, amounting almost, one might say, to an absence of policy, owing to an apparent lack of interest. Throughout that period, Italian energies were almost exclusively devoted to the conflict in the Adriatic, gradually narrowing down its object to the essentials of the Istrian frontier and Fiume. The noise and dust of that dispute served to divert attention from objectives farther from home, not only in popular opinion in Italy, but even among the Italian delegates themselves.

Despite the efforts of the first delegation, the best that could be done, even in that restricted sphere, was a stalemate. By the time of the signing of the German Treaty in June, the former German colonies had all been distributed to Great Britain and the Dominions, France, Belgium, and Japan.[65] That distribution, arranged in the absence of the Italian delegates, evoked no determined protest on their part; merely a reminder by Orlando, for the sake of the record,

---

[62] Finally annexed to Italy in 1924.

[63] No attempt is made here at an exhaustive treatment of these questions, which fall somewhat outside the purview of the present work, and are included for the sake of completeness.

[64] See Chap. VIII.

[65] Mandates were not formally drawn up and assigned until later, but the distribution followed the decisions of May, 1919.

it would seem, of the existence of Article 13 of the Treaty of London. In Asia Minor no final settlement had been reached in June, 1919, but the Greeks had been allowed to occupy Smyrna, which the St. Jean de Maurienne agreement had put in the Italian zone. Even this, a loss more positive than that of not sharing in the division of the German colonies, was accepted by Orlando with surprising meekness.

Africa was therefore no longer a subject for consideration by the Conference, in its purely territorial aspect at least, while Asia Minor remained so. In regard to the former, Italy could only take the position that, by virtue of Article 13 of the Treaty of London, she was entitled to receive certain compensations from Great Britain and from France. Whatever she eventually obtained in that continent, she secured as the result of direct negotiations with these Powers.

The program of the Italian colonial party has been outlined previously.[66] It was far more ambitious than the official program, of which, unfortunately, no precise statement is available. The more extreme claims, such as a Libyan hinterland extending to Lake Chad, did not warrant very serious attention; however, both Great Britain and France recognized the obligation of Article 13 of the Treaty of London.

Jibuti.—According to Tittoni, the Italians asked first of the French their small possession of Jibuti. As early as 1915, during the negotiation of the Treaty of London, the French, in order to forestall this demand, had proposed adding to Article 13 the following clause:

"From these compensations will be excluded the French colony of Obock-Jibuti whose territory is too small to be further diminished and whose situation on the road to Madagascar and to Indo-China is too important to make it the object of complete cession."

On the general plea that France was committed only to the general principle of compensations, and not to any specific cession, the reservation was withdrawn at the time.[67] In 1919 France refused again to cede Jibuti, which therefore had to be excluded from the domain of possible compensations.

Libya.—There remained Libya, with possible extensions to the west, south and east. In the south, the question of French cessions

---

[66] See above, pp. 221 ff. Cf. also C. Fidel, "Le Programme colonial italien et l'alliance franco-italienne," *Bulletin du comité de l'Afrique française,* 1919, p. 32.

[67] Tittoni's speech of Sept. 27, 1919. *Atti del Parlamento, 1913-19, Camera, Discussioni,* XIX, 21305.

in Borku and Tibesti was discussed, but no agreement was reached.[68] In the west, however, the French were willing to make some concessions, and an agreement was signed on September 12, 1919, between them and the Italians. As the result of this understanding, the two French salients between Gadames and Gat, and between Gat and Tummo, were removed, the actual frontier remaining to be determined by a mixed commission in such a way as to give Italy possession of the caravan route from Gadames to Gat, and a good connection between these points in all seasons, and wholly in Italian territory. From Gat to Tummo, the frontier was to be carried along the mountain ridge between these localities.[69] These concessions were aptly described by Tittoni as "surely useful but small things."[70] Several other minor agreements were also concluded between France and Italy at this time.

1. An agreement to join colonial railways, built or building, and to coördinate schedules, rates, and conditions of transportation for nationals and goods of the two countries.

2. An agreement whereby Italian schools in Tunisia were to enjoy the same status as French schools.

3. An extension to Tunisia of the agreement of 1916 for Italians in Morocco in the matter of labor accidents.

4. An undertaking on the part of France to supply from Tunisia Italian needs in phosphates from a yearly minimum of 600,000 tons.[71]

This is the sum total of the compensations which Italy secured from France, not very large, especially if we consider that, save for the territorial cessions, the other agreements could have been negotiated quite independently of the idea of compensations.

Libya and Juba.—With respect to Great Britain, Italy followed the same procedure. As early as June, 1919, Lord Milner had offered a zone to the east of Libya, including the oasis of Giarabub, and a strip of territory on the right bank of the Juba River, including the port of Kismayu (Chisimaio). There was some talk of cessions in British Somaliland, but apparently the offer was not substantial enough to

---

[68] Tittoni sought to minimize the value of this area, which is small indeed, in his speech of Sept. 27. The frontier in that region remained the line of the Anglo-French convention of 1899 until the Laval-Mussolini agreement of Jan., 1935. As the result of this agreement, the Libyan frontier was shifted to the south, parallel to the line of the Anglo-French convention, but beginning from Tummo (see Map IX).

[69] Rouard du Card, *La France et l'Italie et l'article 13 du Pacte de Londres*. See Map IX.

[70] Tittoni's speech of Sept. 27, *loc. cit.*

[71] *Ibid.*

be worth while. Tittoni finally decided to accept these concessions,[72] but it is of interest and importance that the negotiations were not formally closed, so that Article 13 of the Treaty of London remained a potential basis for further Italian claims in the future, so long at least as that Treaty was not denounced or superseded.[73]

Asia Minor—The Treaties of Sèvres

In the face of these rather meager results in Africa, Italy might have hoped, as Tittoni said, for compensations in Asia Minor. And yet Tittoni, speaking in September, 1919, recognized that the problem of Asia Minor, even more than any other, was "a source of dangers and uncertainties." Decision as to the fate of the Turkish Empire in its Turkish portion had been delayed, principally for two reasons. The first was the rivalry between British and French ambitions in that quarter of the globe; or, looked at from another angle, the ambiguous and conflicting commitments of Great Britain, on the one hand to the Arabs, who had been allowed to believe that she would support their aspiration to independence, and on the other to the French as embodied in the Sykes-Picot Treaty. Confronted with disagreement, the tendency had been to put off a decision. There had been considerable discussion during the first half of 1919, and various schemes and plans of partition had been brought forward, as outlined above,[74] none of them definitely accepted. Even at that time, however, the tendency had manifested itself of making light of the commitments to Italy, a tendency which there had been an attempt to justify by recourse to the legalistic argument that the St. Jean de Maurienne agreement was not valid, owing to its nonratification by Russia. The result was only increased friction between Italy and her Allies, the former resorting to unilateral action in the form of unauthorized landings in Asia Minor, the latter retaliating by sending the Greeks to Smyrna.[75] That sore point, Italian occupa-

---

[72] See Map IX. The actual treaty of cession was not signed until 1924.

[73] On this point, cf. Temperley, IV, 335-37.

[74] See above, pp. 218 ff.

[75] In the discussions of the Greek Committee, the French and the British were largely committed to Venizelos' claims, but the Americans steadily opposed these claims in Asia Minor. The Italians naturally opposed these claims also, as they were in conflict with their own aspirations. After indulging in obstructive tactics for a time, they finally ceased to take part in the discussions of that Committee. Cf. House and Seymour, *What Really Happened at Paris*, Chap. VIII: "The Armenian Problem and the Disruption of Turkey." The American

tion, was brought up in sharp language in the Allied note of June 28, 1919, originally intended for Orlando, which greeted the second Italian delegation upon its arrival in Paris. Having replied in unyielding terms on July 7, Tittoni succeeded in regularizing the situation by obtaining the sanction of the Council for the Italian occupation which was to be, officially, like the Greek occupation, Inter-Allied and provisional.[76] The Italian and the Greek zones were then specifically delimited. In July, likewise, Venizelos was called upon to account for the unfortunate circumstances which had attended the Greek occupation of Smyrna. On the twenty-second, the Council decided to send an Inter-Allied Commission of Inquiry. The report of this commission, which placed the blame on the Greeks, was ready on October 13, and was taken up by the Council in the first half of November. Despite its findings, the Greek occupation was confirmed, but a cautioning note was sent to Greece.[77]

The other cause of delay in the Turkish settlement was the fact that the United States had been asked to assume a mandate for Armenia. Wilson himself was not averse to this, but realized that American opinion would not look with favor upon such an entanglement. He therefore refused to commit himself definitely, and, pending his reply, the troublesome question was shelved during the summer of 1919. That reply was forthcoming at the end of October, and, as could have been foretold from developments in the United States, was a refusal to assume the Armenian mandate.[78]

With most of the other settlements out of the way, the Turkish problem had at last to be faced. Despite their mutual differences in the Near East, to some extent because of these very differences, British and French policy had in common, at this time, a marked uncertainty in dealing with the question. At the end of 1919, an agreement had been drawn up by the Foreign Office officials of the

position was weakened by the fact that, although Turkey was mentioned in the Fourteen Points (Point XII), the United States had not declared war on Turkey.

It is of interest that the suggestion of sending the Greeks to Smyrna had been made by Clemenceau as early as February, without apparently any opposition from Orlando. This according to Giannini, "La questione orientale alla conferenza della pace," *Oriente Moderno,* June, 1921, p. 4.

[76] On July 16. Cf. Tittoni's speech of Sept. 27, 1919; also Giannini, "La questione orientale," *op. cit.,* p. 6.

[77] Giannini ("La questione orientale," *op. cit.,* pp. 7-8) gives a detailed account of the report.

[78] Temperley, VI, 505.

two countries,[79] as the result of discussions between Curzon and Pichon. This scheme, approved by Lloyd George and Clemenceau, was based on ousting the Turks from Constantinople and the Straits, which were to be put under some international organization, and maintaining Turkish sovereignty in Anatolia, subject to zones of influence and foreign advisers. The scheme was rejected, however, in January by the British Cabinet as a whole.[80]

At the Conference of Paris, in January, 1920, it was decided to attack the Turkish question at the next meeting in London, in February. As early as January, Nitti indicated that he was in favor of leaving the Turks at Constantinople, but this view did not meet with the approval of the British and the French.[81]

At the London Conference (February 12-23), it was agreed to put the drafting of the Treaty in the hands of technicians, of which six commissions were formed. The Conference itself agreed on two general principles:

1. The Caliph and the Turkish Government should remain at Constantinople.

2. An international régime should be set up for the Dardanelles and the Bosphorus.

Venizelos was heard on the Greek claims on February 16, and again on the twenty-fourth, and it was then decided that Greece should have Thrace, and that Asia Minor should be left (nominally at least) under Turkish sovereignty. However, a special régime was to be set up for the Greeks in Smyrna, and the special interests of France in Cilicia and of Italy in the Adalia region were recognized.[82]

With these directions to guide them, the six commissions set to work and elaborated, after long discussions, the terms of the future treaty; their work was completed at the beginning of April. Events in the Near East were not waiting, however, for the leisurely convenience of the statesmen closeted in London. As early as 1919, it had become evident that the clauses of the Turkish Armistice, in particular those relating to disarmament, were not being carried out in Anatolia. The High Commissioners at Constantinople were instructed to make representations to the Turkish Government of

[79] Vansittart and Forbes Adam for the British, Philippe Berthelot and Kammerer for the French.

[80] Nicolson, *Curzon,* pp. 111-13.

[81] Giannini, "La questione orientale," *op. cit.,* p. 8.

[82] *Ibid.,* pp. 9-10.

Damad Ferid Pasha, who decided to send a personal emissary to Anatolia in the person of Mustapha Kemal. Before the order could be countermanded,[83] Kemal had left for Samsun. Instead of enforcing disarmament, Kemal, together with Bekir Pasha, who was already at work, began to organize the Turkish nationalist movement. His task was made considerably easier by the Greek occupation of Smyrna, which was taking place at this very time, May, 1919. In January, 1920, was issued the Turkish National Pact.[84]

Once sufficiently entrenched in Anatolia, Kemal's nationalists secured a large majority in the Parliament that met in Constantinople in January, 1920. From that time, Kemal was favored by circumstances, and received encouragement from his successful encounter with the French at Marash in Cilicia in March. In May, he drove the Italians from Konia. Neither the French nor the Italians were willing or able to carry on war in the interior of Asia Minor. As early as March 30, Nitti had declared in the Italian Chamber that Italy did not want territorial acquisitions in Asia Minor, but remained interested in the question of the Straits and the access to raw materials.[85] The British were no more in a mood for a military expedition than their Allies. They could easily, however, exert pressure at Constantinople; a note was sent to Turkey on March 8, and the decision to send an expedition was made on the tenth.[86] On March 16 key points were occupied in Constantinople, on the whole peaceably, prominent Kemalists arrested, and Parliament closed. The Allies could easily control Constantinople and press their demands upon the Sultan; their action served only to make the breach final: Kemal merely called his own Parliament at Angora and set up a régime independent of Constantinople.

The treaty drafted in London was examined at San Remo (April 19-26). The same divergences appeared between the Allies, and Nitti

---

[83] Upon representations of the High Commissioners, who at first had given their consent, an order was issued for the arrest of Kemal and his deportation to Malta. Nicolson, *Curzon,* p. 118; Sforza, *Makers of Modern Europe,* p. 353.

[84] For the text of the Turkish National Pact, cf. Mears, *Modern Turkey,* Doc. 18, pp. 629-31.

[85] Giannini, "La questione orientale," *op. cit.,* p. 12.

[86] Venizelos had been consulted on the fifth. Greek troops were readily available in Thrace in case of need. The Italians and the French were lukewarm about this occupation; the preponderance of the British naval force, which would tend to give the British a proportionately dominant influence at Constantinople, was one of the reasons for French and Italian opposition to taking action. There were also rumors of Franco-British differences over the command of the land forces.

pointed out the futility of drawing up a treaty which could not be executed or enforced.[87] The French position seems to have been still one of hesitancy at this time,[88] and in the absence of any prospect of real agreement, the decisions of London were ratified, one might say by default. Venizelos insisted that he could maintain himself in Anatolia, and what amounted to a separate State of Smyrna was set up, with a Greek administration; the zones of economic influence were recognized, and it was decided to ask Wilson to fix the frontiers of Armenia. The Turks, or rather the representatives of the Sultan, were summoned to receive the Treaty on May 11, and were given thirty days in which to submit their observations.

On May 13 Venizelos, perhaps for reasons of internal politics, disclosed the main provisions of the Treaty. This merely added fuel to the Turkish nationalist fire, and in June Kemal's troops showed signs of preparing to attack the British in the Ismid peninsula. The disturbing situation was discussed at the Boulogne Conference (June 21-22). Sforza, who had just come to the Foreign Ministry, took the reasonable attitude that the whole question ought to be reëxamined, and must be discussed with the Kemalist Government. He repeated the suggestion at Spa (July 5-16),[89] but in the face of British opposition and the lack of French support did not win his point. Instead Venizelos was summoned; he offered to extricate the Allies by undertaking, single-handed, to drive the Kemalists from the zone of the Straits, both in Europe and in Asia. British support of this scheme enabled him to put it into effect, and, to the satisfaction of both Venizelos and his supporters, it met at first with complete success: the Greeks encountered no appreciable resistance in Thrace, and in Asia Minor they drove the Turks back and effected their junction with the British forces at Ismid. They could easily have gone on to Constantinople, had they not been restrained by Franco-Italian objections, which the British did not see fit to attempt to overrule.[90] The result was that Kemal, though defeated, was not eliminated, and was enabled to withdraw farther into the interior and to reorganize his forces for a later reckoning, while the Greeks

[87] Giannini, "La questione orientale," *Oriente moderno*, Dec., 1921, p. 386; Nitti, *L'Europa senza pace*, p. 157.

[88] The main reason for this was the French reluctance openly to oppose the British, in order to preserve a united front toward Germany.

[89] Giannini, "La questione orientale," *op. cit.*, p. 386; Sforza, *Makers of Modern Europe*, pp. 164, 165, 358.

[90] Nicolson, *Curzon*, p. 251.

were left in an extended position, bearing the heavy financial burden of an expedition which their depleted treasury could ill afford. The episode is fully in keeping with the previous behavior of the Allies in these regions: in the last analysis, Turks, Greeks, and others were mere pawns in the game of power politics, whose welfare was a convenient commonplace for humanitarian speeches.

The Turkish delegation from Constantinople which had received the Treaty, naturally found many causes for objections, but in this case, as in the case of the other defeated Powers, these objections were, on the whole, not countenanced. The original month's delay was somewhat extended, but finally, on July 16, Millerand, acting for the Council, gave the Turks ten days in which to accept the Treaty as it then stood. This they did, and the Treaty was signed at Sèvres on August 10, 1920.

The Terms of the Sèvres Settlement

Besides the Treaty of Sèvres proper between the Allies and Turkey, a number of other treaties and agreements were signed on the same occasion.[91] These were:

1. Treaty between the Allied Powers and Greece in regard to Thrace (in fulfillment of Article 27 of the Turkish Treaty and of Article 48 of the Treaty of Neuilly with Bulgaria).

2. Treaty between the Allied Powers and Greece for the protection of minorities (Article 86 of the Turkish Treaty).

3. Treaty between the Allied Powers and Armenia, recognizing the latter as a sovereign and independent State (Article 93 of the Turkish Treaty).

4. Accord Tripartite between Great Britain, France, and Italy, recognizing and defining the special interests of these Powers in Asia Minor.

5. Treaty between Italy and Greece in regard to the Dodecanese (Article 122 of the Turkish Treaty).

Taken together, these treaties represent the settlement arranged for the former non-Arab territories of the Turkish Empire, as at-

---

[91] The texts of these various treaties are conveniently collected in Giannini, *I documenti diplomatici della pace orientale.* For an analysis of these treaties, cf. Giannini, "La questione orientale," *Oriente moderno,* Aug., 1921, pp. 132-51; also Temperley, VI, Chap. I, Part I, B; Part II. The Treaty of Sèvres proper is referred to as the Turkish Treaty.

tempted in 1920. It will suffice here to consider their provisions as they affected Italian interests.

Constantinople and the Straits. (Turkish Treaty, Articles 27, 36-61 and Annex, 178-80).—The Government of the Sultan was allowed to remain in Constantinople and to maintain there the capital of the Turkish State. The boundary between Turkish and Greek territory in Europe was placed at about the Chatalja lines. Turkish sovereignty was, in fact, considerably curtailed by the provision that "in the event of Turkey failing to observe faithfully the provisions of the present Treaty," particularly in regard to the protection of minorities, "the Allied Powers expressly reserve the right to modify the above provisions, and Turkey hereby agrees to accept any dispositions which may be taken in this connection" (Article 36).

The zone of the Straits comprised the Dardanelles, the sea of Marmora, and the Bosphorus with islands and shores, partly Turkish and partly Greek, and the Aegean islands of Lemnos, Imbros, Samothrace, Tenedos, and Mitylene. In this area, navigation was to be "open, both in peace and war, to every vessel of commerce or of war and to military and commercial aircraft, without distinction of flag" (Article 37). To insure and maintain this freedom of the Straits, the Turkish and the Greek Governments delegated to a "Commission of the Straits" the control of the waters between the Mediterranean mouth of the Dardanelles and the Black Sea mouth of the Bosphorus, extending three miles from each of these mouths. The zone was to be demilitarized and its existing fortifications demolished. The Commission was to consist of representatives of the United States (if and when willing to participate), the British Empire, France, Italy, Japan, and Russia (if and when it became a member of the League of Nations), with two votes each, and representatives of Greece, Rumania, Bulgaria, and Turkey (if and when these last two Powers became members of the League), with one vote each (Articles 37-40).

The result of this arrangement was in effect to sever Asiatic Turkey from its capital, which was further made defenseless.

Smyrna (Articles 65-83).—The city of Smyrna, with the territory described (see Map XII), remained under Turkish sovereignty in name, but the exercise of the right of sovereignty was transferred to Greece (Article 69). A local Parliament was to be elected and its relations with the Greek administration were to be in accordance with the Greek constitution (Articles 72-73). The territory could be incorporated in the Greek customs system (Article 76), but the Turkish currency remained legal tender and Greece was to abstain from any measures that would depreciate it (Article 77). After five years from the coming into force of the Treaty, the local Parliament could, by majority vote, ask the Council of the League of

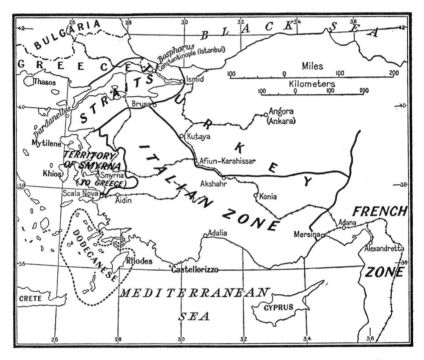

XII. THE PARTITION OF TURKEY ACCORDING TO THE TREATIES OF SÈVRES

The lines in this map are taken from Temperley, *A History of the Peace Conference of Paris.*

Nations for definitive incorporation in the Kingdom of Greece. The League reserved the right to require a preliminary plebiscite (Article 83).

To all intents and purposes, Smyrna and its territory were handed over to Greece.

Dodecanese.—Turkey renounced in favor of Italy all rights and title over the Aegean islands then occupied by Italy as well as Castellorizzo (Turkish Treaty, Article 122).

However, by the Italo-Greek Treaty of the same date, Italy transferred title to these islands to Greece, with the exception of Rhodes and Castellorizzo (Castelrosso) (Article 1). In regard to Rhodes, Italy would accord to it the right of self-determination as soon as Great Britain decided to give Cyprus to Greece, but in any case not before fifteen years (Article 2). The same Treaty extended to the territory of Smyrna the application of all treaties and conventions then in force between Italy and Greece.[92] Italy thus retained in full sovereignty the small island of Castellorizzo.[93]

Libya.—Turkey definitely renounced all rights and privileges left to the Sultan by the Treaty of Lausanne of October 18, 1912 (Article 121, Turkish Treaty).

Anatolia.—Great Britain, France, and Italy had renounced the idea of territorial acquisitions in Asia Minor, to which, in fact, Turkey was now reduced (save for the territory of Smyrna). Instead, they made among themselves the Accord Tripartite, with a view to eliminating friction in the economic exploitation of Turkey. This Accord Tripartite was due to their "being anxious to help Turkey, to develop her resources, and to avoid the international rivalries which had obstructed these objects in the past," and in order "to meet the request of the Turkish Government that it should receive the necessary assistance in the reorganization of the administration of justice, the finances, the gendarmerie and the police, in the protection of religious, racial and linguistic minorities and in the economic development of the country." Under the cover of these high-sounding motives, two spheres of influence, one French and one Italian, were delimited in Anatolia. The French zone (Cilicia) in the east, bordered on the Syrian mandate and Armenia, and had essentially the boundaries of the Sykes-Picot Treaty. The Italian sphere extended from the zone of the Straits in the north, completely surrounding the territory of Smyrna, to a line beginning west of Brusa, running in a southeasterly direction, joining the railway at Kutaya, then along the railway, which was left outside of the Italian zone, to Akshahr, and thence, cutting the railway, due east, till it joined the boundary of the French zone. (See Map XII.)

The railway of Anatolia, the Mersina-Adana railway, and the portion of the Baghdad railway within Ottoman territory, were to

---

[92] This treaty was divulged in the Italian Chamber by Sforza on Aug. 6, 1920.

[93] The reason for the special treatment of Castellorizzo was the fact that that island, separate from the Dodecanese group, belonged more closely to the mainland of the Adalia region, included in the zone of Italian interests.

be operated by a company whose capital was to be British, French and Italian in proportion to the respective interests of these Powers in the whole Baghdad line on August 1, 1914 (Article 4).

When the three Powers were agreed that the provisions of the Turkish Treaty had been executed, the French and the Italian Governments would withdraw their troops from their respective zones.

To this extent were fulfilled at Sèvres the terms of the secret treaties of 1915, 1916, and 1917 in regard to the Near East, in particular the St. Jean de Maurienne agreement.

Despite its elaborateness, the whole edifice of Sèvres never came into use. Nitti, and after him Sforza, had been quite right in pointing out at San Remo, Boulogne, and Spa the uselessness of such a settlement as was being made; in particular the folly of giving Greece a foothold in Asia Minor, than which nothing could have been better calculated to arouse a Turkish nationalism of the Western type, and finally of refusing to recognize the existence of that force and to deal with it in the person of Kemal. Acceptance of the Treaty could readily be imposed upon the Sultan under the threat of British men-of-war, but such acceptance would not be worth the paper it was written on when the Sultan's authority in Asia Minor was no longer existent. Great Britain was the only Power prepared to use force, and even she was willing to manifest it only in the relatively easier and less onerous form of maintaining a fleet in the Bosphorus. That action alone could have little influence in the interior of Asia Minor. When it came to the ultimately necessary use of land forces, which alone could be decisive, the matter was left to Venizelos and the Greek army. Greece alone, even with a British loan, could not conquer and hold Anatolia: in the end, she had to endure a bloody and needless war when she was rather ignominiously abandoned by her Allies. The British Government of the time, particularly Lloyd George, who was most responsible for continued support of the Greek expedition, eventually went down to defeat with the collapse of that policy. In the words of a recent writer:

The policy of Lloyd George in the Straits was almost a complete fiasco. That policy was not only to secure the lion's share in the breakup of the old Turkey, but to dominate and control the Straits and Constantinople. . . . Both Italy and France appear to have understood the fundamental aim of British policy, and from 1921 to the disastrous end in 1922, they held aloof from the futile Greek venture on which Mr. Lloyd George had set his mind and heart. . . . Deserted at home and abroad, on October 19, 1922, Lloyd George was forced to resign the office of prime minister, when the conservatives withdrew from the government coalition—a withdrawal due primarily to the failure of the eastern policy of the government.[94]

If the French gave no support to British policy, and even came to oppose it, yet with their eye on Germany, they dared not break openly with the British. The British, in turn, realized the danger to Europe of open opposition on their part to French policy. The result was the futile settlement of Sèvres in the Near East, and, in Europe, increasingly acrimonious Franco-British coöperation, with ill effects on all concerned—perhaps not least on Germany.

Italy had neither the security problem of the French, nor the far-flung imperial interests of the British. She could, and did, take a saner view of the Near Eastern question. If she could secure the frontier of the Treaty of London in Istria, she would be content for the rest to follow a general policy of coöperation and to concentrate her forces on recovery at home; hence the greater emphasis which the Giolitti-Sforza Ministry placed on economic clauses, and (save in Istria) its very liberal attitude in the matter of territorial settlements. It must be recognized, however, whether this be praise or criticism, that such an attitude is not consonant with being a colonial Power. It is accurate to say that, in 1919-20, Italy was not such a Power, and, what is more, gave no indication that she was attempting to be one.

Looking back over the war period and the events of the two years 1919-20, we can see the difficulties faced by Italy and the effect of these difficulties on her course of action. The dominant principle of European diplomacy had, for centuries, been the maintenance of the balance of power. The great and numerous wars of the past had their origin, in large part, in the attempt of some member or members of the European family to upset this balance in their own favor, and in the effort of the other members to maintain or restore this balance. This is equally true of the last war. The Treaty of

---

[94] Howard, *The Partition of Turkey*, p. 273. Italy and France came to terms with Nationalist Turkey in 1921. Eventually, the French provided military assistance to the Turks against the Greeks, who were expelled from Asia Minor. The Near Eastern question was not settled on a sound basis until the Treaty of Laûsanne was signed with Turkey in 1923.

London was based on this principle. The intervention of America and the unprecedented havoc wrought by the war gave to Sonnino's "negligible expedient of war propaganda" an unexpected reality and force. However, the attempt to set up the much-heralded new order merely ended, so far as Europe was concerned, in a temporary deviation of the time-honored doctrine of the balance of power; at no time did it command whole-hearted and unanimous support among the Governments.

The injection of the new principle in the peace settlement made Italy's position one of particular difficulty and invidiousness. In their dilemma, her first delegation would not agree on a firm line of policy. Sonnino wanted to rest his case solely on the Treaty of London; on the basis of compensations, the Italian demands could hardly be called excessive, and he could have held Italy's European Allies to the letter of that Treaty without great difficulty. But Wilson was in the way, backed by enormous power and prestige. Orlando, less rigid than his Foreign Minister, did not elect at first to appeal to the Treaty, but, willing to compromise though he was, he appeared to demand all the benefits of that Treaty, and Fiume in addition, all the while insisting that he adhered to the Wilsonian principles; on that basis, his case was inherently too weak to carry conviction. That first false move once made, he was no longer free to maneuver. The agitation which he had allowed at home made no impression abroad, and the false hopes encouraged by the delegation in Paris, long after Wilson's opposition had definitely asserted itself, made it increasingly difficult for him to effect the bargain for which he was prepared: Fiume for Dalmatia. Even more serious, his claim to Fiume gave his Allies an opening wedge. By the time matters in Italy had reached such a pass that Orlando had to have Fiume or resign, Great Britain and France, who had never had much affection for the Treaty of London, found it convenient to use the tactical opportunity offered them by this additional demand for Fiume to face Orlando with the alternative: Fiume or the Treaty. They let Orlando fight it out on the dramatized issue of the old order against the new. That conflict, real though it was, must not obscure the fact that Italy was, all the while, seeking to secure adequate compensations to match the advantages obtained by her Allies. That Orlando made tactical mistakes is clear. It is equally clear that the conflict between Italy and Wilson could not have been avoided, save by complete Italian surrender. That any Italian Ministry could have done that, and survived, may well be doubted.

Once in open conflict with America, Italy was evidently not strong enough to enforce her will; nor was she so weak that she could be coerced. Hence the stalemate, which neither Wilson's public appeal nor Orlando's withdrawal could break. The second Italian delegation first exerted themselves with some success in restoring a more favorable atmosphere; however, they too were prisoners of the situation which had developed under the tenure of their predecessors. The Fiume incidents and d'Annunzio's occupation of that city only served further to restrict their freedom of motion and tended to complicate and delay reaching an agreement. Nitti pursued a more strictly European policy, and, in the absence of an American representative in Europe, he secured the consent and support of Great Britain and France to a proposal not very different from the one which Orlando had been prepared to accept. But the three Powers had left Wilson out of their calculations; so long as the American President insisted on retaining the power of veto on any settlement, the Italo-American deadlock could not be broken. The Nitti Compromise had to be abandoned.

That deadlock was, in fact, broken only by the defeat of the Democratic party in the American election of 1920, and the Giolitti Ministry was wise enough to wait until it felt confident of this outcome before resuming negotiations with the Yugoslavs. Once America had disinterested herself in the European settlement, the Treaty of Rapallo was not long in the making. That Treaty, and, even more than the Treaty itself, the tendency of Italian policy at the time toward political and economic coöperation, augured well for the future peace of Central Europe and the Balkans. The attempt to set up for the administration of the whole port of Fiume a *Consortium* in which Italy, Yugoslavia, and the Free State would all be represented seemed the only reasonable way to insure the future prosperity of the town and a satisfactory *modus vivendi* among the three interested parties.

So, at least, it would have been but for the peculiar circumstances of the Rapallo settlement and the unsettled political situation in Italy. When the Treaty of Rapallo was signed, Sforza wrote a letter to Trumbić, according to the terms of which Porto Baross and the Delta between the former mouth of the Recina (Fiumara) and its present mouth were to pass under Yugoslav sovereignty. Unlike the Treaty itself the letter was not made public at the time. The reason for this procedure was apparently the desire on the part of the Government of securing ratification of the Treaty in the Italian Parliament, but the contents of Sforza's letter and the fact that it had been kept secret played into the hands of the intransigent elements in Italy and in Fiume. After d'Annunzio had left Fiume, the Municipal Council recognized the Treaty of Rapallo but with a special reservation with regard to Porto Baross and the Delta of the Recina. The result was continued friction between the Autonomist and Nationalist parties in the city which was the scene of a succession of local *putsches* and of interventions on the part of the Italian Government.[95] In June, 1921, the Giolitti-Sforza Ministry resigned, having failed to put into effect its proposed scheme for the above-mentioned *Consortium*. The un-settled situation continued, and a fresh agreement between Italy and Yugoslavia in October, 1922, proved equally inconclusive. At the end of that month there took place the Fascist *coup d'état* in Italy.

After a time, the Belgrade Government, no less weary than the Italian of the unsatisfactory *impasse*, accepted the solution outlined by the latter as early as November, 1922. Both the Treaty of Rapallo and Sforza's letter were recognized as binding by the Italian Gov-ernment; the very nature of the new régime, no longer handicapped by parliamentary criticism and whose nationalistic devotion was not open to question, enabled it to make greater concessions than had been possible for its predecessors. The Free State ceased to exist and its territory was divided into two parts: the city of Fiume proper and a strip of coast even narrower than that which had been originally assigned to the Free State were definitely annexed to Italy; the rest of the territory, including Porto Baross and the Delta of the Recina went to Yugoslavia. This arrangement was embodied in a Treaty signed in Rome on January 27, 1924, and its terms were put into execution the following month. Whether or not the statement that "at the close of 1924 the Adriatic Question had every appearance of being an extinct volcano"[96] has been justified and will continue to be so, it may be said at least that normal, if not genuinely friendly, relations had at last been reëstablished between the two countries.

[95] It is beyond the scope of the present work to enter into the detail of these events, which are merely summarized here for the sake of completeness, and of which a convenient account may be found in Toynbee's *Survey of International Affairs, 1924*, pp. 408-22.

[96] Toynbee, *op. cit.*, p. 422.

DOCUMENTS

ITALIAN MEMORANDUM OF MARCH 4, 1915[1]

1. Upon the declaration of war between Italy and Austria-Hungary, Italy, England, France, and Russia undertake not to conclude a separate peace or armistice.

2. A military convention shall be drawn up at once in order to establish the minimum force that Russia shall maintain against Austria-Hungary in order to prevent the latter from concentrating her entire effort against Italy, in the event that Russia should intend to turn her principal effort against Germany.

Italy, on her part, undertakes to make every possible effort in fighting Austria-Hungary and Turkey and whoever may assist them, on land and on sea.

3. A naval convention shall be drawn up at once in order to insure to Italy the active and permanent coöperation of the Anglo-French fleet until the destruction of the Austro-Hungarian fleet or the conclusion of peace.

4. In the treaty of peace, Italy shall obtain the Trentino and the Cisalpine Tyrol following the natural geographic boundary (frontier of the Brenner), and in addition, Trieste, the counties of Gorizia and Gradisca, and all Istria to the Quarnero, including Volosca; also the Istrian islands of Cherso, Lussin, and the smaller islands of Plavnik, Unie, Canidole, Sansego, Oriole, Palazzuoli, S. Pietro di Nembi, Asinello, Gruica, and neighboring islets.

5. Italy shall also receive the province of Dalmatia within its present administrative boundaries, including Lisarica and Tribania to the north and extending to the Narenta River to the south, besides the peninsula of Sabbioncello and all the islands lying north and west of Dalmatia proper, from Premuda, Selve, Ulbo, Maon, Pago, and Puntadura to the north to Meleda to the south, including San Andrea, Busi, Lissa, Lesina, Curzola, Cazza, and Lagosta with adjacent rocks, in addition to Pelagosa.

6. Valona and the island of Saseno, with the entire coast surrounding the bay and the territory necessary for their defense, shall go to Italy in full sovereignty (from the Vojussa to the north and east to about Chimara to the south).

---

[1] Salandra, *L'Intervento,* pp. 156-60. Text given in Italian. Author's translation. Cf. Salandra, *Italy and the Great War,* pp. 268-70. (See maps I and II.)

7. Should Italy obtain the Trentino and Istria in accordance with the terms of Article 4, Dalmatia and the Adriatic islands in accordance with Article 5, and the bay of Valona (Article 6), and the central part of Albania being reserved for the constitution of a small autonomous neutralized Moslem state, she shall not oppose the division of the remainder of Albania to the north and south between Montenegro, Serbia, and Greece, should England, France, and Russia so desire, provided that the coast beginning from and including the bay of Cattaro to the mouth of the Vojussa, and from Chimara to Cape Stylos, shall be neutralized.

8. Italy shall retain possession of the Dodecanese islands at present occupied by her.

9. In general, the contracting parties agree in recognizing that Italy has an interest in the maintenance of equilibrium in the Mediterranean, so that in the event of partition of all or part of the Ottoman Empire, Italy shall have her due share in it.

Italian interests shall likewise be taken into account in the event that the territorial integrity of the Ottoman Empire is maintained, only the present zones of interest of the various Powers being altered.

10. Italy shall succeed to all the rights and privileges in Libya at present belonging to the Sultan by virtue of the Treaty of Lausanne.

11. Italy shall receive a share in any eventual war indemnity corresponding to her efforts and sacrifices.

12. England and Italy mutually undertake to guarantee the independence of the Yemen. Leaving the Holy Places free, they undertake not to proceed to the annexation of any part of Western Arabia and not to impose upon it any form of dominion. They do not renounce the right to oppose the acquisition by another Power of rights over the territory of Arabia proper.

13. In the event that the other Powers should increase their African colonies at the expense of Germany, an agreement shall be made to insure to Italy some corresponding equitable compensation, particularly as regards the settlement in her favor of the boundary questions between her colonies of Eritrea, Somaliland, and Libya and the adjoining French and English colonies.

14. England undertakes to facilitate the immediate conclusion, under equitable conditions, of a loan of not less than £50,000,000 on the London market.

15. England, France, and Russia undertake to support Italy in opposing any eventual proposal to admit a representative of the Holy See to the Peace Conference at the conclusion of the present war.

16. The present agreement shall remain secret. As soon as war shall have been declared by or against Italy, the clause relating to the undertaking not to make separate peace shall alone be made public.

DOCUMENT 2

ITALIAN DEMANDS TO AUSTRIA-HUNGARY[1]

THE MINISTER FOR FOREIGN AFFAIRS TO THE ITALIAN AMBASSADOR AT VIENNA

(Telegram.)   Rome, 8th April, 1915.

To satisfy the wish expressed by Baron Burian I here formulate the conditions which the Royal Italian Government considers indispensable if a normal and enduring situation of reciprocal cordiality and of possible future coöperation towards common aims of general policy is to be created between the two States.

Your Excellency will more fully explain to Baron Burian the reasons that support each of the proposals, in formulating which I have taken fully into account the various observations laid before me in the past regarding the needs of the Austro-Hungarian Empire.

I trust that the Imperial Government will grant us with the least possible delay an answer which I hope may be acceptable.

Article I is inspired by an important historical precedent, as well as by obvious reasons of a military character regarding the tracing of the new frontier.

Article II is also justified by military considerations, as well as by ethnological reasons.

Article III represents the only possible compromise between the announced exigencies of the Austro-Hungarian Empire and those of the national principle.

Article IV aims at slightly lessening the painful conditions of inferiority in which Italy finds herself in the Adriatic.

Article V represents the condition *sine qua non* by which any agreement may to-day be concluded; without it no government in Italy could seriously undertake for the whole duration of the war the engagements with which the last two articles, X and XI, are concerned.

Articles VI and VII remove for the future a subject of friction and of

---

[1] *Diplomatic Documents submitted to the Italian Parliament by the Minister for Foreign Affairs (Sonnino). Austria-Hungary. Session of the 20th May, 1915 [Italian Green Book],* Document 64. Scott, *Diplomatic Documents relating to the Outbreak of the European War,* Pt. II, pp. 1299-1302. Cf. also, *Diplomatic Documents concerning the Relations of Austria-Hungary with Italy from July 20, 1914, to May 23, 1915 [Austrian Red Book, No. 2],* Document 141. Scott, *op. cit.,* Pt. I, pp. 263-66. (See map I.)

disagreement between the two States, legitimately safeguarding Italian interests in the Adriatic without hurting those of Austria-Hungary.

Articles VIII and IX explain themselves.

Here follows the text of the articles:

Article I. Austria-Hungary cedes to Italy the Trentino with the frontiers which were those of the Italian Kingdom in 1811, that is to say, after the Treaty of Paris on the 28th February, 1810.

Note to Article I. The new frontier detaches from the present one at Mount Cevedale; it follows for some way the counterfort between Val Venosta and Val Del Noce; then it descends the Adige to Gargazone between Merano and Bolzano, reascends the higher ground on the left bank, divides the Val Sarentina and the Valley of the Isarco at Chiusa and the dolomitic territory on the right bank of the Avisio; excluding the valleys of Gardona and Badia and including Ampezzano, it rejoins the present frontier.

Article II. Italy's eastern frontier is to be corrected in her favour, so as to bring the cities of Gradisca and Gorizia within the ceded territory. From Troghofel the new frontier is to detach from the present one, and to run eastwards as far as Osternig, thence descending from the Carnic Alps down to Saifniz. Thence by the counterfort between Seisera and Schliza it is to ascend the Wirsehberg and then to follow the present frontier as far as the summit of Nevea, and to run down from the base of the Rombone to the River Isonzo, passing to eastward of Plezzo. It is then to follow the line of the Isonzo as far as Tolmino, where it leaves the Isonzo to pursue a more easterly line, which passing on the eastern side of the heights of Pregona-Planina and following the track of the Chiappovano runs up to eastward of Gorizia and crossing the Carso di Comen ends at the sea between Monfalcone and Trieste in the neighbourhood of Nabresina.

Article III. The city of Trieste with its territory, which is to be extended on the north until it includes Nabresina, so as to reach to the new Italian frontier (Article II), and on the south until it includes the present judiciary districts of Capo d'Istria and Pirano, is to be constituted an autonomous and independent State in all that regards its internal [international], military, legislative, financial and administrative policies, and Austria-Hungary shall renounce all sovereignty over it. It is to remain a free port. It should not be entered by either Austro-Hungarian or Italian soldiers. It should assume a quota of the present Austrian Public Debt proportionate to its population.

Article IV. Austria-Hungary cedes to Italy the Archipelago of Curzola, including Lissa (with the neighbouring islets of St. Andrea and Busi), Lesina (with Spalmadori and Torcola), Curzola, Lagosta (with the neighbouring islets and rocks), Cazza, Meleda and Pelagosa.

Article V. Italy should immediately occupy the ceded territories (Articles I, II and IV), whilst Trieste and its territory (Article III) should be evacuated by the Austro-Hungarian authorities and military forces, with the immediate discharge of all soldiers and sailors derived from one and the other.

Article VI. Austria-Hungary is to recognise Italy's full sovereignty over Valona, and its bay comprising Sasseno, together with such territory in the *hinterland* as may be required for their defence.

Article VII. Austria-Hungary is to cease completely to interest herself in Albania as comprised within the frontiers traced by the Conference of London.

Article VIII. Austria-Hungary is to grant a complete amnesty followed by the immediate release of all those prosecuted and convicted upon military and political grounds who are natives of the ceded territories (Articles I, II and IV) and of the evacuated territories (Article III).

Article IX. For the delivery of the ceded territories (Articles I, II and IV) from their quota of responsibility in the Austro-Hungarian Public Debt as well as in the debt resulting from pensions to retired Imperial and Royal functionaries, and against the integral and immediate transference to Italy of all domanial property, movable or immovable, with the exception of arms, situated in the said territories, and in compensation for every State right concerned with the said territories, in all that may refer to them whether at present or in future, without any exception whatsoever, Italy will pay Austria-Hungary the capital sum in gold of 200,000,000 Italian lire.

Article X. Italy undertakes to maintain perfect neutrality throughout all the present war with regard to Austria-Hungary and Germany.

Article XI. For the entire duration of the present war Italy renounces all power subsequently to invoke in her own favour the provisions of Article VII of the Treaty of the Triple Alliance; and Austria-Hungary is to make the same renouncement in all that regards Italy's effected occupation of the islands of the Dodecanesus.

SONNINO.

TREATY OF LONDON AND DECLARATIONS[1]

I. AGREEMENT BETWEEN FRANCE, RUSSIA, GREAT BRITAIN AND ITALY, SIGNED AT LONDON, APRIL 26, 1915

By Order of his Government the Marquis Imperiali, Ambassador of His Majesty the King of Italy, has the honour to communicate to the Rt. Hon. Sir Edward Grey, His Britannic Majesty's Principal Secretary of State for Foreign Affairs, and to their Excellencies M. Paul Cambon, Ambassador of the French Republic, and to Count de Benckendorff, Ambassador of His Majesty the Emperor of All the Russias, the following memorandum:

Memorandum

Article 1. A military convention shall be immediately concluded between the General Staffs of France, Great Britain, Italy and Russia. This convention shall settle the minimum number of military forces to be employed by Russia against Austria-Hungary in order to prevent that Power from concentrating all its strength against Italy, in the event of Russia deciding to direct her principal effort against Germany.

This military convention shall settle question of armistices, which necessarily comes within the scope of the Commanders-in-chief of the Armies.

Article 2. On her part, Italy undertakes to use her entire resources for the purpose of waging war jointly with France, Great Britain and Russia against all their enemies.

Article 3. The French and British fleets shall render active and permanent assistance to Italy until such time as the Austro-Hungarian fleet shall have been destroyed or until peace shall have been concluded.

A naval convention shall be immediately concluded to this effect between France, Great Britain and Italy.

Article 4. Under the Treaty of Peace, Italy shall obtain the Trentino, Cisalpine Tyrol with its geographical and natural frontier (the Brenner frontier), as well as Trieste, the counties of Gorizia and Gradisca, all

---

[1] This is the text given in the British White Paper, Misc. No. 7, 1920, Cmd. 671. For the official French text, cf. *Documenti diplomatici: Accordo di Londra del 26 Aprile 1915*, Rome, 1922. (See maps I and II.)

Istria as far as the Quarnero and including Volosca and the Istrian islands of Cherso and Lussin, as well as the small islands of Plavnik, Unie, Canidole, Palazzuoli, San Pietro di Nembi, Asinello, Gruica, and the neighbouring islets.

Note. The frontier required to ensure execution of Article 4 hereof shall be traced as follows:

From the Piz Umbrail as far as north of the Stelvio, it shall follow the crest of the Rhetian Alps up to the sources of the Adige and the Eisach, then following the Reschen and Brenner mountains and the Oetz and Ziller heights. The frontier shall then bend towards the south, cross Mt. Toblach and join the present frontier of the Carnic Alps. It shall follow this frontier line as far as Mt. Tarvis and from Mt. Tarvis the watershed of the Julian Alps by the Predil Pass, Mt. Mangart, the Tricorno (Terglu) and the watersheds of the Podberdo, Podlaniscam and Idria passes. From this point the frontier shall follow a south-easterly direction towards the Schneeberg, leaving the entire basin of the Save and its tributaries outside Italian territory. From the Schneeberg the frontier shall come down to the coast in such a way as to include Castua, Mattuglia and Volosca within Italian territory.

Article 5. Italy shall also be given the province of Dalmatia within its present administrative boundaries, including to the north Lisarica and Tribania; to the south as far as a line starting from Cape Planka on the coast and following eastwards the crests of the heights forming the watershed, in such a way as to leave within Italian territory all the valleys and streams flowing towards Sebenico—such as the Cicola, Kerka, Butisnica and their tributaries. She shall also obtain all the islands situate to the north and west of Dalmatia, from Premuda, Selve, Ulbo, Scherda, Maon, Pago and Patadura to the north, up to Meleda to the south including Sant' Andrea, Busi, Lissa, Lesina, Tercola, Curzola, Cazza and Lagosta, as well as the neighbouring rocks and islets and Pelagosa, with the exception of Greater and Lesser Zirona, Bua, Solta and Brazza.

To be neutralised:

(1) The entire coast from Cape Planka on the north to the southern base of the peninsula of Sabbioncello in the south, so as to include the whole of that peninsula; (2) the portion of the coast which begins in the north at a point situated 10 kilometres south of the headland of Ragusa Vecchia extending southward as far as the River Voïussa, in such a way as to include the gulf and ports of Cattaro, Antivari, Dulcigno, St. Jean de Medua and Durazzo, without prejudice to the rights of Montenegro consequent on the declarations exchanged between the Powers in April and May 1909. As these rights only apply to the present Montenegrin territory, they cannot be extended to any territory or ports which may be assigned to Montenegro. Consequently neutralisation shall

not apply to any part of the coast now belonging to Montenegro. There shall be maintained all restrictions concerning the port of Antivari which were accepted by Montenegro in 1909; (3) finally, all the islands not given to Italy.

Note. The following Adriatic territory shall be assigned by the four Allied Powers to Croatia, Serbia and Montenegro:

In the Upper Adriatic, the whole coast from the bay of Volosca on the borders of Istria as far as the northern frontier of Dalmatia, including the coast which is at present Hungarian, and all the coast of Croatia, with the port of Fiume and the small ports of Novi and Carlopago, as well as the islands of Veglia, Pervichio, Gregorio, Goli and Arbe. And, in the Lower Adriatic (in the region interesting Serbia and Montenegro) the whole coast from Cape Planka as far as the River Drin, with the important harbours of Spalato, Ragusa, Cattaro, Antivari, Dulcigno and St. Jean de Medua and the islands of Greater and Lesser Zirona, Bua, Solta, Brazza, Jaclian and Calamotta. The port of Durazzo to be assigned to the independent Moslem State of Albania.

Article 6. Italy shall receive full sovereignty over Valona, the island of Saseno and surrounding territory of sufficient extent to assure defence of these points (from the Voïussa to the north and east, approximately to the northern boundary of the district of Chimara on the south).

Article 7. Should Italy obtain the Trentino and Istria in accordance with the provisions of Article 4, together with Dalmatia and the Adriatic islands within the limits specified in Article 5, and the Bay of Valona (Article 6), and if the central portion of Albania is reserved for the establishment of a small autonomous neutralised State, Italy shall not oppose the division of Northern and Southern Albania between Montenegro, Serbia and Greece, should France, Great Britain and Russia so desire. The coast from the southern boundary of the Italian territory of Valona (see Article 6) up to Cape Stylos shall be neutralised.

Italy shall be charged with the representation of the State of Albania in its relations with foreign Powers.

Italy agrees, moreover, to leave sufficient territory in any event to the east of Albania to ensure the existence of a frontier line between Greece and Serbia to the west of Lake Ochrida.

Article 8. Italy shall receive entire sovereignty over the Dodecanese Islands which she is at present occupying.

Article 9. Generally speaking, France, Great Britain and Russia recognise that Italy is interested in the maintenance of the balance of power in the Mediterranean and that, in the event of the total or partial partition of Turkey in Asia, she ought to obtain a just share of the Mediterranean region adjacent to the province of Adalia, where Italy has already acquired rights and interests which formed the subject of an Italo-British convention. The zone which shall eventually be allotted to Italy shall be delimited, at the proper time, due account being taken of the existing interests of France and Great Britain.

The interests of Italy shall also be taken into consideration in the event of the territorial integrity of the Turkish Empire being maintained and of alterations being made in the zones of interest of the Powers.

If France, Great Britain and Russia occupy any territories in Turkey in Asia during the course of the war, the Mediterranean region bordering on the Province of Adalia within the limits indicated above shall be reserved to Italy, who shall be entitled to occupy it.

Article 10. All rights and privileges in Libya at present belonging to the Sultan by virtue of the Treaty of Lausanne are transferred to Italy.

Article 11. Italy shall receive a share of any eventual war indemnity corresponding to her efforts and her sacrifices.

Article 12. Italy declares that she associates herself in the declaration made by France, Great Britain and Russia to the effect that Arabia and the Moslem Holy Places in Arabia shall be left under the authority of an independent Moslem Power.

Article 13. In the event of France and Great Britain increasing their colonial territories in Africa at the expense of Germany, those two Powers agree in principle that Italy may claim some equitable compensation, particularly as regards the settlement in her favour of the questions relative to the frontiers of the Italian colonies of Eritrea, Somaliland and Libya and the neighbouring colonies belonging to France and Great Britain.

Article 14. Great Britain undertakes to facilitate the immediate conclusion, under equitable conditions, of a loan of at least £50,000,000 to be issued on the London market.

Article 15. France, Great Britain and Russia shall support such opposition as Italy may make to any proposal in the direction of introducing a representative of the Holy See in any peace negotiations or negotiations for the settlement of questions raised by the present war.

Article 16. The present arrangement shall be held secret. The adherence of Italy to the Declaration of the 5th September, 1914, shall alone be made public, immediately upon declaration of war by or against Italy.

After having taken act of the foregoing memorandum, the representatives of France, Great Britain and Russia, duly authorised to that effect, have concluded the following agreement with the representative of Italy, also duly authorised by his Government:

France, Great Britain and Russia give their full assent to the memorandum presented by the Italian Government.

With reference to Articles 1, 2 and 3 of the memorandum, which provide for military and naval co-operation between the four Powers, Italy declares that she will take the field at the earliest possible date and within a period not exceeding one month from the signature of these presents.

In faith whereof the undersigned have signed the present agreement and have affixed thereto their seals.

Done at London, in quadruplicate, the 26th day of April, 1915.

(L.S.) E. GREY.

(L.S.) IMPERIALI.

(L.S.) BENCKENDORFF.

(L.S.) PAUL CAMBON.

II. DECLARATION BY WHICH FRANCE, GREAT BRITAIN, ITALY AND RUSSIA UNDERTAKE NOT TO CONCLUDE A SEPARATE PEACE DURING THE COURSE OF THE PRESENT EUROPEAN WAR

The Italian Government, having decided to participate in the present war with the French, British and Russian Governments and to accede to the Declaration made at London, the 5th September, 1914, by the three above-named Governments,

The undersigned, being duly authorised by their respective Governments, make the following declaration:

The French, British, Italian and Russian Governments mutually undertake not to conclude a separate peace during the course of the present war.

The four Governments agree that, whenever there may be occasion to discuss the terms of peace, none of the Allied Powers shall lay down any conditions of peace without previous agreement with each of the other Allies.

In faith whereof the undersigned have signed the present Declaration and have affixed thereto their seals.

Done at London, in quadruplicate, the 26th day of April, 1915.

(L.S.) E. GREY.

(L.S.) IMPERIALI.

(L.S.) BENCKENDORFF.

(L.S.) PAUL CAMBON.

III. DECLARATION

The Declaration of the 26th April, 1915, whereby France, Great Britain, Italy and Russia undertake not to conclude a separate peace during the present European war, shall remain secret.

After the declaration of war by or against Italy, the four Powers shall sign a new declaration in identical terms, which shall thereupon be made public.

In faith whereof the undersigned have executed the present Declaration and have affixed thereto their seals.

Done at London, in quadruplicate, the 26th day of April, 1915.

(L.S.) E. GREY.
(L.S.) IMPERIALI.
(L.S.) BENCKENDORFF.
(L.S.) PAUL CAMBON.

DOCUMENT 4

DENUNCIATION OF THE TRIPLE ALLIANCE[1]

THE MINISTER FOR FOREIGN AFFAIRS TO THE ITALIAN AMBASSADOR AT VIENNA

(Telegram.) Rome, 3rd May, 1915.

I beg your Excellency to convey the following communication to the Minister for Foreign Affairs there, of which you will leave him a written copy:

The alliance between Italy and Austria-Hungary proclaimed itself, from the first, to be an element and a guarantee of peace, aiming first of all as the principal object at common defence. In view of subsequent events and of the new situation arising out of them, the two countries found it necessary to propose a new object no less essential, and in course of the successive renewals of the Treaty, they devoted themselves to safeguarding the continuity of their alliance, stipulating the principle of preliminary agreements regarding the Balkans, with a view to reconciling the divergent interests and propensities of the two Powers.

It is very evident that these stipulations, loyally observed, would have sufficed as a solid basis for a common and fruitful action. But Austria-Hungary, in the summer of 1914, without coming to any agreement with Italy, without even giving her the least intimation, and without taking any notice of the counsels of moderation addressed to her by the Royal Italian Government, notified to Serbia the ultimatum of the 23rd July, which was the cause and the point of departure of the present European conflagration.

Austria-Hungary by disregarding the obligations imposed by the Treaty profoundly disturbed the Balkan *status quo*, and created a situation from which she alone should profit to the detriment of interests of the greatest importance which her ally had so often affirmed and proclaimed.

So flagrant a violation of the letter and the spirit of the Treaty not only justified Italy's refusal to place herself on the side of her allies in a war provoked without previous notice to her, but at the same time deprived the alliance of its essential character and of its *raison d'être*.

Even the compact of friendly neutrality for which the Treaty provides

[1] *Italian Green Book*, Document 76. Scott, *Diplomatic Documents relating to the Outbreak of the European War*, Pt. II, pp. 1316-18. Cf. also, *Austrian Red Book*, No. 2, Document 170. Scott, *op. cit.*, Pt. I, pp. 294-97.

was compromised by this violation. Reason and sentiment alike agree in preventing friendly neutrality from being maintained when one of the allies has recourse to arms for the purpose of realising a programme diametrically opposed to the vital interests of the other ally, interests the safeguarding of which constituted the principal reason of the alliance itself.

Notwithstanding this, Italy exerted herself for several months to create a situation that should be favourable to the reëstablishment between the two States of these friendly relations which constitute the essential foundation of all coöperation in the domain of general policy.

With this aim and in this hope the Royal Italian Government announced its willingness to come to an arrangement having for its basis the satisfaction in an equitable degree of the legitimate national aspirations of Italy and serving at the same time to reduce the disparity existing in the reciprocal position of the two States in the Adriatic.

These negotiations did not lead, however, to any appreciable result.

All the efforts of the Royal Italian Government met with the resistance of the Imperial and Royal Government, which even now, after several months, has consented only to admit the special interests of Italy in Valona, and to promise an insufficient concession of territory in the Trentino, a concession which in no way admits of the normal settlement of the situation, whether from the ethnological, the political or the military point of view.

This concession, moreover, was to be carried into effect only in an indeterminate epoch, namely not until the end of the war.

In this state of things the Italian Government must renounce the hope of coming to an agreement, and sees itself compelled to withdraw all its proposals for a settlement.

It is equally useless to maintain for the alliance a formal appearance which could only serve to dissemble the reality of continual mistrust and daily opposition.

For these reasons Italy, confident of her just rights, affirms and proclaims that she resumes from this moment her complete liberty of action, and declares as cancelled and as henceforth without effect her treaty of alliance with Austria-Hungary.

SONNINO.

DOCUMENT 5

AUSTRO-HUNGARIAN OFFER OF MAY 19, 1915[1]

AUSTRO-HUNGARIAN EMBASSY IN ITALY

Rome, May 19, 1915.

Mr. President,

My Government has realized that the guarantees to be given to Italy on the score of the execution of the cessions which Austria-Hungary is prepared to make, constitute one of the most important elements for reaching an agreement.

It has therefore wished to add to the draft agreement, which I presented yesterday to His Excellency Baron Sonnino, a new article (14) which emphasizes with absolute clarity that the transfer of the ceded territories shall suffer no delay.

Having been instructed to give you this draft agreement thus completed, I hasten to send it here enclosed.

Please accept, Mr. President, . . .

(*Signed*) B. MACCHIO.

Moved by the sincere desire to consolidate the mutual relations between Austria-Hungary and Italy, to put them on a basis of complete good faith, to eliminate any cause of friction between the two countries, and to reach a definite and durable understanding, the Imperial and Royal Government and the Royal Government of Italy have agreed to the following:

Article 1. In conformity with the wish expressed by Italy to come into possession of those parts of the Tyrol whose inhabitants are of Italian nationality, Austria-Hungary accepts a new frontier line, which, leaving the present frontier near the Zufallspitze, shall follow the boundary between the district of Cles and those of Schlanders and Merano, that is the watershed between the Noce and the Adige, up to the Ilmenspitze. It shall then run west of Proveis, leaving this commune in the Austrian Tyrol, and join the Pescara Torrent whose *thalweg* it shall follow up

---

[1] Salandra, *L'intervento*, pp. 292-96. Text given in French; author's translation. This document is omitted in the English translation of Salandra's book, *Italy and the Great War* (cf. p. 357 n.). Cf. also, *Austrian Red Book, No.* 2, Documents 185, 188. Scott, *Diplomatic Documents relating to the Outbreak of the European War*, Pt. I, pp. 311-16, 318-21. (See map I.)

to its confluent with the Noce. It shall then follow the *thalweg* of the Noce which it shall leave south of Tajo, go over the Corno di Tres, follow the northern boundary of the district of Mezzolombardo, and join the Adige south of Salurno. It shall pass over the Geiersberg, follow the watershed between the valleys of the Avisio and the Adige, passing over the Castion, and continue toward the Hornspitze and Mount Comp. It shall then turn south, describing a semicircle, so as to leave the commune of Altrei in the Austrian Tyrol, and continue to the pass of San Lugano. It shall follow the boundary between the districts of Bolzano and Cavalese, that is the watershed between the Avisio and the Adige, going over the Cima di Rocca and the Grimmjoch to the Latemar. From Cornon Pass it shall descend toward the Avisio, crossing this river between the communes of Moena and Forno, and rejoin the watershed between the valleys of San Pellegrino to the north and of Travignolo to the south. It shall join the present frontier east of Cima di Bocche.

Article 2. Austria-Hungary agrees, in addition, to cede to Italy the territory on the western bank of the Isonzo in so far as the population is wholly of Italian nationality.

Beginning from the mouth of the Isonzo (Sdobba), the new frontier shall follow the *thalweg* of this river to a point beyond Gradisca, which shall be included in the territory ceded to Italy. It shall then leave the Isonzo, turn northwest toward Medea and join the Iudrio, whose *thalweg* shall continue to form the frontier.

Article 3. The title of "Free Imperial City" shall be conferred upon the city of Trieste. It shall be provided with a university and receive a new municipal statute which, while preserving the rights of full autonomy which it enjoys at present, shall insure, in addition, the Italian character of this city.

The present zone of the free port shall be preserved and, if need be, enlarged.

Article 4. Austria-Hungary is prepared on her part to recognize full Italian sovereignty over Valona and its bay, as well as the sphere of influence of which it would be the center.

Article 5. Austria-Hungary declares that she is politically disinterested in Albania within the frontiers assigned by the London Conference.

Article 6. As a certain number of subjects of Italian nationality will still remain in Austria-Hungary after the conclusion of this agreement, the Austrian and Hungarian Governments shall exercise special care in safeguarding their national interests.

Article 7. Austria-Hungary shall grant a complete amnesty and set free at once all persons coming from the territories ceded to Italy who have been condemned or indicted for military or political reasons.

Article 8. Italy undertakes to maintain complete neutrality during the present war with respect to Germany, Austria-Hungary, and Turkey.

Article 9. Italy renounces all claim to compensation for any advantage, territorial or otherwise, which may accrue to Austria-Hungary during the course of the present war or from the treaties of peace that shall end it.

Article 10. On her part Austria-Hungary renounces all claims based on the fact of the Italian occupation of the Dodecanese islands.

Article 11. Italy declares herself ready to pay a total sum by way of inclusive indemnity for the cession to her of the above-mentioned territories; a mixed commission shall establish the modalities and the amount of the payment and shall, in case of disagreement, submit the question to the decision of the International Arbitration Tribunal at the Hague.

Article 12. Immediately after the conclusion of this agreement, the Imperial and Royal Government shall proceed to a solemn manifestation in regard to the territorial cession.

Article 13. Mixed commissions shall be constituted on the spot for the settlement of details relative to the cession of the territories in question. These commissions shall be empowered to take decisions which shall be submitted to the Governments for ratification.

The powers of these commissions shall be determined in detail by an additional protocol.

Article 14. The mixed commissions mentioned in the preceding article shall set to work immediately after the conclusion of this agreement.

The transfer of territory shall take place immediately after the ratification of the decisions of the commissions and shall be effected within a month's time.

Article 15. Immediately after the conclusion of this agreement, the soldiers coming from the territories ceded to Italy shall be withdrawn from the Austro-Hungarian lines.

Article 16. Austria-Hungary and Italy accept the guarantee assumed by Germany for the faithful and loyal execution of this agreement.

ST. JEAN DE MAURIENNE AGREEMENT[1]
April 19-21, 1917

Subject to the consent of the Russian Government:

1. The Italian Government gives its assent to the provisions contained in Articles 1 and 2 of the Franco-British agreements of May 9 and 16, 1916. On their part the French and British Governments recognize Italy's rights—on an identical basis as to conditions of administration and interest—to the green and "C" zones indicated in the map attached hereto.

2. Italy undertakes to make of Smyrna a free port in so far as the trade of France, her colonies and her protectorates, as well as that of the British Empire and its dependencies, is concerned. Italy will enjoy the rights and privileges which France and Great Britain have reciprocally guaranteed each other in the ports of Alexandretta, Haifa and of Saint Jean d'Acre (Akka) by Articles 5 of the agreements mentioned heretofore. Mersina shall be a free port with regard to the trade of Italy, her colonies and her protectorates, and there shall be no difference of treatment nor any advantages in port duties which may be refused to Italian ships or goods. Italian goods destined to or coming from the Italian zone shall obtain free transit through Mersina and on the railway crossing the vilayet of Adana. There shall be no difference of treatment, direct or indirect, as against Italian goods on any railway line nor in any port along the Cilician coast and serving the Italian zone at the expense of Italian ships or merchandise.

3. The form of the international administration in the brown zone, which forms the object of Article 3 of the said arrangements of May 9 and 16, 1916, shall be decided in agreement with Italy.

4. On her part Italy adheres to the provisions concerning the ports of Haifa and Akka contained in Article 4 of the same agreements.

5. Italy adheres, in so far as the green and "C" zones are concerned, to the two paragraphs of Article 8 of the Anglo-French agreements referring to the customs system to be maintained in the blue and red zones, as well as in the zones "A" and "B."

6. It is understood that the interests possessed by each power in the

---

[1] Mears, *Modern Turkey*, pp. 619-20. For the French text, cf. *Trattati e convenzioni*, XXIII, 467-69. (See map VIII.)

zones falling to the lot of the other powers shall be scrupulously respected, but that the powers concerned in such interests shall not make use of them for political action.

7. The provisions contained in Articles 10, 11 and 12 of the Anglo-French agreements concerning the Arabian Peninsula and the Red Sea are considered as equally applicable to Italy as if that power were named in those articles together with France and Great Britain and as of the contracting parties.

8. It is understood that, in case it should not be possible at the conclusion of the war to secure to one or more of the said powers the whole of the advantages contemplated in the agreements concluded by the Allied Powers concerning the allotment to each of them of a portion of the Ottoman Empire, the maintenance of the Mediterranean equilibrium shall be fairly taken into consideration, in conformity with Article 9 of the Pact of London of April 26, 1915, in any change or arrangement affecting the provinces of the Ottoman Empire as a consequence of the war.

9. It is understood that the present memorandum shall be communicated to the Russian Government in order to enable it to express its opinion.

DOCUMENT 7

PACT OF ROME[1]
APRIL 10, 1918

GENERAL AGREEMENT AMONG THE NATIONALITIES OF AUSTRIA-HUNGARY

The representatives of the nationalities subject, wholly or in part, to the domination of Austria-Hungary: Italians, Poles, Rumanians, Czecho-slovaks, and Yugoslavs, have agreed, with a view to common action, to the following declarations:

1. Each of these peoples proclaims its right to constitute its unity as a national state or to complete that unity in order to attain its full political and economic independence.

2. Each of these peoples recognizes in the Austro-Hungarian mon-archy the instrument of Germanic domination and the fundamental obstacle to the realization of its aspirations and of its rights.

3. The Congress therefore recognizes the necessity of a joint struggle against the common oppressors until each one of these peoples shall have secured its complete liberation, its complete national unity, and its political liberty.

BASES OF AN ITALO-YUGOSLAV AGREEMENT

The representatives of the Italian people and of the Yugoslav people agree in particular on the following:

4. In regard to the relations between the Italian nation and the nation of the Serbs, Croats, and Slovenes, also known as the Yugoslav nation, the representatives of the two peoples recognize that the unity and inde-pendence of the Yugoslav nation is of vital interest to Italy, just as the achievement of Italian national unity is of vital interest to the Yugoslav nation. The representatives of the two peoples therefore undertake to use all their efforts during the war and at the time of the conclusion of peace in order that this aim of the two nations may be wholly realized.

5. They declare that the liberation of the Adriatic Sea and its defense against any present or future enemy is of vital interest to both peoples.

6. They undertake to settle amicably, also in the interest of amicable and sincere future relations between the two peoples, the pending terri-

[1] Adriaticus, *La Question adriatique*, Document VI, pp. 25-26. Author's translation.

torial questions, on the basis of the principle of nationality and of the right of peoples to determine their own fate, and to do this in such a way as not to prejudice the vital interests of either nation, which shall be defined at the time of peace.

7. To the nuclei of either people which may have to be included within the frontiers of the other shall be recognized and guaranteed the right to have their language respected, as well as their culture and their moral and economic interests.

DOCUMENT 8

AUSTRO-HUNGARIAN NOTE OF OCTOBER 7, 1918[1]

THE SWEDISH MINISTER (EKENGREN) TO THE SECRETARY OF STATE

[Translation]
No. 4978

WASHINGTON, *October 7, 1918.*

EXCELLENCY: By order of my Government I have the honor confidentially to transmit herewith to you the following communication of the Imperial and Royal Government of Austria-Hungary to the President of the United States of America:

The Austro-Hungarian Monarchy, which has waged war always and solely as a defensive war and repeatedly given documentary evidence of its readiness to stop the shedding of blood and arrive at a just and honorable peace, hereby addresses itself to his Lordship (*Monseigneur*) the President of the United States of America and offers to conclude with him and his allies an armistice on every front, on land, at sea, and in the air, and to enter immediately upon negotiations for a peace for which the fourteen points in the message of President Wilson to Congress of January 8, 1918, and the four points contained in President Wilson's address of February 12 [*11*], 1918, should serve as a foundation, and in which the viewpoints declared by President Wilson in his address of September 27, 1918, will also be taken into account.

Be pleased to accept [etc.]

W. A. F. EKENGREN.

[1] *Foreign Relations of the United States, 1918,* Supplement I, Vol. I, p. 341.

DOCUMENT 9

AMERICAN NOTE OF OCTOBER 19, 1918[1]

THE SECRETARY OF STATE TO THE SWEDISH MINISTER
(EKENGREN)

No. 466

WASHINGTON, *October 19, 1918*

SIR: I have the honor to acknowledge the receipt of your note of the 7th instant in which you transmit a communication of the Imperial and Royal Government of Austria-Hungary to the President. I am now instructed by the President to request you to be good enough, through your Government, to convey to the Imperial and Royal Government the following:

The President deems it his duty to say to the Austro-Hungarian Government that he cannot entertain the present suggestions of that Government because of certain events of utmost importance which, occurring since the delivery of his address of the 8th of January last, have necessarily altered the attitude and responsibility of the Government of the United States. Among the fourteen terms of peace which the President formulated at that time occurred the following:

X. The peoples of Austria-Hungary, whose place among the nations we wish to see safeguarded and assured, should be accorded the freest opportunity of autonomous development.

Since that sentence was written and uttered to the Congress of the United States the Government of the United States has recognized that a state of belligerency exists between the Czecho-Slovaks and the German and Austro-Hungarian Empires and that the Czecho-Slovak National Council is a *de facto* belligerent Government clothed with proper authority to direct the military and political affairs of the Czecho-Slovaks. It has also recognized in the fullest manner the justice of the nationalistic aspirations of the Jugo-Slavs for freedom.

The President is, therefore, no longer at liberty to accept the mere "autonomy" of these peoples as a basis of peace, but is obliged to insist that they, and not he, shall be the judges of what action on the part of the Austro-Hungarian Government will satisfy their aspirations and their conception of their rights and destiny as members of the family of nations.

Accept [etc.]

ROBERT LANSING.

[1] *Foreign Relations of the United States, 1918*, Supplement I, Vol. I, p. 368.

DOCUMENT 10

AUSTRO-HUNGARIAN NOTE OF OCTOBER 27, 1918[1]

THE SWEDISH MINISTER (EKENGREN) TO THE SECRETARY OF STATE

[Translation]
No. 5328

WASHINGTON, *October 29, 1918*
[*Received October 29, 4.20 p.m.*]

EXCELLENCY: By order of my Government, I have the honor to beg you to submit to the President the following communication from the Imperial and Royal Government of Austria-Hungary:

In reply to the note of President Wilson to the Austro-Hungarian Government dated October 18 [*19*] of this year, with regard to the decision of the President to take up with Austria-Hungary separately the question of armistice and peace, the Austro-Hungarian Government has the honor to declare that it adheres both to the previous declarations of the President and his opinion of the rights of the peoples of Austria-Hungary, notably those of the Czecho-Slovaks and the Jugo-Slavs, contained in his last note. Austria-Hungary having thereby accepted all the conditions which the President had put upon entering into negotiations on the subject of armistice and peace, nothing, in the opinion of the Austro-Hungarian Government, longer stands in the way of beginning those negotiations. The Austro-Hungarian Government therefore declares itself ready to enter, without waiting for the outcome of other negotiations, into negotiations for a peace between Austria-Hungary and the Entente states and for an immediate armistice on all the Austro-Hungarian fronts and begs President Wilson to take the necessary measures to that effect.

Be pleased to accept [etc.]

W. A. F. EKENGREN.

[1] *Foreign Relations of the United States, 1918,* Supplement I, Vol. I, pp. 404-5. The Note was sent from Vienna on the evening of the twenty-seventh, under date of the following day, and received in Washington on the twenty-ninth.

MINUTES OF THE SUPREME WAR COUNCIL[1]

[Extracts]

October 31, 1918

Clemenceau. I propose that the draft of the military clauses of the Armistice with Austria-Hungary which we elaborated this morning be now read, so that we may discuss it item by item.

Articles 1 and 2 [cessation of hostilities; Austro-Hungarian demobilization] are accepted without discussion.

Article 3 [evacuation of territories].

Vesnić. I accept this article, but I wish to make reservations in regard to it and to the following one, if there are territories to be evacuated. I see no reason for stopping on the coast line of the Adriatic; all the Yugoslav territories must be evacuated.

Clemenceau. I wish to make a remark: we must not confuse armistice with peace conditions. The purpose of the Armistice is to place the victorious armies in such a position that their superiority shall be definitely established. We have no other aim, and our armistice conditions do not commit us in the matter of peace terms; the occupation of the evacuated territories must take place jointly and M. Vesnić's remark will be in order when we discuss peace terms.

Vesnić. I did not mean to say that these were peace terms, but there is at present considerable unrest in all the provinces: our armies may be in this region tomorrow and I do not see why the line of occupation should be limited to that just indicated.

Balfour. The question which is being raised has to do with the preservation of order in the part of the Austro-Hungarian territory which is to be evacuated.

Colonel House. We cannot take this question into consideration for it would raise that of the preservation of order in the whole Austro-Hungarian Empire. What we are seeking is the occupation of certain important points, to insure the supremacy of our armies. (The article is accepted.)

Article 4 [freedom of transit of the Allied armies across Austro-Hungary; occupation of strategic points].

[1] Mermeix, *Les Négociations secrètes et les quatre armistices*, pp. 206-13. Author's translation.

CLEMENCEAU. This must satisfy M. Vesnić; you see that we reserve the right to occupy and cross any territory that we may wish.

VESNIĆ. I should like to specify certain points which I believe should be occupied by the Allied armies.

LLOYD GEORGE. There is much to be said in favor of occupying the two provinces of Bosnia and Herzegovina which have been occupied by Austria for only a short time. Since Serbian troops are in the vicinity, I do not see why we should not occupy them. There is an appreciable difference between articles 3 and 4: article 3 only deals with the occupation of certain strategic points, whereas article 4 enables the armies of the Associated Powers to move freely in the whole country. The two points are different from occupation as such. Bosnia and Herzegovina are inhabited by Slav populations and we must not prevent the Serbs from entering them if they are in the vicinity.

BALFOUR. I think that we would achieve our purpose by adding to the second paragraph of article 4 the words "or to preserve order."

VESNIĆ. I do not wish to be misunderstood: I am not insisting here for Bosnia and Herzegovina alone, but for all Yugoslav countries. There is great unrest in these regions; the Allies have every reason to foster quiet and favorable conditions in these regions during the Armistice, especially as these populations have placed themselves from the beginning of the war in the hands of the Allies.

I also wish to make a remark in regard to the preceding article. It has been said that the regions the evacuation of which was being considered were Italian regions; I do not wish a false impression to appear in this record. It is well understood that the regions in question are to be evacuated for purely military reasons, without prejudice to the future terms of peace. If such were not the case, I should have to make formal reservations.

VENIZELOS. I believe that the correction proposed by Mr. Balfour gives M. Vesnić complete satisfaction, for it applies not only to Bosnia and Herzegovina but to the whole territory.

(Article 4, with Balfour's reservation, is adopted.)

The naval clauses are then read.

Articles 1 and 2 [cessation of hostilities; surrender of submarines] are accepted without discussion.

LLOYD GEORGE. In the next article [high seas fleet] I propose to ask for the surrender of only three battleships instead of four; this is the less dangerous since the Austrians have only six altogether.

Admiral WEMYSS. I am prepared to accept this, but I think Admiral Grassi is better qualified to discuss this article.

Admiral GRASSI. I think that three large ships would be sufficient, provided they were dreadnoughts, the other three being disarmed, and we should have torpedo boats (new type, Kaiman model) in their place.

In fact we could be satisfied with two large ships to replace those which have been sunk by the Austrians.

Admiral DE BON. In that case we should be considering a special situation: our aim is not to replace the Italian units that were sunk, as suggested by Admiral Grassi. That was not what the Interallied Naval Council had in mind: what we were seeking was to reduce the power of the Austrian fleet by taking a complete division of four ships so as to cripple it for a long time to come. Such was the opinion of the Naval Council, and I believe that it should be upheld.

SONNINO. What Admiral Grassi has said was that he would give up a large ship in exchange for a greater number of torpedo boats, of which no mention has been made. These should be of the Kaiman model, which is the latest.

Sir ERIC GEDDES. This is a new proposal which has not been considered by the Naval Council.

Colonel HOUSE. I suggest that we take two battleships and all the torpedo boats of recent design.

SONNINO. We accept, on condition that the torpedo boats be handed over to the Italian navy.

LLOYD GEORGE. We are not examining at present the question of the distribution of ships; we are seeking only to place them under Allied supervision.

In my opinion we must show moderation. To accept Colonel House's proposal would amount to taking everything. We want Austria to accept our conditions: our military terms are already very harsh, and I grant that they must be such; if we impose, in addition, equally hard naval terms, we run the risk of forcing her to continue the war.

SONNINO. I therefore suggest that we take three battleships, three light cruisers, nine destroyers, twelve torpedo boats of the Kaiman model, one mine layer and six Danube monitors, to be designated by the Allies and the United States.

(This proposal is accepted. Article 3 is adopted as well as article 4 [freedom of navigation in the Adriatic for the Allies].)

VESNIĆ. I wish to make a remark with respect to article 5 [blockade]. There are in the Adriatic a large number of commercial ships belonging to Yugoslav subjects who have sided with the Allies from the beginning of the war. I ask that a provision be inserted stating that commercial ships blockaded in the Adriatic and belonging to Yugoslav subjects shall be set free, upon the advice of an Interallied commission if necessary.

CLEMENCEAU. This is covered by article 9, which asks for the return of all commercial ships of the Allied and Associated Powers held by Austria-Hungary. The Yugoslavs may be regarded as an Associated Power.

BALFOUR. That is not my opinion, for we have never recognized them officially as such.

VESNIĆ. I ask you to do it now and to accept the brothers of the Serbs as associates in the same way as the Serbs themselves.

BALFOUR. I am quite ready to do it; but we are then raising, in addition to this particular point, the very important question of the use of the world's tonnage. We cannot allow the Yugoslavs to use their ships for their own needs alone; we must consider, for the future, the pooling of all tonnage to meet the needs of the various peoples. Neither can we allow Germany and Austria-Hungary to use their tonnage in future exclusively for their own needs. I therefore suggest that we impose upon Austria-Hungary the same conditions that we shall also impose upon Germany, namely, the placing of her total tonnage at the disposal of the Allies, under the supervision of an Interallied Maritime Council, which shall be instructed from now on to insure its best use.

Colonel HOUSE. I do not think that this can be considered in the terms of the Armistice, but we can take it up as soon as we consider peace terms.

LLOYD GEORGE. I should also call attention to the fact that, since the blockade remains in effect, we are at liberty to impose whatever conditions we wish for the duration of the Armistice.

ORLANDO. I quite agree, but why confine these exceptions to the Yugoslavs: there are a great many Italian ships at Fiume, which is essentially an Italian city; why not grant them the same privilege?

I propose the following addition: "An Interallied commission may allow certain exceptions."

SONNINO. I propose that the following words be added at the end of article 5: "Save exceptions which may be allowed by a special Interallied commission."

Admiral DE BON. That is covered by the words "liable to capture."

Colonel HOUSE. We might say: "Save for exceptions which may be allowed by the Allies," without specifying any particular commission.

VESNIĆ. I should like it to be clearly understood in the Minutes that this provision applies to Yugoslav ships as well.

CLEMENCEAU. M. Orlando made a very appropriate remark on that score a moment ago.

VESNIĆ. I object to that remark.

Sonnino. It seems to me very difficult to distinguish among Yugoslavs: some are Austrians and Austrophile.

Vesnić. I do not wish to enter into a discussion on that point, but I insist upon entering my reservation in the Minutes for future reference.

Clemenceau. We accept the following text: "With the exceptions which may be made by a commission nominated by Allies and United States of America."

(This modification is accepted.)

Marshal Foch. I should like to make a remark on a question which is not purely military. We are maintaining the blockade until peace, which means until we shall have made a new Austria. That may take a long time; there would therefore result a country condemned to starvation, which might be driven into anarchy.

Orlando. The blockade must continue until the armistice terms are signed.

Lloyd George. Yes, until the peace preliminaries.

Sonnino. In his last note to the German Government, President Wilson said that the terms of the Armistice should be such that the enemy must be forced to make peace; we are covering this condition with our blockade clause. Without this provision we shall not have peace; Austria would, in fact, be in a better situation by not having to care for the populations of the territories which we are to occupy.

Clemenceau. We are agreed then to maintain the blockade until the peace preliminaries.

Article 5, as modified, is unanimously adopted. The remaining articles are adopted without discussion.

MINUTES OF THE SUPREME WAR COUNCIL[1]

[EXTRACTS]

NOVEMBER 1, 1918

CLEMENCEAU. I wish to communicate the text of a declaration which I have just received:

By radiogram addressed to President Wilson and to the commander in chief of the American fleet, the Yugoslavs state that they have seized the Austrian fleet at Pola: on their side, the Italians are supposed to have sunk two ships, one of them being the "Viribus Unitis." The Yugoslavs ask that all the captured ships be placed under the protection of the American fleet or of one of the Allied fleets.

My opinion is that, when the question shall be asked, we should answer that the ships seized by the Yugoslavs, like those seized by the other Allies, must be placed at the disposal of the Entente.

SONNINO. This is just a new Austrian ruse.

Suppose that Germany should tell us, at the moment of signing the Armistice, that her fleet had been ceded to Denmark and that she had nothing left to give us, what could we do? Peace once signed, she would take back her fleet and we should have been duped. Yesterday we agreed on the terms of the Armistice for Austria, which have been sent to General Diaz. We cannot recognize today declarations saying that this or that thing has been ceded to another party.

VESNIĆ. I regret not being able to share M. Sonnino's point of view. The commission which we have set up is concerned with commercial vessels. Today we are confronted with an act of war in accord with the collaboration with the Allies which the Yugoslavs have shown from the beginning. This collaboration is manifested today by the capture of the Austrian fleet, and the Yugoslavs, I repeat once more, Allies of the Allies, take this fleet and ask that it be considered as an Allied fleet. I support this request of my racial brothers and ask the Conference to accept it.

CLEMENCEAU. M. Sonnino has presented an argument that deserves consideration. Yesterday we adopted the terms of the Armistice with provisions for the fleet. Today the latter is in the hands of the Yugoslavs

[1] Mermeix, *Les Négociations secrètes et les quatre armistices*, pp. 234-39. Author's translation.

and their proposal to hand it over to one only of the Allies, President Wilson, does not seem to me a happy one. President Wilson is far away; he does not know the Adriatic and is not in a position to give instructions, whereas we are. The Yugoslavs have accomplished an act of war, for which I congratulate them, but I cannot subscribe to the idea of giving these ships to the farthest removed of the Allies. The fleet must be handed over to the Allies jointly.

Colonel House. The note says: "To President Wilson or to one of the Allies." Why then argue this point?

Lloyd George. I agree; let us not discuss this question now. It is more far-reaching than it seems. We have received this news just this morning, and have not had time to consider it. I think it would be unfortunate to send a reply showing ill will on our part. Yesterday we decided to divide the Austrian fleet, taking a part and interning the rest. Today we receive the offer of the whole fleet to one of the Allies; let us not discourage this coöperation. We are proposing very hard armistice terms to Germany; if she refuses them, we shall need all our resources to overcome her last resistance. The Yugoslavs are a new and vigorous element which could give us valuable assistance in the South; they were within the enemy's house and have helped to destroy it; we must remember that in our reply, which must not be a purely formal answer.

Vesnić. I am happy to hear the words of the British Prime Minister. I ask you to take into consideration that the men who have accomplished this act have risked their lives and that they are not diplomats. They may not be very skilled in the art of drafting notes; what they are saying in effect is: we have seized this fleet and we place it at your disposal or that of President Wilson. We might even congratulate them for having made this distinction; they know that the Government of the United States is associated and not allied with the Entente Powers. Do not hold it against them if they have turned to President Wilson. He is, like all of you, the friend of small nations. I feel certain that I am voicing the deep conviction of the Yugoslavs, with whom I live in close contact. Look upon their request as if they were saying: "We are placing this fleet at the disposal of the Allies; consider us as being your best soldiers." I beg of you to reply in that spirit.

Orlando. We too have received a radiogram; it does not correspond to the one we are considering now. Our discussion is being carried on without sufficient information: the only thing we have is intercepted radiograms; that is not a sufficient basis on which to pass judgment. Since we are speaking of radiograms, I shall give you the one which our commander in chief of the navy in Venice has received from Pola, sent by "Admiral Spaun." M. Vesnić is right; if we were confronted with a revolt of the sailors, who had seized the fleet and offered it to us, we should greet them most cordially, especially as a large part of the crews are Yugoslav or Italian; but most of the officers of the Austro-Hungarian navy are Hungarians or German Austrians, hence loyal officers. It would be surprising if a fleet with loyal officers should surrender. The radiogram is sent from a ship and that fact arouses suspicion. I ask that these two points be examined: if the crews belong to peoples friendly to the Entente, whether Yugoslav or Italian, and wish to surrender, let us assist them in that, for we should thus obtain much more than the Armistice would give us. If isolated ships or the whole fleet wish to surrender, the situation is different; they cannot surrender to any one of the Allies at their choice.

I wish to recall that General Diaz has received our terms of armistice and may have communicated them to the enemy plenipotentiaries. We can no longer change them.

Let us wait until the facts are clear, and let the *pourparlers* continue in the meantime.

LLOYD GEORGE. It is for us to decide; we have received an official request.

CLEMENCEAU. It is not an official request, it is a radiogram.

VESNIĆ. I wish to raise an objection. M. Orlando said that we decided upon the terms of armistice yesterday. Now this news comes as a thunderbolt, a pleasant one I admit. I have every reason to believe, because of information which I had previously received, that it is accurate. We must therefore accept it as official and I ask the Conference not to disregard this offer and not to discourage this good will, which may have repercussions in other provinces.

SONNINO. Yesterday we received a radiogram giving a different impression. I wonder from what source all these radiograms come.

Colonel HOUSE. We need more official information than we have.

ORLANDO. The commander in chief in Venice has received a radiogram saying that he may go to Pola. I have answered him: very well, but take precautions, for Austria is unreliable. I share the common satisfaction at this news.

LLOYD GEORGE. This offer is an improvement upon the Armistice terms, since it gives us the whole fleet. I therefore propose the following:

To ask the American Government or the commander in chief of the American fleet to reply by wireless in the name of the Supreme War Council, asking the Austrian ships to sail at once for Corfu and to place themselves upon their arrival under the orders of the Admiral commanding the Allied forces in the Mediterranean. The Admiral would be instructed to inform these ships of the precautions they would have to take in approaching Corfu and in order to enter the port safely.

If they accept this condition, so much the better; if not, we do not risk anything.

ORLANDO. If we send the telegram proposed by Mr. Lloyd George, what shall I tell General Diaz? I cannot ask him to wait, nor to settle military conditions alone, disregarding naval terms, for the two are inseparable.

CLEMENCEAU. I propose to adjourn this question until tomorrow.

(This proposal is accepted.)

DOCUMENT 13

ANGLO-FRENCH DECLARATION OF NOVEMBER 8, 1918[1]

The object aimed at by France and Great Britain in prosecuting in the East the war let loose by the ambition of Germany is the complete and definitive emancipation of the peoples so long oppressed by the Turks, and the establishment of Governments and national administrations deriving their authority from the initiative and free choice of the indigenous populations.

In order to carry out these intentions France and Great Britain are at one in encouraging and assisting the establishment of indigenous Governments and administrations in Syria and Mesopotamia, now liberated by the Allies, and in the territories the liberation of which they are engaged in securing, and in recognising these as soon as they are actually established. Far from wishing to impose on the populations of these regions any particular institutions, they are only concerned to ensure by their support and by adequate assistance the regular working of Governments and administrations freely chosen by themselves. To secure impartial and equal justice for all, to facilitate the economic development of the country by inspiring and encouraging local initiative, to favour the diffusion of education, to put an end to dissensions that have been too long taken advantage of by Turkish policy, such is the policy which the two Allied Governments uphold in the liberated territories.

[1] Mears, *Modern Turkey*, pp. 626-27.

DOCUMENT 14

PAGE'S REPORT FROM ROME[1]

Rome, Dated December 30, 1918.
Recd. January 1, 1919, 4.30 p.m.

American Mission, Paris.

Italian cabinet situation growing out of Bissolati's opposition to Sonnino's program and consequent resignation still unsolved and uncertain. Reasons for resignation appear to be difference with Sonnino over Adriatic and disapproval over Orlando's alleged half-heartedness in real application Wilsonian principles to Italian national and international problems. As portion of press backing Sonnino and Orlando skilfully avoiding or making issue and as press backing Bissolati is considerably censored in its rather generic expression of views, a confidential statement from Bissolati himself has been given me. Bissolati's actual following in the country is not believed very large. At present the propaganda for Italian expansion along Eastern Adriatic shore is tremendous, but influential, Milan's *Corriere della Sera* is favoring him. Orlando considerably embarrassed will endeavor conciliation, but this not likely without substantial concessions to Bissolati's views. Meanwhile executive committee Italian Reform Socialist Party passes resolution forbidding in effect any Reform Socialist from joining cabinet as Bissolati's successor.

Pro Dalmatian Day celebrated yesterday in principal cities of Italy. Imposing procession at Rome with enthusiastic gatherings largely under organization of Italian universities. Representatives demand freedom of all Italian cities of Dalmatia. Similar gatherings Naples, Florence, Genoa. It looks as though all this is with at least consent of Government which finds itself apparently distrusted [disturbed?] by British election and the favor with which the foreign propaganda is received here.

December 31, 1918.   NELSON PAGE.

[1] Miller, *My Diary at the Conference of Paris*, III (Document 124), 115.

DOCUMENT 15

MILLER'S LETTER TO HOUSE[1]

Opinion for Colonel House

11 January, 1919.

Sir:

In response to your inquiry relative to the Pact of London of April 26, 1915, I have the honor to state as follows:

Pursuant to the correspondence between the President and the Allies, including the memorandum of observations by the Allied Governments, quoted in the note of the President of November 5, 1918, agreement was reached that peace should be effected upon the terms stated in the Address of the President of January 8, 1918, (The Fourteen Points) and the Principles enunciated in his subsequent addresses, subject only to certain qualifications mentioned in said correspondence.

Accordingly, I am of the opinion that any provisions of the Pact of London of April 26, 1915, which may be inconsistent with the agreement above mentioned, reached between the Allies (including Italy, France, and Great Britain) and the United States, were by that agreement abrogated and are no longer in force.

I am, Sir,

Your obedient servant,

DAVID HUNTER MILLER,
Technical Advisor,
American Commission to
Negotiate Peace.

Colonel E. M. House,
Commissioner Plenipotentiary.

[1] Miller, *My Diary at the Conference of Paris*, III (Document 156), 237.

AMERICAN TERRITORIAL REPORT[1]

OUTLINE OF TENTATIVE REPORT AND RECOMMENDATIONS PREPARED BY THE INTELLIGENCE SECTION, IN ACCORDANCE WITH INSTRUCTIONS, FOR THE PRESIDENT AND THE PLENIPOTENTIARIES
January 21, 1919
[EXTRACTS]

14. JUGO-SLAVIA

It is recommended:

1). That an independent federated Jugo-Slav state be established, to consist of Serbia, Montenegro, and the Serbo-Croat-Slovene territory within former Austria-Hungary.

2). That the boundaries of the new state within the former Austro-Hungarian Empire be drawn as on maps 11, 16, and 18,[2] so as to coincide roughly with the language boundary except in two regions—the Banat of Temesvar and the Istria-Isonzo region.

3). That the Serbo-Rumanian, Serbo-Bulgarian, Serbo-Greek, and Serbo-Albanian boundaries fixed in 1913 be confirmed for Jugo-Slavia.

4). That the tentative suggestion be considered of uniting the "High Albanians" in Northern Albania with their own kin in western Serbia and southeastern Montenegro, and placing this homogeneous group of tribes as a self-governing unit under Jugo-Slavia as the mandatory of the League of Nations, with the explicit right reserved to it of appeal to the League of Nations in case of oppression; and of altering the former Serbian and Montenegrin boundaries, as fixed in 1913, according to map 18.

Discussion

1). It is recommended that an independent Jugo-Slav state be established, to consist of Serbia, Montenegro, and the Serbo-Croat-Slovene territory within former Austria-Hungary.

The political and linguistic affiliations of the peoples whom it is proposed to unite in a single state are so well known that a detailed argument is un-

[1] Miller, *My Diary at the Conference of Paris*, IV (Document 246), 235-58. See maps III, IV, and V.
[2] These are maps 669, 664, and 655 of The Inquiry maps.

necessary. It is from every standpoint desirable that the proposed state should not be broken up into its individual fragments along the lines of minor distinctions, as between the Slovenes and the rest of Jugo-Slavia or between Montenegro and Serbia. It is our conclusion that the Adriatic interests of these peoples and the size and strength of their immediate neighbors make it desirable that strong efforts be made to amalgamate the political and economic interests of the group.

But the State should be a federation; with autonomous parts, to accommodate the religious, historic, and minor racial differences of the Serbs, Montenegrins, Croats and Slovenes.

2). It is recommended that the boundaries of the new state within the former Austro-Hungarian Empire be drawn as on maps 11, 16, and 18, so as to coincide roughly with the language boundary except in two regions—the Banat of Temesvar and the Istria-Isonzo region.

[Comment on the Banat intervenes here.]

The Jugo-Slav boundary in the Istria-Isonzo region is the subject of hot dispute because both the Jugo-Slavs and the Italians are eager for the possession of the eastern Adriatic littoral and its ports. The commercial and strategic advantages accruing to the possessor are obvious.

The proposed boundary coincides in general with the main watershed of the Carnic and Julian Alps, and follows the crest of the high ridges forming the backbone of the Istrian peninsula. It gives to Italy all that portion of the Isonzo basin and of the eastern Adriatic coast to which she has any valid claim, together with as much of the hinterland, peopled by Slavs, as is vitally needed on economic grounds. It gives to the Jugo-Slavs part of the Istrian coast and all of the Dalmatian coast and archipelago claimed by Italy, with a fine series of harbors from Fiume southward.

The proposed division would add 6,680 square kilometers to Italy and a population of 715,000, consisting of 345,000 Italians and 370,000 Jugo-Slavs. In Jugo-Slav territory there would be left 75,000 Italians, a very small number as compared with the number of Jugo-Slavs in Italy. The Jugo-Slavs would be left in undisturbed possession of a stretch of coast upon which their hopes have centered for years, and where the Italian claim to majorities is unsubstantiated, except in the case of several of the coast towns, such as Fiume and Zara—there is a small Italian majority in Fiume proper, but a small Croat majority if the suburb of Sušak, in fact a part of Fiume, be added.

The retention of Fiume by Jugo-Slavia is vital to the interests of the latter, and likewise assures to the more remote hinterland, including Austria and Hungary, the advantages of two competing ports under the control of different nations.

Italy is accorded on the east as much natural protection as can be permitted without giving undue weight to strategic considerations. As defined the line affords reasonable protection for Trieste and Pola and their connecting railway, and in fact would leave the Jugo-Slavs in a position of military inferiority if they did not have a protective mountainous terrain and one of the best coasts in the world for defensive naval operations. For almost its entire length the boundary follows watersheds on high and sparsely settled plateaus. It is not without at least remote historical basis, since it follows the frontier between Italy and the Provinces as it existed for several centuries during the Roman period.

3). It is recommended that the Serbo-Rumanian, Serbo-Bulgarian, Serbo-Greek, and Serbo-Albanian boundaries fixed in 1913 be confirmed for Jugo-Slavia.

There is no sufficient justification, and there would be less wisdom, in disturbing the Serbo-Rumanian, Serbo-Bulgarian, or the Serbo-Greek frontiers established in 1913. To do so would precipitate acrimonious and unmanageable difficulties, especially in Macedonia. The same is probably true of all but a minute, extreme northern part of the Serbo-Albanian boundary, although as we elsewhere point out, when Albania is approached doubt enters and lingers.

4). It is recommended that the tentative suggestion be considered of uniting the "High Albanians" in Northern Albania with their own kin in western Serbia and southeastern Montenegro, and placing this homogeneous group of tribes as a self-governing unit under Jugo-Slavia as a mandatory of the League of Nations, with the explicit right reserved to it of appeal to the League of Nations in case of oppression; and of altering the former Serbian and Montenegrin boundaries, as fixed in 1913, according to map 18.

This would open to the Albanian mountaineers the markets, the grain fields, and the winter pastures on which they have relied in the past; it would give to Jugo-Slavia the use of the waterways and harbor which form the maritime outlet for the basin of Lake Scutari. The Albanians involved would be insured a recognized status bordering on independence and an opportunity to be heard in case of oppression.

On the other hand it appears unwise to grant Jugo-Slavia complete sovereignty in Northern Albania, since Serbs and Albanians at present dislike and distrust each other. Doubtless in time the process of absorption of the Albanian population would follow the course it is now running, but the process should not be violently stimulated, and the Albanians should certainly be protected against abuse.

In view of the very primitive societal organization of the Albanian tribes, the separation of the Northern from Central Albania might prove harmless, and even beneficial. By no other device, apparently, can the "High Albanians" be reunited with their brethren in Montenegro and Serbia, for only if Jugo-Slavia is their assigned protector can this be accomplished, and that state cannot, at least cannot at present, be given control of Central Albania.

The area of the Northern Albanian district is 9,800 square kilometers, and the population numbers 275,000. About one-third of this area and nearly half

of the population are from Serbia and Montenegro as they existed before
1914. The people live mostly in the valley floors tributary to the Lake Scutari
drainage system, and about the Lake itself, with bands of population along the
major mountain valleys.

15. ITALY

It is recommended:

1). That Italy be given a northern frontier midway between the linguistic line and the line of the treaty of London, 1915. The proposed line is delimited on maps 12 to 15 inclusive.[3]

2). That Italy's eastern frontier be rectified as shown on map 15.

3). That consideration be given the doubtful claim of Italy to a sphere of influence at Avlona.

4). That Rhodes and the Dodecanese be assigned to Greece.

5). That Libya be given a hinterland adequate for access to the Sudan and its trade, but so limited as not to hamper the French colonial domain or the Anglo-Egyptian Sudan.

Discussion

1). It is recommended that Italy be given a northern frontier midway between the linguistic line and the line of the treaty of London, 1915. The proposed line is delimited on maps 12 to 15 inclusive.

This recommendation would give Italy all that part of the Tyrol to which she has any just claim on linguistic, cultural or historical grounds. It would leave no rational basis for future irredentist agitation in this direction. It transfers to Italy over 10,000 square kilometers of territory and a population consisting of 373,000 Italians and Ladins, 161,000 Germans, and 3,000 others.

The recommended line does not meet those claims of Italy which are based on strategic grounds alone, for the line of 1915, following as it does the main watershed, gives incomparably the best strategic frontier. On the other hand, the proposed line does ameliorate the intentionally bad frontier imposed upon Italy by Austria, and some such amelioration seems essential if the Italians are to enter a League of Nations with confidence in its ability to render their peaceful existence reasonably sure. The weight of this argument would be augmented if Italy were confronted by a united and potentially powerful German State on the north. The task of the League of Nations will be rendered easier and its success made more certain by the adjustment of Italy's northern frontier at least in part along lines which would discourage armed aggression by a powerful German state.

As laid down upon the map the proposed boundary is a good line from the geographical standpoint, since it follows natural lines of demarcation and coincides with the marked topographical barrier between regions climatically

[3] These are maps 656, 642a, 667, 642b, and 653 of The Inquiry maps.

dissimilar. Its position is easily recognizable on the ground, it is capable of clear and accurate delimitation, and is not subject to change from natural causes. Since throughout its entire length it traverses regions of little or no population it does not interfere with the activities of the local population, and the small number of practicable passes makes the administration of customs and other frontier regulations simple.

Finally, it is so drawn as to throw into Austria about 71,000 Germans with a minority of 10,000 Italians and Ladins, forming properly a part of the Austrian realm. Were the line of 1915 to be followed (red line on map 13), it would simply throw the irredentist problem into Austrian territory and would not lead to a lasting peace.

2). It is recommended that Italy's eastern frontier be rectified as shown on map 15.

[The same remarks as under Jugo-Slavia, 2, are repeated here.]

3). It is recommended that consideration be given to the doubtful claim of Italy to a sphere of influence at Avlona.

Probably Italy must be left in Avlona and its immediately adjacent territory, not however, as the final possessor of the region, but as a mandatory of the League of Nations. In this manner any alleged propagandist movements may be reviewed and restrictions imposed in harmony with the spirit of the time in which they arise. Otherwise there will be left in both the northern and southern ends of Jugo-Slavia regions of conflict between two neighboring peoples, the Jugo-Slavs and the Italians, from which there could result only discord and possible war.

4). It is recommended that Rhodes and the Dodecanese be assigned to Greece.

Over 80% of the population of Rhodes and the Dodecanese are Greek Orthodox. They are bitterly opposed to the present Italian occupation, and should be assigned to the mother country.

5). It is recommended that Libya be given a hinterland adequate for access to the Sudan trade, but so limited as not to hamper the French colonial domain or the Anglo-Egyptian Sudan.

The need for such a hinterland is evident, and with the limitations mentioned it is fair to satisfy this need. The proposed action would no doubt be agreeable to France and Britain.

16. GERMAN AUSTRIA

[The only recommendation affecting Italy is the following:]

3). That the German Austrians receive the assurance of an outlet for their trade, either at Trieste or Fiume, or both.

. . .

[The same recommendation also appears under Hungary.]

18. ALBANIA

The Albanian region presents problems so complicated in detail, and the proposed settlements are so experimental in form, and so many interests are involved, both near and remote, that definite recommendations are felt to be unsafe at this time. We merely present the following considerations as of possible aid to the plenipotentiaries:

The boundary of the proposed state of Albania as drawn in 1913 was highly artificial, cutting not only lines of economic intercourse and national affiliations, but even tribal ties, the strongest bond in a society based on kinship.

In fact, the project of a united Albania appears impracticable. The weakness of national feeling among the people, the disruptive forces which spring from backward political institutions, the difficulties of communication, the intrigues of neighboring states—all these are obstacles which can be faced only under the protection of a great Power like England or the United States, and then only by a Power sufficiently imbued with the missionary spirit to be willing to spend its efforts unselfishly. Such a course is no doubt out of the question.

Therefore we suggest that, in Northern Albania, a compact group of Albanians might be segregated, united with their own kin in Southeastern Montenegro and Western Serbia, and placed under the supervision of Jugo-Slavia (see map 17)[4] as the mandatory of the League of Nations, but with the explicit right of appeal to the League in case of oppression.

[Here follows the same comment as under Jugo-Slavia 4.]

The central block of Albanian territory presents a most difficult problem. It should probably be granted nominal independence under some disinterested Power as mandatory of the League of Nations. Italy would be the natural mandatory for many reasons. But it is precisely because of the outside interference of interested Powers that there have been such unhappy developments in Balkan affairs in the past, and Italy therefore seems to be excluded because of the sharp feeling against her in both Greece and Jugo-Slavia.

[Then follows the same paragraph as under Italy 3, referring to Albania.]

22. TURKEY

[The following recommendation affects Italy:]

2). That there be applied to the Turkish Anatolian State the mandatory principle, but no recommendation is made as to the Power to be selected to carry out this principle.

[The report advises that Greece should not be given a foothold upon the mainland of Asia Minor.]

[4] This is map 648 of The Inquiry maps.

ITALIAN MEMORANDUM OF CLAIMS[1]

FEBRUARY 7, 1919

THE ITALIAN CLAIMS ON THE ALPS AND IN THE ADRIATIC

The following pages contain a statement of Italy's claims on the territories of the former Austro-Hungarian Monarchy. They set forth in their whole the various reasons upon which the Conventions regulating Italy's entrance into the war were based. Quite apart from these conventions the Italian claims show such a spirit of justice, rightfulness, and moderation that they come entirely within the principles enunciated by President Wilson and should therefore be recognised and approved by everybody.

Our claims involve the inclusion in Italian territory of a certain number of people of foreign tongue and descent. But similar inclusions have taken place, and on a much larger scale, in the formation of already existing states, and are going to be recognised and legalised in the formation of new states about to be brought into existence. This depends on the fact that the long disregard of natural boundaries by Governments which were the outcome of the policy of equilibrium established by the Treaties of Westphalia, Utrecht, Campoformio, and Vienna, and the interest these Governments had in destroying all proofs of nationality in order to crush political aspirations, have favoured the infiltration and importation of foreign races within the boundaries assigned by nature to the various countries. But the wrong inflicted upon a people can never under any circumstances become a source of rightful claims on the part of those who are responsible before history for the wrong committed.

Thus, according to their national aspirations, Poland, with the additions in Galicia, Danzig, Posen, and Eastern Prussia, would include over 40 per cent. of foreign population; Bohemia, with the addition of Slovakia and Austrian Silesia, about 30 per cent.; Rumania, with the addition of Transylvania, Bessarabia, Bukovina, and part of the Banat, over 17 per cent.; Yugoslavia over 11 per cent., claiming as they do, outside the Italian frontiers, territories in which the percentage of the Slav populations is insignificant; France over 4 per cent.; Italy only 3 per cent.

[1] This text is taken from Currey's *Italian Foreign Policy* (pp. 15-31), which claims to give the official translation. The original memorandum in French is given in Giannini's *Documenti per la storia dei rapporti fra l'Italia e la Jugo-Slavia*, pp. 13-35. There are only minor discrepancies between the English and the French texts. See maps IV and V.

There need be no fear that Italy will create new forms of irredentism, which is always the result of injustice and persecution, since Italy's history gives assurance in this respect. The French-speaking citizens of the Valle d'Aosta, the Slavs of the Natisone, the Germans of the Sette Comuni, have never felt they were living under a foreign government, because Italy has always respected their individuality.

Europe, which has never heard any complaints or protests on the part of these long-standing citizens of the Italian State, will likewise never hear in the future of any injustice inflicted upon Germans and Slavs whom the course of events will now bring within the new Italian boundaries.

Such a conception of the common citizenship of peoples of different tongues does not in our opinion clash with the actual bearing of Mr. Wilson's proposals, in that part in which they ask for a just settlement of long-standing territorial, racial, and national questions, and for the equality of nations on which to lay the foundations of peace.

Italy's Claims

In entering the war in order to face the aggression of the Central Empires, the special aims of Italy were to free her sons still lingering under foreign oppression and to attain an assurance of safety both on land and sea.

The victory to which she contributed by an effort which compares favourably with the efforts of any of her Allies, entitles Italy to formulate her claims on the basis of the principles underlying her resolution to partake in the great struggle by the side of the Entente and against her former allies.

By conciliating as far as possible national rights with fundamental conditions of safety, her aims might be attained as to the land by claiming the boundary of the Alps, comprising the Upper Adige, the Trentino, and Venezia Giulia; and, as to the sea, by so improving the situation on the Adriatic that, without prejudice to the legitimate aspirations of the new states which will border on it, Italy may no longer, as heretofore, be in a position of absolute inferiority and may be relieved of the dangers to which she was exposed up to now.

Italy's claims, in so far as they rest essentially on the principle of nationality, do not call for special explanation. But also those demands, which, while they depart in some measure from the rigorous application of the ethnical principle, aim at securing Italy's future safety, independently of the present or future attitude of the bordering states, are not in reality less consonant with the principles which guide the Allied and

Associated Powers in their actions. It is clear that the foundations of the longed-for League of Nations will be solid and enduring in proportion to the security which the single nations which form it are guaranteed against danger and interference from outside, and definitely—we might almost say physically—against foreign menace.

Italy's claims in this regard constitute no threat to others, they merely protect her against menace from others. Only by their realisation can Italy, without anxiety, put into actual practice the reduction of armaments which should be the greatest benefit mankind will reap as the result of the new world organisation.

The Northern Alpine Boundary

The new Alpine boundary which Italy requires corresponds practically with the line agreed upon in the Armistice signed on November 4th, 1918, between the Allied and Associated Powers and Austria-Hungary. It starts from Pizzo Umbrail to the north of the Stelvio, follows the ridge of the Rhaetic Alps to the sources of the Adige and Isarco, passes through the Reschen, the Brenner, the Oetz, and the Ziller, whence it turns southward and reaches the Dobbiaco (Toblach) mountains and the Julian Alps.

This is the geographical boundary along the Alpine watershed. It is the only boundary which, being formed by an actual mountainous obstacle—the formidable wall which has always been considered Italy's frontier—has any intrinsic value as a necessary and real safeguard. It closes the passes which are crossed by two great highways; it leaves to the populations living in the upper valleys their natural intercourse with the plain; and it follows its course from one landmark to another, all clearly and incontestably defined. The natural development of this boundary should of course include the High Tauern system: but Italy, who has no desire beyond what is essential for her defence, willingly renounces her right to carry it any farther than the Pizzo dei Tre Signori (Ziller Group), diverting thence to the south towards the Hoch-Gall, thence to the summits of the Kreuz Spitz and Hoch-horn Spitz and reaching, after including the whole Sexten Valley with Innichen, the Carnic Alps and the present political boundary of the Kingdom at Cima Vanscuro.

The strategic value of the Upper Adige has always been recognised: in the upper valley of the Adige lies the centre of all the highways for a German invasion of Italy. With it, even if Italy had Trent, the Germans would still hold the gates of Italy in their hands. It is indispensable that Italy should reach beyond Bolzano in order that by owning the side line joining the two great railways of the Brenner and Toblach, the

Germans should not continue to have the actual control also of the Italian side. An Austrian, General Kuhn, wrote: "The Italians must conquer southern Tyrol as far as the Brenner, if they want to defend Venice."

Any other boundary more to the south would merely be an artificial amputation entailing the upkeep of expensive armaments contrary to the principles by which Peace should be inspired. The boundary chosen by Italy ensures equal security also to the peoples living on the northern side of it, because the difficult and impervious nature of the ground makes it practically impossible to carry out military operations of any importance either from the north or from the south. The boundary, which we will call the "Brenner Frontier," is therefore indicated by the very conditions of nature, by the necessities of the people's life, and by reasons of peaceful security. It places the two neighbouring countries on a footing of a perfect equality in every possible way. By reverting to actual natural conditions and by identifying itself with reality, it acquires all the elements of stability.

Compared to the supreme necessity and practical advantage of such a frontier, the fact that it includes about 200,000 inhabitants of German nationality becomes a matter of no significance. Apart from the former historic relations between this region and Italy, commemorated by so many monuments and indelible memories which received eloquent military and political sanction by Napoleon the First's annexation of the Upper Adige to the Italian Kingdom; apart from the fact that the present national conformation of the Upper Adige is the result of violent intrusion and foreign invasions in a basin which geographically, historically, and economically belongs to Italy (even at the opening of the nineteenth century the region was predominantly Italian not only south of the Napoleonic frontier, but in the entire Venosta Valley, and partially in the districts of Bressanone and Sterzen, while the valley of Badia is still Italian at the present day, a total of not less than 45,000 Italians residing at present in the real and proper Upper Adige), it should be noted that the territory lying between the pre-war political frontier and the frontier now claimed, that is, the region of the Trentino and the Upper Adige which form one geographical whole, has a total population of 600,000 inhabitants, of which number even the Austrian statistics admit 380,000 to be Italian, while the correct figures reach 420,000. Even if the reasons of national safety and defence did not militate in favour of the inclusion of the Trentino and Upper Adige in the Italian Kingdom, the mere numerical prevalence of the Italian population (about 70 per cent.), in a region which for evident reasons is indivisible, would necessitate its return to its natural, economic, and national unity.

Then the frontier assigned to Italy departs from the present political frontier near Mount Lodin, so as to include the valley of Tarvis, a cardinal point in the defence of the Tagliamento, a main junction of railway lines of great importance, and the centre of converging roads at the junction of the three ranges, the Julian, Carnic, and Karavank Alps; an open thoroughfare in three directions (wherefrom in all probability its name Treviso is derived) of which Napoleon experienced the defensive importance for the Friuli and for Italy when he united it with the Alto Fella and Weissenfels to his Italian Kingdom. Against these reasons of military security combined with economic considerations—for only in this manner is direct communication between the Alto Fella and the High Isontine Valley rendered possible by a connecting line 17 kilometres instead of 150 kilometres long—no serious national objections exist, as this widening of the frontier would involve the inclusion of barely 5,800 inhabitants of mainly Germanic race.

The Eastern Territorial Frontier

In order to remedy iniquity and error which in 1866 assigned to Italy as her eastern frontier with Austria what in reality was the artificial boundary established by the Government of Vienna between two administrative regions (Lombardy-Venetia and the Austrian Littoral) belonging to the same state, it is necessary, in Julian Venetia also, to follow the indications of nature and the warnings of history and to carry the new frontier of Italy to the watershed of the Julian Alps, from the Pass of Camporosso to the Quarnero.

Here also we must be guided by the same conception of geographical separation, natural defence, historic tradition, and national redemption.

Geographers of all countries and all times have placed the Italian frontier at the Julian Alps. The whole of Julian Venetia has developed historically along lines similar to the rest of the Peninsula, with this difference only, that the movement for the complete national reunion of Italy in a single political organism has hitherto failed to achieve the redemption of this extreme corner of the motherland, just as, previous to 1866, Venetia had remained unredeemed, and as, up till 1859, Lombardy had remained under the foreign yoke. At every step from the sea to the mountains, the tokens of Rome and of St. Mark still fit in with the life of the population, the spirit and habits of which are predominantly Italian, even in those parts where infiltration has in the course of centuries interwoven new elements in their ethnical composition. Documents of the highest eloquence, tenacious sacrifice which did not flinch even from martyrdom, the daily life of the people, which is truly, as Renan puts it, "a daily renewed plebiscite," testify to the spontaneous and harmonious participation of

Julian Venetia in the secular movement of ideals and heroic action for the liberation and unification of Italy, and to the aspiration of this people to unite itself, when the longed-for hour should arrive, with their brothers who had already been liberated. Austria was compelled, on the very day when a state of war with Italy was proclaimed, to dissolve all Italian representations in the Communes of Julian Venetia, because she was well aware that in every Italian she possessed an irreconcilable enemy, dangerous to her existence as an oppressing state.

When the course of disintegration of their State organism forced the Governments of Vienna and Budapest to promise the right of self-determination to the people, this was the signal throughout Gorizia and Trieste, and the whole of Istria and Fiume, no less than in the Trentino, for the populations, uncowed by persecution, privations, penalties, and the internments, to which even old men, women, and children were subjected during the war, to rise and drive out in tumult the representatives of the Austro-Hungarian regime and to proclaim, as with one voice, their annexation to the Italian Kingdom. This occurred in defiance of the armed forces which still held the field, before Italian or Allied troops could ensure protection to the rebels. Thus, Julian Venetia, as President Poincaré said of Alsace, by instinctive impulse, "flung herself weeping with joy into the arms of her recovered mother."

The Italian irredentist movement came into existence on the very day on which the peace of 1866 redressed only in partial measure the great political violence which was committed at Campoformio and reconfirmed by the Congress of Vienna.

In order to give peace to Central Europe and equilibrium to the Adriatic it is imperative to complete the work interrupted in 1866 and to tear up the last fragment of the Treaty of Vienna, which up to the present day has deprived Italy of some of her children, and undermined the security of her Adriatic frontier by sea and land.

To attain this end it is necessary in the first place to carry the Italian frontier to the watershed of the Julian Alps, which from the Moistrovka (east of Mt. Mangart), the Tricorno, Idria, Nauporto, descending by a series of massive ridges as outlined on the annexed map, and following the natural boundary marked by the watershed between Quarnero and the Canal of Maltempo (Croatian coast), plunges into the sea opposite the island of Veglia at the rock which bears the fateful name of St. Mark.

The description of the frontier does not call for elucidation, even with regard to some slight modifications which do no more than define and interpret the summary outline as drawn also in the Treaty of London. Only this frontier will close "Italy's Eastern Gate."

The territory of Julian Venetia has hitherto been assigned to six provinces of the Austro-Hungarian Monarchy. The basin of the Isonzo constituted the "Principality of Gorizia and Gradisca." Trieste and its territory formed a province by itself "directly dependent from the Empire," the Istrian Peninsula (with the Quarnero Islands) constituted the "Istrian Margraviate"; the greater part of the Inner Carso was joined to the Carniola; the town of Fiume with the surrounding district was assigned to the Hungarian Crown as a "separate entity"; lastly, the triangle formed by Fiume, the Polizza Pass, and the Rock of St. Mark formed part of Croatia.

Nature, on the contrary, created Julian Venetia a single and clearly defined geographic whole. The iniquity of events, especially during the last century, has broken up this whole, and divided its ownership, without any regard to the will and interest of the population, thus spreading the seeds of domestic and foreign strife. Here also it is necessary to give Nature its due, to reconstitute the political unity of the region, and decree its ownership to the Italian State, which claims it by right of nature, history, and for economical reasons.

Quite apart from this past history, Gorizia, Trieste, Pola, and Fiume, the most important centres in Julian Venetia, are Italian by the overwhelming majority of their present population, as shown even by official Austrian and Hungarian statistics. The towns and minor boroughs are Italian, and extensive rural districts, of which the economic and civil existence form an indivisible whole with these towns, are Italian also. Even the adversaries of the Italian cause do not also suggest that Julian Venetia should once again be broken up, and that certain of the inland portions should be assigned to a state other than that owning the large centres, which for the most part are situated on the coast. And as these large centres, whether along the coast or in the interior, are all incontestably Italian and lead the moral and material life of the whole region, Italy's claim to the possession of the whole region must be recognised, not only for the higher reasons of her eastern defence, and for those of history and civilisation, but also and more especially by reason of the economic laws of the country and the well-being of its population, without distinction of nationality. Even apart from indispensable reasons of military safety and geographical unity, a frontier of compromise, a frontier not based on clearly defined territorial principles, could neither completely settle the conflicts of nationality, which are apprehended as the result of the inclusion in our frontier of Slav minorities, nor present any economic stability. The natural outlets of the Slavified mountainous zones (which moreover are not densely populated) are the Venetian Friulian plain, and the Italian ports of Julian Venetia, from Trieste to Fiume. If these zones, which are now mainly inhabited by Slavs, were to belong to a state other than ours, they would become centres of anti-Italian agitation, they would inevitably press towards the sea and, supported also by the Slovene and Croatian hinterland, might exercise a vigorous and threatening pressure on our frontier territories, keeping them in a state of continuous agitation and the two bordering states in a condition of perpetual tension. The inclusion of the entire Cis-Alpine territory, also of that part which is partially or entirely inhabited by Slavs, far from creating the danger of Slav irredentism—which Italy knows how to avert by wise treatment of the minority—is the only way to prevent that movement for Slav irredentism which an irrational frontier would foster by the very pressure of that economic necessity which the Cis-Alpine Slavs would, on the contrary, be able to satisfy freely as heretofore in the urban centres and the Italian ports under the common protection of Italian rule.

Given the indivisibility of the region and the necessity that it should form, with its Alpine boundary, the eastern bulwark of Italy, the strength of Italian claims cannot be prejudiced by the number of inhabitants of other languages who are to be found either scattered as a minority among the Italian population in some parts, or even actually in the majority in certain outlying corners of the territory. We have already explained the reasons and the general value of such phenomena—characteristic of the border lands of territories belonging also to others which, however, are not regarded on this account as politically reduced or split. In any case, in order to rectify current impressions, it is well to make it clear that Julian Venetia is only a part which has been severed by violence in recent times from the geographically compact region of Venetia which, taken as a whole, includes little over 40,000[2] Slavs on a total population of 3,600,000 inhabitants. If again one looks only to that part of Venetia which has hitherto been separated from the Kingdom of Italy (i. e. Julian Venetia) official statistics give a population of 482,000 Italians (Italian subjects included), against 411,000 Slavs (including Slovenes and Croats). When it is considered that all the Italian residents (including the majority of Italian subjects) are natives and descendants of natives of the country, while, especially in the towns, the Slavs are mostly of recent immigration, deliberately organised for political aims; when it is considered that official censuses have misrepresented the truth to the disadvantage of Italy, as for instance (not to waste time on examples and details) can be demonstrated by the express statement made by the I. R. Central Statistical Commission, which admitted the artificiousness of the methods followed for some one-side revisions of the last census, it must be recognised that the proportion of nationalities, which official Austrian statistics have acknowledged to show an Italian majority for the whole of Julian

[2] The French text gives 400,000 which is the correct figure.

Venetia, may be presumed to be in reality even much more favourable to the Italians, and unquestionably the reality supports their claims, which are based on geography and on civil and economic predominance.

Without enlarging on records of the political life of the country, it will suffice to mention that in the three administrative provinces of Trieste, Gorizia-Gradisca, and Istria, which according to official statistics count an Italian population of 44 per cent., with 32 per cent. Slovenes and 20 per cent. Croats, the local administrations, that is to say, the fundamental and traditional organs of public life, are in Italian hands in a number of Communes that include in aggregate 70 per cent. of the entire population of Julian Venetia, and this although the electoral system in use is on the widest possible basis. On the contrary, the Communes administered by the Slavs include only 30 per cent. of the total population of the three Julian provinces. Thus the Provincial Diets—even without counting Trieste where the Council Diet counts 68 Italians out of a total of 80 members—are mostly Italian throughout Istria and the Gorizian districts, in spite of electoral regulations which under pressure of the Government have been arranged to favour the Slavs. These clear manifestations of the political life of Julian Venetia prove either that the Italians form, contrary to official statistics, the very great majority and the Slavs, notwithstanding hostile pressure and agitations, recognise Italian superiority and the necessity and utility of living in community with Italian elements; that they speak our language and accept our political programme, concerning which Italians have never made a mystery even in the administrative field. These data acquire special importance when we remember the policy of national persecution carried out by every means, especially during the last fifty years, by the Government of Vienna against the Italian elements, who, regardless of their constitutional rights, have always been deprived of elementary medium and higher schools, while the Slovenes and Croats, in consideration of their unfailing loyalty to the monarchy, solemnly reconfirmed by the motion passed in May 1917 by the Austrian Parliament, and by their military efforts which continued until October 1919, always enjoyed a privileged situation, even in the cities which were purely Italian.

The Defence of the Adriatic

The new boundary of the Julian Alps, which includes in the Kingdom of Italy, the Istrian Coast with Pola up to Fiume, reduces, without eliminating it, the state of inferiority in which, greatly to the danger of the nation and of the peace of Europe, Italy has been placed up to the present in the Adriatic. In order to remove this evil and to eliminate all danger and menace, it is imperative to return to Italy a share on the Dalmatian coast and islands.

Ever since the moment when, on the fall of Venice in 1797, Istria and Dalmatia were handed to Austria, and the natural unity of the Adriatic was shattered into military and political divisions, the problem presented itself, as it does to-day, clear and precise, grave and full of menace: torment to all young Italian democracies called into being by the genius of revolution—remorse to Napoleon who attempted to rectify at Presburg the mistake of Campoformio—nightmare of German and Viennese reaction which from the opposite shore knows that it can still rivet the chains of Italy—clear vision to the thinkers and statesmen, to the people and to the armies of our country, whom only misfortunes and mistakes— up to the battle of Lissa and the Congress of Berlin—prevented from ensuring Italy's welfare and the world's peace.

Times and conditions having changed, Italy can revise her case as regards the Adriatic: instead of demanding absolute rule on this sea her request may be limited to that of freedom, which will not exclude the Yugoslavs from a share in the possession of the Adriatic coast; Italy claiming for herself no more, but also no less, than will ensure her peaceful security and eliminate foreign menace.

Italy's claim is not antagonistic to the laws of geography and history nor to the principles of nationality and economy. The whole of Dalmatia was united to Italy in the centuries of Rome and Venice, for its own good fortune and the world's peace. Indeed, Austria herself considered it Italian territory together with Lombardy and Venetia up to the year 1866 and this even in the geography textbooks written for her military schools.

The Treaties stipulated prior to Italy's entry into the war aimed at ensuring to her that part of the islands and of the mainland of Dalmatia which was considered sufficient to eliminate danger and threat. It was a compromise, not including Spalato, the old town, with the most glorious tokens of latinity, and which therefore could and should be added.

Out of a total area of 12,385 square kilometres, she was to receive only 6,325 of Dalmatian territory, out of the Dalmatian population of 645,000 inhabitants, only 287,000, i. e. only 44 per cent.; of the whole coastline, exclusive of the islands, from Fiume to the mouth of the Boiana, Italy was to receive 117 miles against 647 given to the Slavs, that is to say, only one-sixth. The Yugoslavs would therefore have on the eastern shore a coastline six times the extent of that given to Italy, would possess more than half of the population, and half of the continental and insular area of Dalmatia. Considering that as late as 1909 a Serbian semi-official writer put forward as sufficient for the independence of Serbia a coast on the

Adriatic only 5 kilometres long between Ragusa and Cattaro, one cannot but appreciate the moderation of the Italian claims and her liberality towards her new neighbours, especially when we remember that besides the ports of the Croatian coast (Buccari, Portorè, Segna, etc.), the most important ports in Dalmatia could also be allotted to this state.

As regards nationalities, the Dalmatian territory ensured to Italy by the Treaty includes about 280,000 inhabitants, among whom the official statistics enumerate only 12,000 Italians. This is the result of the most outrageous violence that the political history of Europe records during the last century. Austria did not recoil before any form of artifice or violence in Dalmatia in order to repress Italian feelings, after 1866 in order to check any movement towards annexation to Italy, and after 1878 and 1882 in order to carry out her Balkan schemes.

Even apart from the Illyric-Roman origin, with its Albanian affinity, altogether distinct from the Slav type, of the so-called Morlacchi who form almost one-third of the Dalmatian population, impartial observation supported indirectly by scholastic statistics, election results, and the various manifestations of social life, show the Dalmatian population who come within the boundaries assured to Italy to be of a very different national consistency from what would appear from Viennese statistics. There are no fewer than 50,000 Italians, Italian by name, by fact, and by conscience, of whom nearly four-fifths were artificiously suppressed in the census; the so-called "Slavs for political opportunism" who can neither understand nor speak the Slav tongue and who at home speak exclusively Italian, number at least 15,000. There are then over 100,000 Slavs who know and speak Italian fluently, and to whom life in common with Italians, which is to-day a necessity, will be quite welcome to-morrow when they will be freed from external agitation.

Lastly, there remain in reality not more than 100,000 Slavs in the country districts, who do not speak Italian and remain unaffected by Italian influence, but, as a matter of fact, not even these latter under the pressure of the unbridled anti-Italian agitation which has been going on for so many years, show any genuine aversion to recognise the civil and economic superiority of the Italians of the towns and maritime boroughs. So great even now, in spite of everything, is the vitality of the Italian element on the Dalmatian coast, that the Croats must themselves, in their own papers, openly complain that anybody visiting Dalmatia must receive an impression contrary to their aspirations, that is to say an Italian impression, and they reproach the Dalmatians for their "shameful habit" of speaking Italian. Nor could this be otherwise in a country in which the violence of Austrian rule may have robbed Italians of a parliamentary representation—which in 1869 consisted of 7 Italian against

2 Slav deputies—and of a majority in the Provincial Diet which in the first elections of 1861 had numbered 30 Italian deputies against 13 Slavs, but did not succeed either in impairing the Italian character of Zara which triumphantly asserts itself in Zara's all-Italian Town Council, nor in preventing, for instance, the Chambers of Commerce of the Zara and Sebenico districts from being Italian; nor the constituency of the wealthiest class of the same districts from sending unopposed to the Diet Italian deputies, thus affording clear proof that industrial and trade activity and real estate in the very territory reserved to Italy are still in Italian hands and supporting also in the economic field the Italian character of historic memories and feelings which, since the Italian occupation following on the Armistice, has revealed itself in such a touching and eloquent manner by the spontaneity and persistence of manifestations and aspirations.

But even if historic right did not support it and if racial reality were not actually so different from what the Austrian State has tried to make out in the Slav interest, Italy should still—for the sake of her future safety—not relinquish her claim to the possession of a minimum of the Dalmatian coast and islands. It would carry us too far to go into a detailed examination of the strategic problems of the Adriatic. A single glance at map reveals, however, their essential features already thrown into tragic relief by the recent war.

On the eastern coast of the Adriatic a magnificent advance barrier of rocks and islands protects the mainland and with it the coastal lines of communication. On the western coast is a low-lying beach, undefended and exposed to aggression of all kinds.

On the east side there is the possibility of sheltered navigation, no matter from what direction the wind may blow; on our side there is a complete lack of every kind of refuge, and risky sailing whenever the weather is bad. On the eastern coast, wide recesses and the possibility of casting anchor anywhere; on the west, a lack of anchorages and difficulty of call and refuge.

On the Dalmatian coast high ground offers excellent observation posts which command the wide surrounding horizon; on the Italian coast, on the other hand, low-lying ground and (with the exception of the Gargano and the Conero) no possibility of observing the waters from a height.

It is clear that a Power having exclusive sway over the central tract of the Dalmatian coast from Zara to Spalato, with the military port of Sebenico and the islands, would be free to come out at any moment and give battle.

The Italian fleet, speeding up partly from Venice and partly from

Brindisi, would infallibly find itself exposed to fight with only half its forces against the entire enemy fleet, and to the possibility of being beaten separately before having a chance to join up its forces.

Dalmatia if all in the hands of one Power represents a danger to Italy; a portion of Dalmatia in possession of Italy, especially within the modest limits to which Italian aspirations are confined, represents a danger to no one.

The present war has proved this. Italy with all her fleet was unable to do anything substantial against the enemy's naval forces lurking in the ports and canals on the other shore, and even the co-operation of considerable French and British forces could achieve nothing. Italy was compelled to suffer her naval energies to be worn away in an enervating effort of defence and unaccepted challenge, notwithstanding several acts of individual valour. Austria-Hungary, on the contrary, was able to attack and bombard undefended towns on the Italian coast and then take refuge behind her wonderful screen on the eastern coast, before the ever-vigilant Italian and Allied forces were able to overtake her.

In order to avoid remaining in a state of permanent and absolute inferiority, Italy is, therefore, entitled to ask that, in accordance with what has been set forth above, the coast and islands of the Adriatic which will be allotted to others shall be neutralised; that all fortifications, either on land or sea, should be forbidden and all existing ones dismantled.

As to the zone comprised between Zara and Sebenico, its configuration is such that no form of neutralisation could possibly prevent its being transformed in a few hours into a first-rate naval base by the sudden resort to the latest means of warfare such as mines, submarines, etc., which would make that coast absolutely impregnable. Only by having it in her possession could Italy guarantee her safety.

Italian Rights on Fiume

The Treaty with her Allies which preceded Italy's entrance into the war recognised those rights which, as shown above, are Italy's natural and historic rights and essential to her economic and defensive unity in the mountains and on the sea. Fiume and her district have, however, been excepted, and Italy must now reclaim them not only as an essential part of Julian Venetia, as an indispensable fulfilment of her eastern defensive requirements, but, above all because Fiume is, after Trieste, Gorizia, and Pola, the most important Italian town on the eastern Adriatic. There are in Fiume 33,000 Italians with whom are intermixed only 10,927 Slavs and 1,300 Magyars. Both ancient and modern history show Fiume as thoroughly Italian: the very Croatian Ban Jelačić, who in

1848 forcibly occupied the town by order of Austria and as a punishment to Hungary which had rebelled against the Hapsburgs had publicly to guarantee to the citizens of Fiume "the use of their Italian tongue."

Jealously guarding her Italian culture and teaching, Fiume rebelled against the tendency towards introducing the teaching of other languages in her schools, "thus sowing in the tender hearts of the children prejudice against the Italian tongue, which has always been spoken since Fiume existed, which is the country's own language, and one of the principal elements to which can be attributed her culture and progress both commercial and industrial" (1861).

The mayors, all the members of the municipal council, the deputies, have always been and are Italian and only Italian. Up to quite recently, out of respect to the Italian character of Fiume, the Hungarian Kingdom published the laws in Italian.

Her Italian character and autonomy have been the fundamental elements of the life of Fiume; especially since the day which by her decree of April 23rd, 1779, Maria Theresa declared Fiume to be a separate body of the Hungarian Kingdom, and a town free from all union or connection with Croatia (*separatum sacrae regni Hungariae coronae adnexum corpus . . . neque cum alio Buccarano vel ad regnum Croatiae pertinente ulla ratione commisceatur*). This privilege was confirmed by succeeding fundamental laws and by the "Statute of the *Free City* of Fiume." After the fall of the Hapsburg dynasty, Fiume claimed her right to self-determination and proclaimed, on October 29th, 1918, her adherence to Italy, to whom, according to the tradition of the Italian Risorgimento, she had already been assigned by the programme of the Carboneria (1822).

Italy, in asserting her right to accept and ask for recognition of the spontaneous self-dedication of Italian Fiume, knows too that she is thus meeting in the best way the necessity for a rational exploitation of Fiume's economic value in the interest particularly of the hinterland to which she serves as port. At the same time Italy would have in Fiume, according to the spirit of the Treaty with her Allies, one of the compensations to which she has earned a full right by the greater efforts and sacrifices by which she has contributed to the war, considering also the new conditions created by the disruption of Austria-Hungary.

When Italy joined the Allied Powers her undertaking, according to the military convention then agreed to, was limited by the obligation of Russia to employ against Austria-Hungary a certain minimum force, "to prevent Austria-Hungary from concentrating all her efforts against Italy if Russia should desire to turn her attention in particular against Germany."

The internal political events in Russia which led to a separate peace had the following double consequence: that Austria-Hungary, freed from any possibility of further pressure, was able to concentrate all her forces against Italy and that Germany, also freed from her eastern enemy, was in a position to lend Austria-Hungary that efficacious assistance which at one period had such serious repercussion to Italy's detriment.

In fact, while the unexpected event of Russia's disappearance from among the Entente belligerents was largely compensated to our Allies by the intervention of the American forces, no assistance of this sort came to the Italian Front to relieve the effort of the Italian Army, as President Wilson himself so sympathetically acknowledged and regretted.

The double consequence of Russia's falling out, from which Italy was the principal sufferer, both as regards military effort and sacrifice on the part of the population, would justify Italy in requesting an all-round increase of the compensations which were agreed upon in anticipation of much smaller efforts and sacrifices.

Italy wishes to give proof—even in this case—of the greatest moderation, and limits herself to requesting, as has been stated above, the City and District of Fiume, which racially is in its great majority Italian, and which has of its own accord proclaimed its desire to be united to Italy. Moreover, in the defensive system of our land frontier, Fiume rounds off the extreme, and therefore the most critical point. The border would otherwise be reduced to an untenable line consisting of the administrative frontier between Istria and Fiume, up to now in the hands of one state only.

Fiume in Italian hands would complete, too, the anti-German programme of defence in the Adriatic. Only Italy, that is to say, only a great sea Power, can dispose of the necessary means for carrying into effect this programme which meets the requirements of the combined interests of all the Powers who have fought side by side in the war.

Trieste and Fiume—a French writer warns us in 1915, referring to the terms of the future peace—either under Austrian or Hungarian disguise, are but German ports, southern terminals of a line of domination of which Hamburg and Bremen are the terminals on the North Sea.

Having freed the one terminal, Trieste, from indirect German domination, we must prevent the other, Fiume, from carrying on her German functions under Yugoslav attire even against the desire and intention of the new Slav state, which would be powerless and unprepared to eliminate the old influences and to counteract the German efforts which will be concentrated, especially after the loss of Trieste, on the one possible point of penetration.

Not even an Anti-German Danube Confederation, even if it could be constituted, could replace Italy in this mission without serious delays of which the enemy, with the financial trickery of which he is master, would take full advantage.

The natural aptitude and technical means at the disposal of a sea Power such as Italy are necessary for this purpose. Italy would place this port, as she will place Trieste, entirely at the service of its natural hinterland. She would but reconcile, by means of the best technical and most advantageous economical methods, her own interests with those of her natural customers, avoiding the effects of any political influence or dependence, contrary to the common line of general interest.

To those states Italy could guarantee specific advantages such as bonded warehouses and bonded zones, reserved portions of the general storehouses, special landing places, preferential tariffs for harbour dues, special markets, agreements for cumulative railway and maritime tariffs, agreements for the emigration traffic, etc. She is thus sure of acting also in the interest of her own ports, whose prosperity is intimately connected with that of the hinterland states.

Since Trieste and Fiume must be outlets of German territories (Germany and German Austria), the Czechoslovak State, the Yugoslav countries (Slovenia and Croatia), and of Hungary, the difficulty—not to say the impossibility—is perfectly clear, of any Power other than Italy ensuring to their common outlets on the sea that impartial and objective technical management which is an indispensable requisite of the rapid and economical exploitation of these ports and of the railway and maritime lines by which they must be served. Only Italy could fulfil these functions, as she is obviously outside and superior to any competition either political or economic which may arise between the above mentioned states.

With regard particularly to Fiume, it must be denied that this port is essential to the economic needs of Croatia. The Croatian traffic amounts to only 7 per cent. of the total movement (import and export) of the port of Fiume; the remainder belongs to the other countries of the hinterland and especially to Hungary. Only 13 per cent. of the entire trade of Croatia, Slavonia, Dalmatia, Bosnia, and Herzegovina passed through Fiume, the rest going towards the ports of Lower Dalmatia. The maritime service of the port of Fiume, run so far by companies subsidised by the Hungarian Government, could certainly not be worked by a new state which would bring to Fiume such a small portion of her traffic, which would have many other more urgent demands, and which is in no way prepared for such work. Only a great sea Power, such as Italy, with the necessary traditions, means, connections, and experience could help Fiume to accomplish her mission, although at first some sacrifice would be required which could easily be borne by the Italian treasury in the summing up of the profit and loss which is possible through the cumulative management of so many ports.

Trieste and Fiume in Italian hands could have combined maritime services of wider range, and more economical and perfect in organisation, without giving rise to any conflict of interests and to the mutual advantage of their respective hinterlands.

Maritime services run separately for Trieste and Fiume would be neither rational nor economical. Trieste supported by an important Power like Italy might have them while Fiume has not, to her own detriment as well as to the detriment of her hinterland, which would necessarily pay higher rates for such lines than they would require to pay if Fiume were Italian and could make use of the cumulative services which Italy would maintain for both her ports in the northern Adriatic.

In other words, and not only in this respect, Italy would, to the advantage of both ports and of the producing and consuming districts of the hinterland, exercise a regulating and subsidising function. The other states of the hinterland, and especially Croatia and Yugoslavia, would lack for this purpose the requisite means, technical preparation and impartiality.

The problem of Fiume, so closely allied to that of Trieste, besides being one that intimately concerns Italy—involving, as it does, the interests of a city which is so markedly Italian, and which is, moreover, connected with the other problem of the eastern Italian frontier—is also a European problem in the anti-German sense of the word. Only as an Italian city would the development of Fiume as an emporium be ensured, thus protecting the port itself and the hinterland (especially the Magyar district) from the dangers of the following dilemma: either economic ruin or German help and therefore German hegemony, even if only of an economic character. "Fiume as a Croatian city," as has been written by a French journalist, "means a Hungarian, Austro-Hungarian, or German Fiume, which all amounts to the same thing."

In conclusion, if it is true that the Treaty of London united Fiume to the Kingdom of Croatia in view of its territorial continuity with that region, it is none the less true that the same Treaty did not foresee the fall of the Hapsburg Monarchy, of which the said Kingdom was an integral part. In that case it appeared reasonable that the political possession of an autonomous port on the Adriatic should not be denied to Transleitania and more especially to a total population of 50 million inhabitants, who were quite able to attend to its maintenance and support; whereas, with the fall of the Empire at Vittorio Veneto after the last determining factor of the Italian Army's powerful blow, the need for and the claim to political rule over this commercial outlet ceased to exist.

The history of over a century, from the proclamation of Maria Theresa which declares Fiume to be a "separate body" of the Hungarian state without any "connection whatsoever with Croatia" up to the last decisions of the National Council of Fiume, all goes to prove that only by deforming a material reality in perfect harmony with an inalterable spiritual reality, would it be possible to bind Fiume to the fortunes of a new Slav state.

No one can honestly contest Italy's right to obtain from Peace those fruits which for the most part were assured to her prior to her entry into the war as her due for efforts and for sacrifices infinitely inferior to those which they actually made in the common cause. Whoever disputes or discusses Italy's claims, does not do so from objective or intrinsic reasons, but only from too great a consideration for the pretensions of southern Slavs.

They are the very claims and objections of those Slavs who up to the last moment contributed in full measure to the war, specially devoting their energies against Italy. Only yesterday the most important Yugoslav paper admitted that they had fought *like lions against Italy*—that is to say against the Entente—for what they call *their land*. From the Austro-Hungarian Government, and almost as a reward for the loyalty and dynastic character preserved up to the last by their agitation for a Yugoslav state within the orbit of the Hapsburg Monarchy, they received at the last moment, in the handing over of the fleet, a mandate of confidence which cannot but cause some perplexity as to the attitude to be taken by the Allies towards the future of the new state.

However, Italy foresaw, before allying herself to the enemies of the Central Empires, the possibility that rightful claims might be contested after the victory by companions in arms who might in some respects have political interests different from or opposite to hers.

For this reason she proposed and accepted an equitable compromise implying unquestionable renunciations to complete redemption of Italian land and peoples. Italy thus defined the minimum which, while giving some satisfaction to the legitimate desires of others, would also guarantee that on a favourable conclusion of the war, her hopes would not be rendered vain and illusory as a result of pressure exerted by those very men by whose side Italy had fought.

Having at that time, in order to avoid future misunderstanding, drawn the attention of her new Allies to the possibility of the contestations which have now arisen in a wholly unjustifiable form, Italy is now entitled to anticipate fully that her moderate requests, corresponding to her rights and necessities and having to such a great extent the full suffrage of the peoples involved, should be accepted in full.

YUGOSLAV PROPOSAL OF ARBITRATION[1]

Paris, February 11, 1919

Mr. President,

The Delegation of the Kingdom of the Serbs, Croats, and Slovenes to the Peace Conference has the honor of informing Your Excellency that, having full confidence in the high spirit of justice of Mr. Wilson, President of the United States, and being formally authorized by the Royal Government, it is ready to submit the territorial dispute between the Kingdom of the Serbs, Croats, and Slovenes and the Kingdom of Italy to President Wilson's arbitration.

The Delegation also asks Your Excellency to take cognizance of this fact and to inform the Conference. It has already sent a similar communication to His Excellency, the President of the United States.

The Delegation takes this opportunity to present to Your Excellency . . .

Signed: Pachitch, Trumbic, Vesnitch, Zolger.

To His Excellency M. G. Clemenceau.

Paris, February 11, 1919.

Mr. President,

The Delegation of the Kingdom of the Serbs, Croats, and Slovenes, moved by the fullest confidence in the noble spirit of justice which you have shown in regard to all the questions connected with the Peace settlement, and wishing to contribute to the amicable solution of the territorial dispute existing between the Kingdom of the Serbs, Croats, and Slovenes and the Kingdom of Italy, wishes to inform you that it is ready to submit these disputes to your arbitration. It has been fully authorized to this effect by its Government.

With the assurance . . .

Signed: Nik P. Pachitch, Dr. Ante Trumbic, Vesnitch, Dr. Zolger.

His Excellency Mr. Wilson, President of the United States of America, Hôtel Murat, Paris.

[1] Adriaticus, *La Question adriatique,* Document IX, pp. 33-34. Author's translation.

MINUTES OF THE COUNCIL[1]

[EXTRACTS]

FEBRUARY 18, 1919

SECRETARY'S NOTES OF A CONVERSATION HELD IN M. PICHON'S ROOM AT THE QUAI D'ORSAY, PARIS, ON TUESDAY, 18TH FEBRUARY, 1919, at 3:00 P.M.

PRESENT

AMERICA, UNITED STATES OF	BRITISH EMPIRE	FRANCE
The Hon. R. Lansing	The Rt. Hon. A. J. Balfour, O.M., M.P.	M. Clemenceau
The Hon. H. White		M. Pichon
	The Rt. Hon. Sir Robert Borden, G.C.M.G.	

Secretary	*Secretaries*	*Secretaries*
Mr. L. Harrison	Lt. Col. Sir M. P. A. Hankey, K.C.B.	M. Dutasta
	Mr. H. Norman	M. Berthelot
		M. de Bearn

ITALY	JAPAN
H.E. Baron Sonnino	H.E. Baron Makino
H.E. Marquis Salvago Raggi	H.E. M. Matsui

Secretaries
Count Aldrovandi
M. Bertele

JOINT SECRETARIAT

AMERICA, UNITED STATES OF	BRITISH EMPIRE	FRANCE
Lieut. Burden	Captain E. Abraham	Captain A. Portier

ITALY	JAPAN
Major A. Jones	M. Saburi

ALSO PRESENT

AMERICA, UNITED STATES OF	BRITISH EMPIRE	FRANCE	ITALY
Mr. Lunt	Sir Eyre Crowe, K.C.B.	General Alby	M. de Martino
Mr. Dulles	Colonel Heywood		M. Galli
Maj. D. W. Johnson	Mr. A. Leeper		

[1] Miller, *My Diary at the Conference of Paris*, XIV, 486-501.

For the Serbs, Croats and Slovenes

M. Patchitch	M. Trumbitch
M. Vesnitch	Dr. Zolger

Secretary
M. Vosniak
Interpreter—Professor P. J. Mantoux

Statement of Case for Yugo-Slavia

1. M. Clemenceau in opening the meeting asked the Serbian Delegation to make its statement.

(*a*) *Causes of the Great War.*—M. Vesnitch said that he must begin by an apology. It had not, up to the present, been possible to supply the Conference with a full memorandum. There were certain difficulties due to distance, bad communications, etc., which had rendered this impossible. A memorandum giving general considerations had been supplied. Separate memoranda of a more technical order would be prepared subsequently.

In order to present the problem fully he wished first to draw the attention of the meeting to the origin of the war. This question had been dealt with publicly, but nevertheless he felt it must again be asserted before the Conference that the real cause of the war was the German tendency to expand towards Asia Minor and thereby to acquire dominion of the world. In its road this movement encountered a number of obstacles, the first of which was the Yugo-Slav people. Hence it was decided in Berlin and Vienna that this should be the first fortress to be taken.

(*b*) *Eastward trend of German policy.*—The time-honoured German policy was well-known. Since 1848 and especially since 1878 Vienna under the direction of Berlin had sought to bring under its rule all the Serbians not yet included in the Dual Monarchy. This policy had involved the Great Powers. Since 1848, Great Britain, France and Italy had struggled to preserve the peace of Europe. One stage on this road to the East had been marked by the absorption of Bosnia and Herzegovina. Another critical moment was the Balkan War. Serbia issued from it victorious and became the centre of attraction for all the Yugo-Slav peoples. The enthusiasm shown in Bosnia, Croatia, Slavonia and the Banat was even greater than that in Serbia proper. This had been carefully noted at the Ballplatz, where it was decided that the future must be secured as early as possible. This also was incontestably the reason which had rendered futile all the efforts of the Liberal Powers of Europe to find a peaceful diplomatic issue with the nations of Central Europe. The latter were determined to overcome the obstacle and to set forward on their march

Eastwards in the quickest possible time. It had been impossible to stop them—hence the Great War.

(c) *Action of Yugo-Slavs in the War.*—The Yugo-Slav troops of the Dual Monarchy from the very first day of the war began to hamper the purposes of the Central Powers. When other means failed, they surrendered in large numbers on the Russian and Serbian fronts, and at a later stage, on the Italian front. They felt that this was a war of extermination for their people. Encouraged by the promises made by the Great Liberal Powers, especially by the declaration that the war was waged for the liberation of oppressed peoples, they had contributed by every means in their power to the victory of the Allies. They were now inspired by the confident hope that their expectations of the fulfilment of the promises made by the victorious Allies would not be disappointed, and they felt that their services to the common cause had earned recognition.

(d) *Principles for which the Allies fought.*—Since the very beginning of the war the Great Liberal Powers, France, Great Britain, and with them Russia, had proclaimed that they were not fighting for individual national advantages, but for certain principles. These principles were stated publicly and solemnly and were the three great principles of (1) Nationality, (2) the right of self-determination, and (3) freedom of the small Nations. After the signature of the first Armistice, M. Clemenceau, when welcoming the delegates of all the Allied Powers, had said that from that moment there was no difference between great and small nations, as the small nations had been as great as the greatest during the war. He wished to recall this expression to make clear the difference between the principles of the Allied Powers and those of the Central Powers. Before the war there had been a conversation between Herr Von Jagow and M. Jules Cambon. The former had declared that there was no more room in the world for small nations. This was fully in accord with the feelings of his nation. What M. Clemenceau had expressed to the Allies was the principle which had encouraged the Nations to group themselves and to bring about the triumph of something far higher than the self-interests of individual nations. It was in accordance with this spirit that the peace of Europe and the League of Nations must be brought about.

(e) *Attitude towards secret treaties.*—Adhering to this spirit, the delegation he represented regarded the right of self-determination as an inviolable right. It could not recognise any treaty, public or secret doing violence to these principles, proclaimed by the Allies and latterly endorsed by the United States of America. The Delegation he represented therefore regarded as null and void any agreement disposing of the Yugo-Slav people without its consent. He felt obliged to make this declaration in the name of his Government and of his colleagues present in the room. Had he not made it, he would have betrayed his obligation to the Yugo-Slav people. It was not in the habits of this people to sing its own praises, but it must be declared that if this people had endured martyrdom to assist the Allies, it was because their leaders had assured them that these sufferings were absolutely necessary, that it was probably the last effort required of them, and that the open declarations of the Great Allied Powers were a complete guarantee of the future. The leaders of the people had made themselves responsible for the execution of these promises. The Yugo-Slav people, through them, had put complete trust in the Powers whom he now begged to do nothing which might cause disappointment to the legitimate hopes aroused, and thereby sow the seeds of future deplorable conflict.

(e) *Question of future frontiers of Yugo-Slavia.*—M. VESNITCH, continuing, said that, if it was in order, he would approach the subject of the future frontiers of Yugo-Slavia. The Yugo-Slav people was in a peculiar situation. It had to delimit its territory with six or seven nations. On a former occasion explanations had been given concerning the problem to be solved with a friendly country. In tracing the boundaries separating them from enemy countries it was likely that no great difficulties would arise. But there was another friendly country with which there were problems to discuss. The Delegation would ask that it should be treated on a footing of equality with its Italian friends. He felt that in making this request he was not exceeding the limits of his rights and his duties. He hoped that the Allied and Associated Powers would consider this fair and practical and likely to ensure good understanding between two countries which were to be neighbours, and between which it was desirable that no germ of discord should arise.

(f) *Southern frontier.*—M. VESNITCH explained, with the help of a map, what he proposed should be the future frontiers of Yugo-Slavia. On the south the boundary marched with that of Greece. It was not proposed in any way to alter the boundary laid down by the Peace of Bucharest.

(g) *Eastern frontier.*—On the east the frontier was to be determined with Bulgaria. The behaviour of the Bulgarians towards the Serbians, even before they entered the war, was well-known, hence certain alterations of frontier were demanded.

(h) *Northeastern frontier.*—The Yugo-Slav arguments concerning the boundary to be drawn in the Banat had been heard on a previous occasion. Failing all other means of settlement, the Delegation for which he spoke was ready to allow the populations to make a free choice of allegiance He would like to point out that all invasions of Serbia throughout history had come from that quarter. The latest examples furnished in the course of the late war were enough to prove this point. There were also ethnological, geographical and economic reasons. The divisions of the country made for administrative purposes by the common enemies of Serbia and Roumania were evidence in his favour. No less well-wishing judges could be found than the Magyars towards the Serbian people, nevertheless the division of the country made by them showed the Serbs to be in the majority.

(*i*) *Northern frontier.*—In the North the Delegation proposed a frontier which corresponded not only to ethnic, but to geographical realities.

DR. ZOLGER, continuing, explained that the proposed boundary with the Germans and Magyars was drawn in such a way as to include all the Croats, Serbs and Slovenes along the Drave. The frontier would not accord with the results of the Austrian census. This census could not be trusted. It did not record nationality, but professed to record the spoken language of the people. Workmen serving German employers and communicating with them in German would be represented as Germans. Even German authorities admitted that this method was deliberately devised in order to favour Germanisation. The Delegation therefore proposed to neglect the Austrian census and pin its faith to certain other means of obtaining information. Among these he would cite the ecclesiastical parish registers published yearly, showing the language used in the parish for confessional purposes. The language to which it was necessary to resort to spread the Gospel must be the spoken language of the people. A hundred villages shown in the Austrian census as German were proved by the parish registers to speak Slovene. There were other documents which might be consulted such as the census of 1849-51. This census had been conducted in a less partial manner than its successor, for since 1870 the Pan-German idea had become the official doctrine of the Central Governments.

(*j*) *German attempt to reach the Adriatic.*—In pursuance of this doctrine the most consistent efforts had been made to establish German contact with the Adriatic. In this process the Slovenes had fared perhaps worse than any other Yugo-Slav nation. The process had begun in the 18th Century. The danger had been realised by Napoleon, who had set up the Illyrian Province after the Peace of Schoenbrunn, comprising all Slovene lands, to block the way from Vienna to the Adriatic and to guard the road to the East.

(*k*) *Claims in Carinthia.*—The frontier suggested in Carinthia gave to Yugo-Slavia certain areas in which the Slovenes were not a majority in the population. The justification of this was the forcible Germanisation practised since 1850. Dr. Zolger drew attention to a work called "The

Vilayet of Carinthia," published before the war. In this work it was shown that every means had been adopted of destroying Slovene nationality and the Slovene language. For instance, all writers, even the Germans, admitted that Celovec (Klagenfurt), was in 1850, two-thirds Slovene. At the present time the Slovenes were in the minority. This had been brought about by the educational policy forced on the country. Children were only taught the Gothic script. Where there had been a hundred Slovene schools, there were now but three. From all branches of the public service Slovenes had been extruded. The last Slovene judge died some ten years ago. The last Slovene notary was removed during the war. Barristers were not allowed to plead before the Courts in Slovene. Only one Slovene Deputy was sent to the Reichsrat, though on the population basis there should have been three. The people were afraid of speaking their own language, and a man had been arrested for demanding a ticket at a railway station in Slovene. The war had been used to give the death blow to Slovene life in Carinthia. It was therefore fair to say that the reduction of the Slovene element was not a process of natural evolution, but the work of a deliberate and forcible policy, carried out in contempt of all morality and law. In fixing the frontier between Yugo-Slavia and German Austria, the result of this policy should not be perpetuated. Wherever it was possible to show that 50 years previously the Slovenes had been in possession, he claimed that they should have ownership restored to them. The frontier suggested would be some compensation to the Yugo-Slav people for their losses in the long struggle with Germanism. He would point out that in the course of centuries the Slovenes had lost not only part of Carinthia and Styria, but also the Eastern Tyrol and lower Austria. Wherever it was possible to establish an ethnic claim, he thought that it should be admitted.

(*l*) *Western frontier.*—M. TRUMBITCH said that in the name of the Kingdom of the Serbs, Croats and Slovenes he would place before the meeting briefly, the claims made on the subject of the western frontier, and he would explain the grounds on which the claims were based.

The area in question was that part of the ancient Austro-Hungarian monarchy situated on the Adriatic Sea or gravitating towards it, and inhabited by a Yugo-Slav population. As had been repeatedly proclaimed in public manifestations by official representatives of the people, the territorial claims were based on the rights of nationalities and on the principle of self-determination. It was on this basis that the new state laid claim to countries, the population of which was of Yugo-Slav nationality, desiring to enter into the community of that State. In a general way it must be observed that from the point of view of spoken language and national sentiment, the whole Adriatic Coast of the former Austria-

Hungary from MONFALCONE as far as SPIZZA was inhabited by Yugo-Slavs, in a compact and continuous mass. The whole countryside and hinterland of this coast, with the sole exception of five Italian villages north of POLA, were Yugo-Slav. In most of the towns the Slav element was in the majority, save in some isolated towns such as GORIZIA, TRIESTE, towns on the Western shore of ISTRIA, LUSSIN, FIUME, and ZARA, where the Italian element predominated. The Italian element, therefore, represented enclaves or oases in Slav surroundings, without any national continuity binding it to the Italian peninsula.

The Yugo-Slav majority had always been oppressed. This had been its fate during more than four centuries of Venetian domination. The Slav element, deprived of all national rights, was unable under that rule to obtain any school in its own language whether in the towns or in the villages. Nevertheless, Venetian domination had not succeeded in Italianising any area, and only left behind it along the Adriatic coast a few families and some vestiges of the Venetian dialect, as was the case also in the islands of the Ionian Sea and of the Ægean Sea, where the Venetian Republic had once ruled.

Austria in this province had continued to apply the system she found there. The Austrian régime was anti-democratic, based on the division of classes and nationalities in respect to civil and political rights. Hence, the Yugo-Slav element had always been oppressed and systematically neglected, while the Italian element in the towns received privileges. When, in 1907, universal suffrage was introduced throughout Austria, the first elections showed that the Yugo-Slav element was much stronger than appeared on the surface. The national revival of the Yugo-Slav masses began after the introduction of the constitution in 1861. It was then that the political struggle began between the Yugo-Slav and Italian elements. The Yugo-Slav population, being democratic, had struggled for the freedom of their language and political and social rights. In this struggle the Yugo-Slavs, day by day, obtained further successes and made progress in the acquisition of those rights.

Turning to the application of the principles of nationality and of the right of self-determination, he wished to refer to the regions now under consideration. For greater clearness, he would first mention the regions of the Adriatic Coast from Cape Promontore along the Eastern coast of Istria, past Fiume (Rjeka) and along the remainder of the Croatian coast-line, the Dalmatian coast as far as Spizza (the Southern frontier of Dalmatia), and all Quarnero and Dalmatian islands which, from every point of view, formed an integral part of this coast.

The coast-line just described was almost exclusively inhabited by Yugo-Slavs, both as regards hamlets and villages and most of the towns.

There were sporadic groups of Italian-speaking inhabitants in certain towns, but their number was so small that this factor would have no influence whatever on the national character of such coast-line and islands.

The Yugo-Slav population, which formed the overwhelming majority of the inhabitants, had a high regard for its national unity and was imbued with the unshakeable desire to remain within the bounds of their State as already constituted. Wherefore, in the name of the principle of nationality, they begged that this entire coast-line, with its islands, should be joined to their State.

It had to be remembered that all these regions were poor and incapable of development apart from the State of which their Hinterland would form a part. All the national, economic and commercial life of the majority of the provinces of their State gravitated towards the coast—i. e., of Croatia-Slavonia, Backa, the Banat, Northern Serbia, Bosnia-Herzegovina, Dalmatia and Montenegro, all of whose existing roads and railways led to the sea. The islands on their coast sold all their export produce to the coast towns.

Austria's economic policy did not allow railways to be built in this transverse direction, as would have been to the interests of these regions, but commercial routes were created longitudinally from North to South, with the idea of penetration into the Balkans. It would be the duty of their State to alter this entirely and to build transverse roads and railways which would contribute to the development of commercial relations beyond the sea and primarily with Italy.

The only commercial railway was that which, starting from Fiume, crossed Croatia-Slavonia, Serbia, Bosnia and Hungary. It was built by the Hungarian Government with money belonging to the common Hungaro-Croatian State, at the time when (by falsifying the laws of 1868) Fiume was torn from the Croatians. This port was, therefore, even now the only commercial access to the sea for all these regions, which could not develop normally without Fiume.

To-day, when the Peace Conference was concerned with guaranteeing commercial outlets to the sea even to nations having no direct access thereto, it would be incomprehensible if an attempt were made to take from their nation the ports situate in its territory and on its own coast-line. For these reasons they requested that the whole of the coast-line, including the islands already referred to, might be acknowledged to form part of their State.

The provinces of Gorizia, Gradisca, Trieste with its suburbs, and the Western portion of Istria were situated in the basin of the Upper Adriatic.

The province of Gorizia-Gradisca was composed of two parts, totally different both from the national and economic points of view. The Western part, which extended as far as the line Cormons-Gradisca-Monfalcone, had its own life and constituted an economic unity. According to the language spoken in this region, it contained 72,000 Italians and 6,000 Slovenes, whilst from the geographical point of view it was simply a prolongation of the Venetian plain. As these territories, called the Frioul, belonged according to the principle of nationality to the Italian nation, they did not claim them in any way. The remainder of that province, to the East and North of the line Cormons-Gradisca-Monfalcone, which included the mountainous region, was inhabited by 148,500 Slovenes and 17,000 Italians, 14,000 of whom formed half the population of the town of Gorizia. This town was the economic and intellectual centre of that region.

The Slovenes were a highly cultured people and possessed a deep-rooted consciousness of their national unity with the other Yugo-Slav peoples, and they therefore demanded that this country be united with their State.

Geographically, the town of Trieste and its immediate surroundings formed an integral part of territories which, beyond these limits, were purely Slav. The majority of the population of the said town was Italian —two-thirds, according to statistics—the remainder being Slavs. The Slav element played an important part in the commercial and economic life of Trieste. Furthermore, if national continuity with Italy prevailed in Trieste, they would recognise the rights of the majority in the name of the principle of nationality; but the entire *Hinterland* of Trieste was purely Slav, and 20 kilometres of Slav coast separated the said town from Italian territory. The question of Trieste had, however, to be considered firstly from the point of view of its commercial and maritime importance. Commercially, Trieste was a world port. Its trade was linked with its *Hinterland*, which stretched as far as Bohemia, and in particular with its Slovene *Hinterland*, which absorbed one-third of the total trade of Trieste. Trieste was dependent on its *Hinterland*, and *vice versa*. Should Trieste become annexed to Italy, it would be separated politically from its commercial *Hinterland*, which separation would of necessity prove detrimental to its trade. Since the collapse of Austria as a sovereign Power, the natural solution of the problem of Trieste lay in its reunion with their State, and that was what they now asked for.

The population of Istria was partly Slavonic and partly Italian. According to the latest statistics there were 223,318 Yugo-Slavs and 147,417 Italians, the Slavs inhabiting Central and Eastern Istria in a compact mass. There were a few isolated Italian groups in certain small towns. Judging from the vast majority of the population Central and Eastern Istria were essentially Slav.

The Italian population was most numerous on the Western Coast of Istria, chiefly in the towns, where it occupied only five villages north of Pola. These were the only Italian-speaking villages on the entire Adriatic Coast from Monfalcone as far as Spizza. The Slavs constituted part of the population of some coast towns and of all the remaining villages. Thus the Italian sections of the population could claim no territorial unity. For these reasons, and also because the Istrian peninsula was united geographically with Carniola and Croatia, whilst separated from Italy by the Adriatic, it followed that this peninsula should be recognised as part of their State—which was what they now demanded.

Generally, it should be noted that none of the regions on the Adriatic coast between Monfalcone and Spizza had any vital interests in common with Italy, but rather with their regions, with which they were geographically united. This most important argument should be taken into consideration when this problem was being settled.

After concluding his statement, M. Trumbitch said he would like to add a few words about the population statistics of the areas mentioned. These statistics were made under Austrian rule by the communal authorities. In most cases where the population was partly Italian and partly Yugo-Slav, the communal authorities were Italian. In those cases, consequently, the statistics could not be accused of bias in favour of the Yugo-Slavs.

(At this stage the Delegation withdrew.)

.   .   .

Agenda for Future Conversations

[(a) Discussion of the state of Northern Russia]. . . .

(b) Procedure regarding Yugo-Slav claims.—MR. BALFOUR said that the Council had now heard the evidence of the Yugo-Slavs. Similar evidence had been heard from other nationalities, and in most cases the problems raised had been referred for examination to a Committee, without power to decide on solutions, but with a Commission to report on the facts. In the case of the Yugo-Slav statement, he admitted that there were difficulties, especially by reason of the treaty commitments of some of the Powers present. He wished to ask what should now be done. Was the matter to be left just as it was?

M. SONNINO said that the subject was a difficult one. He wished to be quite frank. Italy could not take part in any Commission or in any discussion outside the Conference, or allow any Committee to make recommendations, regarding questions outstanding between Italy and the Yugo-Slavs. He would also oppose any Committee which was to examine collectively all questions raised by the statements heard that day. The question between the Yugo-Slavs and the Roumanians was already being sifted by a Committee. To this he had no objection.

Mr. Balfour then asked Baron Sonnino to state what procedure he did recommend. He understood that Baron Sonnino would raise no objection to a Committee on the subject of the Northern and Eastern frontiers of Yugo-Slavia. But he would refuse to be a party to any discussion of the frontiers between Italy and Yugo-Slavia outside the Conference. He would point out that the object of a Committee was to furnish the Council with facts, in order that the Council should be in a position to discuss the matter with full knowledge.

Baron Sonnino said that each Delegation was accompanied by its experts and he felt quite sure that at least eight members of the Council must have already consulted them.

M. Clemenceau asked Baron Sonnino whether he raised no objection to the formation of a Committee to investigate the other frontiers claimed by the Yugo-Slavs.

M. Sonnino said that he raised none, provided that the questions pending between Italy and Yugo-Slavia were excluded.

M. Clemenceau suggested that a Committee should be set up and that the Dalmatian Coast should be excluded from the terms of reference. He thought it impossible to entrust this question to any Committee or Commission, by reason of the commitments of the Powers and certain difficult political aspects of the question.

This question resembled that of the Rhine, which also could not be entrusted to a Committee. Such questions must be dealt with in the Council, which was not ill-supplied with the necessary statistics. In this matter, therefore, he agreed with Baron Sonnino. He proposed to name a Committee to deal with the problems raised, with the exception of those pending between Italy and the Yugo-Slavs.

Mr. Balfour then read the following draft resolution:

"It is agreed:

"That the questions raised in the statements by MM. Vesnitch, Zolger and Trumbitch, on behalf of the Serbian Delegation on the Serbian territorial interests in the peace settlement (excepting only the question in which Italy is directly concerned) shall be referred for examination in the first instance to an expert Committee similar to that which is considering the question of the Banat.

"It shall be the duty of this Committee to reduce the questions for decision within the narrowest possible limits and to make recommendations for a just settlement.

"The Committee is authorised to consult representatives of the peoples concerned."

Mr. Lansing suggested that this question be referred to the same Committee as was dealing with the Banat.

M. Pichon said that some of the questions raised were different to the one under discussion in that Committee. It might, however, be convenient that the Committee on these other questions should be composed of the same members.

Baron Sonnino said that he supported Mr. Lansing's proposal as questions of reciprocal concession might arise.

(It was therefore decided that the above Resolution be adopted and that the Committee be the same as that appointed to deal with the Banat. See I. C. 130.)

ITALIAN REFUSAL OF ARBITRATION[1]

Paris, March 3, 1919.

Gentlemen,

By a letter of February 11, you have informed me that "the Kingdom of the Serbs, Croats, and Slovenes" was ready to submit its territorial disputes with Italy to President Wilson's arbitration.

In accordance with your wish, I have communicated this request to the Supreme Council at the session of February 17.

The Italian Delegation declared that it could not accept this proposal.

Please accept . . .

The President of the Peace Conference.

Signed: G. Clemenceau.

MM. Pachitch, Vesnitch, Trumbitch, Zolger, delegates to the Peace Conference.

[1] Adriaticus, *La Question adriatique,* Document XI, p. 41. Author's translation.

DOCUMENT 21

MINUTES OF THE COUNCIL[1]

[EXTRACTS]

MARCH 11, 1919

Request of Serb-Croat-Slovene Delegation to Be Present When Boundaries between Italy and the S.H.S. Kingdom [are] Discussed

4. M. CLEMENCEAU asked permission to read the following letter, dated the 6th March, 1919, which he had received from M. Pachitch:

"Mr. President:

"At the meeting of the Supreme Allied Council held on February 18th, we had the honour to state that in our opinion we ought to be placed in the same situation and have the same opportunities as the Royal Italian Government for examining and discussing the problem of our frontiers. This statement was inspired by the desire to fix our future common frontiers on a basis of equilibrium and in such manner as to ensure neighbourly relations between the two countries of a loyal and friendly character. There was a further and more general reason for making that statement, namely that our Government could only assume responsibility for solutions to which it had given its consent after an exchange of suitable explanations.

"The degree to which we have been animated by a desire to reach an amicable settlement, such as will leave in the future no trace of misunderstanding between the two Governments, has we think been proved by our offer to submit the settlement of this problem to an arbitration by President Wilson which would be sanctioned by the Peace Conference itself.

"In view of the assertion coming from different quarters and diffused by authorised organs of the Press, to the effect that the Council of Ten has accepted the point of view of the Italian Delegation, namely, that the delimitation of these frontiers should be examined and determined simultaneously with that of the frontiers between France and Germany and in accordance with the same procedure, that is to say in the Supreme Allied Council—we consider it to be our duty to bring to the notice of that exalted Council the essential difference between those two problems, a difference which is derived from the fact that the Rhine frontier is to be fixed as between enemy States, whereas that on the Adriatic must be fixed between two Governments whose peoples have been friends in the past, who desire to remain friends in the future and, what is even more important, between two countries which have fought

[1] Miller, *My Diary at the Conference of Paris*, XV, 320-28.

for the selfsame cause of right and justice and have substantially contributed, in proportion to their strength and their resources, to the common victory.

"We are indeed unable to imagine how a problem which touches so nearly the most vital interests of our country could be examined in a practical manner and settled equitably unless we have an opportunity of discussing it with our partners before the Council, nor how the Conference itself can sanction an arrangement which would be lacking in an essential element of validity, namely the participation of one of the interested parties.

"For the foregoing reasons we take the liberty of writing to you, Mr. President, and of requesting your Excellency to be so good as to communicate this request to the Supreme Allied Council with a view to our admission to its deliberations whenever the discussion of frontier delimitation between Italy and the Kingdom of the Serbs, Croats and Slovenes shall be placed on its Agenda.

"I beg, etc.

"P. PACHITCH."

M. CLEMENCEAU, continuing, asked the Conference to say what reply should be sent to M. Pachitch.

MR. LLOYD GEORGE thought that it had been agreed that the Small Powers would be entitled to be present whenever any question affecting their rights came under discussion; and, in his opinion, it made no difference whether the question to be discussed was one between two Small Powers or between a Great Power and a Small Power. He felt sure that the Italian representative would accept that view of the matter.

M. SONNINO said that at the meeting of the Conference held on 18th February, 1919, after the Serbian Delegation had put forward their territorial claims, he himself had proposed, and the Conference had agreed to accept the following resolution:

"That the question raised in the statement of MM. Vesnitch, Zolger and Trumbitch, on behalf of the Serbian Delegation on the Serbian territorial interests in the Peace settlement (*excepting only the question in which Italy was directly concerned*) shall be referred for examination in the first instance to an expert Committee, and that it shall be the duty of that Committee to reduce the questions for decision within the narrowest possible limit, and to make recommendations for a just settlement."

That is to say, it had been decided that all frontier questions in which Italy was directly concerned should be considered by the Conference itself. That did not, however, mean that the representatives of the Serbians should not be present when frontier questions affecting them were discussed by the Conference. The Serbs obviously had the same right to appear before the Conference that other interested States had to appear before Commissions. He agreed, therefore, that the interested parties would have the right to appear before the Conference to express their views, and to take part in the discussions; but the Small Powers could obviously have no voice in drawing up the final decisions.

MR. LLOYD GEORGE hesitated to accept Baron Sonnino's interpretation of the question. He would draw the attention of the Conference to the decision taken at the meeting held on March 5th last, in regard to the admission of Belgians to the deliberations concerning the preliminaries of peace. It was then agreed:

"That the right of the Belgian Government to be represented on the Supreme Council of the Allied and Associated Powers during the discussion of the preliminary Peace Terms should be limited to the occasions coming within the regulations for the Peace Conference when terms for which Belgium was specially interested were under discussion."

In his opinion that decision could not be interpreted to mean that the Small Powers should retire when a decision had to be taken.

M. SONNINO held that in the case of a Commission on Frontiers the Small Powers were heard, but they took no part in the final decision. In his opinion, the Conference when dealing with territorial questions, should adopt the procedure followed by territorial Commissions.

MR. LANSING thought that in justice when the decision came to be taken, either both parties should be present, or both parties should retire.

M. CLEMENCEAU pointed out that the final decision would rest with the Conference itself.

MR. LLOYD GEORGE agreed, but enquired whether both parties should be present during the discussion which led up to the final decision. That was the question under consideration. In other words, should one of the two interested parties be turned out, whilst the other party remained to take part in the final discussion?

M. ORLANDO said that according to his understanding the question should be regarded in the following light. In the first place, he could not agree that the Resolution quoted by Mr. Lloyd George was applicable except on the assumption that the question under consideration referred to a single State, called Serbia, and to a problem affecting that State. Had that really been the case, he would not have ventured to dispute the fact that questions concerning Italy and Serbia should be discussed as between equals and strictly in accordance with the procedure laid down for all other States with particular interests, taking part in the Conference.

But the question now under discussion did not concern the Kingdom of Italy and the Kingdom of Serbia proper. The Conference was asked to consider a question relating to the frontiers which separated Italy from an enemy State, formerly known as the Austro-Hungarian Empire. If, in consequence of the break-up of the Austro-Hungarian Empire, new States had been formed, some of which desired to join Serbia, that meant that the Conference had no longer to deal with the Kingdom of Serbia, but with a new State consisting partly of the old Kingdom of Serbia and partly of other territories which belonged to an enemy State. The correctness of this point of view was evidenced by the fact that the Delegation had sent the communication under consideration not in the name of the Kingdom of Serbia but in the name of the Kingdom of the Serbs, Croats and Slovenes, and one of those members of that Delegation had actually been a Minister of the Austro-Hungarian Empire.

The whole question, therefore, turned on whether this new State should or should not be recognised. Obviously, he (M. Orlando) could not prevent the friendly and Allied Powers from recognising it, even though agreements to the contrary had been entered into. Certainly, the recognition of the new State could not constitute an amiable act towards Italy. But, however that might be, his Allied and Associated colleagues would not hesitate to admit that Italy was entitled to a free choice in the matter; and so far Italy had not recognised the new State. He, personally, did not recognise the Kingdom of the Serbs, Croats and Slovenes. Furthermore, he regarded the Croats and the Slovenes, that is to say the people whose frontiers were in question, as his enemies. As far as Italy was concerned, those people had merely taken the place of the Austrians; and he would ask his colleagues to consider whether the representatives of the Austro-Hungarian Empire could have done anything worse to Italy, had they been present instead of the Croats and the Slovenes. Consequently, as far as he was concerned, the question presented itself as follows. No appeal could be made to a resolution which did not apply to the case under consideration. The question for the Conference to decide was whether matters relating to frontiers between enemy and Allied countries should be discussed in the presence of the enemy. He (M. Orlando) could never accept such a proposition. Italy's allies and associates could naturally do as they pleased, but in regard to matters in which he was concerned, he would never agree to discuss them under those conditions, any more than France would ever agree to admit Germany to take part in a discussion on the settlement of her frontiers.

M. Sonnino, with whom he found himself in complete agreement, had stated that instead of imposing our conditions on the Croats and on the Slovenes, as would be done in regard to other enemy countries, he would agree to their being given a hearing. In agreeing to that, he had made a great concession and it showed how great was their desire to be conciliatory. But beyond that point he could never agree to go and he must absolutely refuse to discuss and to dispute with his enemies.

Mr. LLOYD GEORGE said that he could well understand M. Orlando taking the line he had in regard to the Croats and Slovenes, as obviously they were not in the same position as the Belgians and the Serbs. But he could hardly take that line in regard to M. Pachitch. It would hardly be consistent for M. Orlando to say that he did not object to M. Pachitch or to the other Serbian Delegates, but that he declined to discuss any territorial question if representatives of the Croats or of the Slovenes were admitted on equal terms. Therefore he would make the following suggestion. He thought it would be a very strong order for the Conference to rule the Serbs out when questions relating to their frontiers came under discussion, especially when it was remembered that the King of Serbia was now the King of the Kingdom of Serbs, Croats and Slovenes. The Serbs by the great gallantry displayed by their armies had helped to conquer the countries in question. In his opinion, the Serbs should be granted exactly the same rights as had been accorded to the Belgians to attend when questions affecting their territorial interests were being discussed by the Conference. The Croat and Slovene countries did not constitute separate and independent bodies. They were going to be attached to and to form part of Serbia. He begged M. Orlando, therefore, to consider whether the representatives of the Kingdom of Serbia proper, whose armies had fought on the side of the Allies, should not be present when questions concerning them came under discussion. He thought the Conference could hardly refuse the request of a country who had done its duty to the Allies and manfully supported the common cause during the whole period of the war.

M. CLEMENCEAU thought that M. Orlando's proposal, together with Mr. Lloyd George's amendment, would meet with general approval; that is to say, the representatives of Serbia, an Allied country, should be admitted to the Conference to take part in the discussions whenever questions affecting their frontiers came under consideration.

BARON SONNINO pointed out that M. Pachitch would come to the Conference, not as a representative of Serbia, but as a representative of the Kingdom of Serbs, Croats and Slovenes; and he would presumably be assisted by M. Trumbitch and by Dr. Zolger, the latter a former Austro-Hungarian Minister.

M. PICHON agreed that M. Pachitch had written his letter on behalf of the Delegation of the Kingdom of Serbs, Croats and Slovenes, that is, as the representative of a State which had not yet been recognised by all the Allies. Mr. Lloyd George's proposal, however, was that the representatives of Serbia alone should be invited to attend in connection with all questions relating to their own frontiers. Consequently, he thought a reply should be sent to M. Pachitch, informing him that the Conference would be willing to admit the representatives of Serbia, but it could not receive the representatives of the Kingdom of Serbs, Croats and Slovenes whose constitution had not yet been recognised by all the Allies.

M. Orlando said that the question under consideration might lead to very grave results for Italy. On the other hand, the question was not a very urgent one, since M. Pachitch's letter had only been written on the 6th March last. He begged the Conference, therefore, with the greatest insistence to adjourn the further consideration of the question for a few days, in order to allow him to consult all his colleagues. He was particularly anxious that nothing should be done to prejudge the final solution of the question.

Mr. Lloyd George agreed that the Conference would be bound to meet a request of that kind.

Mr. Lansing said that before the discussion was closed he wished to state the views of his Government, whose views coincided with those expressed by Mr. Lloyd George. The question under consideration concerned Serbia, the same country which the Allies had always known; and the mere fact that the old Serbia had acquired or annexed other territories did not affect the case.

Baron Sonnino, interposing, said that the case under consideration did not merely refer to the acquisition or annexation of territories by Serbia.

Mr. Lansing thought that it did, just in the same way as England had acquired or annexed Scotland and called herself Great Britain. It was all a mere technicality, and in his opinion, it was important to uphold the decisions already reached. Serbian interests were at stake. When questions affecting Rumania and Serbia had been considered by the Conference, both parties affected had been heard. Consequently, he favoured the conclusion that either both parties should be included or both parties should be excluded. In any case one of the contending parties should not be allowed to sit as a judge of its own case.

(It was agreed to adjourn the further consideration of the question to a later meeting.)

Paris, March 12th, 1919.

ITALIAN MEMORANDUM ON THE NAVAL SITUATION IN THE ADRIATIC[1]

THE MILITARY PROBLEM OF THE ADRIATIC

In order to understand fully the unsatisfactory situation, both strategic and tactical, in which Nature has placed Italy on the western shore of the Adriatic, it will be necessary to pay special attention to certain outstanding geographical features which neither the art nor the labour nor the will of man can change.

On the eastern shore there is a magnificent advanced barrier of rocks and islands which form an insurmountable protecting wall for the mainland, and therefore for the lines of communication with the shore. On the western shore there is a low and undefended sea-coast, open to every attempt at aggression or invasion.

On the eastern shore, no matter what wind is blowing, one can navigate at reduced speed in still waters, whereas on the western shore there is an absolute absence of places of refuge and navigation is difficult and risky whenever bad weather arises. On the eastern shore is bereft of landing facilities; so that it is extremely difficult to find places of rest and shelter there.

On the eastern shore the coastlands are high and everywhere have magnificent observation posts which dominate a vast surrounding horizon. On the western shore the land is low-lying, except at Gargano and Conero, so that it is impossible to keep watch from above over the sea, except by means of aerial reconnaissances, which are practicable only in certain weather conditions.

On the eastern shore the waters are clear and deep and difficult to infest with mines, whereas on the western shore they are opaque and shallow, thus favoring the employment of every type of submarine weapon.

On the eastern shore there is a profusion of hiding-places for torpedo boats and submarines, whereas the open and straight coast on the west is entirely devoid of such facilities.

Even the currents are favourable to Dalmatia and unfavorable to Italy. They run from south to north on the eastern shore, turning below the Ancona parallel and running towards our coast, where they bend south-

[1] Miller, *My Diary at the Conference of Paris*, VI (Document 512), 399-406. For this and other documents of uncertain date, the order used in Miller has been adhered to.

wards again. Thus every enemy mine that breaks away from its anchorage, or is launched forth at its place of origin, arrives automatically in Italian waters to spread death and destruction there.

Should the Italians wish to attack the enemy's shore, they must set forth under cover of night and at dawn they would arrive on the field of action; thus they would have the sun in their eyes and the high coast still enveloped in darkness; whereas should the enemy set forth for the Italian coast under the same conditions he would have the sun at his back on arriving there and would find excellent conditions in his favour, with the whole undefended coast clearly and splendidly exposed to his view.

Concealed from view, and in a position where they cannot be attacked, because defended by the bulwark of islands, the enemy's ships can move at their pleasure from north to south, or vice versa, along the greater part of the Adriatic, perfectly sheltered from mines and submarines. But the Italians, the moment they had left Brindisi, would be at the mercy of the enemy, watched and followed and exposed to his attack, all the way as far as Venice, or vice versa.

As a matter of fact, Italy possesses in the Adriatic only two military posts: Brindisi in the south and Venice in the north, separated from one another by a distance of four hundred and fifty miles; and each incapable of accommodating a large fleet. The geographical conformation of the intervening coastal tract makes it impossible to build there any large military port.

The consequence is that in the Adriatic the Italian fleet cannot hold together, united and compact, as demanded by the principles of military science. The British fleet did this at Skapa Flow and the French fleet at Corfu. But the Italians are constrained to divide their fleet between Brindisi and Venice, and even hold a portion of it in the excentric position at Taranto, outside the Adriatic. Not only, therefore, is it hampered by the vast and forbidding distance between its bases, but even if it were all gathered in one base, it would be in an extremely bad position in regard to any eventual field action. For if it were concentrated in Brindisi it could not arrive in the Northern Adriatic in time to ward off an attack there. And, on the other hand, if it were concentrated in Venice, it would not arrive in time to ward off an attack against the southern coast. In both cases he who holds the eastern shore can always select, according to his own judgment, the moment and the point of attack and he could carry out his attack fully and return to safety behind the magnificent barrier of the Dalmatia islands before the Italian fleet would have time to intervene and give battle.

The Italian fleet, therefore, being forced to remain divided between Brindisi and Venice, an enemy in possession of the central tract of the

Dalmatian coast from Zara to Spalato, with the military port of Sebenico, can at any moment come out to sea to give battle. But the Italian fleet, coming partly from Venice and partly from Brindisi, must necessarily be exposed to the danger of having to encounter the enemy with only one section of its forces against the enemy's full strength and have to give battle separately before it could effect its own tactical consolidation.

This state of affairs places him who holds the western shore of the Adriatic in a position of absolute subjection as regards him who holds the eastern shore. This subjection may be defined as *"The impossibility of attacking the enemy on an equal footing,"* or better still, *"The impossibility of avoiding the tactical and strategic superiority of the enemy, even though he be numerically weaker."*

Even if Italy decided to spend millions and millions in transforming the ports of Venice and Brindisi into naval bases, each capable of accommodating a large fleet; and having effected this transformation, if she decided to spend more millions in building a fleet double in strength that of the enemy, she would not even then be on an equal footing. Because the enemy's fleet on arriving off the Italian coast could at any moment bombard densely populated centres, interrupting road and railway communications as well as telegraph, telephone and observation constructions. Thus it might impede the movement of troops to the north during mobilisation and it could land small bodies of invading troops, and, having done so, return to the bases before the Italian ships would have time to arrive at the scene of action. The Italian fleet, however, on arriving off the eastern coast, would find itself before a barrier of rocks and islands and mined canals, all constituting an impenetrable bulwark for the enemy's mainland and allowing the enemy's fleet to move under cover, from north to south or vice versa, at its will, and protected not only against attack, but even against observation. In this way the enemy could always decline to give battle if he felt so disposed. Or if he wished to join in battle he could choose to come out either to the north or the south of his defensive wall, thus taking the Italian fleet in the rear in the open sea, and cutting off its retreat to its bases. And this might happen after the enemy had allowed the Italian fleet to wait until such time as its supplies of fuel, etc., began to run low, and had come out at the opportune moment to prevent its return to the bases. Therefore, it would be impossible for the Italian fleet to attack the enemy's coast or the enemy's ships. And it would be impossible for it to return in time to its own bases if the enemy hit on the opportune moment to come out.

*   *   *

In short, the maritime problem, as regards Italy, can be put in the following terms: *"He who possesses the eastern shore of the Adriatic is the very and absolute master of the strategic situation."*

Nor will the possession of Valona and Pola have any favourable influence upon the very hard conditions against which Italy had hitherto to struggle; for both these strongholds are no less far from the central area of the Adriatic than Venice and Brindisi.

The possession of Pola may well make up for the unfitness of Venice to hold a big fleet, and similarly Valona may well compensate the inadequateness of Brindisi. Thereby Italy may well be allowed not to lay out hundreds of millions to transform and enlarge the military ports of Venice and Brindisi; but, as a matter of fact, the general strategic situation will remain such as it was before, and Italy will still lack a naval base in the centre of the Adriatic.

On the other hand, nature having disposed things in such a way that a central base does not exist on the Italian coast, and that any possibility whatever of creating it is excluded, Italy feels absolutely compelled to seek that base on the eastern coast, between Zara and Cape Planka; in other words, Italy feels absolutely compelled to secure for herself at least the possession of the central part of Dalmatia besides the islands. This is the only way in which the following possibilities can be assured:

(a) That of protecting the central part of the Italian coast, from Brindisi to Venice, by being able to bring the fleet to its defence before the enemy would have arrived from the north or south.

(b) That of preventing the enemy from freely and secretly moving his fleet from north to south, or vice versa, behind the island barrier, without coming out into the open sea, should he wish to avoid battle.

(c) That of changing the present naval strategic situation, in which the enemy can keep his fleet concentrated wherever he will, while Italy must keep hers divided and allow an immense distance to intervene between both its sections; thus permitting the Italian fleet to remain compact in the centre of the Adriatic.

It is no answer to this line of argument to say that with the modern weapons used in naval warfare the disappearance of large ships will render the possession of great fleets useless in future and, therefore, also the possession of large naval bases. What is the purpose of the torpedo boats, submarines, armed motor launches, mosquito craft, and everything else that contributes to-day to supplant the classical battle in the open sea? They have only one purpose and aim, namely, the destruction of the fleets. If the large ships ceased to exist the weapons for attacking them would automatically disappear.

But supposing we confine the question to what we may call the hidden war, or the war of ambush, what then? What would be the position of that Power which possessed an open coast, bare and without places of refuge, with only small channels that could easily be mined, without islands or bays—what would be the position of such a Power facing across a narrow sea another Power that possessed a marvelous labyrinth of bulwarks of every description, of entries and exit by way of innumerable channels, of excellent observation position distributed everywhere along the coast, of deep waters and secure refuges against every adversary, and of conditions that assure calm and safe navigation in all kinds of weather? If the war of ambush and stealth should for a moment take the place of the traditional classic methods, then more than ever would the inferiority of Italy's position be manifest and more unbearable, as against her neighbour possessing the eastern shore of the Adriatic.

The submarine war has only increased the disadvantageous strategical conditions wherein Italy found herself in the Adriatic. Only one way is in stand to reestablish the balance: to secure to Italy the possession of the shore between Zara and the Planka Cape, and of the islands. This was exactly the aim of the London Treaty of 1915, by which Italy fixed the foundation of what was indispensable to her security in the Adriatic.

* * *

Nor will it do to say that the Adriatic heirs of what has been the Austrian Empire will have no fleet and shall not be allowed to build any in the future.

Will anyone state that impositions of a political international character such as the neutralisation of the Oriental shore, the prohibition of every naval armament, the obligation of forbearing from fortification of the shore, will have the power of giving a definite and perpetual solution to the Adriatic military naval problem?

All these measures will, unhappily, never succeed in affording a sufficient guarantee. By the treaties of Campoformio and Lunéville Napoleon imposed the neutralisation of the Adriatic upon Austria; but that did not prevent Austria from becoming, sixty years later, such a Maritime Power as to be able to fight a victorious naval campaign.

But quite apart from this historical remembrance, a close scrutiny of the geographical conditions (which no Treaty and no control would be in stand to change) shows unto evidence that the Adriatic Oriental shore is, from naval standpoint, a perpetual and dangerous threat against the security of the Italian shores. If in a far future political events should drive the Adriatic heirs of the fallen Dualistic Monarchy into making a coalition with some Maritime Power, they would have nothing better to do, even if they lacked a fleet of their own and shore fortifications, than putting their from nature wonderfully fortified shore to the disposal of their Ally; and this would mean the complete reversal of the whole strategic Adriatic situation to the detriment of Italy and despite every Treaty most carefully elaborated. The likelihood of all this is enhanced by the possibility of modern warfare to bring immediately into action mines and submarines.

*   *   *

The London Treaty, acknowledging the good foundation of the Italian Adriatic claims, secured the possession to Italy of the central part of Dalmatia, with its indispensable hinterland and the isles. Fiume, on the contrary, was left to Hungary as an outlet in a time when nothing allowed anyone to foresee that this nation, in consequence of the breaking of the Hapsburg Empire, should lose every territorial contact with the Adriatic on account of her being definitively separated from Croatia.

Now, as Fiume was not included in the London Treaty, and as, on the other hand, the reasons which suggested its exclusion do not exist any longer, Italy is well disposed, in order to get Fiume, to make some concessions of territory and population in that part of central Dalmatia which the London Treaty has allotted to Italy. These concessions are marked by red ink in the annexed little map:

1.) The territory that would be yielded to the Yugoslavs has an extension of some 800 square Km., and as a making up for the 34,000 Italians who would pass over to Italy through the acquisition of the "Corpus Separatum" of Fiume (whose extension is only of 19 square Km.); nearly 42,000 Slavs, would pass over from Italy to the new Yugoslav State.

2.) The Yugoslavs would have the possession of the important road centre of Knin, and this would give them the possibility of an easy and short junction between Knin and Sini by railway. Thereby Spalato, too, would be set in direct communication with the "hinterland" of Bosnia, for that town has already been, some years since, joined to Sini by a railway, and Knin is also already joined to Prijefor and Sunya on the main road which leads from Agram to Belgrad.

3.) The Yugoslavs would have the advantage of seeing Spalato no longer in proximity of a frontier that narrows its hinterland.

DOCUMENT 23

BRITISH MEMORANDUM ON THE TYROL[1]

NOTE ON A SUGGESTED FRONTIER BETWEEN ITALY AND GERMAN AUSTRIA

1. The question of a future northern frontier for Italy involves a conflict between two distinct principles—(a) ethnic justice; (b) strategic security. The problem is still further complicated by the fact that the extreme frontier along the crest of the Rhaetian Alps, which affords the maximum strategic security, was definitely promised to Italy by the Treaty of April 1915 and has received a certain confirmation by the terms of the Armistice of the 4th November 1918.

2. Although the claim of Italy to the Province of Trentino is beyond any doubt, the frontier of the Rhaetian Alps includes in addition the Province of Alto Adige. The Alto Adige is as overwhelmingly German as Trentino is Italian, and comprises (according to the 1910 census) 215,000 Germans out of a total population of over 242,000. The proportion of Germans at the present day is probably still greater. In the Trentino on the other hand there are only some 14,000 Germans out of a total population of 390,000.

3. The line of demarcation between the two races is remarkably clear, and to all intents and purposes coincides with the administrative boundary between the Trentino and the Alto Adige, if we include the Ladins with the Italian population. The German-speaking population of the upper valleys of the Adige and the Eisack are intensely strong in their devotion to Austria, and to bring any large proportion of them under Italian rule would be a distinct violation of the principles of self-determination. The main objection to a frontier approximating to the racial boundary is its strategic weakness as compared to the military frontier along the Rhaetian Alps promised by the Treaty of London in 1915. The linguistic frontier, although resting on the solid flanking buttresses of the Ortler and Monte Cristallo massifs, is weak in the centre where it cuts across the main valley of the Adige between Bozen and Trent, exposing the latter town to a converging attack down the valleys of the Adige, Eisack and Pustertal, since it leaves the passes over the main watershed, *i. e.*, the Reschen, the Brenner and the Toblach, firmly in Austrian hands. It must be admitted that from the strategic point of view the Italians are thus placed

[1] Miller, *My Diary at the Conference of Paris*, VI (Document 513), 407-10.

at a serious disadvantage *vis-à-vis* their old Austrian enemies and the danger is not diminished by the possibility of union between German Austria and Germany. On the other hand, we must remember that a line which would afford sufficient depth of protection to the town of Trent which would dominate the important strategic centres of Meran, Bozen and Brixen, which are vital to the Austrian power of concentration, would afford an infinitely greater measure of security than that provided by the unjust frontier of 1914, which laid bare the Plains of Lombardy to an Austrian offensive.

4. A line is suggested which while violating as little as possible the ethnic principle at the same time affords a definite measure of strategic security, might be traced as follows:

Leaving the Swiss frontier at the Stelvio Pass and following the glacier crest of the Ortler massif, the line would run first east and then east-north-east along the spur which runs via the Zufritt Spitz towards Meran. Leaving this spur at .2607 north of St. Walberg, the frontier would run south-east across the Val Ulten valley to the Laugen Spitz and thence would continue south-east along the crest until it cut the Bozen-Kaltern road at St. Michael. The Line runs thence in a general east-south-easterly direction over the Stadlegg Spur via Deutschen Nofen to Monte Latemar (.2846); thence north to the Rosengarten (.3002) and then eastward to the Sella (.3152). From the Sella the line would run first due north and then north-north-west over the Geisler Spitz (.3027) and the peak north-north-west of it (.2505) overlooking Brixen. The line then turns east-north-east, passing north of Welschellen and Enneberg, thence turning south-east along the Seekofl (.2810) to join the old frontier at Monte Cristallo north-east of Cortina d'Ampezzo. From Monte Cristallo the line would follow the old frontier along the crest of the Carnic Alps to the neighborhood of Tarvis.

The line as above described only includes two small portions of German-speaking territory, namely, the upper portion of the Val Ulten and the part of the Adige valley between St. Michael and Salorno. These inclusions are necessitated (a) to dominate the Val Venosta and Meran; (b) to dominate the important junction of Bozen where the Eisack joins the Adige. By holding this line the Italians effectively flank the approach from the Reschen, Brenner and Pustertal Passes and cover the only road of approach to Trent.

5. Should it be considered that this line does not afford Italy sufficient security, the following alternative line is suggested:

Leaving the Swiss frontier at the Reschen Pass south of Nauders, the line would coincide with the strategic line of the 1915 Treaty, along the main water-parting of the Oetztaler and Stubaier Alps as far as the

Schwarzwand Spitze; thence south and south-east along the water-parting between the Passeiertal and Ridnauntal drainage basins via the Jaufen Pass to the Weisshorn (.2707) in the Sarntaler Alps; thence along the main water-parting of the Sarntaler Alps past the Rittnerhorn (.2261); thence to the Eisack Valley at Waidbruck; thence down the river Eisack to the mouth of the Schwarzgriesbach, which it follows south of Kastelruth to the Rosszahne. Thence eastward along the ridge to the Sella group, where it follows the judicial district boundary around the northern side of the Cortina d'Ampezzo basin, which boundary is with minor modifications the main water-parting between the Inn and Piave drainage basins. Thence the line continues to join the old Austro-Italian frontier at Monte Cristallo.

6. There is no doubt that this latter alternative offers considerable strategic advantages by depriving the enemy of the use of the Reschen Pass and the Val Venosta, a line of approach which will in future be still more useful to Austria when the Landeck-Mals railway has been completed. It confines the concentration of Austrian troops to the use of the Brenner and Pustertal Passes. In addition this second line gives the Italians considerable economic advantages in the important electric power stations of the Upper Adige at Mals, Naturns, Meran, Lana and Bozen, which develop a total of nearly 50,00 [sic] horse-power. On the other hand, we must remember that the adoption of this line would bring under Austrian[2] subjection a population of some 160,000 Germans. This disadvantage could only be overcome by affording the Germans some real measure of autonomous government.

[2] Evidently "Italian" is meant.

DOCUMENT 24

AMERICAN MEMORANDUM[1]

STATEMENT IN RE ITALIAN CLAIMS

On the Adriatic the Italians want: 1) the valley of the Upper Fella and Tarvis, an important railway junction; 2) Julian Venetia; 3) Fiume; 4) the northern part of Dalmatia and most of the Dalmatian islands. This is the territory delimited in the treaty of London with important additions.

1) In the Tarvis region there were at the time of the last census (1910) about 6,000 Germans, 2,500 Slovenes, and 10 Italians.

2) In Julian Venetia (the Isonzo-Trieste-Istria region), the Italian population is almost entirely limited to a narrow zone along the western border. The eastern half of the area is almost solidly Jugo-Slav. The treaty of London line would give to Italy not only the Italian part of the area, but the Jugo-Slav part as well. Italy would receive, in addition to some 400,000 Italians (including citizens of Italy), a total of 455,000 Jugo-Slavs.

Beyond the treaty of London line as described in the published text, the Italians now claim additional areas, partly on the basis of a different interpretation of the position of the line. These additional areas have a population of about 100 Italians and 55,000 Jugo-Slavs.

In addition to extending Italian sovereignty over an area containing approximately 510,000 Jugo-Slavs, the line claimed by the Italians in Julian Venetia would cut the only direct railway line connecting Laibach with Fiume, would involve serious disadvantages as regards Fiume's outlets into the Adriatic because of the extension of Italian territorial waters into the two most important of those outlets, and would transfer to Italy the important quicksilver mines of Idria, located in purely Slav territory. There are only three important quicksilver mines in the world. Italy already owns one of these, and Spain the other. With Idria in her possession, Italy would control more than half the total quicksilver output of the world and nearly half the world's known reserve supplies.

3) Fiume is vitally necessary to the economic life of Jugo-Slavia and is a most important outlet for several mid-European countries. It has no economic significance for Italy. The large business interests of Fiume, the banking houses, and the shipping are mainly in Hungarian and Jugo-Slav hands. Italian capital did not develop the port, and the future extension of the port facilities must depend upon capital furnished by those

[1] Miller, *My Diary at the Conference of Paris*, VI (Document 514), 411-13.

countries which the port serves. Such capital would hardly be furnished by Jugo-Slavia and her neighbors to develop an Italian port. It should be noted, also, that Fiume is the only practicable outlet to the sea for three-fifths of the population of the new Jugo-Slav state, because all other ports are either physically incapable of proper development, or can be reached only by costly transportation across a broad and difficult mountain barrier.

According to the last official census, the Italians constituted a minority of the population of Fiume, even when its artificial separation from the Slavic Sušak is maintained. Out of a total population of 49,806, there were 24,212 Italians, 15,687 Jugo-Slavs, 6,493 Magyars, 2,315 Germans, and 1,099 others. If the statistics be made to include that part of Sušak which is essentially an integral part of Fiume and its port accommodations, the Italians constitute less than 43% of the population. Even in the restricted Fiume the Italian plurality (in neither case is it a majority) is of recent development (since 1880 or 1890), and includes a considerable number who have not given up Italian citizenship. All the areas surrounding Fiume are solidly Jugo-Slav.

4) In Dalmatia the Treaty of London line would give about 285,000 Jugo-Slavs to Italy and only about 14,000 Italians. It would take from Jugo-Slavia the only large area of comparatively low and accessible land on the Dalmatian coast. This area is economically superior to other equivalent areas, includes the most valuable water power and mining interests, and blocks the outlet from the best valley route across the mountains from the interior to the coast. There seems to be no room to doubt the very earnest desire of a vast majority of the population for inclusion within the new Jugo-Slav state.

DOCUMENT 25

AMERICAN MEMORANDUM[1]

THE ITALIAN NORTHERN AND EASTERN BOUNDARY

The red line on the map shows the boundary we recommend where we think it better to diverge from the "London line."

The green line divides Italian and German speech.

On the north, our line offers *good* protection to Italy, though not as good as the London line.

Economically our line is better, as the business of the people we leave in Austria drains to the north and east.

Our line includes 150,000 German Tyrolese in Italy.

The London line includes 220,000 German Tyrolese in Italy.

The Tyrolese are hostile to Italian sovereignty, but, apparently are not especially keen for Austria; they want large freedom to manage their own affairs.

The area between the linguistic line and ours or the treaty of London line might be made autonomous, with a strict mandate, including neutrality, Italy as mandatory, and an appeal to the Court of the League. This alternative has advantages. The Commission concerned recommends a similar plan for the Ruthenians between Czecho-Slovakia and Rumania. Here the plan would not wholly please Italy, but it would give her probation and a chance, safeguard the people involved, and enable them later to ask for another mandatory if the solution worked badly.

Coming to the *Italian-Jugo-Slav frontiers,* the small sketch map shows the territory asked for by the Jugo-Slavs that the Commission concerned does not, on good grounds, recommend for them. The figures in pencil show the number of unredeemed by Jugo-Slavs. As it has been possible, necessary, in fact, for various good reasons, to treat the Czecho-Slovaks and Rumanians much more liberally, the Jugo-Slavs are sore, naturally, if not with justice.

In Dalmatia the situation seems clear. The population is overwhelmingly Jugo-Slav, except in Zara.

Fiume itself, though outside the London line, is Italian, nearly 70%. But if the suburb outside its limits, Sušak, in all vital ways a part of the city, is added, there is a small Jugo-Slav majority. If Fiume is not given

[1] Miller, *My Diary at the Conference of Paris*, VI (Document 515), 414-15. (See maps **IV** and **V**.)

them, the Jugo-Slavs, who will extend north to the Drave, for much of its course, will have no port of their own, with railroad connections north of Spalato, unless they can construct one near Fiume (possibly at Buccari) at heavy expense.

If the Italian majority in Fiume swings the decision, three solutions seem possible, but no doubt none should apply except to Fiume proper:

1) Cede the city to Italy.

2) Guarantee the city *municipal* autonomy, with appeal to the Court of the League, with or without a *municipal* mandate to Italy, but with supervision of the port facilities and commerce in Jugo-Slavia. Much too complicated.

3) Establish a free city *and* port, with Italy as mandatory: internationalize. This would probably involve frequent and difficult contacts between Italy and Jugo-Slavia, but it might meet Italy's present desires, and would have the advantage of enabling the city to ask for another mandatory later on if its interests so advised it.

DOCUMENT 26

MEZES'S RECOMMENDATIONS[1]
March 16, 1919

ITALIAN CLAIMS

March 16, 1919.

To: Colonel House.

From: S. E. Mezes.

As a result of the study I have made of the Italian claims in the Trentino region and on the Adriatic, excluding Albania, and of consultations regarding them with territorial, economic, and legal experts, I have the following suggestions to submit:

It would be equitable and advisable:

1) To assign to Italy the territory in the Trentino region between her frontier of 1914 and the line of the treaty of London, with generous guarantees in the treaty of cession of autonomy, especially in the matter of language, of schools, and of freedom from military service, of the German-speaking population between the linguistic line and the treaty of London line.

2) To move the treaty of London line along the Julian and Carnic Alps, in some places eastward and in more places westward, in justice to economic and topographic considerations.

3) To cede the city of Fiume proper to Italy, subject, however, to a provision in the treaty of cession that it shall constitute a free port, and that equitable treatment in it and on the railway running through Fiume shall be accorded to nations trading with or through Fiume.

4) To cede the islands on the eastern shore of the Adriatic immediately adjoining the territory on the Dalmatian mainland described in the latest Italian proposals, with provisions in the treaty of cession for the generous autonomy of these islands and the mainland concerned, especially in the matter of language, schools, religion, and freedom from military service.

Discussion

1) The treaty of London line in the Trentino gives Italy a security of frontier advantageous in the interests of disarmament, and probably necessary and expedient if German Austria should later on, as she well may, be united with Germany.

The German-speaking Tyrolese in the region concerned seem not to

[1] Miller, *My Diary at the Conference of Paris*, VI (Document 532), 451-53.

have much attachment to German Austria, and still less to Germany. Autonomy would no doubt satisfy them and meet their just needs.

2) The rectifications of frontier suggested would give a better defensive line, following mountain crests, alike to the Italians and the Jugo-Slavs; and would give better railroad communications to Italy, Austria, and Jugo-Slavia and avoid the cutting of railway lines.

3) Fiume proper is an Italian city. Only a small percentage of its commerce is with Jugo-Slavia, probably not more than 10%. As a port it chiefly serves Hungary. The maintenance and development of the port could be better effected by a maritime and relatively rich power like Italy than by an inland and poor power like Jugo-Slavia. The interest of the Italians in Fiume in the development of the port could be depended upon to safeguard it against the rivalry of Trieste, whereas in Jugo-Slav hands Fiume as an Italian city might fare badly in competition with other ports of that country, which even without Fiume are adequate for its own needs, and which are, or can in some instances at least without undue expense, be connected by railways with the country behind them.

4) The western shore of the Adriatic on which Italy borders is exceptionally weak from the naval point of view, while the eastern shore of that sea is one of the strongest in the world. While no doubt Jugo-Slavia by itself will never be a great naval power, the possession of all the islands and ports on the eastern shore of the Adriatic by her would place Italy at a very great disadvantage, which would become much more serious were Jugo-Slavia to become allied with a strong naval power, as is not impossible. The cession to Italy of the Dalmatian islands indicated, and as a necessary corollary a portion of the mainland, would seem to establish a just balance for Italy in this region. The additional safety given Italy would encourage her to reduce her naval armaments.

The mainland region concerned is no doubt larger than is desirable, especially as the inhabitants at present speak a Slavic language, though there is evidence that not very long ago their sympathies if not their speech was Italian, and that the change had been due to the policy of the Austro-Hungarian government. The territory seems an indivisible unit, being low-lying country bounded on the east by high mountains rising abruptly to 6000 feet and over, and cut by passes which themselves attain a height of from 3000-4000 feet; the territory to the east being connected, and being capable of being connected, with the lower lying country only by funicular railways.

In view of the present Slavic speech of the inhabitants of the mainland and practically all the islands concerned, provision for a generous autonomy seems to be necessary, and would probably be sufficient.

If Italian claims are approved, as indicated above, she should be asked to cede the Greek islands of the Dodecanese to Greece and to abandon or abate her claims in Asia Minor and in Albania.

Two maps are enclosed, one being a plan of Fiume showing the area of the city proper, enclosed in a yellow border. It is possible that docks might be constructed by the Jugo-Slavs in the adjoining suburb of Sušak, which would not under the present proposal be ceded to Italy.

The second map shows the ports that would remain to Jugo-Slavia even if Fiume were ceded to Italy under the restrictions indicated. It also shows constructed and proposed railways. I have not had time to verify the statistics that appear in the legend.

JOHNSON'S MEMORANDUM TO HOUSE[1]

AMERICAN COMMISSION TO NEGOTIATE PEACE

Paris, March 17, 1919.

From: Major Douglas Johnson, U.S.A.
To: Colonel House.
Re: Italian Territorial Claims.

1. From confidential conversation with certain individuals already named orally to Colonel House, I understand that:

a. French opinion favors as Italy's northern boundary in the Tyrol a line similar to or identical with that recommended by the American experts; but there is a certain willingness to accord Italy more than she can justly claim (even on strategic grounds) in this region, if necessary in order to secure from her a reasonable solution of the eastern frontier problem.

b. British opinion favors a line in the Tyrol farther south than that drawn by the American experts, but supports the American line as the most reasonable in case considerable weight is to be given to Italy's strategic arguments. A confidential statement prepared by a British military expert is attached hereto.

c. Both French and British authorities have independently reached the same general conclusions as have the American experts with regard to the most equitable frontier in the Isonzo-Istria region. The lines indicated by them differ from the American proposal only in minor details. Both agree with the American experts that Fiume and Dalmatia should go to Jugo-Slavia.

d. It is probable, therefore, that had Italian territorial claims been referred to a commission, as was done in the case of Roumanian, Greek, Czecho-Slovak, Jugo-Slav and other claims, the Commission would have reported in favor of boundaries similar to those already recommended to the consideration of the American Commissioners.

e. Both French and British express an earnest desire that the American Commissioners should insist that the future frontier between Italy and Jugo-Slavia must be drawn only after a full and frank discussion of the problem on its merits.

2. Italy's official territorial claims recently submitted to the Peace Conference include not only the territory allotted to her by the Treaty of London, but in addition:

a. In the Tyrol, the Sexten valley, one of the headwaters of the Drav river

[1] Miller, *My Diary at the Conference of Paris*, VI (Document 534), 457-59.

system, despite the Italian claim that the watershed is the natural geographic frontier of the Kingdom.

b. The important Tarvis area, farther east, also lying across the watershed in the Drav drainage basin.

c. Fiume, and a considerable surrounding area inhabited almost wholly by Slavs.

d. Spalato and adjacent Slav areas.

3. In view of the above facts, it is recommended, with the approval of the Chief of the Italian Division of the Section of Territorial Intelligence:

a. That it be insisted that a free and unprejudiced discussion of Italy's territorial claims is an essential pre-requisite to American participation in any Treaty of Peace which defines the territorial limits of German Austria and Jugo-Slavia vis-a-vis Italy. (This insistence can be based not only on the grounds that America was not a party to the Treaty of London; that the powers signatory to that Treaty later agreed to make peace on the basis of the Wilsonian principles; that the pact of Rome, April, 1918, placed upon the Italian Government at least a moral obligation to have Italo-Jugo-Slav boundary problems considered on other than purely technical grounds; but also on the ground that in claiming territory beyond the line of the Treaty of London, Italy in fact departs from the juridical basis of her claim which she insists upon as against the other parties to that Treaty, and consequently opens the whole question for consideration upon the basis of equity and right).

b. That the American Commissioners might let it be known that they are disposed to consider favorably certain important concessions to Italy not accorded by the Treaty of London, but only on condition that all the Italian claims be considered on their merits. (The Tarvis area should go to Italy for reasons set forth in a separate memorandum to be submitted with maps. Special protection for *all* Italian minorities in Jugo-Slavs areas should be assured instead of permanent control of only a part of those minorities. Support of Italy's proposed protectorate over Albania, if Italy were the mandatory of the League of Nations acting within clearly specified limits; and constituting Italy the mandatory for some colonial possession, might, if these steps were deemed desirable, form additional inducements to discussion. It is not within the province of this Division to advise regarding the two points last named).

DOCUMENT 28

REPORT OF THE AMERICAN EXPERTS[1]

MEMORANDUM

18 March, 1919.

From: Chiefs of the Austro-Hungarian Division, the Balkan Division, the Italian Division and the Division of Boundary Geography, Section of Territorial, Political and Economic Intelligence.

To: The Commissioners.

Re: Dalmatia and Fiume.

The Italians, in their memorandum presented to the Council of Ten on 11 March 1919, demand:

1. That part of Dalmatia granted to them by the Treaty of London, and, in addition,

2. Dalmatia as far south as Spalato,

3. Fiume and the adjacent district.

Every memorandum hitherto submitted to the Commissioners, about which any of the heads of the above-named divisions have been consulted, recommends that Fiume and all of Dalmatia should go to the Jugo-Slavs. We are still unanimously of that opinion for the reasons here set forth.

I. *Dalmatia*

1. The population of that portion of Dalmatia demanded by Italy was divided linguistically in 1910, as follows: 406,100 Jugo-Slavs, 16,280 Italians. The town of Zara had an Italian majority. Elsewhere there was no commune in all Dalmatia with an Italian minority as large as ten percent and only five with minorities of more than five percent. The Austrian statistics may do some injustice to the Italians, but there is no doubt that the Italians are linguistically in a negligible minority. Though in Alsace-Lorraine language may not be a good index of nationality, it is in Dalmatia. There can be little doubt that the national sympathies of an overwhelming majority of the population are Jugo-Slav. The Jugo-Slavs, moreover, have been settled in Dalmatia for over twelve centuries, and for several centuries they have occupied the largest part of the province.

[1] Baker, *Woodrow Wilson and the World Settlement*, III (Document 32), 263-65. A less complete version of this Document is found in Miller's *My Diary at the Conference of Paris*, VI, Document 533.

They are not a recent importation of the Austrian government, as the Italian memorandum implies.

2. Italy has no "historic right" to Dalmatia. Trent and Trieste with their adjacent lands were integral parts of Italy in Roman days, but Dalmatia was not. Dalmatia was merely a Roman province, as were also France and England. In the middle ages, Venice began to establish dominion over the cities of the coast, but her control never extended far inland, except during the last century of her rule.

3. Dalmatia is not now important as a commercial outlet for the interior east of the mountainous coast. It was the Austrian policy to prevent the construction of railways across the mountains. But there are routes by which it is practicable to build railroads connecting the interior with excellent harbors on the coast. The Slavs of the interior would have every incentive to build railways if they controlled the ports; the Italians whose interests in Dalmatia are primarily strategic would be less likely to make the sacrifices necessary for the economic development of the Slav hinterland.

4. Italy claims Dalmatia in order to avoid remaining in a state of permanent strategic inferiority. It should be noted, however, that Italian naval experts (see special memorandum submitted to Colonel House by Major Douglas Johnson) generally agree with the opinion of the U. S. Naval Advisory Staff as expressed in its memorandum on "Problems of Naval Strategy," that secure possession of Valona, Pola and a base in an island group near the central Adriatic, would give to Italy effective control of that sea.

II. *Fiume*

1. In Fiume and the adjacent district the majority is also Jugo-Slav. The Italian memorandum does not delimit the district exactly, but, assuming the smallest proportions admitted by the description, it contained in 1910 a population of 87,248 of whom 24,870 were Italians and 48,886 Jugo-Slavs. The whole surrounding hinterland was solidly Jugo-Slav.

2. For economic reasons it is essential, if Trieste goes to Italy, that Fiume should go to Jugo-Slavia.

(a) No other port could be developed except at great cost, and no other port could handle the commerce of the Jugo-Slav State as advantageously as Fiume. Of the Croatian coast Cholnoky, the Hungarian geographer rightly says: "No bays suitable for modern shipping are open." Dalmatian ports could not be utilized until connecting railways had been built, and they could never supply to advantage the commercial needs of the northern part of the Jugo-Slav State.

(b) Fiume is in no way an economic necessity to Italy. The port's commercial hinterland is on the eastern side of the Adriatic. Fiume in Italian hands would probably have its development sacrificed to that of Trieste.

(c) The commercial interests of Central Europe should be a primary consideration in determining the disposition of Fiume. These interests would be safeguarded better by the competition that would result from the assignment of Trieste to Italy and Fiume to the Jugo-Slavs than in any other way.

We are unanimously of the opinion that neither Fiume nor any part of Dalmatia (with the possible exception of Lissa and its neighboring islets) should be assigned to Italy.

> CHARLES SEYMOUR
> Chief of the Austro-Hungarian Division.
> CLIVE DAY
> Chief of the Balkan Division.
> W. E. LUNT
> Chief of the Italian Division.
> DOUGLAS W. JOHNSON
> Chief of the Division of Boundary-Geography.

DOCUMENT 29

REPORT ON FIUME[1]

SUMMARY OF REPORT NO. 16
BY LT. COL. SHERMAN MILES ON FIUME

1. Col. Miles reports that the people in Fiume desire autonomy of a greater or less degree, but that only propagandists who have no local interests desire absolute incorporation into Italy or Jugo-Slavia. He thinks the desire is based upon the fear that the port will be starved if given over entirely to one state or the other.

2. The "Independent Party" prefers Jugo-Slav rule to Italian, if autonomy cannot be had.

3. The pro-Italians minimize the importance of Fiume's trade with Hungary and Croatia.

4. The vicinity of Spalato is the only location where a port to replace Fiume could be built. But Fiume is a prepared port with loading facilities, railroad connections, etc., while Spalato, or no other port on the coast, could have them for years. Fiume has comparatively easy rail access to most of Jugo-Slavia and Hungary; to build a railroad from Spalato across the Dinaric Alps into the interior would be very difficult.

5. The nationality of the town is poorly defined; families are divided among themselves in their national sympathies.

6. Col. Miles believes that the best solution short of internationalization is to make Fiume a free port under Jugo-Slav mandatory.

7. He recommends that the Italian-Jugo-Slav boundary be run as indicated upon the attached map by the solid black line, but if strategy is to be considered, suggests that the frontier should be the dotted black line.

(The original map submitted by Col. Miles is on a larger scale and displays his lines in greater detail.)

[1] Miller, *My Diary at the Conference of Paris*, VII (Document 610), 172.

DOCUMENT 30

STEED'S MEMORANDUM[1]
MARCH 22, 1919

THE ADRIATIC SETTLEMENT

Since the beginning of the war I have worked to promote a just settlement of the Adriatic question.

As the only Englishman who had worked for a number of years both in Italy and in Austria-Hungary, I knew more of the political aspects of the subject than any of my fellow-countrymen.

During my six years in Rome (1897-1902) and my ten years in Austria-Hungary (1903-1913) I studied closely and at first hand both the aspirations of the Italians and those of the Jugoslavs. I have always kept in close touch with the leaders on both sides and have laboured to bring about an agreement between them.

In the course of this work, many statements have been made to me in confidence by those leaders. The more important of the Italian statements are recorded below.

Early in 1903, the Italian Ambassador to the Austro-Hungarian court, Count Nigra, a collaborator of Cavour, said to me in the course of a discussion on the Adriatic question in which I (having come fresh from Italy) had expressed the hope that the Trentino, Trieste and Fiume would one day be Italian: "The Trentino certainly; Trieste perhaps, but for Trieste we shall have to fight Germany; Fiume, never. Fiume will be either German or Serbo-Croatian; I hope, for our sakes, that it will be Serbo-Croatian."

Frequent visits to Trieste, Fiume, Dalmatia and Bosnia-Herzegovina subsequently convinced me of the wisdom of this view. It was shared fully by the veteran Italian statesman, the Marquis Visconti Venosta, with whom I was on terms of intimate friendship, until his death.

After the Italian declaration of war, when a number of Italian Democratic leaders came to London, they (including Signor Berenini, now Minister of Justice, and Signor Bissolati) assured me that their view of a just settlement would be the attribution to Italy of Trieste, Pola with the Western coast of Istria, possibly the island of Lussin, and Valona. Fiume was not mentioned. Subsequently, at the suggestion of Signor

[1] Miller, *My Diary at the Conference of Paris*, VII (Document 579), 113-16.

Berenini, the map drawn by the distinguished English geographer, Sir Arthur Evans, showing a suggested Italo-Southern Slav frontier, was published in the New Europe, of October 11, 1917, as representing a just settlement. I append this map. The line marked upon it in red has since been generally known as the "Evans Line." Sir Arthur Evans himself now doubts the expediency of assigning the island of Lussin to Italy.

After the disaster of Caporetto in October, 1917, when the Jugoslavs in London were distressed at the misfortune of Italy and argued that if there were no Italy there could be no Jugoslavia, I induced five of the most uncompromising Jugoslavs to meet an equal number of Italians at my house to discuss a basis of agreement. Two days' discussion led to joint recognition of the principles that Dalmatia and Fiume should belong to Jugoslavia, that Pola and as much of Istria as would assure to Italy safe communications by land between Pola and Trieste, and Trieste itself with an adequate *Hinterland*, including possibly Gorizia, should be assigned to Italy. The Italian Military Attaché in London, General Mola, accepted these principles. A further principle in regard to Italo-Jugoslav land-frontiers was suggested by me and assented to by both parties. It was that inasmuch as the joint defence of the Adriatic was a common interest of Italians and Jugoslavs alike, the northern frontier of Jugoslavia should be so drawn as to give the strongest possible line of Italo-Jugoslav defence against an eventual German attack from the North and that the frontier between Italy and Jugoslavia should be drawn so as to give the strongest possible second line of defence north of Trieste and through Istria.

The results of these conversations having been communicated to the Italian Prime Minister, Signor Orlando, in January, 1918, an Italian parliamentary committee was formed to promote an agreement with Jugoslavs. Its delegate, Dr. Andrea Torre, was sent to London where, with my help and that of Dr. Seton-Watson and Sir Arthur Evans, he concluded with Dr. Trumbitch the agreement known as the Pact of Rome, which was ratified in April, 1918, at Rome by the Congress of Oppressed Austro-Hungarian Nationalities.

During the Congress of Rome, efforts were made to sketch a definite territorial settlement. Though Dr. Trumbitch had no mandate to make cessions of territory, he informed Signor Bissolati and other prominent Italians, confidentially, of his personal views on the subject. They were not essentially different from the "Evans Line" and were regarded by the Italians as satisfactory.

In conversation with me at Rome, Signor Orlando repeatedly accepted this line as a basis of agreement. When, towards the end of May, doubt arose as to his fidelity to this standpoint and I wrote him asking whether his views were unchanged, he replied by a telegram which the Italian Ambassador in London communicated officially to me. It ran: "Tell Steed that my views are unchanged and will not change whatever the consequences may be."

At the beginning of last November, when the Armistice with Austria-Hungary was about to be signed, Signor Orlando sent for me in Paris, through General Mola, to ask my advice upon the situation. He said textually, "If I could only return to Italy with the certainty that we shall get the Evans Line, I should be able to tranquillise the whole country and to bring about an agreement with the Jugoslavs."

I assured him that Italy would certainly get something closely approximating to the Evans Line, except perhaps the island of Lussin, but that the way to get it would be for Italy to assist the Jugoslavs to consolidate their unity, and to organize their new State so that its Constituent Assembly, which alone could have authority to sanction territorial adjustments, might make the necessary sacrifices of territory inhabited by Jugoslavs in return for the achievement of Jugoslav national unity by the help of Italy.

Signor Orlando gave me his word of honour that he would pursue this course immediately. Instead, under the influence of Baron Sonnino, he pursued the opposite course.

In all these conversations there was no question of Fiume. The question first arose when the Giolittian opposition taunted the Italian Government with having "abandoned" Fiume, and made itself out to be more nationalist than Baron Sonnino.

When Signor Bissolati resigned on account of his differences with Baron Sonnino, he was generally denounced as the apostle of renunciation. In order to defend himself against this reproach, he claimed that though the Treaty of London ought to be abandoned, Fiume should be given to Italy as compensation. The Italian Government took up the cry for Fiume in order to silence Signor Bissolati and the Giolittians.

Despite the sentimental backing which the cry has since received, the Italian claim to Fiume is specious. The calculation upon which it is really, but not officially, based was recently divulged by a member of the Italian Delegation to the Peace Conference, Signor Barzilai, a Jewish Italian from Trieste, to a prominent French public man. "It will be very difficult for us to keep up the commerce of Trieste," he said, "unless we control Fiume and are able to divert its trade to Trieste. Otherwise we shall have constant difficulties at Trieste."

This seems to supply an additional argument in favour of settling the

Adriatic question in such a way that neither the Italians nor the Jugo-slavs shall be able arbitrarily to divert the trade of Trieste to Fiume or the trade of Fiume to Trieste. Healthy natural competition between the two ports would probably lead to the development of both.

WICKHAM STEED.

Paris. 22, III. 1919.

DOCUMENT 31

YUGOSLAV NOTES TO WILSON AND TO THE COUNCIL[1]

LETTER FROM PACHITCH TO THE PRESIDENT

DÉLÉGATION DU ROYAUME
DES*
SERBES, CROATES & SLOVENES,
À LA
CONFÉRENCE DE LA PAIX.

Paris,
28th March, 1919.

Sir,

I undersigned, President of the Delegation of the Kingdom of Serbs, Croats and Slovenes at the Peace Conference, have the honour of handing to Your Excellency a request on behalf of our Marine Committee concerning the blockade of the Yougoslav coast and ships, and I recommend this important and urgent question to Your kind attention.

Yours faithfully,

NIK. P. PACHITCH.

To the President of the United States,
Paris.

JUGO-SLAV MEMORANDUM

Paris,
28 March, 1919.

Hotel Beau Site,
4, rue de Presbourg.
Sir,

The Shipping Delegates of the Kingdom of Serbs, Croats and Slovenes at the Peace Conference, have the honour of drawing your attention to the paragraph 5 of the naval clauses of the armistice with Austria-Hungary. This paragraph reads as follows:

"The blockade is to be maintained by the Allied & Associated Powers on the existing conditions. The Austro-Hungarian ships found at sea remain subject to capture, *but exceptions will be admitted by a commission appointed by the Allies and the United States of America.*"

[1] Miller, *My Diary at the Conference of Paris,* VII (Documents 630 and 631), 270-72.

The wording *"but exceptions will be admitted . . . etc."* has been inserted at the proposal of Mr. Vesnitch, minister of Serbia, with a view to liberating all Yougoslav steamers from the blockade; it had the full approval of the Italian Ministers, Messrs. Orlando and Sonnino, who added that the same objections [*sic*] should be also granted to Italian ship-owners who were Austro-Hungarian subjects. This clause has therefore received already the full and unanimous approval of all the Allies and the United States Delegates at the Supreme War Council held at Versailles, on the 31st October 1918.

Through unfortunate circumstances, this concession which has been granted to us by the above clause, has never been carried out. A commission appointed to decide on the exceptions has never consulted either our Government or our ship-owners on this important question.

The Commission of 4 Admirals sitting in Rome and Venice during November and December 1918, contrary to the above clause of the armistice conditions, simply ordered the requisition of all the Austro-Hungarian tonnage to be carried out by Italy in the name of the Allies. It placed thus all ship-owners into the same category of enemies, and no distinction whatever was made between German, Hungarian or Yougoslav ship-owners.

The blockade of our coasts continues to this day, and not only are the Yougoslav provinces excluded from all intercourse with the rest of the world, but even Serbia is in consequence entirely isolated, her only line of communication with Salonica having been completely destroyed by the enemy.

The port of Fiume,—the natural outlet for most of the Yougoslav territories and for Serbia, as well—is to-day under Italian occupation, and as long as the occupation lasts there is no possibility for our people to use that only port for the necessary revictualing.

We have made repeated appeals on behalf of our Government to the Interallied Economic Council in Paris in order to release our unfortunate country from the blockade of its Allies; we have appealed so far in vain that the armistice clause above referred to should be carried out so that our steamers may be available to us for our own needs. All our efforts have unfortunately been fruitless, and we appeal to you, Sir, on a point which had already received the unanimous consent of the Allies, but which through carelessness or indifference is plunging our country into certain disaster.

Dr. Ph. Wolff-Viekovic
B. Banac

(illegible)
Coué

MINUTES OF THE COUNCIL OF FOREIGN MINISTERS[1]

[EXTRACTS]

MARCH 28, 1919

NOTES OF A MEETING HELD IN M. PICHON'S ROOM AT THE FOREIGN OFFICE, PARIS, ON FRIDAY, MARCH 28TH, 1919, AT 11:00 A.M.

Raising of blockade of German-Austria

. . .

1. M. PICHON opened the meeting and asked Lord Robert Cecil to make a statement regarding the raising of the blockade of German-Austria.

LORD ROBERT CECIL said that on March 12th the Supreme Economic Council had resolved that all blockade and trade restrictions with German-Austria and Hungary should be abolished and that commerce should be free with all parts thereof, as soon as the necessary machinery of control against re-exportation to Germany had been set up. He was not prepared to ask the Council to affirm the part of this resolution which concerned Hungary. In view of the events that had lately taken place in Hungary he would suggest that this portion of the resolution should be referred back to the Supreme Economic Council. The portion of the resolution relating to German-Austria, however, he would ask the Council to adopt. A certain number of articles susceptible of use for military purposes were to be excepted. These articles were enumerated in the paper forwarded by the Supreme Economic Council (see Annexure "A"). There were also in this paper certain provisions for the establishment of the necessary control, with the object of preventing re-export to Germany. In a word, the general principle recommended was that the blockade should be raised except in respect to articles of military use, as soon as an international control had been established, and was in a position to guarantee that no re-export should be made to Germany.

BARON SONNINO said that he had no objection to raise to the resumption of traffic with German-Austria, provided Hungary were not included.

[1] Miller, *My Diary at the Conference of Paris,* XV, 519-21, 535-36.

He wished, however, to draw attention to a decision taken by the Ban of Croatia-Slavonia, forbidding all import, export and transit of goods between Italy and Yugo-Slav territory. Such a policy, if persisted in, would not harmonise with that recommended by the Supreme Economic Council. Unless these decisions on the part of the Yugo-Slavs were revoked, Italy would be forced to take some counter-action. Up to the present no retort had been made, and he had for the time being stopped any move on the part of Italy.

(For reported action taken by Ban of Croatia, see Annexure "B".)

Mr. BALFOUR said that the matter alluded to by Baron Sonnino was a delicate question, though it had no very direct bearing on the proposal under discussion. The affair, however, was new to him.

LORD ROBERT CECIL said that at the earnest request of the Supreme Economic Council Italy had consented to the complete cessation of blockade in the Adriatic. It was, consequently, a very serious matter that the Yugo-Slavs should answer this with a blockade of Italy.

Mr. LANSING enquired whether there had been any restriction on the passage of foodstuffs to Yugo-Slavia.

BARON SONNINO said that as far as he knew, food had been allowed to pass, even before the removal of the blockade. With regard to the alleged order by the Ban of Croatia, he was not able to vouch for the correctness of the information he had put before the meeting, as he had no official intimation of it and only knew what he had related to the meeting from newspaper reports. He thought, however, that it was right to draw the attention of the meeting to the matter.

Mr. LANSING observed that in view of the presumed action on the part of the Yugo-Slavs, the action proposed by the Economic Council appeared all the more necessary.

Mr. BALFOUR agreed, and expressed the opinion that though there was no immediate practical connection with the proposal under discussion, Baron Sonnino had been right in drawing the attention of the meeting to this matter. It might perhaps be advisable to ask the Yugo-Slav authorities whether they had issued such a decree, and, if so, in what manner they justified it.

M. PICHON agreed that it would be reasonable to adopt this proposal. The Yugo-Slav authorities should be asked to give an explanation and their answer might be placed before the Council.

(It was then resolved that M. Pichon, on behalf of the Council, should undertake to see the Serbian representatives in Paris about the alleged prohibition of trade between Croatia-Slavonia and Italy and to report to the Council.)

BARON SONNINO made reservations regarding the above decision, pending the result of M. Pichon's enquiries. He said that Italy must have the right of taking counter-measures if the result was not satisfactory.

(It was further resolved that all blockade and trade restrictions with German-Austria should be abolished and that commerce should be free with all parts thereof, as soon as the necessary machinery of control against re-exportation to Germany had been set up, with the exceptions and other provisions set out in detail in Annexure "A.")

(Correction in foregoing dated March 29th.)

"The resolution of the Supreme Economic Council was approved, in so far as it concerned German-Austria, with a reservation by Baron Sonnino, subject to the receipt of a satisfactory reply by the Jugo-Slavs to M. Pichon's enquiry.

"The question as relating to Hungary was, however, referred back to the Supreme Economic Council."

. . .

ANNEXURE "B."

Telegram No. 6211 from Rome

Newspapers publish the following text of the proclamation of the Bano of Croatia, published by the official newspaper of Zagabria, the *Narodna Novi:*

The Bano of Croatia and Slavonia in compliance with the decree issued by the Council of Serbian Ministers at Belgrade directs:

1. That all trade with enemy countries, Germany, Austria, Turkey, Hungary, Bulgaria, shall be stopped.

2. All importation of goods for Italy, and the exportation of goods from Italy, across territories occupied by us, is prohibited:

3. A similar embargo is placed on the transit through our territory of goods from enemy countries directed to Italy, as likewise the transit of goods from Italy to enemy countries—all transit across (our) occupied territory is prohibited. This prohibition shall be applied without regard to the circumstances of origin or destination of the goods.

4. The exportation of goods from the Kingdom to occupied territories is allowed when the same are required for the needs of the local population, and are not intended for exportation to Italy, or for the requirements of the Italian troops. Meanwhile publicity is given to this decree and the liquidation and severance is recommended of all business with the said countries, which are excluded from trade relations.

5. All the railway and military and civil police authorities, especially of the stations of Buccari and Koprivnica, have received orders to prevent the importation of goods from Italy or exportation to Italy even in cases where proper transport permits have been issued. They have received similar orders to prevent the transit of goods from enemy countries directed to Italy, through our territory, and the transit of goods directed from Italy to enemy countries.

DR. JOHN PALECK, Bano.

ORLANDO'S LETTER TO WILSON[1]

IL PRESIDENTE
del
Consiglio dei Ministri.

Paris, April 3rd, 1919.

MR. PRESIDENT,

The quite unexpected way in which the Italian questions came up for discussion to-day, made it impossible to examine more thoroughly the many difficult points, including even questions of procedure, which present themselves.

I had not been able to come to an understanding with my colleagues on the Delegation, nor had my colleague, the Minister of Foreign Affairs, Baron Sonnino, come to the meeting, as it had been agreed that he would do, and as was done in the case of Mr. Tardieu when the problem of the French frontiers was under consideration.

As for the very delicate matter of giving a further hearing to the representatives of the Slovenes and Croats,—against whom Italy has been at war for four years,—I would not insist against it, just as I would not exclude the advisability of giving a hearing to the representatives of any other enemy people on whom it is a question of imposing conditions. But, on the other hand, as no such debate has yet been granted, I insist in thinking it advisable to abstain from taking part in a meeting which, as things stand, must necessarily give rise to debate.

I realize, with keen regret, that my absence may give rise to an impression, which I should be the first to wish to avoid, that a misunderstanding has arisen between the Italian Government and the Allied and Associated Governments. I think however that such an impression will not be given, as the meeting this afternoon is not the meeting of the representatives of the four Powers, but a conversation between the President of the United States and the Prime Ministers of Great Britain and France with those Gentlemen.

I earnestly hope, Mr. President, that in this way the reason for my absence will be seen in its true light, i.e. not as an evidence of disagreement, but as an act of consideration towards colleagues, whose wish it is to obtain all the data available in order to form their own opinion on the grave matters under consideration.

Believe me,
Mr. President,
Sincerely yours,
[*Signed*] V. E. ORLANDO.

[1] Baker, *Woodrow Wilson and the World Settlement*, III (Document 34), 272-73.

FIRST APPEAL OF THE AMERICAN EXPERTS TO WILSON[1]

April 4, 1919.

From: Chiefs of the Italian Division, the Balkan Division, the Austro-Hungarian Division, the Division of Boundary Geography, and the Division of Economics.

To: President Wilson.

Subject: Disposition of Fiume.

The following statement of facts and opinions is respectfully submitted for the President's consideration:

1. The port of Fiume is vitally necessary to the economic life of Jugo-Slavia.

2. It has no economic significance for Italy, except as its development would prevent Italy from controlling trade which might otherwise be artificially deflected to Trieste.

3. The large business interests of Fiume, the banking houses, and the shipping are mainly in Hungarian and Jugo-Slav hands. Italian capital did not develop the port. The Italians constitute the small traders and shop keepers and to some extent the professional classes.

4. According to the last official census the Italians constituted only a plurality of the population of Fiume, even when its artificial separation from the Slavic Sušak is maintained.

5. The Italian plurality in the restricted Fiume:

(a) Is of recent development (Since 1880 or 1890).

(b) Includes an unknown but considerable number who have not given up Italian citizenship.

(c) Has probably resulted from artificial encouragement by the Hungarian government, which had a comprehensible interest in developing an alien rather than a Slav majority in the city.

6. The Italian agitation in favor of annexing Fiume is only a few months old. Last summer it was generally admitted in high Italian circles that Fiume would and should go to Jugo-Slavia.

In view of the foregoing consideration the American specialists are unanimously of the opinion:

[1] Baker, *Woodrow Wilson and the World Settlement,* III (Document 33), 266-69.

1. *That Fiume should be given to the Jugo-Slav State without restriction.*

This solution is the only one which in our opinion will prove attractive at the same time to Jugo-Slav capital and to outside capital (Hungarian, Czecho-Slovak, etc.); it will best serve the vital economic interests of both city and state; and in view of the facts regarding the nature and origin of the Italian population, it seems to us the most just morally.

2. *That the interests of the Italian minority of greater Fiume should be assured by the establishment of adequate guarantees for protection.*

Similar guarantees should be extended, in a spirit of equality and justice, to the other Italian minorities in Jugo-Slavia, and to the much larger Slavic minorities in Trieste and other areas transferred to Italy by the recommended new frontier.

3. *That it is unwise to make Fiume a free city.*

Our unanimity of opinion on this point is due to the approximate equality of the two antagonistic elements of the population, the testimony of observers as to the inability of the Italians of Fiume properly to administer the port, the justified sensitiveness of the Slavs toward any infringement of sovereignty over their only good port and chief commercial city, and the serious economic and political disadvantages which such infringement would entail under the peculiar physical conditions which obtain at Fiume (See attached letter by Mr. Miller).

4. *That if for reasons not connected with the best interests of the city and its hinterland it is deemed necessary that Fiume be made a free city, its right of local self-government should be accompanied by the following safe-guards of the interests of the Jugo-Slav State:*

a. The moles, docks, basins and other instrumentalities of the port must be under Jugo-Slav sovereignty as well as Jugo-Slav ownership, and it must be possible for the Jugo-Slavs to acquire the land and other property needed for their extension.

b. The railways and other means of communication with the interior, (e.g., telephones, telegraphs, and postal service) must likewise be under Jugo-Slav control.

c. There must be no discrimination with respect to political and economic rights of any kind, nor with respect to schools and churches.

d. The city (except for a possible free port) must be included within the Slav customs frontier.

e. The organization of the city must be such as to abolish the present artificial division of the port into two parts.

These safeguards are necessary: (1) To ensure conditions of sufficient stability to justify expenditures by the government and by Jugo-Slav and foreign private capitalists for the improvement and development of the port; (2) To prevent Italian interference with the development of the port and with its full use; (3) To give the Slavs a fair opportunity to achieve a position in the industrial and political life of the community strong enough to safeguard their vital interests.

[*Signed*] W. E. LUNT
Chief of the Italian Division.
CLIVE DAY
Chief of the Balkan Division.
CHARLES SEYMOUR
Chief of the Austro-Hungarian Division.
DOUGLAS JOHNSON
Chief of the Division of Boundary Geography.
ALLYN A. YOUNG
Chief of the Division of Economics.

DOCUMENT 35

MILLER'S LETTER TO JOHNSON[1]

AMERICAN COMMISSION TO NEGOTIATE PEACE
OFFICE OF TECHNICAL ADVISORS

6 April, 1919.

DEAR MAJOR JOHNSON:

In our conversation yesterday you asked my views as to the creation of an independent territory comprising, with certain exceptions, the districts of Fiume and Susak under the hypothesis that the territory surrounding these districts was entirely within the limits of Jugo-Slavia, and under the further hypothesis that the entire port facilities of Fiume as well as any land necessary for their extension would likewise be under the sovereignty of Jugo-Slavia, and that the railroads running into Fiume and other means of communication with the interior, such as telephones, telegraphs, and postal service, should be under the control of Jugo-Slavia.

I do not doubt that such an arrangement is a legal possibility, but there are certain legal questions to which attention should be directed as they involve matters of practical importance.

Under the hypothesis the territory in question would be independent but the character of the locus is such as to make it doubtful whether that independence could be more than theoretical.

From the maps which you showed me it appears that what I will call the proposed "free area" while of very irregular shape, would run along the coast for ten or twelve miles, extending into the interior for a very short distance except in the center of the strip where it would be perhaps five or six miles wide, and even from this area would have to be deducted all of the docks, etc., which extend over most although not all of the waterfront. Furthermore, the control of the railroads by Jugo-Slavia would result in dividing the territory to be administered in the free area into three parts: the first what may be called the interior on the land side of the railroad, and the other two small strips of the coast between the railroad and the sea, lying on either side of the docks.

It should be added that under your statement of the hypothesis the area would for customs purposes be part of Jugo-Slavia, and that the population of the area is perhaps 60,000 persons, of whom no doubt a certain number reside in the portion devoted to the docks.

[1] Baker, *Woodrow Wilson and the World Settlement*, III (Document 33), 269-71.

Under any form of agreement it seems to me that the difficulties of the administration of such a very small area as an independent unit would be enormous, and to be successful would require almost complete coöperation and harmony between the government of the free area and the government of Jugo-Slavia. Take for example the question of police The jurisdiction of police over the docks, etc. would necessarily be Jugo-Slav, and also similar jurisdiction over the railroads and their appurtenances, and even if the latter were not technically under the sovereignty but only under the control of Jugo-Slavia. Thus the police of the free area would be over three distinct pieces of territory with the consequent necessity of free passage and repassage over the railroad.

It may be assumed, although you did not so state, that there is one water supply for the territory which would be within the free area, and for the docks, etc. Such a water supply would be under two distinct sovereignties and yet would of necessity be under a single management; indeed, it would be quite important to determine in making such an agreement where the source of the water supply of Fiume was located, for if this source is in the interior outside of the free area a still very difficult complication would be presented.

Without attempting to go into further detail I may mention that somewhat similar questions of administration would be presented in regard to the protection of health, the sewage system, the prevention of fire, and the means of communication between the two areas.

These matters are not mentioned for the purpose of expressing any opinion upon the questions of policy involved, but chiefly, as you suggest, in order, if such an arrangement is to be made, that very detailed knowledge of the local conditions may be obtained so that so far as possible future difficulties may be foreseen and perhaps avoided.

Very sincerely yours,

[*Signed*] DAVID HUNTER MILLER.

MAJOR DOUGLAS W. JOHNSON
  Hotel Crillon
    Paris.

WILSON'S MEMORANDUM TO ORLANDO[1]
APRIL 14, 1919

MEMORANDUM CONCERNING THE QUESTION OF ITALIAN CLAIMS IN THE ADRIATIC

There is no question to which I have given more careful or anxious thought than I have given to this, because in common with all my colleagues it is my earnest desire to see the utmost justice done to Italy. Throughout my consideration of it, however, I have felt that there was one matter in which I had no choice and could wish to have none.

I felt bound to square every conclusion that I should reach as accurately as possible with the fourteen principles of peace which I set forth in my address to the Congress of the United States on the eighth of January, 1918, and in subsequent addresses.

These fourteen points and the principles laid down in the subsequent addresses were formally adopted, with only a single reservation, by the Powers associated against Germany, and will constitute the basis of peace with Germany. I do not feel at liberty to suggest one basis for peace with Germany and another for peace with Austria.

It will be remembered that in reply to a communication from the Austrian Government offering to enter into negotiations for an armistice and peace on the basis of the fourteen points to which I have alluded, I said that there was one matter to which those points no longer applied.

INDEPENDENT STATES

They had demanded autonomy for the several States which had constituted parts of the Austro-Hungarian Empire, and I pointed out that it must now be left to the choice of the people of those several countries what their destiny and political relations should be.

They have chosen, with the sympathy of the whole world, to be set up as independent States. Their complete separation from Austria and the consequent complete dissolution of the Austro-Hungarian Empire has given a new aspect and significance to the settlements which must be effected with regard at any rate to the eastern boundaries of Italy.

Personally I am quite willing that Italy should be accorded along the whole length of her northern frontier and wherever she comes into con-

---

[1] Baker, *Woodrow Wilson and the World Settlement*, III (Document 35), 274-77.

tact with Austrian territory all that was accorded her in the so-called Pact of London, but I am of the clear opinion that the Pact of London can no longer apply to the settlement of her eastern boundaries.

The line drawn in the Pact of London was conceived for the purpose of establishing an absolutely adequate frontier of safety for Italy against any possible hostility or aggression on the part of Austria-Hungary. But Austria-Hungary no longer exists.

These eastern frontiers will touch countries stripped of the military and naval power of Austria, set up in entire independence of Austria, and organized for the purpose of satisfying legitimate national aspirations, and creating States not hostile to the new European order, but arising out of it, interested in its maintenance, dependent upon the cultivation of friendships, and bound to a common policy of peace and accommodation by the covenants of the League of Nations.

ISTRIAN PENINSULA

It is with these facts in mind that I have approached the Adriatic question. It is commonly agreed, and I very heartily adhere to the agreement, that the ports of Trieste and Pola, and with them the greater part of the Istrian Peninsula, should be ceded to Italy, her eastern frontier running along the natural strategic line established by the physical conformation of the country, a line which it has been attempted to draw with some degree of accuracy on the attached map.

Within this line on the Italian side will lie considerable bodies of non-Italian population, but their fortunes are so naturally linked by the nature of the country itself with the fortunes of the Italian people that I think their inclusion is fully justified.

There would be no such justification, in my judgment, in including Fiume or any part of the coast lying to the south of Fiume within the boundaries of the Italian kingdom.

PORT OF NEW STATES

Fiume is by situation and by all the circumstances of its development not an Italian but an international port, serving the countries to the east and north of the Gulf of Fiume. Just because it is an international port and cannot with justice be subordinated to any one sovereignty it is my clear judgment that it should enjoy a very considerable degree of genuine autonomy and that, while it should be included no doubt within the Customs system of the new Jugo-Slav State it should nevertheless be left free in its own interest and in the interest of the States lying about it to devote itself to the service of the commerce which naturally and inevitably seeks an outlet or inlet at its port.

The States which it serves will be new States. They will need to have complete confidence in their access to an outlet on the sea. The friendships and the connections of the future will largely depend upon such an arrangement as I have suggested; and friendship, coöperation, freedom of action must underlie every arrangement of peace, if peace is to be lasting.

I believe that there will be common agreement that the Island of Lissa should be ceded to Italy and that she should retain the port of Valona. I believe that it will be generally agreed that the fortifications which the Austrian Government established upon the islands near the eastern coast of the Adriatic should be permanently dismantled under international guarantees, and that the disarmament which is to be arranged under the League of Nations should limit the States on the eastern coast of the Adriatic to only such minor naval forces as are necessary for policing the waters of the islands and the coast.

These are the conclusions to which I am forced by the compulsion of the understandings which underlay the whole initiation of the present peace. No other conclusions seem to me susceptible of being rendered consistent with these understandings. They were understandings accepted by the whole world, and bear with peculiar compulsion upon the United States because the privilege was accorded her of taking the initiative in bringing about the negotiations for peace and her pledges underlie the whole difficult business.

And certainly Italy obtains under such a settlement the great historic objects which her people have so long had in mind. The historical wrongs inflicted upon her by Austria-Hungary and by a long series of unjust transactions which I hope will before long sink out of the memory of man are completely redressed. Nothing is denied her which will complete her national unity.

Here and there upon the islands of the Adriatic and upon the eastern coast of that sea there are settlements containing large Italian elements of population, but the pledges under which the new States enter the family of nations will abundantly safeguard the liberty, the development, and all the just rights of national or racial minorities and back of these safeguards will always lie the watchful and sufficient authority of the League of Nations.

And at the very outset we shall have avoided the fatal error of making Italy's nearest neighbours on the east her enemies and nursing just such a sense of injustice as has disturbed the peace of Europe for generations together and played no small part in bringing on the terrible conflict through which we have just passed.

DOCUMENT 37

YUGOSLAV PROPOSAL OF PLEBISCITE[1]

Paris, April 16, 1919.

Mr. President,

Our Delegation has had the honor of receiving Your Excellency's letter of March 3, informing it that the Royal Italian Government does not accept our offer to settle the problem of our future frontiers through President Wilson's arbitration.

While regretting this decision, which, in our estimation, eliminates the best way of solving this delicate dispute, and always prompted by the desire to find a satisfactory way of insuring amicable relations in future, we take the liberty, Mr. President, of asking you to inform the Conference that in the event of its being prepared to adopt such a means of settlement, we are ready for our part to accept that the problem of our frontiers with Italy be settled through the direct consultation of the populations concerned. We believe that this means of settlement is particularly appropriate to the solution of disputes between friendly peoples and Governments, as we stated at the session of the Conference of January 31, in connection with the delimitation of our frontier with Rumania in the Banat.

We hope, Mr. President, that this suggestion of ours will be given a friendly reception in the Council over which you preside with such distinction, because it is of such a nature as to insure the harmony of the Allies before the world, which harmony is a precious guarantee of our mutual relations in future. We also hope that the Royal Italian Government will accept this means of settlement, which is in line with its own political tradition.

Please accept . . .

Signed: Pachitch.

To His Excellency Monsieur Georges Clemenceau, President of the Peace Conference, etc., etc. Paris.

[1] Adriaticus, *La Question adriatique,* Document XII, pp. 42-43. Author's translation.

DOCUMENT 38

AMERICAN PROPOSAL ON FIUME[1]
APRIL 16, 1919

DRAFT ARTICLE REGARDING FIUME

1. Hungary renounces in favor of Italy the territory of the city and district of Fiume, as that area is shown on the annexed map, which is a part of this treaty.

2. The League of Nations shall appoint a Commission to govern the area.

3. The Commission shall consist of three members chosen by the Council of the League of Nations, of whom one shall be a subject of Italy, one a subject of the Yugo-Slav State and one a citizen of a third State.

4. The members of the Commission shall be appointed for two years and may be re-appointed; they can be removed and replaced by the Council of the League of Nations.

5. The Chairman of the Commission shall be appointed for two years from its members by the Council of the League of Nations; he can be re-appointed; he will be the executive of the Commission.

6. The Commission shall have all powers of government within and relating to the area, including the appointment and dismissal of all functionaries and the creation of such administrative or representative bodies as it deems necessary. Its decisions shall be taken by a majority vote.

7. The area shall be governed subject to the provisions hereof and so far as possible in conformity with the existing laws; amendments necessary, whether for general reasons or for bringing the said laws into accord with the said provisions, shall be decided and put into effect by the Commission after consultation with the local representatives of the population in such a manner as the Commission shall determine. No law or amendment thereto can affect or limit the provisions hereof.

8. The local civil and criminal courts will continue. A Civil and Criminal Court will be appointed by the Commission to judge appeals from the decisions of the said local courts and to decide all matters which can not be determined by the local courts. The Commission will determine the competence of this last named jurisdiction. Additional courts, as well

[1] Miller, *My Diary at the Conference of Paris,* VIII (Document 802), 372-75.

as changes in the composition, jurisdiction and procedure of the existing courts may be established by the Commission.

9. The Commission will alone have the power of levying taxes in the area. These taxes will be exclusively applied to the needs of the area. Ships and shipping shall not be the subject of taxation, direct or indirect. Subject to the provisions hereof, the present fiscal system will be maintained, with such modifications as the Commission shall deem necessary for the proper administration and government of the area. No new tax will be imposed without consulting the local representatives of the population.

10. Inhabitants will retain their present nationality, but no hindrance shall be placed in the way of those who wish to acquire a different nationality. They will preserve under the control of the Commission their local assemblies, their religious liberties, their schools, and their rights of language. The right of voting for local assemblies in the area will belong to every inhabitant above the age of twenty-one years without distinction of sex. On the other hand there will be no right of voting for any assembly other than the local assemblies within the area.

11. Any of the inhabitants who may desire to leave the area may retain their rights in real property with full power of sale and equitable disposition without restriction, and may remove their personal property free of export and other charges or restrictions of any kind.

12. There will be no compulsory military service, voluntary recruiting, or fortifications. A local gendarmerie for the maintenance of order may alone be established.

13. The customs régime and exports taxes of the area shall be without any discrimination or difference as between any countries or places without the area and shall be determined and established by the Commission, which may modify the same from time to time.

14. There shall be freedom of transit through the area on the routes most convenient to persons, goods, ships, carriages, wagons and mails coming from or going to any point without the area. For this purpose the crossing of territorial waters shall be allowed. Such persons, goods, ships, carriages, wagons and mails shall be subjected to no transit duties or any undue delays or restrictions, and goods in transit shall be exempt from export taxes and all customs or other similar duties.

15. All charges imposed on transport in transit shall be reasonable, having regard to the conditions of the traffic. No charge, facility or restriction shall depend directly or indirectly on the ownership or on the nationality of any ship or other means of transport on which any part of the through journey has been, or is to be, accomplished.

16. There shall neither be imposed nor maintained any control over

the passage of persons through the area beyond measures necessary to ensure that passengers are bona fide in transit and those necessary for police and sanitation.

17. There shall be no discrimination in the charges and conditions of transport of goods or persons entering or leaving the area based on the frontier crossed or on the kind, ownership, or flag or means of transport employed or on the route of places of trans-shipment. The subjects, property, and flags of all States shall in respect of charges, facilities and in all other respects be treated on a footing of perfect equality, in the port of the area and within the area itself.

18. There shall be no impediment to the movement of persons or ships other than those arising from prescriptions concerning police, Customs, sanitation, emigration or immigration, or the importation or exportation of prohibited goods.

Such reasonable and uniform prescriptions shall not unnecessarily impede traffic.

19. In respect of communications by telegraph, cable, wireless or telephone within, into or from the area, there shall be no distinction or preference as to the nationals of any State either in charges or in service, and the charges and regulations regarding such communications and their use shall be fair and equitable taking into account the circumstances without the area as well as those within the area itself.

20. All port charges, dues, tolls and similar charges which may be established in the port of the area shall not be higher than may be necessary reasonably to cover the expenses of administration, up-keep and improvement of the port and shall be applied on a footing of perfect equality to the nationals, property and flags of all States. The foregoing limitations shall be equally applicable to the charges within the area in the use of the various installations.

21. No laws or regulations regarding the railroad entering the area shall be made which shall unnecessarily impede traffic through, into, or from the area and in particular the transport of perishable goods shall be permitted to be promptly and regularly carried out and any customs or other formalities shall be effected in such a way as to allow the goods to be carried straight through.

22. All property in the area formerly belonging to the Government of Hungary shall pass to the ownership of the City and District of Fiume and shall be administered by the Commission, having in view not only the interests of the local population but also the commerce of the port and of the territory to which Fiume affords access to the sea.

23. Italy and the Kingdom of the Serbs, Croats and Slovenes agree that any dispute arising between them, under these articles and also any

dispute the decision of which may be affected by the terms of these articles, shall be submitted to arbitration under rules and provisions established by the Council of the League of Nations, and they agree to carry into effect any award or decision rendered in respect of any such dispute.

DOCUMENT 39

AMERICAN PROPOSAL FOR DALMATIA[1]

PLAN FOR DALMATIA

ARTICLE 1.—The Austrian Government renounces all rights, title and authority over the following territory and its residents in favor of the five Allied and Associated Great Powers:

"The northern part of the present Austrian province of Dalmatia, as far southeast as a line beginning at Cape Planka (between Oran and Sebenico) and following the main watershed in a general northeasterly and northerly direction in such manner as to leave within the territory renounced by Austria in favor of the Five Allied and Associated Great Powers the drainage basins of the Cikola, Krka, and Butisnjica Rivers and their tributaries, and without that territory the drainage basin of the Cetina River; also all the islands northwest of Cape Planka that are at present administratively a part of the province of Dalmatia.

"A commission composed of seven members, of which one member each will be named by the Five Allied and Associated Great Powers, one by the Jugo-Slav state and one by Belgium, will be constituted 15 days after the ratification of the present treaty, to fix upon the ground the trace of the boundary line above described."

ARTICLE 2.—The League of Nations shall appoint a Commission to govern the district.

ARTICLE 3.—The Commission, whose decisions shall be taken by majority vote, shall consist of five Members chosen by the Council of the League of Nations.

The Members of the Commission shall be appointed for one year and may be re-appointed; they may be removed and replaced by the Council of the League of Nations.

In dealing with this territory the decisions of the Council of the League of Nations shall be taken by majority vote.

ARTICLE 4.—The Chairman of the Commission shall be appointed for one year from its members by the Council of the League of Nations; he may be re-appointed; he shall be the Executive of the Commission.

ARTICLE 5.—The Commission shall have all the powers over this territory and its inhabitants hitherto belonging to the Austrian Government, except as herein expressly limited or as modified in their operations by the Constitution to be instituted.

[1] Miller, *My Diary at the Conference of Paris,* VIII (Document 809), 388-91.

ARTICLE 6.—No new taxes shall be imposed without consulting representatives of the population of the territory.

ARTICLE 7.—After consulting the local representatives of the population in such manner as it may determine, the Commission shall draw up a constitution for the territory and its inhabitants, which shall be consistent with the provisions of this treaty, and put the same into operation. The constitution shall protect religious liberty and liberty in the learning and use of languages. Pending the coming into operation of the new constitution, the Commission shall govern in accordance with existing constitutional forms, laws, and usages, as nearly as may be.

ARTICLE 8.—Inhabitants will retain their Austrian citizenship, but no hindrance shall be placed in the way of those who wish to acquire a different nationality.

ARTICLE 9.—Any of the inhabitants who may desire to leave the territory may retain their rights in real property with full power of sale and equitable disposition without restriction, and may remove their personal property free of export and other charges or restrictions of any kind.

ARTICLE 10.—There will be no compulsory military service, voluntary recruiting, or fortifications. A local gendarmerie for the maintenance of order may alone be established.

ARTICLE 11.—The Commission shall have the power to arrange, under conditions which it shall determine for the protection abroad of the interests of the territory and its inhabitants.

ARTICLE 12.—The compensation of the Members of the Commission shall be fixed by the Council of the League of Nations and shall be paid out of the funds of the territory.

ARTICLE 13.—The Commission shall have power to decide all questions which may arise regarding the interpretation of these articles.

ARTICLE 14.—During the year nineteen hundred and twenty-nine (1929), A.D., there shall be held a plebiscite in the above defined territory. In the vote there shall be no discrimination on the ground of sex. None shall be admitted to vote except inhabitants resident in the territory during the five years preceding the day on which such plebiscite shall be held.

The regulation, method, and date of the vote, which shall be free and secret, shall be fixed by the Council of the League of Nations. The vote shall be upon the two following alternatives:

The maintenance of the régime established by the present Treaty;
Union with Jugo-Slavia.

The League of Nations shall decide on the sovereignty of the territory, taking into account the wishes of the inhabitants thus expressed.

If the vote results in the maintenance of the régime established by the present Treaty, the League of Nations will take appropriate steps to adapt such régime to the permanent interest and general welfare of the territory and its inhabitants.

If the vote results in favor of union with Jugo-Slavia the five Allied or Associated Great Powers agree to cede to Jugo-Slavia, in accordance with the decision of the League of nations, all that territory governed thereby.

ARTICLE 15.—As soon after the plebiscite as possible the League of Nations shall make all dispositions and prescribe all regulations which it shall deem necessary for the general welfare and for the welfare of the territory.

ARTICLE 16.—All property situated within this territory belonging to the Austrian Government will pass to the Five Allied and Associated Great Powers for transfer to the bodies or persons to whom it belongs equitably and in accordance with the general interest.

ARTICLE 17.—If and when requested so to do by the Jugo-Slav state, the Five Allied and Associated Great Powers will negotiate an agreement between the said state and the Commission for this territory, granting to the former the right to control, administer, improve, and where necessary construct the railway line running through this territory and connecting Spalato with the said state beyond the mountain barrier, such right being equitably limited, however, by the rights of the port of Sebenico and the interests it serves or can serve in interior regions.

TEMPERLEY'S REPORT ON DALMATIA[1]
April 22, 1919

REPORT OF BRITISH INVESTIGATION IN DALMATIA
AMERICAN COMMISSION TO NEGOTIATE PEACE

Paris, April 22, 1919.

From: D. W. Johnson.
To: Col. House.
Re: Report of British Investigation in Dalmatia.

1. Professor H. V. W. Temperley, the historian who, with rank of major, has been making investigations in Jugoslavia for the British, has just returned to Paris and given me a résumé of his conclusions. I understood Temperley to say that he spent six weeks in Dalmatia, visiting the areas occupied by both Italian and Jugoslav troops. In his opinion, when the Treaty of London was drawn, the Italians sincerely believed that the Dalmatians were so opposed to Austrian rule and so enthusiastic for Italian culture that they would prefer Italian to Austrian domination. He states that upon occupation the Italians were greatly surprised and disappointed to find the strength of the anti-Italian sentiment and the general unanimity of opinion in favor of union with Jugoslavia. The harshness of Italian rule, which he confirms, was not in his opinion premeditated, but developed out of the necessity of suppressing the full expression of the Dalmatians' aspirations. Temperley cites many instances of spontaneous public expressions of anti-Italian sentiment both within and without the area of Italian occupation; and reports that false assertions of the existence of smallpox outbreaks, epidemics of skin diseases, etc., are being used to cover interruptions of communications, segregation of the natives for political purposes, and other similar oppressive measures.

2. Temperley does not believe that the Jugoslav Government would permit at the present time any armed opposition to the execution of decrees by the Peace Conference, giving to Italy sovereignty over Fiume or parts of Dalmatia. He states that such measures will inevitably lead to war, but that hostilities would be deferred for a few years, when the Jugoslavs believe that their own situation would be much strengthened

---

[1] Miller, *My Diary at the Conference of Paris*, IX (Document 844), 12-13.

and that of the Italians less favorable than it is today. He adds that if war comes, large numbers of Englishmen will quite surely volunteer to aid the Jugoslavs in the struggle.

3. Regarding the national aspirations of other elements among the Jugoslavs, Temperley reports that the Slovenes (with the exception of those in the Klagenfurt basin, where he confirms Lt. Miles' report of the existence of many pro-German Slovenes) have an intelligent and wide-spread desire for union in a Jugoslav State; that a considerable minority among the Croatians is affected by their former enjoyment of a certain degree of autonomy and do not want to see it sacrificed for too close a union with Jugoslavia; but that even in Croatia the majority agree with the Dalmatians and Slovenes, desiring union with Jugoslavia.

DOCUMENT 41

ALDROVANDI'S DIARY[1]
[EXTRACTS]

Saturday, April 19.[2]

Meeting at Wilson's residence at 11 A.M. The following are present: Wilson, Clemenceau, Lloyd George, Orlando, Sonnino, the interpreter Mantoux, Hankey, and myself. Wilson has invited me personally "on account of the importance of the question."

WILSON. Sig. Orlando may open the discussion.

ORLANDO. Am I to make a general statement on Italian questions?

WILSON. Yes.

ORLANDO. I consider the Italian question from the point of view of the principles on which the other claims have been based. Since one of the Powers represented here, namely the United States, did not participate in the Treaty of London, as did France and England, I shall now consider the Italian questions without reference to treaty obligations. The three Italian claims are well defined and have analogies in the decisions which have been made for the other Powers. I propose to draw a parallel between the various Italian claims on the basis of the aforesaid principles and their application.

1) In the first place Italy asks for the annexation of the territories on her side of the frontier given her by nature. Italy is a country sharply defined by nature, as few others in Europe, save perhaps Spain and Scandinavia. It is surrounded by the sea on three sides, and in the North it is separated from the rest of Europe by the highest mountains of the continent. That is why we are asking for this line which is our natural frontier; we are asking for the watershed of the Alps. On this side of that line there are populations which are not of Italian nationality. I do not deny it; nor shall I dispute the number of aliens on the Italian side. All those who have spoken of it at the Conference have declared that the Austrian statistics are false; the most extreme statement in that respect has perhaps been made by the Yugoslavs. We could prove with

---

[1] "La settimana di passione adriatica a Parigi (17-27 Aprile 1919)," *Nuova Antologia*, May 1933, pp. 165-86; June 1933, pp. 354-81. Author's translation. This diary gives *in extenso* the Minutes of the meetings at which Aldrovandi was present. These Minutes are not at present available in English, although a résumé is found in Miller, *My Diary at the Conference of Paris*, XIX, 531-39.

[2] Cf. Minutes of the Council, April 19, I.C. 171D.

the aid of absolutely unquestionable documents that the Austrian statistics have been falsified to the detriment of Italy. But that is not the
issue at the moment; the point is not to determine whether there are a
few hundreds of thousands of aliens more or less. Every time that we
have taken up the task of creating a new state we have recognized
that the fact of the existence of several races was not a reason for drawing irregular frontiers, for giving its map the appearance of a leopard's
skin, or for denying it its natural frontiers. It is only a question now
of applying these precedents to Italy. I am not making an analysis at the
moment, but a synthetic demonstration. Istria cannot be divided; it
constitutes an inseparable, homogeneous, and organic entity. If Istria
were to be divided in the manner that has been suggested, its defense
would become impossible. Trieste would remain within reach of enemy
guns. Istria constitutes a unit, as can be seen at once by looking at a
map. Even if the principle of natural frontiers including aliens is applied
to Istria and to all our claims, Italy will have a number of people, of race
different from her own, far smaller than that granted to any other country. Poland, with 25,000,000 inhabitants, will have between 1,800,000 and
2,000,000 Germans. Italy, with all her claims, will have about 600,000 aliens
in a population of 40,000,000. Roumania will have a very large number
of Hungarians; of Serbia there is no need to speak. The Czechs are annexing from 2,000,000 to 3,000,000 aliens, Hungarians and Germans, in
a population of some 10,000,000. Italy therefore believes that she is justified in claiming the frontier given her by Providence. If there had
only been 400,000 or 500,000 Germans between France and the Rhine,
that fact would not have been a sufficient reason for not making that
great river the frontier of France.

2) The second point refers to Fiume. We might say that the question
of Fiume is taken care of by the natural frontier. The Romans used to
call the Monte Nevoso *Limes italicus,* and this included Fiume. For
Fiume we appeal to the right of self-determination of peoples. There is
the historic fact that the question of Fiume has arisen before the conclusion of the Armistice, independently of any action of Italy. On October 18, 1918, the Deputy of Fiume who had been unanimously elected,
declared in the Hungarian Parliament that Fiume, in view of the current state of affairs in Austria-Hungary, claimed the right to be united
to Italy. In regard to Fiume, the question has not been raised by Italy,
but by the city of Fiume itself. It is the duty of Italy to support this demand, which is an illustration of the right of self-determination of
peoples. One may raise the objection that the principles of self-determination cannot be applied to a small entity such as Fiume. This would be
true if Fiume were looked upon as a separate unit, isolated, and outside

the natural frontier; but if we consider that for many centuries Fiume has had its own history and freedom, it must be granted that Fiume constitutes a particular and notable exception, much in the same way that its tradition would give San Marino the right of self-determination. But there is, in addition, the economic question. There is the precedent of Danzig; in the case of Danzig we have not allowed the claim of annexation to Poland on account of the German predominance; we have not allowed economic considerations to prevail against the principle of nationality. If Fiume were to be made a free city like Danzig, it could be said in Italy that the Germans have received better treatment than the Italians. The case of Danzig was even more serious than that of Fiume, for Poland had no other outlet to the sea, while Yugoslavia has many. In fact Fiume cannot be the chief port of Yugoslavia. Yugoslavia has at least six or seven other ports and hundreds of kilometers of coast line. There was a special reason for giving Danzig to Poland, and that reason does not apply for giving Fiume to Yugoslavia. Danzig can serve only Poland, whereas Fiume, along with other ports, serves Yugoslavia. Croatia supplies only 7 percent of the commerce of the port of Fiume. I have seen in the press that Trumbić claims that the figure is 50 percent. Although I was certain of my statement, I have asked further information from the Chamber of Commerce of Fiume, which has replied that the traffic was 7 percent. But whether it is 7 or 8 or even 15 percent, the fact remains that Fiume does not serve chiefly Yugoslavia, but rather Hungary, Galicia, and Bohemia. If in spite of this Fiume is not given to Italy, it will be said in Italy, I repeat, that the enemy has been treated better than the friend. I wish to add a small proof of this historic independence of Fiume. In the coat of arms of Austria-Hungary, different sections of which represented the various Hapsburg dominions, the arms of Fiume appear separately. This shows that in a feudal state like Austria, which attached importance to such manifestations, Fiume was considered as an absolutely separate entity, as a state within a state.

3) The third point refers to Dalmatia.

SONNINO. And the islands.

ORLANDO. I always include the islands in speaking of these territories, just as in speaking of Istria I include the islands of Cherso and Lussin, which are largely Italian. For Dalmatia we must first consider strategic arguments. One need not be a sailor in order to know that the Italian coast is at the mercy of any attack from the other shore. Conditions are such that even if the state holding the opposite shore should be allowed only policing power, and this were reduced to a minimum, it would still be possible for its ships to bombard Italian cities and to return safely to their anchorage. The map shows how this can easily and safely be done; the present war has proved it. The Entente had an absolute preponderance of forces in the Adriatic; but despite the overwhelming superiority of the Italian navy, reënforced by French and British units, our cities have been at the mercy of the enemy's bombardments, without our being able to offer adequate resistance. The situation is self-evident; Italy will never be secure unless she has a defensive base in the middle of the other shore.

But the strategic argument is not the only one for Dalmatia. We have national and historic reasons which cannot but be decisive in the discussion of Dalmatia. There are times when one cannot deny historic reasons. From the beginnings of history until Campoformio, Dalmatia has been united to Italy; first as part of the Roman Empire, later as part of Venice. And this is the consequence of a physical fact, for its mountains separate it from the territory to the east. For this reason, all Dalmatian culture necessarily gravitated toward Italy. Dalmatia has been Italian up to very recent times; until 1881 the majority of the Dalmatian Diet was Italian. Let no one say that we are going back to remote centuries to find a base for our historic right. In an Austrian document of 1887, found at Zara, and of which I have already given a copy to President Wilson, occur the following statistics in regard to the official language (*Dienstsprache*) of 84 Dalmatian communes: 59 used Italian exclusively and 25 used both languages. This Austrian source therefore shows that in 1887 Italian was the language of more than half of the Dalmatian communes. Even now the majority may be Italian in Zara, Traù, and Spalato. This Italianness is flourishing; could Italy, after the sacrifices of the war, let this Italianness be doomed to destruction? What Italy demanded in the beginning, by way of compromise, was only a small part of Dalmatia, leaving to Serbia Cattaro, Spalato, and Ragusa. We think that we are very moderate in asking that this compromise be lived up to.

WILSON. As was agreed with Orlando, I have discussed Italian problems with himself and with his colleagues separately, and I have always told them the same thing. I am now forced to insist on this same point of view. I had the privilege to speak for the associates when peace negotiations were begun. Definite statements were made regarding the principles on which the peace with Germany was to be founded. How could we adopt different principles for the peace with Germany from those for the peace with Austria, Bulgaria, and Turkey? We must act consistently; we must seek a common basis. The whole question comes down to this: we are now seeking to establish a basis for peace, such as was never made in the course of centuries. We must establish international relations on an entirely new basis. A greater issue has never been raised; no statesman has ever negotiated with greater concern, or undertaken to bring about agreements of this kind. Certain arguments must be set aside, among them strategic and economic considerations. Nature has in some cases assigned natural frontiers, as Orlando remarked in the cases of Spain and Scandinavia. Mountains do not only separate waters, but nations as well. I have no objections to make in regard to the question of the frontiers of Italy as they have been outlined in the first part of Orlando's speech. The mountain peaks are easily identifiable; and the frontier of Italy is accordingly determined so as to include Trieste, Pola, and most of Istria. I find no difficulty in accepting the views of the Italian delegates on this point. But further south the argument seems to me to run in the opposite direction.

We are confronted with another national entity belonging to another drainage system.

This brings me to the question of Fiume. Before the war the fate of this region was united to the fate of Austria-Hungary. The latter was ruled by men imbued with the same spirit as the Germans, in whose hands they were mere tools. The consequences would be different if the war had had a different outcome. This difficulty would not have arisen had not the Austro-Hungarian Empire been disrupted. But it has disappeared. It is inherent in the present situation that we must establish new relations among the peoples formerly subject to a political system such as obtained in the Austro-Hungarian Empire. We must do away with the dissensions which were fostered among them. When we were seeking to detach the Yugoslavs from the Austro-Hungarian Empire, we treated them as friends; we cannot now treat them as enemies. Orlando has spoken of Fiume as if it concerned exclusively Italy and Yugoslavia. Fiume is certainly important for the Yugoslavs; but, whatever the proportion of Yugoslav interests in relation to the total commerce of the port, it was primarily an international port serving Rumania, Hungary, and Czechoslovakia. Orlando himself has recalled that the principal relations of Hungary were with Fiume. Hungary was making use of the Italian element in Fiume to oppose the surrounding Slav population. That is why it tolerated the autonomy of Fiume.

SONNINO. The autonomy is ancient.

WILSON. I know it, but I said "tolerated." I must make certain observations in regard to what was said by Orlando with respect to the principles which we have applied in the case of the sovereignty of Danzig. As to Danzig, it has been decided that it should be separated from its former sovereignty; whereas here it would be a case of extending to Fiume a sovereignty different from the one under which it was.

Both economic and strategic considerations run counter to our decision. Both of these indicated that Danzig should be united to Poland;

instead, in order to maintain the integrity of our principles, we have deliberately renounced a strategic frontier, adopting in its place a highly irregular line; likewise in other places we have refused to disregard national considerations when these were in opposition to strategic reasons. Thus we did not allow the economic arguments presented by the Belgian representatives and we denied them a region which would have given them the advantage of a railroad junction, and this on account of the German population. I must say that to give Fiume to Italy would be a decision in absolute contradition to the new principles on which we are endeavoring to base international order. What shall we do? The main point to bear in mind is that Fiume served the commerce of Czechoslovakia, Hungary, and Rumania, as well as that of Yugoslavia. It is therefore necessary to establish its free use as an international port. It is undeniable that the population of Fiume constitutes a mere island, not being united to Italy by a contiguous Italian population. To give Fiume to Italy would be an arbitrary act, so much in opposition to our principles that I could not give my consent to it.

In regard to Dalmatia, I must note that the arguments used by Baron Sonnino when I arrived in Paris were strategic arguments. In this case also, do we or do we not accept the new principles? In the new order of humanity we must unite our efforts to secure territorial integrity and the independence of economic life. Under the régime of the League of Nations, I cannot conceive of a Yugoslav fleet which could threaten Italy.

The only possible danger would lie in a close alliance between Yugoslavia and some other Power for the purpose of attacking Italy.

In this connection I believe that the interference and the control of the Great Powers must disappear from the Balkans. Up to now the Balkans have been a pawn in the European game. Constantinople was notorious as a center of intrigue on the part of the Great Powers, which intrigues constituted a serious and continual menace. The Balkans themselves were not independent; the Great Powers, and particularly Berlin, decided what was to happen there. For that reason I am opposed to giving a foothold in the Balkans to any European Power. It would be fatal to do so; we must eliminate any cause for intervention of the Great Powers in that region. The strategic argument is very dangerous; the treaties of 1815 and 1871 were drawn up by military men; they were responsible for the annexation of Alsace-Lorraine; it is the military men who have led us from one disaster to the other. It would be a threat to world peace if Italy had possessions in the Eastern Adriatic. We are trying to organize a great international association, of which Italy is a part, indeed one of the leading parts. If she claims, in addition, strategic advantages, the question takes on a different aspect: there would then be two régimes, the new and the old. She would hold the new principles in her right hand, the old ones in her left. I cannot drive such a team; the American people would not tolerate it. In America there is disgust with the old order of things; but not only in America: the whole world is weary of it. There would be no support in America for a government that defended it. We are speaking in this room as if we were the masters of Europe; that is childish. If the new order of things is not properly interpreted, a tragic fate awaits the world. I urge this most earnestly on my Italian colleagues. I am trying to be their friend, an intelligent friend; I should not be serving Italy if I granted their wishes. I leave it to history to judge who is serving her better of the two: myself or those who insist on the claim to Fiume and Dalmatia. I am detached from Europe; I was born three thousand miles away, where I have lived most of my life. There was a time when I did not care a snap of the fingers what happened in Europe. Now, however, America has received the task of assisting Europe in creating the new order; I must carry out this undertaking to its conclusion. I can induce the American people to use all its resources for that purpose, but not otherwise. I must recall to my Italian colleagues that, if I am not successful, nothing can be expected from the American people. The question of Fiume has arisen recently; Fiume is only an island of Italian population. If the fate of Fiume were to be decided on the basis of self-determination, that would have to be the case in a good many other places as well. We gave Bohemia and Poland their historic boundaries: Fiume does not lie within the historic boundaries of Italy.

I feel the solemnity of the occasion and I must speak with appropriate deliberation. I have approached this subject in the most friendly spirit; the conclusions that I have reached are those of one who wishes to serve Italian interests, not to combat them.

SONNINO. I shall refer to the point made by President Wilson when he said that I offered strategic reasons for assigning Dalmatia to Italy. President Wilson said that he could not countenance these reasons in the establishment of the new order. I must say that we never asked for conditions of strategic advantage with any offensive in view; but only for necessary conditions of defense and security. We have no aggressive designs against anyone, but only wish to remedy the unfortunate lot of Italy, heretofore open to every aggression. Even with the theoretical guarantees of a League of Nations, a small enemy fleet could conceal itself behind the islands of the other shore of the Adriatic, and from there defy any League of Nations; that has been shown by the present war. If the fleet of the Entente had been able to meet the Austrian fleet, it would certainly have destroyed it; but it was unable to do so, despite its great numerical superiority. If the Italian demand is not granted, there would be left open a temptation to attack us, and likewise a temptation for Italy to make war to do away once and for all with her condition of danger and inferiority. Even though the League of Nations may succeed in creating a situation analogous to that of a civilized state where the courts and the police protect the citizen, the citizen must still be allowed the private safety of his own home. That is our situation and for that reason we cannot do with less than we are asking for.

As to the Balkans we have every intention of staying out of their quarrels. Dalmatia, especially the northern part which we claim, is definitely outside the Balkans. All its economic and cultural relations gravitate toward the Italian shore of the Adriatic. That explains how the Italian element has been able to defend itself despite governmental suppression; it explains how it survived in Zara, Sebenico, and Spalato. Up to 1859 and 1866 the Italian element in Austria was sufficiently large so that the central government found it advisable to take an interest in its protection for parliamentary reasons. After the loss of Lombardy and Venetia, the Italians were persecuted because their diminished numbers carried little weight against Slav pressure. Despite these unfavorable conditions, our people found the necessary strength to survive, owing to the persistent relations of those regions with the Italian shore.

After a war requiring such enormous sacrifices, in which Italy has had 500,000 killed and 900,000 disabled, it is not conceivable that we should return to a worse situation than before the war; certain islands on the Dalmatian coast were conceded to us even by Austria-Hungary to secure our neutrality. You would not even grant us these; that could not be explained to the Italian people. Italy would not understand why she had gone to war; it would be a crime against the Italian people. The result of my policy toward the Allies would be a loss to my country, for which I am ready to sacrifice everything, even my life.

You speak of a League of Nations; but you cannot expect it to accomplish and to organize everything. I should like to know how the League of Nations can be of use in settling the Russian problem. How can we put our trust in it, until it has proved itself fully capable? That will take time; a decree or a treaty will not suffice for it: it will be necessary to change the ways of thinking and of feeling of peoples. It would be criminal of us to accept the settlement which you propose for our problems; our responsibility would be enormous. Italy has been asked to assume great responsibilities in order to guarantee the positions of others, and has received nothing for herself.

WILSON. The same guarantees were given to you as to the others.

SONNINO. As I have explained, we are not guaranteed. On the other side of the Adriatic we are in contact with Balkan peoples, excitable and given to intrigues, skilled and practiced in the art of falsifying documents.

Besides, the League of Nations has no force under its direct control.

WILSON. You are speaking of a time when the Balkans were in a different situation and were used by the Great Powers for their own purposes.

SONNINO. You do not know what the Balkans will be five or ten years from now. I have only sought to do my whole duty, and the final result would be that I have wrought the ruin of my country.

LLOYD GEORGE asks if the discussion must be continued, inasmuch as he and Clemenceau must explain the point of view of those who are bound by a Treaty.

CLEMENCEAU. I think it preferable to continue if you propose to be as brief as I intend to be.

The speech which was to be made by Lloyd George and by myself has been made by President Wilson. We are embarking upon a hazardous but noble undertaking. We are seeking to break Europe and the world away from the old order, which has been the cause of the old conflicts and has finally led to the present war, the greatest and most horrible of all. However, it is not possible to change the whole policy of the world at one stroke. That applies to France as well as to Italy. I wish to recall that, when Italy was gravitating in a different orbit, I always remained a friend of hers. I should be ready to make concessions to our Allies; I want to recall, in this tragic hour, because of the consequences it may have for them, that they are a people who have deserved well of humanity and civilization. Wilson has presented powerful arguments. France and England have their hands tied; we are bound by a Treaty. An agreement was made in London; I was not a member of the Government that concluded it, but it bears the signature of France. That Treaty gives Dalmatia to Italy. That is a fact that cannot be forgotten. However, in that same Treaty, Fiume is assigned to Croatia. At the time of the Treaty, Italy made no claim to Fiume; she gave it to the Croats. Sig. Barzilai has presented to me the argument that, since then, Austria has disappeared, thus altering the situation. That is true, but Italy has none the less signed a document which assigns Fiume to Croatia. I am astonished that Italy should claim, in addition to Dalmatia which we gave her, Fiume which she conceded to Croatia. Under those conditions, there is no treaty any longer; the signatures do not count. It is not possible for Italy to insist upon one clause of the Treaty while denying another. It would be deplorable that the Italians should use this pretext to break with their Allies. I think that our allied friends would be making a mistake: I do not think that they would be serving their cause or that of civilization. I hope that my Italian friends will not rely too much on the first enthusiasm that might be aroused by their action. The cold and inevitable consequences of having alienated their friends would appear later on. We, the French, have had cause, as I have said many times, to complain of the treatment given us by the Italians in the Adriatic. But that is past; we must now overcome another critical period; otherwise we should suffer all the consequences. I cannot speak without a deep feeling of emotion at the thought that peoples who have fought together for years should part from each other. It would hurt us much to be abandoned; but it would hurt Italy even more.

ORLANDO. No doubt.

CLEMENCEAU. If the Italian plenipotentiaries should leave, I hope the power of reason may bring them back to us. I hope that they will make a further effort to reach an agreement. My heart has always been with Italy, with her great and noble history, and I recognize the immense services which she has rendered to civilization. But there is a duty that speaks louder: we cannot abandon the principles which are those of civilization. Italy has our word; but if I keep my word I require that my associates keep theirs as well.

France cannot abide by one provision of a treaty while repudiating another.

ORLANDO. I must make a statement in regard to the Italian demands. At the beginning of today's meeting, I stated that I intended to keep the discussion on the basis of President Wilson's principles, assuming that the Treaty of London would not be taken into consideration. I said, under that assumption. It is evident that if I should demand the full execution of the Treaty of London, I could not ask for Fiume on the basis of that Treaty.

For the rest, in the profound anxiety of my heart, I find the strength to protest against the charge that our attitude may be influenced in any way by a desire to achieve popularity or to arouse enthusiasm. The enthusiasm that will surge in Italy will have other sources.

I fully appreciate the tragic solemnity of the hour. For Italy there are two ways of dying: either to confine her claims to the Treaty, or to part from her friends and remain isolated in the world. If I had to choose, I should prefer death with honor. After Henry III had caused the Duke of Guise to be murdered, when he saw the corpse he exclaimed: "I did not think that he was so *great*."[3] Italy, even if a corpse, would be so great that I only hope that her dissolution may not poison her friends and the world.

LLOYD GEORGE. I shall say only a few words. I have no new arguments to

[3] The point of this remark is in the use of *grande* in Italian to denote physical size as well as moral greatness.

offer; but the situation is so serious that I wish to state the point of view of England, who also signed the Treaty of London.

The English point of view is in agreement with the French. We signed the Treaty; I am in the same position as M. Clemenceau. I recognize the force of President Wilson's arguments, but I must point out that if we had felt hesitations about the Italian claims, we should have given expression to them before Italy had lost half a million heroic lives. I have no reason to express doubts, after Italy has taken part in the war. That is why I say to Italy: England adheres to the Treaty which she has signed. But she adheres to the whole Treaty; and, in the Treaty, Fiume is assigned to Croatia. That is known to Serbia. How can we abolish one part of the Treaty and insist upon the other?

In regard to the principle of self-determination, it must be said that either it should not be applied at all or else it should be applied to the entire territory from Trieste to Spalato. However, that is not what is proposed. As to the self-determination of Fiume, even that is not clear, for if there is no doubt that the Italian population is in the majority on the right bank of the river, that is no longer the case if the population on the left bank is taken into account.

SONNINO. Even in that case the majority would be Italian.

LLOYD GEORGE. Sig. Orlando has pointed to the necessity of not dividing Istria, so as to insure the defense of Trieste, which would otherwise be within reach of enemy guns. How will the similar problem of the defense of Fiume be solved, if Fiume and only Fiume is annexed to Italy, leaving the territory to the east to Yugoslavia?

The Italian argument based on the Italian nationality of Fiume would hold only if applied to the small ancient city where the Italian population really constitutes a majority. But if you wish to annex the surrounding territory in order to secure the aforesaid defense of Fiume, the great majority of the annexed people will be Yugoslav. The population of the whole valley is about 100,000, of which only 25,000 are Italian. I do not see on what principle the annexation of Fiume to Italy could be based.

To give Fiume to Italy would be to break faith with the Serbs, it would mean ignoring the Treaty on the basis of which Italy entered the war, it would be a denial of the principles on which the Treaty of Peace is based.

We grant that the Italian losses have been very serious, indeed frightful. But so have the French losses been very serious. M. Clemenceau could arouse great enthusiasm in France by announcing that the French frontier will be on the Rhine. It is a strategic frontier which would fulfill France's ancient aspirations. There were numerous and powerful elements who advocated this solution, and M. Clemenceau had to take them into account. They can point out that France has lost a million and a half men to defend the principle of the justice of their aspirations. As to strategic arguments, I call attention to the fact that English cities have also been bombarded. The British fleet, like the Italian fleet, was unable to reach the enemy. However, the Germans were unable to transport troops across the North Sea; nor were the Austrians able to transport troops across the Adriatic. In the case of France, on the other hand, except for the Rhine which is a military obstacle, the frontier with Germany is entirely on land. If the principle of security were to be extended, we should have to revise all the principles on which the Treaty is based, beginning with France.

WILSON. France has renounced this principle.

LLOYD GEORGE. How can we apply to Italy a different principle from the one we have applied to France and Poland?

Clemenceau has hinted at the possibility that Italy would leave the Conference. That would be a very grave decision, of which I knew nothing.

For what reason? Because a city of 25,000 inhabitants has an Italian majority. Even this majority would be doubtful if the suburbs were included, and, if the surrounding country is taken into account, the Slav population would have a large preponderance.

I beg our Italian friends to consider the situation which their action would create. What would the Italians do? What would be our position? I think that Italy is wrong and is presenting an indefensible case. If a new war should occur as the result, what would be the situation? I dare not think of it. It would be inconceivable to break an alliance on such a pretext. If Italy should decide to do it, the responsibility would not be ours. We adhere to the Treaty and the responsibility would fall to those who break the Treaty.

SONNINO. But Wilson has not recognized the Treaty.

LLOYD GEORGE. I am speaking only for England. I already told Sig. Orlando some time ago that the British Cabinet has decided to stand by the Treaty.

ORLANDO. I stated that in today's discussion I should not bring up the Treaty of London. If what Lloyd George says means that the Conference recognizes the Treaty, and then reserves the liberty to settle the question of Fiume separately, I shall examine the proposal with my colleagues of the Italian Delegation and give a reply.

WILSON. That puts a heavy burden upon me, which is not fair. I do not know, nor do I feel at liberty to ask whether France and England consider the Treaty of London to be in agreement with the principles upon which the Treaty of Peace is based. But I am free to say that I, for my part, do not think so. To discuss the question on the basis of the

Pact of London would amount to adopting a secret treaty as a basis of settlement. In that case, I should be obliged to tell the world that we are trying to establish a new order from which secret treaties are ruled out. I do not see how peace can be made with Germany on different principles from peace with Austria. The Pact of London is not in agreement with the general principles of the system which we wish to establish. I know very well that the Pact of London was made under quite different circumstances and I do not wish to criticize what has been done. But it would put the United States in an impossible position to make a decision on the basis of the Pact of London.

SONNINO. I only asked for recognition of the contents of the Pact of London.

WILSON. I am ready to explain to the world the reasons for my objections, and I may find it necessary to do so. I cannot ask the United States to subscribe to principles which are in opposition to those for which it entered the war.

SONNINO. Wilson has recognized the principle of Italian security in his statement of May 21, 1918.

WILSON. I did not recognize that Dalmatia was necessary to Italian security. It is not conceivable that Italy should abandon her friends, and I beg the Italian Delegates to reëxamine the situation and not to make a hurried decision, which, if made, would be among the most tragic consequences of the war.

LLOYD GEORGE. I wish the Italians would also take this point into consideration: if they are not present on Friday, when the Germans arrive, the Allies will not be entitled to present demands for reparations on Italy's account.

WILSON. Once more I appeal to the Italians to take time to consider their decision.

CLEMENCEAU remarks that there are urgent questions to be decided in regard to the Treaty with Germany; changes may have to be made in the event of Italy's withdrawal.

LLOYD GEORGE speaks of possible changes in regard to reparations.

The next meeting is set for to-morrow, Sunday, at 10 A.M.

.   .   .   .

The meeting is adjourned at 2 P.M.

Sunday, April 20. Easter Day.[4]

Meeting at 10 o'clock at Wilson's residence. The "Four" and Sonnino, Mantoux, Hankey, and I are present.

[4] Cf. Minutes of the Council, April 20, I.C. 174A.

WILSON (turning to the Italian delegates). I should be glad to know the proposals which you intend to make.

ORLANDO reads the following statement:

"I must maintain all the declarations I have made with respect to the question of Fiume. Reducing it to its minimum terms, I shall point out to President Wilson that from the standpoint of his noble wish to preserve peace in the world, he is too eminent a political man not to realize that one of the essential prerequisites to the achievement of this purpose is to avoid the feeling between peoples that they have suffered an injustice, for that feeling will doubtless constitute the most likely cause of future wars. I assert here that if Fiume is not given to Italy, there will arise in the Italian people so violent a reaction of protest and hatred that it will cause violent conflicts in the more or less near future.

"I therefore believe that the fact of denying Fiume to Italy would be equally fatal to the interests of Italy and to the peace of the world.

"However, since the English and French Allies declared yesterday that they do not recognize the right of Italy to break the Alliance unless she be not granted what is guaranteed to her by the Treaty of Alliance, I feel too deeply my responsibility toward the peace of the world in the event of a breach of the Alliance, and I must protect myself against any possible accusation in this respect. I therefore formally declare that in the event of the Peace Conference guaranteeing to Italy all the rights which the Treaty of London assured to her, I should not be obliged to break the Alliance, and I would abstain from any act or deed which could have this significance."

There follows a prolonged silence.

WILSON. It is incredible to me that the Italian representatives should take this position. At the center of the war there were three Great Powers: France, Great Britain, and Italy. It is they who have borne the main burden of the war. The whole world realizes that it is they who saved it from the designs of the Central Powers; but the war was not won by them alone. Other Powers entered the war, who were not bound by the Treaty of London. I may be allowed to say that without the financial and material assistance of the United States, it would not have been possible to bring the war to an end in this manner or at least at this time. (Clemenceau and Lloyd George express their approval.) Now, when the United States entered the war, she declared what her principles were; these contained certain expressions of sympathy toward small nations, and were also acclaimed by the peoples of the Great Powers. When I made those statements, I did not even for a moment think that they were my own statements, but rather those of the North American people. These would not have had the influence which they had, had they not expressed the feelings of the American people; they do not represent my own personal initiative. But the fact that the principles of right and justice, which first Lloyd George, and then I, proclaimed were considered as interpreting the real significance of the war, led other peoples to enter the war. Now I wish to recall what these principles are, the object of which was not to exclude any legitimate national aspiration. Here are two of the so-called Fourteen Points:

Point XI.—Rumania, Serbia, and Montenegro should be evacuated; occupied territories restored; Serbia accorded free and secure access to the sea; and the relations of the several Balkan States to one another determined by friendly counsel along historically established lines of allegiance and nationality; and international guarantees of the political and economic independence and territorial integrity of the several Balkan States should be entered into.

Point IX.—A readjustment of the frontiers of Italy should be effected along clearly recognizable lines of nationality.

We have sought to accomplish both these purposes. If we do not act in accordance with them, but should adopt instead the Treaty which Italy invokes, we should create antagonisms which would never be extinguished until we had reëstablished matters on a different basis. If Italy insists upon the execution of the Treaty, she will be putting off the conclusion of peace. My attitude would have been different if Austria-Hungary had continued to exist and if Italy were still faced with a great hostile Empire; in that case I would have said that Italy ought to have every guarantee of security; but such is not the case. If the signatories of the Treaty may not withdraw, others are free to do so. I want to ask my Italian friends if they wish to do this: are they determined to reduce the probability of making peace with Germany; to renew the possibility of a general war in Europe; to alienate from Italy the peoples who were her enthusiastic friends; are they prepared to say that they are not willing to enter the new order of things because they are not able to perpetuate the old? I think that what Italy is receiving is a great and glorious thing. Without the Pact of London she secures her national frontiers and she redeems her subjected people. That is a dream which she could not have hoped to realize at the beginning of the war, five years ago. The dream has been made reality through the valor of the Italian soldiers and the united force of the world. I cannot believe that we could part.

That would be the supreme tragedy of the war, if you should turn away from your friends and isolate yourselves. I should deplore it. My heart would be torn. But I am the representative of the United States and I cannot violate the principles which my fellow citizens have entrusted me to defend.

ORLANDO. I must declare to President Wilson that I have made use of the Treaty of London only as a last resort and most unwillingly. I did it in reply to the urgings of Lloyd George and Clemenceau, who appealed to the alliance and said that in breaking the alliance I should be assuming too great a responsibility toward Allies who were ready to fulfill their obligations. President Wilson must do me this justice; I have done what I could to prove to him that the Italian claims were wholly within the limits of justice. If I have been compelled to appeal to the text of the Treaty instead of to justice, I have done it with deep regret. Moreover, Italy is not intransigent. What concession has been offered me? Nothing. What is the situation of Italy? Wilson has pointed to his obligations; but he recognized yesterday that those of his points referring to Austria-Hungary no longer applied, owing to the fact that Austria-Hungary no longer exists.

WILSON. I agree.

ORLANDO. Let us examine the point referring to Serbia which he quoted this morning. Does it give Serbia a claim to Fiume? All the aspirations of access to the sea which Serbia formerly entertained did not go beyond Alessio and San Giovanni di Medua at the most. It would have been beyond her hopes to obtain Ragusa. They are now getting much more. I would ask President Wilson to remember two things:

1) Of all the principles which have been declared inapplicable to Austria-Hungary, after her disappearance, are only those affecting Italy to remain in force?

2) As to the point which affects her, Italy made clear reservations and made them in the presence of Colonel House, who offered no objections. I am therefore not bound by any commitment in opposition to my claims, nor is President Wilson. Wilson says with great feeling that the war was fought for justice and right. I believe that my claims are made on that ground. I make no exclusive claim to absolute truth. The idea of justice is subjective. Jesus said: *Quid est veritas?* I respect the opinions of Wilson, but, on my honor and conscientiously, I believe in the greatest good faith that I am on the side of right and justice. I too have fought the war for right and justice. Wilson concluded by saying how anxious he was at the thought of parting from Italy. I thank him, but I can only say that I am even more disturbed myself. I share his feelings: feelings of loyal and affectionate friendship between the two peoples, and also, I dare say, between their two representatives.

WILSON. Certainly.

ORLANDO. But I also have feelings of extreme anxiety which are not his. I am confronted by terrible difficulties and by the horror of what may happen to my country. But it is because I am convinced that what I am asking is in agreement with right and justice that I must defy everything, even the gravest consequences, and even death if necessary, if I and my country must die for the cause of right and justice.

(Orlando is so distressed that he sobs for a long while.)

WILSON. Sig. Orlando may rest assured that I do not conceal from myself the value of the motives which he has expounded. There is only between us a fundamental political difference. The Italian representatives are not bound by the Fourteen Points. I have recognized that, but I only insist in saying that, so far as I am concerned, I cannot make peace with Germany on the basis of certain principles and with Austria on the basis of other principles. We must apply to all the principle of national self-determination which we have sought to apply in other parts of the world.

LLOYD GEORGE. We are in a more difficult position than when the Conference began. We have had difficulties and have been able to surmount them; but each time we had a choice between at least half a dozen different solutions. Here I see no way out. On one side we hear that Italy cannot agree with her Allies in making peace with Austria-Hungary and Germany because of the questions of the Adriatic and the Trentino. There is the other difficulty that the United States cannot agree to the Italian demands on account of the principles for which it entered the war. On both sides the matter is serious. Personally I am not free to discuss the merits of the issue, for I respect the obligations assumed by my country and which Italy has honored with blood, money, and sacrifices. No one appreciates better than I the Wilsonian principles. It is a serious thing for Italy to make peace and have Germans in the Tyrol and Slavs in Dalmatia, but I have no right to interfere. I have expressed to Wilson the point of view that the Italian political leaders cannot turn back. I am impressed by what Orlando has said. I particularly sympathize with Baron Sonnino. He has been in the war from the beginning. He assumed the grave responsibility of refusing what Austria was offering in order to maintain Italian neutrality. He cannot go back to Italy without having secured what he could have obtained from Bülow without going to war. Italy has lost half a million men and has had a million and a half wounded and disabled. I do not know how Sonnino could turn back. I do not see what we can do.

I suggest that the signatories of the Treaty of London hold a separate meeting to examine Wilson's grave declaration. If we cannot find a way out, England will keep its obligations. I have no suggestions to make, but perhaps we may find something at the meeting of the signatories of the Pact of London. That is all I can say at the moment. What does President Wilson think of it?

WILSON. It is our duty to find, if possible, a means of conciliation. If I were to suggest that Fiume be given to the Serbo-Croats, as is stated in the

Pact of London, and that Dalmatia, as understood in the Pact of London, be temporarily handed over to the five Powers for future disposition, without, however, any guarantee that it will ultimately be ceded to Italy, could the Italian representatives accept this proposal? I recall that there is a strategic point which I would cede to Italy, namely Lissa. I recognize that this is little by comparison with the Pact of London. I should not be candid, however, if I did not tell the Italians that it is highly improbable that the United States would consent in the future to the cession to Italy of the islands and of the rest of the territory designated in the Pact of London.

LLOYD GEORGE. I should like to consider this. The signatories of the Treaty of London might meet tomorrow.

ORLANDO. I see no difficulty in that.

SONNINO. It is our duty.

LLOYD GEORGE. I give notice at once, however, that I have no proposal to make.

SONNINO. I thank Lloyd George for the way in which he has presented the matter, and particularly my own position. We must do everything possible to find a compromise. I do not see any way out; it has been said that there is not any, and that this is the death of me. I do not mean physical death, which is not important, but moral death. I am not in the least concerned by this; I am thinking only of my country. It will be said that I ruined my country; nothing could disturb me more than that. I have sought to do my duty and I have been mistaken; but do not think of me.

LLOYD GEORGE. No, that is an essential point. Italy might not have gone to war, accepting what was being offered her by Austria-Hungary, but she decided otherwise. That must be recognized as of the greatest importance.

WILSON. When I saw him at first, Sonnino told me that Italy had no imperialistic designs. I believe it. I have never doubted it for a moment. The men who govern Italy certainly do not entertain ideas of aggression: as to the Yugoslavs I do not know. I appreciate, like Lloyd George, the tragic situation in which you find yourself, Baron Sonnino. You have fully lived up to the reputation for uprightness, which I had heard ascribed to you. I must say this, for general as well as for personal reasons.

SONNINO. I appreciate the intention. In regard to the question of imperialism, there is nothing in our claims having such a character. There is nothing but the wish to insure the security of our country. What we are asking for is not imperialistic. We do not want anything that constitutes a menace to our neighbors. With respect to Greece, we have already shown that we are ready to accept a conciliating solution. But our claims aim at freeing us from dangers. Take the question of the Balkans. All we are seeking is to keep out of difficulty. We are looking for a settlement that may keep us out of their quarrels: if we do not secure those territories, we shall always have to be mixed up in them. Serbia threatens us: we shall therefore have to ally ourselves with Bulgaria. The purpose of the whole policy of the Pact of London was to keep us from the dangers of being attacked, and to keep from us the temptation to attack others in order to forestall a danger.

LLOYD GEORGE (smiling). Italy has even invaded Great Britain!

SONNINO. Yes, but it has left civilization there.

LLOYD GEORGE. I trust that some of it has remained.

SONNINO. Those are old things. In the course of centuries Italy has been invaded by foreigners: Spaniards, Germans, etc. The present was a chance to free ourselves from any danger.

WILSON. If I thought that what you are asking was necessary to give you security, I should grant it to you.

SONNINO. Ask your experts. You cannot say that Fiume offers any possibilities of aggression.

LLOYD GEORGE. Fiume, in the Pact, is assigned to the Croats.

SONNINO. But the issue of Fiume has appeared as the result of national feeling intensified by the war. Fiume has decided for itself. If you can show that one of our claims constitutes a danger to our neighbors, I shall admit that you are right. Look at the Pact of London. We have given up Spalato with one of the large islands, Brazza; likewise we have given up Veglia and Arbe, which are Italian, and we have yielded on the port of Segna; we have done the same for the peninsula which is in front of Metković. I do not see what more we could do. It would be easy to govern the world with only three principles; but there are enormous difficulties when it comes to applying them in varied circumstances.

It is decided that a meeting of the Heads of the Allied Governments, accompanied by their respective Foreign Ministers, will be held to-morrow at 10 o'clock at Lloyd George's residence.

Monday, April 21.

Morning meeting at 10 o'clock at Lloyd George's, 23, rue Nitot; present, the three Allied Prime Ministers with their respective Foreign Ministers, Balfour, Pichon, and Sonnino. Hankey and I as secretaries; Mantoux as interpreter.

CLEMENCEAU. I spoke this morning with Pichon, and I am confirmed in the opinion that France, having signed a Treaty, will adhere to it. We shall therefore stand together as Allies.

LLOYD GEORGE. There is no doubt about this; but there is no use denying that it would be a serious matter if America did not sign the peace. In the territories claimed by Italy, there are two alien races: the Germans in the Trentino and the Slavs in Dalmatia. If the United States does not participate in the peace, the impression will be given that it is in sympathy with these two strong races, and every time that a difficulty arises between them and Italy, this difficulty will be magnified tenfold by that factor. On the other hand, I do not know how Europe can be rehabilitated if the United States does not remain with us and assist us. After the conclusion of the Treaty, I intend to make a proposal for a general European economic league. If we do not succeed in this, there will occur complete stagnation. I can cite the case of South Africa. After having won that war, the victorious country, while Balfour was Prime Minister, had to spend £30,000,000 to restore the conquered country.

BALFOUR. And this money was never paid back.

LLOYD GEORGE. But if it had not been spent, South Africa would have remained a devastated country. There is a similar situation in Europe. For that reason we must stay with the Americans to the end, and be perfectly honest with them. In regard to reparations, the Americans have moved a long way from their original position. Likewise in the case of the Saar. It might be possible to obtain a similarly favorable result, by being able to show concessions on the part of Italy. If, however, the Italians do not see their way to making concessions, we shall stand by the Treaty.

CLEMENCEAU. That is also my case. I have already discussed the question with Lloyd George, and I subscribe to everything he has said. I thought it might be possible to reach a compromise; but I have lost that hope in regard to Fiume. President Wilson put out a feeler regarding Dalmatia, but I must recognize that the situation is not improved. I saw Wilson again yesterday afternoon in connection with other matters, and, when the Italian question was mentioned at the end of our conversation, I received the impression of a man who has taken a very firm position. A solution might be found if Italy gave up Dalmatia for Fiume, or if, being content with Dalmatia, she tried to obtain some other concession.

The offers made by Austria-Hungary to Italy before her entrance into the war were mentioned yesterday. I looked them up this morning in the Green Book. I was hoping to find there arguments against Wilson; but I found that we could not use that argument because Austria-Hungary offered little or nothing. She did not give either Istria or Trieste.

BALFOUR. Nor Pola.

CLEMENCEAU. What Italy is obtaining now represents a great improvement upon the Austro-Hungarian offer.

SONNINO. The Green Book only goes to May 4; between that day and the twenty-fourth Austria made further offers.

CLEMENCEAU. Yes, but she did not offer Trieste. We cannot find there arguments to convince Wilson. We are here among friends and are giving advice to friends. Even without obtaining the whole of Dalmatia, but only certain points in it, you could secure just as easily a sufficiently strong position. Look at the French problem. I had to give up the left bank of the Rhine, which all the Senators and all the Deputies were asking me to secure. I gave up the idea of having the frontier of 1815 with Cologne, Coblenz, Mayence, and the other points beyond the Rhine. It is true that as the result of these concessions I am not sure that I can save my political life; but I give this as an example. If Italy coöperates with us to the end of these negotiations, she will secure certain advantages. Territorially, she is getting greater concessions than the Italians contemplated at the beginning of the war. I cannot give advice, but it is my duty to say that if we start on the path of compromise a solution may be found; otherwise the consequences will be deplorable. If Italy isolates herself, the work of the Entente will not be complete; the main problems will not be solved; there will be in Europe new dissensions which I should wish to avoid at all costs. In conclusion, we remain Italy's friends and the solution lies in her hands.

SONNINO. That is not quite so. Wilson says that he will not give Fiume, nor does he give Dalmatia. Dalmatia would be given to the five Powers; but he has clearly ruled out the possibility of its being later given to Italy. On the other hand, how can peace be made with an Austria-Hungary that does not exist? You undertook toward us the obligations of a treaty in connection with our entrance into the war, which has cost Italy seventy billions, and a million and a half men, dead or disabled. Why should Italy be frustrated in her expectations? Why did not Wilson speak clearly sooner? When the line of the Pact of London was accepted as the line of occupation of the Armistice, the impression was created in Italy that the Pact of London would also be recognized by America. In fact America did not protest or oppose herself. That was taken to imply approval.

LLOYD GEORGE (to Balfour). Did we give Wilson a copy of the Pact of London?

BALFOUR. Yes. I discussed it with him when I was in America.

SONNINO. What happened since then? And first of all, what did America do for our country? It is true that she gave us money, but she gave us only one regiment and only one American died in Italy.

CLEMENCEAU. That is not an argument.

SONNINO. It is; I am ony speaking in general, not against the United States. Italy knows that she had to face the whole Austro-Hungarian army. She had made definite agreements with the Allies. Now comes a third party who says that we must give up all this. And that, because of new principles in which Wilson believes but I do not. Will diplomats sitting in a room ever be able to change the world? Try to experiment with the Fourteen Points in the Balkans. It would be deceiving our people. When I returned to Rome, I did it as unobtrusively as possible, and when people came to applaud me at my house, I avoided them, because I could see the difficulties which Italy was about to meet. Now President Wilson, after having forgotten and violated many times his Fourteen Points, wants to restore their virginity by enforcing rigorously those which apply to Italy. What will be the impression in our country, after people have been led to believe for five months that their aspirations would be satisfied? All that is to disappear because there is a League of Nations, about which no one yet knows anything. What will happen in the country? We shall have, not Russian bolshevism, but anarchy. I do not know what we can do. I see no solution.

For five years I have not entertained a thought, nor uttered a word to any one—whatever the Emperor Charles of Hapsburg may say—which was not strictly in line with the path which Italy had chosen, and I have led Italy to these results!

LLOYD GEORGE. I do not wish to be misunderstood if I make a new proposal. I have read the memorandum which you submitted, explaining the reasons that make Dalmatia necessary to your defense in the Adriatic. There is no doubt that the arguments presented there have great force. But the main threat comes from the islands of the other shore, behind which an enemy fleet could conceal itself, thus constituting a danger, even though that fleet were small. On the other hand, you will never have peace if you hold the mainland.

SONNINO. There are so many sources of friction in the Balkans that we shall be left in peace.

LLOYD GEORGE. But there are always too many people there that want to cut each other's throats. You would have difficulties for many generations. You would have to maintain a powerful force in Dalmatia. Could you not hold the islands alone, offering to the inhabitants who wished it to transfer them to the mainland? The Yugoslavs are deficient in manpower, many people have been killed in their country. I should advise you to hold the islands and to leave the mainland alone.

SONNINO. I do not say that there may not be agitation in the territories conquered by us if the Yugoslavs foster it. That is inevitable with territorial changes. But if everything is settled definitively, in two years all agitation will cease.

LLOYD GEORGE. Your statistics show that there are 600,000 Slavs as against 40,000 Italians.

SONNINO. In all Dalmatia; not in the part that we claim.

ORLANDO. I wish to say a few things. In the first place, I want to explain the reasons for our resistance, which in some respects we must maintain at all costs. There is a practical reason, of interest to the whole world. If I should go back to Italy with a mutilated peace, which should cause a revolution, that would be dangerous to everybody. If I go back to Italy with Wilson's peace, there will be a revolution in Italy. During the latest manifestations in Rome . . .

SONNINO. . . . and in Milan

ORLANDO. . . . two parties faced each other: the Bolshevik party, of those who deny their country, against the patriotic Fascist party. The latter prevailed. There were two killed and five wounded among the Bolsheviks. The office of the *Avanti* was sacked and burned! The patriotic movement is very strong. What would happen if we have an unsatisfactory peace is that these patriotic elements will work for revolution, and the Bolsheviks will assist them, for their policy—whatever their motive—is to promote disorders and revolutions, in order to exploit the consequences. You may be certain of this. If, on the other hand, Italy receives satisfaction in her national claims, she will certainly remain quiet. I guarantee that. But if there should be a revolution in Italy, in the present state of the world, that would constitute a danger for everybody.

Secondly, I must say that I could not accept the proposal of President Wilson, even as a basis of discussion. I want to add one thing. The line which President Wilson is now giving to Italy is the very one proposed last October by the *New Europe*, which, as you know, is the Yugoslav organ. For the Italians, the Yugoslavs are what the *boches* are for you. To accept Wilson's proposal would be equivalent to Clemenceau's accepting a solution of the war proposed by the *boches*. I had a conversation with President Wilson in January. Showing me a map he said: what do you think of this possibility? The line in question was the one I have referred to. I replied: "I must ask you to consider that, confronted by such an offer, Italy would have no choice but to withdraw from the Conference." Wilson stopped the interpreter and asked: "Sig. Orlando means that in that case he would withdraw from the Conference?" I replied: "Exactly." This happened last January. For three months I have remained in a false position. While I have collaborated with the greatest good will in all the negotiations that have taken place, there has remained between Wilson and myself a fundamental misunderstanding which had its origin in that first conversation. Perhaps misunderstanding is not the word, for each of us knew exactly the thought of the other. Now Lloyd George suggests that we seek a compromise. I would do so gladly, but I see none. I admire Lloyd George in many ways, not least for his inventiveness in finding solutions. If he succeeds in reaching with Wilson a decent arrangement, which I can get accepted in my country, I am ready to consider it. Our joint meetings no longer serve any purpose; we are always at the same point, when the four of us meet, and do not budge from beginning to end. If Lloyd George and Clemenceau, in agreement with Wilson, present to me a conciliatory proposal, which would necessarily have to include the annexation of Fiume to Italy, I am prepared to consider it.

CLEMENCEAU. There is one point I should like to clear up. Would Orlando accept a solution that would eliminate Fiume?

ORLANDO. Definitely the opposite. I think it better to say it explicitly than to allow doubts on the subject to subsist. If possible, so much the better. If not, it is better for everybody to put an end to an embarrassing and vexatious situation. In that case we should have to ask for the Pact of London pure and simple; the Allies have committed themselves to its execution, and until it is fulfilled we shall remain aside by ourselves.

PICHON. Have you not examined any definite proposal of conciliation?

ORLANDO. No. It is up to you to state precisely what we must give in order to obtain Fiume. We must have Fiume.

LLOYD GEORGE. That puts an end to the discussion. You cannot ask for Fiume; that is impossible. The Serbs know that it has been assigned to them and I cannot betray them any more than I can betray the Italians.

CLEMENCEAU. Do you, then, or do you not, stand on the Pact? There can be no middle way. I have given Fiume to the Serbs and I cannot take it back.

ORLANDO. We stand on the Treaty.

CLEMENCEAU. If Orlando stands on the Treaty, so shall we. But I cannot withdraw the promise of Fiume to the Serbs.

ORLANDO. I am asking for a compromise outside the Treaty.

LLOYD GEORGE (presenting an English map attached to the Treaty, in which Fiume is marked yellow and Italy blue). We have agreed to one clause of the Treaty as much as to the other.

SONNINO. Let me explain what President Orlando means. What he is saying is this: if everything is to be put in the balance in order to find the basis of a compromise with you, then I do not insist upon the Treaty only. Otherwise he stands on the Treaty. I recall that when negotiations were taking place with Bulgaria, with a view to her going to war on the side of the Entente, the cession to Bulgaria of certain Macedonian territories was proposed to Serbia, who would then have been compensated with Croatian and Bosnian territory. No agreement was reached then. But that means that at that time you did not consider yourselves bound to Serbia by the Treaty of London. Moreover, the Treaty of London gives Fiume to Croatia and not to Serbia.

CLEMENCEAU. That is the same thing.

LLOYD GEORGE. I do not know that there is any point in prolonging this conversation. It would be better perhaps if Clemenceau and I went to see Wilson to ask him whether and how far he can move from the position he has taken; if he would agree to the cession of the islands for example.

ORLANDO. What about Fiume?

LLOYD GEORGE. Not Fiume.

ORLANDO. Then it is impossible.

SONNINO. Must we then give up Dalmatia for nothing? In regard to Dalmatia I repeat that it constitutes for us a question of security in the Adriatic. But there is also the ethnic question for Dalmatia. It is true that the rural population is predominantly Slav, but the cities are Italian. All that there is of civilization there is Italian.

LLOYD GEORGE. Granted.

SONNINO. We cannot abandon all these fellow countrymen of ours and throw away our historic rights. Wilson said that national reasons must prevail over all others, even over strategic railroad reasons, when he denied to Belgium the annexation of 4,000 Germans. Why should we renounce the 26,000 or 30,000 Italians of Fiume? The same reasons apply for our fellow countrymen in Dalmatia.

LLOYD GEORGE. But in the case of Belgium the Germans were in direct contact with Germany, which is not the case of the small Italian nuclei in Dalmatia, who are garrisoned there, to use an expression adopted by the English for Ireland.

SONNINO. But the Italians represent all the civilization that is there.

LLOYD GEORGE. That is what the English say of Ireland.

BALFOUR. If you consider the difficulties which Wilson has found in solving the Italian question, you must realize that he will have great difficulty in conceding to you the Germans which you would annex in the Tyrol.

SONNINO. He has already given them to us.

BALFOUR. I did not know that; I am very glad of it.

LLOYD GEORGE. I repeat: I do not see that there is any point in continuing the discussion among ourselves. However, the matter seems to me so serious that I think it necessary to broach it again with Wilson.

BALFOUR. There is an important point which does not seem to have been considered. Orlando says that if he goes back to Italy without his claims there will be a revolution.

ORLANDO. Absolutely.

BALFOUR. It should be considered that if Italy alienates America I do not see how her economic life can maintain itself and how, if that is so, the revolution could be put down in that case. Italy would thus have a revolution whether she accepts a treaty that denies her the territories which she claims or whether she refuses such a treaty. She would have a revolution in any case. She would remain isolated and in opposition to all of Europe, which seems to me quite impossible.

ORLANDO. I quite realize the truth of what Balfour has said. The two dangers are equally serious. But Italy is sane. We are familiar with the art of starvation. But if both dangers are equally serious and are both likely to be fatal, I prefer the side of death with honor.

. . . .

Tuesday, April 22.

[In the morning, the Italian delegation approved the text of a letter asking for the execution of the Treaty of London. At 2 o'clock Orlando went to see Lloyd George, to whom he read the letter.]

Having heard the contents of the letter, Lloyd George asks: What does that mean? That you would not come to Versailles with us when the Germans are there?

ORLANDO. Precisely.

LLOYD GEORGE. What will be the consequences? Does it mean that you will not make peace with Germany?

ORLANDO. No, we shall come for the general peace.

LLOYD GEORGE. But in the meantime?

ORLANDO. In the meantime, until our problems have been settled, we shall remain aside.

LLOYD GEORGE. But that will also prevent the rest of us from negotiating, since there are provisions which you have not yet approved and which need your consent, and we cannot adopt them without you.

ORLANDO. Put yourself in my position and tell me what you would do. Our situation is very serious.

LLOYD GEORGE. I recognize that, but you must consider the disastrous consequences to which you would lead your Allies; and besides, it is not conceivable that they should not be able to sign the Treaty with Germany, even without you, and should have to wait for the questions concerning Bulgaria and Turkey to be settled also.

ORLANDO. The Declaration of London establishes that there shall be a single general peace.

LLOYD GEORGE. Yes, but as it is not possible to make peace also with Austria-Hungary which has disappeared, you will not be able to prevent us from signing a treaty with Germany in the meantime.

ORLANDO. I ask you: what would be the position of Italy if I should sign the German Treaty? The same difficulty with which we are confronted at the present moment would not be any different a month from now, and I do not see why, if it is to be solved then, it could not as well be settled now.

LLOYD GEORGE. I wish to point out that the situation is very serious; not only Italy but all Europe needs America. Europe cannot live without America. I will tell you confidentially that President Wilson, who seemed to be very irritated and obstinate last night, is in an absolutely hostile and immovable frame of mind. In order to make him accept the proposal of the islands we had, Clemenceau and I, to have recourse to House, who only succeeded with great difficulty. We were then informed of a document which Wilson wanted to address to Clemenceau and myself, and which would have been given to the press last night for publication this morning, had we not asked the President to postpone it for forty-eight hours in order to find out if some compromise could not be evolved with respect to the Italian problem. You may imagine to what sensation such a publication would give rise, and how the peoples of the various countries would take the side of their own representatives against the others, to the common detriment. Such a step would be irreparable.

ORLANDO. I do not see what arguments against us such a statement from Wilson could produce.

LLOYD GEORGE. I know it, but in any case, the passions that would be aroused could no longer be controlled.

ORLANDO. You have spoken of the possibility of solutions, but will you tell me frankly if a solution has ever been proposed which was even remotely acceptable? Wilson did make some proposals for Fiume (on the order of the statute of Danzig), and for Dalmatia (on the order of the régime of the Saar), but they were subsequently withdrawn. We have three questions to settle; Fiume, the islands, and the Dalmatian mainland.

LLOYD GEORGE. I admit that the proposals were made separately from one another, but do you think that they might become a basis of discussion if they were presented again together?

ORLANDO. We could consider the matter.

LLOYD GEORGE. I shall take it up again with Wilson and I shall try my best to induce him to accept a satisfactory arrangement on that basis, which would involve the line of the Alps to Volosca for Italy as in the Treaty of London; Fiume under a régime analogous to that of Danzig, with its diplomatic representation to Italy, and within the Italian customs system; the islands, at least the more important ones strategically, to Italy; Zara, Sebenico, Traù, and Spalato free cities, pending a plebiscite, under a régime analogous to that of the Saar. I shall speak to Wilson before 3 o'clock and let you know something about 6:30.

Wednesday, April 23.[5]

Thursday, April 24.
At 10:30 Lloyd George comes to see Orlando.

LLOYD GEORGE. I assure you that it was a great surprise to me to see the publication yesterday of the statement made by Wilson, when I understood that it was not to take place until this morning. That is why I sent my communication to you through Kerr at 3 o'clock.

ORLANDO. I have prepared a reply to President Wilson's message.

LLOYD GEORGE. Do you mention Fiume in that reply?

ORLANDO. Yes.

LLOYD GEORGE. You must consider that that puts you in a very delicate position, even toward us. As you know, the Treaty of London gives Fiume to the Croats, and France and England cannot take it away from them and give it to you. You must consider that it would be serious for Italy to insist on the necessity of having this territory and then to have to evacuate it at the request of the Allies. On the other hand, if you did not evacuate it, you would be breaking the Treaty, with all the consequences that this action would have.

ORLANDO. I speak of Fiume only because Wilson speaks of it in his Message, and I answer his arguments with my own. But I intend to keep faith with the Allies, and while I am leaving Paris for the reasons which you know, I do not intend in any way to break the Alliance.

LLOYD GEORGE. Your departure is none the less a very serious fact, for it coincides with the arrival of the enemy, who is coming to sign peace. I consider your action very detrimental and I should like everything done to avoid it.

ORLANDO. I do not see what might be done.

LLOYD GEORGE. Do you not think that a last attempt might be made to try to find a solution during the day?

ORLANDO. It seems difficult to succeed in this in a few hours.

LLOYD GEORGE. I am also thinking of the serious situation which would grow out of a break between you and America. Italy and Europe are in absolute need of America, and a break with you may lead to the most serious consequences. I am afraid that the publication of Wilson's message in Italy may lead to manifestations and outbursts of passion which will be very harmful in the present circumstances. If it could be

[5] Wilson's Manifesto appeared in the evening of the twenty-third. For the meeting of the Three on the twenty-third, cf. Minutes of the Council, April 23, I.C. 175F. The Italians did not attend this meeting.

announced that negotiations have been resumed, or, better still, that an agreement has been reached, at the time of the publication of the message or shortly thereafter, the situation might still be saved.

ORLANDO. I appreciate the weight of your advice and I might find it possible to remain a few days. But it would be necessary to issue a *communiqué* showing that you and Clemenceau have asked me to remain.

LLOYD GEORGE. I see no difficulty in that. It could be worded thus: "At the request of M. Clemenceau and Mr. Lloyd George, Sig. Orlando has consented to delay his departure from Paris, in order to resume negotiations which may lead to the solution of the questions of Dalmatia and of Fiume."

ORLANDO. Very well. I think it would be better to add to the *communiqué* "at the request of President Wilson."

. . . .

[The Italians went to a meeting of the Council at 4 o'clock.][6]

LLOYD GEORGE asks Orlando if he has a suggestion to make.

ORLANDO. I must declare that I have examined the situation, which is undoubtedly serious, with the greatest care. I have already spoken twice by telephone with my colleagues in Rome, and I must say that the situation is very painful. There is, in fact, a question which comes even before the territorial problem, namely that of the effect produced by President Wilson's message. I must say that my high opinion of President Wilson and my personal friendship for him, of which I have sought to give him all possible proof, lead me to believe that his intentions in addressing his message to me could not have been other than friendly. But in politics the public reaction is often more important than the real substance of things. The document contains nothing which is not friendly and courteous, but it gives the impression that this appeal to the Italian people, and to the other peoples concerned, has the effect of putting in doubt—even if it was not intended to do so—my authority as representative of the Italian people. That is the common impression in Italy and in Rome; it puts me in a delicate position and for that reason I must go back to the source of my authority. My decision to leave does not relate to the territorial questions themselves; I have no idea of causing a break, but I must go back to my people to find out what authority I have for remaining at the Conference. The territorial questions are of secondary importance. You might grant what I was asking yesterday, but I am no longer in a position to accept it. I should have to say that I am obliged to go to Rome. I must make sure of what my

[6] Cf. Minutes of the Council, April 24, I.C. 176C.

power is. I am not certain, after what has happened, that I have a right to accept or to refuse anything.

WILSON. Sig Orlando has admirably stated his position, and I can assure him of the reciprocity of the feelings which he has expressed toward me. I can have nothing but respect for what he has said. Nothing will ever be able to influence our relations, but I find very gracious the manner in which he has expressed himself, and I thank him for it.

There is one aspect of the matter which was never part of my intent, and that was making an appeal to the Italian people against him. That thought never occurred to me. I take this opportunity to state the motives which have led me to make this publication. I must recall to Sig. Orlando that my attitude in this matter has been the same from the very beginning. Throughout these months there were doubts among the public who had no part in the discussion. Things were published in the French, the Italian, and the American press which put me and my people in a false light, and it was necessary for me to make this statement in order to show my people what the principles are on which my conduct is based. It was also necessary to consider the impression given to the other states as a result of these arbitrary interpretations. I am very glad of what Sig. Orlando has said in regard to the significance of his journey to Rome, as well as of his intention not to break with the Allies and Associates. It would be a fatal thing if the great Kingdom of Italy should withdraw from the Conference at the moment of signing peace with Germany, and I am glad to know the motive of Orlando's visit to Rome. Once there, he will make his views known. He has given me his impressions and I understand his wish to find out what his people want. I hope and I expect that the reasons for his return to Rome will be made public; that is, his wish to clarify the situation, and not to withdraw from the Conference at this critical moment.

ORLANDO. I thank President Wilson for his noble declaration. It was kind and gracious of him to give me these explanations, since I had already said that I excluded the possibility of any unfriendly intentions toward me, and to appreciate so justly the reasons for my departure. To speak quite frankly, I may add that, even if this situation had not arisen, it might have been well for me to reëstablish contact with my people. I remember that at one time President Wilson himself had suggested my going to Rome to explain there the position of Italy at the Conference. That has now become a necessity. This necessity, which was implicit, has been made public by the publication of the message. We have differences over questions which experience has shown to be irreconcilable. I wish to inform my people, and it is to my interest to put off a solution. I shall explain the situation, from the standpoint of the agreements which would meet with President Wilson's approval and from that of adhering to the Pact of London. I am speaking as friend to friend. Italy had made Fiume into a national issue. America and the Allies have declared that they could not agree. It will thus be up to the Italian people to decide. They will have to see whether they can consent to this sacrifice; the situation remains very serious, but it will have been clarified; we shall at least have that advantage.

WILSON. I should like to ask Sig. Orlando to be so kind as to explain also, in his statement before Parliament, the position of the United States, which feels that adherence to the Pact of London is not in the interest of relations between Italy and Yugoslavia, nor in that of world peace. Much as I may wish to reach an agreement, I must be honest and make this reservation.

ORLANDO. In my statement before the Chamber, I shall not only refer to the terms of President Wilson's message, but also to what I have gathered from my private conversations with him, as well as from the memorandum which he gave me on a recent occasion, and allowed me to use in the Italian Parliament.

CLEMENCEAU. I wish to explain my point of view, which is also that of Mr. Lloyd George, in regard to Fiume. The Treaty of London has committed us to giving certain territories to Italy, but also to giving Fiume to the Slavs. If we cannot break our word with Italy, neither can we do so with the Slavs.

LLOYD GEORGE. I agree. But in addition to this, it cannot be denied that since the signing of the Treaty of London, a new element has intervened: the participation of the United States, which is absolutely free of any agreements with or commitments to the rest of the world. That does not alter our views on the Pact of London; but, under certain circumstances, it might lead to a reconsideration of the case of Fiume. In view of the events that have taken place, I feel free to assume the responsibility of modifying the Pact of London in regard to Fiume. The Treaty of London gave Fiume to Croatia. If Italy consents to a modification on her part in regard to Dalmatia, we shall be free to make a modification with respect to Fiume. This modification would consist in making it a free port, under the control of its Italian, Hungarian, and Slav population, with equally free access for all the hinterland served by the port. Within these limits, I feel free to modify the Pact of London, if the Allies agree. I cannot ask Sig. Orlando not to go to Rome; I myself recently had to go to London for far less serious reasons; but I should like to know what will be the position of Italy in the meantime. If this were an ordinary week, Sig. Orlando's absence would cause no inconvenience, but the Germans will probably be here on Tuesday. Our major enemy, the only enemy still surviving, will be here. If Orlando is away, will Sonnino be here? When will Orlando be able to meet Parliament?

ORLANDO. I could call it for the twenty-eighth.

LLOYD GEORGE. The German delegates may be here Tuesday. Between now and then, will Italy have been consulted or not? There is the question of reparations. Yesterday the English and the Italian experts made some common decisions, but the Italian delegates were not represented at the plenary meeting at which a final decision was to be made. There is to be a decision today. Can we take it without Italy being present? I do not think so. I think that people are essentially more concerned with economic than with territorial questions, which are of importance to newspapers and to certain people who are interested in foreign policy. Then, in the matter of coal, where France is represented by Loucheur, will Crespi be there to represent Italy? Must Italy be left out? There are important questions regarding the exportation of German coal. Have the Allies the right to present demands on Italy's account without her being present? Does Italy wish us to settle these questions for her? Will she agree to what we might accept for her, or will she say that we had no right to accept? Will Italy be present when the questions which affect her economic life are taken into consideration? There is also the matter of a common credit for the reconstruction of the life of Europe. Will Italy participate in this project or not? Who will discuss it for her? Shall we present the claims of Italy? Or shall we proceed on our own account and then add the Italian claims afterwards? Must Italy not make peace with Germany because she is not satisfied with respect to the peace with Austria? These are the problems of a practical nature to which I should like an answer.

CLEMENCEAU. After the events of the last few days, the Germans might perceive a rift in the Alliance, and if the Italians should not be represented at Versailles, that would make the conclusion of peace more difficult.

WILSON. I hope that the Italian delegation will remain. I believe that is the burden of what Lloyd George has said.

LLOYD GEORGE. That is my point.

ORLANDO. I make note of the declarations of M. Clemenceau and Mr. Lloyd George in regard to the Pact of London; but this is not the time to argue its merits. As to Mr. Lloyd George's observations, I recognize their practical importance. There are two questions: the first refers to the period between now and the signing of the Treaty with Germany. That Treaty has been discussed during the last weeks and its provisions have in the main been settled. There are still some very important questions to be decided. However, I trust the Allies, and I feel that when they will encounter Italian interests they will give them even greater consideration than if Italy were present to argue her own case. I trust them as I would a judge who is especially concerned to see that justice shall be done in a lawsuit in which one of the parties has no advocate. However, I might ascertain with my colleagues of the delegation if a remedy can be found. I could leave Crespi, who would remain in touch with his colleagues. There is, secondly, the question of our presence when the Germans come. I have seen in the papers that they have asked for a postponement until May 1.

CLEMENCEAU. I have received no official notice of this. What I have read is that they would not be able to leave Berlin before April 28.

ORLANDO. I hope to be able to consult Parliament very shortly. While I agree with Mr. Lloyd George and M. Clemenceau that it is important not to give the Germans the impression that the Allies are less united than before, at the same time, the fundamental issues involved are so vital to Italy that I think it preferable to ignore the difficulties mentioned by Lloyd George.

CLEMENCEAU. I should like to know whether or not Italy will be represented at the meetings with the Germans.

ORLANDO. That depends upon the decisions to be made in Italy. I ask for a delay.

WILSON. The questions of the Italian frontier do not strictly affect the peace with Germany; I see no contradiction in Italy participating in the peace with Germany while making every reservation for the Treaty with Austria.

LLOYD GEORGE. I still insist that, no matter how much the Italian representatives may trust their Allies, if they are not present, it will not be possible to put forward their claims. If they are not present at the meeting of May 1, if Orlando has not received the consent of his Parliament to participate, how can their claims be put forward?

CLEMENCEAU. It seems to me that we should find it difficult to meet the Germans at that time, for it would be necessary to make changes throughout the text of the Treaty.

LLOYD GEORGE. The Germans will ask who are the representatives of Italy. We cannot present claims on Italy's account unless the Italians are present, or unless Orlando should ask the Allies in writing to present these claims on her account.

ORLANDO. Taken by itself, there is only one answer to Mr. Lloyd George's objections: he is right. I recognize the impossibility of putting forward proposals on behalf of a Power which is not represented. That question must be examined carefully and a decision made, depending upon circumstances. I agree with Mr. Lloyd George that if Italy is not present, she will not be entitled to make any claims against Germany.

I do not agree with Clemenceau that the text of the Treaty would have to be seriously altered, for Italy is interested in only a few of the matters involved in the German Treaty, outside of reparations.

But I wish to consider Lloyd George's objection in connection with the proposal of President Wilson that Italy might participate in the Treaty with Germany while putting off the Treaty with Austria. To this I have two answers. The first is that the general interpretation of the Pact of London of 1915 and Italy's adherence to the Declaration of London of September, 1914, imply that the peace must be a general peace. Such would not be the case if the other Powers were at peace, while Italy was not. It is true that President Wilson is not bound by these Pacts, but I must point out that the question must be examined from the point of view of general equity, not only among the Allies, but also with the Associated Powers; that peace must be general. On the other hand, I must point out to President Wilson that, in signing the Treaty of Peace with Germany, the Covenant of the League of Nations is also being signed. One of the provisions of the Covenant of the League of Nations sets up reciprocal guarantees of the territories of the signatory Powers. It would follow that Italy would undertake to guarantee other people's territory, without herself being guaranteed. Another difficulty would arise from the fact that the Covenant of the League of Nations includes a provision directed toward avoiding future wars and toward solving peacefully the differences between nations. If Italy should adhere to the League of Nations, that would mean that the question of her frontier with Yugoslavia might be considered as an issue to be settled by the League of Nations, rather than an issue growing out of a victorious war. That would prevent me from signing the peace with Germany, if the Italian territorial questions were not settled beforehand.

LLOYD GEORGE. If Orlando leaves, it is important to decide what must be given out to the press.

SONNINO. It is not easy for Orlando to make precise statements in the Italian Chamber unless there are proposals from the other side. I thought that some proposal in regard to the latest point of view of the Allies and Associates would be made today; but President Wilson has expounded the same views as three or four days ago, before certain additional proposals had been made.

Mr. Lloyd George has said that in regard to the question of Fiume, he would consider changing in a certain sense the provisions of the Treaty of London, if Italy were willing to make certain concessions.

Clemenceau seems to have a different point of view, and insists that Fiume has been promised to Croatia.

LLOYD GEORGE. The idea of making Fiume a free city, while taking it from the Croats, is a change on which we are agreed, if Italy is prepared to modify the Treaty of London.

SONNINO. Does Clemenceau agree to this?

CLEMENCEAU. That is my point of view.

WILSON. In the memorandum which I recently gave to Orlando I accepted the idea of making Fiume a free city, as shown in the map attached to the memorandum.

SONNINO. The memorandum of President Wilson indicates other frontiers, as in Istria, which do not correspond with those of the Treaty of London. Does President Wilson agree to leave those frontiers as indicated in the Treaty? I am asking this only in order to make the situation perfectly clear.

WILSON. In the memorandum I stated what must be the position of the United States, from which position I do not wish to depart. I hope that in his declaration in the Italian Parliament, Orlando will adhere to my memorandum.

ORLANDO. I should like to sum up Sonnino's idea. In order to explain the situation clearly to Parliament it is necessary to inform it of Wilson's declarations as stated in his memorandum, as well as the declarations of the Governments who have adhered to the Pact of London. Now Sonnino is asking: can we make a statement to Parliament in regard to a solution to which the two Allies and the Associate are fully agreed? Could I say that there is a solution on which three could agree? If you cannot give me an answer today, you may be able to do so tomorrow. For the moment I can say that the Allies adhere to the Treaty of London.

CLEMENCEAU. I can answer at once and so can Lloyd George.

ORLANDO. But in regard to the statement referring to the Treaty of London I shall be asked: have you President Wilson's consent?

WILSON. I must answer: I am not free to propose modifications in the principles which are the basis of my declarations; but I am free to examine proposals; up to now I have not seen any compromise proposals.

LLOYD GEORGE. That is not what I thought. Clemenceau and myself have sought a middle way in order to support our Ally and to preserve peace, and we understood that Wilson was ready to accept it if our Italian colleagues were likewise ready to accept it. Personally I took the liberty to tell the Italians that such was the situation. I am sorry if I made a mistake. I let the Italian representatives know that if they were prepared to give up their rights on the Dalmatian coast, leaving Zara and Sebenico as free cities, and if they would be content with the islands, excepting those which are virtually part of the mainland, I thought that President Wilson would have concurred and that an agreement might have been reached on that basis.

WILSON. I never committed myself to such an agreement; all I did was to ask Mr. Lloyd George to find out whether the Italians would be willing to enter a discussion on that basis, and the reply was that they were not. In any case I have reserved judgment. I am sorry if I did not make myself clear.

LLOYD GEORGE. The fault was entirely mine. I had the impression that if the Italians had accepted such an agreement, there would be no unsurmountable difficulty on President Wilson's part.

WILSON. I do not want my Italian friends to think that I am not willing to examine every aspect of the question. I am ready to do it a hundred times if necessary.

LLOYD GEORGE. From the way in which President Wilson insisted that Spalato and the islands be left out, I had the impression that he was disposed to accept the rest.

SONNINO. That happened the day before yesterday, when a proposal was made that we could not accept. We examined the question again and found that we could make a counter proposal consisting of the following points:

1. The line of the Alps to the sea, east of Volosca;
2. The sovereignty of Fiume to Italy, allowing great facilities and freedom in its port;
3. The islands of the Treaty of London, except Pago;
4. Zara and Sebenico free cities under Italian mandate.

We received the answer that the point of the sovereignty of Fiume was not accepted, but that the rest was.

WILSON. Did you think that it was a case of common agreement?

LLOYD GEORGE. I understood that to be precisely the case, after the morning meeting, save for the question of the mandates, which I forgot. I thought that the rest was entirely accepted.

SONNINO. Yesterday afternoon, we were informed through Kerr and Aldrovandi that the demand for the sovereignty of Fiume was not acceptable, but that the rest could be. We then wished to find out what would take the place of Italian sovereignty for Fiume. I ask Aldrovandi to say whether we received an answer.

ALDROVANDI. Marquis Imperiali was sent to Lloyd George to seek clarifications in regard to the international position of Fiume. Imperiali was told that Fiume would be a free city under the League of Nations.

WILSON. Lloyd George, who had gone to meet Marquis Imperiali when the latter came to see him while we were holding a meeting, came back into the room where we were discussing with our experts the question of reparations, and informed us of the contents of the Ambassador's communication. He did not consult me, however, on the answer to be given.

SONNINO. The impression I had was that Fiume was to be a free city with a large surrounding zone.

LLOYD GEORGE. That is the proposal contained in President Wilson's document.

WILSON. Baron Sonnino said that a communication was sent to us, during the afternoon of yesterday, while we were discussing reparations with our experts. All I remember is that Mr. Lloyd George left the room to see Marquis Imperiali, and when he came back he merely reported to M. Clemenceau and to me what Marquis Imperiali had asked him. Baron Sonnino said, however, that he had received a communication.

CLEMENCEAU. I did not send any communication.

LLOYD GEORGE. We discussed the matter at length in the morning. I said nothing that was at variance with what had been agreed upon. The only point of difference was that referring to mandates; on this point there was a misunderstanding. Not on Count Aldrovandi's part. It was my fault, as I forgot to mention mandates in connection with Zara and Sebenico. Everything else grew out of the morning conversation. Marquis Imperiali came to ask me what would be the situation of Fiume if Italy did not have its sovereignty. I answered him that it would remain under the League of Nations. The other question of Marquis Imperiali referred to the diplomatic representation of Fiume, and I replied that the inhabitants of Fiume could decide for themselves.

SONNINO. The reply brought to us by Marquis Imperiali was that Fiume would be a free city under the League of Nations. We were beginning to discuss the matter when newspapers were brought to us containing President Wilson's Message. We said that that changed everything, and we decided not to send our reply to the proposals brought by Kerr; we sent, instead, another written communication to the Allies. This morning Lloyd George came to the Edouard VII and spoke of the possibility of reaching an agreement today. We thanked Lloyd George for his intervention, and I thought that when we came here we should find a proposal from the Three. In that case we should have been able to take back something clearer to our Parliament. There is no use in our saying that two of the Allies are agreed to do one thing, but that the third is not.

LLOYD GEORGE. I find myself in my customary unpleasant situation of trying to find a solution between two parties difficult to reconcile. Yet I still hope to be able to offer some suggestion. If I understand rightly, however, whatever may be proposed now, my two Italian colleagues could not accept.

SONNINO. We are in a very difficult position, but I should like to know precisely what is the distance between us.

LLOYD GEORGE. I understand President Wilson's difficulty in saying that he has accepted, when he cannot reconcile such acceptance with his principles. The Italian representatives may go back to Italy with a proposal agreed upon by their three colleagues, but once in Italy they may find themselves in an entirely different atmosphere, in which only one point of view is understandable. I therefore fully understand President Wilson's difficulty in declaring *a priori* to the Italian representatives to what he might consent. I myself have had much experience with labor disputes in industry. I have always said: "Do you, workers, take the responsibility of accepting this proposal if the other side accepts it?" I now likewise ask the Italian representatives: Will you undertake to recommend the acceptance of what may provisionally be agreed upon here?

SONNINO. Yes, if it were acceptable.

ORLANDO. I do not think that I could accept any proposal whatsoever; to do so would be contrary to the declaration which I made at the beginning of the present meeting. I must explain my position in Parliament. I asked the three Powers, two of whom are Allies and one Associate, if they had a proposal on which they were agreed. They answered in the negative. In their last proposal, as I understood it, they spoke of making Zara and Sebenico free cities, giving the islands to Italy, and making Fiume a free city; but they have forgotten one point, namely Istria. It is essential for Italy that her frontier come down as far as Volosca.

SONNINO. The proposal included, according to what we understood had been agreed, all of Istria to the line east of Volosca. Lloyd George has asked whether the Italians were ready to accept a proposal on which the three Powers were agreed. He has asked us whether we should be in a position to recommend its acceptance. I replied that if the proposal were acceptable we should recommend it at home. Lloyd George has explained the difficulty which President Wilson finds in making a definite proposal. The hopes of success are not great if the whole question must be laid before Parliament without our having received first a specific proposal.

LLOYD GEORGE. If the Italian Ministers are not prepared to assume the responsibility of recommending the proposal in Parliament, there is no use in discussing the question further, for then we should not be on a basis of equality with our Italian colleagues.

SONNINO. If we can have a scheme that seems acceptable to us, we could say that we agree to recommend it with all our energy.

ORLANDO. Up to now, however, we have received no such proposal.

WILSON. Orlando will have to explain the difficult position in which the various countries find themselves. Great Britain and France are bound by a Treaty, and the United States by certain principles. He will have to explain the situation before Parliament and say: "Have I the power to go back to Paris and settle everything for the best?" I do not think it would be fair to make a proposal for Sig. Orlando to present to Parliament.

SONNINO. The danger is this. Suppose that Parliament confirms its confidence in us, that we come back here with a mandate to find a solution, and that we do not succeed in finding it. The situation would then be much worse. If, instead, there were a proposal today and we found it acceptable, we should know on what to base our communications and our recommendations to Parliament. Otherwise we shall return here with a mandate, but without the possibility of finding a solution.

ORLANDO. I agree with President Wilson. The events of these past days have clarified the situation. Why should we put pressure on President Wilson? The situation must remain as it has developed. I do not know what Parliament will do. I shall not say: "Decide as you please." The Cabinet must have an opinion of its own, which I shall make known. Either Parliament will confirm its confidence in us or else others will have to take my place. But I hope that just as the Italian people responded unanimously to the appeal which I made to it after Caporetto, it will now likewise manifest its unanimous will. President Wilson will have a clearer basis for his decision.

SONNINO (to Orlando). I do not think so.

WILSON. I think that is an admirable position to take. What would be thought in Italy if Orlando could say that, after having published his proposals, Wilson is now ready to abandon them?

SONNINO. You will admit that we have compromised with Yugoslavia. To do what President Wilson suggests constitutes a danger, for we cannot say to the Chamber: "Give us confidence for whatever may happen." It would be more difficult to find a compromise after having gone before Parliament. If, instead, it had been possible to find a solution now, we should find it much easier to appear before our Parliament.

LLOYD GEORGE. Unfortunately there is here a conflict of principles. There are the principles of President Wilson, with which I agree, and which I have even defended despite certain oppositions; then there is the principle of honoring the signature of international treaties, and that leads us back to the very principle which has been one of the chief reasons for this war. I do not see what danger there is in arriving at a compromise. In such cases it is best to accept the most satisfactory compromise. The proposal which I made did not violate any principle, either of Italy or of Wilson. I do not know what may be the best way of securing parliamentary approval in Italy; but I know the British Parliament, in which I have been for thirty years, and, for my part, I should like to know where I stand and what I should be working toward.

CLEMENCEAU. I agree.

LLOYD GEORGE. For example, in the matter of reparations, I could not go to Parliament and ask for a free hand.

SONNINO. That is just what I am saying.

WILSON. And yet that is not what Lloyd George did in the English Parliament in the matter of reparations.

LLOYD GEORGE. Not at all. I was able to reassure the English Parliament because I knew exactly the solution that was near. Otherwise the English Parliament would not have given me its confidence, doubting that I had confidence in myself.

WILSON. The Italian representatives could go to Parliament and say that neither the Allies nor the Associate can agree to giving Fiume to Italy. The English and the French feel bound to keep their promise as Allies. In regard to the possibility of an agreement, the Italian delegates could say that I understand their difficulties and that I am ready to accept any solution which is in agreement with my principles, even though I have no proposal to make.

LLOYD GEORGE. President Wilson's situation seems to me to be the following: he does not wish to make proposals, but insists that it should be made clear that Fiume must not go to Italy.

WILSON. I must recall to my colleagues that the Italian Parliament has never been acquainted with the position of the Government of the United States as it was stated in my memorandum. My proposals, contained in this memorandum, are not purely negative, but positive as well. They include the necessary measures to guarantee the security of the eastern shore of the Adriatic. They called attention to the necessity of doing so, and included the limitation of armaments, the destruction of fortifications, and so forth, so as to meet these difficulties. For that reason my proposals were positive as well as negative. I should like the Italian Parliament to know what I have said in this respect.

[The meeting was adjourned as the Italians had to leave to take the train for Rome.]

DOCUMENT 42

WILSON'S MANIFESTO[1]

April 23.

In view of the capital importance of the questions affected, and in order to throw all possible light upon what is involved in their settlement, I hope that the following statement will contribute to the final formation of opinion and to a satisfactory solution.

When Italy entered the war she entered upon the basis of a definite, but private, understanding with Great Britain and France, now known as the Pact of London. Since that time the whole face of circumstance has been altered. Many other powers, great and small, have entered the struggle, with no knowledge of that private understanding. The Austro-Hungarian Empire, then the enemy of Europe, and at whose expense the Pact of London was to be kept in the event of victory, has gone to pieces and no longer exists. Not only that. The several parts of that Empire, it is now agreed by Italy and all her associates, are to be erected into independent states and associated in a League of Nations, not with those who were recently our enemies, but with Italy herself and the powers that stood with Italy in the great war for liberty. We are to establish their liberty as well as our own. They are to be among the smaller states whose interests are henceforth to be as scrupulously safeguarded as the interests of the most powerful states.

The war was ended, moreover, by proposing to Germany an armistice and peace which should be founded on certain clearly defined principles which should set up a new order of right and justice. Upon those principles the peace with Germany has been conceived, not only, but formulated. Upon those principles it will be executed. We cannot ask the great body of powers to propose and effect peace with Austria and establish a new basis of independence and right in the states which originally constituted the Austro-Hungarian Empire and in the states of the Balkan group on principles of another kind. We must apply the same principles to the settlement of Europe in those quarters that we have applied in the peace with Germany. It was upon the explicit avowal of those principles that the initiative for peace was taken. It is upon them that the whole structure of peace must rest.

If those principles are to be adhered to, Fiume must serve as the outlet

---

[1] Baker, *Woodrow Wilson and the World Settlement,* III (Document 38), 287-90.

and inlet of the commerce, not of Italy, but of the lands to the north and northeast of that port: Hungary, Bohemia, Roumania, and the states of the new Jugo-Slavic group. To assign Fiume to Italy would be to create the feeling that we had deliberately put the port upon which all these countries chiefly depend for their access to the Mediterranean in the hands of a power of which it did not form an integral part and whose sovereignty, if set up there, must inevitably seem foreign, not domestic or identified with the commercial and industrial life of the regions which the port must serve. It is for that reason, no doubt, that Fiume was not included in the Pact of London but there definitively assigned to the Croatians.

And the reason why the line of the Pact of London swept about many of the islands of the eastern coast of the Adriatic and around the portion of the Dalmatian coast which lies most open to that sea was not only that here and there on those islands and here and there on that coast there are bodies of people of Italian blood and connection but also, and no doubt chiefly, because it was felt that it was necessary for Italy to have a foothold amidst the channels of the eastern Adriatic in order that she might make her own coasts safe against the naval aggression of Austria-Hungary. But Austria-Hungary no longer exists. It is proposed that the fortifications which the Austrian government constructed there shall be razed and permanently destroyed. It is part, also, of the new plan of European order which centres in the League of Nations that the new states erected there shall accept a limitation of armaments which puts aggression out of the question. There can be no fear of the unfair treatment of groups of Italian people there because adequate guarantees will be given, under international sanction, of equal and equitable treatment of all racial or national minorities.

In brief, every question associated with this settlement wears a new aspect,—a new aspect given it by the very victory for right for which Italy has made the supreme sacrifice of blood and treasure. Italy, along with the four other great powers, has become one of the chief trustees of the new order which she has played so honourable a part in establishing.

And on the north and northeast her natural frontiers are completely restored, along the whole sweep of the Alps from northwest to southeast to the very end of the Istrian peninsula, including all the great watershed within which Trieste and Pola lie and all the fair regions whose face nature has turned towards the great peninsula upon which the historic life of the Latin people has been worked out through centuries of famous story ever since Rome was first set upon her seven hills. Her ancient unity is restored. Her lines are extended to the great walls which are her natural defence. It is within her choice to be surrounded by friends; to exhibit to the newly liberated peoples across the Adriatic that noblest quality of greatness, magnanimity, friendly generosity, the preference of justice over interest.

The nations associated with her, the nations that know nothing of the Pact of London or of any other special understanding that lies at the beginning of this great struggle, and who have made their supreme sacrifice also in the interest, not of national advantage or defence, but of the settled peace of the world, now unite with her older associates in urging her to assume a leadership which cannot be mistaken in the new order of Europe. America is Italy's friend. Her people are drawn, millions strong, from Italy's own fair countrysides. She is linked in blood as well as in affection with the Italian people. Such ties can never be broken. And America was privileged, by the generous commission of her associates in the war, to initiate the peace we are about to consummate,—to initiate it upon terms she had herself formulated, and in which I was her spokesman. The compulsion is upon her to square every decision she takes a part in with those principles. She can do nothing else. She trusts Italy, and in her trust believes that Italy will ask nothing of her that cannot be made unmistakably consistent with these sacred obligations. Interest is not now in question, but the rights of peoples, of states new and old, of liberated peoples and peoples whose rulers have never accounted them worthy of right; above all, the right of the world to peace and to such settlements of interest as shall make peace secure.

These, and these only, are the principles for which America has fought. These, and these only, are the principles upon which she can consent to make peace. Only upon these principles, she hopes and believes, will the people of Italy ask her to make peace.

[*Signed*] Woodrow Wilson.

DOCUMENT 43

ORLANDO'S STATEMENT[1]

April 24, 1919.

Yesterday, while the Italian Delegation was assembled discussing an alternative proposal sent them from the British Prime Minister for the purpose of conciliating the opposing tendencies that had shown themselves in regard to Italian territorial aspirations, the newspapers of Paris published a message from the President of the United States, Mr. Wilson, in which he expressed his own opinion in reference to some of the most serious problems that have been submitted to the judgment of the Conference.

The step of making a direct appeal to the different peoples certainly is an innovation in international intercourse. It is not my intention to complain about it, but I do take official notice of it so as to follow this precedent; inasmuch as this new system without doubt will aid in granting the different peoples a broader participation in international questions, and inasmuch as I have always personally been of the opinion that such participation was a sign of a newer era. However, if such appeals are to be considered as being addressed to peoples outside of the Governments that represent them, I should say almost in opposition to their Governments, it is a great source of regret for me to remember that this procedure, which, up to now, has been used only against enemy Governments, is to-day for the first time being used against a Government which has been, and has tried to be always a loyal friend of the Great American Republic:—against the Italian Government. I could also complain that such a message, addressed to the people, has been published at the very moment when the Allied and Associated Powers were in the middle of negotiations with the Italian Government, that is to say, with the very Government whose participation had been solicited and highly valued in numerous and serious questions which, up to now, had been dealt with in full and intimate faith.

But above all I shall have the right to complain, if the declarations of the presidential message signified opposition to the Italian Government and people, since in that case it would amount to ignoring and denying the high degree of civilization which the Italian nation has attained in these forms of democratic and Liberal rule, in which it is second to no nation on earth.

[1] Baker, *Woodrow Wilson and the World Settlement,* IiI (Document 39), 291-95.

To oppose, so to speak, the Italian Government and people, would be to admit that this great free nation could submit to the yoke of a will other than its own, and I shall be forced to protest vigorously against such suppositions, unjustly offensive to my country.

I now come to the contents of the presidential message: it is devoted entirely to showing that the Italian claims, beyond certain limits defined in the message, violate the principles upon which the new régime of liberty and justice among nations must be founded. I have never denied these principles, and President Wilson will do me the justice to acknowledge that in the long conversations that we have had together I have never relied on the formal authority of a treaty by which I knew very well that he was not bound. In these conversations I have relied solely on the force of the reason and the justice upon which I have always believed, and upon which I still believe, the aspirations of Italy are solidly based. I did not have the honor of convincing him: I regret it sincerely, but President Wilson himself has had the kindness to recognize, in the course of our conversations, that truth and justice are the monopoly of no one person, and that all men are subject to error, and I add that the error is all the easier as the problems to which the principles apply are more complex. Humanity is such an immense thing, the problems raised by the life of the people are so infinitely complex, that nobody can believe that he has found in a determined number of proposals as simple and sure a way to solve them as if it were a question of determining the dimensions, the volume and the weight of bodies with various units of measure. While remarking that more than once the Conference nearly failed completely when it was a question of applying these principles I do not believe that I am showing disrespect toward this high assembly. On the contrary, these changes have been and still are, the consequence of all human judgment. I mean to say only, that experience has proved the difficulties in the application of these principles of an abstract nature to concrete cases, thus with all deference but firmly, I consider as justified[2] the application made by President Wilson in his message of his principles to Italian claims. It is impossible for me, in a document of this sort, to repeat the detailed proofs which were produced in great number. I shall only say, one cannot accept without reservation the statement that the downfall of the Austro-Hungarian Empire implies a reduction of the Italian aspirations. It is even permissible to believe the contrary, that is, that at the very moment when all the varied peoples who constituted that empire sought to organize according to their ethnic and national affinities, the essential problem caused by the Italian claims can and must be completely solved. Now this problem

---

[2] Evidently "unjustified" is meant. Cf., e.g., the text given by Temperley, A History of the Peace Conference of Paris, V, 402-4.

is that of the Adriatic in which is summed up all the rights of both the ancient and the new Italy, all her sufferings throughout the centuries and all the benefits she is destined to bring to the great international community.

The Presidential message affirms that with the concessions which she has received, Italy would attain the walls of the Alps, which are her natural defences. This is a grant of vast importance upon condition that the eastern flank of that wall does not remain uncovered and that there be included among the rights of Italy that line from Mount Nevoso separating the waters which flow toward the Black Sea from those which empty into the Mediterranean. It is this mountain which the Romans themselves have called the "Limes Italianus" since the very hour when the real figure of Italy appeared to the sentiment and the conscience of the people.

Without that protection a dangerous breach would remain open in that admirable natural barrier of the Alps; and it would mean the rupture of that unquestionable political, historical and economic unity constituted by the peninsula of Istria.

I believe, moreover, that he who can proudly claim that it was he who stated to the world the free right of self-determination of nations, is the very person who must recognize this right for Fiume, ancient Italian city, which proclaimed its Italianness even before the Italian ships were near; to Fiume, admirable example of a national consciousness perpetuated throughout the centuries. To deny it this right for the sole reason that it has to do only with a small community, would be to admit that the criterium of justice toward nations varies according to their territorial expansion. And if, to deny this right, we fall back on the international character of this port, must we not take into account Antwerp, Genoa, Rotterdam,—all of them international ports which serve as outlet for a variety of nations and regions without their being obliged to pay dearly for this privilege by the suppression of their national consciousness?

And can one describe as excessive the Italian aspiration for the Dalmatian Coast, this boulevard of Italy throughout the centuries, which Roman genius and Venetian activity have made noble and great, and whose Italianness, defying all manner of implacable persecution throughout an entire century, to-day shares with the Italian nation the same emotions of patriotism?—The principle is being adduced with regard to Poland that denationalization obtained by violent and arbitrary methods should not constitute grounds for de jure claims; why not apply the same principle to Dalmatia?

And if we wish to support this rapid synthesis of our good international rights by cold statistical facts, I believe I am able to state that among the various national reorganizations which the Peace Conference has already brought about or may bring about in the future, none of these reorganized peoples will count within its new frontiers a number of people of a foreign race proportionately less than that which would be assigned to Italy. Why, therefore, is it especially the Italian aspirations that are to be suspected of Imperialistic cupidity?

In spite of all these reasons, the history of these negotiations shall demonstrate that the firmness which was necessary to the Italian Delegation was always associated to a great spirit of conciliation in the research for a general agreement that we all wished for fervently.

The Presidential message ends by a warm declaration of friendship of America towards Italy. I answer in the name of Italian people and I acclaim with pride this right and this honor which is due me as the man who in the most tragic hour of this war has uttered to the Italian people the cry of resistance at all costs; this cry was listened to and answered with a courage and abnegation of which few examples can be found in the history of the world. And Italy, thanks to the most heroic sacrifices and the purest blood of her children, has been able to climb from an abyss of misfortune to the radiant summit of the most resounding victory. It is therefore, in the name of Italy, that in my turn I express the sentiment of admiration and deep sympathy that the Italian people has for the American people.

[*Signed*] V. E. ORLANDO.

Paris, April 24, 1919.

BALFOUR MEMORANDUM[1]
APRIL 24, 1919

FIUME AND THE PEACE SETTLEMENT

We learn with a regret which it is difficult to measure that, at the very moment when Peace seems almost attained, Italy threatens to sever herself from the company of the Allied nations, through whose common efforts victory has been achieved. We do not presume to offer any opinion as to the effects which so momentous a step would have upon the future of Italy herself. Of these it is for the Italian people and its leaders to judge, and for them alone. But we, who have been Italy's Allies through four anxious years, and would gladly be her Allies still, are bound to express our fears as to the disastrous effects it will surely have upon us, and upon the policy for which we have striven.

When in 1915 Italy threw in her lot with France, Russia and the British Empire in their struggle against the Central Powers, Turkey and Bulgaria, she did so on conditions. She required her Allies to promise that in case of victory they would help her to obtain in Europe the frontier of the Alps, the great ports of Trieste and Pola, and a large portion of the Dalmatian coast with many of its adjacent islands. Such accessions of territory would enormously strengthen Italy's power of defense, both on land and sea, against her hereditary enemy, and would incidentally result in the transfer of over 200,000 German-speaking Tyrolese and over 750,000 Southern Slavs from Austrian to Italian rule. Under this arrangement Fiume was retained by Croatia.

Such was the situation in April, 1915. In November, 1918, it had profoundly changed. Germany was beaten; the Dual Monarchy had ceased to exist: and side by side with this Military revolution, the ideals of the Western Powers had grown and strengthened. In 1915 the immediate needs of self-defense, the task of creating and equipping vast armies, the contrivance of new methods for meeting new perils, strained to the utmost the energies of the Allies. But by 1918, we had reached the double conviction that if the repetition of such calamities was to be avoided, the Nations must organize themselves to maintain Peace, as Germany, Austria, Bulgaria and Turkey had organized themselves to make War; and that little could be expected, even from the best contrived organization,

[1] Baker, *Woodrow Wilson and the World Settlement,* III (Document 37), 281-86.

unless the boundaries of the States to be created by the Conference were framed, on the whole, in accordance with the wishes and lasting interests of the populations concerned.

This task of re-drawing European frontiers has fallen upon the Great Powers; and admittedly its difficulty is immense. Not always, nor indeed often, do race, religion, language, history, economic interests, geographical contiguity and convenience, the influence of national prejudices and the needs of national defense, conspire to indicate without doubt or ambiguity the best frontier for any State:—be it new or old. And unless they do, some element in a perfect settlement must be neglected, compromise becomes inevitable, and there may often be honest doubts as to the form the compromise should take.

Now as regards most of the new frontier between Italy and what was once the Austrian Empire, we have nothing to say. We are bound by the Pact of London, and any demand for a change in that Pact which is adverse to Italy must come from Italy herself. But this same Pact gives Fiume to Croatia, and we would very earnestly and respectfully ask whether any valid reason exists for adding, in the teeth of the Treaty, this little city on the Croatian coast to the Kingdom of Italy? It is said indeed, and with truth, that its Italian population desire the change. But the population which clusters around the port is not predominantly Italian. It is true that the urban area wherein they dwell is not called Fiume; for it is divided by a narrow canal, as Paris is divided by the Seine, or London by the tidal estuary of the Thames, and locally the name, Fiume, is applied in strictness only to the streets on one side of it. But surely we are concerned with things, not names; and however you name it, the town which serves the port, and lives by it, is physically one town, not two: and taken as a whole is Slav, not Italian.

But if the argument drawn from the wishes of the present population does not really point to an Italian solution, what remains? Not the argument from history; for up to quite recent times the inhabitants of Fiume, in its narrowest meaning, were predominantly Slav. Not the arguments from contiguity; for the country population, up to the very gates of the city, are not merely predominantly Slav, but Slav without perceptible admixture. Not the economic argument; for the territories which obtain through Fiume their easiest access to the sea, whatever else they be, at least are not Italian. Most of them are Slav; and if it be said that Fiume is also necessary to Hungarian and Transylvanian commerce, this is a valid argument for making it a free port, but surely not for putting it under Italian sovereignty.

There is one other line of argument on this subject about which we would ask leave to say a word. It is urged by some, and thought by many that the task of the Great Powers is not merely to sit down and coldly rearrange the pieces on the European board in strict, even pedantic, conformity with certain admirable but very abstract principles. They must consider these great matters in more human fashion. After all (so runs the argument), the problems to be dealt with arise out of a great war. The conquerors in that War were not the aggressors: Their sacrifices have been enormous; the burdens they have to bear seem well-nigh intolerable. Are they to get nothing out of victory, except the consciousness that State frontiers in Europe will be arranged in a better pattern after 1918 than they were before; and that nations who fought on the wrong side, or who did not fight at all, will have gained their freedom through other peoples' losses? Surely the victors, if they want it, are entitled to some more solid reward than theoretical map-makers, working in the void, may on abstract principles feel disposed to give them.

There is something in this way of thinking which at first sight appeals to us all; and where no interests are concerned but those of the criminal aggressors, it deserves respectful consideration. But in most cases of territorial redistribution it is at least as important to enquire what effects the transfer will have on the nations to whom the territory is given, as upon those from whom it is taken: and when, as in the case of Jugo-Slavia, the nation from whom it is taken happens to be a friendly State, the difficulty of the problem is doubled.

We do not presume to speak with authority on the value of the strategical gains which Italy anticipates from the acquisition of the islands and coastline of Dalmatia. They seem to us to be small; though, small as they are, they must greatly exceed the economic advantages, which will accrue to Italian trade from new opportunities, or to the Italian Treasury from new sources of revenue. We cannot believe that the owners of Trieste have anything to fear from Fiume as a commercial rival, or the owners of Pola from Fiume as a Naval base.

But if Italy has little to gain from the proposed acquisition, has she not much to lose? The War found her protected from an hereditary enemy of nearly twice her size by a frontier which previous Treaties had deliberately [rendered] insecure. Her Eastern seaboard was almost bare of harbours, while Austria-Hungary possessed on the opposite side of the Adriatic some of the finest harbours in the world. This was her condition in 1914. In 1919 her Northern and Eastern frontiers are as secure as mountains and rivers can make them. She is adding two great ports to her Adriatic possessions; and her hereditary oppressor has ceased to exist. To us it seems that, as a State thus situated has nothing to fear from its neighbours' enmity, so its only interest must be to gain their friendship. And though memories belonging to an evil past make friendship difficult between Italians and Slavs, yet the bitterest memories soften with time, unless fresh irritants are frequently applied; and among such irritants none are more powerful than the constant contemplation of a disputed and ill-drawn frontier.

It is for Italy, and not for the other signatories of the Pact of London, to say whether she will gain more in power, wealth and honour by strictly adhering to that part of the Pact of London which is in her favour, than by accepting modifications in it which would bring it into closer harmony with the principles which are governing the territorial decisions of the Allies in other parts of Europe. But so far as Fiume is concerned, the position is different. Here, as we have already pointed out, the Pact of 1915 is against the Italian contention; and so also, it seems to us, are justice and policy. After the most prolonged and anxious reflection, we cannot bring ourselves to believe that it is either in the interests of Jugo-Slavia, in the interests of Italy herself, or in the interests of future peace—which is the concern of all the world,—that this port should be severed from the territories to which, economically, geographically and ethnologically it naturally belongs.

Can it be that Italy on this account is prepared to separate herself from her Allies? The hope that sustained us through the perilous years of War was that victory, when it came, would bring with it, not merely the defeat of Germany, but the final discredit of the ideals in which Germany had placed her trust. On the other hand, Germany, even when she began to entertain misgivings about the issues of the campaign, felt sure that the union of her enemies would never survive their triumphs. She based her schemes no longer on the conquest of Europe, but on its political, and perhaps also on its social, disintegration. The Armistice might doubtless produce a brief cessation of hostilities; but it would bring no repose to a perturbed and overwrought world. Militant nationalism would lead to a struggle between peoples; militant internationalism to a struggle between classes. In either event, or in both, the Conference summoned to give us peace would leave us at war, and Germany alone would be the gainer.

This or something like this is the present calculation of a certain section of German politicians. Could anything more effectually contribute to its success than that Italy should quarrel with her Allies, and that the cause of quarrel should be the manner in which our common victory may best be used? We are calling into being a League of Nations; we are daily adding to the responsibilities which, under the approaching Treaty, it will be called upon to assume; yet before the scheme has had time to clothe itself in practical form, we hasten to destroy its credit. To the world we supply dramatic proof that the Association of the Great Powers, which won the war, cannot survive peace; and all the world will ask how, if this be so, the maintenance of Peace can safely be left in their hands.

For these reasons, if for no other, we beg our Italian colleagues to reconsider their policy. That it has been inspired by a high sense of patriotism we do not doubt. But we cannot believe either that it is in Italy's true interests, or that it is worthy of the great part which Italy is called upon to play in the Councils of the Nations.

[Initialed] A. J. B.

Paris

24. 4. 19

JOHNSON'S MEMORANDUM[1]
MAY 8, 1919

From: Chief of Division of Boundary Geography.
To: The Commissioners.
Subject: Formula for Adriatic Settlement.

Referring to Ambassador Page's telegram of May 5 suggesting construction of a Jugoslav port at Buccari in order that Fiume might eventually be ceded to Italy without injury to the economic life of Jugoslavia, attention is directed to the accompanying formula which might offer to the Italian plenipotentiaries a means of emerging from a difficult situation without humiliating the Italian people. Adoption of the formula would result in the solution supported by the American territorial specialists and proposed by the President in his public memorandum of April 22nd, and hence is not a compromise solution; but the ends sought would be attained without needlessly wounding Italian sensibilities.

The following comments will make clear the intent of the formula:

Paragraph 1. If Italy is to receive all of German Tyrol south of the Brenner watershed, as seems to be implied in the President's published memorandum, the addition of this small but strategically important gateway into Italy would not appreciably increase the injury done to German sentiment in the Tyrol, and would materially strengthen Italy's northern frontier.

Paragraph 2. In an earlier memorandum the American specialists have already recommended assigning the Tarvis district to Italy on condition that Fiume goes to Jugoslavia, and have set forth the considerations which make this desirable from the point of view of the central European countries. Possession of Tarvis would favor Italy's scheme for a Predil Pass railway and give her a better natural frontier on the Carnic Alps-Karawanken Mountains crest.

Paragraphs 3 and 4. The area shaded blue, between the line recommended by the American specialists and the extreme Italian claims' line, is solidly Jugoslav, is attached economically to Jugoslavia, and would undoubtedly vote for union with the Jugoslav State. The Jugoslavs accept in principle decision by plebiscite, and while the Slavs west of the

---

[1] Baker, *Woodrow Wilson and the World Settlement,* III (Document 40), 296-302. The spelling "Jugoslavia" is used throughout this document. "Jugo-Slavia" appears in the second half of the document as given in Baker.

recommended frontier, who for economic and geographic reasons are not permitted a vote, may object to this discrimination, the Jugoslavs in general would not strongly contest a solution which would give them the area in question. The Italian Government should find satisfaction in a solution which granted part of their claim immediately and which merely postponed final decision for a few months as regards the remainder; and the Italian people, their passions cooled, would find it difficult to press their case in face of a decision of the population in question to become Jugoslav.

Paragraph 5. A plebiscite in Fiume would, in the opinion of competent observers, show a majority in favor of Jugoslav sovereignty for economic reasons under present economic conditions. It may be regarded as certain that when asked to choose between Jugoslav sovereignty on the one hand, and on the other Italian sovereignty after a rival port has been built at Buccari, even the Italians of Fiume (about 50 per cent. of the population) must in their own interest vote in large numbers for Jugoslav sovereignty; the total vote in this sense would presumably be an overwhelming majority. Thus the provisions of paragraph (b) would never be called into operation. Even if they were, the practical impossibility of constructing an adequate port at Buccari would be forced upon the Italian Government as soon as it began to study the problem and to count the cost. The government's decision to abandon the project would come when passions were less aroused, and the artificially stimulated campaign for Fiume had subsided. Since Italy claims that Fiume has already manifested its unanimous desire to be Italian, and also claims that Buccari can serve Jugoslavia as well as Fiume, the formula is fair to the Italian claims.

Paragraph 6. Lussin and adjacent islands are Italian in population, and while they dominate the entrances to the Gulf of Fiume, under the League of Nations such a condition may not be so serious as to prevent giving the islands to Italy if such concession is deemed necessary in order to secure a proper solution of the much more important Fiume and Dalmatian questions. Lissa has already been tentatively offered to Italy. The Pelagosa group could be given to Italy without appreciable injury to Jugoslavia.

Paragraph 7. There are objections to making Zara a free city, but these may be overbalanced by the advantages of making a concession to Italian sentiment at this point, provided the town alone is involved. If the area were enlarged to include the commune of Zara, a Jugoslav majority would be included.

Paragraph 8. A plebiscite in the Dalmatian coast and islands will give that area to Jugoslavia by an overwhelming majority. The area should vote as a whole, to avoid difficulties due to possible small Italian enclaves. The islands of Pago and Cherso, included in the Treaty of London line, are omitted from the proposed plebiscite area. The Italians have themselves suggested relinquishing their claim to Pago. Cherso, partly Italian in population, would together with its territorial waters practically close Fiume's two best outlets to the Adriatic; it may therefore be wise to avoid complications which might result in the improbable event that a majority on this island should vote for Italian sovereignty. The chief value of the plebiscite would lie in the fact that it is a popular decision which the Italian people might be induced to accept in view of their claim that the majority of the population not only speaks Italian but is attached to Italy by cultural and economic bonds; and that it is a postponed decision which would materialize only after the present excitement in Italy had abated.

Paragraphs 9 and 10. Here may be inserted such provisions for an Italian mandate in Albania, Abyssinia or elsewhere as may be deemed wise.

NOTE

The attached formula has been examined by the territorial specialists concerned with the Fiume and Dalmatian problems (the Chiefs of the Italian Division, Balkan Division, Division of Economics, Division of Boundary Geography, and Chief Territorial Specialist,—the Chief of the Austro-Hungarian Division, being absent) and has their unanimous approval.

SUGGESTED FORMULA FOR ADRIATIC SETTLEMENT, WITH PRESIDENT'S RECOMMENDATION

1. Italy to receive the Sexten Valley (shaded green on accompanying map), a strategic gateway into northern Italy (not included in Treaty of London).

2. Italy to receive the Tarvis district (shaded green on map), a railway junction of much strategic and commercial importance (not included in Treaty of London).

3. Italy to receive the natural geographic frontier in Julian Venetia shown by heavy black line on the accompanying map.

4. Italian troops to be immediately withdrawn from areas east of this line. A plebiscite to be held within a period to be fixed by the League of Nations, and under appropriate safeguards, to determine whether the area shaded blue on the accompanying map shall belong to Italy or to Jugoslavia.

5. Italian troops to be immediately withdrawn from the vicinity and city of Fiume, which shall be administered, within the Jugoslav customs régime, by the League of Nations until its future status is determined.

The city and district of Fiume, together with its moles, docks, basins and other port instrumentalities, to be ceded to Italy when and if the following conditions are fulfilled:

(a) By a plebiscite held within a period to be fixed by the League of Nations, and under appropriate safeguards, the city and district of Fiume by a majority of all votes cast manifests its desire to be annexed to Italy under condition that and as soon as the provisions in (b) have been satisfied.

(b) Within six months after the plebiscite provided in (a) has been held, and in case the plebiscite results favorably to the annexation of Fiume to Italy under the conditions specified, Italy shall proceed to the construction in and about the bay of Buccari of all the port works, including moles, docks, basins, warehouses, office-buildings, railway tracks and all other port instrumentalities, necessary to provide for Jugoslavia and neighboring states a port whose facilities and possibilities of future development shall not be inferior to those of the present port of Fiume; and shall construct rail connections between the new port and the Fiume-Agram and Fiume-Laibach railways not inferior to the existing rail connections between Fiume and the interior. Construction shall proceed under the supervision of an international commission of experts appointed by majority vote of the Council of the League of Nations, which shall certify that the port works, when completed, are not inferior to the present port of Fiume in facilities, possibilities of future development, and rail connections with the interior. The works to be completed within a period to be determined by majority vote of the Council of the League of Nations, and to be transferred without encumbrances to Jugoslavia under such conditions as to free port provisions as the Council of the League of Nations may by majority vote determine.

(c) Italy shall assure in perpetuity, to all nations concerned, the free and unhampered transit across the city and district of Fiume of persons and goods en route between points outside the territory of said city and district. (None of the territory to be ceded to Italy in accordance with the provisions of Section 5 was promised to Italy by the Treaty of London.)

In case any of the above conditions remain unfulfilled at the end of a period to be fixed by majority vote of the Council of the League of Nations, Fiume shall be transferred to Jugoslav sovereignty with such restrictions as to free port provisions as the Council of the League of Nations may by majority vote determine.

6. Italy to receive the islands of Lussin, Unie, Sansego, Asinella, Lissa and its adjacent islets including Busi and San Andrea, and the Pelagosa

group (Pelagosa Grande, Pelagosa Piccola, Cajola, and immediately adjacent islets), (enclosed in green circles on accompanying map).

7. The town of Zara to be made a free city.

8. Italy to relinquish claim to, and immediately withdraw all troops from, those parts of the Istrian and Dalmatian islands and the Dalmatian mainland not mentioned in paragraphs 6 and 7.[2]

(*If further concessions to Italian sentiment are considered essential: Change paragraph 8 to read:*

8. Italian troops to be immediately withdrawn from all parts of the Istrian and Dalmatian islands and Dalmatian mainland not mentioned in paragraphs 6 and 7. A plebiscite to be held within a period of one year from date of this Treaty, under appropriate safeguards [*prescribed by a majority of the Council of the League of Nations*][3] to determine whether the area shaded red on the accompanying map shall, as a whole, belong to Italy or to Jugoslavia).

9. Italy to receive Valona and a sufficient hinterland for its defense.

10. Italy to receive mandatories in such regions as may be agreed upon, and to be assured such equitable economic safeguards as are justifiable in view of her special situation.[4]

(See next page for 11, added after conference with Trumbitch, and 12, added tentatively by me (Professor Johnson) to sound the President on this point.)

11. The entire east Adriatic coast, from the former Austro-Italian frontier to the northern frontier of Albania, to be neutralized under the League of Nations. No fortresses to be allowed on any part of the coast, and no war vessels of any kind to be permitted in the waters bordering this coast. This provision to be accompanied by guarantees for the free passage of Jugoslav merchant vessels through the southern Adriatic and Straits of Otranto, even in time of war.

(If further concessions to Italian sentiment are necessary, change first sentence to read: "The entire Jugoslav coast to be neutralized.")

The effect of this provision would be to render a Jugoslav navy impossible, and to give to Italy absolute control of the Adriatic Sea. On the other hand, the Jugoslavs would have the protection of the League of Nations against any attack by sea.

12. The American government, as an evidence of its friendship for Italy, engages to loan to Italy, on favorable terms, all funds received by the American government by virtue of the terms of the Treaty of Peace with Germany.

[2] This paragraph was ringed in the original document by President Wilson.
[3] Handwritten notation by President Wilson.
[4] This paragraph was ringed in the original document by President Wilson.

MINUTES OF THE COUNCIL OF FOREIGN MINISTERS[1]

[EXTRACTS]

MAY 9, 1919

Territorial Frontiers of Austria

(*ii*) *Frontiers between Austria and Jugo-Slavia.* M. TARDIEU said that the Committee had carefully studied the Jugo-Slav claims to the Austrian provinces of the valley of the Drave. After examining the ethnographical, historical, economical and political conditions, it had decided upon the following solutions for the two boundary regions which formed distinct basins, having as their respective centres, Marburg and Klagenfurt.

(a) District of Marburg.

The United States, British and French Delegations noted that the district of Marburg was inhabited by a population in which the real Slovene element possessed the majority. On the other hand, the Italian Delegation considered that Marburg, of which it recognised the German character, depended on the Austrian economic system, and could not therefore be detached from it without disturbing the economic life of the region and compromising the maintenance of peace.

In consequence, the United States, British and French Delegations proposed to assign to Jugo-Slavia the basin of Marburg; whilst the Italian Delegation opposed to this proposal the reservation of principle formulated above.

(b) District of Klagenfurt.

The United States, British and French Delegations noted that the basin of Klagenfurt was inhabited by a mixed population, composing important Slovene elements, particularly to the east of Klagenfurt. This basin, moreover, constituted a geographical entity separated from the south by the natural barrier of the Karawanken mountains. For this reason, the basin, and not particularly the town of Klagenfurt constituted an association of economic interest more closely connected with the districts situated to the north than with those situated to the south. Nevertheless, the United States, British and French Delegations considered that the information at present in their possession did not appear to be sufficient to allow them

[1] Miller, *My Diary at the Conference of Paris*, XVI, 235-42. See map VI.

to determine with certainty the natural aspirations of the nations of this district. On the other hand, the Italian Delegation considered that the Klagenfurt basin formed an integral part of the Austrian geographical system from which it could not be separated, without disturbing the life of the region and compromising the general peace. For the above reasons, the Committee proposed that the frontier between Jugo-Slavia and Austria should follow the course of the Karawanken mountains from a point southeast of Eisenkappel as far as the Klagenfurt-Laibach road. At the same time, the United States, British and French Delegations proposed that a local enquiry or consultation (under conditions to be determined by the Allied and Associated Governments) should be held, in order to afford the inhabitants of the Klagenfurt basin an opportunity of protesting, should they wish to do so, against inclusion in Austria, and demanding union with Jugo-Slavia. The Italian Delegation, however, opposed to this proposal the reservation of principle formulated above. It declared, moreover, that in its opinion, any question of a consultation or enquiry, as well as of a plebiscite, bore an eminently political character which removed it from the competence of the Territorial Committees.

M. DE MARTINO invited the attention of the Council to the importance of Marburg as a railway centre. In his opinion, the questions of Klagenfurt and Marburg were intimately connected. Consequently the two problems should be studied together and the study should be continued right up to the Italian frontier.

MR. BALFOUR said that before accepting M. de Martino's proposal he wished to enquire whether the arrangement in regard to the boundaries in the district of Marburg had not been something in the nature of a compromise, whereby it had been agreed that a triangle situated to the north of Luttenburg should be left to Austria in exchange for Marburg and the adjoining territory, which was to be included in Jugo-Slavia. As a result, he considered that the Council could not consider one question without the other, as it was by taking the two questions together that a compromise had been reached.

M. TARDIEU agreed that the question should be considered as a whole.

M. PICHON enquired whether the Commission should not be authorised to study the question up to the Italian frontier.

M. SONNINO considered that this could be done then and there. The Council of Four had charged the Council of Foreign Ministers to accept the proposals submitted by the Committee for the study of territorial questions relating to Jugo-Slavia, or to put up their own recommendations in regard to matters requiring amendment.

M. TARDIEU explained that the Committee had thought that a study of the frontiers beyond the Klagenfurt-Laibach road must involve the consideration of Italian claims which had been reserved by the Council of Ten.

M. Sonnino said that if he had correctly understood the question, the Committee in fixing the frontiers between Austria and Jugo-Slavia had given careful consideration to the position of the existing railway lines in these regions, with the result that it had decided to leave the railway line between Klagenfurt, Assling and Trieste free, that is to say, outside the territories allotted to Jugo-Slavia. Now, to give effect to this principle, it would be necessary that the frontier which had been delimited up to the Klagenfurt-Laibach road should thence proceed in a southerly direction, remaining east of Assling, until it met the Italian frontier. In other words, it was essential that the whole of the railway line from Klagenfurt to Trieste, via Assling, should remain in Austria until it reached the Italian frontier. In his opinion, that was the idea which the Committee had meant to follow in accordance with the principle accepted in regard to railway communications by other Commissions. Under this arrangement one important direct railway line of communication would exist between Trieste and Vienna, whilst the other railway lines more to the east would pass through Jugo-Slav territory.

Mr. Lansing said the Council of Foreign Ministers had received no specific reports on these various questions. The Committee for the study of territorial questions relating to Jugo-Slavia had not reported on the particular questions under consideration. He proposed, therefore, that these should first be referred to that Committee for examination.

M. Sonnino said that he would be prepared to accept Mr. Lansing's proposal. He would point out, however, that the Council of Four had directed the Council of Foreign Ministers to report on these very questions. Should his colleagues, nevertheless, insist on referring these questions to the Committee, he would bow to their decision, but only on the understanding that the terms of reference to the Committee should clearly lay down the principle he had just enunciated, namely, that the main line of railway communication between Trieste and Vienna, via Assling, and Klagenfurt should pass wholly through Italian and Austrian territory.

M. Pichon enquired whether the Commission should also be charged to deal with the question of the Italian frontiers in these regions.

Baron Sonnino replied in the negative. He invited the attention of his colleagues to the fact that the Supreme Council had decided that all frontier questions affecting Italy should be settled by that Council. Consequently the reference to the Committee would relate only to the part between the Klagenfurt-Laibach road, where the Committee had previously stopped, and the frontier of Italy. Now, the principle which governed the Committee appeared to be⁴to leave the railway line between

Trieste and Vienna outside Jugo-Slav territory. He thought that question could, therefore, be accepted at once. Otherwise it should, in his opinion, be referred forthwith to the Supreme Council and not to the Committee on Jugo-Slavia.

Mr. LANSING maintained that there was nothing either in the report or in the maps submitted by the Committee for the study of territorial questions relating to Jugo-Slavia, which supported Baron Sonnino's contention.

Mr. BALFOUR said that he understood Baron Sonnino to state that the Councils of Foreign Ministers were not competent at present to decide questions relating to the Italian frontiers. In this view he entirely concurred with Baron Sonnino, at all events as far as Great Britain and France were concerned, since there existed the additional complication in regard to the Treaty of London. On the other hand, for the Council to decide at this stage that a certain railway line must be left out of Jugo-Slavia and included in Italy and Austria seemed to him to be hardly justifiable with the information at present available.

BARON SONNINO agreed that the Committee would be quite unable to discuss such a question, especially if the Foreign Ministers themselves could not do so. Consequently in his opinion the question should be referred to the Supreme Council.

M. PICHON remarked that Mr. Lansing had not said that the present Council were not competent to consider the question. He had merely asked that the question should be referred to the Committee for study and report.

Mr. LANSING agreed. He explained that he felt himself at present incompetent, because he had received no advice from his experts either on the ethnological aspect of the case or in regard to the railways.

BARON SONNINO said that he asked himself what the Committee would do when it reached the Italian frontier, since it would not be competent to deal with the question further. The Committee could, therefore, only deal with another 20 kilometres of country beyond the Klagenfurt-Laibach road.

Mr. BALFOUR enquired whether it would not be an advantage that the question should be examined by a Committee before it came under consideration either by the present Council or by the Supreme Council. So far the question had not been examined by the Committee because the Italian Delegation had held the view that for political reasons Committees should not do so. He quite agreed with the view put forward by the Italian Delegation in regard to the question of international policy; but the Committee could give the ethnologic and economic aspect of the case which would greatly help the Council to deal with the larger questions.

For instance, the area which the Italians desired should be given to Austria and not to Jugo-Slavia was, he understood, largely inhabited by Jugo-Slavs.

That was a question on which the Committee could furnish a statement.

Again, the Italian Delegation maintained that for economic reasons a direct line of communication between Trieste and Vienna and Bohemia should pass wholly through Italian and Austrian territory without crossing Jugo-Slavia. That constituted partly an economic point. Surely the two questions could be looked into by a competent Committee of experts. He understood that to be the suggestion made by Mr. Lansing.

MR. LANSING agreed that Mr. Balfour had correctly interpreted his proposal.

M. SONNINO said that provided the Council of Ministers were willing to accept the lines proposed by the Committee on Jugo-Slav Affairs, he would, himself, withdraw the reservation made by the Italian Delegation in regard to the districts of Marburg and Klagenfurt.

M. TARDIEU pointed out that two reservations had been made: one by the Italian Delegation in regard to the Klagenfurt Basin, which the Delegation considered should remain Austrian on account of its forming an integral part of the Austrian geographical and economic system. On the other hand, the United States, British and French Delegations considered that a local enquiry or consultation should be held in order to afford the inhabitants of the Klagenfurt Basin an opportunity of protesting, should they wish to do so, against inclusion in Austria and of demanding union with Jugo-Slavia. It would be seen, therefore, that the Committee had not made any definite proposals. The Italian Delegation considered that the Klagenfurt Basin should be included in Austria, whereas the other three Delegations proposed that a line should be drawn south of the Klagenfurt Basin up to which the enquiry or consultation should proceed.

MR. BALFOUR enquired whether the procedure adopted in the case of Malmedy could not be followed in the present instance. Malmedy had been incorporated in Belgium, but provision was made in order to allow the inhabitants to protest against their inclusion in Belgium within a certain time; reference would then be to the League of Nations, which would decide. He thought that procedure might be found a convenient method of dealing with the problem of Klagenfurt.

M. SONNINO pointed out that the two cases were very different. In Malmedy there was a question of bringing Germans under Belgian sovereignty; whereas the people of Klagenfurt already formed part of the Austrian State.

M. PICHON interpreted the views of the Council to be that the question should be referred to the Committee on Jugo-Slav Affairs to report as soon as possible, giving precise details to enable a decision to be taken.

M. Tardieu pointed out that the Committee could give ethnic and statistical data relating to this region but it could not give particulars relating to the railway line which would join the Italian frontier at an unknown point.

Mr. Lansing agreed that the Council only required the Committee to give ethnological and economic information.

(It was agreed that the Committee for the study of territorial questions relating to Jugo-Slavia should submit recommendations in regard to the frontiers between Jugo-Slavia and Austria, up to the Italian Frontier, based on ethnic and economic considerations; the Committee should submit their report on the morning of the 10th May, 1919.)

MINUTES OF THE COUNCIL OF FOREIGN MINISTERS[1]

[EXTRACTS]

MAY 10, 1919

Frontier between Austria and Jugo-Slavia

1. M. PICHON asked M. Tardieu whether he had any additional explanations to make to the Report. (For Report see Annexure A.)

Consideration of supplementary report by Committee on Jugo-Slav Affairs.—M. TARDIEU said that the Report had been circulated and that it explained itself.

BARON SONNINO said that in his opinion the solution finally proposed by the Committee in Part II of the Report appeared to him somewhat complicated. Italy, in the interest of the port of Trieste, wished that there should be uninterrupted communication between that port and German-Austria and Bohemia. For this purpose the railway line should not pass through the territory of any third State which had no direct interest in the development of the line and possibly an adverse interest. Similar considerations had been given weight in dealing with Poland, Czecho-Slovakia, Hungary, etc. No doubt this might involve the delivery of a certain number of Slovenes to Austrian rule, but similar instances were not lacking elsewhere. For instance, the town of Marburg had been given to Jugo-Slavia though it contained from 18,000 to 20,000 Germans. He did not wish to delay peace with Austria, and for that purpose, he would, if necessary, agree to the solution proposed, but he pointed out that it was no real solution; it was only a postponement.

M. PICHON said that it had the advantage of rendering an early signature of peace with Austria possible. The ultimate attribution of the territory could then be settled among the Allies.

BARON SONNINO said that the alternatives were to give the territory in question, namely: the triangle surrounding Klagenfurt, to Austria or to Jugo-Slavia. If it were to go to Austria, why not decide at once? Were it to go to Jugo-Slavia, either at once or later, the economic trouble to which he had alluded would inevitably ensue. There was a third possibility, to attribute it to Italy; but this was not desired by Italy, who wished to avoid

[1] Miller, *My Diary at the Conference of Paris*, XVI, 258-63. See Map VI.

the inclusion of non-Italian populations, except in cases of territories required for Italian safety.

Mr. Balfour said that he did not wish to express any strong dogmatic views, but he wished to suggest a few points. He felt some difficulty in meeting the views of the Italian Delegation, and in disregarding those of the French, British and American Delegations. The Italian solution involved not only the separation of some Jugo-Slavs from the bulk of their nation, but their surrender to an enemy State. It was difficult to justify the handing over to an enemy of the natural subjects of a State it was intended to create. Secondly, he understood that the frontier proposed by all but the Italian Delegation followed the crest of a high range of hills. This crest formed the natural frontier between Jugo-Slavia and Austria. The Italian proposal would bring the Austrians south of the range. This, on the face of it, was an extraordinary thing to do in dealing with a hostile State. The proposal appeared to violate both ethnographical and geographical considerations. It was not a parallel case to that of the Brenner, the acquisition of which by Italy could be justified on geographical grounds, though open to criticism on ethnological grounds. In this case both ethnology and geography agreed, and both were to be violated. The only answer to these objections was that one of the two railway lines connecting Trieste and the north passed through this tongue of territory. It was assumed that if this tongue of territory belonged to Jugo-Slavia, it might be utilised to obstruct the trade of Trieste with the North. This was a serious argument, as undoubtedly all the Allies wished to promote the trade of Trieste. There was, however, one qualification to this, namely: that there was another railway line connecting Trieste with German-Austria. This line it was true was inferior to the more easterly line. Still it existed and was an element in the situation. A further qualification was that the Allied Powers in dealing with Poland had been faced by a similar, but yet more vital, railway problem. The arrangement with Germany made it possible that the only main line of communication between the capital of Poland and the sea would be intercepted by German territory. This possibility had been contemplated, and in the event of its being realised, arrangements had been thought out to safeguard the traffic. The Polish case was obviously a stronger case than the one in question, as the most vital interests of the whole country were in jeopardy. It could not be held that the railway line from Trieste to the North affected Italian interests to this extent. If, therefore, the provisions made for Poland were sufficient, similar provisions ought to be adequate for Trieste. Lastly, he wished to draw attention to a very serious aspect of the delivery of this territory to Austria. It would give the Northern powers access to a region from which they could advantageously invade Jugo-Slavia. He did not think that Italy would readily grant such an advantage to any of her own enemies. The Council could not, he thought, decide this case against the Jugo-Slavs until this military problem had been studied. The remarks just made represented the reflections suggested by the report just put forward by M. Tardieu. Before concluding he wished to say that he sympathised most cordially with the Italian wish to develop Trieste. All wished to see Trieste prosperous, and possessed of free access to all the countries North of it.

Mr. LANSING enquired whether he was wrong in understanding that both of the railway roads were single tracks.

M. LAROCHE said that both lines had a single track, but that tunnels had been made on the Eastern line (Trieste-Assling) for a double track.

Mr. LANSING said that he had little to add to the very full consideration given to the subject by Baron Sonnino and Mr. Balfour. As to the principles on which the solution ought to be based, he agreed with Mr. Balfour. In the case of the Brenner Pass the Council had decided to give precedence to topographical over ethnographical considerations, and had given to Italy territory including a large number of Austrian-Germans. They were now asked to change their principles, and to decide against a natural boundary. It seemed to him that a similar argument might be used in the case of Fiume. If this territory must not be Jugo-Slav, because the Jugo-Slavs might use it to interrupt communications with an Italian port, the Hinterland of Fiume, it might equally be argued, must not be Jugo-Slav because the railways feeding the port might similarly be interfered with.

BARON SONNINO said that he did not admit the cases were parallel. In this instance the railway was to pass through a band of territory about 20 kilometres broad. The Jugo-Slavs would not be interested in the railway at all; and if they possessed this strip they might seize the opportunity of neglecting the line in order to favour traffic to another part. In the case of Fiume, however, the whole trade must come through territory which no one suggested should be withheld from Jugo-Slavia. The contest was really between two ports, and the natural flow of commerce to each should be kept as far as possible separate, and no entanglement between them should be allowed. This was the only way to secure the development of both.

As to the ethnological point, in Poland, some 300,000 Germans were to be made subjects of the new Polish State, and about 280,000 Hungarians were to be Roumanian subjects, as the inevitable accompaniment of some hundreds of kilometres of railway.

Mr. LANSING observed that the process of giving to friends rather than to enemies was being reversed. This territory was being taken from the Jugo-Slavs to be given to the Austrians.

BARON SONNINO observed that the Slovenes were not his friends in a greater degree than the Austrians.

MR. LANSING retorted that America regarded them as friends.

BARON SONNINO said that the new States should be considered neither as friends nor foes. Should German Austria, for instance, join the Danubian Confederacy, the Austrians might come to be regarded as friends. Should they join the German Confederation, the Austrians would be counted among foes. The question was really one of permanent commercial relations. Further, if the question of friendship was raised, he claimed a share for Italy.

MR. BALFOUR said that he heartily endorsed the last sentence.

MR. LANSING agreed, but pointed out that the question was an Austrian rather than an Italian problem.

BARON SONNINO said that it was an Italian question in as much as it concerned Trieste, Istria and the Adriatic.

MR. LANSING said that he was struck by the fact that if Austria were brought so far south, she might feel she had a claim to reach salt water.

BARON SONNINO observed that she would only be brought some 20 kilometres nearer the sea.

M. PICHON enquired whether any practical solution could be found.

BARON SONNINO said he was ready to accept the proposal made by the Committee at the end of the second section of the Report. He was ready to do this in a conciliatory spirit to avoid obstructing the signature of a Treaty with Austria. He would have, however, a small amendment to make. He would stipulate that the triangle, the ultimate fate of which was to be reserved, should not be made so wide as to include the western line from Trieste, and thereby to leave in suspense the whole of the railway communications between Trieste and the North. In other words, the triangle should not include the line from Trieste to Villach via Udine and Tarvis.

MR. LANSING proposed that the formula suggested by the Committee be accepted with a proviso that the limit of the territory be to the east of Tarvis.

M. TARDIEU observed that the Committee had constantly kept in view the desirability of preserving uninterrupted communication between Trieste and Austria.

MR. BALFOUR said that he was ready to accept the view that it was the business of the Conference to see that direct and free railway communication be assured between Trieste, German Austria, Bohemia and the North generally.

BARON SONNINO said that on this understanding he would agree to the draft of the Committee.

MR. BALFOUR said that his remark should not be interpreted as a prejudgment on the question of territorial sovereignty. By direct and free communication, he did not mean necessarily to imply that railway lines were not to pass through ground belonging to a third State.

BARON SONNINO said that he accepted the proposal of the Committee on the understanding that due consideration was given to the necessity of preserving the railway communications of Trieste towards the North. He would make no concession in advance regarding the question of territory just mentioned by Mr. Balfour.

MR. LANSING pointed out that the Report of the Committee proposed that the frontier line should pass north of the tunnel of Rosenbach. He thought that it would be better to have the frontier line along the ridge over the tunnel.

(After some discussion it was agreed to omit the last clause of the first paragraph of the Committee's recommendation in Part II of the Report.)

M. PICHON suggested that the Committee should formulate a proposal, after taking into consideration the above discussion, for reference to the Council of Heads of States, and that no further reference need be made to the Council of Foreign Ministers, should the Committee reach a unanimous decision.

(This was agreed to.)

(The meeting then adjourned.)

Paris, May 10th, 1919.

BALFOUR MEMORANDUM[1]
May 16, 1919

THE PROBLEM OF ITALY AND TURKEY IN ANATOLIA

The scheme provisionally accepted on Wednesday last at a meeting of the "Three," contemplates the final destruction of the Turkish State. This is already condemned, and I think rightly, to the loss of its European possessions, its Arab-speaking population, and Armenia. It is therefore in any case reduced, as far as the area of its Empire is concerned, to a mere fraction of its former self; this fraction, however, we originally proposed to preserve, thus leaving to the Sultan the great block of Anatolia lying west [east] of the meridian of Constantinople, which is not merely inhabited by a population the vast majority of whom are Turks, but which contains within its boundaries most of the Turkish race. For this scheme has now been substituted one which cuts this region into two separate states, with different capitals, different sovereigns and different mandatories.

I look with much misgiving at this proposal. It will not only deeply shock large sections of Mohammedan opinion, but I think it will also be made the subject of a great deal of very unfavourable Christian commentary. We are all most anxious to avoid as far as possible placing reluctant populations under alien rule; but ought we not to be quite as careful to avoid the opposite fault? Is it a greater crime to join together those who wish to be separated than to divide those who wish to be united? And if the Anatolian Turks say they desire to remain a single people under a single sovereign, to what principle are we going to make appeal when we refuse to grant their request?

I think we must admit that no such scheme would ever have been thought of, if it had not been necessary to find some method of satisfying Italian ambitions. Unfortunately, this necessity haunts and hampers every step in our diplomacy. The Italians, armed with the Treaty of London, and supported by a passionate public opinion, will never be content with fragments of Tyrolese and Jugo-Slav territory in Europe; with French and British Colonial concessions in Africa, and with the Caucasus in the Middle East. We have also to find something for them out of the Turkish

---

[1] Baker, *Woodrow Wilson and the World Settlement*, III (Document 41), 303-7. The document appears as an Appendix to the Minutes of the Council of May 17, 1919, C.F. 15A.

Empire in Asia Minor. Now I believe there are only two kinds of scheme possible by which the latter operation can be accomplished;—the scheme of partition advocated by the "Three," and the scheme which I ventured to lay before them. This last has not, perhaps, in all respects, been very clearly understood; which is not surprising, for it was very hastily written, and not very fully explained. But the matter is so important that I may be permitted to return to it.

Under my scheme Turkey remained an undivided State without a Mandatory. Its status was substantially that of the historic Turkish Empire. Its territories were, indeed, much diminished; it could no longer count as a Great Power; but in other respects the Sultan would reign at Brussa or Konia as his predecessors had formerly reigned at Constantinople.

Now it must be remembered that even at Constantinople representatives of the Western Powers had special positions in his administration, justified, and, indeed, rendered necessary for various well-known reasons. The public debt, the customs, and in some cases the police, were under the control or supervision of foreign advisers. This system I do not propose to alter, but rather to perfect. The Turks are familiar with it, up to a certain point they welcome it, and they do not deem it inconsistent with their unity or their independence.

The alternative scheme, which found favour on Wednesday, destroys both; for it cuts Turkey into two halves; and puts each under a separate Mandatory. What are its compensating advantages? It is said, in the first place, that it avoids the evils of a Condominium. A Condominium, we are told, is never a success; it is slow moving, ineffectual and the occasion of endless friction between the controlling Powers;—a friction so acute as even to endanger the peace of the world.

But the plan I propose is not a Condominium. A Condominium, as I understand it, is the joint Government of a single State by many Powers acting collectively. Under such a system, the Powers first agree upon a policy, and then impose it upon the subordinate State. They control, actually or potentially, the whole administration. If they differ, the administrative machinery stands still. If their differences are due to their being moved by inconsistent interests, they may become acute and even dangerous. The subordinate Government is perpetually tempted to play one off against the other, and the whole country becomes the theatre of rival intrigues. Everybody quarrels, and nothing is done.

Now nobody will pretend that the Constantinople Government was a good one, but it was not as bad as all this. There were, of course, endless intrigues, political and financial. There was a perpetual struggle to obtain influence with the Sultan and his Ministers. There was much corruption; there was much mal-administration. But it was never a Condominium.

The Sultan appointed his ministers; he appointed the Governors of his Provinces; he raised and commanded the Army; he directed the foreign policy of his country, and was in these and all other important respects, an independent sovereign. Certain branches of his administration were no doubt controlled, not by a foreign Condominium, but by foreigners. He remained, nevertheless, in quite a different position from that which he would have held either under a Condominium or under a Mandatory.

Another objection raised against my scheme is that it gives special privileges to Italy in the southern part of the Turkish state. This is quite true, and of course I should greatly prefer that it were otherwise. But inasmuch as the whole plan is primarily devised in order to do something to satisfy Italian appetites, that is, I am afraid, inevitable. From an administrative point of view, the scheme would no doubt be much better if the Italians played no part in it. I freely admit it—but I submit that the argument is irrelevant. The Italians must somehow be mollified, and the only question is how to mollify them at the smallest cost to mankind.

Then it is said that to give the Italians a first claim to concessions in any district is to violate the principle of equal opportunities for all nations. Again, I am not prepared to deny the charge. My whole object is to give the Italians something which they will really like, and it seems that they have a great liking for concessions. I remember, when the Marquis Imperiali was comparing the advantages which the French would get out of Cilicia with the advantages which Italy was likely to get out of her share of Asia Minor, he was wont to dwell upon the wonders of a certain copper mine, which he said, I am sure quite truly, was to be found somewhere in the French zone. In the same way, I observe that Baron Sonnino's eyes are lovingly fixed upon a very indifferent coal mine on the Southern shores of the Black Sea. Personally, I regard these hopes and expectations with considerable scepticism. I doubt the existence of these hidden riches in Southern Anatolia. Even if they exist, I doubt whether their exploitation is going to make Italy rich; and I have a strong suspicion that even if these industrial enterprises are started under Italian patronage, they will be found after no great lapse of time to be under German management. But all this does not seem to me to be to the point. The object is to find some privileged position for the Italians in Southern Anatolia; and I particularly beg the "Three" to remember that she has already got the germs of such a position by a pre-war arrangement which she made with the Turks, in respect of the region neighbouring on Adalia. My suggestion only extends and emphasises her privileges. It does not create them.

In any case, as Italy is not, under my plan, intended to occupy the position of a Mandatory in these regions, the general principle—that no

Mandatory has a right to exceptional trade advantages in the country which it controls—is not violated. The only difference that I can see between what would happen under my plan, and what would happen if nothing were done for the Italians in Asia Minor, is that in the first case Italy would without question or controversy have the refusal of all concessions within a certain area: in the second case these concessions will be scrambled for at Brussa by the rival company-mongers of every country under Heaven, supported, no doubt, by their respective Ministers. The first plan may be an infringement upon the liberty and equality, nominally at least, secured by the second; but I do not know that these most excellent things are seen to the best advantage when they are enjoyed by corrupt administrators and greedy speculators.

But once again, this is relatively unimportant compared with the main objects of the scheme I am endeavouring to support. This is designed to do two things: to maintain something resembling an independent Turkish Government, ruling over a homogeneous Turkish population; the other is to find a position for the Italians within this Turkish State which will make a sufficient appeal to the ambitions of the Italian Government. From every other point of view the plan is, I admit, a bad one; but from this point of view—which is the one at the moment chiefly occupying our thoughts—I still think it worthy of serious consideration.

[*Initialed*] A. J. B.

MINUTES OF THE COUNCIL OF HEADS OF DELEGATIONS[1]

[EXTRACTS]

SEPTEMBER 15, 1919

Two.—In accordance with his promise made at the meeting of the morning M. Tittoni handed his colleagues copies of the following memorandum regarding the question of the Adriatic.

ONE.—Fiume. The City (corpus separatum) shall be placed under the sovereignty of Italy. There shall be no independent State of Fiume. Jugo-Slavia shall receive all the territories included in this State according to President Wilson's line (Cherso included and Albona excepted).

All the territories that would have made part independent State shall be permanently demilitarized.

The port of Fiume with all facilities for its development, as well as for the railways terminating there, shall be given over to the League of Nations which shall make such arrangements as it shall see fit both for the country of which this port is the outlet and for the City of Fiume itself.

The rights of ethnic minorities shall be guaranteed.

Two.—Dalmatia. All Dalmatia shall go to the Jugo-Slavs except the City of Zara which shall be a free city under the guarantee of the League of Nations, which shall recognize and encourage its intimate connection with the Italian State and Italian culture. The city shall be represented diplomatically by Italy.

Every facility shall be given to the commerce of the hinterland. The economic interests of Italy existing in Dalmatia and the rights of Italian minorities shall be guaranteed.

THREE.—Islands. The only Italian islands shall be Lussin and Unie and Lissa and Pelogosa.

FOUR.—Albania to be independent with a mandate given to Italy.

FIVE.—Vallona. Italian sovereignty over the City with the hinterland strictly necessary to its economic life and its security.

SIX.—Railways. For the Assling Railway Italy no longer makes any territorial demands, but demands only definite guarantees for the use of the line in Jugo-Slav territory. On the other hand no territorial cession shall be granted to the Jugo-Slavs in the Valley of the Drin, but they shall receive there, as to the use of the railway to be constructed, the same guarantees as are given to Italy for the Assling Railway.

[1] Miller, *My Diary at the Conference of Paris,* XVI, 518-21.

[SEVEN].—Neutralization. Italy demands the general neutralization of the entire coast and of the islands from the southern point of Istria to Cattaro, inclusive.

EIGHT.—A Commission appointed by the Conference on which each of the Five Powers shall be represented by a delegate and an expert shall as soon as possible trace the frontiers on the maps and draw up all details.

He also explained that he proposed to adopt the sixth (?) to Italy already telegraphed to President Wilson, as he was unwilling to agree to a plebiscite in the Free State. In reply to a question from Mr. Lloyd George regarding Point Six of the memorandum, he explained that if the guarantee of the League of Nations were to be considered sufficient for the last administration as regards the Assling triangle the Serbians should be satisfied with the same guarantee for the Drin. Mr. Lloyd George suggested that it would be more advisable to say that Zara should be able to choose its diplomatic representatives. Nothing would prevent its entrusting its interests to Italian agents. M. Tittoni said that he had no objections to this solution. He also claimed that his suggestion had appeared in the proposal approved by President Wilson on June seventh. Mr. Polk observed that the proposal in question had been submitted to the experts for examination and as a basis of argument. As regards Fiume he desired to say that he had received a telegram from President Wilson from which it appeared that the President was disposed to accept the solution of the Free State. He feared that the President would be surprised to receive a new proposal. Mr. Lloyd George said that he agreed with Mr. Polk in thinking that it would not be fair to the President. After some further discussion M. Tittoni suggested that the Conference wait the President's reply. As regards the Valley of the Drin, Mr. Lloyd George said that it was not his intention to cede this territory to the Serbians, but he believed that it was necessary to give them the right to construct a railway and facilities for a port. He thought the case different from the Assling triangle where a railroad already existed.

Three.—Regarding the reported incidents at Fiume, M. Tittoni stated that the Italians were blockading the City from the land side. He asked that the Allied and Associated Powers should assist in engineering the blockade from the sea. M. Clemenceau accepted this and proposed the following communication to the press:

On the request of the Italian Government the Principal Allied and Associated Powers have agreed to participate in the maritime blockade of Fiume which the Italian troops have already surrounded on land.

M. Tittoni asked that publication be suspended until he should have an opportunity to communicate with M. Nitti. This was agreed to.

BIBLIOGRAPHY

BIBLIOGRAPHY

Certain works, though not available to the author, have been included for the sake of completeness. These works are indicated by an asterisk.

Adami, Vittorio, Storia documentata dei confini del regno d'Italia. 4 vols. in 5. Rome, Stabilimento poligrafico per l'amministrazione della guerra, 1919-31. Vols. 3-4.

Adriatic Question, The, see United States, Department of State.

Adriaticus (*pseud.*), La Question adriatique. Paris, Imprimerie typographique, 1920.

Aldrovandi, Luigi, "La settimana di passione adriatica a Parigi (17-27 aprile 1919)," *Nuova Antologia,* May 16, June 1, 1933.

Almond, Nina, and Ralph Haswell Lutz, The Treaty of St. Germain. Stanford University Press, 1935.

Amendola, Giovanni, and others, Il patto di Londra. Rome, La Voce, 1919.

Ancel, Jacques, Les Balkans face à l'Italie. Paris, Delagrave, 1928.

Angeli, Umberto, Guerra vinta pace perduta. Rome, La rivista di Roma, 1921.

Annunzio, Gabriele d', Contro uno e contro tutti. Rome, La Fionda, 1919.

———— Italia o morte! Rome, La Fionda, 1919.

———— La Reggenza italiana del Carnaro; disegno di un nuovo ordinamento dello stato libero di Fiume. Rome, La Fionda, 1920.

Antonelli, Étienne, L'Afrique et la paix de Versailles. Paris, Grasset, 1921.

Atti parlamentari, see Italy.

Austrian Red Book, see Austro-Hungarian monarchy.

Austro-Hungarian Monarchy, K. und K. Ministerium des Äussern, Diplomatische Aktenstücke betreffend die Beziehungen Österreich-Ungarns zu Italien in der Zeit vom 20 Juli 1914 bis 23 Mai 1915. Vienna, Staatsdruckerei, 1915. (English translation, 1915.)

———— Diplomatische Aktenstücke zur Vorgeschichte des Krieges 1914. Ergänzungen und Nachträge zum österreichisch-ungarischen Rotbuch. Vienna, Staatsdruckerei, 1919. 3 pts. in 1 vol. (English translation, 1920.)

———— Österreich-Ungarns Aussenpolitik von der bosnischen Krise 1908 bis zum Kriegsausbruch 1914. Edited by L. Bittner, A. F. Přibram, H. Sbirk, and H. Uebersberger. 9 vols. Vienna, Staatsdruckerei, 1930. Vol. VIII.

"Aventure de Fiume, L" [anonymous], *Revue des deux mondes,* Jan. 15, March 1, April 1, 1921.

Bainville, Jacques, Les Conséquences politiques de la paix. Paris, Nouvelle librairie nationale, 1920.

Baker, Ray Stannard, Woodrow Wilson and the World Settlement. 3 vols. New York, Doubleday, 1923.

Beer, George Louis, African Questions at the Paris Peace Conference. New York, Macmillan, 1923.

———— Diary. Unpublished.

Benedetti, Giulio, Fiume, Porto Baross e il retroterra. Rome, Maglione e Strini, 1921.

—— La pace di Fiume. Bologna, Zanichelli, 1924.

Bernardy, Amy, and Vittorio Falorsi, La questione adriatica vista d'oltre Atlantico. Bologna, Zanichelli, 1923.

Bertotti, Emilio, La nostra spedizione in Albania. Milan, Unitas, 1926.

Binkley, Robert C., "New Light on the Paris Peace Conference," *Political Science Quarterly*, Sept., Dec., 1931.

Bissolati, Leonida, La politica estera dell'Italia dal 1897 al 1920. Milan, Treves, 1923.

Bowman, Isaiah, The New World. Yonkers-on-Hudson, World Book Company, 1928.

British Documents on the Origins of the War, *see* Great Britain.

Bülow, Prince von, Memoirs of Prince von Bülow, translated from the German by Geoffrey Dunlop. 4 vols. Boston, Little, Brown and Co., 1932. Vol. III: The World War and Germany's Collapse, 1909-1919.

Burián von Rajecz, Stephan, Graf, Austria in Dissolution, translated by Brian Lunn. New York, Doran, 1925.

Caniglia, Benedetto, Italia e Albania. Rome, Brocato, 1925.

Cappa, Alberto, *see* Sforza.

Cirić, Slavko M., *see* Tchiritch.

Colonna di Cesarò, Giovanni Antonio, L'Italia nell'Albania meridionale. Foligno, Campitelli, 1922.

Coppola, Francesco, La pace democratica. Bologna, Zanichelli, 1921.

Correspondence relating to the Adriatic Question, *see* Great Britain, Foreign Office.

Currey, Muriel, Italian Foreign Policy, 1918-1932. London, I. Nicholson and Watson, 1932.

Cvijić, Jovan, La Péninsule balkanique. Paris, Colin, 1918.

Daily Review of the Foreign Press, *see* Great Britain, War Office.

D'Annunzio, Gabriele, *see* Annunzio, Gabriele d'.

Depoli, A., Il confine orientale di Fiume e la questione del delta della Fiumara. Fiume, 1921.*

Diamandy, C., "Ma Mission en Russie," *Revue des deux mondes,* Nov. 15, 1930.

Di Cellere, *see* Justus.

Fay, Sidney Bradshaw, The Origins of the World War, 2d ed. 2 vols. in 1. New York, Macmillan, 1932.

Federzoni, Luigi, Il trattato di Rapallo. Bologna, Zanichelli, 1921.

Fidel, Camille, "Le Programme colonial italien et l'alliance franco-italienne," *Bulletin du comité de l'Afrique française,* 1919.

Gauvain, Auguste, La Question yougoslave. Paris, Brossard, 1918.

—— L'Europe au jour le jour. 14 vols. Paris, Brossard, 1921-24. (Vols. XIII-XIV).

George Louis Beer, A Tribute . . . New York, Macmillan, 1924.

Germany, Auswärtiges Amt, Die deutschen Dokumente zum Kriegsausbruch

1914, edited by Max Montgelas and Walter Schücking. Berlin, Deutsche Verlagsgesellschaft für Politik und Geschichte, 1927.

Giannini, Amedeo, Fiume nel trattato di Trianon. Rome, Libreria di scienze e lettere, 1921.

―――― Gli accordi di Santa Margherita. Rome, 1923.

―――― I documenti diplomatici della pace orientale. Rome, Edizioni di politica, 1922.

―――― "Il compromesso Tardieu per la questione adriatica," Aperusen, July, 1922.

―――― "Il progetto Miller per la questione adriatica," Le nuove provincie, fasc. ii, 1922.

―――― Il trattato di Rapallo al parlamento italiano. Rome, Edizioni di politica, 1922.

―――― Il trattato di Rapallo nei comenti della stampa. Rome, Tipografia del senato, 1921.

―――― "L'annessione di Cipro all'Inghilterra e l'equilibrio nel Mediterraneo orientale," Oriente moderno, Sept., 1922.

―――― La questione di Porto Baross e gli accordi di Santa Margherita al parlamento italiano. Rome, 1923.

―――― "La questione orientale alla conferenza della pace," Oriente moderno, June-Dec., 1921.

―――― Trattati ed accordi per la pace adriatica. Rome, Edizioni di politica, 1924.

Gigante, Silvino, Storia del Comune di Fiume. Florence, Bemporad, 1928.

Giolitti, Giovanni, Memorie della mia vita. 2 vols. Milan, Treves, 1922.

―――― Memoirs of My Life. London, Chapman and Dodd, 1923. English translation of the preceding book.

Glaise-Horstenau, Edmund von, The Collapse of the Austro-Hungarian Empire, translated by Ian F. D. Morrow. London, Dent and Sons Ltd., 1930.

Great Britain, Foreign Office, British Documents on the Origins of the War, 1898-1914, edited by George P. Gooch and Harold Temperley. London, H. M. Stationery Office, 1926 to date, Vol. XI.

―――― Correspondence relating to the Adriatic Question. London, H. M. Stationery Office, 1920. Miscellaneous, No. 2, 1920.

―――― War Office. Daily Review of the Foreign Press, Allied Press Supplement, 6 vols. Issued by the General Staff, War Office, 1916-19. Vols. V-VI.

Haskins, Charles Homer, and Robert Howard Lord, Some Problems of the Peace Conference. Cambridge, Harvard University Press, 1920.

Herre, Paul, Die Südtiroler Frage. Munich, C. H. Beck'sche Verlagsbuchhandlung, 1927.

House, Edward Mandell, The Intimate Papers of Colonel House, arranged as a narrative by Charles Seymour. 4 vols. Boston, Houghton Mifflin, 1926-28.

House, Edward Mandell, and Charles Seymour, eds., What Really Happened at Paris. New York, Scribner, 1921.

Howard, Harry Nicholas, The Partition of Turkey, 1913-1923. University of Oklahoma Press, 1931.

International Review, The, April-May, 1919. London, The International Review Office.

Intervento dell'Italia nei documenti segreti dell'Intesa, L'. Rome, Casa ed. Rassegna internazionale, 1923.

Italia e Jugoslavia [by a group of Italian and Yugoslav writers]. Florence, 1917.*

Italian Green Books, *see* Italy, *Ministero degli affari esteri.*

Italy, Ministero degli affari esteri. Documenti diplomatici presentati al parlamento italiano dal Ministro degli affari esteri (Sonnino). Austria-Ungheria. Seduta del 20 maggio 1915. Rome, Camera dei deputati, 1915.

—— Documenti diplomatici presentati al parlamento italiano dal Ministro degli affari esteri (Scialoja). Accordo di Londra del 26 aprile 1915. Presentati alla presidenza della camera il 4 marzo 1920. Rome, Camera dei deputati, 1920.

—— Documenti diplomatici presentati al parlamento italiano dal Ministro degli affari esteri (Sforza). Negoziati diretti fra il governo italiano e il governo serbo-croato-sloveno per la pace adriatica. Presentati alla Camera il 20 giugno 1921. Rome, Camera dei deputati, 1921.

—— Parlamento. Atti del Parlamento italiano. XXIVa, XXVa, XXVIa legislature, Sessioni 1913-19, 1919-21, 1921-23. Camera, Discussioni; Senato, Discussioni, Rome, Camera dei deputati.

—— Relazione della commissione parlamentare d'inchiesta per le spese di guerra, 6 febbraio 1923. Rome, Camera dei deputati, 1923.

—— Trattati e convenzioni fra il regno d'Italia e gli stati esteri, 1865 to date. Rome, Tipografia del Ministero degli affari esteri [for more recent vols.] Vols. XII, XV, XVI, XVII, XXIII.

Justus (*pseud.*), V. Macchi di Cellere all'ambasciata di Washington. Florence, Bemporad, 1920.

Kautsky Documents, *see* Germany, Auswärtiges Amt.

Lansing, Robert, The Big Four and Others of the Peace Conference. Boston, Houghton Mifflin, 1921.

—— The Peace Negotiations, a Personal Narrative. Boston, Houghton Mifflin, 1921.

Lémonon, Ernest, L'Italie d'après-guerre. Paris, Alcan, 1922.

Maranelli, Carlo, and Gaetano Salvemini, La questione dell'Adriatico. Rome, La voce, 1919.

Marinelli, Olinto, "The Regions of Mixed Populations in Northern Italy," *Geographical Review,* March, 1919.

Mears, Eliot Grinnel, and others, Modern Turkey. New York, Macmillan, 1924.

Mermeix (*pseud.,* Gabriel Terrail), Les Négociations secrètes et les quatre armistices, avec pièces justificatives. Paris, Ollendorff, 1921.

Miller, David Hunter, My Diary at the Conference of Paris. 20 vols. Privately printed, 1928. Vols. I-X, XIV-XVI, XIX.

—— The Drafting of the Covenant. 2 vols. New York, Putnam, 1928.

Miller, David Hunter, "The Adriatic Negotiations at Paris," *Atlantic Monthly,* August, 1921.

Nevins, Allan, Henry White, Thirty Years of American Diplomacy. New York, Harper, 1930.

Nicolson, Harold, Curzon: the Last Phase 1919-1925. Boston and New York, Houghton Mifflin, 1934.

———— Peacemaking, 1919. Boston and New York, Houghton Mifflin, 1933.

Nitti, Francesco Saverio, L'Europa senza pace. Florence, Bemporad, 1921.

———— The Wreck of Europe. Indianapolis, Bobbs-Merrill, 1922. English translation of the preceding book.

Noble, George Barnes, Policies and Opinions at Paris, 1919. New York, Macmillan, 1935.

Orano, Paolo, L'Italia e gli altri stati alla conferenza della pace. Bologna, Zanichelli, 1919.*

Orlando, Vittorio Emanuele, Discorsi per la guerra e per la pace, ed. by A. Giannini. Foligno, Campitelli, 1924.

Ossoinack, Andrea, Perchè Fiume dev'essere italiana. Fiume, 1919.*

———— Perchè Fiume dev'essere porto franco. Fiume, 1921.*

Paresce, Gabriele, Italia e Jugoslavia. Florence, Bemporad, 1935.

Paris Peace Conference Delegation, A Catalogue of . . . Propaganda in the Hoover War Library. Stanford University Press, 1926.

Piazza, Giuseppe, La nostra pace coloniale. Rome, Ausonia, 1917.

Politica, *see* Tamaro.

Pribram, Alfred Francis, Austrian Foreign Policy, 1908-18. London, Allen and Unwin, 1923.

———— The Secret Treaties of Austria-Hungary, English edition by Archibald Coolidge. Cambridge, Harvard University Press, 1920-21.

Ribarić, J., and others, La Question de l'Adriatique: L'Istrie. Paris, Imprimerie Graphique, 1919.

Rouard du Card, E., La France et l'Italie et l'article 13 du Pacte de Londres. Paris, A. Pedone, 1919.

Salandra, Antonio, I discorsi della guerra. Milan, Treves, 1922.

———— La neutralità italiana. Milan, Mondadori, 1928.

———— L'intervento. Milan, Mondadori, 1931.

———— Italy and the Great War. London, Edward Arnold and Co., 1932. English translation of the two preceding books.

Salvatorelli, Luigi, "La triplice alleanza," *Rassegna di politica internazionale,* May, 1936.

Salvemini, Gaetano, Dal patto di Londra alla pace di Roma. Turin, Gobetti, 1925.

Scialoja, Vittorio, "La posizione giuridica di Fiume," *Rassegna italiana,* 1919.

Scott, James Brown, Diplomatic Documents relating to the Outbreak of the European War. 2 pts. in 2 vols. New York, Oxford University Press, 1916.

Seton-Watson, Robert William, The Balkans, Italy and the Adriatic. London, Nisbet, 1916.

Seton-Watson, Robert William, The Rise of Nationality in the Balkans. London, Constable and Company, 1917.

—— The Southern Slav Question and the Hapsburg Monarchy. Constable and Company, 1911.

Sforza, Carlo, Makers of Modern Europe. Indianapolis, Bobbs-Merrill, 1930.

—— Pensiero e azione di una politica estera italiana; discorsi e scritti di Carlo Sforza, with an introductory note by Alberto Cappa. Bari, Laterza, 1924.

—— "Sonnino and His Foreign Policy," *Contemporary Review,* Dec., 1929.

—— Un anno di politica estera, ed. by A. Giannini. Rome, Libreria di scienze e lettere, 1921.

Shotwell, James Thomson, At the Paris Peace Conference. New York, Macmillan, 1937.

Silvagni, Umberto, and Achille Richard, Fiume ville italienne. Paris, 1919.*

Šišić, Ferdinand, Abridged Political History of Rieka [Fiume]. Paris, Imprimerie Graphique, 1919.

—— Jadransko pitanje na Konferenciji mira u Parizu, zbirka akata i dokumentata. Zagreb, Matica Hrvatska, 1920.

Solmi, Arrigo, Le origini del Patto di Londra. Rome, Edizioni di Politica, 1924.

Sonnino, Sidney, Discorsi parlamentari di Sidney Sonnino, pubblicati per deliberazione della Camera dei deputati. 3 vols. Rome, Camera dei deputati, 1925.

—— Discorsi per la guerra, ed. by A. Giannini. Foligno, Campitelli, 1922.

Speranza, Gino, Daily Reports for the American Ambassador in Rome (unpublished), October, 1918-March, 1919.

Steed, Henry Wickham, Through Thirty Years. 2 vols. New York, Doubleday, 1924.

Stickney, Edith Pierpont, Southern Albania or Northern Epirus in European International Affairs, 1912-1923. Stanford, Stanford University Press, 1926.

Stojanović, Stojan, La Question de l'Adriatique et le principe des nationalités. Grenoble, Aubert, 1923.

Susmel, Edoardo, Fiume attraverso la storia dalle origini ai nbstri tempi. Milan, Treves, 1919.

—— La città di passione. Milan, Treves, 1921.

—— La marcia di Ronchi. Rome, Libreria del Littorio, 1929.

Tamaro, Attilio, Il trattato di Londra e le rivendicazioni nazionali. Milan, Treves, 1918.

—— La Vénétie Julienne et la Dalmatie. Histoire de la nation italienne sur ses frontières orientales. 3 vols. Rome, Imprimerie du sénat, 1918-19.

—— "Raccolta di documenti della questione adriatica," *Politica,* Vol. IV, 1920.

Tardieu, André, La Paix. Paris, Payot, 1921.

—— The Truth About the Treaty. Indianapolis, Bobbs, 1921. English edition of the preceding book.

Tchiritch, Slavko M., La Question de Fiume. Paris, Jouve, 1924.

Temperley, Harold William Vazielle, A History of the Peace Conference of
    Paris. 6 vols. London, Frowde, 1920-24.
Terrail, Gabriel (*pseud.*), *see* Mermeix.
Thompson, Charles Thaddeus, The Peace Conference Day by Day. New York,
    Brentano, 1920.
Tittoni, Tommaso, and Vittorio Scialoja, L'Italia alla conferenza della pace,
    ed. by A. Giannini. Rome, Libreria di scienze e lettere, 1921.
Toscano, Mario, Il patto di Londra, 2d ed. Bologna, Zanichelli, 1934.
—— Gli accordi di San Giovanni di Moriana. Milan, A. Giuffrè, 1936.
Toynbee, Arnold Joseph, Survey of International Affairs, 1924. London, Oxford
    University Press, 1926.
Trattati e convenzioni, *see* Italy, *Ministero degli affari esteri.*
Trevelyan, George Macaulay, Grey of Fallodon. Boston, Houghton Mifflin,
    1937.
United States, Department of State, Papers relating to the Foreign Relations of
    the United States, 1918. Supplement I, The World War, 2 vols. Washing-
    ton, 1933.
—— The Adriatic Question, Papers relating to the Italian-Jugoslav Boundary.
    Department of State, Division of Foreign Intelligence, Series M, No. 167.
    Washington, 1920.
Voinovitch, Louis de, and others, La Question de l'Adriatique. La Dalmatie.
    Paris, 1919.
Wegerer, Alfred von, ed., Das Zaristische Russland im Weltkriege. Berlin,
    Deutsche Vorlagsgesellschaft für Politik und Geschichte, 1927.
Yugoslav Memoranda Presented to the Peace Conference in Paris.
    1. Memorandum Presented to the Peace Conference.
    2. Frontiers between the Kingdom of the Serbians, Croatians and
        Slovenes and the Kingdom of Italy.
    3. The Territories of Goritza and Gradiska and the Town of Goritza.
    4. Istria.
    5. Memorandum on the Dalmatian Question.
    6. The Town of Ryieka (Fiume).
    7. The Town of Triest.
    8. North Frontier.
    9. Albania.
    10. The Military Effort of the Serbians, Croatians and Slovenes in the
        War 1914-18.
    These memoranda are also available in French.
Zanotti-Bianco, Umberto, and Andrea Caffi, La pace di Versailles. Rome, La
    Voce, 1919.
Zoli, Corrado, Gli sbocchi naturali della Jugoslavia all'Adriatico, 1919.*
—— Le giornate di Fiume. Bologna Zanichelli, 1921.

INDEX

INDEX